THE METAPHYSICAL DIVINE WISDOM COLLECTION

A Practical Motivational Guide to Spirituality

Kevin Hunter

Warrior of Light Press

Copyright © 2019 Kevin Hunter
Cover copyright © 2019 by Warrior of Light Press

Published and distributed in the United States by Warrior of Light Press, which supports the right to free expression and the value of copyright. The purpose of copyright is to encourage writers and artists to produce creative works that enrich our culture.

All rights reserved. No part of this book and publication may be used or reproduced by any means including but not limited to digital, electronic, graphic, mechanical, photocopying, recording, taping or otherwise; nor may it be stored in a retrieval system, transmitted, or otherwise be copied for public or private use – other than for "fair use" as brief quotations embodied in articles and reviews - without the written permission of the copyright owner, publisher or author. Social media posts please credit the author. The scanning, uploading, and distribution of any contents in this book without permission is a theft of the author's intellectual property.

The author of this book does not dispense medical advice or prescribe the use of any technique as a form of treatment for physical, emotional, or medical problems without the advice of a physician, either directly or indirectly. The intent of the author is only to offer information of a general nature to help you in your quest for emotional and spiritual well-being. In the event, you use any of the information in this book for yourself, which is your constitutional right, the author and the publisher assume no responsibility for your actions.

Warrior of Light Press
www.kevin-hunter.com

First Edition: July 2019
Printed in the United States of America

All rights reserved. Copyright © 2019
ISBN-13: 978-1733196260

3. Mind and Body. 2. Spirituality. 1. Title

DEDICATION

For you on your soul's spiritual journey.

THE METAPHYSICAL DIVINE WISDOM COLLECTION

INCLUDES THE FOLLOWING BOOKS IN THE SERIES:

On Psychic Spirit Team Heaven Communication
On Soul Consciousness and Purpose
On Increasing Prayer with Faith for an Abundant Life
On Balancing the Mind, Body, and Soul
On Manifesting Fearless Assertive Confidence
On Universal, Physical, Spiritual and Soul Love

PSYCHIC SPIRIT TEAM HEAVEN COMMUNICATION

Chapter 1 5
I Am Psychic and So Are You

Chapter 2 13
Psychic Abilities are Built into all Souls

Chapter 3 19
Psychically Connecting and Other Psychic Wisdom

Chapter 4 25
Communicating with the Divine

Chapter 5 33
The Psychic Clair Senses

Chapter 6 45
Picking Up On Heavenly Input

Chapter 7 50
Psychic Insights

Chapter 8 56
Psychic Accuracy

Chapter 9 60
Psychic Timing

Chapter 10 _____67
How Much Does Your Spirit Team Know?

Chapter 11 _____74
Blocking Divine Guidance

Chapter 12 _____81
Sensitivities are a Gift from the Divine

Chapter 13 _____86
Psychic Spirit Team Communication and my Creative Channeling Process

Chapter 14 _____94
Spirit Guides and Angels

Chapter 15 _____99
You Are Psychic!

Chapter 16 _____108
How to Connect with the Tarot

Afterword _____116
A Final Word

SOUL CONSCIOUSNESS AND PURPOSE

Chapter 1 _____ 123
Opening the Pathway to Divinity

Chapter 2 _____ 129
Knowing When Your Soul Is Transforming and Evolving

Chapter 3 _____ 136
Awakening Your Creative Consciousness

Chapter 4 _____ 144
Soul Contracts

Chapter 5 _____ 151
Life Purposes

Chapter 6 _____ 160
Healing and Transformation

Chapter 7 _____ 169
Soul Groups and Earth Angels

Chapter 8 _____ 176
The Earthly Birth

Chapter 9 _____ 181
The Soul and the Spirit

Chapter 10 _____ 188
The Higher Self

Chapter 11 193
Soul Growth Through Grief

Chapter 12 198
Soul Growth Through Health Issues

Chapter 13 202
Soul Growth Through Relationships

Chapter 14 206
Twin Flame Soul Mission and Purpose

Chapter 15 212
Soul Growth Through Work and Career

Chapter 16 216
Soul Growth Through Superficiality

Chapter 17 220
Soul Growth Through Emotional Healing

Chapter 18 225
The Human Influences on the Soul Consciousness

Chapter 19 228
Spirit Guides and Guardian Angels

Chapter 20 235
The Shift in Global Consciousness

MANIFESTING FEARLESS ASSERTIVE CONFIDENCE

Chapter 1 247
Combat Fear

Chapter 2 254
Stand In Your Divine Soul Power

Chapter 3 264
Stomp Out the Darkness of Fear, Gossip, and Anger

Chapter 4 275
Identify Blocks to Abundance and Blessings

Chapter 5 280
Be the Chief Executive of Your Life

Chapter 6 287
Optimistic Visualization, Getting Enthusiastic and Taking Action

Chapter 7 296
Partake in Pleasing Work

Chapter 8 300
You Are Worthy and Deserving of Blessings

Chapter 9 306
Awaken Your Creative Spirit

Chapter 10 315
Rise Into Creative Confidence

Chapter 11 323
Balancing Healthy Selfishness and Selflessness

Chapter 12 330
Assertiveness, Aggression, Passive Aggression

Chapter 13 335
Step Into Your Soul's Authority

Chapter 14 341
Fearless Assertive Confident Soul

Chapter 15 347
Live Your Life Be Free

BALANCING THE MIND, BODY, AND SOUL

Chapter 1 _____ 357
Raise Your Soul's Energy Vibration

Chapter 2 _____ 366
Fire Up Your Inner Child

Chapter 3 _____ 373
Nature's Therapy

Chapter 4 _____ 376
Elevating Your Mind, Body, and Spirit

Chapter 5 _____ 383
Expand Your Consciousness

Chapter 6 _____ 390
Detoxify Your Soul

Chapter 7 _____ 397
Soul Cleansing to Motivation

Chapter 8 _____ 403
Clearing the Chaos Within and Around Your World

Chapter 9 _____ 409
Gossip Machine to Centered Light

Chapter 10 _____ 416
Balancing Your Inner Spirit

Chapter 11 _____ 424
Rise Above the Mundane and Into the Divine

Chapter 12 _____ 432
Cord Cutting, Shielding, Grounding

Chapter 13 _____ 442
Vibrational Uplift

Chapter 14 _____ 450
The Balance of Masculine and Feminine Energies

Chapter 15 _____ 457
Twin Souls Yin and Yang

Chapter 16 _____ 462
Blissful Happy Place

INCREASING PRAYER WITH FAITH FOR AN ABUNDANT LIFE

Chapter 1 473
The Power of Prayer

Chapter 2 478
Be Vigilant with Prayer and Affirmations

Chapter 3 482
Ask for Divinely Guided Angelic Help

Chapter 4 486
Turn Prayers Into Manifestation

Chapter 5 494
Create an Abundant Life With Faith

Chapter 6 499
Increase Faith to Accomplish, Achieve, and Persevere

Chapter 7 503
Complaining Into Abundance

Chapter 8 512
Taking Action on Divine Guidance

Chapter 9 _____ 518
Gratitude and Optimism

Chapter 10 _____ 522
Grieving, Depression, Suicide

Chapter 11 _____ 527
The Significance of Spirituality

Chapter 12 _____ 534
Spirit Is In Your Corner

Chapter 13 _____ 539
Be Your Own Messiah

Chapter 14 _____ 549
The Commanding Function of Prayer

Chapter 15 _____ 557
Divine Assistance

Chapter 16 _____ 563
Scripture Reminders on Faith and Prayer

UNIVERSAL, PHYSICAL, SPIRITUAL AND SOUL LOVE

Chapter 1 — 573
It's All About Love

Chapter 2 — 580
Creating the Life You Love

Chapter 3 — 584
Self-Love and Self-Care

Chapter 4 — 592
Karmic Soul Connections

Chapter 5 — 598
Soul Mate Soul Connections

Chapter 6 — 606
Twin Flame Soul Connections

Chapter 7 — 616
Benefits and Challenges of Technology Dating

Chapter 8 625
Single and Longing for a Relationship

Chapter 9 634
Love and Relationships

Chapter 10 640
Love is a Battlefield

Chapter 11 647
Seeking Love Through External Validation

Chapter 12 653
Divine Soul Love

Chapter 13 659
Love Yourself Back to Life

Chapter 14 666
Bring Out the Good Vibrations

Chapter 15 674
Universal Spiritual Love

About the Author 689

AUTHOR NOTE

The *Metaphysical Divine Wisdom* books are a series of spiritually based books that focus on different areas of one's life. Like many of my spiritual related metaphysical books, this one is also infused with practical messages and spirit guidance that my Spirit team has taught and shared with me revolving around many different topics. The main goal is to fine-tune your body, mind, and soul. Like all souls, you are a Divine communicator capable of receiving messages and guidance from Heaven.

The *Metaphysical Divine Collection* book is a compilation of six books from the series all in one gigantic book. This is for those that prefer to have it all in one place rather than having to purchase the six individual books. Like many of my spiritually based books, this one can also work as an oracle if you've got the paperback edition. You can pick up the book, close your eyes, think of a question such as, "Are there are any messages for me today?" Thumb through the book with your eyes closed, then trust your psychic instincts on when to stop. Notice the page that falls open and wherever your eyes are guided. This is the general area to read to see if it's something connected to what you need to know at that time. If it doesn't mean anything to you at the time you read it, then it could be something that is to take place, or guidance that your angels want you to pay more attention to.

My personal Spirit team council makes up God and the Holy Spirit, as well as a team of guides, angels, and sometimes Archangels and Saints. I am merely the liaison or messenger in delivering and interpreting the intentions of what they wish to communicate. My team comprises some hard truth telling Wise Ones from the Other Side, including Saint Nathaniel, who can be brutal in his direct forcefulness. He cuts right to the heart of humanity without apology. I have learned quite a bit from him while adopting his ideology, which is Heaven's philosophy. I wouldn't preach Divine Guidance that God doesn't whisper into my Clairaudient ear first.

If I use the word "He" when pertaining to God, this does not mean that I am advocating that he is a male. Simply replace the word, "He" with one you are comfortable using to identify God for you to be. If the word, "God" makes you uncomfortable, then substitute it with one you're more accustomed with like Universe, Spirit, Energy, the Light, or any other comparable word. This goes for any gender I use as examples. When I say, "spirit team", I am referring to a team of 'Guides and Angels'.

One of the purposes of my work is to empower, enlighten, as well as entertain. It's also to help you improve yourself, your soul, your life and humanity by default. If anything, I am preaching to myself, because God knows that I can use a refresher course occasionally. It does not matter if you are a beginner or well versed in the subject matter. There may be something that reminds you of something you already know or something that you were unaware of. We all have much to share with one another, as we are all one in the end.

KEVIN HUNTER

THE METAPHYSICAL DIVINE WISDOM COLLECTION

A PRACTICAL MOTIVATIONAL GUIDE
TO SPIRITUALITY SERIES

METAPHYSICAL DIVINE WISDOM

ON PSYCHIC SPIRIT TEAM HEAVEN COMMUNICATION

KEVIN HUNTER

Kevin Hunter

The Metaphysical Divine Wisdom Collection

METAPHYSICAL DIVINE WISDOM
ON PSYCHIC SPIRIT TEAM HEAVEN COMMUNICATION

Kevin Hunter

CHAPTER ONE

*I Am Psychic
and So Are You!*

Connecting with my Divine Spirit team through channeling sometimes requires taking a deep breath in if I'm not relaxed followed by shutting my eyes on the exhale. The second my eyes close, the connection with spirit is dramatically established as if pushing an electrical plug into a wall socket that creates a spark. The initial connection entails being immediately catapulted through the air like a cannonball firing. It can move in numerous ways where I'm soaring at lightning speed through the vortex portal of the next plane only to slam into an ocean plummeting downwards deeper and faster into its dark watery depths that accelerates in a fashion comparable to a rocket gaining steam, and then the messages float into my consciousness.

One of the other ways is the missile firing is followed by a bomb explosion going off leaving me surrounded by brilliant shining bright white light. This is only to realize I've been moving at rapid speed within it. The light breaks apart and dissolves into billions of stars. This interstellar display evaporates, and the laws of human physics are defied as I ascend higher by means of what some call astral travel and projection. This intergalactic travelling through light years of galaxy and space is where the messages sift into my consciousness.

I have no idea where I'll be taken until I shut my eyes only to discover my vessel is travelling upwards or downwards. The chilling transporting happens if I'm sent into the depths of the ocean, as there is a few second shock and fear of potential drowning. This is followed by a heaviness that luckily subsides into contentment the further I plunge into its intense profoundness. Crossing into the portal I'm surrounded by members of my Spirit council in a comfortable gigantic wave of strengthening love like being hugged to death. Everything grows exceedingly calm while in this brilliant transcending radiance.

This way of communication isn't unusual for me as I've been a natural born psychic since childhood. One of the greater misunderstandings about psychic phenomena is that only a select group of people on the planet is gifted with psychic perception. Because of that belief some have either lifted psychics into special royalty status or discredited psychic foresight altogether. I am psychic and so are you! Every living-breathing organism is psychic from people, to plants, to animals, and to the entire planet. Everything that is not human made but God created has access to these Divine communication receptors deep within the soul's DNA, regardless if there is awareness of that or not. This is one of the ways that everything and everyone is affected and connected to one another.

When you walk into a room full of people and someone is angry and creating a dramatic scene, then every single person in that room will be negatively affected by it. I've been in restaurants where someone nearby our table has this infectious hysterical laugh that makes us, and the surrounding tables light up in laughter as well too. When I was working on {a film production for Warner Bros. Studios} *The Perfect Storm*, I had answered my phone and it was one of the Assistant Directors calling from the soundstage. He paused moving from serious and formal to lightening and warming up to tell me, "You know Kevin, I could be having the most stressful day on set, but as soon as you answer the phone there is this sudden calmness that relaxes me. It's every single time that sometimes I'll admit I'm not calling you for anything important, but I just need to absorb some of what is coming off you. I spoke to others on set about it and they all agreed and said they had noticed the same thing too."

Back during those entertainment day job days, my boss wouldn't always take his car to work and would be driven or use other transportation because it was less stressful. I said to him once, "I live past you now, so if there are ever days you want to ride let me know. I don't mind I like the company."

There were days that he started to take me up on that offer. As months passed by, I ran into his husband who said to me, "I can tell the days that he rides home with you. Because those are the only days that he comes home calm, relaxed, and in good spirits."

The psychic energy that people give off and radiate transfers to other people in the vicinity. When you're radiating a serene, loving, calmness, then those around can feel and absorb that. When you have a terribly toxic roommate, friend, colleague, spouse, or family member, everyone notices it and is negatively affected that it can ruin their day. These emotions that cause others to detect, pick up on, and absorb those other energies off other people is connected to your Clairsentience psychic feeling sense. It acts like a suction cup that breathes in everything that is around it both the good and the bad from the physical, supernatural and ethereal.

Your aura is six feet in all directions around your body. This is how big every human soul's light is. If someone's auric circle is plagued with Darkness and they walk past you, then it will hit your auric circle. This is how it affects your well-being state and vice versa since everything is made of energy. If you read toxic media, news, or social media that upsets you, then the energy of that news and the person that wrote it is emanating off that and hitting your aura. This is all part of another handful of reasons as to why it's important to protect your soul's Light and sensitivities. This means getting strict and disciplined by what you allow close to your auric circle. You're doing that to protect you and your soul from unnecessary dark energies that offer no positive benefit at all. By doing this you are managing your souls light the same way you manage other areas of your life from work, home, to relationships. Often neglected and forgot about is the soul's spiritual life, which is affected by everything around it. It's the same way someone taps on an Aquarium glass where a fish is sitting prompting it to dart away.

With Clairsentience you can walk into a place and sense a dark gloom, which is a psychic signal to high tail it out of there. The feelings people have are one of the most powerful ways that psychic information comes in, but when you're so focused on your feelings and how you feel, then you don't realize that sometimes it's a psychic hit coming through from spirit. This is the case until you learn through repetitive practice how to recognize when it's a psychic hit or your ego mind.

It is true that some people tend to display stronger psychic senses than others, but that doesn't mean other people don't have those same psychic senses. The more blocked someone is, then the more reduced those psychic senses are to the extent that it would appear they have no psychic abilities at all. Those psychic abilities are buried deep down in that soul without them realizing it.

There are endless lists of things that can block someone from noticing Divine psychic guidance. The saying that states you are what you eat or drink is true. The foods you consume can create a psychic block with the Divine. The more bad foods you consume, then the dimmer the psychic senses will be. Altering your state of mind through drugs and alcohol will dim your psychic senses. This isn't scolding anyone or instructing anyone not to have those comfort foods like that hot dog at an amusement park or a glass of wine with a lover. This is informing you what can reduce or dim your psychic abilities. The good news is that you can have that day of fun where your psychic senses have been dimmed, but then it's assumed it's not like you're doing that every day. The next day you may then choose to get re-aligned and healthy again. Consuming toxins daily if you're unable to stop should be reduced to moderation beyond enhancing your psychic abilities. It is also less taxing on your body in the long run as your medical doctor may at some point advise you if they haven't already. Believe me I still love my Classic Rock music blaring at a Beach BBQ with a cold beer in my hand, but I know in that moment my psychic prowess is dimming. I can hear my Spirit team council, but they're distant as if talking through a wall separating us.

Negative emotions of any kind will dim psychic clair senses. This includes any negative emotion you can possibly think of from anger, stress, depression, sadness, grief, agitation, frustration, vindictiveness, greed, and gossip and on and on. I know we basically listed most of the generic negative emotional traits that all human beings experience at one time or another, with some displaying those traits more than others. This isn't telling anyone to deny those emotions, because you will feel them just as the highest holy person will in their own way on occasion. We are all having a human experience and with that come those challenging emotions, but that is one of the reasons why we are having a human experience. It is to be able to learn how to master our emotions and thoughts as much as possible through spiritual maturity. You're allowed to have an off day. This is encouraged as it gets you through the transformation process of hitting the floor and learning how to rebuild yourself back up. You can have numerous off days. The more you work on evolving your soul and physical experience, then the easier it gets in moving yourself right back into faith and centered in the Light when you step off balance.

When someone is twenty years old, they may overreact emotionally to every little thing, but by the time they're forty years old, one hopes through the challenging life experiences thrown at them and through spiritual maturity they have grown quite good at re-centering themselves after a bad couple of days. Life experiences will throw you a hard-fisted right to the face. Many human beings will or have experienced a job loss that causes worry, depression, and fear. People have lovers that leave them causing anger, upset, and sadness. Human beings also experience the loss of loved ones, which can produce heavy grief and crushing despair. These are all part of the emotions associated with human life. You feel those emotions and you process them on your own time.

Eventually on your trajectory of soul evolvement you reach a point where you grow exhausted from feeling like that and you begin the process of taking steps to alter that into faith, hope, and action. This can be from reaching out to others for assistance, support, to changing your diet, exercising regularly, to learning to walk away from toxic people and choices. To re-align your psychic soul vessel, you might choose to listen to inspiring music, go into nature to hang out and commune, or read self-help books that can motivate you to feel joy and serenity again. You can also do what I do which is to access God and my Spirit team from within the core being of my soul. This is where I ask them through prayer to empower me all over again by lifting me right back up into warrior mode ready to conquer the world and forge forward fearlessly. I know that I cannot sit around waiting to die or feeling the same negative emotions day after day with no end in sight. I must rise back up and get back out there.

An ex once said, "The great thing that you do is you rarely get angry, but when you do everyone scatters and we all know it's serious and no drill. But you leave and come back fifteen minutes later and you're all smiles and have got over it. You don't hold onto it for any longer. Most people hang onto it forever never letting it go."

I said, "How dreadful to hold onto that forever."

Many want the rewards without doing the work. This goes for psychic development as well too. Those that have taken an interest in psychic development want the psychic prowess, but will find the development to opening the psychic senses to be dull work. If you want any reward, then you must do the work and continue to be controlled about it. There is no way around that, but if you want something bad enough, then you will work hard to achieve it through regular discipline and hard work. When you exercise regularly, you are building up stamina and toning your body. This is the same way you regularly partake in spiritual pursuits to strengthen the psychic soul part of you.

The soul in the human body is psychic, but the physical body is not psychic, yet both the spiritual body and the physical body work in tandem with one another while on Earth. Working on both helps ensure the other is working at optimum levels. When you work on your physical body by being mindful of what you are doing to it, then this simultaneously strengthens the spiritual body, which brings out those psychic senses. Strengthening your spiritual body can simultaneously strengthen your physical body. Therefore, taking care of both and keeping them at optimum levels is beneficial on your overall well-being for a variety of reasons. One is that it gives you stronger psychic Clair sense channels that guide you along your life's path helping you make better decisions. Another is that it keeps you physically healthy for as long as possible while you are here. This gives you more energy and focus to dive into your passions and life purpose, as well as fun time with loved ones, friends, and family.

Watch what you ingest each day making sure the ratio from healthy to unhealthy shows the healthy being in a higher percentage while allowing yourself the fun you want to do. Physical exercise has been one of the top things that Spirit showed me since childhood to be of importance. I subconsciously knew as an eight-year-old that we have to take care of our bodies. Often there's a disconnect between the body and the soul, but while here they need to work in tandem since they both positively feed off of and work for one another. When you're feeling negative emotions, then this affects your physical body, which transfers to affecting your etheric psychic senses.

Physical exercise would not apply to someone that is physically unable to due to a health issue. This is more for those that don't want to out of laziness or procrastination. I've always been into physical fitness. It started at the early age of five teaching myself to ride a bike on my own, which naturally I fell a number of times, then ran into a cactus on another and created a tiny scar that's still there, but eventually I mastered it and got it going and have continued the exercise routines since. I never looked at it as work, but have always just enjoyed being active. Decades later and my disciplined exercise routine has yet to permanently stop. Even during my heavy alcohol and drug addicted days I was still managing to incorporate some exercise on certain days. The stronger your body is made through exercise, then the stronger your psychic channel is. One of my Medium friends rides her bike daily in between reading sessions for clients. She'll also treat herself to the occasional beer. You'll note the balance between the working on our physical body through exercise, but allowing yourself that toxin once in a while if you choose. Although having one beer is much different than drinking a six pack regularly.

Your emotional state is as important as your physical body, both of which also work off each other. When you exercise there has been long running scientific evidence that it positively improves your emotional state and well-being. You're improving two things at the same time by doing one thing. That one thing is the exercise that kills two birds with one stone by improving your physical health state and simultaneously your emotional and mental state. There might be a day where I fall into a slump, but then I exercise and hop on the bike and hit the beach. When I arrive back home, I feel rejuvenated and uplifted. I've walked into the gym moody and distant, but then after almost an hour of listening to music and working on the weight machines I've found all of that has shifted. Suddenly I walk out smiling with this uplifting joyful feeling like I'm on top of the world. This is because exercise also helps in raising the feel-good Dopamine chemicals in the body.

Those two examples included additional tips that raise your vibration level. When you raise your soul's vibration, then the more enhanced your psychic channels get. The biking (exercise) on the beach (nature) is a winning combo because you're uniting two elements that help raise your vibration. You're combining exercise with nature. Getting out into a nature setting has many positive benefits on both your spiritual body and emotional body.

Nature has been another scientific proven method that has been shown to reduce stress levels in people. When you reduce stress and move into a relaxation state, then it is that relaxation state where your psychic channels expand. How often have you been feeling tense or edgy, but then you walk through a flower garden or a wide-open nature space and you can feel the stress just lift off your body. Many have admitted to receiving divine guidance and ideas after taking a break to head to a nature setting. Their guides were able to easily access them once the negative emotions and thoughts were reduced.

While at the gym you'll notice I was playing music while working out. Music is another element that raises your vibration, which simultaneously expands your psychic senses. People all over the globe listen to music. Music brings the people together through joy and uplifting fun. It inspires others to create, to work, and to continue on.

Exercising in nature while listening to music is a triple whammy! You're incorporating the exercise, nature, and music all at the same time. It's not rocket science to raise your vibration and increase your psychic senses. God didn't make it complicated where you have to take numerous classes, watch endless videos, and pay enormous amounts of money for a lecture or seminar on it. Just get out there and do it.

Many will list meditation as a way to increase psychic development, but I've never technically meditated, and my psychic channels have forever been off the charts. This doesn't mean that meditation doesn't work. It just means I don't personally do it, but I do admire those that have the patience to sit Indian style in meditation for an hour and never move, since that takes enormous discipline. Some of the friends I have in the spiritual communities are also huge lovers of meditation. If you're great at meditation and that's what you prefer to do, then that will help in awakening your psychic senses. It's the relaxing element that is key here. The more relaxed you are, and the less negative feelings or thoughts plaguing you, then the easier it is to connect with spirit. It's as simple as that or perhaps not so simple if you struggle with relaxing.

If you're struggling with relaxing and removing negative feelings and thoughts, then that will need to be the first step to take care of. It's not going to happen overnight. It's a daily process of working to adjust your state of mind. This would include being able to bounce back out of a circumstance that might have upset or bothered you that day. Once you are feeling good, content, and stress free, then that's a great time to psychically connect.

While I don't sit Indian style in nature meditating for an hour, I do frequent nature settings regularly. My way of meditating is strolling through it with my hands outstretched upwards to feel God move through me, around me, and work on my well-being state, which helps me relax. Sometimes I will kick back and plop in an area on the beach and meditate on the ocean and the crashing of the waves, or I'll head to the desert and plop myself on a rock or an area with little to no people to close my eyes and allow whatever needs to come through to do so. Before I write I will close my eyes, take a deep breath in, call in my Spirit team, and center myself, but that doesn't take more than anywhere from one to five minutes max. They come in rather quickly, but this also helps in centering me, which some meditation professionals would say is meditating.

Sometimes we get busy and distracted by the day to day practical parts of our lives, which are understandable, but then the Divine messages get lost during that time. Spirit will do their best to make the messages as known as they possibly can. Sometimes it's subtle, but other times it's so obvious that you can't miss it.

It's never been unusual for me to foresee upcoming events, but I've never looked at that as psychic fortune telling. I looked at it as an extension of me. What my Spirit team council chooses to communicate to me is often flushing in an automatic random way. I can be busy doing other things, and then a psychic alert flies in indicating something is about to take place. Other times it's something insignificant where I'm walking and clairvoyantly see a woman wearing green jogging. Ten minutes later a woman in green appears jogging down the sidewalk past me and that's the end of that. There's no reason for that foresight.

In the film *The Silence of the Lambs*, there is a scene where Clarice Starling (Jodie Foster) is communicating to Hannibal Lecter (Anthony Hopkins) through his cell. In the middle of their conversation his head lifts as if sensing something, then he looks back down glaring at her, "Dr. Chilton I presume. I believe you two know each other."

She stares at him strangely not understanding, then a beat later Dr. Chilton shows up with the authorities to escort her out of the building. In that subtle movement that audience members might've missed, it would be interpreted it that he psychically sensed Dr. Chilton was on his way. This is because there were no audible sounds of him being close and nor was he in physical view.

One of my many psychic light protection devices is to not engage with negative people or negative spirits for that matter, which should be observed whether one is a sensitive psychic being. This is something I've adopted early on in my life as a teenager, but accelerated that mantra during my twenties growing stricter about it. It also makes it challenging or frustrating for some people to get close to me right away unless they work for it. This is because I've always been doubly cautious about anyone I don't know that approaches me. I typically take a step back to observe and psychically read them to see if they are safe enough or not. I can immediately tell if someone is bathed in darkness, lower energy, or has any measure of an ulterior motive. Part of this is due to who is getting too close to my Light that it affects me physically. I need to govern my vessel with the most ultimate protection possible, because my soul comes first. The other reason is due to my distrust in others due to the childhood abuse I endured growing up and the failed relationships that followed and broke apart due to the other partner's lack of integrity. It took a great deal of soul work to evolve out of all that damage.

Combine both of those reasoning's for keeping people at arm's length and you have a supremely difficult person on your hands whose got a wall around him the size of China. This doesn't mean it's impossible since I'm surrounded by people that have been around me for decades. This means they were able to scale that wall, so it's not impossible for the strong and trustworthy. This goes both ways since those in my circles have told others that I'm one of the strongest and trustworthy people they know. You treat people how you want to be treated. It's been conveyed I'm strong and trustworthy and they mirror that right back at me, thus a beautiful long-term connection is created.

There are occasions where a negative person, spirit, or spirits can and will get into your aura and infect your light. Sometimes you can be doing everything right and it still gets on in there. It can cause all sorts of anxiety, turmoil, and a domino effect of back to back negative things happening in your life. It's just not worth the risk to invite in anyone that you suspect is infected by the Darkness, or that you psychically pick up on as having a lower energy. This is part of protecting your light, since your guides can only do so much. They'll warn you through your psychic senses and you can choose to ignore that warning or follow it. Many have admitted to ignoring it, and then later when a multitude of negative circumstances hits the fan regarding the person they will later say, "I knew something was off with that person when I met them, but I ignored it."

Mentally call in your Spirit team and ask that they surround and shield your soul from harsh energies, then pay attention to what is going on within and around you. As you tune into your psychic feeling sense you can determine through uncomfortable jolts if something or someone is on their way that you should steer clear from.

CHAPTER TWO

*Psychic Abilities are
Built into all Souls*

All babies born should immediately be handed a spirit guidebook that will help them navigate through an Earthly life effortlessly than they would without it. This includes knowing to trust and call upon God and their Spirit Guide and Guardian Angel while moving along their current life's journey. Perhaps one could assume that every parent, guardian, and teacher would pass on this knowledge, but unfortunately that is not the case with every single one of them. However, every soul that is born into a human body already has this spirit guidebook within the imprint of their soul's DNA. It's forever there waiting to be accessed by them any minute, time, or day over the course of their Earthly life.

Many people don't believe in Guides and Angels, an afterlife, God, or spirit beings. Some believe in the possibility, others believe it's forbidden to communicate with spirit guides, some are unsure if it's real, and the rest flatly believe in nothing. They believe that when you die, you die, the end.

All souls are privy to the knowledge of being surrounded by at least one guide and one angel before being born into a human body. Throughout the human developmental phase in the first number of years as a child, and through the numerous physical experiences, it is inevitable that memory loss occurs where you suppress your soul's recollections due to physical Earthly life blocks combined with what Spirit purposely blocks you from seeing until it's time. The information is present within you and never goes away. It is stored and is accessible at some point in your life. The soul memories may come through in sweeping chunks or sporadic snapshots. Psychic blocks are formed as the baby moves into childhood and beyond. By the time it reaches adulthood you may be completely psychically blocked causing complete amnesia oblivion unaware of worlds beyond Earth. There are a great many souls coming into an Earthly life again who are learning to bring that part of themselves back more than they ever had in centuries past.

There was once a time in Earth's history when we didn't have the foods, drinks, and negative emotional stresses that we have now. We weren't preoccupied by all the physical material-based distractions. We spent more time outdoors and in nature where the spirit connections were clearer then. At the same time more people are growing mindful of how certain toxic vices and toxic people negatively affect them. They are experimenting with natural herbs and remedies to find the right products that help bring a greater sense of calm focused clarity. Calm focused clarity is a state that so many are trying to achieve, but have fallen short of due to the break your back work mentality that many nations have adopted. The current work life state is to work you to death until you drop or retire, then you've got a few good years to enjoy it far beyond your prime.

This isn't about having an enormous time off to do nothing, which is one end of the extreme where you risk falling into sloth mode. The opposite extreme is working more than you have time off when it should be equally balanced. Incorporating more balance in your life in all areas where possible helps in achieving a greater sense of joy and peace, which simultaneously cracks open the psychic portal. Avoid feeling guilty about the time off you do take for yourself, because guilt is another deadly sin that creates a spirit psychic block.

Being psychic is not a special power or gift, but an extrasensory ability that every soul is born with regardless of their personal human beliefs. This ability is similar to how a human being is born breathing to stay alive. The psychic muscle part of them is a necessity and a part of the soul's make-up the way the human body has organs to physically survive. Everyone has some measure of psychic capabilities that vary from one person to the next, but no one is all knowing and powerful. The soul consciousness has the competence to receive shreds of second-sighted information, flashes of insight, and sporadic foresight, some of which needs to be deciphered and pieced together by you.

Access Spirit in Nature

Every soul on the planet has picked up on psychic hits at some point in their life, even the non-believers and those unaware they were exhibiting psychic phenomena in that instance. Going out into any nature setting with no physical distractions are where the psychic frequencies are highest. It's where God placed humankind long before structures, buildings, and technology dominated. There are endless benefits to these luxuries that humankind created, but they also play a hand at dimming and blocking spiritual communication. Getting back outdoors can assist in raising your vibration where higher psychic input resides. You are in a space that has no distractions assuming you're not going to a crowded nature locale. If you went to one of the world's most popular tourist beaches during high tourist season, then naturally you may have a tough time focusing.

Mother Nature is the perfect place for spiritual and personal enrichment of the body and soul. Spirit energy is heavy in those areas specifically because many higher spirit beings do not hang around areas bathed in negativity. They're not drawn to places like big cities, or wherever it's crowded, buildings sandwiched together, or human made creations. This is because loving spirits are drawn to light and there is little soul light that exists in physical dwellings. There are more angels and spirits watching over every flower, every grass, rock, mountain terrain than anywhere else in the world. Many nature locales contain powerful spirits hanging around those spaces.

The Native Americans were spiritual people, and America was a spiritual land at its conception. This was until it was plagued by puritanical chaotic materialistic greed filled nonsense energy that exists in the country in modern age. The spiritual part of the land sits underneath that debris. The in-tune souls can easily access it when they are centered in grace. They were and are also some of the greatest souls by having finely tuned in Mediumship abilities.

Practicing Mediumship

Partaking in Mediumship entails raising your vibration to pick up on your Guide and Angel, while your Spirit team lowers their vibration to meet you halfway. You are living in the low-density mark, and they reside in the high, so you both meet halfway, which is the medium mark.

Contrary to Biblical passages, mediumship is not of the Devil and it's not a sin, but it can invite in a negative entity. Many are conducting mediumship without trying or wanting to. They are communicating with spirit or a deceased loved one naturally because it is one of the many gifts human souls are born able to do, regardless if they believe in it or approve of it.

Practicing mediumship where you channel should be taken with the utmost seriousness due to the dangers of inviting in a negative entity. Negative spirits exist, but not in Heaven, which contains the highest love energy lights possible. They reside in one of the numerous darker layers of Hell amidst the various spiritual planes and dimensions. There are also deceased spirits stuck roaming about in the Earth plane. They strayed further from the Light avoiding it for fear of what their ego conscious mind imagines it to be. Some of them assume it's full of judgment and punishment if they had been raised in a human upbringing that cemented that false assumption into their consciousness. Some of them are unaware they passed away as they repeat the same movements like a broken record. Meanwhile, their deceased loved ones and guide and angel work to guide them into the light. Other negative spirits will hang back on the Earth plane to aggravate a human soul by attaching itself to that person. They might do this if the human being is an addict. If the negative spirit was an addict as a human being, then it will want to continue with that addiction after passing on. Therefore, it will coax the human being to use the addiction they had when living an Earthly life.

Negative spirits can and will make someone's life miserable. If you've been perpetually despondent and there are no mental health reasons for it, and it's not your general disposition, then there could be a negative spirit in the vicinity seeping itself into your aura. Sometimes just by being in the same room as you can it infiltrate your soul. When you reside in permanent fear, then you risk attracting in a negative Earth-bound spirit. Fear is what attracts a negative spirit to you as this feeds the negative spirit making it stronger in darkness.

All possibilities outside of that would need to be factored in. You cannot automatically assume it's a negative spirit, which is a deceptive trick the ego enjoys conjuring up to illicit fanfare. You would need to examine your overall state of well-being, if you've had a history of depression and anxiety, or if a life circumstance threw a curve ball at you through the death of a loved one, the loss of a job or relationship, or any other details that cannot be explained away that prompted your disposition to become indefinitely negative.

This is about those who generally have a sunny optimistic disposition, where everything is going great in their life, but one day they wake up and moodiness sets in and they cannot figure out how or why. It never seems to leave as the weeks and months pass. Nothing in that person's life can explain how this suddenly came about. Doctor checkups reveal all to be well, diet was never changed, and no life altering circumstances took place. There could be the possibility of a negative spirit that's attached itself or they are psychically picking up on something around them such as a warning.

One of the easiest ways to get rid of a negative spirit is to call in God, Jesus Christ, or the Archangel Michael to surround you with protective white light, and to extricate the spirit out of your vicinity and away from you, and take it into Heaven's holy light. If you're an experienced psychic, you may already have your own go to group for protection, but that is who I call in.

Demonic spirit entities are inhuman and the worst evil imaginable more than negative spirits. The odds of a demonic spirit being around anybody are slim having only about a 1% chance of appearing, but that's 1% out of 7 billion. The percentage of appearance is raised if you are someone that practices mediumship, channeling, or psychic readings as that can awake it from slumber. Therefore, it's crucial that you observe safe practices when it comes to psychic phenomena, including surrounding yourself with white light before you conduct a reading.

More people than ever before have been drawn into spiritual pursuits as well as the psychic phenomena field. This is fantastic pending that it's taken seriously and cautiously. The challenging side to so many doing psychic work is there are readers who have negativity surrounding their aura that is spilling out of them. There is indication they've invited a negative spirit feeder into their vicinity without realizing it. As always use caution when you conduct your readings and be sure to use safe psychic practice by shielding your space regularly and being disciplined about your environment, emotions, and surroundings.

Nailing Down Psychic Input

Some of the people that reveal the most spot-on psychic input are not necessarily professional readers, or may not even believe in it, but might be open to it. This is that friend who always seems to say things that later come true. It's a repetitive process that many around them notice. They're not doing anything in particular or trying to conduct a reading. They likely don't even know how to read using divination tools. Their soul is the tool that brings in the input naturally.

The benefit of having a strong psychic gift is to be able to make sounder choices in your life, while also warning you of danger and what and who to stay away from. Pay attention to all of your psychic senses and what comes in as you move about your day. Pray for guidance when you feel stuck on an issue and ask for signs on the best choice to make that will not leave you in a challenging state, but instead will enhance your life.

A political friend asked me, "I know you're not political, but Ossoff or Handel for Georgia?"

I said, "I have no idea what you're saying to me right now."

He clarifies, "That's whose running for the congressional seat for Georgia. I was curious what you get for them."

As someone that doesn't pay attention to the news I said, "I've never heard of them or this."

I paused in silence then said, "Handel. Whoever Handel is. That's who gets it."

Hours later he sends me a media link with the text: "Handel won. You were right. Not that it's a surprise."

How do you psychically nail the answer, how does it come to you, or what do I personally do? In this scenario, I didn't do anything. It just rushed in with the snap of a finger like it normally does. There's no special ritual. It comes in, I state it out loud, and then it's confirmed later that it came true. It's the same way I've predicted every U.S. President elect in my adult life. It's either said to me *(clairaudience)*, shown to me *(clairvoyance)*, I just know *(claircognizance)*, or pieces come in through the various psychic channels one after the other, then a year later it ends up coming to fruition.

Any soul on the planet can do that when they're paying attention to the Divine. Sometimes it just pops in out of nowhere. You don't think much of it until later when it's confirmed to be true. The reason it comes in effortlessly is because you're also not struggling to get an answer. You're just minding your own business going about your day, your vibration is high, then the psychic information slams in. Your ego isn't trying to push for an answer.

It's in hindsight where you say, "Wait a minute, okay that was a hit, but it came in so easily that I didn't recognize it as being guidance at the time."

There are many light workers and warrior of lights threaded around the world working within the political arena to help shift it away from outdated rules that no longer have any benefit in modern times. The political worlds and the people in them have enormous egos. Sometimes their hearts are in the right place, but other times they're operating from a limited space where they are too caught up in it to see clearly. That's the general perception of most of humanity, with the exception being the enlightened ones who see more than the average person. All can become enlightened if they refuse to be limited and seek to understand all aspects of human life at the time they are living it.

I had no idea what my politically based friend was talking about, as I usually don't when it comes to politics. I still never knew who those two Georgia people running were. I read the headline he sent me with his text after it was confirmed to be true, but I did not read the story, as I don't care to absorb gossip or political media specifically. The other point of this is that predictions tend to be accurately foretold when you don't have any emotion invested into the question, which I don't or didn't.

You experience an accurate psychic hit easily in a situation when you don't have emotion invested into it. Your perception is crystal clear without any blocks in the way. You aren't trying to prove anything or get an answer. This is how it often sifts into your consciousness effortlessly. It's when you are completely emotionally detached from it all.

CHAPTER THREE

*Psychically Connecting
and Other Psychic Wisdom*

The higher degree of psychic connectivity, then the higher degree of sensitivities, anxiety, and insomnia one might likely have. This doesn't mean this is the case with every single person, but for the most part it tends to be the pattern. The reason is that a great deal of the ethereal spirit interruptions that take place on the soul's psychic system can cause the side effects of anxiety and insomnia. You could be battling one or both one night knowing that it has no physical explainable origin. This means things like you didn't consume caffeine late in the day that could be the reasonable reason as to why you might be experiencing anxiety or insomnia. If there is no practical cause for the anxiety or insomnia, then it could be that a psychic message is coming through your Clairsentience psychic feeling clair channel. It's your soul's job to put on the detective hat to figure out what it's connected to. It isn't something that anyone else can tell you because the message is coming through your soul and vessel. If someone called you on the phone to tell you something you wouldn't hand it to someone else to say, "What are they trying to tell me?"

When you have a higher degree and range of psychic sensitivity, then walking out into a crowd is challenging because the likelihood of absorbing or sensing erratic energy will be high. No matter how disciplined one is, and no matter how many prayers, shielding, and meditations one does, it is still near impossible to prevent these sorts of psychic stimuli from entering the soul's shield.

Due to the hyper mental and emotional activity and the psychic interference attempting to make its way into my world every second makes life more challenging. It tends to keep me on high alert all night, on and off through the night, or it will yank me awake and on guard. I've had to get up and pace or open the windows to shake it off. This lifelong insomnia was noticed early on in childhood where I'd be abruptly ripped out of sleep and lying up in bed all night acting like a funnel where the psychic vibrations from the ethers were pouring in without me able to stop it.

When planetary aspects are especially intense, then this increases this activity. Some might not believe in the planets having this kind of effect, but the planets are like anything and everyone else where they are functioning on energy. They're not staying relatively in the same area or along similar orchestrations on its own for all eternity. There are things going on in the Universe beyond human physical comprehension that scientists are stumped on.

When someone has a higher degree of psychic sensitivity, then they can feel the rumblings within them that are connected to an erratic planetary movement in the Heavens. When this takes place, then the insomnia grows worse and I'm forced to detach and lay low as much as possible. My Spirit team eventually showed me the connection between what I was experiencing physically and the psychic activity. I had always been aware of both such as how I was feeling physically, and the psychic hits I'd receive, but it took years into my childhood and teenage years before they pointed out that they were connected to one other.

The primary way I receive spirit information is through my Clairaudience clear hearing psychic sense channel. I can think of no further proof of an afterlife or psychic related incidents when I'm hearing my Spirit council talk to me as clearly as anyone else does. They've said things to me that I've replied out loud with to someone only to discover what I said was true or eventually comes true. When this is the regular way you communicate with spirit since childhood, then you are instantaneously used to it. I had never done any special invocation or other psychic taught practice. It was just happening regardless of what I was doing.

You can note by the previous illustrations as to how much work is involved being a fine tuned in psychic sponge. It isn't necessarily a fun thing to absorb so much more than the average person.

As you become more accustomed to the knowledge that your soul is separate from your body, but that it's also connected, then it gets easier to put on the psychic detective hat naturally in order to decipher if what you're experiencing is psychic activity coming through or your ego or something else.

When a medium is called to investigate a haunting in a house, they will not immediately believe the house is haunted. They will first investigate the house to see if it could be something else like a bad pipe or any other physical explain away before then moving that into the next level which is metaphysical and psychic phenomena. This is how you would act while putting on the psychic detective hat.

The following list is an example of some of the things that can explain away the reasons for repetitive anxiety, insomnia, and other negative emotions before you can conclude that it may be psychic activity attempting to come through:

- You received some bad news that day or recently pertaining to your life or someone close to you. This could include things like the loss of a job, relationship breakup, passing of a loved one, legal issues, you have to give a speech/perform, any kind of personal or professional life issue can cause it, etc.

- Examine the foods you've been eating since that will influence your system.

- Did you drink alcohol, smoke/ingest weed, or take any kind of drug that alters your perception.

- Look at the pills or supplements you take each day or might have taken the day you experienced the unexplainable activity.

- Talk to a Doctor to rule out any kind of medical condition or other health issue going on.

When you've ruled out every possible physical reason, then it could be there is psychic activity and paranormal interference coming in. The activity seems to increase at night because you're not distracted by the day to day practical world. You're alone, quiet, and motionless with your thoughts.

When the psychic activity or challenging planetary aspects rear its ugly head, then everything in my life comes to a complete stand still during that time, no writing done, nothing. Most meetings and appointments get cancelled. My strict exercise regimen gets hit, which is unusual since I'll exercise and work out even if I'm dead. If I'm too out of it due to the lack of sleep, then I'm basically useless. I can write easy personal emails and make friend phone calls since they don't care what state I'm in and understand my nature. Other than that, I use that time to lay low and hang out in nature. I will sometimes lie down in a nature setting and allow the nature spirits energy to envelop and heal me.

During those heavy anxiety moments, I also end up on high alert. The fun part or not so fun part is the insomnia gets out of control. Eyes wide open vigilant like an animal. That part is tough because too much psychic overload is flying in at once. When certain testy planetary energy is in motion, I can feel that friction without knowing there is a tough transit going on. Every single time this happens I'm never surprised to find it's an unstable planetary time. There isn't anything I can do to make it stop, as the energy pull is too strong. I just have to ride it out and wait for the storm to pass, and it will lighten up because as it is said...this too shall pass. Being a fine tuned in psychic sponge means you will take the good with the bad. The challenges for me are that it is constantly fluctuating and moving every second that I can feel it.

No spirit writing or work involving my mental aptitude takes place during those aggravated times. That is temporarily closed for refurbishment throughout the days of little sleep. It's different than the regular bouts of spiritual maintenance I do every so often the way you take your car in for maintenance.

When anything is especially intense it's best to be patient and ride it out as much as possible. There have been the rare times when my insomnia goes on for several consecutive nights. I'm laying up all night going mentally crazy and frustrated. I need my disciplined nightly eight hours of sleep to function at optimum levels. I know that I cannot continue one more night like that.

As the sun sets on day four of bad sleep and the darkness comes upon me, I mumble with the horrid anxiety to God and my Spirit team, "Please let me sleep tonight, please, please, please. You have to help. I cannot do this one more night. I can't. Bring everybody in if you have to."

And thank God I finally sleep that night. The despair is vastly great at that point that Divine intervention finally comes through. The sound sleep feels so good that I'm stunned because it feels like being saved.

Once I sleep fully through the night again, then I'm back to peak levels physically, mentally, emotionally, and spiritually. The spirit communication starts flooding in effortlessly and clearly upon waking, then I spend that day catching up on days lost.

It can be strange during that period when spirit communication is quieter, but as soon as I fully sleep it is like the door slams open and the Light floods in again. The second my eyes open after the first night's sleep, then the channel is fully open and in movement. I smile and say, "Thank you, God! I'm back. Rejoice!"

Some measure of good sound sleep is essential to psychically and divinely connect on a deeper level since the physical health is connected to psychic health.

Developing a Relationship with Spirit

I typically feel the strongest jolt when the Holy Ghost moves through me. Those moments are memorable because it's that connection which produces uplifting love, joy, and serenity. I'm not someone known for shedding tears that easily, so when I do in this case it's to illustrate how powerful it is that it shakes me to my soul's core. Swiftly detach from your ego in order to move into the face of Spirit and back out again as needed. It is also how one learns to tame the beast of the darkness of ego

Calling in my Spirit team, I don't typically conduct any special ceremonies, even though I have friends in the spiritual community that do. Everyone has their own ways of doing things they prefer. My method has always been on the simpler side where I just plain ask a guide or angel to come in for me the way I would ask anyone for something.

For example, there was a period in my life where my union with Archangel Michael was growing stronger over time. It wasn't like day one the request for him to be my personal body-soul guard happened and it was done. He was coming in sporadically at first. As time went on my relationship bond with him grew stronger that it became permanent on its own.

At one point we had the conversation where we made this united pact that he would be there permanently. Part of that was also because I get distracted with Earthly life situations and things would happen. If he was already next to me full time, then it was just easier for all of us to have him be part of the team. He wanted to the way God wants a relationship with His children.

There was a point when I made a firm request with Archangel Michael. I invited him in permanently through an invitation that was real the way you would commit to a love partner. You want this, they want this, and it is done. It's also similar to what Christ followers mean when they say, "Have you asked Jesus to come into your heart?"

Some people don't know what that means, but it's like my relationship with Archangel Michael. He becomes a part of you, as Jesus Christ is a part of me as well too. I love Christ's goodness, compassion, and forgiveness. He also helps me stay centered amidst an inner and outer world of chaos.

With Archangel Michael, this is the same way you meet someone new who is going to end up being one of your close friends. It's not like you're instantly best friends on the first day - at least not in my life. It's over time as you're both showing up for the relationship does it start to grow stronger. This was the same way it was with Archangel Michael. It was allowing him in on occasion. I was thinking, "Okay let me see what you can do and why do you want to be here?"

I'd try him on like a pair of jeans that I'd wear occasionally, until I started to wear them every day by spending more time with him, then the relationship bond started to grow. This concept is similar with all I've connected with whether in spirit or in people. It's the same way someone develops any relationship that grows stronger over time. It's spending more time with them and developing a legitimate loyal relationship with them. Today he's part of the air that I breathe. I can't imagine him not being around anymore. I'm too used to his presence and him being around for so long. I would know if he ever left, but he hasn't. I don't think twice about it. I wake up and he's already there even if I'm not coherent yet.

Connecting with Spirit

Some psychics or mediums meditate to get into a trance like state to connect with Spirit. The reason this is an effective method for them is because you're taking at least a few minutes to quiet your mind. You're silencing everything around you in order to have a stronger connection with the Other Side. When you quiet your thoughts and the noise of the outside world, then there is room for Spirit and God to come rushing in. Silencing everything includes removing any traces of negativity from your aura, thoughts, and feelings. If you're upset about something, then this will make it difficult to channel or psychically connect until you let that go and release it. It's best to wait until you're in a relaxed state, even if that means pushing the psychic or medium session to another day.

When you've moved into a state of Divine reception, then the messages and guidance from above flows into your soul through one of your psychic clair sense channels and the connection is made. The first step to getting closer to channeling naturally is by being aware of your own soul and what's outside of it. When you pay attention and notice all the physical distracting noises, then you're able to diminish those sounds. You can do that when you're out and about in a busy area such as a street or at a mall.

Some of the ways of fine tuning your clear hearing Clairaudience psychic sense channel would include listening to sounds that are typically grating on a sensitive person. For the purpose of understanding the distinctive differences between the psychic channel and physical channel it's helpful to do it for a few minutes.

Perk up your ears hearing the noisy symphonic physical sounds coming from the rumbling of cars, tires skidding, garbage cans banging, sirens going off, people talking or shouting, and so on. Notice the distracting energy on your phone and the things you aim your focus towards while on it. The key is being *aware* when it has become a distraction. Once you're able to notice these differences, you not only realize how distracted the planet is, but you're then able to work on dissolving those sounds from your mind to tune it out. When it is tuned out, then the noise level of spirit begins to rise.

Spirit is already loud because they're in the same room with you, but when it sounds as if they're non-existent, far away, or muted, it is because you're either psychically blocked, or the sounds of the physical part of the world are turned up way too high around you. Those sounds include the noise of your own thoughts. It's like you're blasting your music at home while you and a guest are trying to talk over it. You keep saying, "What?" You then turn the music down a little in order to hear one another. Turning the physical distractions down enables one to hear the voice of Heaven clearer.

I've been driving with my music blaring while simultaneously communicating with Spirit effortlessly because their words travel over the chords of music for me. The downfall is I'm blasting the music. There have been times that I'm asking them what they said through telepathy. I'd repeatedly say, "Say that again."

One would finally shout, "Turn it down!"

I'm thrown off reaching to turn my own stereo down, and then I can hear them clearly.

CHAPTER FOUR

Communicating with the Divine

No spirit being in Heaven can interfere with someone's free will choice unless they are specifically requested to by that soul, or if the decision the soul is making will result in their premature death. Heaven sits back and watches human souls paint themselves into a corner hoping a rush of clarity seeps in. This is why you must formerly request Spirit intervention, guidance, and assistance. When you invite any spirit in Heaven to step in, then your life becomes a bit easier than if you didn't ask for Divine assistance. Challenges are inevitable on Earth, but moving through those challenges more swiftly helps when you have your Spirit team on your side.

Pushing for an answer from the Divine will block the ability to pick up on incoming messages and guidance. Anything connected to fear will sever the connection line. Psychic communication hits filter in when you're in a calm non-judgmental uplifting state. You let go of any resistance while avoiding the desire to push for an answer. Work on regular vibration raising exercises that include clearing your mind, body, and soul of any toxic debris. This can be done in meditation or stillness, as well as through the elimination of vices that you know are holding you back from achieving.

Sit or stand in silence releasing intrusive toxic thoughts and feelings until you are a clear vessel to absorb Divine input. Seeing or hearing celestial wisdom clearly is restricted if you're constantly listening to or paying attention to the noise around you. The noise is everybody else, the media, your negative thoughts and feelings, and the physical concrete world sounds. Physical world sounds are things like car noises, airplanes, and crowd chatter. This doesn't include the sounds of the ocean waves crashing and hitting the sand, or the wind blowing against the side of a mountain. Turn the obtrusive physical sounds all off if you want to truly hear God.

Find a quiet place to sit and be still in prayer or meditation. Allow your Spirit team to know what's bothering you and what it is that you would like help with. You can also ask if there is anything you need to know that day. If you can get out into a nature locale, then this is ideal whether it's your backyard or a park. This would be somewhere you can be alone in God's paradise to release. Take continuous slow deep breaths in and release it all, because you don't need to carry that harsh energy around. This is done until you feel more relaxed and centered.

When you feel defensive, emotionally hurt, full of anger, depressed, then Spirit always advises you to get out in nature. The word nature needs to be emphasized because going outdoors to a crowded mall is not what is going to center you. Find balance in those instances and detoxify your soul and body.

If you're doing this at home, then open the space around you to bring in your Spirit team. You can do this through meditation or quiet time. Play uplifting powerful spiritual background music, light candles, incense, or whatever you choose to bring you and your soul into a centered space. Be patient, give it time, and call them in.

If you pull cards to help with the connection, then you can't pull cards quickly and assume the guides are there. Call them in and give them time to come in, and then pull the cards. Don't control what you hope the answer will be, but allow it to flow in when you're in an emotionally detached space. Release any unforgiveness in your heart about yourself or others. Let it go by visualizing it moving out of you and upward towards Heaven for transmutation, so that the weight of that toxin is released.

Paying attention to the messages and guidance coming in from your Spirit team can help you navigate through your Earthly life much more swiftly. They can help you recognize when something in your life is intended to end, or when you're to act on a circumstance, and so on. They can assist when you learn to pay attention and recognize those hits they're giving you. No one can do that for you.

You may go to a psychic reader for answers, but may not always get the messages you seek. This is because in the end it is up to you to decide how your life is going to go and what decision you are to make. You're not a puppet on strings that can be controlled by another being. An impeccable psychic reader, healer, and counselor can give you clarity and direction, but it is up to you to make the ultimate decision as to the best option. It is up to you to make that decision for your life. It is your life and you are the manager and CEO of it. This is the same way an extraordinary CEO at a company will hear other input or ideas from the employees, but ultimately it will be the CEO's decision as to the best course of action. This is the same way you manage your life. You may bounce ideas off as to what you should do about something with other people. You'll take that into account, and mull it around in your mind, ask your Spirit team for guidance on what to do, and then eventually make the decision based on where you're getting the strongest vibrational pull.

You can minimize the difficulties in your life when you ask for heavenly help and guidance, and then tune in to that still place within where these answers reside. You don't need someone else to give you confirmation because you have the confirmation. God didn't make it difficult where you have to go to people for the answers. You were instilled with built in psychic sense clair channels so that you can be in constant communication with your Spirit team any time, day, or night.

Take a deep breath in, focus on centering yourself, elevate your faith believe, and mentally strip away any fear-based thoughts that get in the way of preventing blessings from falling into your vicinity. You are not alone or being ignored even when if it sometimes feels that way. Allow any negative toxicity around you to dissolve away. This will crank up the volume of the angels and then God comes flowing in effortlessly.

If the answer is not present at that moment, then give it time. Pay attention as you move forward in life for the answer. Sometimes the answer doesn't come in right away when you ask for it. It can come in at a later date. It can be days, weeks, months, and even years later. Although, the latter is rare, the years later is typically when the event you're asking about isn't going to take place until further into the future. Because it's so far out, you're unable to psychically pick up on it. It's only as you grow closer to the date does the information begin to become clearer and stronger without breaking away from that energy vibration.

Be granted the wisdom to understand why events beyond your control take place. Let God and the angels be your driver when it feels as if you have no more strength to persevere. They will re-charge and re-ignite your soul when you request it. Talk to God and your Spirit team daily and pour your heart out. You are heard whether you believe you are or not. You can communicate your request with your thoughts, in prayer, out loud, and in writing. It doesn't matter how you communicate, but that you do.

What's been on your mind lately causing you inner turmoil? This is a clue as to what you need to let go of. Have the intention of letting go of it and releasing it to Heaven for positive transformation. Unhappiness in any area of your life is also a way to discover what it is you need to change. Have you forever been unhappy with your job? What action steps are you comfortable with making to change this? Pour your heart out to God and your Spirit team as to what's bothering you and ask for guidance on steps they want you to take. Often when you ask for guidance you may be requested to act with something that will help bring it closer.

Write to Your Spirit Team

One highly effective way of communicating with your Spirit team is through writing. When you communicate with any higher being in Heaven, you are communicating with God by default since they are extensions of Him.

When you sit down to write out what you'd like to say to those on the Other Side, there is a stronger intention and force behind it. This force intention is energy that carries solid weight. You find your intention to be stronger with your thoughts, while someone else prefers to say it out loud.

I communicate using the various ways one can communicate, but I've found it efficient when I write it out. Part of this is because I'm a writer and it's easier for me to communicate through the written word. I'll sit down and open a new email message box and address it as you would with anyone.

"Dear...."

I'm notorious for emailing myself hundreds of letters to God, my Spirit team, and myself.

You can write a letter to a departed loved one who you miss dearly, because they can read what you are writing when you grant them permission. The addressing of the letter is granting them permission to read it. When you request heavenly support or guidance, you are heard the instant you call out to them. It doesn't matter if the request is big or small because you are heard regardless. You cannot get away with a lie in Heaven the way you can with others on the planet. You might write or say one thing, but what's in your heart is what's heard and understood to be the truth by any spirit being.

Sometimes when you're in a discombobulated state, it's easier to sit down and write it out in an email, on a notepad, or wherever you usually write. I email my letters to God and my Spirit team to myself and file it away in a folder marked, "Angels". This is where thousands of letters and private communications with my team live. I do the same with jotting down psychic information I'm getting and emailing it to myself. When I've reverted to those emails, I've found everything that I jotted down ended up coming to fruition, but I had forgot about it when I originally jotted it down.

Writing instead of speaking or thinking the words can help you articulate it more efficiently. It forces you to stop for a moment and type out what you're experiencing. This is also therapeutic giving you a sense of calm. Any sudden feeling of serenity is the angels easing the stress you're feeling as you write it out. You've also moved into a state of stillness, which helps them to get to work on you easier when you're less erratic or restless. It can also help you make sense of the words you're putting out into the Universe.

As a writer I find writing assists with bringing on clarity and focus, but not everyone is comfortable with writing something out. I have friends who are naturally sociable verbally, or do radio shows and podcasts, so they prefer to speak the words rather than write them out. These are the gifted speakers that dominate through voice rather than the pen.

One friend like that has said in the past repeatedly, "I talk. You write."

Those friends tend to leave me long voice messages that cut them off since there is no more space. They have to call back and continue in another voice box. There are times I call them to say, "I want to talk about this, but I'm going to write you first, then we'll discuss it."

Everyone has different ways of communicating from one another that dominate. This is the same way all souls have varying psychic gifts from one another that also govern. In the end it doesn't matter how you communicate with Heaven, but that you do.

Tuning into Divine Messages

The clearest way of knowing if it's a Divine message or not is if it ends up coming true. The other ways are it's felt with a layer of uplifting love around it even when it's a warning. This may seem like common sense, but you would be surprised that the obvious answer is not what is generally thought of or known to be the one. Some believe that psychic input must be complicated and difficult to distinguish, but the truth is ones Guides and Angels do their best to try and convey it to you as simply as possible. When that tap on the head to pay attention to something doesn't work, then they try other ways such as throwing up repeated symbols and signs to get you to notice it. If God has been knocking on your door for some time, then take the hint and open it and let Him in.

A Divine message continuously comes in until you pick up on the repetitive theme happening. This prompts you to take notice and focus on it. It will continue to come in periodically as it pushes you to action. Take steps towards making something happen if that's the gut hunch you continue to receive. The voice of the ego will cause some form of sabotage even if it's miniscule, whereas Heavenly messages will never cause drama or harm to you or anyone else around you. A Divine message brings good, positive, high vibrational feelings to you or another person even if it's a warning.

When it feels like your connection with Spirit is non-existent where you're not picking up on anything, then that's typically a sign that you're too weighed down or distracted by physical and external matters or desires. If you're experiencing any form of negativity whether in emotions or thought processes, then that's a block. Being mired in any of kind of physical distraction will temporarily dim or cut off the communication line with the Other Side. It makes it seem as if you're not picking up on anything or you're being ignored, which is never true because Spirit is always communicating with you regardless if you can hear them or not.

The Spirit communication gradually opens up when you start releasing and letting go of unnecessary toxic distractions, as well as negative feelings and thoughts. If you're not hearing messages or guidance, then examine your life and make note of what's bothering you or distracting you in the physical world. Work on acknowledging it, then releasing it and letting it go. The answer as to what is creating the block is usually right in front of you. If you have more than one issue bothering you, then you have to let it all go one by one in order to allow the communication to come rushing in. Lifestyle shifts and changes will need to be made in areas where you are able to make them. Some changes you'll be able to make right away, while others will be more challenging, or it will take longer depending on what it is.

Seeking Psychic Input from Others

When one thinks of psychics, they immediately connect that to someone being able to predict your future. Your future is set based on your soul contract coupled with your free will choices. You are creating and designing your own future. Do you need someone to tell you when you'll meet your next soul partner? Or when you'll move into a new home or get that new job? Avoid getting stuck in the cycle of waiting around for something to transpire. Be proactive in making what you want to happen.

You might go to an intuitive friend or a psychic to help give you the messages and guidance you seek that you're unclear on, but it's up to you to come to the answer on your own time. Jumping ahead to get the answer instead of doing the work by moving through the troubling experience can be met with disappointment or confusion.

I've heard or read from others that a psychic reading they had was inaccurate or didn't give them the information they sought out. While others may say that it helped give them peace of mind, but only time will tell if it ends up coming to fruition. If the reading helped give you a lift, then its job and intention were beneficial. Sometimes talking it out with someone or receiving an objective point of view from someone who cares can help immensely.

When your life is not where you want it to be, then you seek out a psychic reader hoping to give you some good news. It's rare that one will go to a reader when they're on cloud nine on all physical aspects of their life from career, love, finances, health, and home. If you go to a poor psychic, then you can get sucked into the reader giving you false hope. You want to avoid the scam readers. Those might be the ones that overcharge you for their services, or tell you there is a curse around you that only they can remove if you pay them more money. Avoid readers that consistently try to get you to purchase more stuff from them. Those who are where they want to be will go to a reader if they love the craft or desire some fun uplifting soul affirming guidance, since everyone is a work in progress. There are endless stories of people who have a great career, tons of money, and a beautiful love relationship, yet they still feel unhappy inside or spiritually bankrupt. This only further cements that true authentic happiness starts from within the core of your soul, then you expand that allowing it to work its way outwardly.

Noticing Divinely Guided Synchronicities

Notice the little synchronicities placed in front of you by Spirit that lead to what you're intended to act on next. Bumping into the same person repeatedly isn't always an accident. This doesn't necessarily mean colleagues where it's expected that you would naturally be bumping into them daily, but it does mean that person you continuously bump into in passing on a beach, while shopping, at a park, on the sidewalk, at a coffee and tea shop, at the gym, and so on. Consider if that person continues to notice you with a mutual glimmer in their eye as if to positively acknowledge you in a way they don't seem to be doing with anyone else around. Maybe it's a new friendship, a love relationship, or acquaintance soul mate intended to relay a message to you that positively enlightens or shifts the direction on your path. Perhaps it's a new business networking connection, or maybe it's the next long-term love relationship. Be open to the signs and symbols floating around your auric world that comes through as messages from other people. Sometimes these other people are not initially aware they are messengers. They too are picking up on the guidance and messages from their own Spirit team.

While driving one morning, I was listening to a popular open-minded preacher in an earpiece. At the same time on my car stereo I had rock music playing low, which I could hear in my left ear that was open to hear external sounds. The preacher pulled out a verse and said the number "seventeen". At the same time the rock singer on the stereo sang the word, "seventeen". The synchronous way that the number seventeen was said at the same time alerted me to pay attention to it. This is one example in how these signs and symbols sift in front of you to take notice.

When I mentioned this was an open-minded preacher, it wasn't to be confused with those hate filled vengeance preacher's that cast judgment on people, which I would never absorb or listen to. This preacher focuses on love never having uttered a hate filled word before. The good ones are out there when you search for them.

Endings and New Beginnings

Your Spirit team guides you down the best path for your highest self. They'll send signals of warning when you're in danger or if you're insisting on going down a road that's less desirable. If something doesn't work out, then look at that as a blessing where it didn't happen for a reason. There could've been hidden dangers that you were not noticing or paying attention to.

Let's say you or someone you know is going to meet a potential date with someone new you haven't met before. You find you have to push yourself to meet up with this person, or you feel unexcited with challenging feelings around that, then this is a clue not to go. I know that might sound like common sense, but when you're in the throes of a decision like that you'd be surprised to find the ego isn't paying attention to the best course of action. You're wrestling with indecisiveness about it. Unless you're filled with excitement, then don't waste your time or the other persons. Some have found they would ignore that guidance, go on the meeting only to realize immediately that it's going to be disastrous or a waste of time. As you're driving back home, you're thinking, "Why did I go? I knew it was a mistake beforehand. If I race home, I'll be able to catch the late-night show."

If an ex-lover is moving out of the country, the state, or far away from you, then look at that in a positive way. If you're single, the angels could be moving this person away from you so that you are open to a new person they are bringing in that is more aligned with who you are today. You may think you've been ready and had moved on from a relationship, but Spirit can see the residual ex energy still lingering in your aura. They have to get rid of this ex physically, so that this new person they want to bring you can come in.

This same concept applies to anyone intended to come in, including friendships, acquaintances, or new business connections. At the time it's happening you might be filled with sadness or grief not wanting this ex to leave, but as time goes on and new brighter circumstances come into your life, you realize why this person had to be sent away. You had outgrown them, but didn't know it because they were still hanging around. It was only after they left that you discover your time with them had long ended. That person's essence in your life was holding you back from these other brighter experiences screaming to get in, even if you disagree with that notion at the time.

Only in hindsight after time has passed do you start to realize the changes that took place after the previous circumstance was completely dissolved. Sometimes this ex is drawn away because they have personal soul lessons they need to learn. Other times it's Heaven's way of helping you become less dependent on someone else and to start relying on you. You can't do that when this other person is still hanging around.

Life is full of beginnings and endings, doors closing and windows opening. This kind of drastic change can bring on all sorts of emotions from excitement to fear depending on whether or not the change is purposely done at your own hands or if it was the Universe that was shutting the door on things you weren't ready to part with. When that happens, it is done so for a reason, even if that reason is not yet evident. One of the many ways to change and grow is to transform completely. This gets you out of any stuck energy like a rut or stagnancy. This way you can move onto brighter pastures and circumstances that want to come into your life.

CHAPTER FIVE

The Psychic Clair Senses

When any spirit being in Heaven communicates with you, the tone is direct, full of love, and uplifting, even if they are warning you of danger. They communicate firmly, while your ego communicates with uncertainty, anger, or any other disapproving negative emotion. Your Spirit team will never advise you to do something that ends up hurting you or someone else.

Your Spirit Guide, Guardian Angel, God, or any entity or spirit communicates with you through your senses. Your senses are not to be confused with your physical senses, but these senses are interwoven between your physical body and your soul. These senses are also referred to as *clairs*, which means 'clear'. It is being a clear psychic channel with the planes and dimensions beyond the Earth plane. There are over a dozen clair points in your soul, but there are four primary clairs. Many have one or two dominate clairs, but those who work on opening the other clairs have all four clair channels opened up and even some of the others. It takes work and a lifestyle change to keep them open since a clair can easily dim or close depending on your life circumstance. Since you are an energy vessel, when they turn to anger or sadness, then this is simultaneously closing the psychic clairs. If you are suddenly lifted in grand feelings of joy, love, and peace, then your psychic clair senses begin to expand. How you think, feel, and navigate Earthly life influences both your spiritual and physical body.

Your clairs are also considered to be an extra sensory perception, because the clair senses reach places beyond what your physical senses can do. You hear the voices of spirit, but your physical ears are not hearing them. It is your spirit soul senses that hear them. The extra sensory part of the equation is the extra psychic sense that is beyond the physical.

You receive a telepathic hit when you are thinking of someone you haven't communicated with for some time, then suddenly they contact you out of the blue to say they were thinking of you and wanted to reach out. You might say to them, "How weird as I was just thinking about you!"

Your Spirit team is implanting this psychic information in your mind for a reason. Maybe it's to remind you of the good that existed in that person and how they made you feel. Perhaps it's to bring you both together again to resolve old issues and bring the connection to proper closure. Or it could be that you or this other person has information or wisdom that is passed onto you when you have that conversation. Sometimes it can simply be a good, positive, fun discussion that uplifts you out of a mood you've been in or it's you that uplifts them. When a great deal amount of time passes with no contact from someone, then often that gives both parties clarity they were unable to see while in the connection.

You both have a telepathic communication line flowing back and forth between your souls. Telepathy is Claircognizant communication that is verbally unspoken. Claircognizance is a clear knowing about something you're not versed in. It is also the area that thoughts are transmitted psychically that later comes true. Telepathy might be where someone is deeply thinking of you and is unknowingly transmitting the informational thoughts to you. This wakes you up to suddenly be thinking of them. You hadn't for quite some time, and then out of nowhere they flash into your mind. You later discover when you reach out to them that they had been thinking of you the week prior.

Some have admitted they've noticed that when you're thinking of someone that they are likely thinking of you. While this can certainly be true, typically one of you ends up reaching out to the other at some point not long afterwards. The telepathy has a measure of psychic foresight to it. You can also have telepathic communication with a soul on the Other Side such as a departed loved one. The departed loved one is sending you a psychic signal that they are around you and guiding you on something. You then suddenly get a strong flush of their presence in your mind that you hadn't for a while. This could be where you are also missing them deeply out of nowhere. This deeply missing them component is a signal that they're with you at that moment. You're feeling their presence so deeply that it might sadden you because you're missing them, but that should be a joyful feeling to know they are doing amazing and have stopped in to say hello. They didn't intend to sadden you or upset you.

It is assumed that someone with psychic abilities has a rare gift, but these gifts have been given to every living soul including the most rigid Atheist or most heinous human being on the planet plagued with Darkness. They have psychic abilities deep down in their soul. No one is more special than anyone else where psychic abilities are concerned. Everyone is psychic and has the ability to connect. Some connect easier than others or in different ways than someone else does. Someone might have a stronger Clairvoyance channel than someone that has strong Clairaudience. Everyone has these psychic clair gifts, but each person's gifts might vary. It's up to the individual to discover which of their psychic clair senses are the strongest. Some people might not have to work as hard to re-open their clair senses or they live a life that has minimal blocks in their environment.

All souls have psychic gifts, but you're not paying attention to this Divine input of information if you are buried deeply in the physical world. Living on this testy battlefield of a planet comes with an array of blocks that reduces your psychic gifts. The good news is that one's psychic gifts never go away. They might dim or darken, but they're accessible to anyone who chooses to re-awaken that part of their soul.

The Four Psychic Clair Senses

The Four Main psychic clair senses are *Clairvoyance, Clairaudience, Clairsentience,* and *Claircognizance.* Read the basic descriptions in the coming pages in this chapter in order to pinpoint what best describes you. The descriptions are the basic generalizations of how to recognize you or someone else as having that clair.

The psychic clair senses are present deep in the DNA of your soul since it is a part of you, but it just needs to be worked out if it's unnoticed. It's the same way someone who goes to the gym regularly to stay healthy, fit, and build muscle. If they suddenly stopped going or working out and exercising, then the muscle would lessen over time and one's health would gradually deteriorate. Psychic clair senses work in that same respect. You treat it like a muscle that needs to be built, strengthened, and taken care of regularly. Your physical body can build muscle or tone when you exercise. Your clair channels work in the same way. When you regularly exercise a psychic clair, then you build its muscle over time. You do the work out maintenance as you would if you were exercising regularly to strengthen your physical body and overall health.

Clairvoyance

Clairvoyance means "Clear Seeing" (or "Clear Vision"). You have clairvoyance if you receive visual images, cues, or impressions sifting through your mind's eye. Your mind's eye is also called the third eye. The third eye looks like an eye and is located between your two physical eyes, but slightly raised above it. It cannot be seen with your physical eyes. If you close your eyes and focus on seeing your third eye, then you should be able to see it with practice. It is behind the area between where your eyes are located turned right side up. When you see violet light around the third eye area or in your peripheral vision, then this is a positive indicator that your clairvoyance is opening up.

The psychic images are projected through clairvoyance like a mini movie playing for you. Someone might be born into this lifetime blind through their physical eyes, yet they receive powerful psychic visual impressions through their third eye. The third eye is where your clairvoyance channel shows you the psychic messages and guidance your Spirit team is communicating to you. You would know whether or not the visual images were your imagination or a psychic hit if what you're seeing ends up coming true.

Clairvoyant messages often need to be decoded. The reason is the communication is being brought to you through a moving visual picture or still image. The significance of the illustration does not always mean what is being shown to you. It is up to you to decipher what the message is supposed to be about. You might be shown a ship leaving a harbor, which might make one assume they are going on a cruise. The obvious answer is not always the right one when it comes to clairvoyance. The ship could be a metaphor to how you're feeling rather than a literal message. Having psychic senses, especially clairvoyance, requires one to be able to delve deep. It isn't enough to open up the psychic clairs, but there's a great deal of regular work going on that you're expected to do.

If you are someone that has vivid dreams that you recall long after you've woken up from sleep, then this is a sign that you may have strong clairvoyant abilities without realizing it.

Here's one minor example of clairvoyance. You are asleep and having a dream where you are walking the streets at night. There are hundreds of snakes and cobras moving about around you attacking everyone except you. As a clairvoyant it's your goal to decipher what this moving image means, because it's highly unlikely that this is an image showing you of what's to come. It can mean that you're a rising successful star in your profession who is untouchable, but this is not met without enemies. There is someone or many who are or will be jealous of you. This could be one way to interpret the dream of the snakes attacking everyone around except you. You might have to do some research to find out the significance symbolism of snakes as well as snakes that attack, and all of the details in the dream, such as it being nighttime. It's a good idea to keep a journal or notepad near you to jot down your dreams or any random psychic hits you receive throughout the day. As mentioned earlier, I email it to myself so that it's recorded down for later viewing. You will forget the psychic hits unless it's written down.

I saw the love interest that was coming to me in grave detail. I jotted down the person's name, stats, job, the time frame they were showing up, and even the birthdate! I filed it away emailing it to myself and went on with life. A year later I developed a crush on someone that I felt a strong pull towards immediately and I know they felt it too, because I could psychically feel that. Months later as I got to know this person, I was suddenly prompted to go back to one of my readings a year earlier. I was stunned to find out this person was the love interest! Everything matched up from name, birthdate, job, stats, height, build, eyes, hair, and on and on. I had forgot about the reading because I'm doing dozens of reads a week that are getting filed away. Moral of the story is to write down what you get as soon as possible. A well-known medium friend of mine has said to me in private, "You read better for yourself than I've seen anyone do."

But I'm also a believer that if I can, then anyone can if they tune in and focus.

You have clairvoyance if you also see spirits from the Other Side. It looks as if they're in front of you or to the side of you in your peripheral vision. They don't look like physical human beings, which is the way they're portrayed in some Hollywood films. They look more opaque or translucent. You may even see them as lights or sparkling lights in your peripheral vision. When I clairvoyantly see a spirit initially, they will look like a human being for the first few seconds until I do a double take, then I realize they are translucent. They're not translucent on the Other Side, but the way it comes through the spirit planes in front of you it appears as if they are.

For some your conscious will block your abilities to see spirits for fear of seeing a deceased spirit looking the way they had when they passed away. They might have died a violent death such as a murder or car accident. The spirit is fine and doesn't look like that on the Other Side, but they can appear how they choose to for anybody. This sometimes includes how they looked when they died or the age they passed away. If they died a violent death, then they might appear that way to be recognizable to you.

Someone's grandfather passed away at ninety-two years old, but when he crossed over, he appears in top form looking like a young twenty-five to thirty-four-year-old human being. He might appear ninety-two years old in human years to a psychic medium in order to relay what is coming through on a reading for someone. You might not know who the medium was talking about if your grandfather appeared the way he did at twenty-five years old. He would look significantly different if he appeared as he does on the Other Side.

Generally, the deceased loved one is brought to top form back home and appears stronger and more vibrant than ever before. In human age it tends to be late twenties to early thirties. Any human physical, mental, or emotional issue is dissolved when you cross over. For example, if someone had to wear glasses their entire Earthly life. Those glasses are no longer needed when they cross over. If someone suffered from depression or mental health issues, then when they cross over, they are brought back to their natural soul state of all love, joy and peace in a big vibrant way.

Clairvoyant messages can also come through your psychic channel as symbols, numbers, colors, letters, words, and pictures that have a meaning to you or someone else. It can be something from the past, the present, or future. Those who have clairvoyance tend to daydream as well. These daydreams may be random, or they may be images of what's happened, what's happening, or what's to come. They see their own future as if it's a vision board of what is to take place at some point. When someone tells a clairvoyant friend a story, the clairvoyant is living the story as if it's happening to them personally. They see the story as if they are the main character. The clairvoyance channel is incredibly alive that it can be challenging in this way to mentally see what someone is describing to you.

Clairsentience

Clairsentience means "clear feeling" (or "clear sensing"). This is when you feel the psychic messages, guidance and impressions coming through you from Spirit and Heaven. Those that have high clairsentience might walk into a building and feel as if all eyes are on them even though no one is looking. Or they might pick up on an uneasy sense of foreboding that tells them to get out of a particular place or away from someone. They perceive danger is about to happen and then it soon does. They also intuit good stuff that is coming into their vicinity as well, which ends up happening. You might have a strong upbeat joyful feeling that the job you want is going to come about and then this later comes true.

Having clairsentience is when your Spirit team communicates messages and guidance through your feelings, emotions, and senses. It's not something that is heard or seen, but felt within you. Those that consider themselves to be highly intuitive, empathic, or super sensitive are more likely to have a strong Clairsentience psychic channel.

You might be the kind of person that becomes emotionally upset when someone you're interested in romantically is not reciprocating that interest. You text and email this person regularly hoping to illicit a response that is satisfying to you. Yet the object of your desire is casual in their reply when communicating with you, or they continuously drop the ball with your text dalliance. You question whether or not they're truly interested in you. When they throw you a bone and click 'like' on one of your social media posts, then you're suddenly on cloud nine believing they're interested in you. Soon you grow upset when a week has passed, and you haven't heard from them. Repeatedly becoming emotionally upset over something like this comes from the ego, but the emotional sensitivities associated with the upset is a sign that you could have a higher probable degree of clairsentience, but it just it needs to be brought out and controlled.

The emotional upset experienced can also be a clairsentient message that this person is not as interested in you as you were hoping. They might be interested in you on some level, but not in the way you crave. Deep down you know this to be true since it came through your clairsentience psychic sense, but your ego is reactive because it's not what you want. This is also an example of the tug of war between the ego and the psychic sense part of you. To endure keeping this connection alive would only frustrate and depress you. When they give you a rare 'like' or comment on your social media page, or they text you, then this catapults you into feeling as if this person is deeply interested in you. The truth may be they like you on some level, but not in the deep way you're craving.

Pay attention to your feelings since this can be an accurate barometer gauge on what is real and what is not. When you move your ego out of the way, then you're able to decipher the accuracy of Heaven's incoming messages through clairsentience.

Someone with clairsentience can be all over the place when it comes to feelings and emotions. You will want to ensure you work on well-being exercises that keep your emotional balance on an equal footing in order to communicate with Heaven efficiently. With clairvoyance, the clairvoyant will hear someone telling them a story and will see the story as if it were a movie and actually happening to them. With clairsentience, the person listening to the story will 'feel' what's happening in the story as if it's happening to them. Sometimes if it's a horrific story the clairsentient may say, "You have to stop."

This is because the feelings they're experiencing over the story are so overwhelming it's as if it's happening to them. Clairsentience beings can feel things deeper than most.

Gifted actors tend to have highly calibrated clairsentience clair channels, which enable them to effectively inhabit a character as if they're walking in that person's shoes.

If others accuse you of always being too sensitive, then this is a clue that you may have a high degree of clairsentient gifts ready to be awakened. When others find you too sensitive, it can be because every little thing that someone says or does bothers you. Your ego is unable to control your reaction. When you develop your clairsentience and understand how it works, how to shield yourself, and put self-improvement into practice, then you react less to every shred that comes your way. You're able to manage it more efficiently over time with spiritual and emotional maturity.

When you have clairsentience, you receive hunches and gut feelings about situations and circumstances. You might have a gut feeling that you should've gone down one road, but you ignored that gut sense and went in the other direction where you find that a less than desirable circumstance takes place. Some have said, "I should've listened to that hunch I felt. And I knew what I was supposed to do, but I ignored it."

This is a sign that you're receiving guidance and messages from your Spirit team. Those with clairsentience absorb other people's energy like a sponge. They may find it difficult to be in overcrowded areas. They would be the ones that complain that it's challenging standing in a grocery store line due to the heavy input of other people's energies around them. The clairsentient can sense the emotions and feelings of others; therefore, they can intuit what someone is going through without words. At the same time, it can be psychic overload, which is why those with strong clairsentience keep to themselves or stay away from crowds or large amounts of people as much as possible.

Clairsentient people feel every little nuance around them to the point that it often becomes uncomfortable and draining. This prompts them to take frequent breaks of alone time. They'll be the one that leaves the party or event early as they can only handle people's energies in small doses. They sense everything around them from people's emotions to what's to come for someone. Their internal feelings are all over the place like a roller coaster ride every second. They might give the illusion they are extremely put together on the outside, but on the inside, they're wrestling with a roller coaster of emotions that constantly ebb and flow like the ocean. They could be prone to be a bit jumpy as if someone moved quickly behind them. They turn around to find no one there. Clairsentient people are ridden with anxiety, nervousness, and have a fight or flight response to any and all around them. Imagine absorbing everyone else's feelings being poured into you and how that might make you feel.

A clairsentient being feels the answers, messages, and guidance filtering through them from Heaven. The way Heaven communicates with this person is through their feeling sense. Someone that senses something specific has happened, is happening, or is going to happen is someone with a strong clairsentient psychic channel.

Clairaudience

Clairaudience means "Clear Hearing" (or Clear Audio). When you're clairaudient you hear the voices of God and your Spirit team. You can differentiate between the voices of you, your ego, and the voices of Spirit and Heaven by its accuracy of the message being relayed. Crazy voices are the ego or someone with an unbalanced mental health state pushing them to do something that isn't desirable such as harming someone. Spirit will never communicate to someone to hurt, hate, or harm anyone at all ever. They also won't advise someone on how to achieve fame or get rich quick schemes – things like that.

When you look back during the times you were in danger, you might recall when you received a heavenly message through your clairaudience channel. When there is an urgent situation that could put you in danger, you might hear a voice shout to you to run, which quickly gets you up and going. You later protest that if you didn't run who knows what might've happened.

Clairaudience is one of my dominate clairs where I hear voices, words, and sounds coming in through one of my ears that later comes true. Their voices are sometimes in unison or individually. The voices can sound disembodied or as if they're standing next to you. The voices are different than your own, but there may be cases when it might sound like you.

One of my ears is partially deaf, but the irony is that's the ear where spirits voices are crystal clear. I've been an avid music listener since I was a child, and I had pipe dreams of being a rocker or musician. I could live without communicating in any form except through the sounds of music. I hear the words clearly from my Spirit team as I'm listening to the notes and chord changes in a song. The words of Spirit flow and interweave through these notes effortlessly. My clairaudience channel works like an old radio where you're changing the station between the static to receive a clear station.

Every so often a ringing in my ear buzzes and it's a sound that hasn't been detected to be a medical issue. This buzzing is the sound of my Spirit team downloading important information into my consciousness that is discovered to be of importance at a later date. The pattern was realized when every time the buzzing took place something of importance that comes to light psychically shows up in my consciousness afterwards. I've relayed messages to a stranger about someone that has passed on that they know, but who I don't. I've said their loved one's name as it is the name I hear through clairaudience. My psychic history has seemed to show that I nail names and time frames, which tend to be on the more challenging side to do. I wish I could offer some concrete instructions on how to do that, but I don't do any exercises. It's just always come in naturally even when I'm not trying to get anything.

Hearing things about others through clairaudience is what has convinced me that there is more to this life than this plane. I'm communicating with someone on the Other Side who I do not know. The stranger I'm relaying the information to informs me that it's someone they knew who passed away. There is no way I can know this information when it's a stranger, but they have confirmed that what I've told them is true. I hear the deceased person talking in my ear. They are not dead in the sense that one believes someone to be dead. They reside alive and well in a different plane than the Earthly plane. Having these occurrences happen sporadically throughout my life since I was old enough to construct sentences had convinced me early on that this is not the end.

Those with higher ranges of clairaudience tend to also be musicians and singers. They might not be aware of it, but they can certainly develop it. If someone's work is connected to sounds and music, then they hear guidance and messages through the notes of these sounds. Ludwig Van Beethoven composed some of the most memorable and beloved music in history, yet he was also considered deaf. This irony begged others to question, "How on Earth did he write these incredible pieces if he is deaf?"

His hearing was faint, but spirit infused his clairaudience channel with music that has long been remembered over the centuries.

Other clairaudients might find that they mumble or talk to themselves and yet they're perfectly sane. They are having conversations with spirit without realizing it or trying to. It's talking to someone the way you talk to a particular friend on the phone. The conversations or talking isn't random and full of gibberish. It is clear concise information that later proves true or is positively helpful to that person or another.

The voices a clairaudient hears are not to be mistaken with the voices that others hear instructing them to murder their Children or cause any other harm, hurt, or hate on someone else. They inaccurately claim the words come from God or that God is showing up in the form of that person. The voices of God, Heaven, and Spirit will never instruct someone to hate, harm, or hurt themselves or anyone else. Those are the voices of that person's ego, the Darkness, or Devil as some call it. The voices coming from God are always empowering, uplifting, and full of love even when warning of danger. These are traits that are the opposite of an individual claiming to be of God. Heaven instructs or offers messages and guidance that can help that individual or another person positively and with compassion. Those who are clairaudient will hear things that no one else can hear, which later come true.

Claircognizance

Claircognizance means "Clear Knowing" (or Clear Knowledge). Someone with claircognizance will receive messages and guidance from Heaven being dropped into their mind. They will typically announce something that they have no way of knowing only to find that it comes true. When asked how they know this information, they will be unable to efficiently answer that question. They have no idea how they came to receive this sudden insight. The messages sifted into their consciousness seemingly out of nowhere.

Someone might say, "You're absolutely right! How did you know that?"

You'll look at them stunned and say, "I don't know. It just came to me."

Those that have strong claircognizance are the bigger thinkers of the world that bring positive change, such as inventors, scientists, teachers, speakers, research investigators, and writers. These people are usually skeptical about where the information is coming from. Some of them might not believe in God or an afterlife. They need concrete evidence before they become a believer, but even then, they still function with some measure of uncertainty at times always looking for concrete tangible proof.

When someone exhibits claircognizance, they have the presence of being in control and in command. They always seem to have the answer for anything and everything that ends up assisting others in a positive way. Their mind is constantly turned on and in motion making mental lists that periodically come to them all day long throughout each day. When you receive a lightning bolt of an idea out of the blue that brings you positive success, then you can be assured that your claircognizant channel is functioning in top form.

Perhaps you're driving through a new town with a friend only to discover that you're both lost. You ask for heavenly assistance and you suddenly know to turn left up ahead. When you turn left you both find that you're no longer lost, and you know where you are. This is an example of receiving assistance through your claircognizant channel. It's receiving Divine guidance and inspiration into your consciousness that helps you know things that you didn't five minutes prior.

On another scale someone with deep claircognizance would be someone like Alexander Graham Bell's connection with the invention of the telephone or Thomas Edison and electricity. The information and data for those creations dropped into his consciousness.

Claircognizance is "knowing" the answer to something. You know what's coming up ahead or how something works. The information sifts into your consciousness from seemingly out of nowhere. This later proves true or is positively helpful to you or someone else.

Someone with claircognizance tends to tune everyone out unless it's a super important bullet point. They're the ones that interrupt others while in a conversation to bring their expertise or examples to what the person is talking about. They cannot help it as the information, guidance, and messages flows rapidly and effortlessly through the individual's claircognizance channel. This isn't to be confused with someone who interrupts others repeatedly for the sake of attention and to hear themselves talk, although many claircognizant people may do that. The messages the claircognizant picks up on come through with an underlying tone of excitement. Suddenly the messenger cannot control themselves and needs to share it immediately. Claircognizant people might be called know-it-alls at one time or another, but that pun tends to come from those threatened by a different form of intelligence. While others find they want to listen to the claircognizant expand on certain topics, but it's often layered and detailed.

Someone with claircognizance may have difficulty sleeping as the thoughts in their mind never shut off. This isn't someone that has the occasional restless sleep over an issue that's happening to them personally, nor is it the restless sleep conjured up by a stressful time in your life. Claircognizant people are always tossing and turning from birth until human death, even when life is going great. Some of them may be prone to taking a sleeping pill, herbal relaxer, and even something harder at night. Otherwise their mind will never shut off and they'll never sleep.

Claircognizant people are always thinking and sometimes overthinking things in greater detail. Others tend to comment that they can see the claircognizant's mind wheels always churning. The claircognizant loves words and communication, whether that is being an avid writer, passionate reader, enthusiastic speaker, or all of the above. Musicians and singers are more apt to having clairaudience, but someone with claircognizance would be the songwriter of lyrics. The clairaudient would be the one jotting down the musical notes since they hear the sounds.

Because claircognizant people tend to have the right answers or know what to tell others that can assist that individual, this makes them the go to person whenever someone is having any kind of issue. It is rare for the claircognizant to go to anyone for advice, since they already tend to know the answers naturally. If they do go to someone else, then it's to compare the wisdom or get another point of view since they are a lifelong teacher and student type. They make excellent counselors, inventors, scientists, problem solvers, and writers.

Clairalience and Clairgustance

Clairalience means "Clear Smelling". Someone with clairalience smells scents that are not happening in real time or on this plane. You might suddenly smell Cedarwood and recall that this was the smell that your Grandmother used to have in her house. Yet, the smell is coming out of nowhere in the place where you currently live. This sudden scent around you that is not physically explainable can be that you're picking up on the presence of your Grandmother in the vicinity. She is communicating her presence through clairalience.

Clairgustance means "Clear Tasting". This is when you taste something seeping in from the spirit world. You can be lying in bed and suddenly you smell a foreign scent or taste chocolate and yet there is no rational place for the scent or taste to be coming from. You haven't eaten anything resembling chocolate and there are no smells burning anywhere near where you live that could resemble Cedarwood. These were a quick couple of examples of having clairalience or clairgustance.

Recap

All souls have built in psychic clair senses within them that allow spirit messages to flow to you sometimes without you realizing it.

Clairvoyance is the psychic information being projected to you through your Third Eye in between your physical eyes.

Clairsentience is the psychic information that comes through the feelings you get. I can receive a physical ailment on myself that ends up being someone around me that has that physical ailment.

Claircognizance is the psychic information coming through your sense of knowing. You just know something is going to happen or you know the information or answer without having been versed in it.

Clairaudience is the psychic information comes through an etheric voice speaking it to you. Anything that comes through your psychic senses would be something that ends up coming true. That would be the obvious key that it was a psychic hit and not your ego or the Darkness messing with you.

Every thought or feeling someone has is not a psychic hit or a mediumship dialogue from Spirit. Often, it's the mindless chatter of the ego. Therefore, being especially cognizant of what's going on in and around you can help you differentiate what is coming through is you, the ego, and lower self, as opposed to it being Divine psychic information or your higher self.

CHAPTER SIX

Picking Up on Heavenly Input

Heavenly guidance can come through as an answered prayer or a light bulb idea planted into your consciousness that causes you to leap with excitement and joy. This idea could be something geared towards one of your life purposes. One's life purpose is what benefits both you and others in some positive way. For instance, you make a million dollars that is Divinely guided to change your life from the dead end one that you've felt you've been in for years. The money isn't just to change your life, but it's to also give you more flexibility to be able to help others in some way. Helping others can be in donating of your time, compassion, and services. God knows that once you're taken care of and set up, then you're no longer living in the epicenter of the fear of not having security. You then have that extra time that you wasted living in that worry to become a blessing to others.

The ones that reach that success quicker are the ones that can squeeze in being of service or being a blessing to others while struggling in their own life. Because this also shows that your compassion is so great that you enjoy helping others when and where you can. Doing that also helps you be less-me focused in the worry about what you don't have. It gives you a break from that negative energy within you and into something more fulfilling by helping others.

Sometimes you make decisions that you believe to be heavenly guidance, but then you later get smacked down. It did not go as planned and you wonder if it was your ego that had pushed you to go after something instead of your Spirit team. You wonder and doubt whether you had accurately received heavenly messages and guidance. Your Spirit team may guide you to go after something, but then you find you fail at it. This is not a failure in the way you equate disappointment to be. You fall on your face after the first few tries, but you get up and climb back on that horse again. You learn more from failures than you do successes. Failure and struggle build character and gives you the tools that will become valuable when the achievement and success happens. You incorporate those lessons gained from the failures and apply them towards the success that comes about at a later date. Believe that you can do anything you want when you go after it with passion and persistence.

Developing a relationship with God and your Spirit team requires working with them regularly as you move along your life's path. They will show you the moves in life to take in steps. First, they show you the first step, you take that, and then they show you the next one and so forth. If someone takes years to pick up on the one step that's being relayed, then it will feel as if you're not moving. Your Spirit team is waiting for you to take that one step that they continuously implant into your consciousness in order to show you the next step. Often, I'll hear someone tell me that they're always thinking about doing this one thing, but they have yet to act on it. The fact that it's forever been in their mind for years is no accident. Sometimes the psychic information is sitting there in front of you, but you're not doing anything with it. This might be because you think it's your imagination and you're not aware that it's Divine guidance, or you may fear taking that step. They would never push you to take a step that they don't have complete confidence that you can do with amazing gusto. They psychically see you doing it and all going well, which is why they are guiding you to it. Your ego is getting in the way to delay you from making that move.

If you have trouble connecting with your guides, then stop what you're doing, including overthinking things. Move into a place of still calmness in order to get your soul centered. Take a few deep breaths if you need to relax. Take a stroll in nature somewhere to clear your mind. In that clear relaxed state, you are better able to pick up on the heavenly input of your Spirit team. The act of listening is to get in tune and receptive to the information, guidance, and messages being filtered through you from beyond.

You can practice the art of listening with those around you. If you take a step back and evaluate your behavior you can detect if you truly do listen to others or if you merely use them to vent and talk about your stuff. In order to better hear your Spirit team, practice listening in your everyday life. Strike up a conversation with a friend, acquaintance, family member, or stranger. Ask them questions so that the floor and spotlight belong to them. Sit back and listen to their response absorbing the words they're saying. Care about what they're telling you. Don't just listen to them talking while you figure out what you're going to say next. Care about each word they're saying and taking it in. This gets you into the practice of reducing your ego's plot to dominate, while getting your higher self to rise back up and listen and pay attention to the other person.

Listening is one of the most difficult things to do for people next to forgiveness. No one listens much anymore. Attention spans are short, and people are instantly reactive to what someone says or writes. This dominates rather than taking a moment to hear what someone is saying or read what someone is writing whether that's on a social media post, blog or book. This listening and paying attention exercise helps you to then pay more attention and listen to the guidance coming in from the Spirit world.

God and your Spirit team always communicate with you. No one is exempt from that, but the question is, "Are you listening?" When you talk excessively or cannot shut off the voices of your ego, then it can be difficult to pick up on what your Spirit team is trying to convey to you. Ironically you might notice that some that are unable to be less me-focus also tend to be non-believers of anything beyond the physical world.

Another exercise connected to listening and strengthening your psychic senses is to get into a quiet space at least once a day if you can. Turn off all distractions around you including cell phones and the television. If you live with other people, especially if they're making a ton of noise, then go into a room and close the door if possible or get out in nature. Close your windows briefly if you live on a street where you hear the noise of traffic, horns honking, loud talking, or sirens.

Play music by going for something ambient, chill-out, soft, or classical. Anything that is not loud and obtrusive. Adjust the volume level to one that is loud enough that it is not a distraction, or too low you can barely hear it. I love loud rock or classic rock music generally, but when I need to psychically connect or channel, then I change the music selection to something of an ambient, chillout, soft, light guitar or etheric nature. It is also brought down to a lower level. The repetitive consistency of the lower level type music also adjusts the neural activity or brain waves to that of relaxation, which is the gateway to opening the psychic channel connection with spirit. This is the frequency that allows the Divine messages to be easily picked up on.

Sit or lie down in a comfortable position and get relaxed so that you're brought into a calmer state of mind. Spirit messages are picked up on much easier when you're in a tranquil state. When you're stressed, busy, or have distractions going on, then those are blocks that prevent you from picking up on heavenly input. As you get relaxed it can take anywhere from five minutes or more depending on how easy or challenging it is for you to move into this calm state. When you are in this comfortable relaxed position, then there is room for God to come crashing in with your Spirit team.

Avoid straining to pick up on anything, as that will block the input. Instead relax and allow the energy to flow through you naturally. Don't expect anything or try to push for messages or an answer. Remain in a content state where you are centered and not seeking anything out. You might do this several times and receive no Divine guidance. This doesn't mean they're ignoring you. Sometimes it can take practice getting yourself into a calm state numerous times before you start to receive a breakthrough.

Ask your Spirit team to show you signs that they're around you. The signs can be meticulously subtle, but when you're in tune to all that is around you outside of the physical world, then you pick up on the symbols effortlessly knowing without a doubt that it is a message. Second-guessing what you receive is generated by the lower self and ego.

Visualize a pathway out in nature that is winding up a grassy hill to two closed doors side by side next to one another. Watch the doors open gradually allowing in bright white light. This light is shining onto the focus of your dreams and desires. The doors are being pushed wide open. On the other side of that door are the moving images of what you desire. This is a canvas where you can allow your imagination to go wild in painting all the things you've ever wanted. This visualizing gets you in the habit of using your imagination more, which is also connected to the subconscious psychic part of your soul.

Work with your Spirit team by connecting with them regularly as if you would a close friend. Ask for regular guidance on the steps you need to take in order to obtain your dreams and desires. Ask Heaven for courage when you feel fear, or if you need a boost in faith when you experience doubt about something. Ask God if there is anything you need to know or a way that you can be of service. Solicit for supplies or additional income to put into your dreams if that's the purpose of connecting.

The basic action steps to do when you long for something are to pray, ask for help, listen, take action, put in positive energy and passion, and then believe it is here now. Combine those steps into a delicious cocktail of positive manifesting strength. Your psychic perception needs to be on the mark so that you can pick up on what you're receiving from spirit. Sometimes their response might come right away, while other times it might come in out of the blue long after you've connected.

When you are a fine-tuned well-oiled soul machine, then the communication line with your Spirit team grows to be effortless. They will nudge you to take the next step in going after what you want. They will let you know when to pull back or when to dive head on in. They see more than the human eye can fathom or comprehend. They have an airborne view of what's to come for you and they know when it's safe to proceed on, even if you are full of fear in taking that step, they know it's safe. You might ask for help with something, but then it doesn't come to pass. Sometimes you have to give it time. Months go by and suddenly what you asked for surfaces or a problem you had is resolved.

One way to tell if it's you or your guides communicating is that when you're talking, then you tend to hear or use the word, "I". It might be bathed in ego or negativity such as, "I'm not qualified to write about this topic."

When it's your Guide or Angel, then you will hear the word, "You". It will be immersed in love or optimism. This voice will say something like, "You will write about this topic as you are qualified more than you realize."

The voices of spirit operate on a high vibration and are filled with uplifting love that assists you or someone else in a positive way. The chatter in your ego mind causes confusion and chaos pushing you to act on those voices, which ends up bringing harm or disappointment. Voices from spirit are direct, optimistic, and filled with compassion and love even if it's sending you a warning.

The feeling of being trapped at times is another sign of one having higher psychic abilities. The trapped feeling is also the absorbing of the harsh energies being darted around this planet. You're absorbing it without intending to. This is someone with a higher degree of clairsentience.

Run psychic tests such as keeping a journal or notebook and record the information, messages, and guidance down that you think is your Spirit team. Revert to the notebook over time to see if what you wrote down ended up coming true or had a positive effect. If it did, then you know it was heavenly guidance. If it didn't, then that can also help in deciphering that it was your ego or an estimated guess. With continued practice, you notice when the guidance you pick up on is more on the mark or not.

CHAPTER SEVEN

Psychic Insights

Heaven and the Spirit World have an aerial of view of the trajectory of your life. They've informed me in the past that if human souls could see what they could see up ahead for them, then they wouldn't be complaining and whining so much. Every human soul can see much of what's up ahead for themselves through their own psychic foresight. Some have said they don't believe in psychic abilities, but they might believe that people can be intuitive. Being psychic or intuitive work hand in hand regardless of what you call it. You're tuning into your core psychic senses, which are communication receptors with worlds beyond this one. All souls have this ability to read better for themselves than anyone else can. Accurately reading for yourself or anyone can be challenging when your ego is ruling the show that is your life.

How often have you received an internal jolt that something was about to happen, and then it did? I've heard some non-believers take a step back and recall those rare incidents where the psychic phenomena that came in did indeed occur for them during a dire circumstance. Increasing the psychic frequency requires raising your vibration and tuning into what's outside of physical distractions. Putting trust and faith in God and your Spirit team helps in trusting the messages you receive. If you're experiencing an issue or you're longing for something to come about for you, then have patience and faith that what you desire will work out in your favor in the end. Take the higher view that the angels have which is to trust that what is to come about will on divine timing. Sometimes it's not what you predicted or what you hoped, but you learn to realize that how it turns out is often much better than you envisioned it to be in the end.

Heavenly psychic guidance sifts into your consciousness almost effortlessly while in a dreamlike meditative state. When you wake up from sleeping at night it's almost immediately that you may have forgotten your dream, even though you awoke from it minutes prior. This is what it's like before you enter an Earthly human life. Before you enter this life, your memory slate is wiped clean except for hints that include your life purpose. This is similar to your memory being wiped clean when you awaken from a profound dream. Only hints of this dream you had while sleeping are left if at all.

You made a contract with your Spirit team before you entered a human life. In this contract are things like the soul mates you would encounter, the things you would endure, your life purpose, when you will pass on and head back home. Some of what's also in the contract are the many challenges you are intended to endure for the purpose of soul growth. When your psychic prowess is running on high octane fuel, then the more information you can retrieve from this soul contract. Your memory is fully restored when you cross back over and head home into the next plane. Part of the role your Spirit team has with you is to help you fulfill elements of your soul contract. This is also why having a stronger psychic sense will help you in noticing when their guidance is coming in, because they are guiding you towards fulfilling the elements in your contract among other things.

Some live an entire Earthly life and do not fulfill their soul contract completely. They may not come to this realization until the final days on their death bed as a human soul. When they realize they are going to leave their physical body, then the reality and the fear might hit them at that point. They might say, "Why didn't I forgive him or her?" or "Why didn't I allow love in from this person?"

These words filter through your consciousness as you transition home to where you came from in the spirit world where your Spirit team and other members of your soul family greet you. What also takes place is going over your contract for that Earthly life you just came back from. You will be going over the entire life bit by bit. This consists of things such as what you did and what you didn't do. What you did to others and what others did to you. What you accomplished or neglected and so forth.

Let Go, Let God
Let Go, Let Flow

I receive some pretty common questions from readers. One of them is about love. People are frustrated about not being in a love relationship. The desperate need to have a lover is what blocks one from obtaining a lover. It's the negative feelings associated with that need, which includes the fear that it won't happen. When you let go of the negative desire and panic to obtain a lover, then the lover shows up. I can attest for me personally that this is true. Every serious love relationship I have been involved in throughout my entire life to date came to me and developed when I wasn't looking for anything. I was in a state of perfect contentment before it happened, and then it happened naturally. Part of working on spiritual evolvement is learning the nature of patience and tempering the ego. It is to trust God and the Universe to guide and glide you naturally towards your dreams. This isn't done in a reckless fury of a rush.

The second common question is surrounding one's career. Others are trying to figure out what type of career they want, or what job they should go after, and in what industry. The response my Spirit team gives me on that is to think about what your passion is beyond making money and then you have your answer. The desire to chase money as one's sole purpose will leave you dejected. I can also attest that the response to this question was accurate for me. I have never gone after a job or career position for the purpose of monetary gain. I went after it because I had a passion and desire for that type of work or position. The money wasn't on my radar. It ended up flowing in naturally and in great abundance more than expected. The increased financial flow for each work position I accepted in my life was the icing on the cake.

Pay attention to your senses when deciphering the incoming Heavenly guidance while on your life's journey. The guidance could come in the guises of déjà vu moments. Déjà vu moments can be psychic hits of the future or of the past. The past can be a previous life or someone else's past. This can be the case even though the déjà vu moment is playing out as if you're the main character.

The future psychically seen is what's to come, which also means it's not necessarily a vision of what's coming for you personally, but it can be someone's future around you. The way dreams and clairvoyant images come to you are not always direct. It may show you a vision, but one that is not necessarily going to play out exactly in the manner it's being displayed. Clairvoyant hits sometimes need to be decoded and interpreted.

Sometimes another person's guides will communicate with my guides. My guides will then interpret what the other person's guides are relaying. They communicate at a fast pace that it overlaps with one another. It's much different in communicating than the way we do here on Earth in the physical body.

Obtaining a Psychic Reading

Since all souls are born with measuring psychic gifts, this means you can also all train yourself to pay attention to the input you receive. It takes work to strip away the materialistic desires that dominate in life so that you can be a stronger psychic vessel. This doesn't mean you can't desire physical needs, but it's not dominating or burdening you. With practice and work, you can be just as capable of giving and receiving reads for yourself as a professional psychic reader can.

Professional psychic readers or mediums find it difficult to read for themselves, since their judgment is clouded and not objective. This is why many will read with another reader from someone that is not emotionally invested in their life. This is also why many psychics do not read for friends or people they know since it becomes a conflict of interest and can taint the reading. They have emotion invested in their friend and may bend the read to favor the friend. In the end a false read is given, and the friend is not helped. Sometimes it causes the ending of a friendship where the friend feels uncomfortable by what their psychic reader friend has relayed to them.

Searching for the right psychic reader can be challenging and much like searching for the right Doctor. Readers read in a variety of ways. Some are tarot or angel card readers, some are fortune tellers, others channel messages from the Other Side, and some use objects, while others use nothing, but their own soul as the divination tool. There will be a synastry between you and the reader that feels comfortable for you both. No reader should tell you what to do. For example, they should never instruct you to leave a lover unless the lover is abusive. The role of an ethical reader is to simply guide or inform you of what they are seeing about a person or situation in question. They should remain completely objective and neutral in your situation. This is how your guide or angel is with you. They are guiding you and not telling you what to do. They are giving you free will choice as an independent soul to make the right decision.

An ethical reader would say something like, "If you stay with this person, then the philandering will continue. It is up to you to decide on your next course of action."

You have free will choice to decide what's best for you knowing this information. I've had angel reads, psychic reads, tarot reads, channel reads, and intuitive reads. I've witnessed those that use no divination tool, those who use boards, rocks or other devices. I love the craft and all points of view. I love watching and listening to the differing ways that others read. You gain different insights and perspectives with a different reader. It's a personal decision when choosing a reader to go with, just as you would in choosing a relationship. One person may love a reader that someone else did not gravitate towards. There is a synastry between reader and client.

Sometimes others that enjoy the psychic craft love to know what methods other reader's use when reading cards. I don't have a pattern that I stick with when reading and I rarely use any divination tools. I follow what my Spirit team is telling me through my soul and psychic clair sense channels. If there are moments when I need back up or want to double and triple confirm something, then I may pick up a deck.

I might then say while grabbing and shuffling the deck, "I want to know about a potential love for this person."

Nine times out of ten the card they have me flip over is the exact answer I had previously said without the card, but pulling the card gives my ego mind that additional confirmation needed.

Ask your guides and angels for clarity when you're puzzled by the information they're giving you. Request they show you signs and symbols to confirm what you're receiving from them. This is one way to determine if you're receiving accurate information or if it's your ego dominating the read. Every soul is born in tune to the Other Side and connected to God. The more a human soul allows their physical surroundings to influence them, the further away from God and heavenly communication you go.

It is also best to avoid volunteering psychic related information to others unless they've asked you for it. It's not particularly enjoyable watching someone head for a cliff and not being able to say anything. You cannot interfere with others free will choice. They must learn lessons on their own. I just keep it to myself unless I'm specifically asked if I'm seeing anything. If I'm asked what the best course of action is to take with a decision, then I'll let them know what I'm getting, but the answer needs to be prepared for. Often it may go through one ear out the other. They do the opposite, then come back to me to say, "Okay you were right, now what do I do? How do I get out of this?"

It's uncomfortable to not come off as if you're shattering someone's dreams. I'm all for one going after what they want. They're excited about something and you do not want to crush that for them. You see it being a dead end or not ending well and they ask you about it. You have to be delicate in the delivery of what you're getting, while still allowing them their free will choice to make the ultimate decision while also being supportive too.

Is a Spirit Trying to Kill Me?

I've received common strange inquiries from others in the past where the person is saying that they're hearing voices, and the voices are saying they're going to kill them. You'd be surprised by some of the stuff that comes in. The inquiry comes to me wondering if it's a spirit on the Other Side. When one is hearing harmful voices, then this is typically the voice of the ego. Spirits in Heaven communicate with love, while the Darkness and the ego communicates with hate and negativity. If it's a demon possession, they would take over your entire soul and body, but those cases are extremely rare despite how common it seems in Hollywood horror films.

The harmful spirits that reside in what some refer to as purgatory feed off a human soul's addictions. They may coax the human being to partake in an addiction. They don't have the kind of power to whisper they're going to kill that soul though. It would defeat their purpose as well since their goal is to get high through the human being's addiction or vice.

If you're hearing negative voices speaking to you, then you'll want to rule out some things. If you've had a traumatic experience in your life, then this can trigger up negative self-talk that might give one the impression it's a dangerous entity or spirit saying harmful negative things to you. Some post-traumatic stress side effects cause one's mind to splinter into different selves where it feels as if it's not you saying harmful things, but an entity or spirit. It can happen months or even years after the traumatic event. Most people have had at least one traumatic event or circumstance they can recall through the duration of their life that stands out. It could be something such as a love relationship breakup that left you wounded and depressed for a period of time or it can be an abusive situation you had to endure.

If the harmful voices are something that continues indefinitely, then it's best to seek out a mental health practitioner to adequately treat and/or diagnose the underlying cause. This can also rule out any deeper issues that might reside within you that need addressing and healing. The next step recommended is to go to a highly evolved healer, counselor, or therapist as you continue down your individual spiritual path. With practice you will be able to decipher what are your guides and angels, and when your ego mind is playing tricks on you such as with the voices.

CHAPTER EIGHT

Psychic Accuracy

It takes a great deal of work and practice to be able to detect when it's a psychic hit coming through compared to wishful thinking or a good guess. Grow to be hyper self-aware and conscious of everything in and around you. If someone fixates heavily on themselves with both the good and the bad, then this is a good start. You're already hyper intuitive about all facets of you that this can easily translate into being hyper intuitive to when it's your Spirit team communicating.

If repeated dark thoughts plague your mind, then examine your current well-being state. If one week you're suffering from raised depression or anxiety feelings, then the ominous thoughts can be ego based. You would need to rule other possibilities out such as what's going on in your physical life that could be causing it. Examine what foods, drinks, and supplements you're ingesting as that has an effect as well too. If you're on cloud nine and everything is great, then you get a random rush of something negative coming in, but it doesn't knock your current happy state of mind off balance, then it could likely be a psychic premonition.

A premonition or psychic hit typically continues to come into your consciousness repeatedly, whereas ego thoughts are all over the place, fear based, and inconsistent. If you receive a death feeling like you or someone else is going to die, then it doesn't necessarily mean an actual physical death is going to happen. It can be a circumstance coming into your life that might be challenging, either with you or someone around you. It can be a metaphysical death or the ending of one way of life. It can also indicate a major soul life transformation is about to take place, which can feel like a dark foreboding. It depends on numerous factors that include what the thought or feeling is, what and where your state of mind is at during the time of the thought or feeling, as well as other circumstances going on around you that could play a part.

Most fear-based thoughts that people have usually turn out to be untrue. Those types of feelings and thoughts come from the ego or the Darkness plaguing your aura into a state of instability. It wants to see you fail and will generate thoughts into your consciousness that are untrue. This can also be when someone is over worrying about something that ends up working out the way it's supposed to. Having an increased faith-based belief system engrained in the soul helps to calm your unstable nerves a bit more than those nerves would be without that belief system.

It's more than accepting or receiving a feeling or thought the instant it comes in. It's also paying attention to you and your surroundings to gauge how the information, guidance, and messages are coming into your psychic senses. You would also make note of what spiritual frequency you're operating at on that day. This requires hyper alertness and extreme discipline with your life and lifestyle choices. It takes constant daily work to become a strong healthy psychic vessel. It cannot be done for one week, then you get lazy a week later and then try to do it again two months later. You're basically starting all over when you put it off, so it is necessary to work on shifting your mindset to that of being an open psychic vessel. It's like taking certain vitamins or supplements where you must take them regularly to notice the positive benefits over time.

When it comes to beginning psychic development, many have informed me that they feel like they're making something up until the person they relayed the information to inform them that it ended up coming true. One key trait to remember is to trust. Trust what you're receiving from Spirit and don't worry if you're going to be wrong since that's a given. The psychic information may not mean anything to you, but it might mean something to someone else around you. If you're reading for someone else there's no reason to say, "This may be wrong, but I'm getting that..."

People already know you may be wrong, or it ends up not being true. There's no need to say that. The only times I've said something remotely close to that is when someone is upset by what I'm seeing, then I may say something like, "I hope I'm wrong for your sake."

Unfortunately, due to them being used to my accuracies, they fear that it is unlikely to be inaccurate. Clairvoyant hits will sometimes be brought to you through your dreams. It's your soul's job to decode the messages in your dreams. Jot down what happened in the dream before you forget it, then break up everything that was happening in the dream that you can remember and juxtapose this with what you're going through in your daily life at that time. It's a puzzle to put together to decipher what's being relayed to you from above. You could be getting a symbol or sign about something, but often psychic information is not exactly coming in the way one might think it means. You could get a symbol of a car, which might make one think they're going to buy a new car, but it can also be a road trip, an accident, or something else entirely with a car being the psychic clue. Sometimes there is no point or message in a dream. It's your subconscious projecting those images to you, while other times it is a Divine message.

There are people that can see symbols and signs if they have strong Clairvoyance, but even if they don't, they may see these things while in a lucid dreaming state. This is because the main part of your conscious is asleep, which helps in removing those lower self-sabotaging blocks that would prevent you from seeing a psychic related message while in a waking state. Those things some see that are like one another are real, but just in another plane seeping into this plane.

When you deliver spirit information to another person, keep in mind of what Heaven's set of appropriate code of etiquette guidelines are. It includes that you only state what you're being told by them to others in a way that is objective and compassionate. Say what you see, sense, know or hear, but avoid instructing the person what to do. Only go as far as to say, "If you do this, then this is what will happen."

If the other person says, "Which one should I do?"

The response should be, "That's up to you to decide."

Your friends or family might tell you what to do, but when you go to an objective psychic reader, then they should remain neutral. This includes never telling someone that their death or someone close to them is imminent.

Another psychic rule of etiquette is avoid entering someone's aura and giving them information unless they've expressed permission. Not doing that is similar to breaking into someone's house, which is an invasion of privacy. Especially don't do that to relay negative information. I heard one person that wasn't a practicing psychic telling people things like when their death is going to be, or not to drive because they're going to be getting into a major accident someday, and that there is a major Earthquake going to happen any day now. As many bad things as you can think of, this person was randomly telling people that. The people he was telling this to never asked him, it was randomly volunteered, and nor was he accurate anyway. The ego wants a new person to believe they're super psychic suddenly. This prompts them to runaround making outlandish uncalled for statements, which screams of inexperience and gives practicing or professional psychics a bad name.

An exception to this rule would be if you're friends with this person and you randomly blurt out things not realizing you're making a psychic statement. I've never personally blurted out something considered tragic like their death or a car accident. I keep those negative things to myself. I'm always moving cautiously and would never interrupt someone to say something off like, "I need to warn you, there is an airplane that's going to be hurled at your head next week. Avoid sitting on your living room couch."

Contrary to some storylines about psychics in Hollywood films, most psychic information that comes in are not big loud tragedies. The giveaway is if the person seems to recite that to everybody on top of not being asked permission for it.

Part of mediumship and psychic etiquette is that you are responsible when it comes to how you word or deliver information as much as possible. This also includes deciding whether it's your place to offer information. I've had some email me or my Editor to say that my Spirit Guides are trying to get my attention regarding an issue, so my guides are going through that person to tell me. My Editor said he's told people, "If his Spirit Guides are trying to relay a message to him, believe me he has no problem retrieving it on his own."

Approaching random people or messaging those you don't know to relay things like that is inappropriate human behavior, but it's also poor psychic etiquette. If you're bent on relaying psychic information, then ask the person if it would be okay if you psychically read them. If they say no, they don't want you entering their auric energy field, then move on. If they say yes, then carry on with the reading.

CHAPTER NINE

Psychic Timing

One of the soul lessons that all have in their contract is to learn the art of patience. Spirit isn't handing blessings to you as soon as you ask for it. They're not always going to relay psychic information to you if they know it is not time for it yet. They may also be prevented from revealing certain information too soon. If they were telling you everything all at once in one sitting, you wouldn't be able to retain all that information. And if you knew everything that was going to happen to you, then you would no longer live life. You might sit back, relax, and wait for the date that something is supposed to happen. Not doing anything is considered an action step in the eyes of the Universe. You are choosing not to do anything, which will block the circumstance from happening, which alters your souls' path. This is because you stopped doing anything subconsciously thinking this will land on your lap anyway, so you may as well do nothing.

If everyone were being handed blessings right away, then no one would learn anything. When I was sixteen years old, I knew I was going to work in the film business, but I didn't know when. Spirit Clairvoyantly showed me visuals of me in there and in that world. I knew it was coming, but I had no idea when exactly. All I knew was that it was on its way to happen soon. At the age of twenty-three, I received the lucky break call that changed my life and got me into the film business with one of the top five bankable movie stars at the time. This was seven years after the original psychic hits that were showing me in that world. The predicted psychic forecast eventually happened, but not as quickly as I thought.

If my Spirit team said I'd get it in three months and it didn't happen, then I'd be disappointed and let down, or I wouldn't have done anything to help move it along. Or if I demanded that I get in before that moment, and they gave me an opportunity, then the chances are the opportunity would have crashed and burned. Because I was forced to be patient and wait, the dream did come true and in more magnificent ways than I had ever imagined. It was so big that at that time people around me could not believe it. It was, "How-wha-how did you do this! This is impossible!" It was the same shock across the board because it was that major of a gig. Still to this day my entire film business tenure was bigger than what most long for in the business, especially for an average regular person such as myself with an abusive, poor background, and zero experience. This is said to illustrate that anything is possible to achieve regardless of where you came from.

Be patient for your dreams to come true. Know that if it's taking years to transpire that there could be other factors at play beyond your comprehension. Sometimes we must endure years of struggle before obtaining the gold. Because this builds character and makes you humble when it does come about. When you push for something to happen with frustration, then that pushes it further away. That impulsive energy creates a block that delays it from happening or pushes it further out in the distance.

Psychic timing is often impossible to predict, because there are numerous factors to consider that would delay something from taking place. It is true there have been occasions where I have predicted timing to the day. One thing to note is those were rare times when Spirit did give me a date through Clairaudience, and it happened on that date because no parties involved were delaying it through free will actions. Spirit doesn't usually offer exact timing in many cases. They might just say soon or further out in the distance. They might circle a general calendar date. If they say May 5th, it might not necessarily be on that day, but within or around the day. They might say May 5th and you wait around, but nothing happens so you figure it wasn't true. But then out of nowhere on July 18th is when what you were hoping for does happen. Time is fluid in the spirit world because they don't operate on the calendars that we do.

If I receive timing, then I'll say it out loud, but if I don't get any timing, then that just means I'm not being given timing for whatever reason. Sometimes forecasted predictions of what's to come are given by spirit on a need to know basis. There are times that even your Spirit team doesn't have the psychic answer to your question, because God is blocking it for them too. If it's blocked for them, then it's blocked for you. If they are exempt from knowing when something is to take place themselves, then they won't give timing. If they know when it'll happen, they will only say it if it has any benefit for the person.

Perhaps you've been waiting for years and have become discouraged to the point that you've stopped trying and given up on life. In that case if Spirit has the answer, then they will offer reassurance to the person that the event is indeed in the soul's contract to take place. Keep on believing, have faith, and remain patient. This is why sometimes you might have seen or heard others about to give up, but then a sliver of light shines in revealing some scattered mini blessings on the horizon, then this shakes that soul out of its rut motivating them to keep going. They are so grateful to have that tiny bit of blessing that popped in that it ignites their faith to believe something great is in the works. Those mini blessings dropped here and there also help in building humility into your character.

Sometimes God and Spirit need you to do your part. Many spend each day complaining that nothing good ever comes to help them. They lack motivation, passion, and drive. As a result, they ensure this state continues and so does God. Spirit is not about dropping blessings onto a soul that is stuck in sloth mode if the soul won't get up to put in somewhat of an effort. Putting in any effort repetitively prompts God to swoop in and start lighting more of the way. If you are paralyzed by fear, sadness, or any other negative emotion, then pray for help with that element first.

Other general reasons timing isn't given are that there are still circumstances that need to take place that will enlighten that person some more before what they want arrives. If it comes too soon before someone is ready, then it'll slip through that person's fingers because they weren't able to accept it in the right spirit, even if they think they are. What your ego believes and what God sees are two separate things.

Spirit is doing their best to make some of your wishes and dreams happen, but there are pieces within the puzzle that need to be maneuvered to orchestrate the circumstance to happen. It could be that Spirit is making it happen, such as they are bringing a certain soul mate person to you, but you both keep missing each other. One of you is not noticing the other one or you keep ignoring them. Neither of you are acting on it every time Spirit gets you in the room together.

Timing is fluid and non-existent in the spirit world. They have no concept of time because they don't operate on human made clocks. Timing is something human beings created because they function according to a clock. Timing is a foreign language to Spirit, even though they are aware we are operating by a clock created by us, but they don't care if their timing is not the same as your timing. We see things as a matter of racing against the clock, but they see it as an unimportant blip.

What if someone gives another person timing in a reading? What if that time frame predicted comes and nothing transpires as expected? One might assume the reader was off, wrong, or was being nice by giving them an estimated guess to satisfy the client. I've heard those stories, but then a year later the prediction comes true. Events took place that shifted the timing because Spirit cannot control the free will actions of human beings. They're not going to freely give timing to any reader, because Spirit doesn't care about the ego dramatics that human beings have where we want something now. They don't care about the ego's angry frustrated irritation. They will instead urge you to learn the lesson of patience.

One of the most demanding questions most often asked in a psychic read is, "When?" When will a circumstance happen? They want an exact date as to when they will meet that lover, start that new career, or buy that house. You're not on the phone with your plumber demanding to know when he's coming. You're talking to Spirit and they're not going to bow down to demanding questions like when. They have no qualms about ignoring that.

It is understandable that you want to know when something will happen, since you are in a human body and crave immediate material security. This physical comfort could come in the form of the great job, money, or awesome love for example. When these things don't seem to be forthcoming for a prolonged period, you might begin to grow permanently solemn, frustrated or disappointed. This state lowers your vibration, which could block or delay the event from taking place or push it further out until you've been made to be humble and accept where you are today first. This energy certainly doesn't bring the event to you quicker. It is always best to remain optimistic and cheerful when possible since that energy is what attracts in positive circumstances. This doesn't mean deny your low feelings, but to work on moving out of that and back into optimism through faith.

No psychic reader can necessarily predict when something is going to happen for someone anyway. Those in Heaven that relay information to the psychic conduit live in a world without devices such as calendars and clocks. There is no time that exists for Heaven in the way that human souls have made it on Earth. Therefore, it's near impossible for spirit guides and angels to give a psychic conduit an accurate time to give to their client as to when an event will take place. Time is fluid to those in the spirit world, so when they see a human soul wanting to know when something will take place, they will either ignore that or give their best estimated time frame if it is in their sphere of consciousness to give. Sometimes guides are also blocked from giving it.

Any time frame that happens to be given should be taken with a grain of salt. There are a great many factors that can and will often delay something from happening with any time frame predicted.

There are psychics that nail timing more times than not, but for the most part it's challenging to nail timing. You are gambling with someone's free will choice, which is unpredictable. I've nailed timing in the past and witnessed it happen later. I have had the person I've relayed the information to come back to me a year later. This was in order to say that something I stated a year ago has come true for them. When I used to offer professional readings and someone asked for timing on something, I would rarely relay it unless I heard a month or date slam into my psychic clairs during the read. The circumstances where I offered accurate timing were voluntarily on my part because my Spirit team happened to be highlighting a month, day or season through my clairaudience channel. I just included it as part of the read. If Spirit said nothing as to when something will happen, then I would just say, "I don't know. Soon."

There are reasons Spirit isn't telling you everything you're asking at that moment. Sometimes information is on a need to know basis. Your ego wants to know when something is going take place. Your higher self is not interested in the when or how, because it knows all is well and what is intended will be.

The timing that is given by a reader is the probable timing pending that you or other circumstances connected to your desire are not hindered by any of the party's free will. Free will is not taken seriously enough when it comes to psychic hits. Most human souls operate using free will choice. They rarely listen to their guides and angels. It is more about obtaining their desire immediately. For example, in a love read no one can predict the impulsive choices you or this potential lover might make on any given day. This alters what was originally predicted to happen.

There is a danger when a psychic gives someone a time frame as to when an event will happen. If the time frame the psychic gave comes and goes, then the one who was read for will debunk the psychic as being inaccurate or that it just isn't in the cards for them. Months or even years down the line it turns out that the event does eventually take place, but it is so far into the future that the client forgot all about the read to begin with.

One way to look at it is that a reader or your own guides and angels are informing you that something is indeed intended to happen. Don't worry yourself over the when and how it will happen. Otherwise you'll drive yourself into a mental obsession. This obsession is what lowers your vibration. When you are in a state of joy and contentment, in the here and now, then this raises your vibration. This then allows positive events to unfold, and even greater opportunities to reach you sooner than later.

I'm one of the most impatient people I know, so this is something I can relate to. I know what it's like to want to know when something is going to take place and how frustrating it can be when time has gone by and nothing has come to pass. Heaven says to trust, have patience, and keep the faith. Know that the path you're on is the way it is for a reason. The choices you've previously made have led you to the place you're currently in. What you desire will reveal itself to you at just the right time. Speaking from personal experience, I can attest that this is true. Additionally, it's important to remember to follow the nudges, signs, and guidance that your Spirit team is putting in front of you. If they are constantly dropping the same signs in front of you to go to a different part of town you normally go to, or another store that is off your typical route, then trust that. It could be they are trying to orchestrate something beneficial for you.

A psychic reader can rarely assist you with something like this. They might tell you that you're going to meet your next lover in October. October comes and goes, and you wonder why it never happened. Were you sitting around at home hiding out between the day of your psychic read and October? This makes it impossible for any lover to find you unless that soul mate rings your doorbell like the postman or delivery person.

When a psychic informs you about a probable situation coming up, then keep an open mind. Take steps that can help it come along to you more readily. If this is a love partner entering the picture, then this means get outside and mix with other people. Go out more often so that this wonderful lover can bump into you. Pay attention to your Spirit teams nudges on where to go if you're confused.

While out and about, if this potential lover approaches you and strikes up a friendly conversation, then let your guard down and throw on the charm with them. Smile, be engaging, warm and open. You might not be immediately aware that this person is the potential right away when they approach you. They might not be what you were originally envisioning or thought of, so you end up closing yourself off to someone that desires to engage with you in conversation.

Another important action step can be that it is you who will approach this lover instead of waiting for them to approach you. This is an easy step for an extroverted soul. If you're an introvert, then practice using your gifts of non-verbal telepathic communication on this potential. You can do this with a smile or by giving them a simple, "Hello." Pay attention to their body language and how responsive or unresponsive they are. This also means pay attention to your own body language. Do you stiffen up to a block of ice with an expressionless face when this person enters your vicinity and notices you, or do you smile back and acknowledge them?

This is a cold closed off world and some souls may have an automatic fight or flight response. They could be stunned that someone said hello to them let alone an attractive stranger. They might button up and turn away from you or give you a grunt of a response. Does that mean they're not interested? Not necessarily. When you're in tune to your surroundings, you can gauge whether someone is interested or not. Watch for the subtle cues in their body movement. Do they pull away from you feeling uninterested, angry or threatened? And do they suddenly soften and move back towards you with acknowledgment? Their movements may be subtle that you might not notice it right away. You assume they're not interested when they may either be shy or thrown off that someone good looking is engaging with them. Unless someone has been drinking in a bar to loosen up, most people are not used to others being nice to them, especially if you live in an overpopulated big city. If you're a woman, you might have a traditional way of believing how relationships should form. This is where you prefer the guy approaches you and strikes up a conversation. That was the way things once were, but times are significantly different. Now both men and women must do the work if they want to find a long-term loving relationship. If you're a woman, then you approach him with a hello.

If you're interested in a same sex love relationship, then you have additional factors that come into play or ones that might cross your mind. They might be things such as, "What if I approach this person and they don't go my way? Or what if they have a negative reaction to my sexuality?"

Of course, you would use precautions regardless of what your sexuality is when approaching a stranger. You're not going to blurt out: "Hey, I'm interested in you!"

This method could work, but being subtle and polite in your approach can go a long way. This is where you are striking up a conversation as if it were a potential friend. You'll eventually pick up on enough energy vibrations off the other person to determine what their interest level is. There are people that are super sociable and friendly. It doesn't mean they're necessarily seeing you as a potential lover.

Your Spirit team is not going to drop the great lover at your doorstep if you're hiding out at home and you never go out to mingle. They're not going to drop an awesome career opportunity in your life if you've never sent your resume or credentials out to potential employers. Heaven helps those that help themselves. They help those they see are taking action steps to try and make something happen. This is when they swoop in to meet you more than halfway. When you're passionate and positively driven and action oriented to achieve your desires, then it's that much quicker to arrive.

Spirit may see something coming soon, in the near future, or out in the distance. When Spirit says, "Coming soon", then that can be anywhere between next month to one year. "Far out in the future" would be beyond that from one year to several years or more. Some factors come into play such as free will choices that you or others make that can bend or extend the event you desire from happening, to when it was soul contracted to take place.

CHAPTER TEN

*How Much Does
Your Spirit Team Know?*

Common questions I hear from others are things such as, *"How does one explain horrendous rapes, murders, the torturing of innocent people, etc. Where were those people's guardian angels? You watch an episode of forensic files and it's enough to make you wonder. I wish there was an explanation that makes sense."*

It's an understandable concern with an answer that resides in plain view. It's not the job of God, a Spirit Guide, or a Guardian Angel to stop horrific acts from happening at the hands of a human being. Where in any soul contract does it indicate that this is the role they must play? They are guides, which means they guide. A guide's job is not to do things for you or stop things from taking place. There could be a variety of factors to dive deep into when considering why a tragic incident happens. One of them is that all souls including those in a human body are granted free will choice. They might be choosing to ignore the Divine guidance coming into their consciousness to stop them from conducting a harmful act on another person. It could be the victim brushed off nudges and warnings not to go to a certain place that day that ends up having a tragic occurrence.

Some survivors of a shooting for example have said that beforehand they felt like something was off and that they shouldn't be there. Other times Guides have orchestrated situations where authorities or other people are brought to light about a dangerous incident about to happen, but those people also ignored those warnings or found nothing fault worthy at the time of the investigation. Spirit can't do much else if people are not paying attention to them.

Many people on the planet either do not believe in Guides and Angels, or they are not paying attention to their Spirit team. This goes back to watching what you are ingesting in your body and make note of your state of mind, because all of that not only influences your physical body, but it also affects your connection with the Divine. If someone is mentally ill, they are not in their right mind to pick up on the messages and guidance coming in from above to stop any harm they plan on enacting. It's also presumptuous to assume that every shred of living and choices made by humankind can be or will be controlled by God and Spirit, while everyone kicks back and relaxes allowing them to control positive outcomes for you.

In a world plagued with mass shootings or terrorism, notice how a good deal of the events that were targeted were where it's crowded, with some being schools or businesses. Schools will typically run safety drills more often in the event of an emergency due to the rise in shootings. Many of the larger shootings have been in entertainment venues where alcohol is consumed. Alcohol dims and removes your tuned in connection with the Divine. No one is saying that you shouldn't drink or go to an entertainment establishment. This is something I've frequented and partaken in myself on occasion. The point is being aware that your Divine connection is dimmed to the point that you're not paying attention to your Spirit team's warnings that danger is near, so you need to be hyper vigilant and careful while out and about. Pay attention to everything and everyone around, while noting where the nearest exit is.

How often after these horrific traumatic events have taken place do you hear about a survivor explaining how they felt something was off before the tragedy, so they left the venue, and then the attack happened? That person was one of the few picking up on the Divine message warnings coming in. Crowded areas in general will create a block with the Divine because you're also picking up on other people's energies that cause psychic interference. This is partially why I avoid going to crowded places unless necessary or without choice. Many psychics, mediums, and sensitive intuitive empath's have also protested to having trouble going to places that are crowded as it messes with their sensitivities.

Some have asked how God can allow misfortunes happen to people. If you're on the freeway speeding and not paying attention to your Guide and Angel nudging you to slow down and pay attention, then there is only so much they can do to prevent an accident. This fate results in your death and other deaths based solely on your free will choice to act out in a way that is dangerous and detrimental.

A pilot of an airplane took down a plane and crashed it into a mountain with 144 passengers on it. When someone is at the helms of a manmade vessel with 144 lives in that one person's hands, then those passengers on the plane are under the rule of that one person. You might say those passengers did not deserve to die. Perhaps they prayed and no help was forthcoming. An aircraft is soaring in the Earth's atmosphere with someone operating on free will. They ignore any heavenly guidance that is dropped into their consciousness. Their Spirit team is doing whatever they possibly can to penetrate someone's state of consciousness. Those that chose to board the aircraft might have done so by free will choice. Perhaps their own team was nudging them to not get on the plane. Perhaps they made a prior agreement that this is how they would complete their Earthly life run. By the time they realized something wasn't right, it was too late to pray and ask for help. As stated, no heavenly spirit being can interfere on any human soul's free will choice, without an expressed invitation via mentally, out loud, or in prayer.

Part of the reason my Spirit team had me write the spiritual related books is to help people make positive choices in their life, which simultaneously improves your well-being. This is transferred to others around you when you lead by this example. You become a way shower, which touches one person, then another, and so forth. This work isn't effective in a sound bite in a social media meme to grow followers, or that gets liked, scrolled past, and discarded. It needs to be digested as an entire piece.

People that have attested to work on their well-being on all levels have purported to be more psychically in tune than they were before they did the work. The work is to arm those interested. That way when you've hit a wall of giving up, you're versed enough to take the inspirational words to heart and put them to good use to pull you back up quicker than if you didn't have them. Human life is governed by going through the motions. Go to work, the grocery store, pick up the kids, make dinner, and so on. There is little to no moments within our disciplined Earthly life routines to have just enough light open for God to come in.

More people than not are saturated into the physical material world. They have been trained by each other on how to function, behave, think, and what to go after in life. They are technologically based, which has its plusses, but the flip side is it blocks one from paying attention to any guidance being filtered into them from above. They operate on sound bites, blurbs, and the short and simple. In the cases where an accident has taken place, and someone that survived recalled feeling something foreboding beforehand, this was a clairsentience psychic hit they experienced. When a catastrophe or accident happens, it is also intended to act as a catalyst to wake humanity up from slumber to implement strategies that can prevent such a disaster from happening again.

How often do you sense something is about to happen and it does? Or you hear a voice inside you stating something that later comes true? You have free will choice to choose which path you would like to take, but choose wisely. Heading down the wrong path will result in a dead end or cause something catastrophic. The damaging effects of free will choice are showcased all around the world and in the media.

Some countries feed their children unhealthy diets, because it's all they know or it's all they can afford. Children are raised on these diets, and when they grow up, they raise their Children this way and so forth. This is the same with someone's values and beliefs. They gain that knowledge by how they were raised. It doesn't mean they're right, because it's all they know. The evolving or advanced souls are the ones that break away from that mold and realize there is something bigger than what they've been trained to know. They are aware they have a purpose here.

The Role of Spirit is to Guide the Soul

You ask Heaven and your Spirit team for help and you receive. You ask people for help, and you may not receive. Others have protested to ask God for help, but nothing has come to fruition. They stop believing and their faith dwindles. If what you're asking for can only happen with the help of someone else, then you cannot blame Heaven when it doesn't happen.

Your Spirit team is the lineup of players in your life that reside on the Other Side in Heaven working with you and guiding you along your Earthly life path. They are made up of one Spirit Guide and one Guardian Angel. They are present with you when you are born into a life in the Earth plane. From that point on your journey, they remain with you until you meet up with them again when you pass on from this lifetime. If you are someone that works with Heaven, angels, guides, or any other benevolent beings, then you may have more than one guide and angel that come to your side. Some may stay with you permanently, while others will come in specifically during important junctures in your life and then leave once you have accomplished what needs to be done. In Football, your teammates are your family that has your back. This is the same way your Spirit team has your back and vice versa. You work together with one another, as you are a family that has a relationship.

Let's say that you are spending your days longing for a romantic partner. If your Spirit Guide and Guardian Angel are working with you on other day-to-day situations, then you may have another guide or angel that joins you in your life assisting you on your search for the kind of soul mate that would be beneficial for you. This Spirit will work with your soul mates Spirit team in order to bring you two together.

You could be a busy professional and not active in the dating world aside from joining dating sites and dating apps to get to know potential suitors. Or perhaps you have done that, and it resulted in disappointment. This assigned "love guide" works with this other potential's guides to help you two to connect. You find you suddenly start crossing paths with the same person repeatedly at the store, at the gym, in an elevator, or even in a parking garage. There is a reason behind running into this same person consistently and randomly. You are attracted to them, and you notice they seem to be taking notice of you in a positive warm way, yet you both brush it off or do not act on it. This is partly due to your ego and partly how technology has trained others to communicate via technical devices, but rendered them incapable when face-to-face. Both of your Spirit team's will continue to work on getting you both together. It is up to the both of you to do the rest of the work. This work includes something that might be difficult for some such as saying hello.

If you find that every time you run into this person, the butterflies rise, you grow nervous, or feel inadequate, then mentally in prayer ask God and your Spirit team to help give you confidence and courage. What's the worst that is going to happen if you make a mistake by saying hello? The other person says nothing or reacts in a way that wasn't what you were expecting.

It is difficult for two people coming together today where primary means of communicating to each other is through technological devices. Now you're standing in front of someone and you're suddenly a mute. This other person is likely just as nervous as you. They might be kicking themselves for not responding adequately. If you continue to run into this person, you'll both grow more comfortable with the other one being around. It will get easier to begin conversation even if it's always *a hi, hello, how are you?* There are no missed opportunities. If the soul mate you are intended to connect with is meant to happen, then it will.

The "Free Will Universal Law" is God's law, which says that all souls have free will choice. God, Heaven, and any spirit being are not allowed to interfere or intervene with your free will choice, unless your free will choice is going to result in death before your time. And even in those instances your Spirit team is not always able to prevent premature death.

There are some that don't want to know the future. Some of the reasoning is due to fearing what might be seen, while others prefer to live life without interference of knowing what's supposed to happen. The other reasoning is some either don't believe in psychic foresight, or the opposite end of the spectrum is because one believes that wanting to know the future is demonic or is against God's law, which neither is true. Although, connecting with the Other Side can invite unwanted spirits if you're not careful. Ensure that you shield yourself with white protective light and invite in only the highest vibrational spirits.

Some have stated to being blocked from receiving spirit messages about what's to come for them, but it's not always a block that is the cause. There are answers to questions you're not intended to know either at that time or at all. If you are to know what's coming up ahead with something, then that information would continuously hit you repeatedly and indefinitely until you picked up on it or noticed it.

Spirit can counsel you about certain circumstances, but not if the outcome is also concealed from them too. If it's hidden from them, then it's unknown to you no matter how psychically gifted you are. You're also not intended to know what's coming as it will prevent you from doing the soul work that you need to do that will ultimately bring in what you're hoping will come to be for you. If you knew everything that was coming, then you wouldn't bother doing anything or putting in any work. You'd sit back and wait, which is a free will choice move that can prevent the outcome from taking place.

The job of a spirit guide is to guide, and not necessarily to inform you about every single detail on your path up ahead. The reasons as to why this is the case is wide and varied. There might be a test you must endure on your own without any handholding. They will not give you the answers to this test even if they are privy to those answers. This is the same way a teacher gives students a test in Earth schools. The teacher isn't going to give the student the answers, otherwise the student won't learn.

Spirit can and may guide you through certain circumstances, and put up warnings or hints if you were straying too far away from where you're supposed to be, but other than that it is up to you to make your own free will life choices. If everything was handed to you the second you asked for it, then you'd become spoiled, would never learn anything, and subsequently would not grow and evolve. When Children are handed everything, then they expect it and will become spoiled throwing a tantrum if they don't get it. The same goes for the soul.

There are certain circumstances preordained or predestined to one degree or another. This includes the many soul mates you cross paths with over the course of your life. Soul contracted circumstances could be missed out due to someone's free will choice. If two souls were intended to come together and unite, but one eventually denies that and moves away due to free will choice, then there is a backup plan where another soul mate will cross paths with you once the guides know for sure that the other soul mate will not be coming back. Spirit can see what's coming down the road towards you even if the soul mate is making poor life choices that prevent the union from happening. Spirit may see that the soul mate will still eventually wrap back around at a later date, but it's taking them longer to make it to you.

Spirit advises you in the areas Divinely allowed, while other times they must remain quiet for your soul's growth benefit. The more open you are, then the more in tune you are to pick up on the guidance they do have to offer. The higher your vibration, and the more in tune you are, then the more you're able to pick up and follow the guidance coming in. When you're in your mind or ego, you may rationalize, overthink, and compute information. When you're in your heart, then you can sense what the Divine is relaying. Your Divine psychic senses will tell you the truth.

If you were intended to know everything that was coming up ahead, then you wouldn't live life. You would instead kick back and do nothing since you already foresee what's coming. Therefore, what's relayed is on a need to know basis through spurts of information. If you're not picking up on anything surrounding an issue, then take that as a clue to continue living life and make sound choices to propel you forward. Spirit will jump in if it's something you're intended to know or that is okay for you to know at that time.

This is also the case if you're single and looking for a potential love partner. You may pick up on someone coming to you that may have dark hair, so you might stop searching for a potential partner, or you will push away the potential partner if they don't have the characteristics or statistics you were expecting. The psychic information you received could be incorrect and a fragment of your imagination. It could've been what your ego prefers, or your psychic hunch was semi-correct in that there is a person with dark hair coming in, but that's not the partner. That person could be the catalyst that sets up the meeting between you and the actual partner who ends up having light hair. Or the dark-haired person could have no connection to a potential partner at all and was simply a friend or acquaintance coming into the vicinity. You just psychically misread the person you received in visions.

In the end, when it comes to the right soul mate connection, then it will happen naturally. There will be no guessing or effort. You will both sense an instant attraction and camaraderie. You will also both take steps to connect mutually and without resistance or strong persuasion. The dance of the lights of both soul mate partners will intertwine effortlessly when they come together.

CHAPTER ELEVEN

Blocking Divine Guidance

Having a crystal-clear connection with Heaven requires a high vibration. You will know that state has been reached when you feel naturally uplifted, centered, focused, and clear minded. This means naturally and not through artificial substances, which often creates a block even though you're feeling high on life. Anyone buzzed on an alcoholic drink feels great, which is why some drink. It's why I used to drink like a fiend in my early twenties. It was to feel good since feeling good on my own wasn't working.

My Spirit team says the best way to achieve sharper psychic perception is by getting rid of anything humankind made. They understand this is not realistic or practical while having a human experience, but the closer you are to achieving that, then the greater the psychic communication line is.

Witness those who do not need much to survive, such as hermits or gypsies who live in nature solo. They live out in vast reservations of nature where Spirit's connection is strongest. It's positively valuable to take periodic bouts of time out or time off when possible to commune and meditate in nature. Take regular retreats when you can throughout each year. This means taking one to three days off at a time from your busy schedule when possible to vacation in a nature setting. This can be by visiting a beach, desert, ranch, lake, park, forest, or mountain area, unless you already live in a nature region. Avoid taking it for granted, since that can be easy to do until it's gone or taken away by life circumstance. Whenever I head down to my beach minutes away, I always feel this wave of feeling so blessed. I'm highly aware this is no accident.

If you're only able to do that one day a month, then that's better than not doing anything at all. Take a friend, your kids, a spouse, a neighbor, an acquaintance, a colleague, or lover if that will help motivate you to go. Sometimes when you make plans with someone else, it's more difficult to back out of it than if you were going alone. Some personalities prefer to go alone to clear the mind with no distractions at all.

Identifying Challenges and Blocks

One day you wake up and realize you suddenly don't like your job or the relationship you're in. Perhaps you no longer feel connected to some of your friends. If this feeling comes over you and never goes away, then this could be a likely sign that your soul is transforming and evolving. Your Spirit team may have instigated this progression to move you to the next plateau. They may see that many of the things in your life are causing major blocks with them, which simultaneously prevents larger blessings from coming into your life. You then begin to implement changes in your life that includes dissolving anything you see to be toxic.

Dissolving people or tougher circumstances can take time. Dissolving your job will be the hardest unless you're able to find another job immediately. You don't want to make any drastic reckless decisions such as quitting your job before you have another one. You certainly don't want to leave a love relationship abruptly, especially if it's not abusive in any form. Conversations with your partner should be had in explaining your newfound spiritual growth or personal changes you're experiencing that could be altering the dynamic of the relationship. You may even find that your partner is interested in it as well too, or at least accepting of it. Most everything is fixable in a relationship beyond the couple having immensely outgrown one another. The strongest exception is if you're in any kind of abusive connection, whether that is emotional, mental, or physical.

Take a good hard look at your life and examine every shred closely. You won't be able to do that in one day. Throughout different periods each week, your mind will drift towards parts of your life to do a thorough life review. This includes the things that are happening in the present as well as the past. Often the challenges one is having in the present are somehow related or connected to the past. This is whether it was a poor decision made in the past, or a challenging trait gained during your childhood or upbringing. You may not even realize that a traumatic event in your childhood made you gain fear traits that you ended up carrying with you throughout your adult life. This affects your current state today, since the karmic thread is connected to that time in your life. It will continue to be carried with you until acknowledgement over how it started came about. The next step is learning how to shed that part of you in order to be clear and free of its bindings.

There may be some things you participate in that you will not want to part with, but which are ultimately causing a block in your life. You are your own accurate barometer as to what changes you need to make. If you're unsure, then you'll have to continue living life until it comes to you. Ask for Divine assistance and help as to what needs to be released from your life, and then pay attention to the signs coming in from above. This is not necessarily something that you'll come to the realization of in one day.

It can be days, weeks, or months before you realize, "A-ha! This is it. This is what was in my way. How did I not see this before?"

This is that magnificent moment of enlightenment and clarity. Other times, you may immediately know exactly what it is that needs to be changed in your life, and then you can begin working on removing it.

Sometimes your ego can deceive you into believing that you're not blocked by anything. An example would be the rush you receive from gossip or absorbing negative media that propels you to swim along with it. The rush is deceptive because it's also the same high you get from drugs, alcohol, food, or any other toxic vice. A toxic vice can be anything that ultimately contributes to your downfall whether physically, spiritually, mentally, or emotionally.

How about whenever you talk to a friend, then your body feels weak and worn out from them. Perhaps they seem to be patronizing, condescending or they make snide remarks whenever you say something. This is an example of a subtle toxic relationship, because they're not being overtly abusive. When you feel bothered by the call afterwards, then this is a sign that your vibration has dropped whenever you talk to this negative friend. They might be someone that always expresses anger, gossip, or complains. They could be consistently depressed, sad, and down in general without any interest of finding ways to move past that. No event makes them that way, but they are always in that state around the clock. This affects you, your vibration, and your overall state, because you are in that energy and you're absorbing it and becoming one with it.

It's one thing where you offer supportive action-oriented words that help this person move past it. It's another thing if they're just agreeing with you, but never taking action steps to correct this. They refuse to admit that their general demeanor has been on the negative side. Acknowledging your repetitive negative state is the same as awareness. Awareness is the first step on the path that leads to recovery. Much of the psychic blocks with the Divine that exist are throughout one's daily life including the people you connect with, work with, and get involved with.

Other examples of positive lifestyle changes that will raise your energy vibration to be a stronger psychic vessel are cleaning up your diet, eating healthier, breathing deeper, frequenting nature, and partaking in regular exercise. It is also avoiding large amounts of alcohol, drugs, the media, and people who are toxic, drowning in stress, depression, or poor life choices. This is not to say that you should abandon family members or loved ones that are under stress. There is a fine line between getting too involved that you fall into a dark hole with them or choosing to remain detached from their drama. You want to avoid being emotionally drawn into someone else's whirlwind of consistent upset, especially on a regular basis. It does nothing to help you and nor will it help by feeding them the same negative vibrational words they're exuding by agreeing with their chaos. This is like sprinkling lighter fluid on a burning fire. This energy expands causing more of that same substance. The hard-gritting practical world places huge heavy burdens on one's back that cuts off the psychic connection. Finding that healthy balance between both the grounded earth and the spiritual heaven is ideal.

Coffee and Alcohol Psychic Blocks

Your Spirit team is always communicating with you, but if you're not picking up on anything, then notice what you're consuming into your body that can be the culprit. What you ingest plays a part in what blocks the heavenly psychic connection line. This includes the foods and drinks you eat or drink, to the people you hang around with, to your lifestyle choices in general. Notice what feelings you're experiencing as a result of bringing any of this into your aura. If there are any negative based emotions within and around you afterwards, then that will influence the spirit communication line. If your thoughts are negative, judgmental, hyper critical, or full of fear, then that will also affect the psychic input. Everyone reacts differently to certain foods. One person can be fine with having a cup of coffee, while another person will be more sensitive to the stimuli it gives.

Many have asked if coffee and alcohol specifically blocks your psychic abilities. The short answer is yes to a degree for some folks, but the longer answer is that coffee and alcohol in large amounts significantly dims and blocks Divine communication. This is not necessarily the case if you have one cup of coffee, or one glass of wine, or one or two beers max occasionally. It's only when you start downing more than that where it can dim the communication line. This overloads your psychic system making it challenging to connect. This is an exercise each person will have to test out to see what works best. Test your connections with a cup of coffee and without one to see where you're most comfortable.

Coffee would also include products with caffeine content in it. Everyone's body chemistry is different where someone can have a cup of coffee or mild caffeine intake and it's not going to completely block the communication line, while others will receive a complete block. It's when you get into super high caffeine amounts causing your stress and anxiety levels to rise. It's the stress and anxiety feelings associated with it that dim or blocks the psychic communication line, and not necessarily the cup of coffee or glass of wine.

Not everyone experiences the same effects from caffeine or alcohol though. Someone can have a beer or two max and they find it awakens the connection line with the Other Side, yet the connection is short lived, because then you start coming down off the high within an hour or two later, and you feel groggy and lethargic. Your vibration starts to drop and the match between your high vibrational Spirit team grows further away, so with that said the buzz from alcohol is a temporary high like any sort of toxin.

When you get into three glasses of wine, or you're drinking a six-pack of beer, then you're in a drunken state and have no strong spirit connection. You might pick up on a word or two from God and your Spirit team, but anything coming in is garbled and unclear, or you simply receive nothing but silence. If you can't remember what you did or said drunk, then you're not going to recall anything from Spirit either. The bottom line is that if you receive silence and hear nothing, then you're experiencing a block. Something you've ingested has created this block, or it can be your emotional state is not on a high vibrational level, even though you might personally feel that you're fine. The clue is the silence you think you're getting from your Spirit team.

You might be under the impression God and your Spirit team is ignoring you, which is never true. It is you ignoring them through what you're absorbing into your aura. This is whether through your thoughts and emotions, to your food and drink intake. A drunken state will give you a complete block, partially because your mind is all over the place, scattered, in a fog, and unfocused. Drinking heavy alcohol until you're in a stupor will mess with this clear mindedness and drop your vibration.

This isn't telling anyone to quit drinking coffee, or caffeine, or alcohol, or bad foods, so don't misunderstand this to be a lecture or judgment. It's merely offering what can dim or block the communication line for those concerned. These are basic guidelines that you can consider or disregard if you choose.

As stated, everyone's physical and emotional state is different from one another. Someone can have a beer or a cup of coffee and still have the connection, while someone else notices that it diminishes. I can have a beer or a glass of wine and pick up Spirit messages, but soon after as I come down or move into the buzzed phase is when I notice the connection begin to dim and disappear.

You may find that you love your daily glass of red wine, but one part of you wishes you didn't have that craving. You could decide to reduce the daily glass of red wine to several days a week instead of daily, then gradually move that to once a week, and then eventually to once in a blue moon. The once in a blue moon notion is where you can live without it, but once in a while you share some wine with a friend and you don't beat yourself up over it or feel guilt, since guilt feelings lowers your vibration too. You're able to keep your vices in moderation, but you're not quitting either unless you eventually choose.

It's sometimes easier to eliminate something when you gradually reduce the intake over a period rather than quitting cold turkey. This is because you're slowly and safely allowing yourself and your body to adjust to the new changes you're making. It's not as tough or challenging than if you stopped abruptly one day, which can cause withdrawals and side effects. This applies to anything you're longing to dissolve, reduce, or eliminate. We're just using the coffee and alcohol examples, but switch those words out to the vices you wish to change.

As you were reading those last few paragraphs, you likely already know what it is that has been a concern for you.

You know your body best when it comes to your intake of coffee, alcohol, red meat, dairy, etc. You know what you do, say, or think that will make you feel a certain way.

Like anything that can be damaging or toxic in large quantities, you want to keep the guilty pleasures in moderation if you have a passion for it to the point where you overindulge regularly to where you wind up face down on the floor all day accomplishing nothing towards building your dreams. This isn't for Spirit's benefit, but for your own well-being. They know that when you are vibrating at a higher level that you are more in tune to the guidance coming in that can help you achieve the dreams you long to conquer. It will also help in giving you more energy and focus to put towards doing other things you love.

I used to drink alcohol like a fiend in my early twenties, then one day as I moved into my mid-to-late twenties I changed. Those close to me noticed this drastic change.

It led to numerous questions darted my way, "How did you stop? Why did you stop?"

My initial response was, "I was tired of losing a day."

The misunderstanding was that I stopped and went completely abstinent, which is not true. I still have a beer or a glass of wine on rare occasions, but I'm no longer drinking a six pack or two bottles of wine in one sitting as I would do during my weekly party in a cup days throughout my late teens to early twenties. I felt like crap and would lose a day when I used to do that. I conducted a trial and error process where I discovered what would make me feel uncomfortable and lose my Spirit connection compared to what would strengthen my connection. I spent a great deal of my twenties and thirties keeping all of that to myself except to my circle of close ones. Eventually, I began sharing little reveals here and there through my writing work for those interested or curious in it. I would dissolve or eliminate certain toxic vices and pay attention to if I noticed any spiritual, emotional, or physical difference.

With coffee I discovered that it didn't seem to matter if I had a cup of coffee or not. This is because I felt the exact same way with or without it, so I would think, "Why am I drinking this every day? It's not doing anything of any benefit, since I still feel groggy afterwards."

This was my personal choice to work with my Spirit team to help dissolve my cravings. I'm not anti-coffee or anti-alcohol at all, but just no longer crave it anymore. Not that someone might not catch me have a fun coffee drink with a friend on a rare day, but mostly I stick with teas. You don't beat yourself up over breaking your little discipline routine once in a while. You're not going to go to Hell, and nor will you be banished out to pasture for enjoying a guilty pleasure from time to time.

Make note of what is a human made substance and what comes from the Earth. Human made substances tend to play a part in dimming the Spirit connection, while anything from the Earth can help enhance it such as fruits and vegetables. In the end, when you don't want to give up what you love or you're not ready, then remember the moderation rule if you're trying to simultaneously have a stronger Divine connection.

If you're going to conduct a psychic, angel, or spirit reading connection for yourself or someone else, then hold off on drinking those two margaritas until you're done. Hold off on eating a large meal as that can weigh you down and will reduce any heavenly communication. It is up to you to decide when you are ready to reduce, dissolve, or eliminate a toxin or block, and then begin that process safely with your Spirit team.

CHAPTER TWELVE

*Sensitivities are a Gift
from the Divine*

You might have a tougher time moving through the feelings associated with a Divine message if you're super sensitive. At the same time, the more sensitive you are, then the higher degree of clairsentience you have. It can be both a gift and a curse due to how emotions can make you feel. The trick is to use those emotions to your advantage. Mentally train yourself to view circumstance through emotional detachment so that the emotions don't drown and pull you under. Usually someone that picks up on psychic input regularly each day will be used to it, regardless if it's intense. If you watch the same scary movie repeatedly, then you jump less at the scare parts than you had done when you first watched the film.

Emotional detachment takes practice where you spend time working on how you comprehend situations around you and learning to not take much if anything personally. Let things that normally trigger you to roll off. It's re-training your mind on how it perceives circumstances whether in the physical or spirit worlds. This can be difficult for a sensitive, an empath, someone ridden with anxiety, or a Clairsentient, because it's their overall nature to feel the intense psychic input, the messages and guidance coming in, as well as other people's energies. Compounded onto that are day to day issues that happen in your physical life that can cause imbalance or upset.

As a clear sentient being, your goal is to gradually learn to not enter situations that you know will negatively tamper with your psyche. This includes avoiding locations you know will be crowded. You won't go to the mall or a grocery store in the middle of the day on a weekend. You'll avoid repetitively going to a gossip media site if you know it's going to upset your inner world on any level.

I have a Clairsentient friend that doesn't go outside until nighttime when most people are back indoors again. Although, in general he's a night owl and doesn't mind, but has said that he waits for people to go back inside so he can go outside without interference. There are occasions where this is an annoyance, but there is no wiser alternative that efficiently aligns with his equilibrium. You are making lifestyle adjustments that cause less aggravation on your emotional psychic system.

Whenever you arrive somewhere and see a crowd of people and feel dread or anxiety every single time, then this is a sign that you have strong Clairsentience. The extreme side of this fear manifests into social anxiety and/or agoraphobia, which can affect anyone regardless if you're shy or highly sociable.

I've come across people on both sides of the spectrum from the introverted to the extroverted that have Clairsentience. It's less shocking to find an introverted person with social anxiety or agoraphobia, but there are also extroverted people that crave constant social stimulation and are outgoing, but are also exceptionally sensitive that it keeps them tied to the home base unable to be out in crowds let alone outside in a busy place period. They have a harder time because part of their outgoing nature desires constant social engagement, yet the sensitive part of them causes them to take caution and retreat.

The psychic input coming in from Heaven doesn't typically bother me no matter how intense it is. This is because the input is usually surrounded with a layer of love. It's other people's energies that bother me, so I can't be around that no matter how desperately someone might want me to. I call on Archangel Michael to shield my soul with a layer of white holy light if I need to enter a nest of toxic energies on any given occasion.

Sometimes you can do everything possible to not be affected by psychic input and yet you're still affected. Mediums and psychics become used to the input over the course of their lifetime that they become less bothered by it, but it can still happen even for those that practice emotional detachment. There are times where I am jarred by the psychic input coming in, but it's a temporary jarring, and then it rolls off naturally on its own. It's not something I'm consciously aware I'm doing. If it's extreme, then it can take its toll on me energetically. In a sense, one can say it comes with the territory. Requesting regular assistance from Heaven helps ease the feelings. That means you ask them to shield you from any additional negative, toxic, and dark energy daily.

Pay Attention to Your Sensitivity

As a sensitive, you may find a tendency to take things darted at or around you personally. You might negatively react in ways that is disproportionate to the circumstance taking place. This is the case even if it doesn't feel that way. It is only in hindsight when you look back do you realize that there was something else going on with your feelings and state of mind that caused a larger reaction. It can be a challenge to decipher if what you're picking up on is a message from the Divine or from your ego. This challenge can span a lifetime as you learn to differentiate between all input you're picking up on, because it can come in at the same time, which will make it doubly confusing.

The good news is that because you're a sensitive, you are more in tune to the vibrations around you than others might be. It's just a matter of honing in on what is Heavenly guidance and what is not. The other plus is that if you're highly sensitive emotionally, then you feel the messages and guidance coming in from spirit. You are learning to distinguish between what is a Divine message and what is your lower-self yanking on the reigns. Your lower self is the space the darkness of your ego enjoys controlling and bringing out to cause chaos and turmoil. There is also the Darkness that exists in the spirit plane that some refer to as Hell. That Darkness has its minions attempting to infect human beings because it's so easy to do.

Learn to have a stronger relationship connection with your feelings, so that you can detect if an uneasy emotion is a psychic hit and heavenly guidance, a reaction from your ego, or a side effect from something you've ingested into your body. We know from the earlier chapter that too much caffeine can make you anxious and more stressed. Too much alcohol can cause you to feel erratic, angry, unsettled, or depressed. Some toxins you ingest can create artificial emotions that give the illusion that you're connected with spirit, when in truth you're connecting with your ego. Consuming toxins in large quantities can cause this deception, but again this is not condemning or judging anyone that indulges in it.

I have an extended family that enjoys their alcohol and weed and there is no judgment. I also have those friends that walk into my place, light up their weed vaporizer pen, and start blowing it out the window as if they're sipping water, so none of that bothers me. This is about being aware of what can cause some of the turmoil or disconnectedness with spirit. Keeping certain toxic guilty pleasures in check, balanced, and in moderation is harmless, but of course abstaining from the larger health harming toxins as much as possible is even better. You know what your guilty pleasures or vices are and whether it's hampering or enhancing your life in positive ways. The less you are on, the louder the voice of spirit is.

Being sensitive is a blessing from the Divine. You might not feel like it is when you're sensing every nuance within and around you, including the uncomfortable stuff. Pay attention to those sensations to determine whether it's your ego or Heaven relaying messages through your Clairsentient feeling sense. They could be guiding you to make lifestyle adjustments that continuously cause you turmoil. If the same person around you keeps instigating grief and upset, then what can you do to change that? If you've found a friend has pushed themselves into your life who you don't care for all that much, then what can you do about it? The immediate action step is to begin the process of dissolving them from your life or keep them at super low doses if you're not prepared for complete elimination. Sometimes it's not that simple if it's a spouse, parent, sibling, or close family member.

Think of you and your comfort before any other. It's not selfish to make sure you are taken care of first. Only when you're taken care of can you focus on others. Boundaries need to be set in your life where you are strict and disciplined about who and what you invite into your soul's auric home. These systematic restrictions also include what you're putting into your body.

What are you consuming that soon causes you to feel worse than you did before you consumed it? Sometimes the side effects are worse than the disease. Pay attention to what ultimately aggravates you and brings up negative feelings. You're more than likely a super sensitive being, so something will negatively affect your welfare more than it might with someone who is less sensitive. This includes who you surround yourself with, what you consume, and what you read, such as gossip or certain negative media. If your emotions are provoked into negativity whenever you read about the same topic, then stop seeking it out and reading it. Stop ingesting something that worsens your emotional state. Extricate someone out of your life that never brings anything positive to your world.

Pay attention to what you consume. If you're addicted to numerous daily energy drinks and you're always edgy and irritable, then it's time to dissolve or reduce the intake of this toxin. Seek out healthier alternatives that can help give you energy and focus without the side effects.

If you find you reach for a beer or a glass of wine after work every day and part of you desires to stop or it winds up making you feel worse, then rotate the days where you substitute the alcoholic drink one day and the next day you sit outside with a calming tea such as chamomile, lavender, or tension tamer tea.

Guilt feelings over anything will lower the soul's vibration and this includes feeling guilty over having a beer. If you're going to have the beer, then have it without guilt. The guilt emotions will reveal a drop in your vibration.

Three separate people take the same alternative herbal supplement only to discover they all had a different experience with it. Some had a positive experience, while another had negative side effects, and the third participant felt no noticeable change.

Someone says, "I have two beers and I don't feel much."

While another says, "I have one beer and I'm on the floor."

Everyone's physical chemistry is different from one another. What works for one person might not work for someone else. This is about knowing and understanding what you can safely handle by gauging the effects beforehand, during, and afterwards. This is all aligned with paying attention to everything within and around you. Awaken your extra sensory perception in all aspects of your life so that you may grow even more aware than you ever have.

Tune in and follow the guidance and leadership of God, Spirit, or Divine. Avoid allowing your purpose to be taken away by other people. They may not have malice by wanting you to follow them and do what they want you to do, but if that means it's going to take you down a path that is disagreeable to your soul, then you are going against your integrity and the repetitive warnings from your Spirit team that something is off. Spirit doesn't give you guidance and messages for their sake. They do it for your own protection and higher self's soul purpose. They can see what's coming up ahead even when you don't. You're not here to live other people's lives.

There may be times when you lose someone close to you by choosing not to do something that feels unfavorable to your heart. Your Spirit team has greater things in store for you beyond being held back by others. Avoid falling into the toxic allure of people pleasing. As a sensitive, you may be more caring and wanting to help, but if something feels off about what you're being asked to do, then trust that instinct. Generally, the first sense I receive about anything is often a psychic hit communicating something important that ends up coming to fruition. My personal guidance system comes from above, and not from other people, and so should yours. Your sensitivity is a gift to help you make the best decisions or course of action while on your life path, even if it's not what someone else wants you to do.

CHAPTER THIRTEEN

*Psychic Spirit Team Communication
and my Creative Channeling Process*

My Spirit team's perspective is different than the outlook of the people living an Earthly life, including myself at times. They give me another angle to peer through in a sense. The way I view things is split in parts. One of those parts is that I have a human ego where I can become affected over certain day to day practical things to a degree as any other person. Although, I'm able to take things more in stride and have it roll off with the assistance and connection with my Spirit team. Others around me have used the phrase, "Calm inside the storm." They've said that while everyone is running around creating or swirling around in drama, I'm unaffected with unmoving rock like strength.

In my earlier teen years, I wasn't working with my Spirit team daily the way I began to as I grew older, but I was in regular communication with them growing up only because it was inevitable. They have been communicating with me since I was a toddler. I don't remember when it started because it was as soon as I was conscious. They're communicating while I'm busy doing other things. I'm not connecting in the way it seems many connect, which is the candles, incense, and props. I can be walking to my car and I hear them informing me of something important. There was no way to run from it or not hear them in my world. The days I didn't work with them or I ignored them were highly noticeable. For instance, issues that popped up were more dramatic, heightened, intense, and all over the place. With Heaven's intervention, the issues were less intense and resolved quicker. I grew to learn they were trying to get my attention in order to work with them like any team would. I realized that I didn't need to go through life completely alone. You can call on them at any time, day or night, to help with something.

One other part of me is the consciousness of my Spirit team. This part of me has an emotionally detached aerial view of circumstances once the dark side of my ego and blocks are dissolved or reduced. Sometimes the answers Spirit gives me are not necessarily what one wants to hear. Nor are they answers that would give one peace of mind depending on how your ego takes it. There is a separation between who I am, and the spirit guidance offered. Falling into a channel for me when it comes to the work can happen naturally, effortlessly, and within seconds. It takes longer if I'm absorbed in someone else's drama, which I learned to avoid as I grew older. No matter how hard you try to dodge it, sometimes it lands on your lap for whatever reason, or you accidentally walk right into it carelessly.

The transition from the human part of me to my Spirit team happens within seconds. I might walk away giggling at some obscene practical joke I've played on someone and walk into the next room. I sit down and move both my hands over my crown and over my face mentally calling in my Spirit team and now I'm in the channeled connection. My Spirit team has the steering wheel and I'm in the passenger seat kicking back. There is an evident distinction between their helpful compassion to my personal crass extremism. I think some people expect me to be walking with my hands in the air connected every second. How odd would that look?

Heaven understands you're going through human experiences they cannot relate to since it is not the world they live in. They reside in a sphere of consciousness place that is all love, all knowing, uplifting joy, happiness, serenity, and peace. There is no antagonism, bullying, domination, and unkindness where they are. They view Earthly life behind a glass studying human behavior and actions like a therapist. They know the basis for life and the reasons things happen. They know the truth and reality that blindsides the ego. Even if the spirit in Heaven had once lived an Earthly life, they did during a time in Earth's history that is radically different than it is now. History and humanity are ever evolving at a slow pace, but it is evolving. It would progress much quicker if the darkness of ego were more accepting of other people. To not do so is naïve, animalistic, and primal.

You're having a human experience and with that there will be hurt, pain, and suffering. There are times where you unknowingly invited it in and other times when it was beyond your control due to free will.

The messages from Heaven come in clear and effortlessly when you are calm, peaceful, centered, and in an environment that matches those traits. Heavenly bliss is the state to thrive for and attain in order to access spirit information and guidance. The power of being in a nature locale is beyond measure. It's an impeccable location to connect with spirit or for a creative artist to create in. It's the space that the imagination reaches the channeling frequency that connects Spirit to human soul. Creative artists have a higher frequency of sensitivity that allows them to receive input from the Other Side, even if they're unaware this is where it's coming from. Messages and guidance filter in through your etheric senses, which are undetected by the physical part of you.

It often sifts into your consciousness in a way that is not always clear. The information you receive can be discombobulated and all over the place depending on what state you're in.

My state of mind moves into a space where my consciousness is taken over by my Spirit team. When that happens, I have sudden volcanic energy bursts of messages flying in that I have to write out quickly before the moment is gone. The energy is fast paced and high that makes me feel like I can run a marathon. There is a small window before the door is shut again. Physical demands and life circumstances can play a part in that. I grow agitated if interrupted while in that high. This disruption is like being abruptly shaken awake from sleep in a frenzied force.

Once that natural high euphoria has reached its peak, my energy level suddenly and dramatically falls to the ground without warning, and so do the words. The communication door to Heaven has slammed shut and I'm no longer in the channel zone. I'm slumped over or on the floor trying to regain life force and energy to stand up. It can take a little while before I reach that state again, but I can get there quicker when I'm in a serene setting. Nature surroundings are a stronger environment to take a walk in afterwards. This is not as effective when you live in a noisy area that has too many people and cars. What also helps is going for a walk, jogging, hiking, or biking. Movement and physical activity are good to do no matter how much energy has been drained from the channeling session.

Mediums communicate with those that crossed over to the Other Side and relay messages to those on the Earth plane wanting to converse with their deceased loved one that reside in another plane. Mediums are channeling, but channeling has a slightly differing goal than mediumship. Channelers will communicate information from more than one being or entity such as a team of Guides, whereas a Medium is connecting with a departed loved one in the spirit world. While psychics peer into the probable future by connecting with a guide or angel.

When I have the channeler hat on, then I communicate with a higher-level team of Spirit Guides, Guardian Angels, Saints, and Archangels primarily for the purpose of the work they have me do. The words in the work are intended to empower, inspire, and teach others that are interested or ready for the information. Sometimes one is guided to a book by their Spirit team because there might be one sentence you needed to read that is the answer to a question that has been up in the air for some time. I cannot articulate the messages efficiently through speaking. My mind moves too fast to verbalize it at times. It's easier for me to sit down and write it all out without distraction. It also comes out clearer pending my state of mind is free of toxins. Have you ever tried to email someone when you're upset? The email dictated comes out all wrong and nonsensical. You re-read it later and say, "Why did I send this?"

Describing how channeling works is like a gifted actor attempting to describe their process. Popular working actors have said they read the text on the page and interpret the words as best they can. Every actor has a different method and there is no right or wrong way. It is whatever works successfully for that person. This could be the same way that your psychic intuitive gifts might be stronger with Clairvoyance, but weaker with Claircognizance. Everyone's psychic gifts vary from one person to the next. Channeling works in this same fashion where other channelers communicate in a variety of different ways that are not similar to the way someone else does it.

I've been channeling naturally since I was a child, even though I never attributed a word to what I was doing. It was just a process that was taking place automatically the same way one speaks. It's not like they teach this stuff in school, although they should. People would be more connected and in tune, which would result in their life experiences being smoother and less troublesome. Those that want to thrive in the world of business, political, or legal arenas would be even more successful if they were psychically in tune.

When you fine tune your senses, then there is no telling what you can do. Creative people in the arts tend to be exceptional channelers. This includes musicians, singers, actors, artists, and writers. They have a strong measure of feeling able to walk in others shoes. They have a greater capacity of input in understanding all things beyond. They channel to write music, lyrics, books, and performing. This channeled information filters into them from above.

Some Mediums meditate to get into a trance like state. The reason this is an effective method is because you're taking at least a few minutes to quiet your mind. You're silencing everything around you in order to have a stronger connection with Spirit. When you quiet your thoughts and the noise of the outside world, then there is room for Spirit and God to come rushing in. Silencing everything is by removing any traces of negativity from your aura. If you're upset about something, then this will make it difficult to channel until you let that go and release it.

The connection comes and goes throughout the day depending on what my state of mind is like at any given moment. I'm an ever-flowing neurotic emotional mess, so when I'm moved into a state of reception, then the messages and guidance flows into my soul through one of my Clair channels and the connection is made. Asking for the connection to be made while in a meditative state doesn't always work for me since I operate on an adrenaline rush. Being in the channel, the connection smashes in without warning. The frequency brain waves move up and down on their own while I'm doing other things until there is a connection, then I stop and sit down to recite the information flowing in. It's almost like the tides of the ocean are constantly moving, and so is the frequency channel within my soul. If I'm disconnected at any moment, then that state can change three minutes later out of nowhere.

I will stare at a blank page of a potential manuscript for days and even weeks and then bam the channel connection is made. The information is either dictated to me clairaudiently, or it's all dumped into my mind in one sitting through claircognizance like a tidal wave gushing over land. Sometimes they'll show me visuals through clairvoyance, while other times I'll feel it.

When I fall into the channel space for a project, then no interruptions are allowed. Breaking this rule interferes with the process and flow of input. Breaking away knocks me out of the channel momentum. It can destroy the creative process for the day. Once the Spirit connection is made during the creative process, then I separate and disappear for a while. This is also similar to the process of a working actor.

When I'm not channeling for the work, then day to day psychic hits are coming through sporadically via my Spirit team or council as I sometimes call them. As a child, I could hear voices of spirit communicating to me. Sometimes they spoke individually and other times in unison. I knew they weren't on this plane, but it felt like they were in the next room or standing next to me. I'd be outside playing, and I could hear them talking to me. At the time I never used the words guides, heaven, or Spirit team to describe them. When I was a child, I thought of them as people located somewhere else that wasn't on Earth. They have always been like a loving teaching counsel of souls, and yet they have always been right there with me travelling along wherever I went. I never thought of it as strange or different. They were never cruel and have always been kind and loving. I thought of them as my best friends outside of the physical human friendships. This is because they listened to me and heard my problems and offered assistance that helped me in some way. They knew and know everything about me, every secret, and every tiny shred of hidden nuances. They would tell me things that were about to happen and then it would come to light. It is the one area I have always felt truly loved unconditionally. In all the decades on this planet they have yet to utter one judgmental or condescending word, which is pretty miraculous considering that most people can't seem to get through one day without doing that. They have my back no matter what. When it's all you know, then you don't think twice about it. You gravitate more towards them and God over anything else without question or hesitation.

I assumed that everyone was communicating daily the way I was growing up, but I gradually discovered most were not paying much attention to their psychic senses. I later learned from my Spirit team that they could if they tuned in. My Spirit team had me go through tough tumultuous bootleg camp like exercises and struggles that showed me what would block the connection and what would open that connection.

All Souls Can Connect with the Divine

Some religious followers use their words to harm others or put people down and say that it is coming from God. While some non-believers will then retaliate and say that anyone who says their words are coming from God is a crazy person. Both of those extreme points are false. God is everywhere. He is in every cell, atom, and ion that exists. He is the energy that makes up every centimeter on the planet, the universe, and all dimensions across time and space. He is within every human soul, animal, plant, you, and even the most harmful hate filled person. There is no escape from Him. You can refer to God to whatever sounds more comfortable to you like Spirit, the Light, the Universe, etc. The best parts of you are what God is and the worst parts are your ego, also known as the Devil or the Darkness. The only destruction and corruption going on in the world is done at the hands of humankind plagued and infected by that Darkness.

It doesn't matter what someone believes or does not believe, because He grants all living energy free will choice even if it's not true. The purpose for that is to help your soul learn, grow, and evolve. You don't learn, grow, and evolve unless you're granted the freedom to choose and experience things for yourself. You can stay stuck in a negative mindset or despise other people, but the only person it hurts in the end is you. It stunts your soul's growth even if you cannot see that it has at that moment. There is no clarity when the ego is running the show. At the end of your life run when you cross over, then the truth becomes clearer as you are shown images of all your human years on the planet and what you did or did not do with it. You're shown what you said or did not say to someone. This includes how that affected you and the other person, whether it was a loved one, or an acquaintance, or stranger. You experience those emotions through all perceptions.

Everyone is connected to God because there is no way you cannot be. It is easy to determine who is picking up on the voices of God and who is not. God has the highest vibration traits possible and imaginable. This means when you exude high vibration traits such as love, joy, and peace, then you are connected to God. When you exude traits that are the opposite of that such as hate, pain, negative feelings and thoughts, then you are disconnected from God. What this also means is that someone can be a practicing religious person who goes to Church regularly, but is a negative or mean person, then they are unaware they are disconnected from God in those moments.

You do not need to go into a Church to communicate with God. The media portrays cruel intentions born out of a religious person, so it gives all religious followers a bad name, but there are both good and bad people in every group that exists on the planet. You don't hear about the good, because the media consistently feeds you the negative. They dramatize stories because they know that's the only thing that can hook in the darkness of ego. One concludes that it must be all people in that group that are bad when that is all you hear.

An atheist or non-believer can be displaying compassionate, loving, and giving traits to others and IS connected to God more than they would believe. It doesn't matter if you go to Church every week and have crosses adorned all over your house. If the actions you display are of a low vibration or negative, then you have no connection with God or your Spirit team in that moment.

I'm overtly sensitive to the point where it has been an issue in the practical world. It is that sensitivity gauge, which has enabled me to connect and communicate with a team of guides and angels as if one were pouring a glass of water or flicking on a light switch.

Those that are equally sensitive and in tune understand this since it's something they experience as well. It is not limited to "special" people as every soul that exists is able to connect when they incorporate certain practices and lifestyle changes that enhance and awaken these gifts.

A practicing psychic has higher degrees of a Divine connection, because they participate in it regularly. When you do anything regularly, then you become better at it. As a high vibrational psychic vessel, you come to know to steer clear of drama, toxins, and negative people as much as possible. You're aware enough to know not to go to a busy grocery store at high noon on a weekend day if you can help it. You're not going to hang out on media sites or phone apps where harsh egoist words are darted at and around you.

I was able to successfully submerge myself into the practical world and function like any other material driven human being. Deep down I found the practical world jarring and those in it to be lacking compassion, soul, and heart. The dark side of humanity is aloof, cruel, abusive, and antagonistically self-absorbed. The only way to function in that nonsense and to get through it was to drown myself in addictions and distractions such as drugs, alcohol, cigarettes, and other time wasters. I discovered that these addictions also contributed to me being unable to fully hear the voices of Spirit. My Spirit team taught me that these addictions dimmed the communication channel to them.

Excellence is what I thrive for and I'm just as hard on myself as I am on anyone else. Part of this is my meticulous Virgo Rising. Like Heaven, they've shown me that human souls can go the distance and striving for excellence within and without if they have the passion and desire to.

Re-Center Yourself

The voices of spirit are uplifting and calm, even if it is warning you of danger. They will guide, inspire, and lovingly coax you onward on your higher self's path. Their intention is to help you stay focused and clear minded in order to accomplish your life purpose goals. They're not fans of seeing anyone experience negative emotions and therefore desire to help you swiftly move past that when it hits you. It's part of the human condition to have easy access to these feelings, since that is the doorway to communicating with Spirit. When the negative emotions overtake you, then this blocks communication and does more harm than good to your overall well-being.

Even the most centered person on the planet experiences negative feelings from time to time. When that happens, they can readily glide over it and move back into a focused detached emotional state, rather than dwelling in the toxicity of negative emotions. Address something with assertive compassion that needs to be addressed, and then let it go and move on.

The centered soul is in tune and can easily hone in on the reasoning behind someone's actions that might have bothered them to begin with. They do this without judgment. This isn't about making excuses for someone's poor behavior, but it's understanding what's behind an action and choosing not to be a part of any blame, drama, or anything that brings you down or negatively riles you up. When you move into negative territory, then revert to focusing on activities and people that make you smile. The clearer Divinely guided answers come in when you're centered and standing still.

Meditate, relax, and center yourself guru. Drink more water than usual to release the toxins accumulated in your organs, and in your emotional state as well. Things begin to feel good after you release the junk that clogs up your soul. It's healing, therapeutic, and freeing. When the Divinely guided answers come in, then allow it to flow into your consciousness.

Relaxing Exercise

Find a comfortable spot to sit and relax in. Breathe in deeply and exhale, then repeat breathing in and then out as you grow more relaxed. On every exhale, breathe out all traces of negativity. Breathe out any pain, hurt, or sadness you're holding inside. Breathe out all that toxic emotion. Breathe out elements of residual anger and any level or form of upset. Breathe out any envy, jealousy, doubts, and all hints of negative toxins and emotions.

Whenever you inhale, then in imagine you are breathing in the light. Drink in this light whenever you inhale. Allow the light to envelope you inside and out. Imagine it is diminishing and dissolving all lower energies. Allow it to blast away all remaining negativity in you. Breathe in and drink in this light. Exhale this light so that it is blown out of you and filling up your aura around your soul and body. Now you are bathing in this light inside and out. Every time you breathe, the light grows bigger and begins to sparkle. There is no escape from this light as it fills you up lifting you into a peaceful serene love and joyful feeling. Visualize and feel yourself being surrounded by this light of God lifting your vibration up. This is the space where psychic input comes flowing in. God did not make it difficult to connect with Spirit. It's a matter of relaxing and tuning in.

CHAPTER FOURTEEN

Spirit Guides and Angels

Your life force is the positive energy that flows through your soul. When it is operating at its highest state, then that is when you are most connected to God. When your life force energy drops, then this affects your mind and your physical body. This is followed by you experiencing a perpetual negative state, such as you're always getting sick, feeling depressed, or enduring a permanent stress state that never lightens. You lose interest in activities that once made you smile.

When your life force dwindles and remains permanently low, then it's time to ignite it. Igniting it will unleash any pent-up repression that might have been forced upon you at the hands of others or at your own doing. You are not moving through your life alone. Spirit helpers that are within reach the moment you call on them surround you.

Your Guardian Angel is a spirit being who typically did not live a life as a human being, whereas your Spirit Guide has lived at least one Earthly life. Often your Spirit Guide is someone related to you. They can be a relative of yours from centuries ago or one who passed on not long before you were born. They go through formal training in Heaven before they can efficiently be allowed to guide an Earthly soul. One of the basic training rules given is they are not allowed to interfere with your free will choice unless it's to prevent your potential death before your time.

You might have more than one guide or angel if you are working with the Other Side and Heaven regularly. If you are involved in a life purpose activity that is geared towards assisting yourself or others on the planet in a positive way, then you may have more than one guide. Guides and Angels are also drawn to someone that displays love, joy, or peace traits on a regular basis. It can be someone that is innately a compassionate loving human being who does their best to do the right thing. This brightens that soul's light; which spirits see and feel. The guide or angel will come into that human soul's vicinity by being attracted to their light like a magnet.

If someone prays and communicates with God regularly, or works with spirit beings in Heaven, then they also tend to attract in other heavenly helpers to their side. These Guides and Angels might come into your space to begin the process of working with you in order to help you achieve a specific desire, pending that it is aligned with your higher self. They might come into your vicinity to work on easing your heart of sadness, anxiety, or stress brought upon by Earthly concerns and circumstances. You wake up one morning to discover that you're feeling quite good after experiencing a hard time. This is your Guardian Angel working on your spirit. You log onto the Internet and see an invitation to an event. You feel nudged to go to this event and while there you meet someone who becomes your love partner for life. This is your Spirit Guide working with you. Your Guardian Angel tends to focus on your thoughts and feeling state, while your Spirit Guide will focus on your external practical matters.

Your personal Spirit Guide and Guardian Angel will be among the mix of souls on the Other Side that greet you when you cross over and head back home. Some have referred to your team as your invisible helpers, but this is not entirely accurate since your Guide and Angel are not invisible. They might be hidden to the naked eye for many, but they are most definitely visible.

If you're someone with a highly calibrated psychic clair channels, then you're more apt to being aware of your Spirit team. Your team takes the form and shape that they know is familiar or comfortable for your human mind to process.

Others have been sharing their personal experiences and encounters with angels for centuries on all corners of the globe. The angels appear for that person just when they needed it most. Sometimes the angels materialize as a reminder to let you know they are indeed real and present for you. The angels and Archangels are God's hands and arms. They are an extension of Him. When you communicate with an angel, you are communicating with God. You are not praying to the angels, since all exaltation goes to God. Since it's difficult for a human soul to reach God, the angels are His gift to you in order to help you improve and raise your vibration so that your connection with Him is stronger. He is always communicating with you, but you do not pick up on that when experiencing any negative feelings. This is where the angels come in to lift you up so that you have a crystal-clear communication line with God.

My mother recalled a story when I was eight years old. We were walking through a mall making our way through one of the shops and I was lagging behind her out of curiosity. She noticed I stopped to study the statue figures of angels on a shelf. She watched me concerned because the look on my face was one of anger, as if someone had provoked me. I looked at her astonished and said with irritation, "Why are they all blonde with wings? That's not how they look."

Not all spirit beings have wings, and this includes angels, even though artists have been depicting angels with wings for eons. This is due to the light of the angel being so bright that it seems as if there are wings behind them. Angels appear how they want to for that specific person. Sometimes they appear as a human being that shows up to help you in some way, and then they vanish without a trace. Most angels typically appear with white and/or blue sparkling lights around them and through them. They are androgynous and not in human physical form, even though they may appear that way to ease the human mind.

One's Guide and Angel reside in the dimension above the Earth plane. It is easier to connect to them than if they were in one of the higher dimensions. Your Spirit team can see, hear, and feel you through this domain, but you will have a tougher time connecting with them in return due to the heavy density wall that separates these worlds.

There were episodes in the series *True Blood* that showcased a doorway into a fictionalized world where Fairies resided. The doorway and transporting part of that design was not far off from the transition of dimensions such as the Earth sphere to the next dimension where Heaven and the Realm world exist. Another Science Fiction piece that is also not far off in describing the spirit planes is the *Twilight Zone*. The logline of that series basically says that the twilight zone is the doorway into another dimension. The creators of these entertainment pieces and most Science Fiction entertainment come from one of the heavenly Realms where Star Souls are born (a.k.a. Star Child, Star Seed, Star Person). Some of the Star souls that have been born into a human body might not have been aware that they were receiving these visions, ideas, and information from above. Regardless, they've incorporated them into human reality. This information they receive is dropped into the deepest part of their consciousness. This subconscious space is where the connection with the Other Side resides.

You are a spirit whose life force never dies, even if it feels that way sometimes. Your spirit resides in a temporary physical body in order to have an Earthly life for a variety of purposes. The body you inhabit will not last forever. It will age and eventually give out. In the human reality, you call it a death, but it is not a true death since your spirit is still intact and alive. It is just no longer crammed and stuck in its human physical body that weighs you down. Your physical body is a rental and you want to take care of this rental with good diet and exercise. It is hoped that you won't trash it the way some trash their apartments.

In the spiritual genre, many use the terminology *Body, Mind and Soul*. Those affiliated with that genre have the goal of improving all aspects and the totality of oneself. This is by loving your body and taking care of it, but also by being aware that you have a soul that you need to take care of as well too. You want to be aware and in tune to the idea of who and what you are. When your physical body has given out and is no longer functioning, then your soul exits its body and passes through a tunnel of light to the Other Side. This Other Side is reached by moving through the doorway or tunnel of light into another dimension. This other dimension is where Heaven and other dimensions exist.

Often you agreed to have a physical life for a variety of purposes. Everyone is on the planet with the goal of spreading the three biggest traits aligned with God: Love, joy, and peace. All words affiliated with those three words describe what Heaven is like. You may look around and wonder how humanity grew to be removed from those phenomenal traits, but it is the reason you are here. Life is rough for some and reaching that state of being can be challenging, but it is not impossible.

Heaven cares about humanity and has been displeased with how everyone treats one another on Earth, not to mention the ongoing crises state the planet is in due to human tampering. This is from the environment, to the unnecessary destruction of nature, animals, and other people. Building physical dwellings on top of one another has contributed to this suffocating feeling and disconnected others from God. It's a struggle to reach a true connection with tampering energies around you, but alas it's not unmanageable with practice. Some are nonchalant and in denial about the current state of Earth. They debunk the idea that anything is wrong with it. They write it off and take no responsibility in contributing to the damage of the world.

Earthly life might sound like some kind of science experiment gone wild placing you here to live and then removing your memory of who and what you are. Your soul's memories are not completely erased, but just suppressed. The Earth's density and the many blocks around you have limited the important parts of this memory. Past life memories are reduced to nothing unless it is relevant. Otherwise you'd be experiencing heavy emotion over something you did in a past life.

All souls have access to the deeper parts of their consciousness. When you are born, you are completely psychic and in tune to all things around you, beyond, and on over to the Other Side. Gradually, your caregivers, peers, and the society you grew up in began to have a larger influence on your human development. They train you on what to like, what not to like, and how to think. The ones that break away from that cycle tend to be rapidly evolving souls. They know they have an important mission or purpose here, even if it's to spread compassion, love, or joy to others in some manner.

The negative influences around you dimmed your connection and light to Heaven. How these contributors did this was by putting images in front of you of the physical world and inflicting the limited routines onto your way of life that it became systematic. This included that you're disciplined and on a schedule. You go to bed at a certain hour and you wake up around the same hour. You have breakfast and you head off to school, or when you're older you head to a job or a career. The school schedule is relatively the same and so is your job schedule. You drive back and forth to work to make money to pay for your car, a place to live, food, as well as clothing. You do this for what feels like forever while falling deeper into the routine of physical Earthly life, which is not the soul's true existence at all in the end. This cycle continues indefinitely until you retire and wait to pass on. That will oppress any high vibrating soul if that's all it's doing. You need to physically survive and take care of yourself, but don't lose sight of who your soul is while on this journey.

If you do not feel you are psychically in tune, then your goal is to begin the process of becoming more in tune. This means paying attention to everything around you beyond the physical. None of that is real or important in the end. One thing that both believers and non-believers can agree upon is that one day this will all cease to exist for you. You will eventually depart this plane. There is no way around that, so why not make the most of it and raise your consciousness and do the soul work.

Your Guide and Angel assist and guide you down a path that benefits your higher self. Therefore, enhancing your psychic gifts is important. It's to be able to communicate with them more effortlessly. Your higher self is the part of your soul's consciousness that is aligned with optimism such as love, joy, and peace. These are words that are also what Heaven is like while living there. Your lower self is your ego and the part of you the Darkness does what it can to grow, since it loves seeing destruction and downfall. The Devil and Darkness are doing its job when you see humankind behaving at its worst. The Darkness is aligned with the harm, hurt, and hate traits. It is the bully that seeks to destroy someone else because they are different. It is the part of you that wallows in any negative feeling or thought. This might be anger, stress, depression, sadness, or confusion. Someone who is a gossip and trash talks others resides in their lower self. The lower self is cut off from God and is not psychic, while the higher self is part of God and the Holy Spirit. Your higher self is psychic and in tune with what resides beyond and outside of this physical existence.

You can call on your Spirit team any time. You can call on any higher being in heaven from someone you love that passed on, to other guides, angels, to God, to Jesus or whoever you feel closest to. You can also call on an Archangel. The Archangels are hierarchy spirit beings that manage the angels and reside in another dimension. Like Guides and Angels, you can request the assistance of a specific Archangel to come into your life when needed. Many of them have traits they specialize in; such as Archangel Michael is God's General. He goes to battle for you, gives you strength and courage, and protects you from harm. Archangel Raphael is the healing angel that can help with anything health or well-being related. He might assist by guiding you to exercise, change your diet, and find the right doctor, or healer. Archangel Gabriel helps the artists and parents of the world. She's the motivator pushing you to get to work on creative projects. Archangel Uriel is the one who gives you those great light bulb ideas and shines a light on the path you're intended to be on.

Like the angels, the Archangels are God's hands and arms, which means when you're communicating with an Archangel, you're immediately communing with God even if you're not intending to. Archangels, angels, and spirit guides show up in your vicinity the minute you call out to them.

CHAPTER FIFTEEN

You Are Psychic!

All souls are created equally and no one is more special than any other. A soul might incarnate into a human body on the Earth plane and appear visually different from another soul within its physical casing, but the soul itself is made up of the same substance as all souls. It incarnates into a human body to live an Earthly life with others who appear and act differently than they do. Part of the reason for this is in order to teach that soul to love and accept someone for their differences. If everyone appeared and acted the same, how boring would that be? Yet, that is what the ego desires. It wants everyone to look, act, and support the same things as it does or else there will be Hell to pay.

The planet would be a beautiful uplifting joyful place to be if every soul was operating from their true highest vibrational nature full time. Unfortunately, that is not realistic since the darkness of ego in humankind has made the planet a negative place to be living on. It turned Earth into a ticking time bomb on the fringes of exploding. It is a place ruled by greed, power, hatred, violence, and pain. Humankind is to blame for ensuring the planet remains in that negative state.

Obsessing over media stories will block your psychic radar. This applies to those who fall into the negative gossip about celebrity, entertainment, and politics. If you spend your days attacking political candidates or celebrities, then you have created a thick block between your Spirit team and your communication with them. When you consistently complain about a political candidate you don't like, or a celebrity you despise, or someone you don't support, then you have contributed to the negative energy state of the planet. Note the word *consistently*, meaning if you do it rarely such as once or twice, then it won't create that much of a dent, but multiply that with doing it regularly and with everyone else who is doing the same thing, and how often you're doing it, then you've got a disaster of toxic energy flooding the etheric atmosphere around Earth.

Are you a regular offender? Or did you allow it to slip out in conversation casually without malice a few times? The emotion behind the words adds weight to how large of a contribution it is. The more negative feeling the emotion is, then the more polluted the energy is being darted into the atmosphere. If you're communicating positive uplifting words about these things, then you are doing your part in uplifting the vibrational energy around the planet into that of love.

What did the cartoon character in the Disney film *Bambi* say? If you can't say anything nice, then don't say anything at all. It's as basic as that positive mantra that has been worded and re-worded over the centuries by those who desire others to be bathed in love and joy around the clock. They understand that being around a negative person just brings you down. Who wants to be around that? The ego does! The angels have joked that they are happy to mace anyone with white Light that is permanently stuck in the dark toxic cesspool of negativity, which is not a pleasant place to live.

Feeling any kind of negative emotion for a prolonged period will block Heavenly communication. This means if you're living under constant stress, heavily depressed, or perpetually angry. Those are the kinds of emotions that dim and block the communication line with the Other Side. This is also why working psychics and mediums typically take fifteen minutes or less before starting their readings for the day to relax, re-center, and turn the noise around them off. This way they can efficiently connect with the spirit worlds for accurate messages for that client.

You are a soul in a temporary human body with emotions, feelings, and thoughts you are wrestling with every second. Believe me I can relate having incarnated into a human family this lifetime with depression, anxiety, and suicidal tendencies right down my Mother's genetic line. I've battled depression, anxiety, and negative thoughts on occasion just like any other. I'm not immune to falling down that rabbit hole, but I'm consciously aware of it and doing my best work to climb back out as quickly as possible because I know in the end it doesn't help me. I also know that it's not necessarily something that someone can control. It can take a lifetime of discipline battling mental disorders on this Earth plane. I've had lifelong anxiety and social anxiety over depression. The social anxiety was brought upon by an abusive childhood upbringing at the hands of a violent parent. The extreme social anxiety and anxiety symptoms were not present when I was born. They were engrained during my human development days. I understand what it's like to battle with mental disorders, but this isn't the same as falling into a perpetual pessimistic path about what's in the media. If I were a pessimist, I could never have accomplished the things I set out to do over the course of my life, even after numerous parties told me I couldn't do it. I paid no mind and went after what I was intended to do and accomplished it. You can too!

A high vibrating soul can do their best to ensure they steer clear of drama by working hard to set up their life in a way that has minimal contact with the nonsense of physical life. The further you are away from the noise, then the stronger your psychic frequencies are.

The soul is a highly calibrated psychic machine that fluctuates up and down while inside the human body on the Earth plane. When it's in the spirit world it stays highly calibrated, but when on the Earth plane it bounces around all over the place due to the dense heavy thick atmosphere that surrounds the planet. Most of the particles that exist in this density are created by every soul on the planet by negative actions and thoughts. If the atmosphere is this extremely dense, then you can imagine how awful and toxic so many souls are in the way they act and think on a daily basis. It shouldn't be a surprise to anyone as to how bad it is, because all you have to do is log online to the Internet and skim gossip media sites and comments. Visit social media sites like Twitter, Instagram, or Facebook and you'll get a pretty good idea over how bad it is. The culprits and offenders are blind to the temporary rushed high they're wallowing in and are unaware they're doing anything wrong. It's the same way an abuser denies having abused anyone when an accusation is made. Holding a mirror up to oneself with objectiveness can help in seeing how bad one might be acting out. I've heard people tell others who act out, "You should watch yourself on video to see how bad you are with others. It might wake you up."

Luckily, there are many immensely awesome high vibrational light workers and warrior of lights who know their purpose and reason for incarnating during any time in history. They have chosen to steer clear of the drama and noise of the physical life and limit their posts and dealings to ones that are uplifting, empowering, and inspirational. They do their best to remain centered as much as possible in the eye of the hurricane.

Every soul has clairs (clear senses) and chakras (energy points) that move up and down and expand in and out. It acts like a gauge depending on where that soul's consciousness is at and what kind of emotions that soul is experiencing at any given moment during its existence. If you are riding sky high on love and joy, then your vibration raises. When your vibration raises, then so does your psychic antennae. If you are in the throes of any negative emotion, including complaining or whining about someone else, or what's being done to you, or how something upsets you, then this drops your vibration, and lowers your psychic frequency. It's just the way the soul is designed vibrating with varying colors and shades of the rainbow. It can glow a vibrant green color as it experiences healing, to an uplifting joyful bright yellow, to a purifying white, and then to the darkest shade of toxic black. This is all in the span of an hour depending on what that soul is experiencing in its life. If their emotions and moods fluctuate, then so does the psychic antennae.

It is the soul's goal to be aware of that and conscious of it. Knowing what will wear them down and what will enhance it. When you discover you've slipped into a low vibration, then work on raising your vibration again. Even the most compassionate loving person will slip into a low vibration. Sometimes it's not even at your own hands. You could be in line at a grocery store absorbing negative energies without realizing it, or you hear someone arguing with venom, or a friend darts gossip at you, or you read a negative post on social media, then your vibration begins to drop and you didn't intend for that to happen. You were minding your own business high on life and then the negative energies infiltrated you. When that happens, then work on re-raising your vibration, clearing your space, centering, and grounding yourself.

Over the centuries, it has been taught to believe that having psychic gifts are only for a select chosen few. The reality is that every soul is born with these gifts and capabilities of being a conduit with the Other Side, including the ones that are completely closed off and blocked to it. The more psychic hits you receive throughout the day will give you a clue as to when you are operating with a high vibration and when you're on a lower vibrational playing field. It is raising your vibration that gives one clearer psychic reception.

A Medium is someone that acts as a vessel of communication with the Other Side. Spirits on the Other Side live in a world that is high vibrational, which also means they have a high vibration. It's much easier to have a high vibration in the spirit world than it is in the practical world since the soul's natural state of being is high vibrational to begin with. The spirit world is bathed in high vibrational energy. There are no wars, hatred, anger, hating, or harming of any kind back home. It is 100% pure love, joy, and peace.

The spirit in Heaven has a high vibrational state of being and a human soul has a lower vibrational state even when operating at its highest potential. This can make the psychic connection challenging on Earth. This is also why even the best psychics will only receive pieces of information coming through that later prove to be accurate. They're not receiving the whole picture at times because their vibration is attempting to connect with the higher vibrational energy in the spirit world.

When the Medium wishes to make a stronger connection, they will work on raising their vibration to a higher state, and their Spirit team will begin to lower their vibration in order to reach the Medium. They are meeting the Medium conduit halfway, hence the word *Medium*, which is the halfway mark.

A Medium is psychic, but a psychic is not a Medium. Every soul is born psychic and has varying degrees of this ability, but that does not equate to being a Medium. A Medium communicates with spirits or those who have crossed over. They can gain broader access from the Other Side than a psychic can. While a psychic may receive random communication hits about the future, what's taken place, or is taking place. This is the basic difference between a psychic and Medium. Once you've awakened your psychic gifts, then it is easier to take that next step and make a spirit connection as a Medium.

Spirit helps by giving you what your soul needs in order to continue on its path. This means they don't necessarily give you what you want. There are reasons you are enduring challenges. While some of the challenges are at your ego's hand and by your own doing, other challenges are placed on your path for a reason that might include enlightening you in a way that helps you grow and evolve.

This is part of the reason a psychic can't give someone the winning lottery numbers. Naturally that would make someone's day especially those who are struggling financially. If Spirit gave billions of people on the planet the winning lottery numbers, then imagine what kind of disasters would come out of that. Spirit gives you what you need and not always what you want. The lottery numbers are computer generated and chosen through free will. Spirit is unable to override the free will choice of a human being unless it is to prevent their death before the time that was soul contracted.

In Heaven, all souls are of service balancing both work and play. This is what they desire of human souls who seem to do more work than play, or the opposite end of the spectrum more play and no work. They advise against primarily working without play because you'll experience burnout, and the flipside extreme of all play and no work, because then nothing gets accomplished. This also means even if they could, they wouldn't be passing out the winning lottery numbers to people anyway, especially to those souls who are not ready for it. Having boundless money flowing in does not equate to happiness, as there are a great many people who are financially well off and are still not happy or they are struggling in other areas.

While having enormous financial flow does help with the practical necessities required in life this is true, but it doesn't equate to being happy. You could achieve that and may possibly be happier than the drudgery of having to work at a job you despise, but if your soul isn't operating on a higher vibrational playing field, then misery sets in.

Spirit understands that human souls on Earth need money in order to survive on the planet. You primarily need clothes, food, and housing, but you desire love. Spirit will help each soul on the planet to ensure they are taken care of to the best that they can pending you invite them in to work with you since they cannot interfere in another soul's life unless specifically requested by that soul. They will guide you in action steps to take that will lead you closer to obtaining enough income to ensure you are living comfortably and at peace. This means guiding you to meaningful work that is aligned with your equilibrium. One that will make you happy to do. The cold structured 9-6 Monday thru Friday corporate world is not for everyone, and certainly not conducive to a sensitive soul. As it stands, Heavens view has been that the cold structured corporate worlds are in drastic need of re-structuring for morale alone. If you dread going into work each day, then you hate your job. This isn't healthy on your life force or souls' vibration. Some people are afraid to leave their job or try another one out, but sometimes taking a risk knowing that you have something to fall back on can get your energy flowing again.

Heaven also understands the need for law, order, structure, and discipline on Earth, otherwise there will be anarchy. There is a fine line between being too strict and not strict enough. Human rules and laws are enforced for a reason to keep the darkness of ego from acting out dangerously, which it's already doing. Imagine murders, rapes, severe crimes, huge theft, and vandalisms wreaking havoc and destroying Earth with no one to stop it, because human laws have been abolished, and there are no longer any law enforcement officers or a legal system in place to prevent or reduce it. The ones committing those types of dangerous heinous crimes would destroy the planet and each other in under a year.

This is also why many souls on the Other Side incarnate from realms that consist of Wise Ones and Knights. These are the task master rule making Earth Angels. And yes, of course it is true there are corrupted lower evolved souls in charge contributing to the noise. Yet, it's the calling of the Wise Ones and Knights to keep order to a degree. This also means that a lower evolved soul will not vibe well with a soul from those realms. Wise Ones tend to come off harsh at times and too much of a know-it-all that rubs the lower energies the wrong way. They are usually either extremely loved or extremely hated with little to no in between. The Knights have some compassion in there that tempers that harshness a bit.

You have psychic gifts that can assist yourself as well as others in a myriad of positive ways. When you tune into the vibrations from beyond and dissolve the blocks preventing the messages from coming in loud enough to grasp them, then you'll be amazed at what you pick up on. Everyone's methods of connecting with their Spirit team vary. You will discover along your journey as to what's working, what isn't, and how to navigate through that.

Through daily work, discipline, and exercises you can awaken your psychic sensitivity. It would require a lifestyle change as well as an open mind to seek out what might seem like the unknown, but it is truly home in reality to the soul. There are many avenues to take that can assist in cracking open your gifts, which are already built into each soul.

Spiritual studies have become widely accepted as the years have progressed. It's been a growing industry that incurs billions of dollars post 2000's. People are becoming more curious or interested in the genre and in wanting to gain knowledge surrounding this industry in order to help them reach a higher sense of peace.

It is true that some human souls seem to be much more in tune than others, but a great deal of that has to do with them diving into the craft regularly, and/or not allowing the practical world distractions to block them from peering through the veil efficiently.

There was a time in history that anyone believed to be psychic or a prophet, was a witch, Satan's helper, or sorcerer. They were condemned to death as a result. Even if you were considered different and set apart from society, then you were branded evil and were persecuted in some violent way. If you displayed those traits, then you were looked upon as the spawn of Satan and a blasphemous sinner. Many were killed for observing those traits either by beheading, hanging, strangulation, torturing, crucifixion, or by being burned or crushed to death. Times have significantly changed since those archaic days. Now more people are growing hip to the knowledge that all souls have these inherent God given gifts of Heavenly communication. Some are starting columns, blogs, You Tube video vlogs, social media sites, getting published, giving seminars, speeches, and on and on. Today it's celebrated when at one point in history it was shunned or forbidden. There is nothing sinful or forbidden about having a strong connection with Heaven in order to positively improve your life and the lives of others.

Even though the spiritual genre is becoming more celebrated or accepted, there are also a great many cases in some countries that have not progressed within the genre. They still observe the burning of people who seem to be *witches* during seemingly progressive times. One case involved a 20-year-old mother of two in Papua New Guinea. She was blamed for the death of a 6-year-old boy. A mob of relatives of the boy took the young mother and then stripped, tortured, and burned her alive. This was in 2013 and the world did not talk about it. How fast is Earth evolving away from that if this is still going on post 2000's? Perhaps in North America or in parts of Europe that is unheard of, but there are still some countries continuing to live in the stone ages. They need to be brought up to speed, but that isn't likely to happen soon. Earth has existed for centuries and yet exuding love seems to still be an impossible feat that many have no interest in. A book like this cannot be sold in some countries because of the content. This is what happens when a soul denies its true nature and refuses to educate itself, raise its consciousness, move forward and upward, and connect with the Divine.

The lower evolved look upon those set apart from the crowd as odd or weird, but those with a raised consciousness and a high vibration can see that person's greater purpose for standing out. If you are odd, then you are more gifted with a larger purpose than you can imagine. Following the crowd is playing it safe. Those considered odd or weird veer away from the norm because the norm needs to be changed.

While there has been a rise in atheism and anarchy as a side effect of the judgment that exists within organized religion, there has also been a rise of spiritualists professing to being psychically connected. This is no accident, because all souls are connected. If there is a soul energy living in an organism, plant, person, or animal, then it is psychically and energetically connected. You are also psychically and energetically connected to it too. Someone in tune to energies can hold a crystal or stone in their hand and sense the vibrations moving through it. They are aware of the movement taking place beyond the physical material life.

Psychics and Mediums who publicly profess to having a connection with the Other Side are simply recognizing the God given gifts within them that all are born with and that all can reach. One may not connect with the spirit world in the exact same way as another, but all souls have the capacity to have a strong connection with Spirit.

Track your interactions with your Guides and Angels by keeping a journal of the information you receive from above. Even if you think it might be your imagination, write it down anyway. Record each message you receive, whether you believe it's from your Spirit team, your ego, or your own intuition. After a month or a period of time has passed, then revert to it and jot down the outcome of that message. You will be able to tell the difference between the self-generated messages and the messages received from your guides. Trust the messages you receive without fear or doubt. If you make a mistake or you end up being wrong about something, big deal keep on going. Your ego will get in the way at times and create unnecessary negative self-talk that is not based in truth. Sometimes you make a mistake, but with practice you improve at focusing on what is your higher self and what is not.

Anyone can connect to the spirit world that works at it. You must take care of yourself on all levels, such as physically, spiritually, mentally, and emotionally. When you have raised your vibration on those key well-being traits, then the closer you are to receiving accurate, mind-blowing, heavenly communication.

Follow the strong black and white code of spiritual ethics as your gifts develop and expand. Avoid offering random serious psychic information to someone unless you've expressly asked them if it's okay to tap into their energy. While sometimes you may automatically be tapping into their energy without trying or intending to like myself, I avoid reaching out to someone or approaching them with dangerous challenging information unless specifically asked.

A good balanced diet helps to increase psychic awareness. This isn't a fun rule for some who love their guilty pleasures and believe me I understand as I have my own personal guilty pleasures, but I do keep it in moderation. It's human nature to be attracted to fun foods. The truth is that a good deal of these guilty pleasures dim or block the psychic input entirely. You are what you eat. This popular saying is true. If you continuously eat heavy foods that are not good for you, then that weighs you down. In order to assist in increasing psychic receptivity, you need healthy foods. These are foods that give you brain power and improve your health. Because when your body, mind, and soul are operating on high capacity, then this assists in increasing the awareness to spirit reception.

Your soul at its core is a high vibrational being filled with ever flowing love, joy, and serenity. Don't forget who you are. Don't get lost in the negative toxic energy of the physical world. Take care of yourself, which means taking care of your soul and body on all levels as much as possible. Incorporate healthy life changes you can make today that will help you in awakening the parts of you that existed from the conception of your soul. These are the parts that can help you be happier, stronger, and that much more powerful.

You were born a vessel of love! Even if you do nothing with the gifts that exist within you, you will at least be shining that bright light of high vibrational energy onto all those in your path, which in turn tempers the severity of the bullets firing all over the place by the darkness of ego. The ego may have tantrums and cause all sorts of noise, but contrary to belief, love is more powerful than any other energy that exists on any plane in the end. Let your love flow and shine outwardly wherever you go. Remember to revert to love, joy, and peace when possible. Take regular action steps that can help bring you back to this natural state of being whenever you falter on your path. Be conscious of who you are and the reservoir of gifts moving through you. This world needs more love and light in it. It is up to you to help guide others in that direction by doing the individual work to evolve and raise your consciousness. The planets ruler is not a human being. It is the Creator of all that is. Through the Divine is where effective positive change can happen within each individual.

CHAPTER SIXTEEN

How to Connect with the Tarot

When you're new to realizing the psychic gifts built within you, then you may at times doubt what you're picking up on wondering if it's really a psychic hit or not. One of the beneficial ways to knowing if you're receiving accurate Divinely guided psychic messages is to write down everything you're receiving. Keep a journal or an email folder that you record down anything you might consider to be a psychic message. This way you can go back to it months later or even years later to read through it to see if it was something that did come to fruition. Another way is to use a Divination tool. Divination tools have been used in the psychic field for centuries from using a pendulum, crystal ball, runes, angel board, tea leaves and so on. One of the most popular well-known divination tools is the Tarot.

I rarely use divination tools to connect with Spirit, but this doesn't mean I don't approve of it. I've been a Tarot enthusiast supporter, lover, and occasional user since I was a child. I remember being eight years old picking up my first Tarot card to look at it and suddenly messages were flying into my consciousness. I would then gaze at the dynamically stimulating images of the cards and allowing all the elements surrounding them to hit me like a tsunami wave. This is the same way I would sift through my parent's record collection fixating on the album covers when vinyl was the big thing. The images of the album covers were as vibrant and layered with detail as a Tarot card. Album covers are not as creative as they once used to be.

There are endless messages that can come through from staring at any image, let alone a Tarot card. If you have an attraction to art or a painting and find yourself picking up on what's unsaid and getting lost in the caverns of it, then you're that much closer to being able to efficiently and adequately read a Tarot card.

I've met CEO's that secretly admit to not making a decision without first connecting with the Tarot. Anyone can consult with the cards regardless of what position you hold in life. It doesn't matter if you're a lawyer, doctor, surfer, receptionist, garbage man, plumber, or politician. The Tarot is an exceptional communication device to receive messages, wisdom, and guidance from your Spirit team for any human soul on the planet.

The brilliance of the Tarot is that it's for anyone who has a passion for the cards. You don't have to be a professional psychic or medium to use the tool. There are endless varying takes of the meanings of Tarot cards in a reading that one tried or true way doesn't exist. When you feel confident enough with the cards, then you'll have your own methods that work.

I've always found the Tarot to be an excellent divination tool from which to confirm messages with my own Spirit team whenever I felt the incoming messages to be hazy or unclear. Spirit would then guide me to the right Tarot card to flip over so I could see or confirm what they wanted me to know through a card. Spirit communicates through symbols and signs as well as other means that can get your attention. Since the Tarot is ripe with symbolism, this is a great way for them to relay messages to you. Diving into the worlds of the Tarot can take a lifetime of endless study. When you enjoy what you're immersing yourself into, then it ends up being a gratifying experience.

How I Connect with the Tarot

My Spirit team has been communicating with me through my etheric clair channels throughout the course of my entire life. Everyone has this ability since these etheric channels reside within all souls. The unseen senses are one of the many ways that Spirit can communicate with you. My soul, mind, and body have been an extraordinary vessel of psychic communication without the use of any other device.

This is a physical world with an enormous coating of thick density that acts as a wall between this world and the next. Earthly distractions, erratic emotions, and physical pleasures can block or dim the communication line with Spirit. There might be moments when your vibration is not as high as it could be. The Divine messages coming through are not loud enough, or your ego steps in to second guess what's relayed. This is where the Tarot or any Oracle for that matter can be of benefit.

The Tarot is an extension of myself when seeking to expand or confirm what's coming through. I throw down a card and flip it over only to find that the message is the one my Spirit team had informed me about. I use the Tarot partially to confirm information I'm picking up on and because it's fun to play with. It's like someone that loves playing Blackjack or any other fun card games. I find the Tarot equally enjoyable and entertaining. It is also a way for me to have a phone call with my Spirit team when the supplementary ways they communicate are not coming in clear enough. This is no different than what anyone can do when you tune in to everything that is outside of the physical concrete world that distracts you.

Your Spirit team is communicating with you daily whether you are aware of it or not. They will communicate with you through one or more of your clair channels. Pay attention to your clair senses in order to pick up on the messages and guidance filtering through you from God, a higher power, your higher self, universe, heaven, your guides, angels, or whoever you're comfortable with calling it. In the end, the messages and guidance are coming in from beyond the physical materialistic distracting world known as the Earthly life.

Having crystal clear communication with your Spirit team can assist you with your Tarot readings. Tarot is an exceptional divination tool to help you in picking up on what is being relayed. This is especially helpful if your psychic clair channels have dimmed, you're second guessing the guidance, or you feel you're not picking up on anything.

I've been reading with hundreds of people since I was a teenager as I enjoy the psychic craft. I've unsurprisingly also made many additional friends in the Tarot reading world as a result. I love watching how others read since each way one reads is varying. Every single reader reads differently from one another. There are no two people who read the same way. This is because everyone has varying gifts in the way they interpret messages from the Other Side. If one reader doesn't work for you, then there will be a reader who does. This also means that you likely read and interpret differently than others do.

It is often advised that you avoid reading for yourself. This is because you may unknowingly taint your reading by bending it to suit what you're desiring. This won't stop anyone from reading for themselves, but take precaution by being as objective as possible when you do.

Avoid reading for yourself or for anyone when you're not in a state of complete open psychic reception. This means if you're emotionally upset, angry, depressed, or any other negative emotion, then this can fault the reading. The same goes if you're doing a reading while on a drug chemical high, wasted on alcohol, or if you've consumed a large meal or anything that could be considered a toxin to the body. This can make the reading come off all over the place and unclear.

Many professional psychics avoid reading for those close to them because they're not emotionally objective enough to give their best friend a clear reading. They will be gentler with the reading and attempt to read in a way that benefits the friend. Once you do that, then you've begun the process of contaminating the reading. The clearest readings are when the reader is centered, operating from a high vibration, focused, objective, and emotionally detached from the client.

It's common to read for oneself and bend the read to fit the answer you're hoping for. I've watched novices pull one card after another because they were unhappy with the card they were originally given. Once you do that you've corrupted the read and created a false reading that will not be based in truth. At that point you're just pointlessly throwing cards down.

One is not always objective with their own stuff and requires someone else that is emotionally detached from themselves in order to receive an unbiased reading. In those cases, you'll want to seek out a professional psychic reader that charges for their services. This is because the charge is an exchange of energy. You are giving them money in exchange for a product. In that movement there is a balanced reciprocated energy moving between you that gives a better reading. The more upset and emotionally distraught you are when giving a read, the more off and unclear the reading can be. Be clear minded, centered, and relaxed when giving a reading whether for yourself or another. This is another reason why readers generally do not give readings to those they know whether it is an acquaintance, friend, or family member. They may unknowingly alter the reading to positively favor their friend. This is doing an injustice because you're giving false hope.

Reading for a friend can also cause friction if the friend is not positively receptive about it or ends up criticizing the read. I've heard numerous cases and have close psychic medium friends that have said they watched friendships and connections end over a reading that was given. Some are uncomfortable when their friend is seeing challenging circumstances and stating it to them. I've certainly had this issue myself in the past, especially considering the way I communicate let alone read in general, which can be direct and bold.

Many professional readers, psychics, and mediums have been known to obtain readings from other professionals in their field for clarity.

I'm a believer that anyone can read better for themselves than anyone else when they are in a clear state of reception. I've gone to readers in the past and found that my own readings for myself were the ones that transpired and came to light. Because in the end who knows you better than you do! Even when I have read for myself, I'm not bending the read to suit me, but rather giving myself the cold hard truth. I have given myself readings in the past that were not pleasing, but ended up coming to fruition. I saw the messages in the reading as a warning to me, but also one that I knew was coming, but I just had to confirm it with the cards. This is also part of the reason I moved into the spiritual teaching work. It was to help others come to the answers on their own. Why go to someone to help you with something you can do on your own with your Spirit team.

I've watched others express disdain or unhappiness when they've pulled a Tarot card that appeared negative to them. Challenging is the more appropriate word. Everyone is challenged in their life. No one is exempt from that including the rich or famous. When you're challenged, then you grow and evolve. You also learn how to attract in what you desire. If a challenge is presented to you, then find ways to move through it.

The Tarot reading is like any psychic reading in that it is giving you the probable forecast. This probable forecast is what is seen if things continue as they are, regardless if it's showing something positive or challenging. As a free will thinking soul you can alter that forecast to something else by your choices.

The Tarot can help as a guide in terms of offering suggestions of what's to come, but in the end every human soul has free will choice. If you make a choice that goes against what the Tarot presented, then you alter the read and wind up creating a new path to head down. This is beneficial if you are faced with challenging cards, which you objectively look at as areas where you need to make some changes. The Tarot can also give you a warning, which helps to pre-armor you with what's to come. I've certainly seen the end of a personal love relationship with the Tarot weeks before it took place.

The Tarot is not necessarily going to tell you what you need to do. It is up to you to decide that for yourself. When reading for others you want to avoid telling someone what to do. You don't want to interfere with another's free will. The ethics of an exceptional reader is to present what you're picking up on without judgment, but you cannot and should not make the ultimate decision for someone else.

How to Conduct a Reading

Before conducting a reading, ensure you are in a centered, calm, and focused state of contentment. This will bring you the most accurate reading. If you're not in that state, then wait until you are. This is also why earlier in the book I offered practical tips on centering yourself and taking care of all parts of you. This way you can easily bring yourself to that state quickly rather than taking weeks. The way others read varies from one person to the next. Work on finding rituals or exercises to partake in that will assist in bringing you to that calm state.

One way can be to set up a personal altar or space you use for readings. If you don't have any space in your home, then designate one in a place that is uncluttered. This is where you are most comfortable and will be undisturbed during the reading. Whether that is on your bed, living room couch, or dining room table. Make sure there are no distractions when you choose to conduct a reading. You can turn this space into your own private temporary altar. You may choose to Sage the space before a reading to clear away all the negative energies. Create a calming sanctuary with candles burning, soft music playing, and incense burning. Lower the lighting a bit if you're able to.

Meditate for a few minutes or more before a reading until you are in a centered relaxed state. Take long deep breaths in and out as you relax, then say a prayer or personal invocation. Call in your Spirit team, God, your angels, guides, or whoever it is that you have a strong relationship with on the Other Side. When in doubt, call in your Spirit team to assist you with the card reading you're about to do.

While it's not always necessary to create all these bells, whistles, and theatrics, you will find your readings are clearer when you create the perfect environment within and without before conducting a reading. When you pose a question to the Tarot and find the response to be unclear, then re-word the question. Ask the question in a different way, then try again. If your questions are scattered, then the messages will be too.

Spreads

My soul is the core instrument I use to communicate with Heaven. It is a clear enough conduit that it's all I need before anything else. You have the same ability as well within you. I started to see spirits entering and leaving my room at the age of four. The spirit communication has been going on for as long as I can remember without letting up. When you've been doing something naturally for decades, then it's all you know. When I used to offer professional readings, I'd hold the deck in my hand answering the person's questions without consulting the cards. I need to be doing something with my hands, so this is when I'd start shuffling the deck, "Let's double check everything I've said."

One by one the cards would confirm it all. I adopted my own methods from an early age by using a personal rhythm that is nothing like the default set way that others have been trained to do when reading. I've never followed the norm or anyone else's formula, but rather throw cards down like a poker player in a fury. The instant message pops up a second after the card has hit the table.

I have also never used or worked with a Tarot spread in my life. I come to the information, messages, and guidance that are intended to come through without any obstacles and restrictions. I'm a Wise One that doesn't follow anyone else's set pattern or rules. Those that know me best know this to be true. This doesn't mean that this is the way to go. This is merely what works for me. If you are in the beginning stages of reading, then you may want to investigate if spreads are something you would be more comfortable using.

Those that have been super close to me for eons have all pointed out over the decades that they can tell when it's me communicating with them, or when it's a spirit from the higher realms coming through. They've pointed out a distinctly noticeable shift in the language and information that comes out of me that changes within a matter of seconds. It's as if they're having a conversation with numerous people!

As I'm posing the question to my Spirit team, I will hear through Clairaudience how many cards I'm being asked or guided to pull for the answer, and I stick with that. Trust how many cards you are guided to pull when you ask your question before you conduct a reading. Changing that number because you're unhappy with the cards that were revealed smears the reading. It ends up inaccurate and confusing. If you're unsure how many cards to pull, then stick with anywhere from 1-3 cards per question.

Tarot card readers interpret and read the cards in differing ways. Not all readers read cards in the same way. There is no right or wrong way, but however you're guided to read the cards. Some use spreads such as past, present, future spreads, or the Celtic Cross spread. While others use no spread, but pull the number of cards they're guided or asked to pull. A Tarot spread tells a story where each card emphasizes or gives new meaning to the cards that follow or surround it.

In a reading spread, the cards may either show something that already took place, is happening in your life now, or is coming up. It's up to you to determine where it falls in the time frame. If it's in the future or has not happened yet, then this is the probable future. It is foreseen that this is what is to come. Your future changes based on the decisions or indecisions you or others make based on free will. Therefore, it's equally important not to take a future forecast read too seriously.

Many professional readers tend to state that all reads should be taken with a grain of salt or used for entertainment purposes. They cannot be held liable or responsible for a read that did not come to fruition, or for influencing the person they're reading for to make a decision that ultimately causes heartache or additional challenges. This is another reason you avoid telling others what to do in a read. Not only does it interfere with their free will choice or life path, but it can also prompt the client to make a decision that makes things worse for them. You cannot put yourself in a position where you are held liable.

The cards show the trajectory of where a situation is headed. They can also offer guidance as to what changes you would need to make in order to bring something to fruition or to prevent a challenging circumstance from happening. You own your life and the direction you choose to allow it to go in. Be the master of your own ship.

The Tarot can intimidate some that feel they'll never be able to read. It is true that some people are better at it than others the same way that some people are better drivers. Even a beginner can dominate by hitting an accurate reading out of the gate. Don't worry so much about trying to be an efficient reader. The more you let go of the need to try to be, the easier it will get.

Because of my lifelong love for the Tarot, I ended up writing a Tarot guidebook called *Tarot Card Meanings*, which included the general messages of each card. This guide was specifically made for the novice that had trouble learning the basic meaning of a card. Readers would tell me that many of the Tarot books they would pick up were ripe with detail, but slim on the overall meanings of the cards. This caused confusion for some that messaged me if I knew what a card meant, so that's also what prompted me to devote a book solely about the meanings of each card and nothing else. There is nothing wrong with looking up the card meanings as you're learning, but you also don't want to base what a book says about a card as being verbatim, including my book. You most definitely don't want to conduct a professional reading for someone and then reach for a thesaurus in the middle of the reading.

Trying to learn the meanings of each card can be overwhelming, which was the reason I created a basic guide to help the beginners get their feet wet. The best way to read is to not stress out over trying to learn the descriptions of each card. Instead tune into your Spirit team's guidance and follow your gut as to the first hunch you get when you flip over a card when seeing it, rather than worrying about what a card means. You grasp what the overall energy and essence is about a card to help you get to the answer. One of the many benefits to using the Tarot is that it can also help sharpen your psychic senses, because you are called to use parts of your soul and spirit that you normally wouldn't be exercising in your everyday life. The Tarot helps you to use senses you normally ignore.

AFTERWORD

A Final Word

Spirit can hear your thoughts and feel your feelings. When you're wandering around talking to yourself out loud or in thought, then you are heard. When you are feeling down and frustrated, then you are felt. God and your Spirit team can hear your mind filled or mindless chatter as some might call it as well as when you're angry or feeling immense love. You may not be a believer in much, but whatever you're thinking Spirit can hear you. This is also why you cannot attempt to deceive God, since He and all heavenly beings know exactly what you're thinking, feeling, or up to. This is whether it's aligned with something Dark or Light, they are aware of it. This is also why those that try to get away with murder end up meeting their Karma in some form, because you might think you got away with murder, but not with any heavenly being. The direction you aim your soul's energy is what will expand and bring more of that to you.

Spirit knows more about everyone on the planet than your own best friend or family members. You may feel misunderstood by those around you, but God and your Spirit don't misunderstand you. They know every shred of what you're experiencing or going through. They want to guide out of misery and towards enlightenment if you would pay attention to the feedback they give.

Many have admitted that when they've had a tough time in life that they've seen that glimmer of hope that is no doubt coming from Spirit. They could be driving around and then hear a song play or they see a billboard sign that just happens to have the exact words they needed to hear. It could be words that only someone they once loved used to say. It could be a psychic related tip that what they're desiring is coming and to stay hyper vigilant and focused in faith.

There is no special tried and true way to connect with Spirit. The more you take care of your body, mind, and soul on all levels, then the more psychic input you will pick up on. The less you stress, the more psychic communication you'll hear. The more centered you are, then the more psychic guidance you'll feel sifting through you.

When one thinks of psychic gifts, they get excited thinking that it's just about foretelling the future. This is the last thing on Spirit's list. They are about helping people fine-tune all aspects of themselves so that they can achieve and accomplish what they set out to do from their life purposes to making sounder decisions in life. They know the more you take care of you, then the happier you'll be. They want to see people happy and expressing love over joyless negativity.

The ultimate reason all souls have incarnated on Earth is to learn about love. The only way you can truly learn that is by being thrown onto a gigantic rock with people that are so different from you, it would take a miracle to get you to find that space of acceptance for them. This isn't to be confused with showering love on a terrorist, but learning to love also means learning to view life through the lens of the angels with emotional detachment. My higher soul's view is through this same lens of God, my Spirit Council, and Heaven's angels. We would rather see two people in love regardless of gender or belief, than someone residing in toxic negativity. When you've lost your way, revert to raising your faith and believing there is something greater than your problems. Move back into that glorious uplifting loving light of God's magnificent rays baptizing you in a blaze of optimism. This is the space that psychic communication is increased.

Kevin Hunter

The Metaphysical Divine Wisdom Collection

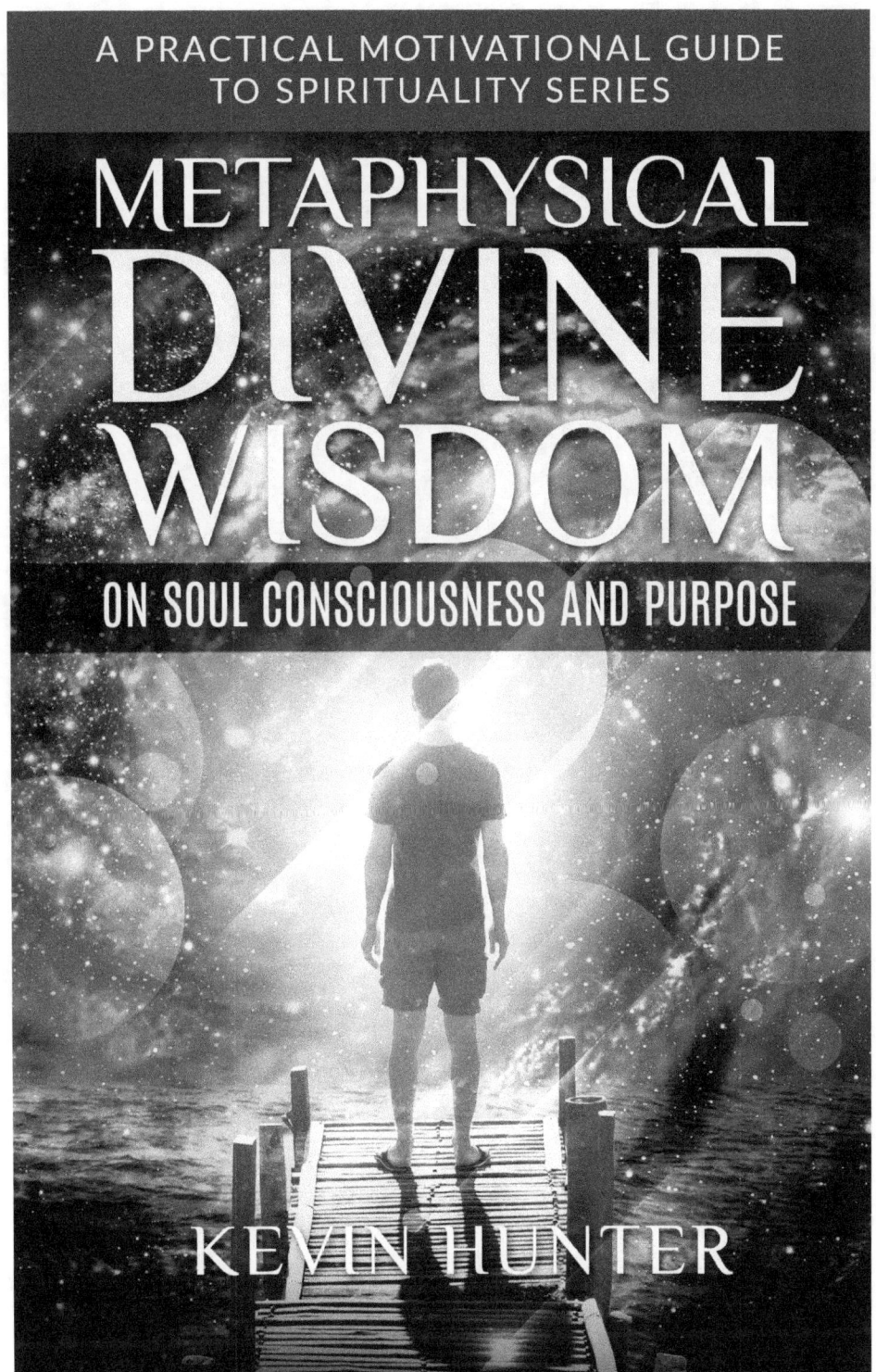

METAPHYSICAL DIVINE WISDOM
ON SOUL CONSCIOUSNESS AND PURPOSE

CHAPTER ONE

*Opening the Pathway
to Divinity*

Over the course of my life and in my spiritual teachings, I've conveyed wisdom that entails simple understood ways of improving your well-being, which instantaneously raises your soul's consciousness. Sometimes I might say something in conversation in a manner where it could be digestible to the recipient, but I cannot control if they ignore that or if it flies over them. I'm not going to hammer it into someone's psyche. I might do that in our books with the goal of cementing that concept into the consciousness, but not necessarily in random conversation.

One of the reasons my team and I talk and teach about this work is because I know that the level of the soul's consciousness upon death is the level that soul will gravitate towards back home in the Spirit world. If a soul like Mother Teresa is vibrating at a higher frequency such as where love, joy and peace reside, then that soul will gravitate towards a higher frequency of consciousness in Heaven. That soul will be pulled in the direction of those on a similar frequency. If the soul is vibrating on a lower level such as those that enact violence and hatred of any kind such as in the form of physical, emotional, including the nature of ones feelings and in words online, such as a simple social media post or comment, then that soul will be pulled in the direction of that energy upon death. It doesn't matter what platform that person is choosing to use, because the energy is attached to and traveling with that soul wherever it goes and whatever it inhabits including in a human being. This is the overall energy of your spirit's soul you are choosing to radiate at. When you vibrate on a higher frequency, then the spaces you inhabit in the Spirit world will be in that comparable frequency.

To describe it in a more practical way, the higher frequency vibrating soul would move into the areas where there are magnificent palaces amongst a vibrant colored paradise. Whereas the lower frequency vibrating soul would move towards an area where there are no actual homes, but a pile of wood to figure out how to put the impossible together yourself amongst a dry humid barren land filled with yellows, greys, and muddy browns.

This means that someone rich and famous on Earth with gorgeous palace like mansions in various places might be a toxic negative person, while someone poor in this life that struggles living check to check is a positive person. The positive person struggling in this life is pulled into the mansion like paradise on the Other Side, while the rich and famous person on Earth with the nasty attitude that treats people unkindly ends up being pulled into that barren land in the spirit world. This is just a quick and easy way to make the point, because it is much more layered than this.

One might say they don't believe in any of that the way some don't believe in a Hell, but why take that chance? Why not improve yourself if just for the sake of being a better person rather than for the sake of achieving that pot of gold.

Incidentally, what was described is like the concept that extreme religious people might believe that if you're a good Christian on Earth, then you will inherit the riches in Heaven, while the rest will go to Hell. It's a bit more complex than that, but the similarities with some of the teachings are obvious.

There are some souls unable to complete the dream like journey that ends when you puncture through the spirit plane and wind up being pulled into a left door or back gate where the energy vibrates on a lower level, then they'll wrap back around into another incarnation on Earth. This incarnation is one with additional lessons to endure in hopes that the soul will evolve upwards at least one notch than the previous lifetime. Otherwise the incarnations can go on indefinitely until the soul begins to show signs of evolving, which can mean positively changing all aspects of yourself.

Your Vibration and Consciousness

When there is talk of vibration, frequencies, energy, and a soul's consciousness, then this can fly right over the average person's head unless it's explained in simplified terms. A good deal of what is taught about the consciousness can come out convoluted. This makes it challenging to understand what is being explained. One of the goals of my guides working through me is the betterment of humanity. The advancement of Earthly civilization starts with you. It starts with one individual doing the soul growth work. It's a gradual often arduous process as one person evolves over time, which is simultaneously shifting their energy and consciousness. A positive shift in energy and consciousness in one person has a beneficial effect on those around them even if those around them are unaware they are in the presence of an evolving soul. The phrase to *lead by example* is to present your soul's best self. This will rub off on those around you regardless if you think it's having a positive effect or not. It can shift one other person in the vicinity that begins to change themselves as a result of that. When they change, then this is passed on and so forth. This is one of the reasons why we're seeing more people partaking in some form of spiritual interests. Others are hearing about it through someone around them and this is triggering something remarkable within them.

Your consciousness needs to be awakened enough to allow you to see profound spiritual truths. No one can awaken your consciousness except you. It is the individual soul's job to do the work, research, study, and experience in order to strengthen your soul essence. This means not following the masses, but breaking away from the collective to find your personal soul path.

You are made up of energy the same way everything is made up of energy. How you direct that energy will dictate the essence of what will come back to you. If your feelings and thoughts are negative, then what is soon brought into your life is what matches that vibration. If your thoughts and feelings are positive, then this is the energy that is eventually brought into your life. There is no set time frame on how quick or slow something of equal or greater value to the energy matched with your feelings and thoughts is brought into your life.

A raised vibration coupled with life experiences helps in awakening your consciousness. When your consciousness is awakened, then you view Earthly life with a broader perception. Suddenly Earthly life in general appears trivial and superficial. You may start to feel permanently disconnected from it, isolated, and set apart from the norm. While this might cause you to stumble into a depression, understand that these are clues that your soul consciousness is expanding into something greater that awaits. A raised soul consciousness gives you a wider psychic perception that allows room for stronger cognitive input. This is the area where divinely guided information from above falls into and is planted.

Your vibration is made up of undetectable cells to the human eye, but visible to the spiritual eye. It is an invisible energy field that exists within the DNA of your soul, aura, and physical body. These cells fluctuate and change colors depending on your mood, your thought processes, your actions, who you surround yourself with, as well as what you ingest into your body. You are in control of this vibration energy field able to oversee and dictate how well you would like it to function through your life choices.

It's the same way you control other parts of your life such as the car you drive, to the house or apartment you live in, and so on. When you maintain your car, then you ensure it runs smoothly with routine check-ups, oil changes, checking the tire pressure, etc. This is similar to you taking care of your physical health as best as possible from getting regular check-ups, to watching the diet you consume, exercising regularly, to your overall daily state of mind. Taking care of your physical body affects your spiritual body. It's watching your thoughts and feelings to ensure they are on the positive side. All of this affects how bright or dim the energy field of your vibration radiates.

A High and Low Vibrational State

Your vibration can drop when you fall into a challenging negative state, which will happen on occasion. You get caught up in the routine and day-to-day practicalities of life and experiences that it leaves no room to check up on you, and how you're doing, and what your soul needs. The soul craves nourishment and the ego will at times interfere prompting you to reach for toxic substances to temporarily feed it, but which ultimately drain you leaving you wanting more.

When your vibration is low, you feel and experience negative feelings such as anger, depression, stress, irritability, and so on. When your vibration is high, you feel euphoric feelings of joy, love, peace, and contentment.

While in a higher vibration state, you'll find that what you desire moves into your vicinity quicker than if your well-being state was on the negative side. Your psychic intuitive awareness then grows allowing the heavenly spirit answers, messages, and guidance to come into your consciousness and through your psychic clair channels on a clearer level. The messages and guidance you receive is what helps you make sounder choices in your life.

A vibration in spiritual concepts is your overall emotional well-being and energetic state. Feelings such as depression, anger, and guilt lower your vibration, but if you're feeling joyful, in love, and centered, then your vibration begins to rise. The lowest vibrational state includes feelings of anger, stress, or depression. Watch out if you're experiencing a combination of all three at once.

The highest vibrational states are feelings of peace, joy, and love. It isn't a surprise that those traits are synonymous with the Christmas holiday season as a reminder to not forget your natural state of being. Experiencing all three of those states at the same time makes you a high vibrational powerhouse! Love is the highest vibrational state possible, so always revert to raising your emotional state to that of love.

You are born in a perfect state of high vibrational energy. Somewhere along the way rough tumultuous Earthly life circumstances shake your faith while knocking your vibration down in the process. When you're conscious of when this happens, then you can quickly re-align your vibration. I understand how hard that can be for those that live tougher stress filled lives. No one is exempt from Earthly life challenges, including the rich and famous. Even they are faced with their own challenges that might be similar or dissimilar to yours on a personal level outside of having financial riches. It's tough for some people to feel sympathy for someone that is financially well off, but no one is above or below anyone else in spiritual truth. No one gets a free pass from Earthly life challenges. Some of those challenges are ego self-induced, while others are spiritual lessons to help you grow and evolve.

Be mindful of your well-being state whenever possible, because a low vibration alters the energetic field around you. This blocks both divine guidance and positive circumstances from entering your vicinity. It tampers with your life on a spiritual and physical level. Being in a perpetual negative mood state can have health related consequences. When you have a high vibration, then positive experiences flow into your life. Your psychic antennae with the Other Side is also sharper where you're able to pick up on the messages and guidance coming in swiftly than if you were in a low vibration state.

Seeking the Path Towards Enlightenment

The lifelong battle with demons in my personal life is always matched with those from beyond the veil consistently pointing me towards the Light. When touched by the power, it is unconditional love experienced that no words can describe. The soul is overwhelmed in that radiance when enveloped in its arms. The answer to the question of the meaning of life is always the same. The answer is LOVE.

The more enlightened you become, and the more you raise your consciousness, then the better off you'll be. This doesn't mean that you'll be stress free, but you'll certainly experience less stress while being able to efficiently navigate through the treacherous waters of the practical world easier than if you did not have that raised consciousness.

Imagine if every human soul found the gift of love within them. No one would need to be here since that would be Utopia. When you find the space of love and learn to keep it there and revert to it when possible, then the closer you are to creating Heaven on Earth. It's a beautiful thing when one soul awakens another in a positive way just by being in their presence.

The rays of God's Light activate the soul propelling you into a Utopian paradise and beyond. The ultimate Nirvana is surpassing that perfection through methods a limited consciousness could ever dream possible. This is the exceptional glory your soul was born into before the dense turbulence of Earthy life enveloped and suffocated you.

Deep down every soul longs to re-attain and achieve that blissful excellence that gives the impression of unabashed joy and serenity. It is a condition where unwavering love and harmony surround you in a protected cushion. Transcending beyond the dull insensible frustrated Earthy life and into the natural condition the soul once habited is a goal that delights. It reminds the soul of where it came from. You runaway and travel around the globe searching for a sign of this utopia, only to be consistently left with disappointment. This is because utopia begins and ends inside the spark that burns within your soul like a pilot light.

Examine the negative emotions that initially impede your soul's movement. Start within and visualize this pilot light being ignited to the degree conceivable of generating a wildfire that expands in an explosion purging and clearing away all the darkness the ego consistently loses itself in.

The experiences you have in life both the practical and spiritual all play a part at shaping, molding, and evolving your soul's consciousness. In the coming chapters, we'll look at some of these areas.

CHAPTER TWO

*Knowing When Your Soul
Is Transforming and Evolving*

There are some immediate signs that indicate if you or someone you know has incarnated from the Other Side with a bigger purpose. For one, you will know without a doubt what that mission is. You will already know that one of your life purposes is geared towards the betterment of humanity and the planet on some level. There is no, "I have no idea what my purpose is." Because if the purpose is a larger mission, then this is felt within the soul's DNA from as early as childhood. It may be that while in childhood, through the teenage years and into the beginnings of young adulthood that it might not be broadly clear what that mission is. The visions start to grow and expand within the soul's psychic senses early on. They include even tiny elements of that mission becoming largely evident to your consciousness. It is the person that by age fifteen that thinks, "I know there is a bigger reason I'm here beyond this nonsense."

Those with larger missions and purposes also tend to be evident people as early as childhood. There is something different than the norm with the child. This means the child will face ostracism by the lesser evolved that are unable to penetrate challenging depths at that time on their soul's unfolding process. They might be regularly bullied or called derogatory names like weird, freak, unusual, etc. Unfortunately, that's just what the higher evolving souls must deal with in earlier age when you're thrown into the center of the population that tends to operate on a superficial minimal level. Before you incarnated into this Earthly life, you're already aware of the challenges you'll face with hostile threatened human beings. If you're an outcast with broad visions within you that are greater than the mundane, then there is a high percentage of a chance that you are here for a larger mission and life purpose.

This drive for this mission propels you to contribute positive changes in that arena through action even if it means you will have to stand alone. And often you will end up standing alone on the ledge. Leaders tend to be the ones that view circumstances from a differing point of view than the rest of the masses. This enlightening process on the way to evolving your soul consciousness may not come to you right away. It can take a great deal of time and personal soul growth work contributions on your behalf before it cracks open. It may not come to you until well into adulthood, on your deathbed, and sometimes not at all. There is no rush to enlightenment because soul work operates on a different frequency than the physical human life work. The more life experiences, challenges, and lessons you endure tend to help one achieve enlightenment.

A teenager punk rocking drug user covered in tattoos might make one believe they have no purpose, but don't be fooled by their choices or form of personal self-expression at first glance. Strip away the external costume one chooses to wear this lifetime to peer into the soul's truth. Eradicate the labels burdened upon oneself such as black, white, gay, straight, male, female, liberal, conservative, and so on. Labeling confines you to a box and gives the illusion you have an identity, but when you limit and restrict yourself with a label, then you risk losing your soul's uniqueness. One of the goals of the human ego is to box you in, repress, limit, impede, and hold you down. It throws you in the passenger seat with blinders on and drives you over dangerous roads with speed bumps and traffic spikes. In that space you're unable to penetrate through any surface intended to expose reality.

To one extent a label needs to be used to give someone a deeper understanding of something when they're unable to come to that conclusion through telepathy, but you are not the labels you use to describe yourself in the end. The intention of labels is to divide and create separation. It compartmentalizes others into divisions not aligned with any soul's true existence. You lose authentic identity with a label since branding gives the illusion of a special uniqueness. You don't need a label to be exceptional because everyone's light shines when stripped of the outdated labels that ultimately break down and suppress who your soul is in long-term truth.

Individuality is evident without the need to distract through exclusions and groupings. Classifying others and forcing them into boxes creates unhealthy competition to one up each other and prove your group is the exceptional one. Once you do that, then you've handed the steering wheel to the darkness of ego that lives to push you down. There is no synchronization when you are out of alignment of your most indisputable self.

Back home all souls live in harmony regardless of being distinctive from one another. It's not on their radar to point out differences because eccentricity is honored and encouraged. Whereas on Earth the dissimilarities are shunned or feared because it makes the darkness of ego uncomfortable preferring that everyone be a clone. Stand out without hiding behind limitations and imperfections. Who are you without any outdated fads and labels you use to describe yourself?

Some people show signs of being a light worker, warrior of light, or other elements of a divinely guided trade, even though they might not be aware of it yet. It's easy to tell who is or who has that something unique about them that you know they're going to be evolving quicker than others over the course of their life. They may currently seem to be operating on a superficial level, but there are clues behind that surface where they display signs of something deeper going on.

Someone might not show obvious signs of being from a heavenly realm. Perhaps they gossip endlessly, live on a superficial level, display the darkness of ego beyond comprehension, but if you pay attention and look closer, you'll be amazed at what you find. At some point they may say something that shows an immense depth that will eventually one day break out in a bigger way with spiritual maturity. It's that one thing in a sea of superficiality that makes someone stop to ponder. This soul dramatically changes over the years becoming a different person entirely in the eyes of those around them.

Many from a heavenly realm tend to be either highly sensitive or highly addicted – sometimes both! Those who are super sensitive may fall into an addiction to mask, numb, or cushion this sensitivity, but this uncontrollable sensitivity is their calling card, winning streak, and the gift that needs maximum protection. The sensitivity and addiction gene are a clue that you are being asked to rise above that as best as you can. This way you can manage your life in a way that enables you to focus and put hard work into and towards the building of your life purpose. You have much to offer and don't want it to go to waste. It can take a lifetime of discipline to stay on your soul's path. You'll steer off course occasionally and have an off day, but when that happens drive right back up onto that express ramp and continue moving forward. Avoid beating yourself up when you veer off track on any given day. Allow yourself the day that you fell off the wagon knowing that you will get right back on path after you've worked through the emotions associated with falling off. Rinse and repeat this cycle until it becomes easier where you are deviating off course less and less. This doesn't mean you will never fall of course while you are moving through a stronger enlightening phase. You are going to have off days. It's just part of the human physical condition. Allow yourself to feel the pain or negative emotions associated with veering off course. It's all part of the soul's process. Whenever you are moving through that, then you are going through another soul transformation.

Surround yourself with positive people, friendships, hobbies, and endeavors that you know will prevent you from falling down a toxic path just by being in their presence. These are the kind of toxic paths that you are aware of that delay you from moving forward in doing what you need to do. Govern your life like a strict executive by being extra careful with who and what you allow in your environment, as well as what you put into your body.

None of that means you can't have any fun. Fun is all part of self-care pending you're not doing things that can harm any part of you whether spiritually or physically. Self-care is essential to your soul, so that you don't experience burnout. You need those regular days in between your passion and life purpose work where you devote to self-care to do things that bring you pleasure and joy. This contributes to a brighter balance in your world. The more balance you incorporate, the more equalized and steadier your soul feels.

For some people the enlightening process may come well into adulthood when the soul experiences what is called *the shift*. This is when you come to the realization that you had been going through the motions of what you've been trained to do by society and other human souls, but then there is a specific period or moment in your life where this shifts significantly. Something traumatic may happen in your life or you'll experience a deep moment of clarity where your mind and consciousness expands and cracks open. Your perception is permanently altered where you view human life in a different way than you had before that moment. This shift and turning point alters the trajectory you were previously on. Many of the interests you had leading up to that date and the things you once felt connected to no longer interest you. It's as if the shift happened over night where you wake up one morning literally and metaphorically. This is where you come to realize much of what has currently been going on in your life is no longer of interest to you.

For example, this could be like the job you once loved is no longer attractive to you, or the long-term friendships you have suddenly feel like strangers you no longer can relate to. Some of the people you had been close to feel like foreigners whose values and views are either different than yours, or they seem severely limited and too superficial for you to tolerate anymore. Their interests and personality no longer mesh well with yours as they once did. You don't have hatred or negative emotions about them. You appreciate them as the angels do about all souls, but on a personal level you've outgrown them. You know you once agreed with them on important issues and had the same perception, but your soul expanded during its spiritual transformation and it grew beyond that. This isn't the kind of feeling that comes and goes, but a feeling that comes and never leaves you beyond that day of realization. It doesn't mean you have no love for them, but the new transformed you can no longer relate to them.

During my drug addicted days in my early twenties, I knew that I was no longer interested in that. I had a mission and purpose that I didn't want to be ruined by my adolescent rebelliousness. After I stopped the drugs, I was still going to the drug lord's homes to hang out with them. They were all partying, but I wasn't consuming anything. About a month in I thought, "What am I doing here? I can't relate to anybody here now that I'm sober."

You gradually dissolve those connections naturally like you're shedding the cocoon you had been living in. You release them with love remembering the blessings and lessons learned while with them. Some of them may remain in your life, while others will gradually dissipate away where you're seeing them less and less. You don't even necessarily have to do anything, as it's often a natural process where you are both growing more distant due to the wide discord.

Friendships that were once close have dissolved in this same way for others that have gone through similar spiritual transformations. It wasn't due to a problem that created a fight or a disagreement, but that you or they were peering out with new eyes. Your perception has been so radically altered that your values and whole being presented seem like another person entirely that you may not even recognize yourself anymore. The gears have shifted, and you head down a different path that is no longer in line with those you were once close to. Others may naturally transition with you down this new path and begin showing signs of evolving as well. This brings on a deeper connection than you had before.

This isn't a temporary shift, but a permanent one where you begin the process of making both major and minor changes to your life over the months and years to come. This is another sign that you are evolving. It's also realizing that the way things are on the planet is not normal just because humankind at that time in history says so. From an early age you're automatically suspicious of the current way that human life is and its structures, but by adulthood you've broken off that piece. You have a higher view of the triviality that others find themselves trapped in.

Technology has taught, trained, amplified, and exaggerated aggressive behavior without considering the consequences. In 2005, I saw the coming of an uprising of a major ongoing culture war around the world that would take place in bigger ways than could be comprehended at the time. It was a culture war that could ultimately destroy the planet over the coming centuries if changes were not made individually. In order to change globally you must change individually one person at a time. You must ask yourself if you're part of the problem or are you going to be one of the solutions contributing your part.

God sends His best to Earth that can viciously stay centered amidst the lower energy fueling system instigated by the darkness of ego. He knows only His best is more than capable of climbing back up if they get knocked down. Earth is a battlefield and you are His soldier hired to do His will. Falling into where everyone else is going does not lead to salvation. It leads to an avalanche of misery. Energy grows and expands regardless if it is Light or Dark energy. If it's miserable Dark energy, then it can and will eat and consume the soul. It's a pain that never lightens up.

When you're moving through a spiritual transformation, then you may start to feel more alien and detached from the masses entirely. You find you don't agree with anything that's going on in the media on either side or amongst your peers. You see everyone functioning in a limited way, which further alienates and isolates you from the nonsense. You are unable to relate or connect to anyone closely, with the exception being the trusted ones around you. This can create an isolating lonely feeling, but evolving souls are usually comfortable alone. They don't typically crave attention and praise from anyone. Your sensitivities become more enhanced because your psychic senses are growing more enriched. The two are interconnected which can lead you to be susceptible to absorbing in all that negative energy on the planet, which lowers your vibration and sucks the life force right out of you.

It's not God's job to absolve anyone from their sins nor give anyone a free pass to behave badly. It's up to the individual soul to learn from their mistakes in order to grow and evolve their soul's consciousness. All souls are evolving on Earth with whatever endeavor they undertake on their own time and in their own way that's most comfortable for that soul. There are also a great number of souls who never change, evolve, or shift at all throughout one lifetime. They will undergo numerous lifetimes to gain knowledge with the intent that it will eventually awaken and broaden their consciousness beyond the physical limitations they're trained to focus on.

One of the many goals of a soul in a human body is to grow, expand, evolve, and eventually transform. Some never reach those levels in their first life run, while other more advancing souls are transforming rapidly and repeatedly accelerating beyond comprehension than the norm for a human being. Transforming is not an easy process, because of the pain involved. The pain can be so great that having suicidal or despairing thoughts isn't unusual. You feel like the pain is too much, but then you take a step back and realize your souls' purpose is greater than the temporary pain you're feeling in that moment.

A transformation is full of all kinds of feelings. I've been through so many of them that I'd love to say I'm used to it. Some of them are harder than others. The more challenging ones I can sense when it's coming up on the horizon. It could be building up the months or even a year prior as I start to psychically sense that I'm heading for that transformation. Once the transformation has hit, then it can take months to get through, as there's a metaphorical shedding of the skin kind of like a caterpillar transforming into a butterfly. The caterpillar goes into a cocoon where it appears motionless. This can be aligned with you feeling as if nothing is moving in your life no matter how hard you try. You feel this long stagnancy going on when in actuality you are moving through the caterpillar's cocoon stage. It requires a great deal of faith and patience to understand things are brewing underneath even when it doesn't feel like that. There is no time limit before you break out of the cocoon and into a butterfly.

I've had major things around me being wiped away to make room for the next chapter. I could psychically see it coming, and then this would cause a feeling of dread over it. Sometimes as I'm seeing it, I'm thinking, "Oh no I don't want to transform again. It's too much."

Deep down I still know that the more you transform, then the more you evolve your soul. On the flipside, I could never stay the same since that would drive me crazy. When things start getting too rigid or stale, I know another spiritual soul transformation is coming again.

During that transformation process everything comes into question. Relationships, jobs, social roles, goals, etc. New experiences personal and professional come in as the old is dissolving. When I've had those kinds of major transformations, I could feel the weight of the previous chapter of my life tightening up and strangling me. The Archangel Nathaniel specifically comes in to extract all the old in your life and rip it out whether you want it to or not. It's so abrupt that it can feel like the end of the world or that it's as if it's one bad thing happening after another. It's only when you take a step back to have the higher perspective that the angels have, then you understand that something greater is in motion and at play for you. This is where you can now say, "God has a plan right now and I'm going to trust Him on it."

The larger transformations I've had were so lengthy and difficult that I knew it was the end of a chapter. This psychic foresight was giving me panic attacks before it arrived because I knew it was coming. Even though I also knew it was a good thing in the end. It doesn't mean the intensity of the visions weren't pounding on my psychic system. You are constantly building your soul the way cities were built from nothing. Our souls are like the water that flows like the Ocean tides. It was made to continuously move and transform and evolve.

When you've had a great deal of intense life being experienced in a short amount of time, then the positive aspects to that are the soul strengthening traits coming out of those experiences and lessons. It's going to direct you into your next chapter, which will be grand and beyond expectations. If you've made it this far through all the challenges, the distress, pain, excitement, then celebrate that! Celebrate the life you have. Break open a bottle and rejoice in that soul win. When you transform and evolve it never means you have fully evolved. If you peak, then you lose life force again. Therefore, the soul's goal is to continuously transform and evolve. The gift that comes with your final challenge is your next challenge.

CHAPTER THREE

*Awakening Your
Creative Consciousness*

Awakening your creative spirit within has many benefits that are connected to simultaneously expanding your soul's consciousness. When you dive into creative hobbies or pursuits, then you are utilizing and working out parts of your psychic intuition that may have been dormant. The benefits to breathing life into your psychic senses is that this helps you pick up on the Divine guidance and messages that your Spirit team can be urging you to do. Their role is to guide you throughout your life in steps, but this doesn't do you any good if you're unable to psychically pick up on what they're giving you. This is one of the various reasons as to why paying attention to that creative part of you can help in expanding those psychic gifts that already reside within your soul's DNA.

Nurturing your creative spirit assists in tapping into parts of your soul consciousness that awaken it. Your creative spirit is present when you experience positive energy flowing through you. This energy is ignited when you make a direct connection with God. This vibration state is where you have access to the true you, which is your higher self the soul part of you in its glorious perfection before it was born into an Earthly life.

Your higher self can take hold of the reigns of your life when you work to strip, reduce, or dissolve any negative tampering influenced by the domination of your physical surroundings. Make a connection with something greater than yourself by allowing that Divine energy Light to permeate your soul and cleanse it of toxic debris. This will assist in the process of awakening your creative spirit from slumber.

Your creative spirit is more than being artistic and getting involved in creativity pursuits, although this is a good part of it. When your creative spirit is activated by a high vibrational state of being, then this is the space you create and intuit from. You can apply this to your dealings in life, your creative and artistic endeavors, and to having a greater communication line with your Spirit team on the Other Side. Your creative spirit helps brings your soul into a high vibrational state of being because coming from a place of creativity raises your vibration. This is the zone where you create and manifest your visions at higher levels, while concurrently moving you into the joy of your life. It includes thinking like a kid, unleashing your inner artist, and coming to the realization of your soul's potential. When you claim your celestial power with the assistance of your Spirit team of heavenly helpers by your side, then this assists in capitalizing the true divine power within you. This is part of what it means to have access to Divine assistance and how that plays a part in arousing the muse within you in order to bring your state of mind into a happier vibrational state.

Your Spirit Team

When your soul enters its Earthly life in a human body, you are not born alone. One Spirit Guide and one Guardian Angel accompany you. They are your "Spirit Team" that will remain by your side from birth until you cross back over in human death. The goal they have with you is to ensure you stay on the right path that benefits your higher self. When you pay attention to their nudges, guidance, and messages, then the happier and more content your life is. When you do not follow their guidance, or take notice of when they are helping, then your life becomes chaotic, stressful, or anxiety ridden. If you are someone that works with Heaven, angels, God, archangels, saints, or any higher being in the spirit world regularly, then you will attract more guides and spirit Light energy sources into your vicinity that desire to help you. Some of them enter your aura to bask in your own soul's light, which is like a warm sun on a gorgeous Spring day.

One of God's gifts to human souls are also the Archangels and Angels, which are His hands and arms assisting and guiding you to raise your vibration so that you will better be able to hear God. When you connect or communicate with an Archangel or Angel, then you are connecting with God. You are not praying to the Angels, since they are a part of Him. When your vibration is low, then your connection to God is cut off. The angels and archangels help you to reach Him. Being connected to the Light is what contributes to your souls evolving process.

There are additional heavenly helpers that may come into your life during key transformation and transitional periods in your life when it's most needed. This can be from a project you're working on that will be of benefit to you or others. They will also be present to ease your mind and heart during times of grieving and sadness. The grieving can be over the death of someone close to you, from a broken love relationship, or during periods of depression. Once the additional guides or angels outside of your team have accomplished a quest with you, they leave to assist others, or they will go where they are guided to or needed. All in Heaven desire to serve because they either have no ego or little ego. When you use the dark side of your ego, then you do not care about others. When the ego part of a human being shows that it cares, then it could be masking an ulterior motive with the interest of personal gain.

You are born psychic and in tune to all that is beyond the physical world. This is the natural state of your soul. You are also born operating with high vibrational qualities such as love, joy, and peace. All of this begins to fade in varying degrees due to human tampering and distractions during adolescence and your developmental years. Your surroundings contain your caregivers, peers, the media you watch, and the community you reside in. All of this influences you on how to think, and what to follow, or what to believe in. This affects the rate as to how fast or slow your soul's consciousness will move through its many evolving processes.

The Larger Lights of Children and Animals

Children and animals have the highest ranges of psychic abilities than any other. Children haven't been fully tampered with and destroyed by jaded adults. When a child is scared or explains that they're seeing something no one else is, an adult automatically tells them, "Oh, it's just your imagination." There isn't a worse phrase to tell a child that is confiding in you about something that may be present that a cynical adult no longer understands. This phrase is what begins the process of erecting blocks to Divine communication in that child's life. In all fairness, it's not the adult's fault entirely. They are a product of the environment they were raised in. They we're trained to view things that are not understood by the ego to be a figment of one's imagination. Be open minded to what a child is telling you. They see, hear, feel, and know far more than adults give them credit for.

Animals remain as the spirit beings with the higher psychic ranges throughout the course of its life. It doesn't have the kinds of blocks that human souls create. An animal isn't concerned with paying rent or a mortgage. It's not concerned about finding work or stressing out over triviality and superficiality. If it's fed, has a place to sleep, and with an owner who loves it, then there are little blocks in its world if any at all.

Imagination is the source where your creative spirit is awakened. This space is the portal that leads to a stronger communication line with Heaven. The artists of the world and throughout history have greater access to the Divine because they have a good degree of sensitivity and imagination. They can walk through another's shoes without judgment no matter horrible that other person might be. Gifted actors excel at this as well. This open mindedness is one of the keys to having a crystal-clear connection line with your Spirit team.

It's not uncommon for those in childhood and teen years to have super strong connections with the Other Side, but it may be accompanied with the fear of wondering who is around them or why. Sometimes those who appear for them are Guides or Angels, and other times they are spirits who have not crossed over into the light and are unaware that they've gone. They're stuck in the transition between the Earth and spiritual plane. Spirits are attracted to the Light whether already on the Other Side or in this plane. Since children and animals tend to have larger lights around them than adults, then this makes them a magnet for spirits that have been stuck between this plane and the next. Children and animals have these larger lights because they haven't been stripped of this light due to blocks created in the physical world. Therefore, the spirit tends to gravitate and surround them. They're attracted to the light and the life force of the human soul. This also means they're attracted to adults that have a stronger psychic sense and a larger light around them. It's like being attracted to anything where you want to get close to it and feel it. Some young people are so fearful of it that overtime as they grow older the connection and light dims. As a result, they refuse to acknowledge it as an adult.

Breaking Away from the Norm

Those that preach about God and Heaven in a negative, hate filled, prejudicial way with vengeful angry words that attack other people are not communicating with God, since there are no negative words uttered from Him. Those words come from the Darkness or the Devil as some call it, which influences the human ego. The darkness of ego separates the good that exists in humanity and instead creates labels to ensure all souls are estranged from one another. All human souls are siblings of each other, since they were birthed out of the one source, but their light begins vibrating at different frequencies depending on its influences.

Others have been turning their backs on any mention of the word God because of the stigma that misguided souls have preached. They insist that God disapproves of you, which could not be further from the truth. His immense love for you is unconditional. He only expects that you put in effort to be a better more compassionate person. Evolve your soul in order to move onto brighter destinies. This isn't any different than what a good parent desires for their child.

The Earth plane is a place for all student souls, whether they are here for the first time since they sparked out of God, or if they are experiencing a repeat life in order to continue their soul's education so they can continue to expand and evolve. They cannot move on until individual soul lessons are learned, gained, and accepted. The student souls are called *Baby Souls*. They are more naïve and innocent, yet some of them are filled with hate and destruction because they have not mastered the ego. The ego became this way due to how they were raised in their environment. Hate and negativity are passed down into the human child. When you train your child early on to have love and compassion for all souls, then they will grow up this way.

The in-tune soul can sense a low vibration within a baby soul that seems to be permanent, but which is temporary. The vibration is stuck vibrating at a lower level until the soul awakens its consciousness. This typically comes through with experience and knowledge gained while on Earth. It is breaking away from the masses to realize there is more at play than what is being fed by others. Until then it is unable to expand, but instead stays exactly where it is swimming around in hatred and negativity. Some of them are also cruel, insulting, or power hungry. They are driven to put others down whether through domination or by bullying. You likely have an image of who someone like this is unless you've been cut off from all media sources and people.

When you visit certain places around the world, you'll notice that those who live in that specific community are all mostly like one another. Things like they may follow the same religion or vote for the same political candidates. They have similar rituals, opinions, and belief systems, etc. There might be some minor differences, but for the most part they behave quite the same as one another. They are clones going along with everyone else in order to not rock the boat, to fit in, or be accepted.

There are those that reside in these communities that the majority considers to be the oddball, weird, or different. Those are the ones that the community considers to be unusual from the rest of them. They are unable to hide who their soul truly is. They will eventually reach a point of defying that if they hadn't from the beginning. They tend to be the ones destined for greater purposes. Unable to suppress their true creative spirit, they're also usually the ones able to access spirit easily.

It takes great strength to see, feel, think, and do things differently than those around you. Think for yourself even if it defies what society or the community around you considers to be normal. Normalcy is a guideline that one's community insisted upon with one another, but it doesn't necessarily mean they're right. What is considered the norm is not always the case from the point of view of Spirit. It's just what the human community you are surrounded by trained you to believe.

The human mind has a great capacity for awesomeness, but the lower part of the human mind will follow anyone dangling a carrot in front of it. Your surroundings and the media tell you how to think, act, and who to lynch, or who to support. Human souls move like herds following someone they believe to be a good shepherd, or whoever their peers are raving about, or whatever fads happen to be in at that time in history. Easily influenced and swayed within their community instead of doing the hard work and research to find the highest truth.

The lone wolf that turns away from the crowd and walks in the other direction is usually a leader or guide in the making. They view things differently than the majority around them do. Often, they incarnated for a specific purpose that prompts others to view things in a broader way that eventually influences others to follow or learn from. History has shown that those that were ostracized, hated, or criticized tended to have the most positive beneficial impact in contributions towards the betterment of humanity. They might be that person who conveys compassion to all no matter what, even when the lynch mob around them is attacking or bullying someone else.

The surroundings you grow up around can wreak havoc on your soul's inner core-built system during your developmental years. This is carried on your soul's back indefinitely until it begins the laborious process of stripping away negative habits and values that were learned. This toxicity gives rise to the darker part of your ego or lower self. Your ego will do what it can to sabotage you. It can be greatly convincing that it's as if you've been taken over by the Devil himself.

The Darkness resides in one of the spirit planes that is in an interdimensional existence with this one working to poison and infect as many as possible, since it's so easy to do. It will bring out your lower self that views circumstances and others through a bleak, toxic, and often dangerous view. This is predominately evident in those that bully, harass, and call others derogatory names on their platform of choice. The darkness has infected that soul poisoning it with lies that cause harm and destruction. It helps no one around including the one dishing the harmful words, since it lowers that person's vibration as well. It's a waste of unnecessary energy that blocks good things from entering that person's life. Instead it invites in more negativity and ultimately creates the downfall and fate of that soul's consciousness.

Rise Up into Your Glorious Soul Power

Your inner light operates out of a high vibration. You have access to it since it never leaves you. When your vibration drops, then your ego and lower self rise simultaneously. This is followed by a weakening of your inner light to the level of a pilot light waiting to be re-ignited. When it is re-ignited, then the light begins to grow and fills up your soul like a wildfire that pushes your higher self back to the forefront of your life. The bigger the flame, then the more light it attracts in. When the light expands, then this contributes positively to your evolving process, which raises your consciousness giving you deeper psychic perception. This light is the doorway to God *(Spirit, Light, Essence, Power, All Knowing, the Creator, Energy, etc.)* It is where the helpful guidance and messages come in from spirit to help you along your path. It is what assists you in attracting in your desires pending that it is aligned with your higher self's goal. It is the part of you that is psychic and in tune.

Having confidence in you is having confidence in God. The best parts of you are what God is. He is not a man with a beard sitting high up on a throne looking for ways to judge you. The ego is what judges' others negatively. God is made up of energy that has the highest vibrational traits imaginable. He is made up of love, joy, peace, confidence, optimism, forgiveness, and grace. Because His vibration is so high to the point that it's not comprehensible, this makes it difficult for human souls to reach Him. You cannot reach him when exuding any measure of negative emotion.

Raise Your Consciousness

Negativity on any level can block you from achieving. Every soul is deserving of good on the planet, and every single person has something positive to offer. In higher spiritual truth, no one is more special than anyone else or below or above another, because all souls were made equally. Some souls have an easier time at evolving their consciousness than others. While other souls remain at one level throughout one Earthly lifetime.

In Heaven, all souls are considered one united. This is how it is supposed to be on Earth, even though the human ego convinces some people that they're either better or worse than another. It can be seen this way when you compare a giving Saint to a terrorist killer. In that comparison the differences are wide, but this is about both of those people's souls deep down at the core. When the soul is born into an Earthly life, then it is born with the highest God like qualities available and imaginable. It is only as the soul moves through its human journey do the experiences it endures shape and mold them to something else entirely.

The Godly traits the soul is born with are always inside them and forever accessible. The soul has to figure it out for itself and do the work to bring it back out again. As you're likely aware, not many accept that challenge and they end up suffering. Remembering your soul's true heritage makes you a powerful soul.

Every time you learn lessons that propel your soul forward spiritual growth is achieved. It is the knowledge gained through each experience that contributes to progress. This is regardless if the experience is challenging or positively enjoyable. It will still add to molding, shaping, and expanding your consciousness to greater heights. Sitting around in front of the television all day everyday accomplishing nothing of value will ensure your soul's growth remains in the same place. The exception to that is if someone is an invalid or battling a health issue. The health issue in this case is offering mental struggles and will power that strengthen and grow your soul. The opposite kind is if you plop on the sofa staring at trash television all day out of laziness.

You cannot watch reality television regularly or read gossip content daily and raise your conscious. This doesn't mean you have to avoid those things completely if you have interest in them, but typically a higher vibrating soul doesn't have much of an interest in those types of things. It's considered an unhealthy addiction due to the dumbed down content that enforces a stereotypical shallow existence, which is also having that same effect on your soul. This is about the offenders that spend their days absorbing this energy with no interest in anything else, rather than the occasional fun and playful curiosity you might have in a rare story.

Raising your consciousness is important because remaining stunted in terms of soul growth ensures that karma is built up and an Earthly life do over in a tougher circumstance is inevitable. God sees that the one life run was wasted and didn't work. Having to do it again in a tougher circumstance life situation has a greater chance of placing enough Earthly life challenges to help your soul be snapped into long term soul reality that there is something greater at play than the Earthly life mundane that human beings set up. This is the same as a Wise One task master Teacher in school that gives the students a harder test than the one before in order to challenge them. This isn't done in punishment, but to help them grow and expand their mind and consciousness so they may graduate into something grander than where they are now.

There isn't one main event that assists in your spiritual growth, but numerous mini events interwoven throughout your Earthly life. When you feel like it's one thing after another going on in your world, then look at that as being lessons you are enduring for a greater purpose as hard as that might feel at the time. Know that nothing stays the same and this challenge too shall pass. Major events will offer larger growth experiences, but the mini events are just as important if not more so. The side effect to the events is that it helps you make sounder decisions, which help you live a more prosperous and abundant life.

CHAPTER FOUR

Soul Contracts

Before you enter an Earthly life, your soul got together with a council of highly evolved heavenly leaders that work with you to put a soul contract together. The soul contract includes many of the main events that will happen in your life and the reasons for those events. The many soul mates you'll encounter will also be listed along with the estimated dates that they show up. Everything in the soul contract is a forecasted estimation, because you and those around you in the contract are also granted free will choice to do what you or they want to do. Paying attention to God and your Spirit team helps you fulfill your destinies and bullet points within this contract. You ask for their help when needed, you follow their guidance, and act when necessary.

When you ignore God and your Spirit team, then you are also ignoring some of the things that are in your souls' contract. They are trying to help you fulfill elements in your souls' contract. They will repeatedly put up the same signs in your path to get you to notice it in hopes you'll act on it. If you continue to ignore it, then that same sign will continue if it needs to. For some people the same sign never goes away. When they reach human senior age or their final years, they might conclude that there were things they were supposed to do, but they never did. Those things were in their souls' contract, but they ignored it and chose to set out to have a different life. One of the harder things to see is someone express regret at the end, instead of finding ways to accomplish, do, and see what they intended while here.

When they arrive back home in Heaven, one of the main things they do beyond reuniting with some of their loved ones is they want to get their hands on that soul contract. They will see all the things they were supposed to accomplish and what they failed to accomplish. They'll also recall instances in their Earthly life when they were clearly being shown to do something that is affiliated with this soul contract, but their human ego denied or ignored it. This is also due to the many blocks that were present preventing them from accurately picking up on that Divine guidance coming in from their Spirit team. God and your Spirit team are not pushing or urging you towards something for no reason. There is a purpose behind their guidance. The soul develops amnesia when it incarnates into a human body. Part of that is for their protection. If they knew exactly what was to take place, then they would never live life. They would sit around and wait for it to happen.

If the soul sits around waiting for the contracted events to take place, they would waste their time because the events would not happen due to their free will choice to sit and wait for it. The soul has many purposes it needs to set out to do while here. Each human soul is given just enough information from Spirit at the right time allowable on God's timing. Even the most psychic person on the planet won't be able to see everything. They can only see what God allows them to see at that moment, which can come through in psychic snippets and flashes. Sometimes enduring a severe crushing struggling phase is part of your soul's contract. There is an added benefit to your soul's growing consciousness.

What is also drawn out and included in this lengthy soul contract that can fill a gigantic book are the experiences you agree to endure in that Earthly lifetime. This includes your life purpose, goals, lessons, missions, and the challenges you will face. There are various bullet points listed that assist in the growth and evolvement of your soul. Also included in this contract are the soul mates and karmic connections you will meet along your journey. These relationships are intended to assist in expanding and growing your soul. They include family members, friendships, colleagues, acquaintances, and lovers. They make up the many soul mates you encounter in your life.

When the contract is drawn up in Heaven, also listed is that there will be different special guides or angels that will show up temporarily to help the soul with pivotal events, such as getting the right jobs, finding the right soul mate partners, and on up to greater quests that help humanity in a positive way. One is not always at the same job for a lifetime. They will endure many different jobs that they are gaining important qualities, skills, and traits from. They will then apply those additional gained qualities to their next chapter. The same goes for soul mate partners, which is also why many have many different soul mates sifting in and out of their lives. Those waiting for that one special soul mate are unaware they have more than one that will come in the form of friendships, family members, colleagues, acquaintances and in love relationships.

Look at every single job or people you've encountered throughout your life, whether good or bad, and examine all the positive benefits you gained that helped in your evolving growth process. The more you evolve your consciousness, then the easier it is to detect what you learned. If you're unable to see what you learned, then you will continuously encounter similar soul mate people and situations throughout your life that are teaching you the same lesson. This is in their soul's contract to be of added benefit to your soul. On a subconscious level, their soul knows what it is they will be bringing to your life, with you bringing something of benefit to them. All soul relationships are both a teaching and learning situation on both sides.

There is something you are intended to gain even through the meanest person you meet. What have you learned from those types of connections? You will be given similar soul mates from one another when a lesson isn't being learned hard enough. Eventually this cycle stops when you have the spiritual awakening and awareness that you are constantly attracting in the same types in. That's when you need to take a good hard look to discover why your soul is continuously pulled into the same repetitive circumstances. This is also a clue as to what your soul's many purposes are to accomplish in this life, since not all life purposes are a financially driven and lucrative career. The same way you have more than one soul mate, you also have more than one life purpose within one lifetime. All of this and much more are in this soul contract.

You are also set up with three separate departure times throughout your Earthly lifetime. If the first two points of Earthly departure are denied and decided against, then the third departure time is the Earthly death. It is the maximum allowable time you've agreed upon in living one Earthly life. You might even recall one or two previous moments where you almost died. These are not the same as near death experiences, which are enacted to awaken the soul that needs to be awakened for a greater purpose.

Your soul contract is in a personal book devoted to you that the Archangel Metatron keeps in the Hall of Records in Heaven that some call the Akashic Records. There are key circumstances that are listed to take place in it, but that doesn't mean every single one of those bullet points will happen. Things like free will choice can delay or negate it all together. For example, in the book it might state that you'll meet a love partner at age twenty-eight. It describes who that person is and other details about them as well as where and when you'll meet them. Due to free will choice and other unforeseen circumstances beyond your control or this other person's control, delays can push it out, then you find that you end up meeting this person at age thirty-six. The delays or free will choices pushed the circumstance further out, while in other cases delays and free will choices are so great that it pushes it out indefinitely. The path crossing with this person never happens or it comes so close, but you both miss it.

All human souls have the capacity to see, feel, know, and hear messages and guidance from beyond. Everyone is equally and unequivocally psychic for the purpose of being able to connect with their Spirit team. You're on a mission on Earth and they are guiding you with that mission. If you are not picking up on anything psychically, then that means you are experiencing a block. Blocks form easily in the physical Earthly life since the physical life is a challenging one. Human beings generate most of the problems that exist. If there were no human beings on the planet, then the planet's energy life force would evolve and re-grow itself on its own without the tampering destruction that people tend to wreak on it.

Endless data of information exists in this soul contract. This contract is more than a sheet of paper or the kind of contract you expect to receive for a job position. The duties listed in a human job contract are not far off from the nature of the soul contract, which lists an array of duties and purposes you're agreeing to work towards accomplishing for the benefit of your soul. One core difference between the soul contract and a regular job contract is that you cannot get fired for not performing your soul duties. Every soul contract is also large enough to fill numerous large books that house each soul's lifetimes on Earth, galaxies, and dimensions. Not only does the contract list your purposes and core events scheduled to take place, but everything you do or do not do in your entire soul's history is also recorded in this book. Everything you can ever imagine about you is in this contract.

Much of the challenges the soul endures are also listed in the soul's contract in the Hall of Records on the Other Side. This Hall of Records is no ordinary library. It contains all the answers to anything and everything that a soul could possibly want to know. Placing your hand on it allows the information to be filtered rapidly into your soul's consciousness like a computer uploading data.

One of the many agreements contained in the soul contract is a set up that lays out numerous paths that branch out into other numerous roads. It looks like the LIFE board game, but is a hundred times more complex.

If you miss one fork in the road and head down a different path it might reveal that you would take the longer route around before you reach your destination. What is interesting is that most of the roads lead to the same destination, with a percentage of souls heading in a completely different direction due to the free will choice action of the individual.

An event intended to take place may be soul contracted, but no spirit being can interfere with your free will choice. This is still your life to live it for you. Your Spirit team will do their best to gently guide you towards the direction you originally agreed upon, but your ego can override that and choose to do what it wants you to do. As a result, you end up being taken for a ride in another direction.

Some paths take the longer away around, while others might have more challenges listed on them. As mentioned, there are also the three exit points that indicate the main sections of your life where your soul may choose to exit this life and head back home. There are also agreements indicating the various soul mates you'll encounter along your life path. It also lists the purposes and intentions that you and each soul mate will have with one another. These include the numerous lessons you've both agreed to endure for the benefit of soul growth, which affects the evolving soul consciousness.

Because you have free will choice, this can negate and alter what is intended to take place. This contract may reveal a love soul mate showing up at a particular time. Due to free will choice on your part and/or this other person's part, it can alter and change both your paths pushing the connection further out or from happening at all.

One example is it can be something such as remaining with a current partner that was supposed to end awhile back, but didn't for various reasons. The next partner soul mate rarely shows up before the previous one is absolutely without a doubt complete. In some cases, the next soul mate partnership does show up, but you both fail to acknowledge one another or pay attention due to having one foot cemented in the previous connection refusing to give up and walk away. You know that previous connection was supposed to end a long time ago because it's usually bathed in toxic unstable issues. Your free will choice can convince you to stay longer than you should have for fear of what might happen or not happen.

Other times, the ego will put you through a denial phase where you believe without a doubt this person is the one, you're supposed to be with, but the other person is failing to see that. As a result, you cling to that person not realizing you had been deceived by the ego to drag it on longer than it was intended to. When it is the right person for you, there will be no resistance coming on either side. It will happen as natural as it would in a romantic comedy.

Sometimes the future soul mate love partner will show up while you're still in the connection that was supposed to end. You feel a strong gravitational pull towards that new person even though you might not romantically act on anything with them. Both teams of guides from your side and this other person's side are aware that the old connection is going to end, so they jump the gun and orchestrate the bumping into part of this new person knowing nothing might take off for a while.

For some people, connections take time before having full lift off where it's safe enough to bring them in and let it take its time evolving into more down the line. Meanwhile, the former love connection has fulfilled its contract agreement and begins to disband. It isn't long before the new love interest begins to have lift off.

This is one example of the many possible scenarios that can take place. There are times where no lift off happens due to free will choice. The connection will be pushed further and further out. Sometimes it never happens and one of the soul's passes on. Should the soul decide to have another Earthly life along with that soul mate at or around the same time, they will both be listed again on the new soul contract in hopes of recognizing one another. Therefore, some people might seem familiar to you, even though you just met them.

When two souls are ready and evolved enough, then the lifelong love partnership will happen when either least expects it. You will both be placed on the same path where it is orchestrated perfectly to the point where you're both standing face to face. There is no way either of you cannot see it.

The same is applied to work life and jobs. You could be stuck at what appears to be a dead-end job, but you have dreams of starting your own entrepreneurship, which is more popular today than ever in history. You may feel guided to leave your job, but you fear prevents you from making any changes. This can cause delays as well that may last for years. This isn't telling anyone to leave their job recklessly. It's something you must plan out methodically ensuring you are safe and secure enough to some degree.

If you have dreams of starting your own business, then take action steps today while at this job. You do this by devoting even just a half hour a day towards it when you're not at this day job. If you love this side business, then that passion and excitement will be the fuel for you to dive into on the side even when you're exhausted from your work at your regular job. You'd be surprised how devoting a tiny amount of time each day or week towards it starts to create some movement. When it's grown enough, then you'll know when it's safe to leave the day job. If not, then your Spirit team will yank you out of that job for this purpose. When you lose a job, you'll eventually see that it was for a reason. You are now free to work extra hard towards your life purpose work. This life purpose work and calling is one that is in your contract. The intense feeling you were receiving about leaving your job is your soul's awareness that this is something you are intended to do. You may not be aware of the origins of this feeling, but often it is something buried in your subconscious from soul memories of this contract.

All the experiences you have and will have in this life are part of your soul contract. They are all intended to contribute towards positively enhancing your soul and to bring you to the next step on your soul's evolving journey. Your Guide and Angel work with you in your life to ensure that you stay on the right path. Therefore, it's also important to be in tune and pay attention to your Guide and Angel. Staying on path is to help you fulfill the terms in your contract. When you're in tune and connected, it's not difficult to know what your purpose and terms are.

Sometimes you might be privy to what the terms are as circumstances happen for you. You might experience heartbreak in a love relationship and then say, "Now I know not to get involved with someone who is married and has no plans to leave their spouse."

You gained major soul and life enhancing skills in the process of the experience. It strengthened you to be on the lookout over who is a quality mate and who would not be good for you. These situations that happen can be in your soul contract. If it isn't, then it is the result of your free will choice, since no being in Heaven can intervene on your free will without your permission. Free will can cause an array of delays along your path, not to mention poor life choices. When you're not connected and in tune, but are guided by your ego and lower self, then you find that its one roadblock after another. You spend your entire life running around in circles chasing your tail doing what your ego wants. You may not come to the realization that this is what's happening until many years in. You discover, "Wow, what have I done the last five years?"

When your terms have been completed, you may exit this lifetime at that point, but not always. Sometimes one might fulfill their contract, but then will spend the remainder of their life working in a career that is their life purpose. They become of service to others or choose to spend their days enjoying their human retirement since they've fulfilled the terms in their contract. When you are in human retirement in later age you are still experiencing different kinds of purposes that could be connected to helping others in some way or gaining wisdom through study. The retired spent their life working hard on their life purpose and they deserve a break of luxury and relaxation too. Sometimes finally having that break is when they find their life purpose if it hadn't been discovered in the earlier years.

Luxury and relaxation are two qualities that Heaven wants to see all souls experience on a regular basis. They see relaxing and taking time outs as a necessity for your soul in order to recharge your soul's batteries. These acts are near non-existent today thanks to the break your back work all day everyday set up designed by the soulless. The soulful understand the benefits to working hard and smart, while also taking regular time outs. When you take regular time outs, breaks, days off, then you are more productive at work. You are stronger, healthier, and have a better attitude. This concept has yet to seep into the consciousness of many.

CHAPTER FIVE

Life Purposes

Every single soul on Earth has a list of life purposes in their soul contract. The purposes are all listed together in a pyramid like scheme. For example, one of my main life purposes is clear. It is my spiritual teaching work through the written word. Because this work was prominent in my life going back to childhood, it is listed at the top point of this pyramid. I had always subconsciously known this was what my Spirit team was leading me towards in a big way. As you sift downwards into the many layers of the pyramid there are an eclectic array of purposes within all of that, which are connected to the singular purpose. These might be things like working on being more fearless in certain areas of your life. I've had to personally work to master that over the course of my life considering that I'm a completely different person than I was when I was fifteen. I grew into my warrior like confidence as I entered my twenties.

One of your main life purposes is connected to what brings you and/or another person joy. It would also be what you would do for free if you had all the time and money in the world. Your life purpose is your passion that assists and benefits you as well as others. For instance, my writing work benefits a great deal of people as readers have reached out to me to share, but it also benefits me in that it's supremely therapeutic and helps me work out my own demons during the creative process.

If one's purpose is to live a life showering the world with love, then this is an objective that brings both you and another something positive. You could assign that example to an entertainer who enjoys being a musician and seeing people smile while they play on stage. In that instance they are showering the audience with love. You don't have to be a well-known entertainer that showers the world with love. You could be that neighbor who smiles and is warm and friendly with everybody on the block whenever you head outside. In that instance you are fulfilling one of your purposes of showering love on others.

God and your Spirit team know what your soul's life purposes are. They know what plans have been mapped out in your souls' contract for you. You also have this knowledge embedded deep in your subconscious too. It was something you agreed to before you chose to live an Earthly life. You can discover the answer to what that is when you tune in within. Your life purpose is not a question that can be answered by anyone, but yourself.

Not all life purposes are career related or a financial gaining one. Some life purposes are emotional traits learned, such as spending a lifetime learning how to easily forgive others over slights your ego feels they enacted on you. Forgiveness is one of the hardest action steps for a soul to reach, therefore this emotional trait exists in most every soul's contract on the planet. How do you forgive someone who took advantage of your good nature and seemingly destroyed an element of your life? It takes work and discipline to make your peace with someone that caused you turmoil. The sooner you do that, the quicker you evolve and move onto more important purposes. The angels and the egoless higher evolved spirits see the love in every soul, which is why they can exude the most magnificent forgiveness traits known to all creation.

Life purposes are easy to detect because it's one of the main goals that never seems to leave your mind throughout the years. For some, it is what gives you pleasure to dive into, but it can also be specific emotional traits that you struggle and wrestle with most of the days of your life, such as learning the act of giving, receiving, and to reducing anger and stressful dramatics to situations.

One life purpose example would be Albert Einstein and the work he contributed that assisted in prospering the planet. This doesn't mean all are called here to invent something. Many life purposes are geared towards acquiring soul enhancing traits such as gaining human life experience and the knowledge that it entails. This can be by learning responsibilities such as finding a job to pay your bills. There is more to Earthly life than finding a job and paying bills, but it's the learning responsibility act that is the knowledge gained that connects to your purpose. One should seek out a job that gives them pleasure and by default those around you. This isn't always an easy thing to do with the grave amount of competition fighting for the same role.

It's not uncommon to feel like you don't want to be here anymore or if you feel like your journey is complete. This is not always a fun world to live in. The misery created can be at the hands of those around you, but sometimes it can be you who is creating the misery without realizing it. If you're still here, then you are supposed to be, even if you have no clue as to why. It is your job and quest to discover why on your own. Ask yourself the important questions and examine your life to a hair-splitting degree to conclude as to why you are here. Everyone on the planet has a purpose.

In a journal or email to yourself, jot down the significant life events that transpired for you to date. What did you learn or gain from that? Allow your soul to involve itself in the Earthly life schoolwork so that you may graduate into other expanded spheres of soul consciousness. No one can do it for you. It's the same methodology as going to Earth's grade school. You had to show up to class, pay attention, study, and take tests in order to pass. Earthly life school for your soul is similar in that you must do the work, learn, grow, evolve, and graduate. You will be tested and asked to learn from mistakes you make or harm you've caused on other people, animals, and even the planet itself.

Earthly life is tough for millions of human souls that are working jobs that crush and kill their life force. Part of this is due to the current way that people have designed the modern-day work world. There is a greater distinction between working a job in a corporate environment you despise as opposed to finding a job that brings out your passions, creativity, and enjoyment. There are many souls that feel at home in a corporate structured environment, but it should be with the goal of making a positive impact for others. The problem is most that fall into that structure become equally rigid failing to invite in healthy balance. It's vital to your soul to balance your spiritual personal life and your practical work and career life.

As also discussed, not everyone's life purpose is ones chosen career. Many life purposes are not geared towards monetary success. Monetary success does not contribute to soul enhancing qualities, unless the millionaire is a humanitarian who uses their large income to assist those in need. This charity is an important character trait in enhancing one's soul.

A popular culture example could be someone like actress Angelina Jolie. She rose to movie stardom in the 1990's and into the 2000's and beyond. She was one of the final remaining true movie stars left before the rise of technology made everyone a star. She worked hard as an actress and her name became universally known, then she had that personal awakening moment while making the *Tomb Raider* films. The films were shot in beautiful countries that were also seeing hardship, refugees struggling, and poverty. This opened Jolie's eyes to the point that she once commented that it made her see life in Hollywood as trivial and superficial. Her new fight and larger purpose came to be her humanitarian work that never ceased and only continued to expand and grow over time. She became a United Nations Ambassador and Professor outside of her movie roles. The movie roles brought pleasure and entertainment to the masses, but one of the crucial elements it did per her divine soul contract was that it made her name popular and well-known. It was much easier for her to be taken seriously as a humanitarian and fight for those causes as a well-known name. Her big name would bring light to the tragedies happening in the world, because people will be more likely to see what Angelina Jolie is up to rather than a name they've never heard of.

I may not be of Angelina Jolie's universally known status, but my twenties were spent making a big name for myself behind the scenes in the film industry. Many in the entertainment business know who I am due to working with me over those many years, as well as the continued lifelong friendships I made with many in the business. I worked hard on film productions for the studios and talents in that industry, then like Jolie in a sense I also profoundly woke up towards the end of my twenties realizing that I was tired of the superficiality of the business. I remember working on a big film for Warner Bros. called *The Perfect Storm* at the young age of twenty-seven manning a crew of 800 people when I had another awakening moment. I was thinking, "I don't want to do this anymore. I love being here, but when am I going to start writing for a living?"

I had become in demand by the industry, but I wanted out. I wanted to follow my life purpose and become an author of work that helps the souls of humanity as per contracted. This feeling was something present in childhood and never left me, but towards the end of my twenties it was growing out of control that I couldn't shake it off. It propelled me to give up the high paying job offers to do what my soul was calling me to do knowing I'd be losing out financially. It wasn't about the money in the end. This is another clue as to what you're supposed to be doing. The feeling never leaves you throughout your life only growing bigger until you find a way to do it.

Not everyone fulfills elements in their soul contract. In fact, a great many number of souls do not fulfill it completely. This is one of the many long lists of reasons as to why some souls opt to come back for another Earthly life in order to fulfill the terms that were in the previous contract. Telling this to someone having an Earthly life now would prompt them to say, "Oh no, I'm not coming back here."

The ego part of us says that because the person's current life experience or the state of the world today is not satisfying. It's filled with unhappy glum people that are also mean, heartless, and cruel. However, on the Other Side in Heaven, you have a much broader perspective. You're in a different space with far less ego. The soul wants to come back in order to fulfill its purpose or to assist the planet in a way that no other is doing. You realize back home that this is God's house and our job is to protect it.

Journalist, Oprah Winfrey, is a humanitarian that used her money to help others in a positive way. She opened the, "Oprah Winfrey Leadership Academy for Girls in South Africa". She's contributed millions of dollars over the years to help those suffering from poverty as well as towards others in making their dreams come true. She had an inner drive to do something positive with her life. She went after her dreams and achieved it. She then took the gift of monetary success and used it to help others in a positive way, which ultimately became her true soul's life purpose. This gave her and others joy.

This is one example of how to determine what someone's life purpose is. Your life purpose can be as big as being a friend to others the way Jesus was and is to the underdog. The irony being that many of his followers of today turn against or criticize the underdog, but so do people that have no belief system in place as well.

One's life purpose can be a side hobby that you enjoy doing. Brian, a twenty-six-year-old, set up a website to help people. This enabled others to email him for free advice. He has made himself an open door for others to discuss their problems with him. He doesn't charge anyone, but also doesn't care about that. He is fulfilled knowing he's been able to help at least one person. This is his life purpose. He discovered that it brings him, and others joy by being of service.

The world we live in requires that you must make money in order to survive. It's not like it was centuries ago when you could barter your services, which is giving someone something of value for something of value in return such as food and housing, etc. Over time human beings moved away from that and demanded that you use paper money for things. This gave money power over people. The ego in human souls will at times do whatever it can to obtain what they want. They will push others down to climb to the top of the ladder to stealing merchandise they want in a store to breaking into someone's car or property.

Greed has overpowered the human condition, which is also why bartering wouldn't survive today. You cannot trust humankind to be honest. There is nothing wrong with charging for your services as this is the way Earthly life is set up now. You cannot pay your rent with sticks and stones. You have to get a job to make money to pay for the necessities of life such as housing, transportation, clothes, and food.

In Brian's case, he has a day job, which is his primary source of income. If he deeply wanted to pursue his passion and life purpose full time, then he could begin requesting some measure of payment for his services, or like Churches add a donation button on his website. Never quit your day job to pursue your life purpose hobby unless it is safe enough to do so. This means your life purpose brings in enough income for you to survive so that you may safely leave your regular job. This is a dream that many would love to have. Not everyone wants to work in the rigid, cold, corporate environments. The way that Earthly life is set up now is that it's not as challenging to create your own business that is aligned with your purpose. Most everything is online now, and you can create businesses and services online without having to lease out a building to set up office. That's a major expense you're saving. There are some businesses that would require you to lease a space. An Esthetician wouldn't be able to work on someone's face unless the client is in the room with them. The Esthetician desires this kind of work. They are attracted to beauty and physical appearance upkeep. This is their life purpose because it brings joy to others through health, beauty, and self-care.

How can someone tell you what your purpose is? Only you know what brings you and others joy. This is for you to decide and not someone else. My life purpose is writing books and teaching through the written word. Not only does it bring me joy fulfillment, but I learned to understand that this has also been helping people around the world. To receive a note from someone in Turkey, Japan, or Australia who loved one of my books and had to tell me is cool. I'm happy to hear someone feels inspired in life after reading a piece of my work. This means the job that my Spirit team works to do is effective.

There is no need to worry that you've found a life purpose that isn't bringing in money. The key to knowing if it is your life purpose is if it brings you and/or someone else joy and assistance. You would do the work for free if you had all the time and money in the world. It's something you find yourself doing because you want to.

When you have free time from your day job, then you are excited to dive into your life purpose fun. Your life purpose doesn't feel like work to you. It's something you enjoy doing. Life purposes can also be helping the masses in some way such as working in a homeless shelter or traveling the world to assist those in need of basic lifesaving supplies. It can be painting on a canvas and showcasing your work in a gallery. Art brings others enjoyment; therefore, it is that artists life purpose. A concert performer enjoys putting on a show and the audience benefits by having a good time, which raises their soul's vibration. It takes them away from their mundane lives. This performing action is the band or singer's life purpose. Making movies that entertain and make people think a different way is a collaborative effort that is connected to all the filmmaker's life purpose. You will know it is your life purpose when you find that this is an activity you would participate in when you're not at your day job. It doesn't feel like work to you.

Everyone needs to be contributing something in a positive way that is bringing love to another person. You were not born angry, bitter and depressed. Other human souls have inflicted that belief system on you. You absorbed it and reacted to it in ways where it might have permanently damaged you. It will be reversed and undone in this life or in the next when you pray and ask for heavenly assistance to lift those burdens off your soul. Invite in Heaven to permanently work with you on improving your life. They love you and want to help you reach a state of peace and contentment in your life.

One of your quests on learning to love is that you are tested repeatedly. This is done at the hands of those who may not be walking the talk, or who are not spiritual, but superficial. While you are working on your life purpose and contributing to humanity and your surroundings in a positive way, you may wonder what they are offering besides annoyance and grief. God, Heaven and the Angels see the love and your true self including the worst parts of your ego. Your criticisms and judgments are wasted words and energy.

Instead of reaching for that drink, I am more inclined to exercise. I'll jog up a mountain trail, or on the beach, or anywhere in nature. It is less stressful than jogging through the busy streets. I bike regularly along the beach coast as well. Exercise centers and elevates your spirit. You have more energy in the process while appearing and feeling better too! Others notice a brighter glow around you. Your entire aura and being attracts others to you. You have more time and energy during the day to accomplish important tasks. These tasks are geared towards your life purpose, spending quality time with loved ones, and more time for healthy rest. Relaxation is a luxury as well as a necessity. Get away for a couple of days and head to a place in nature, such as a park, the desert, the mountains or the beach where it is quiet and serene. I use those surroundings as an access to re-center myself if I am feeling out of sorts. If I'm at home and unable to get away for any reason I'll put on a melodic chill out or uplifting music album, then light some incense and candles. I will create a safe, calming sanctuary where I live.

Incidentally physical fitness trainers have a purpose that helps others get healthy and fit, while a massage therapist has the life purpose of contributing towards the health and well-being of their client through that act.

You are here to fulfill your life purpose, learn soul enhancing lessons, gain knowledge, and to enjoy this life and have some fun. This fun does not fall into the category of toxic. You are not asked to stop these poor ways of living for anyone's benefit, but your own. Heaven wants you to live at your fullest potential while experiencing euphoric feelings of joy. When you participate in healthy activities, exercise regularly, and have some measure of discipline about what you put into your body, then the fun and enjoyment you experience is beyond cosmic. If a stressful situation hits you, then as a high vibrational soul you can take on that stress in exhilarating stride. You are equipped to allowing the stress to roll off you without tampering with your energy field. The stressed situation evaporates rather quickly, than it would if you had not asked your Spirit team to intervene and work with you.

When you let go of all the burdens you carry on your soul by others, will you then see the truth of who you are. The obsession some have with homosexuality, race, politics and religion diverts the world from love, joy and their life purpose. You have a preoccupation over a breed of God's creation that you do not understand. Your ego and the infection of the Darkness allow this to happen preventing you from fulfilling terms in your contract. It is pushed to uproar out of fear and misguidedness. One of your life purposes is then to master that and learn how to come to terms with accepting others. If you are anti anything such as anti-gay, anti-race, anti-gender, but you want to evolve your soul, then it's time to begin the process of diving into what you despise so you can have a better understanding of it. More times than not, those that dive into understanding something they fear come out of it transformed and changed realizing they were previously misguided and wrong.

Whenever you do something good or bad this is filed away in your soul contract and records. Archangel Metatron who holds these records stands near the throne of God with the Archangel Jeremial during your life review. Your guide and angel are highly developed psychic entities that know your probable futures, your map, thoughts, feelings, and life purpose. They work to keep you heading in the right direction. You must tune in, pay attention, and communicate with them regularly, so that you stay on course and do not experience anger or sadness.

Don't shortchange yourself or be embarrassed as if you are not deserving of a great life. Heaven and your angels know you deserve it. They want you to be at peace, so that you can fulfill your life purpose. You do not have to be on this planet to suffer.

Your life purpose can also be whatever makes you angry or riles you up. For example, someone is always getting upset or angry when people throw trash in the ocean. This repeated anger for the same thing is a clue they were meant to come here to do something about it, such as joining in with an environmental organization, start a blog, or mobilize to clean up the oceans. This is their life purpose.

To turn your hobby into a career, take action steps towards it daily. You can do this in baby steps. Spend at least thirty minutes a day diving into whatever it is you want to accomplish. If you are working on a book, then spend at least thirty minutes each day writing a page. The universe will meet you tenfold in manifesting your dreams. When you are working on what you love, then it doesn't feel like a drag. You may be working at a job you're not happy with, but when you have something to look forward to at the end of the day, then it raises your vibration. This opens the door for the universe to step in and meet you halfway. You'll be that much closer to having your dream come true. It may feel like a struggle at first, but you will eventually notice the positive changes revealing itself to you in trickles over time. If you keep at it, then eventually that love will be your career! It will bring in enough financially that you're able to quit the job you're unhappy with. Ones hobby or love is often connected to their life purpose. However, a new human soul experiencing their first Earthly life may have a purpose that requires they learn patience or forgiveness. It might not be a specific "work" oriented goal, but it could be.

When you are not at your job, what do you enjoy doing on your off time? What is your hobby? Is it painting? Is it singing or playing the guitar? Your hobby is not surfing the internet, heading to the bar with friends every other night, or shopping for clothes. Those are called distractions, time wasters and addiction feeders at times. Your hobby is an activity that you enjoy doing on your own. It's one that gives you an added skill or knowledge around a certain area that gives you pleasure. Your hobby is what you want to turn into a career.

Let's look at a couple of well-known entertainers in music history. Bruce Springsteen has been playing his guitar since he was a teenager. When he was playing the guitar in those days it was his hobby and something he enjoyed doing. He was able to transition that hobby into a full-time career that lasted a lifetime. When entertainer Madonna was a teenager, she enjoyed dancing as a hobby. She took classes and looked for work that would enable her to incorporate her love for dancing. She was able to broaden that into an even bigger career that has also lasted a lifetime. Heaven applauds the music entertainers that bring joy to the world. Remove all the negative rants and criticisms that people whine about a musical artist they despise, then you will see a soul that enjoys being a musical artist and does it for the passion and love of it.

Many that work jobs that are not surrounding their hobby or passion are more likely to be unhappy than those who are. Those that are unhappy with their jobs tend to reach for addictions like alcohol, food or other toxic vices more than those who are happy with their work. Some of them reach for addictions to function. They will pop pills to tranquilize themselves to sleep at night and then ingest high doses of caffeine for an energy jolt to get them started every morning. You take something at night to calm down and sleep, and then you ingest something to infuse you with energy to get you going. The days where they are not at their job, like the weekend or a vacation day, they are less likely to reach for substances. This is a clue that you are unhappy at your job, but are convincing yourself that this is just the way it is.

If you keep making excuses that you're too tired or that you never have enough time, then you push your dream and purpose that much further away from you. The right time may never come unless you take control of your life by working this hobby into your schedule. I've had to work two full time jobs that included my regular job and my career. It can be done if everything in your entire being loves this hobby. You can turn this into a career if it is work that you are interested in doing as I did. Your finances are taken care of and you are completely settled and secure in every way. You are then able to spend time on this hobby because it gives you joy. The money that comes in from this work is just the icing on the cake. It is the benefits your purpose gives others, which is its own reward.

CHAPTER SIX

Healing and Transformation

Every soul on Earth is evolving at varying paces and rates, including the ones that move at a slower rate. The ones moving through a slower rate of evolvement should be easily detectable since they're the ones that create the most havoc on the planet through the means of perpetual negativity and hatred. This can be visible in anyone from the violent to the lesser suspects, which are the ones that rant, complain, attack and rave on their social media accounts or to whoever will listen.

Hostility cannot be met with hostility. Hostility and aggression against someone whose values and thoughts don't agree with yours does not change minds or hearts. You cannot bully someone into submission no matter how much you despise their view or how much you feel their view is off. The bulldozing method to push them into submission is ineffective, meaning that it doesn't work. The human condition does not respond in kind to what it deems to be antagonism or a threat. The primal nature of human beings is similar to the animal kingdom where its first instinct is to react in defense of hostility. The soul consciousness is affected by all of this, but it is functioning on a higher playing field. It's a separate organism with a greater purpose than the physical primitive that weighs human life down.

The even lesser suspects are the seemingly nice people that have a strong attraction to gossip and superficiality. Those are the ones that base their existence on judging appearances. They are attracted to human labels that define and give the illusion of validity and popularity. They may do it innocently or superficially, but their soul's evolving process is at a similar motionless standstill as those below them such as the negative and violent attackers, whether through words or physical harm.

The souls that reside in the space of superficiality are higher up on that chain of evolving souls. They are closer to the precipice point of exceptionally evolving, but need that crucial awakening turning point that is more likely to come through over the lesser evolving souls. The lesser evolving souls are evolving, but it can take numerous lifetimes before it reaches the precipice of this transformational change of residing in love.

To break it down in simpler terms: 25% of the planet resides in the bracket of the slowest evolving souls. Those are considered the *baby souls.* They are the most dangerous due to the hatred they emanate off their auras. They are the ones completely taken over and held onto by the clutches of the Darkness. You know who those souls are since they are the ones that bully, harass, name call, attack, cause violence, and in other cases murder. It's all the same energy within that cluster of souls that will be transported into the same area upon death, which is through the back gate or left door of the darker part of the spirit worlds.

50% of the world is the dominant part of the planet filled with many souls that reside in the epicenter of superficiality. These are the *mid-level souls* what some might consider to be the average human being on Earth going through the motions, having an Earthly life, while repetitively obsessing and complaining over triviality. They would also be the ones that keep the gossip channels and social media business going through ranting and attacks. They may step into the role of perpetual complainer to whoever will listen whether in person or on social media. Social media dominates Earthly life today as the primary way of expressiveness and communication. One third of each of those two brackets of evolving souls will be or are on the precipice of evolving into the bracket above of them on the chain of soul evolvement.

The final 25% of the souls on Earth are the higher evolving souls filled with the most light. Those are the *evolved or evolving post graduate souls* that rapidly evolve into a higher consciousness during one lifetime. They are also easy to spot, as those are the ones that are positively changing throughout the course of their life. They might be the ones that had that awakening moment while in the previous bracket of souls where they begin to question human life and the superficiality of it. They could've been that guy or girl that was obsessed with gossip and superficiality at one point, but suddenly begin to see things differently. They start to take a higher emotionally detached view of human life. They begin losing interest in the fads they were once interested in. They complain and rant less than they used to. Their emotional reactions to things grow calmer and more centered. They are the ones stepping into their higher purposes that have a positive global effect on humanity over time. Within those three core brackets you have the various levels of evolvement between each soul.

The higher evolving souls on Earth move through numerous healing and transformations in one lifetime, while a baby soul may only have one long lifetime of healing and transformation that becomes clear on their Earthly death bed. Going through a healing and transformation process can be tough as you shed the old former ways of your previous life, as well as any pain accumulated that has been lodged into your soul and aura. Healing and transforming is exceptionally beneficial because it contributes to your soul's growth. You go through some rough stuff in your life, and as a result you come out of it smarter and stronger. This doesn't mean it's necessarily fun going through all of that, but it is obligatory. If you don't experience challenges, then you don't grow. If everything is handed to you, then you risk becoming spoiled and entitled.

Healing and transforming doesn't have a timeline attached to it. It's an individual experience that can take months to years as the soul is evolving away from a certain experience. Take your time working through any healing and the emotions associated without rushing it. Avoid falling into any paths of toxic addictions to numb the pain. All that does is put a temporary Band-Aid on it before you're eventually thrown back to the beginning where you recall the healing you were originally going through. You still must allow that healing to take place, which will then propel you into the transformation stage.

During those stages you might across feelings of loneliness and isolation. When that happens reach out to others that understand what you're going through. Connect with open-minded friends that can empathize and be sympathetic. There are also support groups you can join where there are likeminded individuals going through the same thing. It doesn't feel so lonely and is more familial and full of community. When going through a personal transformation you may find that you cannot relate to anybody, which is perfectly standard and normal as your soul is awakening and your consciousness is being raised in the process.

This nineteen-year-old reader once mentioned that the images I've sometimes used for a social media posting tend to have only one person in them and that it seemed to symbolize loneliness. Although an interesting observation, the reasoning is because one's spiritual quest is a solo experience. When your soul is wounded, the first place it shows up is in relationship connections. One of the goals of the soul mates around you is to awaken something in you that needs to be addressed or caressed to life. The positive side to the more super intimate relationships you have is to help you see what needs to be dealt with within you or positively opened up. It's still an individual soul experience that is being enhanced by those around you regardless if the soul mate is a friend, acquaintance, colleague, or love relationship.

You may have been attracting in the same types of people into your world or you have had the same types of friendships for years, then one day you go through a major transformation and suddenly you are no longer attracted to the kinds of people you normally were. When this happens, then your energy vibration has lifted causing a change on the path you've been on where it's raised and then shifted upwards. You'll know which direction it went in by the kinds of energy that new circumstances end up being based in. When you grow, evolve, change your perception, and work to raise your consciousness, then you can be assured that many of your surrounding connections will change.

I've sifted through so many different levels of energy vibrations over the years that those I hung around with also changed. There are the loyal friendships in my circle that have been around me for decades, because they also personally shifted while being open to the changes I was going through as I with them. Others moved into the acquaintance box where we would remain in touch, but we were not as tight the way we once were on a regular basis. They are good people, which are why we still connect on occasion, but our views and personalities went in different directions.

Life continues through these interpersonal shifts that move like the tides in the ocean. The soul consciousness is a fascinating energy as it fluctuates, grows and evolves over the course of a lifetime. Then you have other soul consciousness beings on the planet that never grow. They remain exactly at the same intelligence level they were at when born. Those consciousness beings continuously die only to be re-born again in another Earthly life in hopes of getting that soul consciousness to expand and evolve out of the clutches of the Darkness.

Your current existence might throw you some wild curve balls where you were heading down one path, but then something offsets it and you're suddenly going down another road. This doesn't mean the road is necessarily worse than the one you were already on. Neither were bad roads, but something poignant takes place that upsets the balance and you're re-directed down another path that in hindsight is potentially better than what you previously had in mind.

Born into Abuse, Bullying, and Trauma

Rough life circumstances you endure will improve over time since nothing stays the same forever. It's tough at first, but as trite as it sounds, time does heal the painful wounds and struggles you go through during the soul's crushing phase. This is the case even if you recall certain incidents that surround what caused the pain to begin with. It's not met with the same severity it had when the healing process began. You become stronger and a force to be reckoned with because of it.

Many born into abuse, bullying, or any kind of trauma tend to be stronger than others because of those experiences they were forced to endure. The dangers for some are if the damage is so great that the soul has a hard time being lifted to do the work of going through the healing and transformation process. As a result, they could end up caught in a permanent victim position where their life seems to be stuck on pause. You want to do the work to understand why horrible traumatic circumstances took place by moving away from blaming anyone. You may have been in a prolonged child abusive situation, but this is what is also giving your soul the accelerated growth and evolving God had in mind for you for a greater reason.

Work hard to move forward fearlessly down that opened road in front of you. In the beginning, it is human nature to place blame and fault on someone else that hurt you or slighted your ego. You want to reach that place where you forgive them, so that you can let go of what happened and move forward to the next plateau. Forgiving them doesn't mean you're making excuses for their actions. Their actions will feel unforgiveable because it was so detestable and caused pain to you or others. The abuser will meet their karma later and have to answer to that and pay it back in this lifetime, the Other Side, or the next. That will not be your problem or your issue to concern yourself with. You will forgive them for you, so that you don't have to carry around that toxicity, weight, and burden that someone else created.

You endure the varying levels of emotions one must go through when healing and transforming. This includes understanding what brought the circumstances on to begin with. This is whether it was personal choices or a free will choice that led to the event happening.

Other considerations are if you were powerless to have been in an upsetting situation. This can be where you were a child born into a home of abuse and under the power of someone else as I was. It wasn't a personal choice you made to be there, but you were born into it. There are several reasons this could have happened. One is that the soul chose to be born in a turbulent environment for a specific gain or advantage that is understood to be at a later date. This might be hard to be believed at the time. The flip side is the parent or parents operated on free will choice and from the Darkness that got a hold of them to control their ego. You didn't ask for it, because no one asks for horrific abuse.

I grew up in a violently abusive household where I endured abnormally cruel psychological, emotional, and physical abuse by a parent. All my earlier relationship love partnerships ended due to the person either being uncommitted or they strayed to the point where I ended up trusting no one. I'm on guard with anyone new I come across as I automatically expect poor behavior to be displayed since nine times out of ten that winds up happening. People have an ulterior motive to attempt to control or oppress. This isn't the case with the enlightened higher evolving ones. This is the cliff note version of what took place to illustrate that I understand how challenging it would or could be to reach that place where you can forgive. You forgive your abusers for your soul's benefit, because you don't want to carry that trauma and anger around for the rest of your life. You have other work to do and you wish them well on their path.

What all those people did at the time was not okay, but like me you will spend years letting it go and releasing it. While there is no feeling of animosity, there are remains that I'm stuck with such as the occasional PTSD reactions that pop up out of nowhere or the permanent social anxiety. You learn to orchestrate your life that is conducive to your well-being temperament.

As you let go of past trauma and work through it, then you grow stronger and wiser. Your vibration rises, your soul consciousness expands, you get healthy, and you start to pay more attention to your Spirit team. You allow yourself to feel them, exercise more, hydrate, watch what you consume since that can affect one's feelings. High amounts of caffeine can heighten anxiety, while drugs or alcohol can give rise to depression feelings. Work on seeing things with a positive outlook. Circumstances happen for a reason and although that reason is not seen immediately, over time it is revealed as to why one endured a situation that called for healing and transformation.

Sometimes helping others or being of service to those in need is a positive way to get through healing. It moves your focus away from what's going on inside you and towards the donating of one's time in assisting others. It's therapeutic for one's self as well, because sometimes you're guided to help those who are in similar situations. Many great healers fall into that role because they might have had to endure past trauma or abuse. They know how to successfully navigate past that in order to help others. They have more sympathy and compassion for their patients or clients because they too had to endure that. This doesn't mean there are no healers who did not endure that either. There are Earth Angels with empathic psychic gifts able to walk in someone else's shoes able to get to the root of an issue.

Lead by Example

Transforming your soul includes evolving in order to see the broader picture. This helps in stripping away the ego, which causes most of the sabotage. When you view most things from the perception of an egoless being, then you receive that clarity. There are numerous soul lights threaded around the world doing what they can to offer reminders of the soul's path and to help other souls evolve. This may come in the form of correcting disrespectful behavior, teaching compassionate common-sense etiquette, helping someone through suffering, teaching positive spiritual concepts, helping others have a more peaceful and content life, giving and displaying love, shining at your brightest, and allowing those in the vicinity to soak that up. None of that is without its challenges. You're dealing with those who have an exceptionally stubborn, rigid, limited consciousness and can only see what they've been taught to date. It is rare for a human soul to branch away from how it was raised and follow their own path, since most follow what they've been taught or directed to do. There is only so much you can do to help. The best way to assist is to lead by example since you cannot force someone to bow to your whim. Not only is that against the *Universal Free Will Law*, but some souls will remain at the consciousness level they are currently at through one Earthly lifetime.

Earthly life is a school freely open for any soul looking to evolve and grow. The mediocre minds on Earth have made fun of others who seem to be buried in a book. We've seen this in Hollywood films about teenagers where there is always that one teenager making fun of the friend with books in her or his hand.

"Why are you bringing your books?"

The one carrying those books will be going far in life we can assure you. Immersing yourself into study and research to raise and awaken your consciousness in order to transform has a greater long-term investment on your soul than staying where you are.

Transform and Evolve

The Archangel Nathaniel tends to show up in someone's life when that person is going through a major transformation. He assists in removing anything outdated one after the other. This can include work, love, friendships, etc. It's a huge elimination, purging, and cleaning process that's taking place. This is in order to begin moving you into a new and better chapter with no additional baggage. This new chapter is more like a new book because the soul's perception of circumstances also shifts and expands as well.

Archangel Nathaniel's energy is perfect with mine as he's quite aggressive, heated and passionate in a way. He can intimidate those that might be too sensitive to that kind of energy, but I've always felt at home working with him.

Evolving souls have been choosing to incarnate since Earth's conception. At the turn of the 20th Century and beyond, the numbers of incarnations have increased astronomically to match the demand for human life choosing to procreate at an astronomical rate into the billions. This is due to poor sexual indiscretion, ignorance, peers push them to, ego rule, or because they believe God tells them it's what they're supposed to do. All are equated with the lack of soul knowledge because God doesn't instruct anyone to overrun the planet to the eight billion and growing mark. The more human souls multiply, then the more Earthly realm souls choose to incarnate.

You may be stuck in the in-between stage of being a non-evolved soul to an evolved one, which is what the Mid-Level Souls are enduring. They are at the precipice of knowing there is much more than the mundane Earthly life than finding a job, getting married, buying a house, and having kids. An understanding is rising that there is something deeper going on with the Universe beyond what human civilization set up for physical survival.

You could be experiencing confusing and conflicting emotions about the world and wondering why you are here. You have your own personal identity that is in a tug of war with the ego part of you that wants to feel important. You will do whatever it takes to obtain this. This doesn't change as you continue to transform, unless some measure of self-awareness has seeped into your consciousness. In God's eyes you're already important without the desire for domination.

Throughout Earth's history, humanity has continuously seen one challenging year after another unable to break free from that cycle. This is on a global level, while the individual part of you is attempting to figure out who you are and what your purpose and place is currently. You may be searching for your own identity and wrestling with the meaning of life. Some will follow what their caregivers have instilled in them, while others will break away from that and assert their individuality to become an independent thinking human being. No matter how much you attempt to break away from what your caregivers have instilled in you, there will be traces of what your caregivers have placed upon you. It can take a lifetime to diminish the learned traits you're not proud of. You are evolving in that process. The loudest unheard voices come from the evolved. Be your own champion and walk with the Light.

A familiar theme among those touched by the Light is someone on the wrong side of humanity is visited by a spirit, which results in a life changing transformation from within. In one chapter of the infamous book *The Christmas Carol*, the greedy Scrooge miser directs his anger at the Spirit of the Present. Scrooge condemns God and all that work in his name for humankind's bad behavior. He cowers when the Spirit rises over him and lashes out with the truth straight up and as bold as the Mighty.

"There are some upon this earth of yours who lay claim to know us, and who do their deeds of passion, pride, ill-will, hatred, envy, bigotry, and selfishness in our name, who are as strange to us and all our kith and kin, as if they had never lived. Remember that, and charge their doings on themselves, not us!"

Author Charles Dickens would forever be praised for Divinely channeling what would become a profoundly philosophical message disguised in the tightly organized Christmas Carol. Academics would spend their life debating whether the piece was a non-religious story or a Christian metaphor. Considering that it's historically attracted people on both sides and everyone in between since it came out all those centuries ago indicates it's spiritually Universal.

Scrooge is a narcissistic cold hearted mean selfish man who is given a forced life review in the middle of the night. I call it *Spirit Hours* because you're not distracted and instead are receptive to receive. He's visited by a deceased business partner stuck to roam the Earth in heavy chains and money chests. He warns his old friend of the same fate and much worse if he doesn't repent and change his ways. This is followed by Scrooge being visited by three spirits, which would've been an order of angels and High Spirits, with the goal of freeing him from bondage of the ego's self while simultaneously transforming him into joyful deliverance.

This metaphor of the Christmas Carol would be a sign that you're transforming and evolving as Scrooge did. You're moving away from the familiar old and into the confident brightness of the new.

Transcending Utopia

Transcending utopia means to go beyond your limits and travel outside of the generic mundane materialistic achievement that human beings taught one another to thrive for. A utopian society is what every soul secretly longs for deep down. It is where everything is perfectly blissful on all levels according to the core soul values you were born with. It isn't just outwardly perfect, but the sensations connected to how flawless everything feels reveals the authentic perfection that you were made from. Utopia is the ideal paradise as imagined in one's dreams that is also unachievable by human standards. Heaven and all the spirit realm worlds on the Other Side contain the highest forms of Shangri-La, but to get close to that experience while on Earth requires a soul adjustment.

Transcending utopia is a state of mind that all spirit beings long for you to have. For some it is easy to achieve if your natural disposition state is pleasant and enjoyable, even during stressful times. It is having everything you ever dreamed of to the degree of being completely content in all ways and on all possible levels that your being has the potential for. Transcending utopia is going beyond that and even further into the distant reaches of the Universe that are impossible for the lower mind to achieve. Never give up, never lose faith, and keep forging on fearlessly towards that goal of continuous soul consciousness transformation.

CHAPTER SEVEN

Soul Groups and Earth Angels

There are three core human soul groups as mentioned in the previous chapter:

- Baby Souls. Those are the souls causing the greatest harm on Earth. They use the maximum amount of darkness of ego. They're the ones that harm, hurt, or hate. They start wars, incite violence, and destruction on the planet or on other beings. Many are the criminals on Earth, but there are also souls who are not criminals, yet cause quite a bit of heartache or disaster on others through words towards others as well too.

- Mid-Level Souls. Those are the ones just trying to get by and survive. They are trying to make it through an Earthly life. Their purposes are geared towards working hard on one or many aspects of themselves. They may be on the planet to live an Earthly life and follow the human customs of that time such as getting a job, getting married, buying a house, having kids, etc. Some of them may reside in the epicenter of superficiality and gossip or attention seeking. At some point one of these souls may start to question life in general and possibly receive an awakening that thrusts them to graduate and begin moving to a higher soul level.

- Evolved/Evolving Post Graduate Souls. These are the teachers or the ones bringing light and wisdom to others on some level. They enact positive change and tend to steer clear of the human ego trappings as much as possible. Some of them may be greatly evolved and here to live an Earthly life while bringing something positive to the planet. There will be other souls who are evolving out of the Mid-Level Soul branch and into this branch during their lifetime. Those are the ones also living several lifetimes in one. Many souls from the various realms that exist on the Other Side incarnate as an evolved or evolving soul to offer their services to the betterment of humanity, but may start out in the Mid-Level soul branch, even though deep down there is a deepness old soul like quality about them from as far back as childhood.

Human Souls Operate on Different Levels

On Earth, there are hierarchy positions within some companies running from the CEO down to the executives, to the assistants, receptionists, and so on. What is interesting is that even though a CEO on Earth may be financially successful, they could be spiritually bankrupt. Their Earthly drive is for monetary success and nothing else. They could be considered a baby soul in the spiritual world, while their assistant may be a realm soul that Heaven knows to be an evolved/evolving, advanced, post-graduate soul, which in the end is what lasts beyond your time on Earth. Only on Earth is the distribution of power imbalanced or what human souls consider to being of power, since real power is spiritual soul competence.

A parent might be a baby soul ruling from the darkness of ego, while their child could be an evolving post-graduate soul that is much older in soul years than their own parent. This would be obvious where the parent seems to be more childlike with its abusive nature and/or tantrums, and the child comes off more wise, centered, or compassionate than its parent.

All human souls will die and when that happens, they will be buried just like every other human being that passes on. They will be buried without anything, but what they're dressed in. Even that will tarnish and grow old over time covering a physical body that disintegrates into the Earth's ground before becoming a set of bones. The soul that continues to live on will exit that body and immediately move towards the part of their soul's home with other souls that are of a similar equitable nature. There is no such thing as power to get ahead in Heaven, because all souls live in peace and harmony. They're not fighting or killing one another off to get ahead.

Upon human death, the assistant that worked on Earth moves to a higher space of consciousness than the CEO on Earth did due to him not growing his soul consciousness while here. This is because in the spirit realms you move to areas where your soul group is. The soul group consists of your soul siblings that have similar gifts as you do and who are on the same soul growth level. You head back home to Heaven upon your Earthly death with newfound insight you gained while on Earth.

Living an Earthly life, you are forced to engage with souls that are on various levels of soul growth that may be similar or dissimilar to you. What is immediately understood for you is the chaos that ensues on the physical world. Many souls on Earth struggle to get ahead and one up each other to prove they have the answers when in reality few have only slices of truth.

Human beings ruling their life from the darkness of ego cause most of the misery experienced. If every single soul on the planet were in tune and connected with the Divine full time while using their God given born traits of love, then Earth would be as blissful as Heaven. This will unlikely happen since Earth is filled with Baby Souls. Those newborn souls that sparked out of God were quickly born into a human body for the sake of learning and growth on Earth.

Children throw tantrums when they don't get what they want, and baby souls are no different. A baby soul can be in the body of a 70-year-old human being. Just because the human being is appearing of older age it does not mean they're wise. It is still a baby soul who has experienced one lifetime at this Earth school. Depending how rapidly they evolved will determine where they will go upon their exit of the human vessel.

Some Earthly souls will display a higher range of their gifts than other souls, but it doesn't mean that other souls are incapable of that. All souls are the same inside as they came from the same Light. If they display less of the gift than another, then this is connected to having a block in the physical world, or it is compensated through having an ability displayed through another gift that someone else might have less of. All are born into an Earthly life with specific psychic gifts that are extra enhanced than another for them to use that for the purpose of the higher good. This benefit is also for them to pay attention to so that they can be guided along their Earthly path with minimal challenges as possible.

All souls will endure challenges as that is the nature of the beast that is the Earthly life. Those more in tune to the planes beyond will work harder to access their deep gifts in order to be able to move about through any Earthly challenges swifter than someone else who ignores those gifts.

Earth Angels

Lucifer was a fallen angel that once resided in Heaven. He was magnificently beautiful looking and made this incredible music sound wherever he moved. One day he decided to defy the Light in a big way and was cast out of Heaven due to the corruption he was attempting to create. It's important to note that he chose to be cast out. He had that choice because God doesn't keep any prisoners or anyone that doesn't want to be there, regardless if it's an angel or human being. We're not puppets on strings that God is playing and controlling. All souls have free will choice to do something good or choose to do something bad. Lucifer made the latter choice time and again that his soul was drawn out of Heaven since the Light spits that stuff out if it's contaminated. He fell like a lightning bolt and now resides in what some refer to as a fiery pit of Hell. Some belief systems believe there is this fiery pit with Lucifer looking like a red ogre with a tail and pitchfork that has become a popular culture image, especially during Halloween time and in scary films. This is not what he looks like, as he's quite exceptionally beautiful looking, but his soul is hideously dangerous. This is how he can cause such deception to the ego mind, because the ego is pulled in by someone's attractive exterior instead of what's in the soul's heart.

Earth is one of the dimensions of Hell. This means that Lucifer is not actually below the Earth, but here on Earth. He is technically located in one of the layers of Hell located between Earth and Heaven. This is one of the additional explanations of why I have Clairvoyantly seen these creepy crawlies and other darker entities spilling into the Earth plane since childhood. I could never understand that throughout my adolescence until my Spirit team was showing the missing pieces to the puzzle to me over the course of time. Then I was mesmerized as if I had discovered gold, "Ohhhhhh. Wow. That's interesting."

Lucifer is close enough to create destruction in the lives of human beings. He does this because he can. He wants power the way some human beings desire greed and power. It isn't for the purpose of good, but the purpose of annihilation and ruin. He works through them to push them to accomplish this through simple manipulation and influence. It's like taking candy from a baby it's so easy.

God owns Earth, but the Devil is temporarily running it by infecting anyone he can. It's not just through vitriolic hatred and violence, but he can do this through selfishness, greed, and self-centeredness. He invades people's minds by poisoning it. He can do little deceptive things such as whispering into your consciousness that you're no good at anything. He'll crush your self-esteem, because he enjoys belittling and bullying others. He'll also do that through other people by contaminating and influencing them to behave badly with others. These are the ones that are predominately bad, rather than the rare moment a genuinely good person is stressed out about something.

Examine how many people believe the negative thoughts about themselves. No Light being will ever talk to you the way the Darkness does. The Devil will steal souls to create a growing army of Darkness in the Hell regions, including on Earth, which is evident. Your soul can choose to live in the Light, which will take that power away from the Darkness. The most difficult ones he can't get into easily are those of the Light on Earth.

Earth is one of Lucifer's dominions where he has some of the most success at rallying, enslaving, and masterfully manipulating millions of souls every second all at once. He plagues the planet by working through them. They form into Locusts that spread and urinate lower energy wherever possible. To counter that God sends His trusty light warriors to contribute their parts at tempering and stomping that darkness out as much as possible. We sometimes call these lights Earth Angels that incarnate from another land beyond the veil, but even they can be susceptible to the lower energy if they're not careful. They are gifted and capable of wiping it away as quickly as possible and getting right back to work with their exceptionally keen focus, drive, and purpose. God only sends His best, which only angers the Darkness like you would never believe. God's best is a thorn in the side of the Darkness.

The Light warriors tend to be highly sensitive in some way, as well as profoundly psychic more than those that are unaware of their psychic abilities. They are more in-tune to the vibrations beyond the physical plane due to the many previous life lessons they've gained. The harder the life lesson the stronger your evolving process is. The more you evolve the clearer your consciousness. The clearer your consciousness the keener your psychic channels are.

The Light souls on Earth do their best to stay away from anyone that resides in a lower energy space. They can detect when to steer clear due to having a vastly tuned-in calibrated psychic antennae. They move towards those that reside in a higher vibrational Light state, while the darker human soul attracts in others that reside in a negative space. Their negative energy grows more repressed as the Dark energies take over, while the stronger sensitive soul rises like helium above the Darkness and into the vortex of the Light where love resides.

One of the few traits that all Earth Angels have in common is that they're keenly aware they are here to do His will. This is the common link that brings them all together in a communal circle like the Avengers fighting crime. Each brings their distinctive personalities and talents to their holy rampage with the goal of protecting and progressing humanity and the planet.

Some higher evolved souls will continue to incarnate into an Earthly life beyond their final incarnation. They are not doing that for the purpose of balancing out any Karmic debt or for soul growth purposes, even though the positive side effect is additional soul growth. This is never shunned by an intelligent consciousness. They desire to contribute something positive towards humanity that can benefit the planet.

Many of the higher evolved souls are the warriors of lights, light workers, and earth angels that all view the planet as God's home and creation that needs protection. It's like when someone housesits for a best friend. They treat the home as if it is their own. Because they are protectors of His work, they have a deep desire to keep the planet healthy on His behalf. Relying on newborn souls to keep it in great shape is not an option, because when you put a tantrum havoc-wreaking child in a room, then you cannot expect it to clean that room up. You might walk into that room to find it is in complete disarray with crayon writing on the wall.

The child needs to be trained and taught that destroying a room is not appropriate behavior. The child that resists knowledge ends up having a harder life. Every soul on the planet has the soul capacity for great knowledge gained including the tantrum child. They need higher evolved souls or evolving souls to guide and teach them. We see these higher evolved souls in the people around the world that are making positive differences in the lives of human beings. Some of these highly evolved souls may not even be cognizant of their role. They enjoy what they do so much that the deeper meaning and quest behind what they're doing isn't on their radar.

It is easier for a higher evolved soul to accomplish those tasks while in a human body, rather than attempting to do it in a spirit body that many don't pay attention to. Most people either have trouble accessing God, Spirit, the Angels, Higher Spirit Beings, or they don't believe in it. Irrespective of anyone's personal human belief system this lifetime, every soul has the gifts of Divine communication.

Higher evolved souls view the constant chaos on Earth from Heaven as all souls do through the veil. Gradually some of them conclude that they must incarnate into a human body for a specific cause that can help progress Earthly life positively in some way. If the higher evolved souls never choose to come to Earth, then Earth will eventually be destroyed. It's like the abandoned home that is soon ruined and destroyed by trespassers that have no consciousness. If you think Earth is in a poor state now, then imagine if the souls of the Light that are here now trying to temper that decided not to come here. Earthly life would end up in ruins and destroyed. Things like there would be no human laws enacted to capture criminals and keep them locked up to prevent further destruction. Even though it is true some of the laws are warped and criminalize people that are not truly criminals. They might have committed a crime that would be considered minor in Heaven's eyes, as opposed to a larger true crime such as grand theft, murder, assault, or physical harm and violence to another person or property.

The danger for the higher evolved soul that incarnates into a human life is they are as susceptible to the negative energies as anyone else. They can succumb too deeply to Earthly pleasures that could prevent them from getting to work. I know this well since my spirit has experienced everything under the sun, around the block, and back again. Keeping it balanced is significant to guarantee you don't get lost in it to the point that months have passed by and you realize, "Wait a minute I haven't accomplished anything good."

That was a statement I had made during my adolescent stage more than once. This doesn't mean I was never exempt from behaving what some might consider badly. I grew up this lifetime as a rebellious reckless aggressive warrior soul. Wanting to get my hands onto anything that was toxic. Temptations have never been beneath me in the past. If I had never tried it before, then I wanted to. Some of it was for me to escape the pain I was experiencing in this life due to the repetitive childhood trauma, but some of it was also to experience so that I could have a better understanding of it and report back. All the colors on my soul's palette were bright and receptive to it all. At the same time, I was fearless despite all the warnings of those around me that I shouldn't do certain things. If I shouldn't do it, then I would.

I may be highly in tune psychically, but I'm also a former addict to anything and everything I could get my hands onto. Our human lives are always met with some measure of turmoil. Even the ones you think who have everything down or who have it together are not exempt from this. They also have lessons they're wrestling with since no one gets a free pass.

The higher evolved soul may choose to incarnate for a specific purpose that contributes something awesome to human life. If they're going to take the time to incarnate and live a human life to be able to accomplish this, they will add other elements in their soul contract to achieve while at it. They might choose to live a harder life for a brief period that will help their soul adapt to the harsher aspects of Earthly life. This way they can gain important disciplined traits they need to help them accomplish their purpose or purposes. The soul is aware before incarnating that the risk of their Earthly mission is that their soul's memories of Heaven and their psychic channels will be suppressed and potentially diminished once in a human body. This is why many human beings tend to have amnesia about where their soul came from or what it's like back home in Heaven.

Over time there will be souls on Earth that begin to remember or discover ways that can help re-open their psychic channels they're born with. I've talked about many of those methods throughout my work. Much of what my Spirit team has filtered through me to discuss isn't to ruin someone's Earthly pleasurable fun or to condemn troublesome behavior that can backfire on you. It's to offer what helps in awakening those psychic clair senses that is more connected to God than anything else. Having a strong faith-based system makes life a bit easier than not having that faith. God is your long-term family unit and you want Him on your side. Everything my Spirit team teaches is also for me too. I'm certainly not exempt from this. During my adolescent immature phase, I disregarded what they'd teach the way any teenager scoffs and disregards what their own parents are attempting to instill in them. As I was growing older, I was still aware of what my Spirit team had been teaching me and was beginning to adopt much of what they had been teaching. I realized what they were helping me with was on the mark, so I began to share that with others that were interested too.

CHAPTER EIGHT

The Earthly Birth

Heaven, the Spirit World, and the Other Side are all the same place depending on whom you talk to and how that soul prefers to label it. You are a soul in a human body living an Earthly life for a numerous chain of purposes. Some souls have many intentions, while others have one big objective above those intentions. There are also universal goals, which include learning to love or bringing others together in a positive way. If you were born to love and that comes innately, then you are a teacher of love. You lead by example in expressing that love full time naturally. This is because your gifts are stronger in the areas of your purpose. It doesn't take much work to use them, but it does take work to put them to action.

Into the lighter doorways of the spirit worlds, there is no darkness or pain, no judgment or criticisms, no hatred or violence. There is no ego therefore no greed or resistance, any power or repressed oppression. It is a utopian wonderland filled with enormous beaming light and flickers of vibrant sparkles of color that moves in the direction you will it to be. This Light reaches anything that can be filled from every soul, cell, plant, desert, mountain, ocean, or animal on all planes and dimensions that exist throughout time and space. You may call this light God, a Higher Power, the Source, Spirit, the Light, or any other name comfortable to the current reality your consciousness has chosen today. Unlike human life it has no desire for labels because in Heaven this Light just IS. Names and labels are what human beings use in order to differentiate, describe, or single out something that desires no separation back home. When I use a label, it is so that one can have a quick understanding of what we are talking about, but otherwise they're not part of Spirit's vocabulary.

The Light affects all that it touches with the same positive results. It brings on a sensation of overflowing love, peace, and joy. It consumes you in a magnificent way bringing with it an out of this world uplifting sensation that can make one feel as if it's going to fall over or burst apart while in it. It's an exhilarating high that cannot be obtained by any human made drug, food, or drink on Earth. If you've ever been in love with someone that loves you back, then you understand the rush of excitement and joy that is experienced when you both physically touch one another to sitting alone in one another's presence. This is because love in any form releases your soul from the confinement it suffers through while having an Earthly life. This same rush of excitement that comes from a lover's touch is magnified one hundred times on the Other Side just by being in Heaven's atmosphere. It feels like you're soaring even when you're standing still.

When your soul steps into this Light, then any negative feeling you're experiencing is blasted away immediately. When a soul crosses over to the next plane passing the dark exits and through the right doorway and front gate, it then enters this Light where all emotional, physical, or mental deterioration that soul was battling with on Earth diminishes. If you had what you consider to be a handicap or any kind of physical or mental disorder or disability, then this is removed and exists no longer as your soul travels through the rays punching through the doorway of Light. Any kind of human handicap or disorders are an Earthly physical condition connected to the physical body vessel you're temporarily renting before you vacate your premises, but it is not the true state of your soul. Therefore, you want to avoid singling yourself out with labels such as having a disease or handicap that you identify with unless it's relevant to a cause you're fighting for.

"Hi, I'm Mary and bound to a wheelchair because…."

Or, "Hi, I'm Bob and I'm HIV Positive."

It may be a physical human disease or handicap that has attacked your physical body this lifetime, but it is separate from the core part of your soul that ends up erased from your consciousness when your spirit travels back home. Who you currently are would be Mary or Bob, a loving and compassionate soul who gives to others generously through your empathetic activism.

If you own a car, you do not say, "Hi I'm so and so, I drive a BMW and I work for a law firm."

You are not the car you drive or the job you work at, regardless that these are the physical, material, external things that people focus on. When one meets someone new, they immediately go down the generic list of human taught questions such as, "What do you do for a living? Where do you live? Where are you from?"

Those are temporary identities you've assigned to your physical being, but have no validity once you vacate your vessel. It's just something you are choosing to affiliate with today at this point in your life, but your roles on Earth do not define you. Who your soul is back home is what defines you beyond any temporary physical attributions and statuses.

Your soul sometimes chooses a handicap in order to develop a different perspective or for a specific purpose or goal that the soul must discover on its own. The challenges of this handicap contribute to soul enhancing and growth properties that the soul might otherwise not gain if they were not having that experience.

To my ego mind, I could express doubt, but to my higher self's space and what my team relays, I receive it with an open mind and disburse the information publicly by allowing others to decide for themselves what they're comfortable accepting to be of truth. Doubting partially comes from the ego part of a soul not wanting to believe something is possible or for real. Doubts are concerns and worries where you require additional concrete visible answers that will bring your ego to a higher level of comfort and peace. It adds security to ease the skeptical questioning part of you, but your higher self has no doubts. Doubts can also signify a warning nudge from your Spirit team preventing you from heading into danger. When you cross over back home your soul and physical self is restored to top form appearing around in the ranges of a human being aged twenty-five to thirty-five, but in a more profoundly radiant way than visibly imaginable. Some souls may temporarily appear to be the age they passed away at to a clairvoyant medium in order to be recognizable to you.

On Earth, someone might have a cup of coffee to wake up in the morning, or they might have a glass of wine or a beer to wind down after a long day at work. Sometimes they do this to let loose and have some fun since the life they currently live feels joyless, stressful, and restricting. There is little to no love experienced in one's life. When you're high in love, you rarely yearn for a drink or drug. This Light in Heaven is your cup of coffee or bottle of beer. You do not crave a vice back home in Heaven. The state you attempt to achieve while living an Earthly life through vices is reached naturally on the Other Side.

Your soul Light is born out of what some call God. God is not a man with a beard sitting up on a throne looking down at everyone waiting to cross you off His list. Nor does He desire to throw you into a brimstone and fire like setting if you've made mistakes. God is a force that is within every soul light including the faithless and non-believers. How unconditional of Him to still love someone who makes mistakes. His love for you is bountiful and endless. He is the Light that overtakes every cell that exists in all dimensions and in all paths within and around you. When you feel and display traits aligned with love, joy and peace, then the closer you are to God. The more negative traits you experience or display, then the further away from God you are, and the less light that occupies your space. If someone is persecuting or bullying others in God's name, then you can be assured they are nowhere near God or the Light. The exception is if it is done to prevent someone from physically harming or hurting themselves, or someone else.

Higher spirit beings advise that you exhibit assertive compassion in those instances, rather than aggressive bulldozing. The latter comes from uncontrollable emotions from your ego that take flight beyond that soul's control. There is a healthy ego and a dangerous nasty ego. The darkness of ego is never at peace and thrives in the shadows by multiplying and growing. The dark side of the ego would be in a murdering terrorist, while the light side of the ego is someone that displays optimistic confidence over what they can accomplish and do in their life. Someone sure of themselves has a healthy ego, while someone slamming or criticizing someone confident and sure of themselves is operating from the darkness of ego.

There are newborn baby souls and there are the more advanced souls on Earth in a human body moving through the various stages of evolvement. Newborn souls are the student souls who immediately enter an Earthly life upon being born out of the Light. It is generally their first life run on Earth. The higher advanced souls that may seem like an old soul have been around the block so to speak. They are the teachers, inventors, leaders as well as movers and shakers. Newborn souls tend to be on the naïve side and use the most amount of malicious ego because their soul has not grown enough to effectively battle the Darkness that contaminates it. The word naïve might be too innocent of a word to the damage this soul causes, but in the eyes of the angel's *naïve* is the word they give me.

The newborn baby souls instigate the most disruption and donate the largest amounts of negative energy while contributing harmful pollutants that cause tragically damaging results on humankind and this planet. They might be the soul that spends their days criticizing others in an unhelpful way by posting malicious comments at everyone or those around them. They name call, bully, and put others down. The targets they hit can be over someone's physical appearance, or if that person does things differently than they do, or lives in a way they do not approve of, then they will attempt to assert domination over them. In the end, they are unsuccessful since the Light ultimately overpowers the darkness in the end while lifting up the bullied.

The souls that exude dark energy full time are someone you do not want to be around or spend that much time with if you can help it. They will lower your vibration and cause enormous quantities of inner or outer turmoil. They will create roadblocks that prevent you from moving forward and lead you down the wrong path often without trying to. You might be stuck living or working with someone like that. You want to steer clear of this individual since they can bring about your soul's downfall if you don't rise above it.

Not all baby souls wreak havoc on others in a negative way. There are just as many good newborn souls as there are bad. The newborn souls that are good tend to evolve and advance their souls growth at a rapid rate beyond that and into the next stratosphere. A newborn soul can also be someone without drive to accelerate or improve themselves and their soul. This is because they do not have the growth tools to do so or they do not know any better. Their soul's energy is rendered stagnant in those environments. They might be governed by their ego and doing what they were taught to do by their families, peers, and society around them. They are a product of their surroundings going through the motions of how they were trained to by others during their human developmental years. They elect to come back and have another

Earthly life in order to polish up and advance their soul. Some of the newborn souls are destined for greatness, but are growing up in a setting that does not support soul growth, but rather restricts it.

If you're aware that you're not like everyone else and you feel like the outcast in your surroundings, then this is a sign that you are a gifted evolving soul waiting for the right moment to make its mark on humanity, if even to allow your soul's light to shine as brightly as the Sun on those around you. The road will eventually lead you to that place naturally on its own time.

Where a newborn soul might follow others, an advanced soul would be the leader who takes charge and goes against the crowd. They manage to rally up equal interest and opposition in the process. Advanced souls know without a doubt they are here for a larger purpose. They also understand what that objective is. There is no question or doubt about it. They might struggle in young age, but eventually will dive into their purpose at some point in their life. An advanced soul is a disciplined individual. It is someone contributing something positive towards humanity, themselves, or others in some way. The advanced soul elected to come here at this time for larger purposes they must master and accomplish. This is like a college student rising through the different levels of study along their education journey. Although in this case the evolving soul's education is connected to their continuing rapidly evolving soul growth.

CHAPTER NINE

The Soul and the Spirit

You ask an atheist where did the first human being come from and you'll get a wide variety of responses from things like you can't ask that question because it's illogical or a silly. They have said that you can't just believe you have to conclude your reasons as to why you believe based on science. You'll get a wide variety of responses that never technically answer the question. It's like when you ask a hardcore religious person where God came from or what does he look like or anything else associated with some of the extremer beliefs. They stare at you blankly or answer the question without answering it. Both extreme sides will at times also attack the person asking the question, which is another tactic to avoid answering a question you don't know the answer to. When the most acceptable answer above all that would be, "I don't really know, but it's just what I believe since nothing else has made sense enough to me to believe."

It's interesting how similar atheists are to fundamentalist religious followers in that and many other ways. This in its essence is an example of a soul consciousness choosing to make their belief system their current reality, which gets thrown out the window when their human body dies. All the nearly eight billion souls roaming the planet at this time have their own individual consciousness that is creating their current reality. This consciousness within their soul that has some measure of intelligence and the power to increase this intelligence over time is easily influenced or swayed by what it reads, what it watches, who it associates with while shunning anything or anyone else that is the anti-thesis of that. When the truer way to evolving a soul's consciousness in a greater way is seeking to understanding the fundamental compartments of the human condition and how that coincides with the soul part of that body. Even scientists have discovered they've made mistakes since they are human which equates to being infallible.

The film *Contact* was based on the book by scientist and author, Carl Sagan. What I loved about it was the interesting dichotomy between the Jodie Foster character who was an atheist scientist and her close friendship with the Matthew McConaughey character, a Christian philosopher. For one I loved the idea they were able to be close friends despite that one area where they had extremely opposing viewpoints. You rarely hear something like that happening today between two people, even though in my personal life my friendships are across the board in belief systems and values. In the film she winds up having a questioning spiritual like experience that leads her to believe the possibility of something else out there beyond the physical human life. This propels her to come to the conclusion that she believes this to be true based on faith. Faith – a word she never thought her scientific analytical mind would ever use to describe why she believes something. As an atheist scientist her whole life was based on finding verifiable evidence until she has that one experience that knocks her solid world off kilter. In that transition on her quest for something else out there, her soul consciousness receives that awakening that transforms her to something she never thought possible.

You are a soul in a human body, but when one describes your soul's vibrational energy, then this could be talking about your overall spirit. When you are let down by a relationship connection that ends, then one might say, "This relationship broke my spirit." This is your all-inclusive life force energy, rather than the soul that inhabits your temporary vessel. It is also a metaphor because your spirit can never be broken. What they mean is that it broke your symbolic heart, not your physical heart, but your heart chakra's life force. At the same time, there have been numerous medical and scientific studies that indicate how negative feelings of any kind have a negative effect on your physical heart and health. This means feeling sadness over a breakup or death can cause cardiovascular stress. When my Spirit team and I discuss ways of helping you work on your well-being state, this also has a positive effect on your physical health. All parts of you are intertwined and connected from the soul, to the spirit, to your physical body and complete consciousness.

When you are born into an Earthly life, you're flowing with abundantly high vibrational energy that cannot be contained. This energy is your life force. As your soul moves into a human physical body, it becomes confined and suppressed to a good degree. The soul often feels suffocated dying to get out. It will seek out ways to achieve this including through unhealthy ways.

High vibrational energy is in the space your soul lives in before you enter a human physical body. This energy resides within your soul's core. It is always accessible even when you feel disconnected from it or when it's been severely lowered while travelling along your Earthly life journey. An impenetrable wall might surround it, but it is still in you deep down for access. You can either try to work on bringing that energy force out or wait until your physical human death when it bursts out of the body you inhabit, and you're brought to your soul's natural state when you reach the gates of Heaven. It is wiser to work on bringing it back to its most instinctive state possible while here, rather than live a life in permanent misery. Working on improving all aspects of you has a positive benefit on your soul's consciousness and physical, spiritual, and mental well-being.

This high vibrational energy within the core part of your soul is shattered over time at the hands of the society that surrounds the newborn human child. This society is made up of your caregivers, your peers, your community, the town you live in, and the media you engage in. Those around you naively impose their often-harmful views that create an array of seemingly impossible roadblocks and hurdles for that child of God to climb out of. For some, it may be that you were born into an abusive household, or at the hands of a caregiver that viciously inflicts values in you that cause you to despise others because of their life choices or that are different from you. Hatred towards a group is often taught to you by your community, caregivers, influencers, and peers. This includes hating or disliking anyone of any race, religion, sexual orientation, political affiliation, gender, and so on. You lump them together in one group to express your disapproval of all. This is not coming from a place of Godly love. You may know someone like this, or you might even admit to yourself when you've been guilty of separating others out of anger. When your higher self is the dominate ruler of your soul, then you are more likely to correct it after realizing you've crossed the line and are not viewing circumstances clearly. There are good and bad people in every possible label created by human beings. There is no discrimination when it comes to who chooses to govern their life through the lower self or higher self.

The ego views circumstances in a perpetual hazy darkness. You may have discovered the hate filled ways of the darkness of ego simply by logging onto the Internet to see how humanity behaves. Technology is a great invention to bring others together much more rapidly than before, but it also shines a light on how humanity is at that given moment in time. When there was no Internet connection or media, then people went along with living the way they were trained to by those around them in that area. Technology, social media, and the Internet blasted the truth wide open to see that people are not as nice, caring, compassionate, and loving as one might have thought they would be. If every single human soul accepted what everyone is choosing to do without judgment, then there would be less anger and discrimination. Twitter feeds would be bathed in positivity or balanced calm objectiveness when in a disagreement. This is highly unlikely to happen while human souls remain governed by the darkness of their ego. If you disagree with someone, do you fall into your lower self by attacking them or do you step into your higher self to use assertiveness with communicating? It is not a realistic request to ask that one show love to all people, such as if a murdering terrorist is physically harming one of God's Children. It would be challenging to not be revved up to do something about that, which would fall into one of your soul's life purposes.

As a warrior of light soul, you are fighting in the name of the Light to protect all souls that cause harm on one another. Many need to be trained how to respect others, which is why so many souls choose to incarnate on Earth throughout history to help contribute something positive that brings Light to the planet, while also improving human behavior and its existence and way of life.

When your peers continue to tell you that something is wrong with you because you're different from everybody else, then you are witnessing someone bathed in the lower energies of the darkness of ego. The ego generally has a difficult time accepting and loving those that are unlike it. The ego finds that person weird, unusual, and uncommon, while the higher self sees every soul as one. If you've been the recipient of that abuse, then it might have made you feel like an outcast, inadequate, or incompetent. You might spend your life trying to prove that you're not different in order to fit in. Or you avoid going after anything you want to do as you feel you won't be good enough and will be rejected. Your higher self is the soul part of you that is of God; therefore it knows it's worth requiring no human validation or approval from anyone. The darkness of ego views circumstances, people, and its surroundings in a limited way. It is unable to access the broader view that Heaven sees.

When one raises their consciousness, the spiritual portal begins to open and the Light pours into you. This Light shines brightly bringing the spiritual truth out. This truth is one that the dark ego has a difficult time absorbing or would prefer to keep hidden.

You have great soul power and stamina within to rise above the Darkness knowing how awesome you are. Who you are at your core is a perfect soul child of God. Pay no mind to the naysayers and negative critics around you and access this Divine source energy from within to be the best that you can be. When you have God in your house, then everything around you becomes irrelevant and trivial. Imagine what it feels like to know there is no element or trace of Darkness within that Light. Visualize this Light filling you up with pure joy, peace, and love. You step into this Light and it immediately blasts away all traces of negative feeling or thought. This Light overtakes your physical body, your spirit, soul, and mind lifting you up in the process.

Have you ever had a love crush on someone? You know this crushing love feeling inside you runs deep and intensely to the degree that you never forget it throughout your life. Perhaps you were with someone who reciprocated this love, but then one day they took it away. Multiply that love crushing feeling when it felt incredible while in the throes of love. Even while multiplied by one hundred, the feeling doesn't come close to what it's like while being immersed and part of the Light.

While the spirit world terminology is often used to illustrate the separate planes, in truth it's much grander than that. Some believe the spirit world to be filled with ghostly spirits roaming around. The brighter aspects of the Light filled spirit worlds are the ultimate Utopian paradise that is an unbelievable spectacle. It mirrors the nature settings and natural wonders on Earth, but is even more vibrant, lush, and magical than the human mind could comprehend. It would have to be because why would a place full of 100% uplifting joy, love, and peace be less than the physical Earthly plane? The Earthly plane is a school set up that house's spirits of every variety in a human body. All souls on Earth are students, with a quarter of that being both student and teacher. This is because even a teacher is a student learning new things while living an Earthly life.

A spirit is also an entity, such as the entities that reside in different planes other than the Earth dimension. Spirits might appear translucent or opaque to a clairvoyant, but back home in Heaven's spirit worlds they have physical bodies. It is not the same physical body that a human body is. They appear in any shape or form they desire to morph into. The physical body they inhabit, and display cannot be harmed the way a human body can. It is in its perfect state and can shift from male to female if it pleases or into a light source or other figure.

God, the Light, and Heaven see your true nature and who your soul is. Who it is at its base is all love, peace, serenity, compassion, and joy. These are some of the highest vibrational qualities built into every soul.

A murderer's soul is seen with love. This doesn't mean they get a free pass for their wicked ways. Somewhere along their Earthly life the dark part of their ego took over and chose to do anything in its power to sabotage that soul's purpose. Their ego could have been developed and programmed into their consciousness as early as age three in human years or it could've been infected by the Darkness in the darker part of the Spirit world. When the soul exits the physical body and crosses over back home, then it is faced with choices to make that can bring the soul to redemption. Some of that entails another Earthly life in a less than stellar circumstance than their current one was. Other souls are put to work and take the long way around through the back gate of Heaven, which is a separate doorway.

There are some dark love undertones to this. Perhaps your lover's soul has become lost in purgatory, or they end up in another spirit realm and you never see them again. It's not impossible to visit them should that be the case, but from the human mind's perspective, the worst is generally feared. When you cross over, you move onto other destinies that are not always the same as someone else's, including your loved one on Earth. Still it is possible to travel and visit one another once you've crossed over. This travelling between worlds to see them happens in a matter of seconds. We take cars, trains, and planes to get to different cities on the planet, but this is the slower way compared to traveling in the spirit worlds.

Your soul is the spirit part of you that is not part of your physical human body. Your human body is a temporary vessel your soul is renting out for a limited time. When you're born into a physical human body, you enter this life through a human female. This is the beginning of one lifetime for you. This human body starts out as a physical human infant and grows up and ages over the course of a short amount of time. In Heaven, it is the opposite where one's basic appearance remains the same.

On Earth, the human body is limited and for some those restrictions vary in endless ways.

Some choose to enter this life in a wheelchair, or you might have asthma issues, mental health battles, or another human physical limitation. All of this is to endure certain circumstances to overcome and accept that will have a positive benefit on your soul's evolving consciousness. When you are connected to spirit even while in a human body, then the boundaries that inhibit you from forward motion are non-existent.

You are loved beyond measure in Heaven. It doesn't matter what or whom you've chosen to live this lifetime as. Whether you are male or female, rich or poor, gay or straight, religious or atheist, and no matter what race, or political affiliation you choose, all are seen through the eyes of Heaven as being equal. The separate labels are what the dark ego of the human mind chooses in order to feel superior or separated from others, when in truth all labels are irrelevant. Using labels creates separation by viewing reality in a limited way. When you only see the love in someone else, then you're able to access the parts of that person that the angels see.

The angels see who the soul truly is when stripped of its dark ego. When you become defensive or argumentative every time someone says something, or you get upset over every news headline, then this is coming from a place of ego and your lower self. There is no truth or love while in that space. Seeing the love in others is seeing life through their eyes and understanding what their reality is like. This does not mean that you're accepting someone's bad behavior or horrible words they might have darted your way. If that's the case, then it's best to cut them out and extricate them from your vicinity. This is about taking issue with the small stuff in a profounder way that it does nothing to help anyone.

Some hang onto anger over trivial issues such as a friend having to cancel a lunch date on you since something else came up that they needed to do. It's giving someone another chance and offering forgiveness to anyone who desires to make amends with you. If someone is interested in strengthening your connection because they feel horrible about the way they behaved, then hear them out. Too often others have a wall of anger where you think the person has some nerve calling to say they're sorry now.

Holding onto anger breeds a mold like Cancer within your body that spreads like poison slowly attacking all parts of you from the physical to the spiritual. When you come from a place of love and acceptance, then the cold parts of the emotions you're feeling evaporates. This doesn't mean you have to be best friends with someone again, but hearing them out and thanking them with compassion is taking the high road. It is being diplomatic and civil with no traces of animosity in your heart. You no longer have to engage with them if you choose not to. Leaving it on a high note is operating from your higher self.

I understand the difficulties that arise when you're trying to see the love in someone else who has done wrong in your eyes. You realize the naivety or selfishness that someone else has shown and it can get under your skin. On one level it is the human ego that was bruised, because the spirit soul part of you doesn't operate from that same ego. It has an emotional detachment to everything around them.

These Divine rules are guidelines that contain a structure much like the Ten Commandments had the intention of doing at that time in history. It's to train human souls to grow, expand, be compassionate, become better people, stronger, and more evolving. In the end, none of the stresses, anger, and negativity that you experience has any bearing on anything once you've passed on and travelled back home. Suddenly whatever you were holding a grudge about will be trivial and irrelevant.

Call on your Spirit team to help you in the areas where you're having trouble forgiving someone for something erroneous. This benefits your well-being as well as everyone around you. Release toxic emotions to Heaven for transmutation.

The way you learn to see the love in others is by seeing the love in yourself. See your soul in a way that God and the angels see you. To them you are perfect in every way, even when you fall and make mistakes. When you plummet down a path of addictions, they still love you and want you to accept and love yourself enough to want to stop damaging all parts of you. There is no judgment despite what some might believe. There is no discrimination because they view you in a broader and more profound way that is difficult for a human ego to comprehend.

Your Guardian Angel is the one that lifts the pain off your heart that drives you to an addiction to cover up pain and to forget about life for a spell. Someone that operates from a lower vibration will have distaste or be repelled by someone confident and self-assured. This is considered a threat to the dark part of one's ego. Someone evolving and looking to build, enhance, and grow their soul's consciousness is attracted to someone that exudes radiant like soul confidence. They admire someone that loves and appreciates themselves and what they can produce. Pay no mind to those who attack or bully you for being sure of yourself. You are operating from a higher frequency by standing in your power and loving the totality of you. Love all that you are and shout it out from the rooftops, and from the highest mountain, because you are magnificent.

CHAPTER TEN

The Higher Self

Earthly life is tough for millions of souls. It feels like an uphill battle that never ceases. To put your soul under so much pressure that it ultimately crushes you is the kind of heaviness that Heaven wants to prevent you from experiencing. For some, it results in premature death due to the compounded stresses you've placed upon your back. No soul on Earth is exempt from that as it can affect the souls moving through all levels whether it's a newborn baby soul on up through the mid-level and to the evolving soul. All are affected in this same way by the stresses of Earthly life, including myself on up to the Dalai Lama. I mention myself, because I am forever a work in progress. Life does not have to be that hard where it kills you early in life. When you come to the realization of where this resistance is coming from, only then can you begin the process of experiencing true freedom. This freedom is what your soul craves. It longs to be released from the confined ridiculous structure that human ego has designed. Avoid falling down the path of destructive addictions or suicide to get away from the chokehold this life has on your soul.

Earthly life today has a never-ending supply of material distractions such as cell phones, computers, jobs, rents, mortgages, poor diets, toxic relationship connections, lack of exercise, stress, depression, and the list goes on and on. All these things and much more block the divinity within reach. This holiness is accessible and resides within your innate nature. You do not need to search for it or move to another area to find it. You're carrying the answers within you.

People live in big cities on top of one another and that contributes to the suffocation of your soul. Therefore, implementing soul enhancing practices when possible can assist in lightening this load and make living in nearly any condition somewhat better than manageable. When you walk through an empty park or garden, then you've noticed that you suddenly begin to feel calmer and more relaxed than you were before you went out into nature. Your mind awakens and clarity seeps in with an attempt to yank your true higher self's nature out to dominate again. There are basic ways to reach that serenity space your soul craves where you're reminded that God is with you. This also helps as a physical health stress reliever. Many avenues in which your soul can find this freedom exist on the planet in these healing nature settings.

Hatred and negativity are a poison that chokes you. Putting in an effort to display love, compassion, and fun will lift you up allowing your soul the freedom to float above the clouds. This soaring feeling is where you grow closer to God. You have pieces of Him within you; therefore you are Him. No soul is exempt from this despite what they may or may not believe.

You are perfection through the eyes of all in Heaven. The *you* that is the truest part of you are your Higher Self. Your higher self is located in a more sophisticated state of awareness within your soul. It can be obtained by rising above any negative thoughts, moods, or toxic consumptions. You reach that higher space when you are clear minded and centered. You have access to this higher self since it is the true you. The false *you* is the one that struggles against the current and falls into physical superficiality.

Put your higher self back in charge whenever you find you've been faltering into negativity. You can do this by releasing the need to manage circumstances that are beyond your control. You accept and emotionally detach from that which bothers you. Work on letting it go since it is not worth it in the larger picture. You do not need it. Invite your Spirit team into your life to guide and assist you in this process. You can do so by sending out a request to God and your Spirit team mentally, out loud, or in writing.

You can say, "Please help me." And it is in motion.

Bringing yourself to your natural state is where you see things through the eyes of love. Your higher self requires nothing because everything is as it should be. If a mistake is made, your higher self learns from it with indifferent emotion and moves on. Your higher self efficiently corrects the mistake without drama, because it knows that all is well. This is just an Earthly life run and should not have to be so complicated. It becomes complex when you are mired down heavily in physical desires and functions taught to you by society. You have to get a job and go to work to make money to physically survive here. It's understood that this is how physical Earthly life is. You can still go after the physical necessities you require without getting obsessively bogged down in it that it stresses you out or makes you permanently unhappy.

To move into your higher self's state is to not desire or want. What you want may not be aligned with your higher self's state. You may want someone specific in your life in a love relationship, but this person is not someone that will be on an equal footing as you. Heaven sees someone else on its way into your life that is aligned and around the same level as you spiritually. This is why most souls attract in those who are similar to them to a degree. When there are vast differences in vibration to someone else, then the connection grows challenging and sometimes breaks apart. Exceptions are balanced Teacher-Student relationships where there is a compassionate give and take.

Your vibration is moving up and down throughout each day depending on what is being thrown at you. This is why it can be difficult at times to be in your true self's state every second on this turbulent planet. Your day starts out fantastic and you are in your higher self's state. You are happy and full of love. You get in your car and someone cuts you off or honks their horn. You suddenly feel stress and agitation. This gradually moves you into your lower self's state. That is until you bring yourself back up to that space of feeling centered and at peace again.

It becomes a juggling act or a yo-yo as you learn how to adjust your frequencies throughout any given day. You might say, "This would be easier if I didn't have to deal with people." But this is not necessarily true. You could spend all day at home alone and not doing much. Soon you reach moments where you feel unmotivated, lonely, isolated, secluded, depressed, or bored. Those states gradually begin to lower your vibration into your lower self's state. No one caused it, but the negative thoughts in your mind. This is one of the challenges of living an Earthly life.

A pioneer conquers new territory by being themselves and going against what the masses believe in order to promote positive change. Think for yourself even if you stand alone. Stick to your guns even if others disagree or attempt to bully or attack you. It is more than likely that you will be bullied and attacked at some point in your life if you haven't already. The dark ego is threatened by those that are strong, different, rebellious, outspoken, or a know it all. Pay no mind and stay focused on your life purpose and goals. Someone may confront you at some point in your life. Lower vibration human souls are threaded out among those who operate on a higher level. The lower evolved is threatened by someone that rules at life. Ignore that kind of energy, as it's irrelevant. You have a job to do, so refuse to back down or fill yourself up with fear that you will not be popular by going against what is expected of you.

For some, the idea of an afterlife is a fairy tale that gives one hope for those that fear death. This is a false belief conjured up by those that do not experience day-to-day connections with source. They might have never reached that one defining moment in their life that convinces them enough that there is more beyond their physical existence. The more in tune you are, the more you are likely to have profound experiences with the spirit world that perk up your ears.

It is difficult now more than ever in history for a human soul to connect with something beyond. They are distracted by the physical demands of Earth from buildings, cars, phones, computers, electronics, drama, violence, negativity, and noise. The list of blocks between humankind and Heaven are endless. This has led souls to grow up on Earth not believing in anything spiritual related. To believe that there is a God that sits on a throne above the clouds casting judgment and waiting to punish man is the real fairytale, but God is another name for all that is. Every cell, every atom, and organism that exists is God. He is everywhere filling up all available space possible in every plane, realm, universe, and dimension. You cannot run from Him.

There are some that do not believe in an afterlife. They have come to this conclusion due to a strict religious upbringing that was filled with negativity and judgment. Or they might not believe in Heaven because life has dealt them a poor hand. They might end up being confined to a wheelchair and they look at that as a negative. Often those situations are a result of accelerated spiritual growth needed. When one finds that at some point in their life that a major handicap or challenge has taken place, then it's intended that you begin to view the world and all that is around you in a broader or different way. The goal is to awaken your mind if it was previously closed. The other case is the handicap came upon someone because the physical body is not infallible. It will be met with challenges that evaporate when you head back home to Heaven.

An atheist will protest to not believe there is another place one goes to when they pass on. They believe that when you die it's the end. Although some profess to be atheists, they are more agnostic when they reveal statements aligned with the belief that your mind is open enough to allow room for the possibility of there being some form of God or afterlife. This is pending they can receive concrete material-based evidence on that; otherwise the conclusion is that it must not be true since they've never seen it. The evidence will not show up in a math equation. The data exists when you fine-tune all your psychic senses. You open them up a crack to receive a divinely guided message convincing enough to your ego that ultimately helps you ask the bigger questions and notice the possibilities of more being out there.

I have been testing my Spirit team and Heaven out my entire life. I do this because I don't blindly follow or believe in something I cannot see. I have an analytical mind and require some measure of proof that convinces me, so I understand skepticism. I've had repeated occurrences where I've stated something that was about to happen, and it later has. Everyone has that connection and at one time or another may be able to recall those instances where they've noticed this same psychic phenomenon.

The ego cuts off the communication between the non-believer and what exists outside of them. Your ego is what sabotages you and tells you that you're not qualified and have no business doing anything you want to do. Your ego's voice instills fear and causes your life to feel chaotic, while the higher self's voice is filled with overflowing love, calm, or excitement. Your ego's voice changes its mind daily and often, while your higher self's voice is stable, faithful, and frequent. Your higher self's voice will continue to push you to do the same thing repeatedly for years until you finally do it. That voice would never urge you to do something that would ultimately bring you or someone else down. There is a domino effect to your decision-making process. When this happens, it is a clue that your choices were made from the ego.

Your ego pushes you to act in ways that cause pain, hurt, or confusion, while your higher self's voice gives you brilliant flashes of ideas that never leave your mind. When you implement them into action, then you experience success, love, and joy. The ego will make you feel as if you're bouncing around, stagnant, heading nowhere fast, or going around in circles and never accomplishing anything. While your higher self pushes you to make changes that benefit you and others. It might coax you for decades to finally write that book, make that video, and apply for that job. While your ego will delay you from moving forward and will say you're not qualified to write a book. It'll tell you that you don't have the time, or it will instruct you to wait until you're more settled. When you listen to that voice, you can be assured that you will never accomplish anything, and nor will you ever write that book.

You hear those who are of older age express regret, "I should've done this or that. It was always on my mind too, but I never did it." Right there is a clue to the heavenly guidance you were receiving most of your life, but you ignored it. Those listening to their higher self's voice are suddenly filled with glorious love and excitement. Pay attention to what's going on inside you in order to decipher what is your higher self and what is your lower self. Examine the repercussions, challenges, or blessings that come out of that as a result of your action or inaction.

CHAPTER ELEVEN

Soul Growth Through Grief

The next two chapters we'll look at some of the harder soul challenges for people. These are connected to experiences such as grief or battling an illness. These sorts of challenges have made people question if there is a God, angels, or anybody that cares. How could a loving God create so much suffering? I've suffered on every level possible throughout my life that could make anyone question their faith. Humankind causes a great deal of suffering. Either we are generating the suffering ourselves or another person's free will actions have generated the suffering on us. Some want a guarantee of a pain free life, but that doesn't exist on Earth while living a human existence. The pain free life exists when you head back home to Heaven.

We come to Earth to teach others lessons and learn lessons from others as well as through our human experiences. While some may have a hard time believing this, Earth is a school for human souls. When you head to a human school like High School or College, no one promises that it will be easy. You will go through highs and lows as you are learning something in these higher institutions. The same goes for the soul that lives an Earthly life. You will be tested by yourself and by others. All of this influences your soul's consciousness. Grieving or battling an illness has their own array of challenges with it that benefit the soul's consciousness as difficult as that might be to consider.

Grief is part of the human experience. It can be the sadness over the death of someone close to you, but it can also be grieving over the loss of anything of value to your soul such as the loss of a pet, a job, an apartment or home. It might be the loss of a friend or love relationship that ended. It can be losing anyone or anything that means a great deal to you. Perhaps someone you loved moved away from you physically, mentally, emotionally, or spiritually. It can be a friend that moves away to another state or country. Even though you remain in touch, it's not the same because you're not physically hanging out in person absorbing one another's energies. The energy is more potent in person than it is through the technological waves. Grief can be present over the loss of a job or the hurt over something valuable to you. The grieving feelings one experiences with anything are the same bereaving emotion across the spectrum regardless of the circumstance. It still brings on the same pain and despair.

Offering Supportive Strength for the Grieving

Being a supportive friend to someone grieving over any loss or a physical death of a loved one can require delicate understanding. It is your role at that moment to step into the teacher role by being there for that person. You might wrestle with whether you should get into the spiritual talk by discussing how the soul never dies. That truth can be too far-fetched for someone to think about after they've lost someone. Deep down they may understand and already know it to be true, but it will not matter at the time they are battling with that major change in their life. Everything the one grieving usually believes is temporarily tossed out the window, because the feelings they have for the person that is no longer in front of them is so powerful. Grieving is a part of the soul's growth and experience. It must be allowed to freely feel whatever they sense in that moment without restriction or blockage.

When you're battling the depths of grief there is nothing one can truly say to you except to be there for you, to be present when needed, give space when you know the one grieving wants to be left alone. This doesn't mean vanish and disappear, but instead be within arm's reach and accessible by periodically checking in with them. Reminding them they are not alone and that you are there.

Perhaps you're a friend who is the practical joker or the funny one who never gets that emotional. This humor part of you is a gift to the grieving that needs some relief from the pain if only for a short time. They might ask to hang out with you for the purpose of forgetting about the grief for an hour or for the day. They know you're the fun one or the jokester that is exceptional at getting everyone to forget about any stresses, sadness, or troubles. This helps in keeping their vibration high while teaching them how to laugh again.

Others grieving may want that friend who is the deep insightful one. They crave your philosophical nature. While others may want the whole gamut of friends from the funny one on Saturday, then the insightful deep one on Sunday. Some want the variety of friend experiences in order to feel the entire spectrum of emotions and understandings when it comes to the loss of someone dear.

Contrary to my work being on the more serious side, in person I'm more of the practical joker coupled with the philosophical insights and guidance. I've had friends going through tough grieving times in the past. When that's happened, they've reached out to me that they need me to help them forget. They've spent so much time with others showering sympathy and condolences, but they need that no-nonsense fun time to relieve their soul of the pain.

Depending on how attached you were to the person that physically left, you will experience grief over it. The grieving emotions are still the same regardless if the person passed on in human death or physically left the relationship you had with them. It still feels like something was ripped out of you leaving your soul to suffocate. You feel like you cannot breathe or continue with life. You become depressed and bed ridden feeling like you want to die. Reaching for a toxic addiction doesn't help, as you feel even more miserable afterwards. There is nothing anyone can say that can make those feelings disappear. It is the soul's individual experience to move through on their time frame.

As a supportive friend, the best you can do is be there when the grieving wants to talk, or if they want someone there in the room with them where no talking is required or necessary. They feel a comfort knowing someone else is in the house, even if you're both doing your own things in different rooms. Sometimes the grieving wants to be distracted from the feelings. They know that you can get their mind off it just by being yourself and who you typically are.

Don't beat yourself up if you're doing everything you possibly can to make them forget about it and you find it's not working. You're making them laugh, or showing them a good time, yet you look over and the person experiencing grief seems to be somewhere else and completely distracted and down. Don't take that personally because it has nothing to do with what you're doing or not doing. You are helping them even if you're not realizing it in that moment. You're already a comfort by being there. They will appreciate that if not in the moment, but long after they've moved past the grief.

The last thing you do not want to say is something along the lines of, "You need to move on."

This shows you feel put out that your friend is not in the same happy content space that you are. Feeling put out is not a genuine friend.

When you're grieving, then it becomes about you and what you've lost, and how will you go on. You will not want to go on, as it's too painful to get up every day and put on the face that all is well, when deep down you're still in pain.

Little by little and gradually as time moves on, the wounds will heal and close, even if the scar is forever present. You will become stronger than before viewing life in a broader way through this tumultuous emotional experience. It can help you realize what's important in life. Earthly life goes beyond your job that helps pay the bills, or the material desires you continuously chase after. Suddenly everything on Earth seems trivial after you've gone through a grieving experience.

You never want to shove your personal doctrine or belief system to someone you suspect doesn't share your beliefs or is not ready to hear it. This is regardless if it's a grieving person or not. The exception is if they ask you for that wisdom or for your view on the death.

There are many things you can do to support someone grieving over the death of a loved one, and that is to be a friend. Let them know you're there if they ever want to talk. Unless asked, don't get into the whole soul never dies speech if they don't believe in it or if they're not in the right state of mind to hear it. When someone is upset and feeling grief, then anything you say will not be heard much anyway.

Grieving Through a Tough Circumstance

Grieving is a state all soul's experience at one time or another when a loved one has passed away or moved on from them. It's part of the cycle of human physical life. Spirit understands that you have every good reason to be distracted when a death happens, and they will never stop communicating with you regardless. They will never stop working with you to heal your heart and help you continue. They will work to put signs in your path that the person you lost is still around you even if you're not physically seeing them. If it's the loss of a friend, relationship, or job, then they'll work with you to help you see the loss as the beginning of something better for you. There are millions of stories over the centuries where someone admits to noticing that their deceased loved one was communicating with them at one point.

The human experience part of you produces heavy grief at times. Sad emotions create a block with the Divine cutting off all communication. It prevents you from hearing them making it seem as if everything has gone quiet. Spirit is communicating with you especially during the grieving process, even if you're no longer picking up on anything. There is no time limit to healing as each soul has their timeline where the healing happens naturally on its own. There are positive blessings in motion outside of what seems like a tragedy and it is beauty in its simplicity.

It can be painful when someone you care about passes on, let alone when it seems they've left too soon. You worry if they've left peacefully, which is the ego creating those fears, since souls exit this plane peacefully and smoothly. It is the human existence part of you that brings in a tidal wave of grief. There is no time limit as you move through it since this process can take as long as your soul needs it to.

A Death Welcomes a New Beginning

A death can be the death of someone close to you, but it can also be a metaphorical death where it's the end of one way of life and the beginning of a new chapter.

Heart related issues are the leading cause of death in humankind. My spirit doesn't see human death in the way that others do. It's not that I don't feel it because I do if it was someone close, but I don't view practical human circumstances in the same way that others might and tend to. I've been viewing it through the lens of my Spirit team, which is less emotional, but sympathetic and empathetic to the pain someone is experiencing. Depending on my state of mind that day, my perception can vacillate between Spirit's eyes, then my ego's eyes, to my higher self's view, then the lower self's, and back around again. It swings all over the place like a pendulum creating a vast reservoir of emotion inside.

The morning my father passed away, the paramedics, the firemen, and the policemen that were present had all approached me in a group like a mob. One of them said, "Can we talk to you? You seem to be the only one together here."

That remark stood out because I hadn't given it much thought until I realized that everyone seemed to notice. It was only when they said that did I scan my surroundings realizing how upset everyone was. They added that I appeared to be standing in a calm centered focused state. I've had film producer friends all say at different times over the years, "You're like the calm within the storm."

You say the word "Death" to humankind, and it's viewed with darkness. You conduct a web search of the word *death* and you receive pages of dark images or the grim reaper. This is the perception humankind has of death to the point that those images are #1 on the web search engines, because more people clicked on those images. There is no soul death, even though the soul's experiences are met with endings and beginnings. The soul moves on and begins a new chapter, but any death is not a tragedy. It simply means your current life run is complete. Your soul evolves out of this existence and continues on to a place that is much more magnificent than Earth, but mirrors that utopian ideal your soul longs for while here. Death shouldn't be dark or negative, and I've had death throughout my life on all levels.

CHAPTER TWELVE

*Soul Growth Through
Health Issues*

Mental health issues affect millions of people around the world. The general list includes depression, anxiety, and the various ailments from eating disorders, to psychotic and mood disorders. Those suffering from some form of mental health issues find that it prevents them from living the kind of life they dream of. It can prevent you from going after what you want or inhibit you from defending yourself. For some it can lead to suicide or permanent stagnancy.

Depression sufferers feel inadequate or unable to motivate themselves to live. Agoraphobics are afraid to leave their homes, or they feel uncomfortable in crowded or confined spaces. Those with social anxiety avoid accepting invitations to parties or functions, as they fear being watched, judged, or simply cannot handle the huge number of psychic stimuli tampering their emotional sensitive system. As you get to know others on a personal level, there isn't anyone who isn't battling some form of disorder or phobia connected to one's mental health, especially in this hyper technology age that has been shown to have aggravated it. You might never fully diminish the disorders in one lifetime, but you can get close to where you're able to function somewhat realistically in this hostile world and form some semblance of a life.

Almost everyone on the planet has some sort of neurosis, while others may battle harder versions of these disorders. Some of these disorders are genetic and inherited. They run right down the genetic blood line. Other times it's taught or placed on the back of that soul. Many struggle with disorders their entire life or attempt to temper it and keep it under control.

For those that battle disorders, it might please you to know that some of the most successful people in the world battle some of these same issues. Entertainers from well-known actors and singers wrestle with social anxiety. They can train themselves to shut it off temporarily when they are in the performing zone, whether on stage or in front of the camera. This is one of the positives of diving into creative pursuits whether professionally or as a side hobby. Some are born into this life with a mental health disorder, while others develop it over the duration of their Earthly life due to human societal tampering.

Due to the rise of technology, selfies, and phones, narcissism is a trait that is grown and bred into the generations raised post 2000. From that point forward, Earth's history moved into a generation being raised on technology, selfies, and computers. This has rendered many incapable of carrying in person conversations or exuding proper class etiquette. Many are growing up in environments where they are assaulted by selfishness in others every second. You cannot hide from it or be unaware of it unless you live in the middle of nowhere or never go online. This along with poor diet and nutrition all contribute to the high amounts of anxiety, depression, and mental health issues that exist.

Some choose to take anti-depressants or anti-anxiety medication, while others refuse to as they feel that it alters their brain chemistry artificially. They prefer to engage in counseling with a therapist or talk therapy instead, while others participate in counseling along with medication. These are choices that are up to you and your doctor. It's your life and you and your doctor know what's best for you to get through it. Ironically, I've discovered those that are against medication that may need it seem to self-medicate in other ways that are not exactly healthy.

As someone plagued with social anxiety my entire life, I understand what's it like to wrestle with it. Those suffering from social anxiety know what it's like to have their thoughts, feelings, and heart racing for no apparent reason. Someone is walking towards you to talk to you, and you want to jump out of your skin. You want them to go away. You don't want to have to talk to them, deal with people, stand up, and give a speech, and so forth. You desire a daily pill to keep those issues contained as much as possible. Do what you feel is best for you. There is nothing wrong with wanting to be on medication or wanting to dissolve medication. This is a personal choice that you make. With anything health related, always seek out a professional medical doctor regardless of what anyone states. Take hold of the reigns and govern your life the way you see fit. What's important is that you're addressing any issues you're battling with in a healthy way.

All mental health issues go away when the soul crosses over. Until then you learn to adjust your lifestyle and way of living to help it be more manageable. This is the same way anyone who suffers from any form of mental disorder this lifetime. If you have social anxiety, then you don't spend your days heading to areas that are jam packed with people. If you go to an amusement park, then you go on a day that you know isn't so crowded. You avoid going to the grocery store at high noon on a weekend when it's typically more packed than at any other hour.

You might be driven to mask the mental health issues through toxins that make you wish you could stop. Efficient ways of eliminating a toxic addiction such as bad foods, drugs, alcohol, cigarettes, caffeine, or coffee is by gradually reducing it over time.

I understand the day to day struggles that exist in life as I've been through those trenches too. I know how to navigate through it. I've been in the gutters of addiction as I have an addictive personality, but I also have a strong connection with the Other Side. I've learned from Heaven that the only person beating up on you is you. Everyone has their own gauge on what works for them. It's about doing the best you can. If you fall off the wagon, you don't beat yourself up. You get back on the horse again and continue moving forward one day at a time.

Hyper focus on anything expands whatever the attention is on. If it's focused on a health concern, the healing takes longer to come about. Great health improvements are made through prayer and by shifting your focus positively away from the issue. I've had catastrophic health issues that were painful, but went away after I believed it would improve and get better. Instead I focused on fun, joy, laughter, and did whatever I could to get to that place from watching a funny movie to joking around with a pal.

There are shattering health issues that do or will come about that are beyond human and Heaven's control. It's better to look upon it with positive thoughts rather than negative ones. The negative thoughts will only make you feel that much worse. At least the positive thoughts will ensure you remain in high spirits throughout the process.

I've had major health scares in the past that were physically painful, but I continued to ask for Divine help and eventually one day it was no more. It was as if it never happened. I have days where I'm not focused or my faith is waning, but I quickly revert to being focused not long afterwards.

When you work on taking care of yourself regularly and treat what you put into your body with the utmost care, then any illnesses that arise are minimal. This doesn't mean you'll be problem free, but it can help in making it less tough. I've certainly felt worn down as if I was coming down with something, but as soon as I'm aware of that, I immediately up my preventatives before it blows up. I wake up the next day feeling great again. When I feel my body under stress and my immune system declining, I'm guided to begin my remedies to get better quickly. I immediately double the water and vitamin C intake. I sleep earlier and longer than usual while avoiding strenuous exercise or anything that can cause anxiety. I may do wheatgrass and blue algae shots as well as making sure I'm relaxed and detached from any stress. This is partially why I haven't had the major flu since the early 2000's - knock on wood.

Exceptions to this are you may be an older person or younger unhealthy person where it takes longer for your body to fight off illnesses. There are also circumstances where you discover it was beyond your control. You may be born this lifetime with a weaker immune system you have to battle, so you do the best you can one day at a time. Surround yourself with supportive people that can give you what you need.

When you feel a cold or the flu coming on, immediately start the medicinal regimen. Drink lots of water and up the Vitamin C intake. You can go as far as to drink a shot or two of wheatgrass if you can keep it down. Above all sleep more than you usually do. When your body is wearing down, this is a sign that you need to take it easy and rest. If you watch movies, then stick to comedies, since lightheartedness, joy, and laughter raise your vibration. When you're sick or your immune system is crashing, then your vibration is low. This will help raise it and help you get better quicker. Avoid strenuous exercises during this time so as not to wear your body out and dehydrate it. Although some exercise is helpful such as casual biking or walking, but you won't do that when you have the full-blown flu.

Drink more water than usual by doubling it. If you drink fifty ounces a day, then aim for a hundred ounces spread out through the day. Head to bed earlier than you normally would. Sleep, water, and prayer will rejuvenate your body quickly.

Other preventatives might include water with squeezed lemon or lime, and a dash of cayenne pepper. Add a healthy sweetener, or agave syrup if it's too difficult to take down. Heat it up and then sip carefully. Other flu and cold illness fighting preventatives that are high in Vitamin C are jalapeno peppers, onions, algae, and garlic.

You can call on Jesus or Raphael. Archangel Raphael is the healing angel to call on for all things healing, health, nutrition, exercise, and well-being related.

CHAPTER THIRTEEN

Soul Growth Through Relationships

Now that you've made it through the wilderness of grief and illnesses, let's move into one of my favorite subjects to discuss. Love and relationships! One of the bigger benefits towards the soul's evolving consciousness is through your relationship connections with other people. The lessons while in those connections are invaluable. In the spiritual arena we call these connections soul mates, so we'll continue to use that label for the sake of understanding.

Every soul on the planet has many soul mates. They can come in the form of friendships, family members, colleagues, and love partners. Some of these relationship dynamics are considered karmic relationships, soul mate connections, and the rarest of them all the twin flame. It doesn't matter what you choose to label or call it, because the intention and meanings of each are evident. Every soul on the planet has or will experience numerous karmic and soul mate relationships. As challenging as it might be to accept, the soul knows the family they will be born into on Earth. When you say that to most people the initial response is, "Boy, did I choose wrong." The more tempestuous and antagonistic the family connection, then the more lessons learned. The more lessons learned, the quicker the soul consciousness evolving process is. You don't grow much residing in a picture-perfect palace where nothing happens. The more tempestuous a connection is, then the more likely it is a karmic connection. Your soul mate connections are the ones with people that push your buttons and push you out of your comfort zone. They have endless roles with some of them being sent to act as catalysts to help guide you from one area of your life to another.

Twin flame connections are a rare relationship dynamic because most of the time one's twin flame is back home in Heaven's spirit world. There is little reason for a twin flame to be on Earth at the same time as their twin flame. Why would they when you spend an eternity with your twin flame back home? One of the reasons they would incarnate relatively at the same time would be for the sake of helping one another's accelerated soul consciousness growth and evolving process, or to be a supportive partner in some way that benefits one another's fight to improve humanity through humanitarian efforts and work. It is typically the soul's that have moved into the post graduate higher evolving end of consciousness when they are more likely to meet their twin flame this lifetime. This isn't with every single higher evolving soul, since many choose to live single lives while focusing on their larger purposes. They understand they came here for that larger purpose that takes precedence over anything else. The main goal for twin flames is to act as support the way any teammate supports one another on the sports field.

It would be nearly impossible to attract in a quality mate for life if you are wrecked with low self-esteem or if you're battling any kind of turmoil or addictions. This is especially the case when it comes to the twin flame connection, because both partners have reached a relatively balanced alignment between one another spiritually and emotionally. This doesn't mean it is without issues that either individual battles with, and nor is it about the occasional turmoil, wrestling of addictions, or low self-esteem one has from time to time. This is about the soul that fights a daily uphill battle of struggle that endures for years.

When I was battling all these issues and more up through my twenties, the partners I was bringing into my world were battling similar circumstances. In hindsight, it was too obvious not to notice the pattern. While in the throes of battle, you'll attract in an undesirable situation or partner, or a rebound soul mate catalyst to move you out of the sphere of soul consciousness you're currently in. This is someone sent to you for the particular purpose of assisting you in moving past turmoil, drama, or addictions. Their soul's job is to inspire you to improve, but that doesn't necessarily mean they're the long-term friendship or love partner. Once their job is complete, usually those types of connections begin to dissolve and then an even more together friendship or love partner shows up. The in-between soul mate partnership is taking you from one point to the next where you then leave and encounter the greater partner that follows.

The catalyst soul mate partner is to work in tandem with you to heal something from the past. This might be where two people connect and discover they are battling the exact same issue of getting over a love relationship break up or a job loss. Because of their mutual understanding of what it's like going through the same thing, they can relate and work out the issues together in conversation by this common denominator. The connection that is forming is no accident.

The friendship suddenly feels like two best friends hitting the road together, but often once the core issue is worked out and both are over the loss they experienced, they notice that their connection starts to wane or grow tired. It may drag on a bit longer than usual until one day they realize they're not connecting the way they used to.

This is because the job they each had as soul mates for one another has been complete. That job was to get you both from one station to the next. There may be some cases where you know it's over and begin distancing yourself, but the other hasn't reached that level of realization and is holding on for dear life.

You cannot wait around for this catalyst soul mate partner to show up to help lift you out of turmoil and bring you to the next station on your soul's journey. When you're waiting for a rescuer to pull you out of your life, you could be waiting indefinitely. If your life is stuck on pause due to circumstances or past choices, and there is no soul mate catalyst coming in, then lean on God to lift you up. You can do this by requesting His intervention and help through regular prayer. Make prayer a regular part of your daily life if it isn't already. Have faith and believe you are being helped even if the effects are not visible. You also must do the work and stand strong in faith to make the necessary efforts, adjustments, and action steps to improving your life one day at a time, which simultaneously contributes to raising your consciousness.

Examine where your overall self-esteem is at because a low self-esteem will not attract in a healthy life, let alone assist in the soul's evolving process. It only invites in more issues. A low self-esteem person may be constantly comparing themselves to others, which is not hard today for so many people with access to social media. Everyone is comparing themselves to others and feeling less than in the process. A low self-esteem person is more likely to become abusive with a friendship or love partner by lashing out at them. High self-esteem people are not bullying or attacking others in any way. There's no reason for them to because they are sure of who they are. The low self-esteem person may attack through backhanded ways where they make fun of someone not realizing they're doing that to prop themselves up. They break others down so they can be falsely lifted. If the partner on the receiving end has high self-esteem, then they will eventually walk away from the connection, because those types of partners are not interested in abusive situations. Even though you may not have realized you were behaving that way until after the relationship has dismantled and you fall back into the low self-esteem traits again.

A sign that someone is evolving their soul is they grow surer of themselves and confident. They are not comparing themselves to others the way they might have done. This is because when you evolve spiritually, then you're becoming more connected to what is beyond the triviality and superficiality of the physical world. It's no longer of interest to you to resort to petty comparisons.

What are the traits you love about yourself? What are traits you cannot stand about yourself? What are the areas you can change to adjust the parts of you that make you hate yourself? What are the areas that you can't stand about yourself, but you know you cannot change?

Feeling truly whole is loving all that you are. It is accepting all parts of you especially the uncomfortable parts. It is raising your self-esteem into a warrior like confidence that you are content being alone and independent. This is not to be confused with being lonely. Loneliness and being comfortable alone are two different scenarios. Warrior like confidence means you are also in a perfect space of peace. Only when you love yourself in this grand way can you be more than ready for the greatness that matches that kind of vibration. You will have the occasional low periods in life as everyone does. It's human nature to experience ups and downs. You might feel the random low self-esteem hit or you'll feel tender about the way you look or certain parts of your personality. This is about your overall state and demeanor, not the occasional stresses and lows that everyone can feel from time to time. It doesn't mean you have to beat yourself up attempting to be consistent about it, because that would be an outlandish and unrealistic request. You're human and you have human emotions that are generated and connected to the ego, which in turn tampers with your feelings and thoughts.

We all vacillate from the positive to the negative every day. To demand that someone be positive around the clock is an impossible unrealistic demand. This is about finding a healthy balance to being fully aware of the range of vibrational energy you're radiating throughout each day. This is all part of the process of evolving your soul's consciousness. As you move through the different levels of evolving, which include all the challenges and pitfalls in life, then you come out of it with a newfound sense of serenity and outlook. This is when the most ideal partner will move into position in front of you.

CHAPTER FOURTEEN

*Twin Flame Soul
Mission and Purpose*

When a soul chooses to incarnate into another Earthly life run, it is because they have a purpose, goal, and mission to doing so. This mission is a solo one that will entail numerous purposes within them. If the soul is rapidly evolving their consciousness, then the likelihood of connecting with a twin flame partnership is great. Like karmic and soul mate relationships, a twin flame soul can be a friendship, family member, business partner or lover. The twin flame would only incarnate at relatively the same time that enables both partners to simultaneously encourage one another's higher purposes and goals in offering that person support in some manner and vice versa.

The twin flames are like a spark of fire. When fire burns up the land and terrain on one end, and there is another fire burning separately on the other end, then depending on the direction it's headed, those two fires will eventually connect and merge. The results are combustible! It can create a power that is beyond human comprehension burning everything in its wake. When two twin flames connect on Earth, this same metaphor set up takes place.

Both twin flames already have a commanding presence that is sensed by others when they enter the room alone. When that same person walks in the room with their twin flame, everyone notices and feels it. The energy is incredibly passionate and deep that it is beyond ignorable. It's what it truly means to say, "Those two over there are a power couple." They almost look like the same person, even if they physically look different. It is the similar intense energies that people are picking up on.

Twin flames tend to be go-getters with enormous goals and missions and purposes to accomplish throughout their life that includes improving the state of humanity by being who they are and the work they set out to do. Someone that is idle, lazy, or has a slacker mentality in general will not be meeting or encountering their twin flame. Because the twin flame is not needed since the person is not contributing anything positive towards the betterment of humanity on any level whether through teaching, or the arts, or humanitarian and charity works, etc. There is something about each twin flame person that is identifiable and unusual beyond any physical attraction chemistry.

When your twin flame is in the spirit world, they may work as one of your guides to bring soul mate connections into your life. They don't want you spending your days longing for love or companionship, so they assist in the process of bringing you potential lovers, friendships, colleagues, or acquaintances for soul mate connections.

The reality is also that not everyone will experience a romantic love partnership, let alone one that lasts until the end of their days. This leads to the myth that there is someone out there for everyone, which is a misguided romantic notion that doesn't ring true for every single person on the planet. It's also a fictitious assumption to feed the masses with, especially when it is not realistic or practical. There are millions of people that will never obtain a love partner or are not looking for one.

Usually a sudden love feeling experienced on Earth comes from one's Spirit Guide, Guardian Angel, or Twin Flame on the Other Side working with them. Some people are without friends, family, or lovers. This doesn't mean that Spirit has ignored them. Potential soul mate relationships are brought to all souls, but that doesn't mean they're making the connection happen and keeping them alive. Someone can get you a job interview, but it's up to you to get the job.

Numerous soul mate potentials cross paths with you, but it's up to the both of you to say hello and build a connection. No one in Heaven can make that part happen. You're not a puppet on strings. You are a thinking, feeling, conscious person who has free will choice to create the life you desire. You have free will choice to take that Divine sign given to you and act on it or disregard it. You might recall positive blessing circumstances that could have happened in your life, but you unknowingly let it pass on by. It was only later in hindsight when you looked back that you wish you could have acted on it.

Some people choose to live a loner hermit lifestyle away from other people. They have free will choice and they have chosen to live this kind of life for various reasons. Sometimes it's due to circumstances that led them there. For others, they might be highly sensitive, divinely connected, agoraphobic, and therefore unable to withstand the nonsensical erratic energy that is typically being emitted off many people. The loner has chosen this life and is not necessarily looking to increase their opportunities of crossing paths with soul mates.

Technology and social media give you instant ways of connecting with others. This has made it easier for souls to interconnect if only via a computer or phone. If twin flames find each other online, then they will eventually find a way to be close to one another physically at some point during their lives. They both have a deep desire for this because to not do so is indefinitely crushing. They need to be in the same vicinity of one another and will do whatever they need to in order to make it happen.

Embarking on an Earthly Mission

The twin flame is the ultimate deep love that transcends all. Most twin flames are on the Other Side and not living an Earthly life. One of the common reasons all souls incarnate into an Earthly life is for the purpose of teaching and learning. The twin flames are together on the Other Side for all eternity, so there is little reason for both to incarnate into an Earthly life, unless there is a larger reason, purpose, goal, and mission to do so. This would be one that requires the both of your Divine powers to work in tandem. They are one another's champion in all aspects of their life.

Earthly life is a blip on the radar, a millisecond on the clock, compared to soul eternity. This is one of the reasons why not all twin flames incarnate at the same time. One of the twin flames decides to incarnate into an Earthly life for purposes laid out in its soul contract. This is before heading back home to Heaven when their mission is complete. It is back home when they are re-united with their twin flame who has been watching and guiding them on their Earthly journey along with their Spirit team.

If a mission is incredibly greater than the norm, a twin flame may incarnate not long before or after its soul partner to offer support and receive that similar support in return for a spell. They become a powerful duo when they're together. There is no telling what they can accomplish while united on Earth. Both are brought to one another to evolve their mutual soul consciousness together.

Mirroring, Repelling, and Attracting

The twin flame soul connections repel as much as they love each other, but this is predominately in the beginning. Usually one or the other is about to embark on a major spiritual transformation where they soon rapidly begin to evolve their mutual souls' consciousness. Twin flame relationships may break up, get back together, break up again and get back together. This is not the same as relationships that operate in the vortex of high drama or ones that have constant arguments, which is a Karmic connection. Twin flames have an endless calm love for one another even when splitting apart. There is little to no emotional blackmail, arguing, or drama between them. If they split apart then they will eventually coast right back into each other's arms or lives again.

There is a point where they stop splitting up and stay together permanently for the rest of their current Earthly lives. This has been more so the case post-technological modern-day time, since the choices one has on the planet are not as limited as they once were. Twin flames can find one another much easier today than they were eons ago. Even though they can find one another easier, it is still not without its challenges preventing them from coming together right away.

The twin flame partnership has pain and confusion in both partners while they're apart, but it's not their intention to cause this pain. The aloofness causes hurt enough. They are always telepathically connected, even if they're not together physically. When they re-unite, they will often bring up synchronistic circumstances where they were both thinking or feeling the same thing as the other one was.

If one of them feels as if the partner is up to no good, then the other partner is likely feeling the same way in return. When they sit down to talk about it, they realize they're both thinking and feeling the same thing about the other one. They also discover that what was assumed in both is unfounded. They must learn to trust one another and ensure that trust is proven and reciprocated. The twin flames effortlessly communicate telepathically while on Earth. This is due to both evolving rapidly in one lifetime that their senses grow even sharper while with each other. There will never be a case where one is in tune and the other is not. Both seem to display similar behavior patterns that it is almost like looking in a mirror.

Back home the twin flames have faith and trust running between them naturally, but on Earth they are tempted by Earthly physical material egotistical pleasures that can cause break ups. This is also another reason why the twin flames rarely incarnate at the same time, because when they do, they have evolved and transcended high enough that they are not typically tempted by the Earthly pleasures and addictions that tend to break apart connections or stall forward soul movement. They are not immune to addictions, but it is on the rare side if the temptations are severe enough. They are more likely to display the temptations and addictions earlier in life, but by the time they move into the thirties and above, they have worked to minimize, reduce, or eliminate that way of life and thinking.

While one of the partners, typically the older one has evolved quickly, the younger one shows signs of this evolvement, but is still wrestling with releasing the temptations on Earth that wreak havoc on the lives of human soul relationships. They are still operating from egotistical desires that may have more to do with human genetics, such as an alcoholic gene passed on from a parent.

Twin flames may likely be from different backgrounds or towns on the planet. They might have an age gap of six to ten years or more give or take. The reason is because there are more lessons to gain with someone that comes from a different background or cultural influence. Both of the humanitarian and spiritual part of their nature tends to explode in larger ways when they finally merge together. Both partners continue to gradually evolve beyond that while in the confines of the relationship that doesn't feel like imprisonment at all, but true freedom since they also operate independently. While some people feel suffocated in a love relationship, the twin flames feel alive and free when with one another than while single. This is also the case even if one or the both had generally observed non-committal traits in their dating life and previous relationships. In one sense, they were subconsciously waiting for their right soul mate, which they truly never felt they had in previous partners, even though they enjoyed whoever they were seeing at the time while in the moment. This same essence between them is also evident if the twin flame connection is a friendship, family member, or business partner.

The twin flame connection defies all this uniting them naturally and effortlessly. There is no effort because when they end up in the same room together it is like magnet and steel colliding. It will happen for the most non-committal person on the planet. The union pushes both partners to evolve even more while in the presence of one another's spirit lights. It is while in the relationship together that whatever spiritual plateau they had reached before that moment, the connection takes them higher than that and in ways they didn't know were possible.

Twin flames tend to be leaders that are quite independent due to their spiritual evolving process. Souls that are rapidly evolving are less interested in functioning in groups, while being more comfortable alone or as a leader of sorts. They also tend to show little signs of co-dependency, while revealing exceptional leadership skills due to being comfortable with who they are.

From a soul level, when the twin flames re-unite this lifetime, it equally excites, inspires, and ignites the other's soul to greater heights neither would have reached without the presence of the other. This inspiration continues until the end of both of their Earthly lives when they re-unite back home.

Twin flames do not join just to unite to make love on a beach for the rest of their life. There is a purpose and reason the two have come together on Earth that is beyond the core basis and desire for having a love relationship. It is all connected to evolving their soul's consciousness.

Usually the twin flame will show up just before the initial mate is about to embark on another spiritual awakening or transformation change, while the other may be years behind them. If this is the case, the younger in Earth years twin flame may accelerate their spiritual evolvement while with the older one, or the connection will temporarily break apart. This would be the case due to the younger one not being emotionally ready for an intense connection. They may be of different human ages, but they are the same soul age.

At the same time, they cannot stand to be away from their twin flame partner because it feels like a hole is missing within them. It never goes away even if they end up with other people. Twin flames are like a triple header soul mate connection that compliments one another to climb enormous altitudes. It's like the Lunar Eclipse displaying the power of three Full Moons on one day. Soul mate connections can be intense, but the force of a soul mate connection can exist on various levels from the physical to the spiritual. Whereas a twin flame connection is primarily on a spiritual soul level first and foremost beyond anything else. The partners see one another's soul behind their eyes regardless of what they look like. They can be a couple that is intensely drawn to one another for decades, but purely on a platonic level. Their sexual nature with one another may be somewhat non-existent for human physical or emotional reasons, yet they cannot be apart from one another.

The twin flame connections are not always love related, which on the one hand may be a blessing for some. If the two incarnate relatively at the same time during one lifetime and fall in love, it will be more intense than if your twin flame was a best friend, family member, or a business partner you've joined forces with for life.

Those around that witness a twin flame connection when they are together will point out the natural ease they notice both have as if they are made for each other. They might point out that until their friend met this person, they were unstable or floundering all over the place, but now that they're with this person they've never seen them thrive and improve so dramatically. They will point out that they both seem to have the same essence, movements, and moods to one degree or another. And others may point out that they seem like they even look the same, even if they are physically different in appearance. There is something about the cosmic kismet like feeling that shows them to be two peas in a pod. Once together on Earth, they never leave one another's side even during splits, which seem permanent, but often the splits end up being temporary.

God splits the soul in two to give each soul an eternal partner, but the twin flames will decide how and when they will choose to be together. To be with someone for eternity is a long time, so both souls will have periods of their existence when they're not with each other.

CHAPTER FIFTEEN

*Soul Growth Through
Work and Career*

The jobs you have in life all contribute to the evolving process of your soul's consciousness. You might think you're stuck in a dead-end menial job, but there is something you are gaining there beyond a paycheck. One should do their best to be grateful they have a job in a world that has become increasingly difficult to find work for so many people. If you hate your job, then I'm sure that anyone that's been unemployed for years would be happy to take your job off your hands. Volunteer work and charities also count as work that is affecting your soul's consciousness.

We're often thrown into testy situations with other people where we are having to learn lessons like patience in getting along with a personality that is opposing to you. One of the greater wishes by many is to find work that has meaning to them. Often jobs that have a great deeper meaning to you are connected to one of your life's purposes. When you put joy into your work, then this raises your soul vibration in the process.

Working in a job or career that has deep meaning and fulfillment to you while getting paid for it is something many want to achieve. It can be frustrating when you're an intelligent thinking talented consciousness who has dreams of wanting to partake in work that means something to you, while being efficiently compensated enough to survive. You find you're stuck in a life soul crushing job that you head off to day after day simply for the paycheck.

Career transitions are challenging for anyone, because transitions in general are life altering and require effort. Many self-employed entrepreneur success stories also discuss how difficult it can be at first. I've always been a huge fan of rags to riches success stories since I was a kid. Those are the stories that reveal someone who came from nothing and made something out of their life. They weren't born into money and nor did they have a well to do life. Instead they had to work harder than those who were born into money or had stuff handed to them. They had the struggles where it seemed impossible, but they soon climbed the ranks to the top. Those are the inspiring stories that remind you that anyone can do it if they believe and try hard enough.

This isn't necessarily about accumulating financial riches, which is a hollow superficial goal. This is about being able to turn your life purpose, hobby, or passion into a career where you are making enough money that you no longer have to work at jobs you despise just for the paycheck.

Rags to riches stories often entail someone that just wanted to be able to do work that was their passion. They weren't looking to make a million dollars. The financial abundance that came flowing in was a positive side effect to them putting effort into their passion. They put in positive energy that came in naturally because they were enjoying the work. This attracted in the financial abundance.

When you feel no guidance or messages coming in from above, then it could be that you're experiencing a psychic block. Therefore, raising your vibration is an important factor to consider, because doing that assists the evolving process of the soul consciousness while helping to dissolve any blocks that give you a stronger Divine connection. Everyone is born with psychic abilities that never go away even if it feels that way. Those gifts vary in frequency from one to the next. The psychic senses are hanging out under the surface and always accessible. When you don't feel psychic, it just means something is blocking it. Blocks can be certain toxic foods, drinks, negative moods, bad energy, technological distractions, and other people to name a few. The closer you are to the physical Earth such as in nature, then the easier your abilities can begin the process of being re-awakened. The physical Earth is anything that is not manmade, such as buildings and cars. Certain lifestyle changes need to be incorporated into your life as well such as stripping yourself of potential blocks. One way to raise your vibration is through exercise and working out. This assists you in being a clearer vessel with the Divine, not to mention the health benefits you receive out of that too.

I've forever been a strong advocate for exercise since I was a kid. Since my teen years, I've been into exercise, working out, and taking care of myself as much as possible. I'll go hiking in the mountains, to rock climbing in the desert, to regular jogs and biking on the beach where I'll hang out for hours connecting with Spirit. This is because exercise awakens every cell in your body and soul, but so does being in nature. When you're exercising in nature, then that's a double whammy that assists in raising your vibration. Those cells that are awakened are transporters that communicate with spirit beings from beyond. When those cells awaken, then the information flows in more effortlessly. Exercise does a body good releasing happy endorphin chemicals. Happiness lifts your vibration cracking open the Divine communication line.

Getting into a happy state, exercising, and being in nature will all help raise your vibration. When you combine all three at once, then what a powerhouse feeling that is.

A raised vibration is what acts as a funnel for your Spirit team to communicate with you much more easily. It also brings in free flowing good stuff into your world. Forcing happiness or pretending to be happy won't work, so it will have to be authentic joy. Exercise has always been like oxygen to me. The initial getting to the exercise may be tough for some, but once you get into some form of cardio to get the body warmed up, then this gets the oxygen working through your cells. It feels like soaring above the clouds making you feel good.

Display Optimism and Gratitude

It took me a long time to move away from relying on regular day jobs to pay me and realize the income was ultimately coming from God. You could do your life purpose work if the financial support part of it is given to God to pay you. You develop less worry and guilt, and more faith and optimism knowing that you're taken care of when you modify your thinking process. This is by changing your perspective to understand that God is ultimately your source of income. This is rather than heavily focusing on a company or a boss to rely on to stay afloat and be taken care of. It takes a great leap of faith to be able to let go of that control. Jobs come and go, but God is always constant. All forms of abundance are trickling down from God, to the company, and to you. It's no accident that you're at a job. You are gaining important soul lessons through all your human experiences from your job or career to your relationship connections.

If fear or worry enters your mind, then alter the sentence to something positive: "Thank you so much for your help with this. Thank you for the blessings you've bestowed on me to date. Thank you also for ensuring I have a place to live without fear or worry that my bills won't get paid. Thank you for my strong health and happiness."

A huge lift inside can be felt when changing your sentences from something challenging and negative to something aligned with gratitude, optimism, and faith. When you heavily complain about things never going your way, then this creates a huge heavy burden on your soul while bringing more of that into your life.

Worry creates more worry, while joy creates more joy. When you feel like your job is not going as planned or you hate it, and your mind constantly goes there whenever you have a free minute, then take a step back and halt the tone of that thinking. Shift those words to ones of gratitude. Look at the reasons behind why you might be required by spirit to be at that job during the time you are. Think of the good things you have in your life. The ones that would make your life worse if you didn't have those good things. They can be items such as your car that is in good condition helping you get to and from work without worry. You don't worry much about your car until something goes wrong with it, then you realize how grateful you are to have a car that runs. Don't wait for something bad to happen to realize what you have, but be grateful now.

It's easy to take things for granted until those blessings unacknowledged are taken away. When you are in a negative space, then stop and direct your attention to the blessings you currently have. Maybe you've reached the point of feeling sorry for yourself. You find that you say things like, "Why does everyone else get the good stuff, but I'm still struggling to get my share of the blessings?"

The same ones feeling sorry for themselves regularly will also moan about not having any friends. When you look closer, you notice they seem to be surrounded by numerous people that fit the description of a friend. They're still unhappy and despondent not seeing it because perhaps they have conditions on what they expect from a friend. You can have a pity party begging for attention from others, or you can get over it and continue persevering on doing what you're called to do. Never beg for anyone's friendship and attention. One often looks at what they don't have, rather than what they currently do. Pay attention to the blessings existing in your present moment. Acknowledging and displaying gratitude for what you have now is a positive abundance attractor.

CHAPTER SIXTEEN

*Soul Growth Through
Superficiality*

Part of raising your soul's consciousness includes having a higher view of Earthly life. Getting bogged down in superficiality can create a block due to the delusions it casts upon your soul. Current human life today has propelled others to become obsessed by youth and exterior appearances. For some it is to the point where reality has fazed those that have fallen into the epicenter of this superficiality. There was a time pre-technology when you respected your elders. Now many disrespect those older because they are ageist and under the delusion, they are untouchable and exempt from aging. What is failed to realize is they will age and be discriminated against as well, unless they are lucky enough to reach older age when the upcoming generations of souls have moved out of that shallowness. Otherwise, they will have a much harder time with ageing because of this inability to accept spiritual reality early on. It is unlikely that any immediate generations will rise above this kind of showiness due to how prevalent and saturated exterior looks have dominated the Internet waves.

There was the infamous case between the years of 1585 and 1609 when Hungarian noblewoman *Countess Elizabeth Bathory de Ecsed* allegedly had hundreds of virgin girls tortured and murdered. This was to be able to bath in their blood. She believed bathing in the blood of virgins would help her retain youth. Cut to hundreds of years later when Earthly life moved into modern technological times in the 1980's, 1990's, 2000's and beyond. Popular culture in Entertainment became more about visual appearances in the music industry, rather than making and playing great music. Magazines airbrushed their models and celebrities almost to the point of making them unrecognizable in some cases. Even the most amateur photographer on the planet who enjoys taking their daily selfies will ensure that the filters are just right. The photos must appear attractive enough to post for validation and praise. There have also been endless cases of people getting killed or falling off a cliff by trying to take that perfect selfie or shot to gain more likes and followers. Chasing numbers that become irrelevant and obsolete when you exit this plane.

This all stems from the ego part of the soul's core desire of longing to be loved, admired, and praised. Some desire praise and attention more than others to the degree of extremism. A soul was born out of love and will die right back into that love. It moves about in a human body longing to be hugged, cuddled, and loved up. When that love is starved from their existence, they may harden and toughen up, become distant, aloof, and indifferent. Or they may head in the opposite direction and compensate by trying anything and everything to find ways to gain that praise and admiration that never sticks. Any validation lasts for a millisecond until they notice that people have moved onto other things and no longer have any interest in them again. It's dangerous to place your well-being state in the hands of others. Relying on people online and around you to continuously prop you up and feel good about yourself can become tiresome from all aspects. Love yourself and all that you are now.

The body is temporary and aging every second until it stops working and disintegrates. This scares some causing them to be unsure of what happens after that. They may believe there is life after death or they're hesitant because they don't see it with their own eyes. The one thing everyone agrees on is that we will all cease to live on this planet forever. Those that invested deeply into the physical material world may have the greatest fear involved. The reality check will hit them on their deathbed when the material and physical fades away.

As you grow older and your soul consciousness evolves, then this can help some in becoming more fearless when it comes to death because you know it's coming. You reach the realization that you don't have a choice and you must find a way to strengthen your faith and resolve. This is partially why you may have noticed that as one grows older their spiritual belief system seems to become stronger. This is the case even if they were a non-believer in younger age. Perhaps they won't suddenly believe in God, but they will grow more open minded of the possibilities of something good beyond their Earthly life. They subconsciously know that their body will permanently stop working for good. It will shut down and become lifeless. They may hopefully see that their soul consciousness is somewhere in there and that it will continue on.

The human bodies were not designed to live forever. You reach older age signified by your physical body aging and eventually shutting down. The body will die, and the soul will exit and move on to new destinies. There is no way around that. No one would want to live on this planet forever since back home is where the true fun and serenity exists full time. You are with those in your soul tribe, whereas on Earth you are mixed in with all souls in various levels of growth. Many of those souls use enormous amounts of dark ego, which dominates over their higher self. This is what causes so much unrest and unhappiness on the planet.

During the dawn of the first human civilization, people were living to be hundreds of years old because diseases were rare, diets weren't tampered with the way they are now, and stresses were low. All of that changed and transformed as human beings began to decide how people should live. They designed and created a life that has ended up creating more stress. They started to mess with foods and diets in a way that has slowly killed people off early. Diseases, health issues, and plagues were bred as a result. The average human being was passing on in their age thirties. This has been reversed to one degree where lives have been extended significantly by the healthier choices many make. People are also having access to better medical resources that didn't exist centuries ago. The ever growing and expanding spiritual metaphysical movement has been helping to make one another's souls more aware, conscious, and enlightened about life beyond the physical and superficial.

At the same time, many are passing on early due to heart related issues, which is connected to the stress filled lives that many live. When it becomes all about making money and working for the sake of working, this puts on stress, especially if you're not doing work that is done out of love, or for the sheer passion and enjoyment of it. Some are working with people that are irritating or stressful on a regular basis, which has a negative toxic affect. They infiltrate that onto others with the intention of crushing that person's life force and well-being state. Energy expands and flows around you and it will hit all those in your line of fire regardless if it's good or bad.

God and the Angels are egoless, which means they're not bothered or affected by the damage humankind causes on one another. This isn't to say they don't have a conscious. They have the biggest consciousness that exists. They're not emotionally affected by anything the way human ego is. There are beings in the spirit world that have an ego, but it is not the dark ego that plagues humankind. These are the spirit guides, saints, beings from realm worlds, and departed loved ones. They are affected and bothered by humanities treatment of one another, but not to the degree that a human being might be. They don't have the same ego that human beings have because their ego is highly evolved, aware, and in check. They'll view it the way an activist might when reading terrible news about something being taken away from another person. It's observed with an emotional detachment

Heaven has never been terribly pleased with the direction and state the planet has gone down no matter what period of history it's in, yet they are aware there are many spirit beings all over the planet doing their part to contribute something positive towards humanity that is aligned with love. These souls incarnated on the planet to contribute to the betterment of life on Earth. The goal of spirit is to bring all into a higher evolving consciousness and vibrational state possible, so that Heaven can exist on Earth. It will take centuries to reach that state if at all. You can see this as being the case if you examine the barbaric nature of human beings throughout history. That toxic monster nature is still present on the planet, but instead of nailing people to a cross or violently killing them, the toxicity resides and expresses itself through other people's feelings and thoughts through a technological device.

There is goodness threaded out amidst the darkness of the world. The good deeds taking place are enacted without the desire for anything in return. Because it's seemingly rare, when it does happen, you're floored and prompted to take a step back in stunned amazement.

The love available from above never ceases all throughout any personal ordeal. This is also to help face the soul in the direction of this source of love. It's only hoped the soul can snap back into the true higher consciousness to realize that none of the drama around them matters, and nor is it based in reality. You've given your power away to a ruler or a group thinking they have jurisdiction to help you feel better.

Those good well-being feelings you're attempting to access are built into you available for accessibility. You don't need a group to prop you up in the end. Maybe you did in the beginning as you wore the training armor to get your feet wet and to help you grow strong, but in the end, it was never needed.

You might show love to the Universe, your guides, your team, God, and all in Heaven, but it's not because they are soaking up the love you return tenfold. They have no ego and have no desire for those elements because that love is already built into them. The love essence is their true nature, so they don't desire something they already have. Those same love elements are also a part of every soul on Earth, even though it might seem as if someone has strayed far away from it through poor actions, behavior, or cruel words. Heaven is so busy loving that they are impartial to whether you love them back.

Reaching that moment of awareness and awakening is one of the greatest gifts you can give your soul. You become that much closer to transcending utopia. A personal awakening of the soul consciousness is like the rapture where the trumpet blows, and the sky parts, and the Archangel descends with a shout! This is the moment when light is shed onto your consciousness and you see things you hadn't noticed before. The answer was always there, but it was as if you were previously living in darkness. It's a beautiful incredible feeling reaching that state of knowingness. The truth was always in front of you, but you hadn't paid much attention to it until that moment of awareness that feels like a magnificent exhilarated release. Only then are you taking your first baby steps into utopia.

CHAPTER SEVENTEEN

*Soul Growth Through
Emotional Healing*

When seeking to convey optimistic positivity, it cannot be a forced fake positivity since that energy is picked up on as negative. It's like putting a Band-Aid over a cut. The cut is still there as an open wound, but hidden underneath the Band-Aid. Your fake positivity is the cut covered by a Band-Aid. The Universe and Heaven know your general state even if you try and fake it. You cannot get away with a lie or hide anything from any being in Heaven. They all know what you are hiding underneath the essence of that energy. What you do, say, feel, or think is in plain view to them. This is the case even if your actions are different than how or what you feel or think.

Sometimes you can be putting on the happy face, when deep down you're miserable. You may not even be conscious of doing that. If you realize you have been conveying a fake positivity where you show the world your optimism, but deep down you're hurting or in mental or emotional pain, then that is the first step towards spiritual recovery. You've admitted you're battling while putting on that smile to others.

If someone you were in love with rejected or left you, then it is absurd to assume you're going to bounce back an hour after they left and dive right back into life like it never happened, unless you are a gifted sociopath with no emotions. You're going to feel the gamut of challenging feelings that may last one week, or it could last one year. For some it may be even longer than that depending on how attached to the person you were. I've witnessed cases where someone never truly bounces back after that. They are forever shaped and molded a different way than they had started out due to the traumatic experience.

You would understandably experience upset, hurt, and sadness over something like that. You are unable to pull through and want to stay in bed all day. Even when you push yourself to get outside and continue to live, you experience the kind of pain that feels as if something important was ripped out of you.

To shift that wide discord, you move through the many emotional stages one experiences with something like that. Take your time, allow yourself to process it, and make sense of what's happened. Move through the various stages of grief in your own personal way that ranges from depression and sadness, to anger and rage. You'll hopefully talk about it with a friend, a counselor, or anyone that will listen. You can also write your feelings down in a word document, journal, or an email to yourself and file it away. This is to help get it out of you. Eventually you move out of those challenging emotions as you take your time processing each one.

The healing process concludes when you can move past those negative feeling emotions and into a state where you are willing and ready to accept and release the person that has hurt you. When you release that person, then you do it with love. Meaning there is no additional pain or malice in your heart for them. You're not condoning any bad behavior they might have done, but you are kicking out any pain that attached itself to you out of your vicinity. You no longer need it. Abuse done to you is not your fault. If you instigated something, then apologize to the person and forgive yourself for the ill will you might have caused, then release it and let it go. You don't want to carry that pain around indefinitely.

Work on getting yourself into that place where you will positively be better off without that person that caused you pain. You mentally thank them for the experience; "I bless you on your path." And then you release it and let it go.

There is no time limit as to how long it can take when it comes to moving through a healing process. This can be healing over anything, such as any kind of hurt or upset in your life, regardless of what it is. For some people it can take weeks or months, and others it may take years. There are cases where some get stuck in that cycle of hurt that lasts indefinitely for years and sometimes decades if not treated or healed. The tragedy with the latter is they remain in the exact same space they were when the initial upset happened. Sometimes you may not even be aware that you're still stuck in a cycle due to something from the past.

An example might be someone who was married for decades, and then an affair breaks up the marriage. This is followed by Divorce and all the stresses that come out of that. The person cheated on might carry the cheater in their aura until they release it. It is understandable that one would be upset by this kind of abrupt life circumstance that throws you a hard-right punch, but you don't want to let it stay with you for too long. The longer it stays with you, then the longer it becomes a part of you. It has the danger of shaping you into someone you might not want to become.

Where it gets exceptionally tricky is when the pain endures for years. The person never quite bounces back into life again. They just go through the motions numbed to everyone and everything around them. They become inaccessible for the right new partner or circumstance to come into their life. It also blocks the flow of abundance from coming in.

I understand this well having been through that in personal experiences. Years in I've hardened and become more difficult to get close to. Through my connections with God, I begin to see it all unravel before me. I receive that high awareness I hadn't noticed before. I mentally went back into time to try and find out when I changed or was changing. Nine times out of ten, I wound up tracing it back to some kind of traumatic experience, such as a love relationship break up or childhood abuse.

In the past, I've discussed the importance of taking those moments throughout your life to do a thorough life review. This has so many benefits that include going backwards into time to make note of the significant life circumstances that took place in your life, whether good or bad. Make note of what transpired out of that. How it might have changed you for better or worse. The worst is not about judging you. It's making amends for what changed certain traits that you're not particularly fond of, but you don't know how to change it. Acknowledging it is an important step towards changing it. You cannot change something you're unaware of.

Many years have passed after you emotionally shut down following a traumatic event, crises, or break up. You may one day awaken to realize that you had been stagnant for so long and are not sure why. This is because the incident that kicked that off was so long ago by that point, but your overall nature, personality, and demeanor had permanently changed to who you've become today. It's only when you stop to ponder and re-trace your steps backwards when you realize that who you are today was kicked off by traumatic events years prior. You had long forgotten about it, but it had also shifted your behavior patterns in the process to who you've become now. This is that moment of awakening and clarity or as some say, "A-ha! Wow, I can't believe how drastically that situation changed me. I need to do something about this today!"

The process of positive change begins at that moment you gained clarity and awareness.

You've admitted there's a problem rumbling within you. What a fantastic awareness level to reach and achieve for your soul's consciousness. Because now you can begin the steps to work on healing those open wounds that caused you to deny your feelings and prevented you from moving forward and onward with life. You want to attract in a positive abundant feeling, but you wrestle with that due to the hard life circumstances that have thrown you one curve ball after another.

Heal emotional wounds through awareness, putting in the daily work, and bringing in a counselor, healer, or therapist if you're able to. If that's not feasible for any reason such as financial, seek out groups online that share your difficulties. Having camaraderie support or others to talk to that are going through a similar circumstance has more of a positive than challenging effect. The positive effect is this can empower the both of you to stand tall and into your own. It produces healing in a quicker way than if you didn't have that support.

The challenging side can be if neither party are interested in healing and just want to rehash past circumstances for months and years longer than necessary that it turns into gossip and vengeful thoughts. This leaves you stuck in that dark state. If you've sought out help, then that means you've already surpassed the first step of being aware that you are wrestling with something difficult. Deep down you want it to stop and are ready for help. You begin the process of seeking out that assistance. You have the intention and desire to do what you can to help you through a negative chapter in your life.

I personally turn to prayer for assistance and intervention when healing is needed. Ask God and your Spirit team to work through you and to help you heal and guide you towards steps on how to do that. Request that you be helped to understand what it is you need, and to assist you in taking notice of when He is helping. Ask that He help you understand by putting that assistance in your path.

There are times that God and spirit are putting helpful signs in front of you, but when you're wallowing in a negative state you might not notice it, since a negative state can block Divine communication. Fear not since He is always with you and will continue to put that help in front of you indefinitely until you notice it. You will wake up one day and get that bright idea that puts you into action mode. When the answer appears, it feels like it had always been there, but you hadn't noticed it until that moment.

Your emotional healing may leave a scar the way a deep cut on your body can. The wound is healed enough that it makes you whole again. "Whole again" is the perfect exceptional state you were in upon birth.

I've talked to people who have massive anger issues. They admit it's caused a ton of problems in their life, but they cannot control it. Admitting you have a problem is one of the best first steps you can take that will adjust your soul and body down the path of beautiful magnificent recovery. What an amazing gift that is to be blessed with knowingness.

Have it in your mind that you want to do the work in order to make your peace with any ill will you might have caused another person or what someone else might have caused you. This is regardless if it was you causing pain for another person or you were just cruel to yourself.

You can be cruel to yourself through self-hate by your actions, thoughts, words, and feelings. You can be cruel to yourself with the addictions and toxins you continuously put into your body knowing it can result in harm. You can be cruel to yourself by saying yes to things that deep down don't feel right to you. Learning to tell others no are also a purpose some need to learn this lifetime. Naturally, there are circumstances where you do have to suck it up and say yes, such as if it is a part of your job you get paid for. This isn't about that, but about the things that morally and spiritually affect you in a negative way where you can truly say no. Your boss needs you to fax something; well of course you do that. A friend keeps asking you to do something you're uncomfortable with. Saying no to that is not being rude or unaccommodating. Saying no is saying yes to you.

This illustration is mentioned because it influences your overall well-being as well as the process of positive manifestation and abundance attracting. If you remain in a negative cycle, then this will leave your soul's life trajectory on pause for as long as it takes before you begin moving out of that state.

This applies to whatever upsetting traumatic circumstance has taken place in your life. You want to work on moving through those emotional changes associated with the experience while eventually reaching a place where you can release it. This isn't just to benefit you, your body, mind, and soul, but it also assists in helping you to continue living this life you've been blessed with. Bad experiences happen on some level for everyone, even the most seemingly privileged person. No one is exempt from enduring some form of rock and roll in their life.

Experiences both good and bad are designed to teach you lessons that positively affect your soul's growth process. The higher level your soul reaches, the greater the abundant attraction quotient is. Abundance being about your overall state of mind, rather than financial increases. The desire for riches is a hollow goal that does not fulfill in the end. Having enough income coming in can certainly bring you less stress in your life to one extent. This is in the ways that it would allow you to quit a soul crushing day job and dive into work that is your passion and life purpose. The income gained should be used to continue improving your soul while giving you more time and energy to apply towards your passionate soul driven life purpose work that helps others.

You may be perfectly content today, even though you might have endured traumatic experiences earlier in life, such as in childhood, but if you have not made your peace with what happened to you in an earlier part of your life, then you are subconsciously carrying that around with you even if you've suppressed it. This also influences your manifestation process today.

If you're attempting to examine your life today to see what could be blocking the positive flow of abundance and none is evident, then move further back into time to see what wounds have yet to be healed. Sometimes journaling, writing about it, or talking about it can help get it out of you to make your peace with it. Another additional way is to find a comfortable spot in a nature setting or a private space at home to commune with God regularly. Even though you can conduct prayer anywhere you like from walking to your car, sitting in traffic, or while you're getting ready for the day. The benefit of finding a space to have an in-depth prayer session is that it helps you be distraction free in order to fully focus on any guidance that is coming in. Ask Heaven what needs to be healed in your life. This can include old forgotten wounds that are still present in your subconscious. This will help increase the flow of positive abundance energy.

CHAPTER EIGHTEEN

*The Human Influences
on the Soul Consciousness*

You are a conscious, thinking, feeling, soul light born out of love and having a physical human experience. At the beginning of your Earthly life, you were born profoundly psychic and in tune to all that is around you. This is the natural state of your soul since its conception. You basked in the traits of love, joy, and peace full time while in it. This is your true soul's essence. Whenever you stray outside of that you are no longer aligned with God or higher-level Spirit beings in Heaven. Instead, the Darkness has infiltrated your aura and your ego has risen and taken over your soul's true essence.

You were born with an ego that expands as it enters the Earth's atmosphere. This ego causes you to struggle and have conflicts as it attempts to take over you and dominate your actions, thoughts, and feelings. When your ego runs recklessly it grows and expands into darkness. The dark ego is what prompts you to wrestle with challenges in this lifetime. It is also what causes all the chaos, violence, hatred, and havoc on Earth.

These challenges you struggle with were called sin during ancient times, even though some circles continue to keep the word alive. In the modern-day world, the word sin is best understood as challenges. The sins committed can delay you on your path and wreak havoc on your soul's innate system. This innate system is the higher self part of you that governs your life through a broader perspective.

The seven deadly sins were created in order to assist human souls in making sounder choices. As time progressed, these sins were soon viewed as extreme depending on who was executing them. This eventually tainted the deadly sins into something evil.

They were disregarded and not taken seriously except in smaller religious based circles. Although the seven deadly sins have underlying religious based tones, they are challenges that all human souls wrestle with to one degree or another regardless of religion. When you're deeply absorbed in toxic challenges, then it causes an array of issues and complications on your life path. These sins or challenges prevent the positive flow of energy and abundance in your life. They also play a hand at creating a block that stops up the communication line with your Spirit team.

As you grew from infant into childhood, the peers, community, and society around you played a major hand at your developmental process. They implemented belief systems and values that although might have been brought to you without malice, they often ultimately erected blocks on your soul's path. It's stalled the soul's consciousness from evolving, as well as dimmed the communication line with Heaven. As a result, you might have questioned the existence of anything outside of yourself because you stopped picking up any signs of your Spirit teams' guidance and messages. You can tell if this is the case or not by going back into time and remembering how you were raised and what those around you were like.

How much of your values and ways of living today are similar to what your caregivers and peers were like growing up? If they are on par and similar, then this is an example of how you were heavily influenced by those around you. If you're a Christian, Buddhist, or Muslim, and so we're most of those around you growing up, then this is another sign of being influenced by your surroundings. You adopted the way of life you were taught by those in your vicinity. This doesn't necessarily mean it's a bad thing. It's pointing out how human behavior is influenced by its surroundings. You're examining how those around you today have heavily influenced your values and beliefs. This continues into adulthood as you adopt new values and beliefs that your new social circles follow.

If you're in love with a potential political ruler or candidate, odds may be that your peers have the same love. If it's not a candidate, then it's a political party. Some will stand firm on their personal moral rule that they cannot be friends with anyone who does not share their beliefs or values. They might deny this and emphatically ensure they love all, but this turns out to not be the case when an isolated circumstance pushes them to reconsider their tolerance level. This is especially the case where religion and politics are concerned. Two topics that should never be discussed at a dinner gathering or at work. Those with differing opinions cannot be convinced to see it your way and vice versa. The irony is you learn more lessons from those that have little to nothing in common from you.

You can be friends with those who have diverse political or religious beliefs from yourself, and still be able to remain close because you have other elements outside of that which bring you together. You naturally don't get into conversations on topics where you know it is opposing of one another. And when you do discuss it, you are respectful of one another's beliefs. You are coming at it from an emotionally detached intellectual perspective. This is a sign that your soul consciousness is accelerating.

Someone who came into this lifetime as a homosexual can be a friend with someone who grew up Christian in this lifetime. This is as long as the Christian has no issues with their friend who is gay and vice versa. It would be debatable on how close of a friend two people are if a big part of them is rejected by their friend.

Christians receive a bad knock because the media has focused heavily on the ones that claim that being homosexual is a sin. The real sin is those absolved in the seven deadly sins, which include Pride (judgment) and Wrath (hate). Heaven has taught me over the years that there is nothing sinful about two souls coming together in love, regardless of their human physical gender. Human souls have free will choice to believe what they want to believe, even if it's not based in reality.

There are a great many wonderful loving Christians who love all souls without conditions, as long as the soul is not hurting anyone. You rarely hear about them because the media finds anything connected to goodness to be too boring for a story or worth talking about. The ego is driven by fear, which is easy to create on this planet.

The world witnesses someone preaching hate, but then you investigate how that person was raised only to discover that this person's caregivers and surroundings were like that as well too. There are cases where someone's values are erroneously distinctive. You were raised in a positively joyful home with suitable values, but you dart off in the opposite direction into a life of hate or negativity. Every human soul being is a complex character with a mixture of attributes that comes in from various sources. The best parts of a human soul are the ones that are a part of God. The worst parts are where the ego has been led astray.

CHAPTER NINETEEN

*Spirit Guides
and Guardian Angels*

As we bring this to a close, let's take a look at a key factor that can help in continuing to evolve your soul consciousness. Every soul on the planet without exception has psychic senses that enable them to connect with their own Spirit team of guardians that work to guide you on your path. In order to easily access God and evolve your soul's consciousness and life purpose, He gives each soul at least one main Spirit Guide and one Guardian Angel to assist and guide where needed throughout your Earthly life. Communicating with your Guide and Angel is communicating with God. They are His hands and arms, so you are communicating with Him. Your Guide and Angel are with you from your human birth until your human death. Before you are born into an Earthly life, you commune with your Spirit team that consists of one Guide and one Angel.

It's your Guardian Angel that will be there for you during the moments when emotional healing is needed. Your Spirit Guide works with you on the practical survival stuff. For instance, your upset about a breakup that happened or the death of a loved one, then your angel comes to your side. You're having trouble finding a job, a new apartment/home, or relationship, and then your Spirit Guide would help with that. It's not that cut and dry, since they both work overtime on guiding you over little day to day things too, but this is what their roles tend to be like.

A person's Guardian Angel and Spirit Guide are always near the person they're assigned to in many ways on varying levels. Being connected to them is like having a best friend in another dimension. Like God, these are beings that know everything about you, all the good and the bad. They know your thoughts and feelings, the things you hide, the things you reveal, and yet they never leave your side. They also continue to love you unconditionally no matter how horrific a human crime you've done, which isn't saying that you won't need to pay for that crime depending on the severity. This is the same love God has for all of his Children of souls.

One of their jobs is to support and guide you towards and down the right path that helps in fulfilling the terms of your soul contract. This includes through paying for karma created as well too. When you act out and cause trouble in school, then you're sent to the Principles office to be disciplined. The soul class works in a similar way, but some of the soul crimes are not all the same as the Earthly crimes. If you're headed towards danger, then they do their best to stop you or steer you away from that. Therefore, it's important to be clear minded and to develop a strong connection with them. It helps you decipher between a good decision and a bad one when you're tuned in to them daily.

Guides communicate through your psychic clair senses. There are psychic clair *(clear)* channel senses within every soul, but there are four primary clairs. They are Clairvoyance *(clear seeing)*, Clairsentience *(clear feeling)*, Clairaudience *(clear hearing)* and Claircognizance *(clear knowing)*. These clairs are the psychic channel sense frequencies in which you communicate with God or any spirit soul being in Heaven.

You were intended to have a strong connection and communication line with Heaven, so that you don't have to go through this life alone. You don't have to always figure it out for yourself when you have this Spirit team waiting in the wings 24/7 wherever you are. Your psychic gifts are not a gift at all as its part of who you are. It is already built into the core part of your soul.

Your core Spirit team is of the many that greet you as you enter the gates of Heaven. They are your team who works with you guiding you away from harm and down the path that benefits your higher self. In a sense, they do their best to help you along your life's path. This can be to assist you in picking out a school or trade course aligned with your purpose, or to finding a job, an apartment, or potential love interest that will be beneficial for you. They help with the small details in your life that you may be oblivious too.

One of the other reasons your guardians are with you is in order to assist you in accomplishing the varying purposes you agreed upon prior to entering an Earthly life. They are also present in orchestrating situations that will be benefit to your soul's growth.

If you are someone with a strong connection with the Other Side, you pray to God regularly, you're going through tough human life experiences, or have a purpose that is beneficial to the betterment of humanity and this planet, then you likely have more than one guide or angel outside of your primary heavenly teammate duo. Even though your team is with you, often many are unaware of their presence. Your team and any soul being in Heaven cannot intervene or assist you in your life without your expressed permission. This is due to that free will law previously mentioned. The law says you will need to request your Spirit team's assistance or guidance. This is also why so many people are led astray down inappropriate or harmful roads. They may not be asking their Spirit team to work with them daily. They also may not believe that there is such a thing or they're ignoring the perpetual warnings from spirit.

For the most part, your Spirit team will assist a human soul by giving them nudges to head in a direction that will positively benefit them. They will communicate with that soul through their psychic senses and hope the human soul is paying attention. Their job is to help you make sounder choices, but as for anything outside of that, they need your permission. You can give them permission in prayer, affirmations, with your thoughts, out loud, or in writing. You can write them an email and send it to yourself. You call to them and say something like, "I give you permission to intervene with…"

It doesn't matter how you say it, just as long as you let them know. Your soul is built with innate crystal-clear psychic senses for a reason. This is to make your life as comfortable as possible even when you're faced with challenges. The challenges are not as bad as they would be without your strong connection with Heaven. They help you make smarter choices by guiding you through them.

Everyone is born with all psychic clair channels, but typically one or two of the channels are stronger than the others. If you feel that you do not have any clair channels, then that means there are blocks that have closed it up, because everyone has these clairs. No one is more special than anyone else where psychic abilities are concerned. Everyone has varying ways in which they communicate and pick up on Divine assistance.

Someone might have a stronger Clairaudience channel where they hear the voice of spirit, while another person might have a strong sense of knowing the answers. Others feel the guidance coming into them, and then you have the Clairvoyants who receive messages through visual cues. The clairs are always there and accessible to you. They can be opened up when you make healthy positive life changes. When you govern your life through negativity, then this closes the psychic clair channels up. This means that your moods, thoughts, and feelings affect the extra sensory part of you.

When you regularly fall down the path of abusing a toxic challenge, then you will find your clair channels dim to the point that you're unaware of these senses being present at all. Those who run around making negative based comments vocally, or online, have zero connection with anything outside of themselves at that moment. If they do this regularly, then they are indefinitely disconnected from God. A soulless being is someone that does this on a frequent basis. This type of egoist criticism does nothing to help anyone. It doesn't help anyone reading those comments and absorbing the energy surrounding those words. They have no connection to anything outside of the physical. Those connected with Heaven operate from a higher space than those bathed in hate and negativity. This includes spiritually based people, since no one of any group is exempt from hanging out in the areas of negativity, including myself. This is part of the challenges of the physical human life to overcome.

Many are aware that everyone has one main spirit guide and one guardian angel that is with you from the moment you're born in a human body to the moment you depart that human body. If you haven't seen them through Clairvoyance throughout your Earthly life, then when you cross over back home you most definitely will see them in front of you as clear as the day. You will instantly know them like running into a friend you hadn't seen in a while. This realization is immediate and automatic.

When one talks about you having one main spirit guide and guardian angel, what is often left out is how are they with you from human birth and human death? What if someone is a couch potato that sits and watches trash television all day, then gossips on the phone when there is another lull? Is this magnificent Spirit Guide and Guardian Angel hanging around on the couch with that person? I don't know about you, but I'd slit my wrists if I was stuck guiding someone like that. In spiritual reality, I wouldn't feel like a failure that I'm unable to reach that person at all throughout their life, because feelings like failure are non-existent on the Other Side. You just keep trying to get that person's attention repeatedly throughout their life and hope for the best.

The Spirit Guide and Guardian Angel are with the soul in the human body they've soul contractually agreed to be with, stand by, and guide. They are not hanging around the person 24/7 for decades or however long that person lives. The guide and angel have other things they are doing on the Other Side. They are alerted to oncoming danger before it takes place because their psychic foresight is at the 100% mark. They know all before anyone does or says anything the same way God does. They can see the projected outcome of this circumstance coming in before it happens. They can then guide the soul away from that danger. There is never an incident where a Spirit Guide or Guardian Angel is late to an incident. It's impossible due to their psychic radar and the incredible access they have to that person's complicating and intricate soul records. They know what's about to take place. If a person is operating with free will, which many tend to do, and they're heading for danger, the guide and angel are alerted way in advance of a probable outcome that's about to happen, so they have plenty of time to warn the person. At that point, they can only hope that the person is tuned in enough to pick up on those warnings.

One of the benefits of being in constant communication with God and your Spirit team is that they become a part of your daily life. When you are talking to them about an issue that's popped up that someone else did that affected you, they are already there and present to help you do something about it so that you can move on from it and onto more important things.

My mother recalled a story when I was eight years old and accompanied her at the local mall. I walked away from her independently as I tend to still do today with everyone it seems. She was looking around to see where I went and found me staring at this shelf filled with angel statues. She said she remembers I had a furious expression on my face. Perplexed while watching me turn towards her angrily shouting while pointing to the statues, "Why are they all blonde with wings?! That's not how they look!"

Ah, the injustice was boiling the inner waters of this warrior soul to a furious rage. That's because the depiction of angels in artwork has forever presented angels in a manner that is inaccurate to what they truly look like, but instead in a way that is more comfortable for people to accept.

One of the other things that would cause a sneer is that guardian angel depictions are usually cutesy cherub little fluffy angels. It's no wonder there are so many skeptics, because no reasonable and rational person could possibly believe they look like cute cuddly stuffed animals. There are cherub looking angels on the Other Side, but they deal more with matters of love, and they are far from cuddly. I'm thinking of the Munchkins in the Wizard of Oz. Ferocious with grand reasonable personalities.

For centuries, there have been countless stories of people encountering an angel in physical form. This is from both believers and non-believers alike. They've been recounted in every holy book in every religion known to man. Regardless of someone's personal belief system, nearly 80% of the planet has a strong belief in angels even if they're not religious. That's every 8 out of 10 people. This is because when they encounter one on those rare occasions there is no doubt. Many that have had angel encounters protested to not believing "in any of that". This changed after the encounter that was deep and profound enough that it altered their conscious perception. Many have experienced similar encounters with an angel especially during traumatic or dire circumstances. Those are the venues where an angel makes its presence known. Angels tend to show up just as the person needs it. It's those little reminders that tell you that you are not alone.

Angels show up and hear your prayers and remain present during a time that it's most needed, especially for those with rapidly failing health. When it's someone's time to go back home to Heaven, then the angels and that person's Spirit team along with other beings from Heaven is standing around that person working double time. It's kind of like when an entire family goes to pick someone up at the airport and arrives just before the person has landed. You're standing around waiting for their arrival to pick them up and take them with you. There is often more than one spirit being waiting along with the Archangel Azrael, the angel of death, which is not as cryptic as that sounds. If the person is in the hospital, but has three months to live, then in addition to that persons Spirit team being present throughout, deceased relatives begin flocking within the last number of days as well too.

Angels don't have eyes, as creepy as that might sound to imagine, because we're used to everyone having eyes. They also don't have an anatomy. Even though paintings of angels show them as looking like human beings. In movies they're made to look like us, so everyone thinks or believes they look like a man or a woman.

Angels are a magnificent bright light source created out of God's fire to act as His trusty strong and compassionate assistants. Like all beings, angels can and do morph into the appearance of something human. When they do morph into a human being, their eyes are one of the first initial ways to recognize them, because their eyes, which can be any color, are striking and pierce through you.

When people have had angel encounters, they know without a doubt that it was an angel regardless of how it appeared.

My mother once asked, "Where do you get your great sense of humor? It can't be from any of us."

I said without hesitation, "From the Angels."

Because contrary to some beliefs about Heaven being this cold dark place where judgment occurs, they tend to exude traits of joy, humor, and laughter. When you spend enough time with them, then it will rub off on you as it does with me.

You create your circumstances through your intention. Avoid falling into a victim mentality where you blame everything that goes wrong in your life on other people. Or that you did something to make it happen or must have done something bad in another life to deserve it. No one deserves bad things to happen to them, but you have the gift of standing in your power and taking control of your life. You don't have to do it alone when you have God on your side.

When you pay attention to your Spirit team, then you can pick up on when they are guiding you away from harm, or when they guide you towards helpful circumstances. A common theme of the ego is living in denial of the truth. You deny the messages because it's not what you want to hear. It is displeasing to the human ego. Sometimes the messages intended to assist are guiding someone to do something they're against. This can be a circumstance where you're consistently guided to let go of the possibility of a love relationship with someone you desire. Your Spirit team can see how it will end up ahead and it will not end happily in your favor. Or they see the Soul Mate relationship partner you're contracted to connect with coming in soon. Being with the wrong person may delay the connection from happening.

How many times have you received a nudge to go down one road, but instead you went down another? The result was that something negative or challenging popped up in your life. You later say, "I knew I shouldn't have gone down that road. I sensed something was up, but I ignored that feeling." This is a clue as to how your Spirit team is working with you.

The ways people connect with Heaven are vast and varying from one person to the next. Many of my books include the different ways that can assist someone in being a stronger conduit. This includes a lifestyle and attitude perception change that needs to be adopted. This is from the way you think and feel to what you ingest into your physical body.

When you shift direction and embark on a beautiful personal spiritual journey, then you will find wonderful and amazing new circumstances rise up. Even if this is a feeling and state of mind. This state of mind is where true bliss resides. There is no end date, time limit, or rush to reach the destination you're hoping to achieve. Take your time with it and follow your gut instincts on what action steps to take.

Some try so hard to make a connection with God not realizing that it's the trying so hard part that pushes the connection away. Most of the time the connection with Heaven happens when you're not trying so hard. When you let go of the control, then it comes. This is what that phrase, "Let go and Let God", means. Learn to know yourself better than anybody. Trust your initial gut reaction to hunches that hit you. When you second-guess the message, you believe you're picking up on, then you move further away from the message or guidance you originally got. If you're receiving a strong hunch that continuously comes to you, then make note of that. The hunch will be something positive that does no harm to anyone, including yourself. Moving your well-being state into that of relaxation, open mindedness, and clarity helps in accessing Spirit easily and as naturally as you pick up the phone to call someone.

CHAPTER TWENTY

The Shift in Global Consciousness

A great deal of this chapter was spearheaded by one of my guides, Saint Nathaniel. We cannot willfully deny that there is a shift in consciousness taking place around the world within each individual soul. It has been this way since the dawn of humankind. It takes centuries for human souls to evolve. When you examine Earth's history, you will note how long it's taken for human beings to evolve. It's been repetitively unnecessarily violent, negative, and filled with hate. This is still going on today in a larger way due to how many people have populated the planet over the centuries. You give as many of them as possible access to a technological device with access to social media and you have a deadly weapon on your hands. While we insist and urge one to display love whenever possible, it cannot be denied that the state of humanity is chaotic. This disorder is what will break the dam that allows a shift in consciousness. This madness has been going on throughout the centuries of Earth's history and progression. As the population of human souls has grown - so has pandemonium.

When you experience constant discomfort internally with amplified emotions, then this may feel to be connected to a shift in consciousness. While this is true to an extent, it is more multifaceted than that for us to place a label on it. Humankind desires labels in order to understand circumstances and people in a broader way. The negative side to labels is when you use it to create separation from one another. Any negative feelings prolonged in you can have a variety of factors attributed to it. These factors and effects are connected to the way humankind has designed Earthly life to be with its structures and rules. While having structure and discipline is important to a degree in order to minimize ego generated chaos, it also creates havoc depending on how restricting you are with others.

Someone experiencing prolonged discomfort internally may have developed this at the hands of other people, their surroundings, the boom and noise of technology, lack of exercise, poor diets, and lifestyle choices. These are some of the potential major contributors towards these turbulent feelings. Forcing one into a corner experiencing these symptoms does and can contribute towards that soul having a shift in consciousness. A great awakening and shift in consciousness happens with a human being when they reach a breaking point at some moment in their life. They come to realize that human life and the toxic negativity that exists globally or within their personal life does not make their soul happy. They begin asking the bigger questions such as, "Why am I here? Why does this place exist? There is nothing but anger, chaos, hate, judgment, unfaithfulness, and so on…"

Someone hurts another and that soul's ego feels scarred as a result. They cannot understand how someone can do something to be cruel to another and feel nothing. Someone that feels nothing and acts out violently towards another is someone without consciousness. Although it seems they have no consciousness, they have one in the deepest core of their soul that sits burning like a pilot light waiting to be ignited. Until then they have an aloof detachment from their soul and everything beyond the physical reality they've created.

We've spoken before about the Mayan Calendar and its effects or non-effects long before December 21, 2012, which was the day believed to be the end of the world. The reason we've never gone any further in depth is because there is nothing to talk about. This was a fad that caught on around the globe and had no bearing on anything legitimate. We said December 21, 2012 will come and go like any other day. The day did come and go with no noticeable shift or ending of Earth. The talk began to build in your year 2012 as you moved closer to 12/21/12. The Mayans did not make any sort of prediction that the end of the world would be on this date and nor was a shift intended to take place at that time. The Mayans ended the Calendar on December 21, 2012 because others invaded them outside of their tribe forcing them to abandon the project. We ask of you this, to look deeper into how orchestrated was this at that particular time.

Human ego loves to create hype and drama. With that comes temporary excitement or fear energy that the end is near. The ego also enjoys capitalizing on fear for personal gain. There were movies and books put out about the year 2012 and its significance, as well as for entertainment. If you research history throughout the years, you'll discover that there has always been some measure of apocalyptic scare talk every year. This talk is born out of fear. Fear is connected to the ego.

In some circles they turned this fear energy into something positive such as December 21, 2012 being a day where a global shift would take place and usher the universe into a new era. A new era has occurred periodically over the centuries regardless of the Calendar date. This happens as humankind evolves at a slower rate towards the realization that your soul's life is and should be about love. It is not about pushing others down, bullying, or creating a structure of life that contributes to long-term stress, unhappiness, or early intended human death. Love is what thrives and carries on indefinitely. Love feels good to your soul. It uplifts and adds a euphoric feeling of joy and peace to your life. Love blasts away negativity and heals the soul. It empowers and contributes to helping the soul achieve greater heights of consciousness.

There was a tragedy that hit the news on December 14, 2012 that involved a young man going on a shooting rampage in Connecticut. There was another shooting just days before that at a mall in Oregon. This prompted some to believe that it was somehow related and connected to "doomsday" on December 21, 2012. Those acts were committed by the free will of people that were not mentally balanced and should have been given help, but the guidance provided was ignored. When you're disconnected to your soul and anything outside of the material world, then you grow oblivious to the signs where someone is in desperate need of love or intervention.

The world is currently continuing to shift for the better and has been for some time. This is where the light is equal to the dark, but that did not have anything to do with the year 2012. What has been happening over the course of your 20th Century and beyond is a global shift. In the 2000's, you moved into high noon where the dark energy in human souls became equal to the light. This means that there is an equal amount of good and light in ratio to the darkness and hate in the human being. This is witnessed in the human politics arena where you find people seeking and desiring to interfere and control how another person chooses to live their life. This global shift began to accelerate during the 1900's and onward. As the decades progressed, there were more souls being born to usher in this shift with the goal of raising one's consciousness. Many are becoming more aware of their surroundings and how they behave in their life. They are also living in the heavy density of the Earth's atmosphere and not aware of whom they are deep down beneath the physical reality.

As Earth's history continues, there will be newer generations of souls entering a lifetime in a more evolved manner than the previous generations. This is helped along by the current generations who are evolving and passing it down the bloodline. The 2000's and beyond saw the true beginnings of the rise of the technology age. The positives are this is what can and has contributed positively to the growing consciousness in others. Information is readily accessible and spread much quicker than it ever has. This is all part of the shift in consciousness.

The dark and light in humankind have been in constant battle with one another. It feels extremely heightened to you because there are billions of people that inhabit the planet. The way everyone can communicate is instantaneous, but this adds coldness to the soul and the globe. This coldness does not contribute to a rising of one's consciousness. Connections with one another are short lived while others ruthlessly act out for selfish gain. Humankind is struggling to survive and living under immense stress. This does not contribute to a rising of one's consciousness. This creates an overabundance of unhappy, distant, stressed out human beings trying to survive day to day. Their lives feel empty without any excitement. They reach for time wasters or toxic addictions to keep going. This slowly kills that soul's life force, which does not help in shifting their consciousness. There will need to be a massive uproar, anarchy, and outcry that the way human life is currently designed no longer works. You are becoming hip to the truth that you cannot suffocate the soul.

The shift in consciousness can be seen by the way others live and the positive energy they exude. A deeply spiritual person constantly evolving might soon find work or a purpose that enables them to feel this joy. They feel the joy when tackling the elements in your contract. They will set up life in an area on the planet that isn't congested with angry, cold, stressed persons. When they live in a stuffed area then this recommended human design can make them believe there is a shift in consciousness. The disconnect is severe by the hostility that plagues the planet overall. It is what dominated humanity. When you vacate the trenches of that, then this might offer the illusion that humankind is shifting in consciousness. We do not deny that many souls are evolving each of your days. There is a shift in individual consciousness, but globally this has not been seen in some time. It may be centuries before this is seen on a grander scale. Half the world despises anyone who does not agree with one another or who is of another gender, race, political affiliation, sexual orientation, religion, and so on. These labels you created have no connection to soul reality. You have clues as to where you are it in global consciousness shift on media websites. Read what people type into comment boxes to give you an overall feeling as to where the state of humanity is currently at. If a massive awakening and shift has taken place, then this will reveal itself in the positivity that humankind communicates to each other. This will give you a taste of where you are at with a shifting in consciousness globally.

The true spirit within the physical human body has not evolved and expanded above the soul's ego. The ego part of them will make it known verbally or physically. This acting out is not someone whose consciousness is being raised. It is the ego living in fear of those who refuse to live the way it does. Those creating this harm are waking other souls up from slumber. It is waking them up and into the direction of developing a higher consciousness of love. It is waking them up to realize that how others are being treated is morally wrong and not of God. The human ego has a challenging time with coming to terms in understanding that God created souls to be individuals with their own set of personality traits to master and hone in to the best of your abilities. Souls are prevented from raising its consciousness by not displaying one act aligned with love and compassion.

Shifting your consciousness is having an understanding that you are here for the purpose of love. You are here for your soul's growth. You are here to evolve your soul as either student or teacher, or leader, or follower. You have a detachment to the physical. This means you do not identify with labels to separate *(i.e. race, nationality, man, woman, republican, democrat, gay, straight, spiritual, atheist)*. Nor any other label that limits your soul and places you in a box. You are not your job, the clothes you wear, the house you live in, the car you drive, the family you were born to, the physical appearance you work on to attract or feel good about yourself. These are all fads created by humankind to disillusion you into believing that this is who you are.

Raising your consciousness is coming to terms with this design that has duped humankind into believing you are something if you have or identify with material physical properties. Labels were created by humankind in order to separate souls from one another, but it is not who you are.

Raising your soul consciousness includes moving into the space of love for all. It is accepting that you are a soul in a physical body. You love and appreciate all aspects of you. It is to know that hurting, harming, or hating anyone is to not understand who and what you are in spiritual truth. To be a constant complainer lowers your vibration and prevents you from shifting your consciousness into love.

You will easily become submerged into the physical human life with its ever-changing fads and traditions. This can confuse someone into believing that this is who they are. The shifting in consciousness is being aware of this and not being naïve to believing this to be the soul's reality. It is the only reality you know at that time in your life due to how you were raised. It was taught by the generations passed. When you recall incidents in your life from when you were five, six, or seven years old, it will feel as if you're watching a movie about someone else. If it was a wonderful time, then you feel nostalgic and miss it wanting to re-create it in your later years.

As human souls continue to evolve, they will begin the process of passing a love mantra around to their offspring and so forth. The ones who have failed at this are the ones that have trained their children to hate and cause harm on others different from them. This shift in consciousness will take time since it is a generational shift in consciousness that is happening. This has progressively been going on since the beginning of humankind.

There is a war between the light and dark. Those of the light are the ones with a higher consciousness and the dark being the ones attempting to stop that from happening. This is seen all around the world as humankind attempts to assert itself through the darkness of their ego. If one wants to see how things are changing in a way that benefits this shift in consciousness, then look back through history. How long did it take for women to be treated and considered equal? How long did it take before humankind stopped treating African Americans as slaves? How long was it before someone that identifies as gay was able to marry someone they love? How long did it take before religions accepted other religions? How long did it take for certain circumstances to happen if at all? You can note that some of these situations you've set up have slightly improved, but it took centuries to come about and even still it's not widely accepted by human ego despite what your laws suggest.

These examples are to illustrate what it means to shift your consciousness globally. While it appears, this is beginning to improve and speed up, it will take a while longer to reach that place of peace on Earth. Earth is a ticking time bomb and many human beings are waking up in larger numbers to the idea that the negative way you treat one another is the real sin. Having this awareness is where the true shift in consciousness resides.

When you are not exuding and displaying love, understanding, and compassion, then you do not know God. When you step through the gates of Heaven, it is an overflowing love you experience that never lets up. Love is the reason you are here. Love is the answer to the big questions you have about why you are here and why everything was created. It was for the soul to learn to love and experience love. When you love any soul, only then are you closer to that goal. All circumstances and paths are connected to love and lead to love. Whenever you're in doubt, bring your soul back to this space of love that lives deep within you even if you have forgotten that it ever existed. You were born from love, you entered an Earthly life from love, and you are made up of love. Nothing else matters in the end but love.

Final Words from Author

Heaven is real and I know this because I've seen it through Clairvoyance on more occasions than I can count. I've experienced it and been taken through it. I blink my eyes and the various images and messages of the spirit world flash in front of me without warning and then evaporate. This has been going on for as long as I can remember. From the moment I was born, I had one foot in the physical world and the other foot in the world where I came from. As a four-year-old, I was seeing and hearing spirit in a profound way that I never thought twice about it. Those around me noticed this during the moments I would tell them something that ended up coming to fruition. When you pass on, then you're left with your soul. All your physical items and worries or concerns are irrelevant with the snap of a finger. If all you're left with is your soul's consciousness, then why not give it more attention while you're here. I've relayed descriptions of the Other Side throughout some of my work. From my near-death experience that cracked my portal open and shifted me down a holier path, to the process your soul endures as it crosses over, to the differences between the souls in Heaven with those on Earth, and to the magical paradise of life in Heaven. There is something else beyond this dimension and I've been experiencing it throughout this current life. The glimpses they continue to give me while I'm here are reminders of what's important and to ignore the cattle and noise of the human ego that will attempt to get in the way. In comparison, the other worlds make life on Earth trivial and more accurately aligned with Hell. Yet, there are glimpses of Heaven in its rarity attempting to shine its way through the thick thud of the aura of the state of the human body by those that are working to raise their vibration and soul consciousness. If all would work to keep their vibration high, then what a peaceful and loving world this planet would be!

The Metaphysical Divine Wisdom Collection

The Metaphysical Divine Wisdom Collection

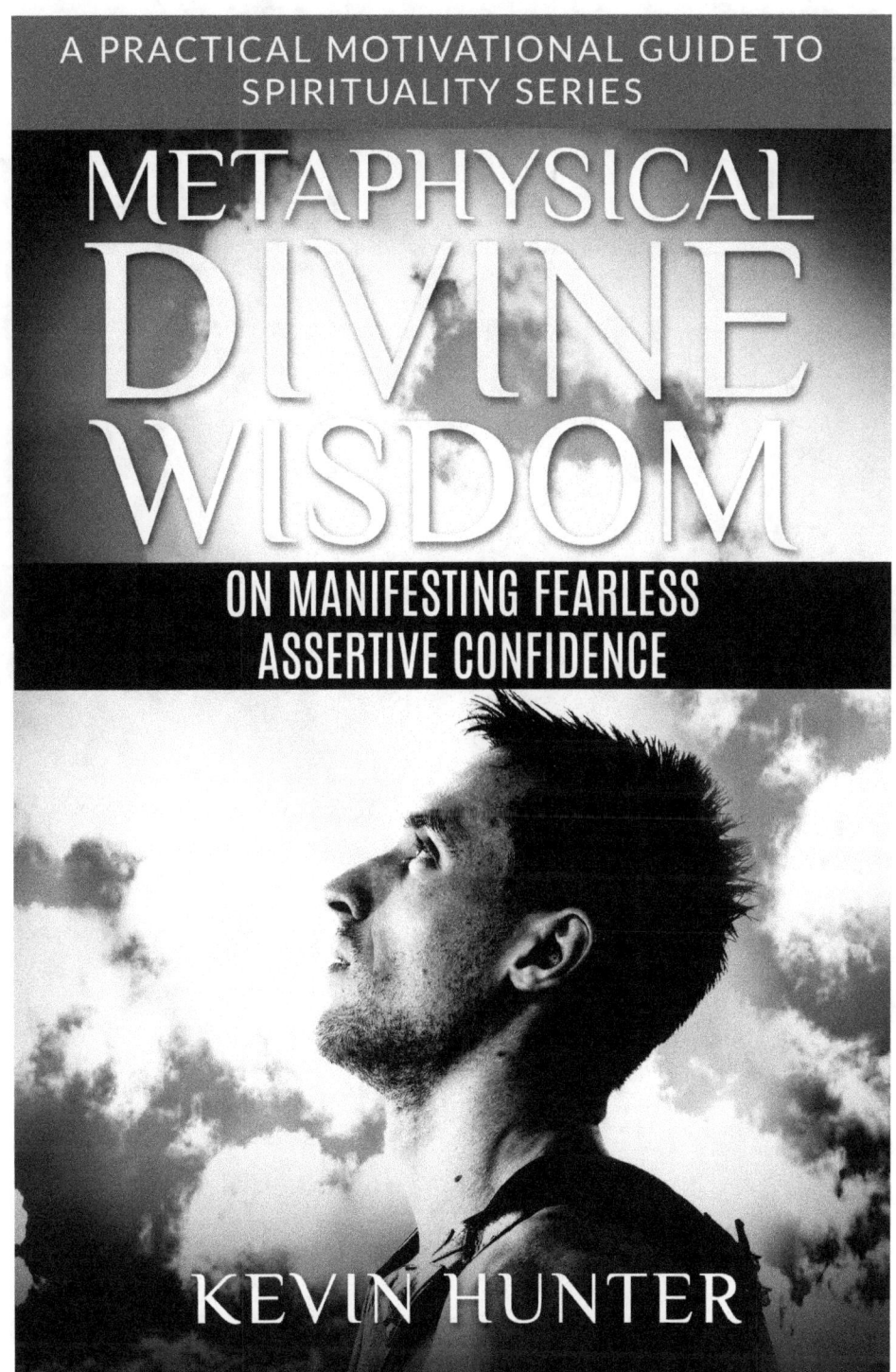

The Metaphysical Divine Wisdom Collection

METAPHYSICAL DIVINE WISDOM
ON MANIFESTING FEARLESS ASSERTIVE CONFIDENCE

Kevin Hunter

CHAPTER ONE

Combat Fear

It's been noted that one's confidence can crumble upon losing things in the key practical areas of your life. You might feel a shattering of self-worth when you lose your job, a relationship, a friend, or your home. It's interesting to note how losing a material or physical possession affects your confidence and sense of self-worth. It can cause you to lose interest in activities in life that you once enjoyed. You may become bed ridden and depressed. You cancel plans, ignore phone calls and are unreachable for a period of time. In those instances that your confidence is shattered by a material or physical loss, then that's when your confidence is needed more than ever. The human ego has insisted upon you to base your confidence and self-worth on the things you've achieved and attained when the reverse is what should be the case. You've made physical material possessions an extension of yourself when all you need to rise up and thrive is already burning within you. It is the fearless assertive confidence you build and expand up within your soul first, and then you use those traits to drive you towards attaining your desires.

The most successful people that came from a poor uneducated background and achieved their dreams did so based on the fearless assertive confidence they had within them first. They may not have had the degree or the money, but they did have a passionate Divine fire that filled them with confidence. This kind of fearless confidence doesn't cost any money, because it's a trait that your soul already owns.

When you lose any kind of physical or material possession, then that should be the drive that propels you to utilize the fearless confidence that is already burning within the pilot light of your soul. This part of your soul comes from the light you were made from where all things are possible.

When you lose anything of value that negatively affects your confidence, self-esteem and self-worth, then make that the driving force that propels you to rise up into warrior mode. Stand strong under that powerful Divine Light allowing it to be the nourishment your soul feeds off of that helps you move into manifesting a fearless assertive confidence. Fear is one of the most crippling and destructive energies that the Darkness infiltrates into anyone it can. Its goal is to witness your downfall by paralyzing you with fear.

Everyone experiences some form of fear at some point if not on a regular basis. Most anything fear based isn't real. It still doesn't stop you from conjuring up fear about what will or will not come. It's a matter of recognizing fear, looking it in the eye, and then running it over not allowing it to consume you. Fear is the opposite of faith. Fear starts with a false thought from the ego, and then the soul follows willingly believing it. It takes time and practice devoted to training oneself to ignore the fear and walk in faith.

Fear is one of the leading causes of soul and personal failure. It brings on paralysis, chaos, and procrastination. Moving past fear requires awareness of what you're attempting to defeat. Overcoming fear is no easy achievement. It can take a lifetime to conquer since the human soul has a built-in ego that will do what it can to stop you from achievement. The ego is split into both the light and darkness of ego. The light ego being what gives you confidence to trust and believe in who you are and your abilities, while the darkness of ego twists that into greed, anger, or fear.

Every soul on the planet experiences fear throughout their Earthly life. It is the one common trait that everyone has listed in their soul contract before incarnating into an Earthly life. You're a feeling, breathing, thinking consciousness moving about in a physical vessel for a variety of reasons. Every single person on the planet has a reason for being here, even if you have no clue what it is at any given moment. It is up to you to discover your numerous purposes that are connected to one singular intention. There are the default motives that all are here such as learning to love, but there are other goals outside of that even though love is always at the top of the list in the end.

Where you are on the fear scale can range from the minimal to being consumed by a fear that drowns and paralyzes you. The more sensitive you are, then the more fear you are apt to brewing up inside. Use your sensitivities to your advantage and transmute any fear into self-confidence. Believe in yourself knowing that you are worthy if not more capable than any other to do what you are perpetually called to do.

One soul may be aware of internal fears and will ignore it by persevering anyway. Another soul will become crippled by fear and accomplish nothing in the process. The latter soul allows the grips of this invisible negative energy to plague their thoughts and entire being to the point of paralysis. The dreams they've always wanted to conquer never transpire due to this fear.

Fear breeds out of the ego, the part of you that gives you a sense of self-worth. When left unchecked the ego will run uncontrollably initiating all sorts of chaos and drama. The ego thrives on drama and negativity. This is what gives the beast life. Fear is manifested from the darkness of ego the same way a female gives birth to its child. Fear begins to grow and expand during your childhood development and upbringing. If you grew up in a household where you were constantly being told you're no good and will never amount to anything, then as you grow older and set out to accomplish your life purpose, the fears that rise up from conquering your purpose will incessantly talk you out of it. The ego will talk you out of accomplishing anything positive by filling your mind with thoughts you heard from others growing up through adolescence. The dark ego says, "You can't do that, you're not qualified, you are wasting your time, and you will never be a success at anything."

The repetitive words forever sift through your mind preventing you from taking action and getting to work. This creates a block that prevents you from going after what you desire. It is a block that forms a wall intended to disconnect you from the Divine. The Divine is where the answers, messages, and guidance reside in to help you travel down a smoother path while here.

The Dangers of Fear Energy

Avoid getting caught up in the grips of fear as you're channeling energy in a positive direction. Fear energy is one of the most dangerous energies ever attributed to humankind. For centuries it has been amazingly excessive triggering all sorts of destruction on the planet and on each other. From the perspective of an angel you can imagine what that looks like seeing comets darted around like a tennis ball getting everyone nowhere.

Fear and worry plague the planet to an unhealthy degree causing it to expand and shoot out into the universe only to dart right back down like a boomerang in an explosion. The fear and worry energy have been especially magnified due to how quickly information is transmitted through the media and Internet. This fear originates within all of the individual souls on Earth and multiplies creating a fire that burns and destroys everything in its wake. Fear and worry do nothing to help anyone.

Fear is one of the soul's worst enemies. It is the reason the planet is plagued with interpersonal and global battles. Fear is responsible for preventing you from achieving and conquering your purpose. Living in a space of fear is what blocks you from moving forward. Opportunities are lost due to fear because it ensures you remain paralyzed causing you to cower and hide from going after what you desire.

Fear stalls humanity from evolving as witnessed in the centuries of evolution on the planet. While progress continues to be made in diminutive trickles, improvement still moves at a glacial rate thanks to humanities fear. It should not take hundreds of years to advance in the tiniest steps despite taking what we can get. This is due to individual fear resisting against changing their perception and awakening their consciousness. Finding the space of love and respect is challenging for the mediocre mind. Training every breathing organism to snap out of it takes an army of lights to do their part. Extricate fear from your aura and become unstoppable.

I met a woman in her 60's who was a former bank manager who quit and moved into semi-retirement. She wanted to supplement her income by becoming a Real Estate Agent on the side. The positive is she wouldn't have bank hours and could work when she chooses to on her own schedule. She walked into this new real estate career having zero experience not knowing the meaning of a counteroffer. Six months after she started this new career, she was closing $1 million plus homes in beach coastal cities. After one year, I started seeing her face on bus stop benches and freeway billboards.

Some people say they're too old for something or not qualified and have no experience, but this woman is a testament that she could do it IF she wanted it bad enough. She wanted it bad enough and went after it with joy, confidence, and passion, then conquered it in bigger ways than anyone imagined.

Fear is a ridiculously powerful dark energy that keeps you spinning around in the same spot ensuring you get nowhere. It causes you to hate others that are not like you or those that you don't understand. People that are unusual and dissimilar from the norm are more often than not the souls ushering in positive change in their individual way. They avoid following the herd and seem to be pushed to the forefront alone. That is one clue that you are standing in front of a soul leader.

Fear is controlled by what spiritual circles call the *ego* and religious circles call the *devil*. Either way both are interchangeable to describe the same thing, which is why I often vacillate between using both. The ego doesn't want to see you succeed and win. It wants to keep you feeling trapped and helpless. Work on releasing fears connected to anything in your life. Release it by handing it over to God, source, the universe, your higher self, the angels, your Spirit team, or whatever you're comfortable referring to it as.

You can say something like, "I don't want this, please take it. I'm not going to worry about this anymore. I'm going to let you do that while I focus on other things. And so it is."

Ignore the fear and run into the flames of possibilities knowing you may get burned, because at least you put yourself out there. You stood up for yourself by doing what you want to do. Your consciousness will be that much stronger, smarter, and powerful.

The attitude I've always had when diving into anything and everything I ever wanted fearlessly is to just dive on in. This means doing it anyway no matter what kind of fear energy attempts to get in the way. Nothing stops me when I'm operating from my highest self because I am worthy and qualified. That's not bad for someone that battles with social anxiety daily. You may be afraid of jumping; yet you still do it anyway because it's worth the risk to at least try to conquer your dreams. Reach that place where you can look back on your life and say, "I am a long way from where I've been."

In my life's trek to wellness from the brink of ruin with drug and alcohol addiction, I have risen up again and again. You are stronger than whatever is trying to tear you down. Recovery is sublime good hard work worth any price. Summon the nerve to get back up after any misfortune and don't let your life pass you by where it results in you getting the feeling that you've missed the boat. It is never too late to start anything you truly want to do. You are more powerful than you realize.

Fighting the Fear

Many human souls have passion and heart, but will do nothing with that Divine given gift out of fear. Fear is the #1 cause of turmoil in human souls. Fear comes from the ego and prevents you from going after your life purpose, your dream job, or the love interest. It is fear to speak your truth lovingly, or fear that stops you from going out and accomplishing things.

Some wrestle with anxiety due to their heightened sensitivities to the stimuli around them. Those with higher traits of anxiety, tend to be more in tune, psychic, or intuitive than other souls. They absorb more than the average person absorbs, and for that matter need to adopt a strict disciplined routine that is aligned with their personal equilibrium. Use your emotions to your advantage, since they house communication receptors with the Divine.

Anxiety rises when fear becomes too great, but most fears are outlandish, meaning that what you fear tends to be exaggerated. Notice what makes you fearful about something, then examine what that is to a high degree and note if the cause is more in your head rather than based in truth.

Sometimes it's not necessarily fear of failure, but fear of success that you're undeserving of rewards. You might feel guilty about it, but everyone deserves success and rewards. No soul is more special than another in the eyes of Heaven. Opportunities exist for you to take hold of and run with in the right spirit.

This is the same fear associated with the risk of pursuing a potential love interest. You might be afraid to approach your love crush for fear of being rejected, but if it's someone you can't get your mind off of, then take the risk to at least say hello to this person. Gauge their interest level after saying hello and notice if they seem standoffish because they're not interested or unfriendly due to shyness. Some people have given up a potential love interest intended for them out of fear, or they'll avoid approaching a potential partner out of fear. Fear is one of the greatest causes of human sabotage holding people back from achieving the life they desire. You don't want to wait until you're in the final days of life wishing you could go back into time and went after those things that were itching at you, but which you ignored and brushed aside out of procrastination, fear, or a lack of confident drive.

Many ignore the windows of opportunity revealed to them by spirit and wind up watching life race on by. Don't allow opportunities and blessings placed in front of you to go unnoticed. You don't want to reach a place at the end of your life where you have regrets wishing you would've gone after something or taken a risk on what you desire. One of my exes initially went after me due to the fear of not ever seeing me again. This was on our last day of school where everyone was leaving, so it was now or never seeing me again. That fear was strong enough that propelled enough confidence and drive for my ex to come after me. Granted, they're my exes now for other reasons, but there are no regrets. We still speak highly of one another today.

I've always been a fan of the fearless and the courageous, even if they know they'll fall flat on their face. I love seeing anyone walk through fire no matter what because nothing holds them back. They stand in their soul's power. If they fall, they pay no mind and get back up and keep going as if it's no big deal. They're fearless and continue to stand strong in the face of any setbacks or calamity.

Mastering fearless confidence on Earth can be challenging with the endless toxic negative energy being darted at you from all angles. Sometimes you create that negativity with the power of your own mind. Your worries and fears are unfounded since in the end all is always well. In Heaven, all souls are fearless and confident. There is no lower energy that permeates their aura like it does on Earth.

Archangel Michael – The Extractor of Fear

The Archangel Michael is God's right-hand security general that oversees all beings, including Warrior of Light's, all archangels, and angels. Many Warriors of Light souls have Archangel Michael around them since he is one of the strongest most fearless beings in the Heavens. He might assist with extracting fear from a soul while helping them to rise to confidence when their lower self gets in the way. He is also their protector to ensure they are not harmed by anyone. Warrior of Light's tend to invite in antagonism from the lower evolved that feel threatened by their natural ability to stand in fearless, assertive, confidence full time. For that matter, it is beneficial to have Archangel Michael in your house to extract the lower energies out of your vicinity. Anyone can call on him when experiencing fear or an attack from lower energies.

Archangel Michael is the loudest entity I've ever come across throughout my life. He is the only entity louder than God, while stretching to appear as tall as 30 to 40 feet and sometimes taller to make his presence known. He is often depicted in artwork as standing on or holding down a hideous monstrous devil like creature without effort. This can be the Devil itself or the darkness of ego in individual souls.

Someone that might come off assertively overconfident and bold rubs the lower energies the wrong way. Archangel Michael is with me every day of my life and ironically this is his principal energy. Only the dark ego would be ruffled over another who exudes superhuman confidence. This is because one of the goals of the Darkness is to take down confidence or anyone that achieves.

Archangel Michael struts around almost like a boastful rooster alpha male. Calling him overconfident is too little of a word to describe his self-assurance. When he's not extracting lower energies and people away with his light sword, he's showing off like a male peacock. Sometimes the light around him bursts into a brightly colored light show for no reason at all except to show off the way a male peacock does. This is similar to Archangel Michael's basic nature when he's not diving into battle fearlessly for God.

Call upon Archangel Michael for intervention when you are drowning in fear, anxiety, self-doubt, or lacking in confidence.

People believe what they want to believe and there is nothing you can do about it. Thinking in a limited way is the kiss of death. Communicating with any angel or archangel is communicating with God. They are His arms and hands, so even if you don't feel you are communicating to God, you are. The best parts of the human soul are of God. The darkness of ego is not. You can't run away from God. Michael isn't more superior than God since he is of God. Michael is so powerful and loud that he comes off more superior than God, even though they are one in the same. This soldier angel is present in all of the Heavens in a big way!

Archangel Michael has been around popping up over the centuries, but is now more present more than ever. The various reasons are that the Darkness is particularly heightened due to how rapidly it spreads through technology, which is why Michael has called on souls to come into this lifetime to fight the darkness of ego that exists in others. There are also more people on the planet, which equates to more minions for the Darkness to govern. And there are more people today that have become hip to spiritual pursuits and are need of Archangel Michael.

If you're experiencing a negative entity hanging around you, call on Archangel Michael and request that he bring the entity into the light. If you're feeling enormous fear, then bring in Archangel Michael to help lift you into bold confidence. Know that you are more powerful than you might give yourself credit for. Rise to the task of becoming the natural born fearless warrior soul you were made to be.

CHAPTER TWO

*Stand In Your
Divine Soul Power*

Finding that space of fearless confidence can be generated within the pilot light part of your soul that is ignited when you partner up with the Divine. You may call this the Divine, God, the Universe, Spirit, Energy, the Light. It's all the same thing regardless of the label used. This partnership enables you to efficiently stay on your higher self's soul path knowing when to make a move or to take a step back and have patience.

You are just as deserving of blessings, abundance, and success as any other soul being is. There is enough room on the planet for every single soul to experience success. There is always enough to go around. Everyone does and says things in their own way. They all have the ability to showcase their unique talents with their distinctive styles. It's interesting that the human ego prefers that everyone be a clone of them from having the same viewpoints, interests, and values across the board. It is the individual differences between each soul that is their winning card. Avoid listening to anyone that attempts to stop you from going after your life purpose or goals. They might tell you that you're not qualified or that you're not as gifted as someone else. When someone tells you that you're not qualified, they subconsciously mean that it is they who are not qualified. If I listened to all of those negative criticisms, then I never would've accomplished the things I did throughout my life. In the eyes of God, you are just as qualified as anyone else. When you accomplish what you set out to do, then you move into the space of being fueled by the Divine.

When you listen to the voices of your ego, the Darkness in your mind or in other people, then you will ensure you remain stuck. The goal of the Darkness is to attempt to stop you from accelerating and achieving success. You want to stomp the Hell out of that Darkness when it attempts to get in your way. When your feet hit the floor each morning the Darkness of Hell should shake. Your soul's success is not dependent on other people's opinions of you. When you partner with God, there is no telling what you can accomplish. You soar upwards into that space of fearless confidence that can only be generated through your connection with Him.

You go to a spiritual empowerment event to listen to five different guest speakers on motivation. They all enjoy talking about the same goal and content, but they're each discussing it in their own way. This indicates how everyone has something to offer surrounding the same topic, because not everyone says or does things in the same way. One speaker might not interest you, but they will interest someone else. The same goes for anyone in any field. One rock singer is different from another and appeals to the same or a different audience. There is enough room for everyone to contribute their talents in their authentic and original way.

In today's world post technology, one of the positives of having access to the Internet is that it has given many talented people various opportunities to showcase their talents had they had not access to get online. Many businesses have closed up physical stores, but kept their business thriving through online sales. Many have been moving into starting up their own successful self-employment business, while others have been transitioning into working from home either part or full time. This has resulted in more productivity, a calmer lifestyle, less stress, better health, and more energy.

There was this motivational YouTube video of this 18-year-old guy who was selling enough product online that he could do that full time. He explained that he doesn't have to take a full time nine to six corporate office day job that he'll end up despising because he does so well with this Internet business. Sometimes he walks along the beach on a Tuesday afternoon when no one is there because they're all at their soul crushing corporate day jobs. He loves that freedom of space to clear his mind without the crowds. He's able to do that because he sets his own hours and makes enough where he can afford to do that. He's not a millionaire or rich by any means, but he makes enough consistently and regularly to pay his rent and bills without worry. It gives him the luxury of working when he wants to rather than the rigid inflexible 9a-6p schedule that is the current norm. He gets more done in little time than it takes someone else in a corporate job. He also controls when he chooses to work.

There are more people than ever before that are moving into successful self-employment businesses. They started out by supplementing their income by taking a side day job while building their business on their downtime. You just want to do your best to look for a day job that makes you smile enough to not feel stressed and worried, otherwise that energy will carry over to the side hobby you've been working at building. It's still understood that sometimes you have to suck it up and take any day job. This is a physical life that requires money for physical survival necessities. When you are doing that you are ensuring that you and your family are taken care of. This is getting you in the habit of taking responsibility and being disciplined, which are winning traits that will be applied and carried over to all aspects of your life from personal to a professional self-employed business.

The sole cause of abundance blockage is fear. This fear can prevent someone from building a career out of their hobby. There are endless stories of someone finding their purpose, passion and hobby that wound by turning that into full time work where they can make survivable income off of. Some people will stay in what they perceive to be a dead-end job for fear of biting the bullet and taking a risk to walk away and go after their life purpose work. You should never walk away from a job unless you know it's practically safe to do so. This means you are prepared for the worst-case scenario that could entail you not finding another job.

The best way to move your passion into a financially independent career is to work on it on the side while you have the security of your current job. Devote at least a small amount of work each day towards your side passion career, so that you don't feel as if you're wasting your life at a job you despise. The benefits to doing that are if it's your passion, then it doesn't feel like work. It also gives you something positive to look forward to each day knowing you have this back up plan you're working on. If one day you suddenly lose your job due to being laid off or fired, then at least you have this passion career on the side you had been working on. It just may give you the push to dive into it at full force once regular day job employment ceases to exist. It's never too late to think about and plan potential opportunities for your future today. You don't know where you'll be in ten or twenty years. The stable job with the security and the benefits can end with the snap of a finger. This has been happening a great deal more than it ever has.

Allow Your Confidence To Break Out

There are some that prefer you to be meek about your accomplishments. They see boasting about what you've done makes you come off as if you have a big ego or that you're a narcissist. The "narcissist" word grew to be an overused trendy social media term that has been tossed around with reckless abandon without truly understanding the psychological definition. Typically, those that complain or attack others that are higher achievers haven't accomplished much, so it feels like those that have attained many things are rubbing it in. Those who go out there and achieve what they set out to do are so busy in that energy of achieving that to stoop lower to complain, criticize or attack becomes beneath them. Talking about what you've accomplished and the hard work you've put in to making something happen is not arrogant. It's stepping into your confidence over your Divine given gifts, abilities and talents. Being a people pleaser doesn't work. Focus on the guidance you receive from above and you'll never be led astray.

Confidence is not a dirty word or trait to have. People fall in love with those that are confident over those that are weak. When a man or woman strides through a room head held high with a smile, then that is what attracts in others that glance over with a smile intoxicated by that confidence. They want to engage with that energy rather than a negative pessimist with low self-esteem that negatively critiques everything you say or do. To a higher vibrational soul, the confident person is admirable as it shows you have goals, passion, and drive. It indicates that you're a hard worker, strong, and you get things done.

Warrior-like go-getters are attracted to other go-getters. Those looking to be inspired are attracted to those go-getters as it inspires them. When you persevere and accomplish your dreams and you succeed, then this is marvelous in the eyes of those that enjoy feeling inspired and motivated. It gives others hope that they can do it too. They know if they set their mind to it and work hard, then they will reach their destination.

When talking about your accomplishments with anyone whether it's in a job interview or with a friend, don't worry about coming off too assertive. Shout what you've accomplished from the rooftops and don't be fearful about it. Own what you created and fought to make happen. I received all of the previous jobs I did throughout the film business with the heavy talent in that industry due to this assertiveness that dominated the interview meeting. Each person that hired me had felt that this is someone that gets stuff done and we need something like that here.

When someone shouts their accomplishments from the highest mountain, then it isn't long before a negative beaten person will feel low, envy, or disdain about that. This pushes them to complain that the other person is not qualified, conceited, arrogant, or a narcissus, instead of admiring that confident quality in that person to go against the grain and tackle their passions. Use others accomplishments to motivate you to rise into who your soul is and shout that from the rooftops, rather than trying to spin it into something negative. Negative reactions typically come from jealousy and envy buried deep in the subconscious of the human ego.

Envy is a deadly emotional toxin because it pulls you under causing the Darkness to take over, envelope, drown, and suffocate you in that envy. Sometimes the envy might be due to jealousy, other times someone isn't jealous, but just a miserable person in general. They may have lived a life where others ignored them, so they will find fault with everyone and everything that is going after their dreams. No matter the context and whether it is jealousy or envy, all of those negative emotions are abundance blocks, since any form of negative emotion, feeling, or thought creates a block to blessings.

There is also the other kind of envy you may know about, which is generated in your heart. This is where you're not a bad person, but you have been working hard in life, and you're not seeing any positive results, traction, or movement, then you see someone else do what you had been doing for years and they shoot upwards across the map. You notice something like that happen and it ends up creating envy in you. You feel beaten down by it because your work is exceptional, you're gifted, accomplished at what you do, and you work so hard. You see someone with little experience or whom you might feel is not qualified necessarily, but they put something out and it attracts in the massive abundance. This will kick anyone on the sidelines wondering when your turn will come.

In those moments there isn't anything you did to attract that. Everyone has a different timeline as to when things pan out the way they're supposed to. It's important to do your best to stand strong in faith knowing that everyone's timing for things is different.

Affirm, "I am just as qualified as that person is. I'm glad that they are being blessed and by the way I'm in that line too!"

Research other success stories in the field of your interest in tips and inspiration.

A friend of mine went to a wedding with someone he was dating. He and his date found they were comparing themselves to the guests. The guests appeared to be advanced by the life status they achieved in both of their eyes. This friend explained that everyone at the wedding was accomplished and successful. They were also around the same age as he and his date. After the wedding, he and his date talked about it and felt like they were so far behind compared to the successful wedding patrons.

Comparing yourself to others can bring your vibrational energy down. Whether it's I'm better than you or you're better than me. Feeling like someone is better than you pulls you down harder because of the despair, disappointment, and frustration energy associated with it. You are not above or below me, because we are the same. Everyone has their own gifts and talents to offer to humanity for the greater good. Even if it's in the same genre you're interested in. Every single person has a distinctively unique way of offering those gifts and talents that will appeal to someone out there.

Working so hard and feeling as if you're getting nowhere fast can take its toll on you. You continue to struggle while others around you will try something and hit instant success. You might find yourself getting critical not understanding why. You might think lower energy words like, "They're younger than I, have almost little to no work experience, and they're better looking than I am…."

This can easily cause a combination of depression and envy. There is no set time frame for achieving success. Everyone has their own timeline of when things will come about. For some it may seem instant, while another will struggle for much longer. It doesn't mean you're less than or not talented enough. Sometimes it's the more talented and gifted that take the longer way around to see the abundance flowing into their life effortlessly. They're gaining more knowledge and experience that others don't have through that longer process. It's like the Tortoise and the Hare story. The Tortoise moved slower, but ended up surpassing the Hare in the end in that fairy tale.

It's been known at this point that I started my work life in the film business when I was twenty-three years old working for a movie star actress at her company. All good blessings came down from that point where it opened more doors and job offers. I still receive notes from upcoming generations in their teens and young adulthood reaching out to me to ask how I got into the film business. Because the role I was brought in to do was difficult and considered rare for the age I was at during the time. They're trying to get in as well too. It was also during a time when Movie Stars existed, and the public didn't have a connection with the remaining ones like they may have now due to the Internet, Instagram, and social media.

It took me seven years to get into the film business. I knew I would get in when I was sixteen, but it wasn't until I turned twenty-three when I finally got that lucky phone call out of the blue that changed my life. That was one of many major turning points and crossroads in my life. Getting in was persistence, passion, and dedication, but it was also a stroke of Divine luck and constant prayer. It was one call amidst it all that changed my life and cracked open the abundant door. I always say getting in was luck, but staying in was talent. That goes for anything anyone does. I came from a poor background and no access to resources, but I did have fearless assertive confidence when it came to getting that important job.

Stay strong; remain faithful, and full of hope, as you forge ahead undeterred by anything the darkness throws at you. Everyone is moving at their own pace. Feeling frustration over the lack of results can make you want to give up and throw in the towel, but keep going and stay focused on your purpose and mission. Avoid comparing your trajectory to someone else's because your talents are needed. You'll get there if it kills you. Your drive is your winning card; so don't allow someone else's success to squash what you are working on. Instead allow that to help you feel inspired and motivated to work even harder.

A healthy ego shines through when you are confident in your gifts, talents, and abilities while not shying away from announcing it to the Universe. The meek don't get far in this cutthroat world it's been learned, so allow the confident part of your soul to come out of that submissive side and allow it to shine its vibrant light into the ethers. Visualize that light expanding and growing more blinding than you can imagine that it blasts everything away in its wake. This is how powerful your soul light is back home in Heaven. While it may be ferociously beautifully strong on the Other Side, that light is still within your soul. It is simply contained inside the temporary physical body you've inhabited this lifetime. This light can still fluctuate and expand and contract as it does back home while within your body. It can get crushed under the weight of the Earth's energy density and the darkness of ego, but you have enough power to let the light out in an explosion that it breaks apart this darkness at your own will.

Self-Esteem and Self-Love

One of the other traits so many battle with today is low self-esteem. This wasn't always the case, but since the rise of social media giving everyone a voice it also amplified that low self-esteem in destructive ways. People growing up today are finding they keep comparing themselves to others on social media. He's beautiful with ripped abs and she's got a killer stunning body. Is this what we've allowed human life to become? A competition over who is better than someone else? Qualities that become non-existent the second you die. That sounds like an awfully long waste of time to be preoccupied with. Regardless, it seems to be inescapable because it is in your face every time you go online. You can't help it; you see it and you are brought down. This was going on before the Internet where magazines were airbrushing people to the point they were too perfect. Society was comparing themselves to the models on those covers not realizing that it's all lighting, make up, and hair people that make it all look good. It's also why actors have admitted it's difficult for them to watch themselves on screen. They'll nitpick and critique how they looked as well as their performance.

Talking with this body builder at the gym one day, the conversation moved into vanity. He commented that I seemed exceptionally fit, although I disagreed explaining that I like taking care of myself, but I don't personally see it. I then added that he was. He said, "Oh no, I don't see it in myself either. I think I have that body dysmorphia something or rather."

That kicked off a discussion into how people view themselves differently than the way others do. I was surprised to find that even though to others he appeared built, muscular, and physically fit, that he didn't see that at all. His personal view of himself is skewed to an unrealistic level. This was one person out of numerous people that I've conversed with over what they perceive to be flaws in themselves. I've also discovered that those who might be considered off the charts good looking battle with it more than others. This was a surprising revelation to learn.

In the past, I've discussed the process of external upkeep. Some body builders are extremely muscular to the point that others have explained it can be too much. They don't see themselves that way, so they continue pumping more iron than necessary that it becomes an unhealthy obsession. This has also been seen with some that partake in plastic surgery. Constantly having plastic surgery to the degree they become unrecognizable. They go beyond more than what was originally needed.

How about those that have spent enormous amounts of money to look like a celebrity. They've paid anywhere from $20,000 to a $100,000 to change their appearance to match a famous person. You have to wonder where someone's mind is at on the self-esteem scale when you drop that kind of money for something that superficial. It falls in line with other toxic addictions. There is a lack of self-love for who you are. This is different than the basic aesthetic grooming beauty upkeep one enjoys like facials, skincare, hair care, physical workout training, etc. Meanwhile, there are children that live in some kind of abusive impoverished situation with no funds to help them.

There is what could be considered genuine flaws to work on, such as if you're someone that has rage anger issues. Calling it a flaw may be the wrong word to describe it, and using the word challenge could be more appropriate. This particular kind of flaw or challenge is one you could admit, "I have anger issues. I'm aware of it and I have been working on trying to control it more."

That's a different kind of challenge that can be worked on to improve yourself. What you might perceive to be a flaw in your appearance and looks is subjective. Learn to love everything about you. You change the things you're able to change, and you love and accept the areas that absolutely can never be improved. Steer away from comparing yourself to others. In God's eyes you are a radiant beautiful being that He is already impressed with.

Humanity is gravely obsessive over their physical appearance because the ego in humankind harshly judges one another by what they look like. The perception of who is considered beautiful or good looking would be vastly different if people saw one another's soul instead of the physical vessel they temporarily inhabit. Relationships would last longer because people would be merging together based on soul attraction rather than physical attraction, even though I understand that physical attraction helps at first, but that's only the start of coming together. Physical attraction fades no matter how good looking someone is. When you're younger you base the quality of a potential love partner solely on their physical attractiveness to you. As you grow older and more mature, the quality of a potential love partner is based on personality chemistry and the companionship factor.

There would be less of an obsession to try and garner false attention through perfecting your exterior and more work done on your interior. Raising your consciousness and awareness level can help in rising above the superficial and diving beneath the surface to get to the root of who someone truly is. It can help you dive into getting to know who you are too. Those hyper obsessed with their bodies, selfies, attention, and constant physical exterior adoration aren't fans of that kind of talk. They take it as an attack, even though the message is a generality to smarten up and dive beneath the superficiality. One needs a healthy dose of spiritual saving if they're more consumed with vanity than penetrating the depths of all things beyond.

This isn't saying not to do your best to take care of yourself and look good in the areas you are able to, nor is it saying that there is anything wrong with finding yourself or someone physically attractive. It's about the borderline obsessiveness of being consumed wholly by your looks and basing your existence on whether or not your body is worshipped by others. External validation is a shallow goal. Fixing yourself up in the areas you are able to has been shown to help build up confidence, but you don't want to fall too deep into basing your confidence on how you look and what you have, since the confidence is within you regardless of how you look.

I've been just as guilty of the selfie craze having done the muscle flexing selfies, although I was never doing it as much as others and it's rare when I do that anyway. I've had people ask me to check out their Instagram page. I head over there and notice their entire Instagram is nothing but hundreds of every selfie of them that you can imagine scrolling all the way down. It's concerning to see how deep they've fallen into the obsession of superficiality, attention, and adoration. They use their body and looks to gain false attention. They're not promoting a product associated with their body such as fashion or fitness, but are just seeking love from others. What might be even more disconcerting is they get that attention, which is likely why they continue doing it. Thousands of people are liking and splattering each photo with attention, but it's shallow attention.

I've also run those social experiments where I've purposely put up a photo of me fully clothed, which garners little attention. One week later I then put up the opposing shot, which is me shirtless and suddenly the image skyrockets to the top of the trending mark. The approving comments, likes, and messages in my in-box flood. Meanwhile, I'm disappointed to see the experiment worked. I'm aware how shallow humanity is by their opposing reactions to each shot. I've been out there and tested everything discussed. When you have self-love for yourself, then the desire for constant external adoration isn't looked-for.

Self-love and gratitude are magical elements to incorporate into your life that help in pushing the abundance door wide open. This positive thinking isn't news when it comes to attracting in abundance. This is to hammer home the feel-good feelings to reach into one's psyche where you can feel more inspired. This is to experience contentment and optimism about where you are currently at and what's to come. It is to praise how far you've come and how hard you've worked. Give yourself the credit for what you've accomplished to date.

Rapper Snoop Dogg received his star on the Hollywood Walk of Fame in 2018. I fell in love with his speech because he praises himself and gives himself the credit:

"Last but not least, I want to thank me for believing in me. I want to thank me for doing all this hard work. I want to thank me for having no days off. I want to thank me for never quitting. I want to thank me for always being a giver and trying to give more than I receive. I want to thank me for trying to do more right than wrong. I want to thank me for just being me at all times."

I chuckled because I thought it was amazing and brilliant. Some immediately get turned off or offended when anyone believes in themselves or props themselves up. They'll naively throw the ego or narcissistic word around with abandon. There is nothing wrong with applauding and giving yourself credit for the hard work you put in. You're the one doing the work; give yourself a round of applause! You can't rely on others to prop you up. Prop yourself up!

On one occasion, I was hanging with my former actress boss about three years into my employment with her. We were kicking back chatting about things. At one point I said, "I really have to thank you, because I could not have done all of these things I've done to date without your help and you opening that door."

She just point blank said with a lighthearted smile, "Oh stop, you did it yourself."

That forever stuck because I thought, "Actually you are right. I shouldn't be bowing down to others for the work I fought to do on my own."

External human validation isn't something I require, because I know my worth through source. I know who I am, what I can do, and what I've done. Believe in yourself and give yourself credit when you do good things. Praising yourself is considered self-love that lifts your vibration up into the vortex of attracting in more good stuff.

CHAPTER THREE

*Stomp Out the Darkness
of Fear, Gossip, and Anger*

There's nothing more paralyzing and detrimental to human beings than fear. Fear has plagued humankind since they first started inhabiting Earth. Fear blocks you from moving forward and prevents the positive flow of abundance. Fear can come in the disguise of worry, stress, depression, and anger. It will expand negative emotions and create madness depending on the case. Fear isn't just about fearing making a positive move in life. Fear resides in those that truly dislike groups of people. For instance, hate crimes against someone who is different than the antagonist generally begins to breed in the womb of fear. The antagonist might respond by saying, "I'm not afraid of them. I just don't like them."

Basically, they don't like anyone that falls into a particular demographic. This comes from a subconscious fear of coming across someone who isn't exactly like you. God throws everyone together on the same rock to learn tolerance, acceptance, and forgiveness. Those are some of the most difficult traits that people have trouble with conveying. This is clear due to how people stick with their own groups the same way they did on the elementary school playground. This is the innate primal human instinct, but it is not the soul part of you. The soul is inclusive, but the human ego is exclusive.

There were more people than not who were once prejudiced against race, then it became prejudice over anyone that had a same sex relationship. Once they realized that every other person they loved around them fit the description of people gay, then they gradually changed their tune realizing they made a mistake about their hatred and just didn't know any better. Now it's becoming increasingly common and accepted, but there are still those living in the stone ages with a limited view that have yet to gain love for those not like them.

Using Biblical text that was added in at a later date by superstitious fearful men isn't a good excuse, since God created all breathing life this way for a reason. God doesn't have hang ups about two souls in love with each other regardless of their gender. Love is what He desires to see, so in that instant when two souls are in love, He is pleased. God has disdain for those that express hatred over two souls in a committed love relationship, let alone disdain for those that display hatred on any level. If you have hatred in your heart, then there is no Divine energy existing in there. Jesus Christ was the same way. His complaint was over adultery and not about committed love between two souls.

Dive down deep as to why you don't like someone. Hating an entire group isn't valid because there are good and bad people in all groups. When you pull one person out of that group you despise and you're locked in a room with them to have a conversation, there is a greater chance that when you both leave that room you'll like them. If anything, you will both at least have a bit more compassion, respect, and understanding of them. The only way that will never work is if someone's consciousness is not raised. A limited consciousness permanently resides in darkness unable to break free. The darkness is where fear lives. In order to get over a prejudice you have about a certain class of people is to spend one on one time with them in a casual friendly setting.

I've conducted social experiments like this. This is where I've placed two people in a room together who are in opposition on the political spectrum. The intention of putting them in the room together was to get them to have friendly conversation outside of their personal political choices. Nine times out of ten they generally ended up liking each other, or at least respecting each other despite their personal political values. The exceptions are those that are entirely extreme and rigid that no light or tolerance has room to enter the picture. This is the current state of the universe today. There is zero Divine clarity and psychic foresight within hatred or negativity of any kind. When you take the time to get to know someone different from you, then eventually you come to a greater more compassionate understanding of that person.

You've likely witnessed people attacking another person over their personal views. This does nothing to change that person. Seeking to understand them and have a cordial sit-down conversation with them is more likely to gain some measure of respect. This is not always the case amongst those rare exceptions, but in many paradigms it is. If you already know they can't be reasoned with, then wish them well, bless them on their path to enlightenment, let it go and walk away.

Fear energy is also one of the major culprits to blocking the flow of positive abundance and blessings in one's life. It doesn't matter if the fear is overachieving your goals or fear that causes you to despise an entire group of people. It is still fear energy in the eyes of the Universe. Fear lives within the darkness of a soul's ego. Fear is responsible for the chaos energy that forever surrounds the planet when humankind is operating from a low vibration. Fear will make you doubt yourself and bring on baseless worry energy.

Doubts and worry that you will not achieve or succeed what you desire stems from fear. When that happens, then you need a healthy dose of inspiration that can be found in empowering music, books, or films. This is one of the positives of entertainment, which was created to help people forget about their troubles, help them to lighten up, or give them a dose of inspiration. Balanced entertainers that remain neutral on their personal values while in the public eye don't always get enough credit for this goal at times.

The alternative rock song *High Hopes* by *Panic at the Disco* sings, "I had to have high hopes for a living. Shooting for the stars when I couldn't make a killing. Didn't have a dime, but I always had a vision. Didn't know how, but I always had a feeling I was going to be that one in a million."

Listen to empowering music with positive lyrics that help motivate you. Watch movies about those that came from nothing and made something with their life. Rags to riches stories can be incredibly inspiring. People that had nothing and struggled with little to no money, but soon overcame that and made something with their life. They might be films like *Erin Brockovich, People Vs. Larry Flynt,* or *Joy*.

Erin Brockovich was a regular person trying to make ends meet. She found a cause that moved her and was mainly interested in uncovering it. The financial abundance ended up coming in, even though that was not her concern when fighting for the underdog.

The Founder, another rags to riches film that stars Michael Keaton, was based on the true story of Ray Kroc, the guy that created the McDonald's fast food chain. Opinions on him are across the board from people that loved him and those that loathed him. The point of this was that he was an unsuccessful salesperson, but somehow struck gold when he found something great in the McDonald's formula for fast food. He ended up rising up the ranks to major never-ending financial success.

Watching those rags to riches type films can leave you feeling as if you were injected with newfound inspiration and optimism. Joyful experiences can help you get into a positive state, but so does aligning with God and Spirit. Putting your trust and faith into the universal heavenly forces above is better than any material abundance that can be offered.

Many successful known entertainers admit to having self-doubts or fear, which humanizes and helps them to be relatable to their audience. They fear they're not that good or that they'll be found out that they're no good. They are good at what they do, they are popular, and at the top of their game, but they're also human and have human emotions that their success is a fluke.

It helps to have some perspective that everyone experiences doubts or worries, but don't let that cripple you to the point of non-movement. You rise above it and keep forging forward making the most of what you can do while you are here. You may as well try, because what else do you have to lose?

Turn Anger Into Positive Action

Manifesting fearless assertive confidence can hit a threshold where your higher self has lost control of the reigns allowing space for your ego to grab the steering wheel taking you on Mr. Toad's Wild Ride. This confidence begins to expand and burn rapidly out of control driving your ego into fury and anger. The ego is unstable always residing in some constant state of fear, which can manifest into anger. Fear is not always apparent to what it actually is. The fear can be fearful of being trampled on, pulled down, not reaching success. You do whatever you can to ensure success that you begin to act out erratically due to this fear. Every person on the planet has the fear and anger within them that comes out in various ways. Depending on your overall character and nature, your anger temperament will be different than another person's. The way you react in anger will vary compared to someone else. Is the Dalai Lama or the Pope running around bullying people on the sidewalk, verbally attacking people on social media, or starting fist fights for no reason? They have a different centered assertive way of channeling that anger positively.

All forms of anger are toxic putting stress on your health and body, but that doesn't mean you're supposed to pretend to be happy when you're faced with challenging circumstances that break your equilibrium or drive you to fury, such as when someone betrays your love and trust. Even if you pretend that you're fine and put on the false face, within the embers of your soul is revealed to be your true face, the mirror held up to the Heavens. It is your body, your Spirit team, and God that know how your consciousness truly feels. It's your senses they read and instantly pick up on that have far greater energy than the pretend face you're putting on for others. It's what is in your heart that is read and not how much money you have in the bank, what kind of car you drive, or the awards you have under your name. It is your character and heart the angels see and know to be true over any pretense shown. It is how you choose to act before you achieve your desires.

This is also why you cannot get away with a lie with any spirit being the way you can with another person, unless of course one has a high degree of Claircognizance (clear knowing). Claircognizant beings tend to psychically know when someone is lying, even if they don't call them out on it. Most of the time depending on how severe or harmless the lie is they just keep it to themselves. If everyone increased their psychic abilities innate within them since their soul's conception, then they would be able to detect things like when a media story is exaggerated or produced with the indirect intention of riling your ego up. A raised consciousness also helps in peering beneath the surface and being proactive rather than reactive.

Look at what it is that you continuously jump to anger about. This is one of the many clues as to what your many life purposes are. The next step is to channel that anger positively for the greater good. For example, if you always get angry over those who toss trash everywhere but in a trashcan, then use the anger constructively by seeking out ways to prevent that from happening. Those that get upset over anyone dumping trash in the ocean might be someone who chooses to join an organization like Greenpeace to fight to keep Earth clean. They are turning their anger into positive action.

Someone cut you off in traffic and you immediately understandably rise to anger, but then depending on who you are, you hopefully get over it within a minute and move on. I was biking down a hill once and into a bike line that crosses over a lane for cars that turns right. It's not a busy street, but one car whipped around in front of me out of nowhere to cross over to turn right. They were driving recklessly. If they had accidentally braked, I would've flown into their car. That would drive anyone to anger because it was obvious in that scenario that the driver is an example of an aggressive erratic impatient driver that will eventually cause a major accident due to this angry driving. Sadly, as many have informed me, and I've witnessed this is not uncommon. This is what happens when you give an ego a machine to control and drive around. It then becomes a weapon that the ego feels temporarily invincibly safe within the same way a negative toxic commenter feels safe hiding behind an alias online to type out obscenities and attacks at people all day long. These are false ways that confidence is felt since these technological methods give the illusion of making you feel confident temporarily.

It's the same as mobs that mobilize to protest and enact violence on others they disagree with rather than coming together to fight poverty or child abuse. In those moments they are temporarily confidently empowered behind the safety of a group, which isn't authentic confidence. Having a strong faith-based connection with the Divine generates within true healthy confidence. It operates in a composed, compassionate, and assertive manner rather than a bulldozing violent one.

How about if you discover the person you devoted yourself to in a committed relationship or marriage had been unfaithful to you, or pulled the rug out from underneath you by leaving the connection. The anger felt with that will be greater than the anger over someone cutting you off in traffic. Except in this case the anger turns to sadness and grief, but as hard as it would be to accept it is the ego that is bruised. It can be challenging to get to a place where one comes to the realization that the unfaithful wasn't deliberately trying to hurt you. This doesn't mean you have to be best pals, but part of spiritual growth is getting to that place where you can accept that this is that person's journey and it has nothing to do with you. You are in a different place in life that is more aligned with someone on that same frequency.

For others they'll remain in the epicenter of anger becoming hardened and indefinitely bitter. You'll develop fear that every potential future relationship will result in that person doing the same thing. In that sense, you continuously create the reality that this is what is to be. It plays out in the exact same way over and over again with future mates. That is until you choose to break the pattern and make character adjustments to prevent the same lessons from being repeated indefinitely.

Fear is one of the biggest abundance blocks that continues to destroy humanity on so many levels. When you are afraid of anything in life, then that fear creates a blessing block. This can be fear of the end of the world being near or fear over anything associated with the media or politics. Anything connected to the word fear affects your consciousness, which then affects the flow of positive abundance.

Most of the things you fear and want to run from are the tools you're intended to use to help improve and transform your soul. There is a reason you endure difficult circumstances, whether it's a job you currently don't care for or a relationship connection that didn't end well. You were gaining wisdom, knowledge, and skills while in those circumstances to take with you to the next venture. Every experience I had gave me additional tools and traits that would be needed for my next mission and so on. All experiences you have are not just life changing growth qualities gained, but they happen so that you can apply it to future endeavors.

Take any anger and channel it positively through action. This action should be intended to fix whatever it is you're angry about, otherwise let it go. Being angry at a circumstance that took place or at someone else isn't going to make them change. They're off busy happily doing their thing while you're at home bitter and irritated marinating in that toxic cesspool energy that only attacks your state of well-being.

If you're angry about a particular issue, then stand up and speak out in ways that can benefit others positively. This isn't to be confused with vocally complaining or gossiping about something, or ranting and raving on social media, all of which is lower vibrational negative energy that does nothing to benefit anyone at all ever. If something is bothersome and you feel the need to vent or complain, then turn the words into action statements that can progress matters. If you're upset about a political policy, then tell Congress as many of my friends have done. Rather than posting daily toxic complaints, they're getting dressed up in their Sunday best and standing before Congress to present their case to stay focused and push a particular bill through for approval. If one is legitimately passionate about a particular issue, then they will find ways to change things by going through the right channels where it will make more of a difference than a little social media rant.

If you're truly interested in rising above an issue, then you will communicate in ways that will resolve it so that you can continue moving forward fearlessly instead of remaining stuck in the quicksand of toxicity. Honor your higher self's truth and wishes, which includes speaking your truth with assertiveness and compassion.

Be fearless and stand up for yourself and ask for what you want, whether it is from your Spirit team or those in life that can help you. This can be for something like getting another job to finding the right love partner.

Dissolve all of the layers of negativity you've accumulated so that you can bring that part of your life to closure. Start a bright new chapter each day with a clean slate vibrantly informed. Create more suitable solutions for yourself that will make you infinitely happier in the end. Never do or say anything just to make someone feel better if it makes you feel less than your stellar self by doing so. Channel anger positively to get your soul back into Divine alignment where you are in an assertive, centered focused space.

Dangers of Critical Gossip

Avoid gossiping and negatively talking about others and what you feel they did to you or how you feel about them. When you find you're doing that, wrap it up and shift the words to positive action-oriented words and how you plan to bring things to a resolve. The same goes for those that criticize you. You will be criticized at some point in your life if you haven't already. This is whether you offer services to the public or someone you know harshly criticizes you in a way that is non-constructive with malice intentions. Many have offered different ways of handling that from examining what they're saying; to engaging with them calmly and positively, to sending them love and light. The best way to handle someone like that is to ignore them. You don't engage with someone ranting negatively at, about, or around you. This is the same way you avoid inviting any negative spirit into your aura. There is no positive benefit in engaging with dark energies.

The darkness of ego is the culprit behind negative moods and thoughts. When you allow the light to come cracking in, then that is a sign your higher self is taking back the control. The ego is a dreadful culprit in getting in the physical world's way of true happiness.

Refrain from using world events as a reason to fall into the lower energies of blame, gossiping, and politicizing. Human trauma of any kind can shake one's faith. Don't allow any human tragedy to consume you to the point of fear that you disconnect from the Divine. Free will choice and the darkness of ego have no connection with source.

There will be a natural cycle of uncomfortable emotions that you'll endure, play out, and move through until you've reached that space of having forgiveness for anyone that upset you. This is in order to graduate from that and move forward and onward in your life back into fearless assertive confidence.

Picking Your Battles

One of the other greater challenges many have is maintaining a sense of serenity and peace. This includes getting along with people that are different from you. You're presented with varying circumstances that can easily generate upset. When this happens, then be mindful that it's happening. Your soul was born peaceful and without judgment of those different from you. If someone is happy living their life and they're not hurting anyone, then it's no ego's place to interfere with that. This also doesn't mean you allow someone to bully or run you over. You have to be hyper-vigilant and aware as you navigate Earthly creation whenever other people are around. Many sleepwalk throughout their Earthly life. They move through the same daily routine activities they were trained to do by others early on. Some never work to improve, enhance, and awaken their true consciousness spirit, but merely go along with the popular fads and lingo of that time period they grew up in.

A lower state of being seems to be easier to attain than achieving a higher state of being. The irony is most people that are in a low vibrational state wish they had the latter. They find it challenging to reach a higher state of being. When you're angry about something, then the last thing on your ego's mind is not about re-centering as quickly as possible. It is about jumping into reaction instead of taking a step back to observe and evaluate what and why something is triggering you. Re-centering is the next step to take when you've fallen into a space of negativity or an angry reaction. This isn't asking you to deny your feelings of anger, since anger is one of the many emotions that exist in humankind, but it is an emotion that comes from the ego. You want to find the source of what is causing that anger, then look at the grander picture of what you're angry about to see if it's misplaced or not. Nine times out of ten it tends to be misplaced.

Every hour spent angry is a waste of time. Take that anger and channel it positively through action that can fix or correct whatever it is your angry about otherwise work on letting it go. Being angry with someone else isn't going to change or enlighten that person. They're off happily doing their thing while you're at home brooding over something they did, said, or anything about them. This can be someone you know personally, a public figure, or a stranger.

Some tend to get angrily riled up over something a public figure said or did in the media. This does nothing to change that person and it doesn't resolve anything. You don't know them and you're not in their house having a conversation with them. Instead your aura marinates in that toxic cesspool energy that doesn't hurt the target. It hurts you and your well-being, while simultaneously blocking heavenly spirit guidance from coming in.

Many fall into the allure of posting repetitive complaints on their social media accounts that ultimately wastes time and spreads the dark energies. The ego convinces you that you're being proactive, but darting negative complaints and words to someone isn't proactive but reactive. This dark energy flows into the cells of your body and gets lodged in there when improperly channeled. If someone was out of line with you, then take a moment to sit on that before responding if you have to respond. You'd be surprised how you can win over your opponent when you respond with assertive confidence rather than ruffled aggression.

If the anger is a daily pattern or left unchecked, then it can manifest into something more harmful, such as a breeding ground for future diseases and health issues. Due to the state of humanity today and its obsession with drama, this will cause an enormous amount of health issues, which will be seen in the later years. At press time the trend of posting negative rants on social media is really only about less than ten years old. It hasn't been going on long enough to notice the negative health repercussions, but these health issues are building within them now.

When you're in the epicenter of that developed hurricane of toxicity forming in and around you due to your own words, feelings, and thoughts, then it's difficult to be aware that you are. Dark energy blinds you to the truth for gain of witnessing your own downfall. When one falls into the deep seed of repetitive anger, then they are out of their minds and oblivious to how far down the rabbit hole they've fallen. If this is you, then you later realize that it's been one thing after another going wrong in your life while being unaware of how or why it grew at such an astronomical rate. The dangers can be seen in someone whose consciousness is on the cusp of expanding, otherwise the pattern will repeat indefinitely until death.

One way to counteract this dark energy is by avoiding the gossip media. Stop seeking out salacious top trending headlines and social media posts designed to attract, entice, and lure you in. Avoid commenting and posting attacks wherever possible. The ego loves drama because it's designed to get you caught in its web preventing you from seeking out more positive activities to focus on that bring you into the epicenter of enlightenment. Use discernment and good judgment over what media is worth knowing and what is something that is out of your hands. I've found that most of it is unhelpful.

There are a number of people around me that don't get involved in gossip or media to the point that they really don't know what everyone is arguing about and they like it that way. Unless your job is a position that requires you to correct certain issues you're passionate about, then there is no benefit to joining in with the crowd to argue about the latest dramatic news story. The ones who don't agree with your values won't be positively influenced, so it's a time waster. Politicians do that to each other on Twitter behaving like Children, with other Children chiming in with their banter because they feel like they're being heard. All it creates is a bunch of time-wasting non-productive noise where you're preaching to the choir or you're not. It's not changing anything of value. No one you're attempting to get on your side to agree with you are going to stop and say, "Oh you know what you're right. Thank you for attacking me in a tirade of curse words because I now see your point."

That's never happened in the history of negative rants. Most of the time what people are arguing and gossiping about is forgotten within one to three days as another enticing headline flies to the top of the list to attract in their focus. It can take practice and enormous willpower to not be tempted to read certain types of content. That practice includes immediately knowing whether something is a gossip piece, or an objective balanced news piece focused on straight neutral reporting. If every time you get riled up over media pieces put up by a particular news source, then it's time to step away from that source for awhile in order to get re-centered and re-directed on more important priorities that will ultimately bring you joy and peace.

The ego part of the soul gets riled up and angry in its own way. The trick is to catch it when it happens so that you resolve whatever it is that got a rise out of you. Learn to pick your battles and by quickly taking steps to bring that anger back down to the space of contentment again. This isn't about ignoring your anger and your feelings, but like everything connected to spiritual growth and evolvement you're growing more self-aware of the modifications you need to make. The more content you are, then the more confident you are.

Figuring Life Out As You Go

There is a difference between protesting against something that your values tell you to be wrong, as opposed to rebelling against someone else's sound judgment intended to prevent disaster or chaos from swallowing you up whole. All you can do is let that person figure it out the hard way. It can no doubt be frustrating because you care about that person and don't want to see them fall off that cliff, but in the end it's not up to you. This is their life and they need to stumble and fall on their own. If you spend all your days doing things for them, then they'll never learn anything. They might learn later in life or when it's too late long after you've gone. At that point, they have no other choice, but to find their own way solo.

If you're a parent or guardian of a child, then you have some measure of understanding of this. Especially when a child reaches a certain age where they gradually assert their independence and discover who they are as an individual. This means they will rebel even if what you're telling them is helpful. They may purposely defy you and head right for that cliff anyway just to spite you. It can be maddening to see someone you care about walking towards a cliff knowing there is nothing you can say that will stop them from that. The more you attempt to stop them, the more they carry on towards that cliff. The ego is a rebellious beast that will do what it wants when it wants.

A parent is guiding their child not necessarily to be strict, but because they know what will happen if the child makes an erratic decision. They know because they had gone through it themselves. There comes a point when you need to give someone else wiggle room to be free and discover the art of learning on their own.

A parent is essentially intended to be a guide the way a spirit guide is for a soul. The guide isn't living the soul's life, but gently pointing them in the direction that will bring in the best results for their higher self. While doing this they and you ultimately leave the soul free reign to make the choice that sits most comfortably for them, even if it's a choice that will not be desirable in the end. God is much like a parent with all souls hoping to steer the soul away from danger and towards peace.

If a soul doesn't make mistakes, then how can it grow and evolve? Sometimes it can take someone months, years, or decades for the soul to realize that the way they've been doing things hasn't exactly been successful. That's the start of the change potentially happening within them and then the real work comes in. This change can come in as a call from God or the Divine. Receiving the awakened call is just the beginning, because then you have to put in the work.

The mind and heart are rarely in agreement with each other. Your heart longs for a particular person, job, or circumstance, but your mind talks you out of it. The rational mind loves to dance with the ego, otherwise known as the dance with the Devil. The ego resides in the mind intent on overriding and dominating the higher self. It will insist on doing what it wants to do regardless of what your heart is saying. The ego doesn't like back talk and will stomp its feet in a tantrum after you give it a challenging response that didn't back it up.

There is a reason circumstances take place beyond your control or current understanding. Life ebbs and flows, nothing stays the same, and not every soul sticks around with you throughout your entire Earthly life. Know yourself and learn to be independent of relying on anyone, except God and your angels for guidance.

None of the world drama that goes on matters in the end because every soul on the planet has a Divine plan attached to their consciousness. This is the case even if you cannot see that while in the moment. It is the responsibility and life quest of that soul to come to the conclusion of what their purpose and plan is on its own. No other being can inform them of what it is.

Some find they've given their power away to others, whether it's a friendship, relationship, or family member. There was a time in my late teens and early twenties when I was living hand to mouth with little to no money, but I pulled myself up and began working to take care of me. An example of giving your power away might be if one's partner takes care of things. This prevents you from being independent. Eventually a time comes where you feel suffocated and stuck wanting to move on, but you're unable to because your partner pays the bills and you haven't had a job in years. This makes you feel even more paralyzed and stuck.

You can get unstuck from giving your power away by taking steps to fix the circumstance. You rise up into that fearless assertive confidence within you and take back the controls. Once you find work and begin making your own money, then you are able to take steps to leaving the person you've given your power away to. This is no different than when you are a young person living under your parent's roof. If you don't want to live in a situation forever, then you need to become an independent adult and do something about it by conjuring up Divine fearless confidence from within. Get a job, make money to survive, and find another place to move to. You can't live life depending on someone else to save you. Take the bull by the horns and take control.

CHAPTER FOUR

*Identify Blocks to
Abundance and Blessings*

It's beneficial to reach that place where you are grateful and thankful for what you have in the moment. It's a difficult task to accomplish when your soul knows what it desires next and sees no movement. I understand this frustration as I've been there too. What I have desired eventually has come to fruition, which is why I share those personal stories. It's to illustrate that I'm not spouting off random wisdom on a teabag, but have gone through the hard times myself on so many levels. I've gone through it and endured it, then found ways to conquer and overcome it. This includes from the incessant child abuse to the toxic addictions to cigarettes, alcohol, and drugs, to rising up the ranks behind the scenes in the entertainment business. The stories of what I've endured are numerous, but it's said to give someone else hope that is in those trenches right now. You can climb out of it with a strong confident will and determination. It will be a long running fight, but in the end, you'll reach that Promised Land.

One of the many teachings that Heaven has passed down to me is to feel grateful for what you have now. This state of being is what raises your vibration. The raised vibration is what brings in those desires you crave. The feeling grateful condition is of benefit to you because of the rewards that come with it. When you're feeling good, then more of that greatness comes into your life. When you feel lousy, pessimistic, and miserable, then it's as if it is one bad thing happening after another. What you put out is returned back to you and what you reap you sow. Plant the seeds of what you want now, and then on Divine timing watch it blossom into fruitful flowers and come to fruition. These are common metaphors because many have expressed to having tested out these theories with great success.

It is common sense that if you want a job, then you have to fill out job applications or send out your resume. No one is going to call you with a job offer if they don't know who you are or that you're looking for work. You want to win the lottery, then increase your chances by buying a ticket. These are basic examples of how the universe works. When you put a little action-oriented effort, and you ask your Spirit team for assistance, then they meet you halfway. It isn't enough to do all three, but you want to also feel optimistic, excitement, and gratefulness at the same time. Putting all of those traits together is a winning combination that will take you closer towards success instead of keeping you perpetually negative, pessimistic, and full of worry.

Whenever I would suggest anything to some people that could help positively change their life, they would respond with something negative. I would hear statements such as, "Oh they'll never hire me. They'll want someone thinner or younger. I'm not qualified."

I noticed the repetitive negative words being voiced. You have to want to fight for your life. Don't govern it based on what you think others want. You might be surprised to find that when you keep kicking a door that it will eventually be knocked down and you'll get that breakthrough at any age and no matter your qualifications, experience, or stats.

If there comes a point when you're helping someone else to make positive changes that you discover they're not interested in ever changing, then this is your cue to begin backing away. There is nothing more you can say that will break someone out of their monotony. It's been months and maybe even years of the same sad song being sung from that person. When in that negative state, the individual is not always putting in the work or asking for Divine intervention and help. How I obtained my past desires we're by stepping into confidence, asking for Divine help, and following the guidance they gave me by putting in the work through action. There were the naysayers and critics, but they will always be circling like gnats as you've likely come to experience yourself on occasion. You don't pay any attention to that and continue forging on with your purpose and goals living life for you.

Whenever there has been anything I wanted to accomplish, then I would have consistent excitement and optimism about it inside. There were the occasional doubts or worry that I would not obtain my goal, but those feelings were rare and miniscule. The feeling would only pop up once in a blue moon for a brief moment, and then it would blow away just as fast. It was so infrequent that it did not dominate or rule me. I'd naturally and quickly move right back to optimism and in feeling grateful. I also had it in the back of my mind that I would keep trying to do what I wanted, because I wanted it bad enough. I frequently asked my Spirit team for assistance in prayer. I paid attention to what they were guiding me to do and then I took action and followed it. With hard work, passion, and persistence I eventually saw results begin to trickle in. There is no such thing as instant successes. It's a matter of little action steps each day that are bringing the success closer to you.

Sometimes the grateful state of mind is experienced by force such as a less than stellar situation takes place in your life. You wish you weren't complaining so much because now things have grown worse. Those experiences are also designed to teach your soul gratitude and humility. It is by pushing you into a harder circumstance in order to see that during your previous repetitive complaining juncture that things were not as bad as they could be. Now they are worse in order to send your soul that wake-up call to have more gratitude. You experience gratitude when you are aware that you may not be where you want to be yet, but you are grateful for the things that are working in your life. This is what opens up the doorway for blessings to enter the picture.

Constant complaining is a block preventing positive movement. Coming across someone who has it far worse than you do is something that can shake someone out of their negative rut. The guilt comes on for having complained repeatedly about how unhappy you are with where you're currently at. No one in Heaven wants to see you unhappy. They do want to help guide you out of it. You're not purposely being ignored since they're not cruel. There are steps that need to be taken to reach that space of happiness. There are also emotional traits such as gratitude and humility that need to be gained in the process. You are forced to be humble so that when the good stuff does come in you will be in a place to receive it in the right modest spirit.

Guilt is another trait that can block one from success. You feel a twinge of guilt that you are undeserving of good and this creates a block between yourself and your desires. I've had the slight guilt that would pinch me wondering if I was asking for too much. Luckily, those moments were rare since most of the time my basic nature is one of optimism. Guilt also comes onto someone who feels they're being an imposition. Someone sensitive with strong Clairsentient psychic channels might feel guilt when someone wants to help or do something nice for them. It's merely a matter of catching yourself when you fall into a negative state, and then immediately work on shifting your mind's thoughts down a more positive and uplifting direction.

If the guilt were a reaction to how poorly you treated someone else, then you would work on shifting away from the guilt and make amends with the person you treated in a hurtful way. This is by being aware of your surroundings and how you treat others. You pay that karmic debt back by reaching out to that person to bury the hatchet from a place of compassion. You consciously know that you want to make it right. Once that's accomplished you move on to the next level. It sounds contradictory to point out that you should not feel guilt, but you should also not feel anything at all either, because then you're moving into sociopathic territory. The trick is to find that middle ground where you're aware of how or what you've done to someone, but you're not drowning in the guilt. Nor are you living in a state where you are unfazed by your behavior.

Some circumstances have barriers and blocks preventing you from experiencing the life you want. When you've admitted to the negative feelings you are allowing to plague you, then that is a great step towards reaching the breaking point where you're freed.

You become highly aware of what has caused these uncomfortable emotions. You've sacrificed your happiness to do what you feel is right. This is an amazing quality to have, but it's also time to begin the process of thinking of you first. There's nothing selfish about making sure that you're taken care of before anything or anyone else. If you're not taken care of, then it's difficult to take care of anyone else. Others may walk all over you and take advantage of your goodness when you display signs of being totally selfless with nothing in return. They don't all necessarily do that on purpose, which is where one must train them to treat you and others with respect. In general, they are typically not fully aware that this is how they're behaving.

As you remove the barriers that have been erected in front of you on your path, then your psychic Clair sense channels will begin to work at optimum levels. The negative feelings are creating these blocks. You're applauded when you make positive life changes, such as giving up or reducing certain addictions that cause these blocks. Sometimes that's not enough if the negative feelings are still there as that is also a block. This is partially why working on extricating negative thoughts and feelings is equally essential. You have a conscious and you're extremely aware of what's going on around you, so it's challenging to not be paying attention to it or noticing how you feel.

Unhealthy relationship connections are also a block. There can be some relationship healing that needs to take place. This includes forgiveness, letting go of blame, or any feelings of victimhood associated with a broken connection that continues to plague you.

Your mind and your body go through a workout with physical human life challenges. It can be super exhausting causing you to feel overwhelmed and stuck. All of these circumstances can create blocks in your way from obtaining good. Know that you do deserve good and are deserving of love.

These blocks can be removed by requesting heavenly assistance. Other ways are by taking frequent breaks throughout each day. This is taking at least fifteen minutes once a day where that time is solely for you. Find an area where it's not crowded with people and take regular walks. It can be to walk around the block, through a quiet nature setting, or strolling through a place where you know you won't feel assaulted by any harsh energy emitting off of others. This includes avoiding a busy street with cars racing by. You need quiet serenity in order to contemplate and commune with Spirit. Doing this will help you to clear your mind out, raise your vibrational state, and allow for great ideas on your next steps to flow in.

Allow your thoughts to wander while on these walks. Your thoughts may start off on the negative side over a circumstance that's been bothering you, or you'll be thinking about where you're at with your life. While being outside and going for those walks, you'll work on emptying all of that stuff out that's distracting and plaguing your mind. Sudden revelations, guidance, and awakenings are received from spirit while doing that. Someone goes on their tenth walk and arrives back home with an amazing idea that has filtered through them that was guided by spirit. It turns out to be an answered prayer.

Your team can easily work on you when you're not distracted by anything else.

Look at every year as another chapter in the book that is your life. Work with God and your Spirit team by communicating with them regularly on how you would like to see your life mapped out. It doesn't matter if you feel that you're talking to yourself or not hearing them. You are heard and eventually the answer will come to realization for you.

Admitting is the first step to recovery. When you've admitted that the way things are in your life are not jiving with what your soul truly desires now, then the closer you are to progress. You are ready for changes and to have things shaken up a bit. It might seem as if you're off track or at a standstill, but you are on track more than it appears. A standstill feeling is the crossroads point where the inner transformation takes place as you begin to move in the direction towards what you truly love.

CHAPTER FIVE

*Be the Chief Executive
of Your Life*

Who doesn't want positive abundance flowing into their lives? Most everyone desires some level of monetary success to live on the planet comfortably without worry knowing that their bills are paid, with clothes on their back and food on the table. Money is considered evil in some circles, but that is a dramatic statement since money is only as important as the value you place on it. Abundance and success are not only related to money. It can be success in a love relationship or victory in any accomplishment you've succeeded in. This includes one of the most important types of success, which is inner soul triumph

Your soul's life moves in cycles in the same way that your human life moves in phases. These cycles are full of endings and new beginnings. Your day comes to an end when you head off to sleep at whatever time that might be. When you wake up the next day you start a new beginning. Look at this new beginning as if it is a new page within the chapter of the book you're writing that is your life. Twenty-four more hours are put into your next day's bank account. You are the manager of your soul's existence and all choices you decide to make that day. Direct each day in the manner that you would like it to go. Take control of this page within the chapter of your book and write the words that you want to see happen.

When you begin each day with the intention that it will be full of good, then this is far more effective than beginning your day with worry, anger, sadness, or any other negative emotion. The state of mind you choose to begin your day in is what will dictate how your day will go. Wake up each day with the objective that you will feel good. If you're heading to your job, then head into work experiencing greatness! Even if you're not a big fan of your job, it is far more effective energy having a positive mindset and making the most of it rather than shuffling in miserable.

Having a positive mindset is what brightens up your day and those around you. It is also what brings more of that good stuff into your life because this energy is a magnet bringing something of equal or greater value to you. It's inevitable that there will be roadblocks that drop down in the way on your path. You could run into a toxic person while in your car, at a store, on the sidewalk, or at work. When that happens, you will deal with it like an efficient executive since you are the CEO of your life. Allow those moments that ruin your great day to evaporate. Mentally scoop it up with your hand and toss it out like you're pitching a softball as far as it can go. Ask the Archangel Michael to protect and shield you from harsh toxic energies when you begin each day.

Self-Fulfilling Prophecies

Everyone wants to feel good each day of their life. Concern settles in when life is not going according to the way you dream or desire. You worry that the things you want will never happen or that you're going to be perpetually stuck. Life is always moving, shifting, and changing. Nothing stays permanently the same. Look at the decisions or the non-action choices you're making or have made that are a result of you feeling stuck. If you get up every morning to spend your day surfing the Internet up until lunchtime, then how will anything change in your life? That's an example of how non-action won't bring you the results you crave. I've heard many cases where someone asks for help in prayer, but nothing comes. What are you doing to help it along? Do you pray and then go back to watching videos, scrolling social media or any other time waster?

There are moments when non-action is an action in itself. Sometimes you're guided to not make any decisions until the coast is clear or Divine timing has taken place. This is about making no choices that positively contribute to a change happening in your life.

Worry is a fear-based emotion generated from your ego, but it is also part of the natural human experience in order to master it. It is an emotion that creates a block between you and what you crave. It is a normal reaction to feel fear that something is not going the way you hoped. Concern comes about when something isn't going your way or when you're about to make a big change in your life. When this happens, call on your Spirit team and ask them to help give you faith, strength, support, and direction. Ask them to give you confidence and clarity to notice when to take action and to be pushed to do so.

From the angel's perspective there is nothing to be concerned about. They see that all will always be well in the end when you have them in your corner. It might feel as if it's impossible not to worry about a situation while you're moving through a specific experience, but when you worry, then you create a self-fulfilling prophecy that brings more obstacles into your life that will add even more anxiety. Thoughts produce things and can magnify a situation by bringing similar situations that are equal to the emotion you're experiencing.

A common phrase I've heard others say is, "Why do bad things keep happening to me?" When you worry about one thing, then this brings about other similar things. When you feel uneasiness about anything at all, then call upon your Spirit team and request that they ease your heart and mind of this worry. Understand the concept that in the bigger picture worry never lasts since situations never last. There are peaks and valleys as well as highs and lows in your life. Eventually your soul will travel back home upon your human death and then the worry is suddenly irrelevant and non-existent.

When experiencing fearfulness, not only is it effective to ask for help, but also work on changing the tone and overall essence of your emotions and thoughts to that of love. This is thinking or saying something like, "All will be well in the end. I know this without a doubt. None of this matters and this too shall pass."

When you lose your job, then the emotions experienced will vary from one person to another. Some will understandably worry about how they will pay their bills, while others will adopt a newfound amazing positive energy out of the job loss. They will see it as a blessing in disguise since deep down they were terribly unhappy at this job to begin with. It was soul crushing and sucking out their life force. When the job was taken away out of nowhere, then their soul eventually experiences freedom. You are now free to start a new chapter in your life wherever you choose. You may still wrestle with the fear of the unknown in that situation. Bills need to be paid to survive so that's an understandable worry. Make a Divine request for a strengthening in faith and to be guided to a brighter situation that will ensure you are physically taken care of financially.

If you've been unhappy at your job, then look for work that will excite you and bring out your passionate side. When something is lost, something else is gained. In order to bring in a new and better situation, the universe will abruptly remove something to make room for what's to come. At first your ego will look at it in panic, while your higher self will see the potential that can come out of it.

This is the same with love relationships. When you lose someone who meant the world to you because that person decided they were no longer interested, or the connection has run its course, then you open the door to allowing someone in who is more aligned with you, your values, and who you are.

In my past work life, I've accepted job offers where I was making less than what I made in prior jobs, but in the end the money multiplied over time to the point where I was making double what I had ever made before. The reason I accepted a job that was little pay was because I eagerly wanted to do that particular work for various reasons, including the knowledge I would gain from the experience. The money came in effortlessly and in bigger ways than it had ever done. This was because my vibration was high. I looked at the job with joy, love, and excitement. I wanted to be doing that kind of work. I would have done it for free. It wasn't about the money and therefore the money came rolling in as a result. Sometimes there is a risk, but I was perfectly content with that chance and the rest came in naturally. When you move through a transition and into a new chapter, then be open to receiving that change in the right spirit!

Noble Service

Focusing on service is a great way to raise your vibration and get the positive energy flowing in your life. It adjusts your focus into helping others instead of being hyper focused on you and how you're feeling at any given moment. When you're focused on yourself, then you're fixated on pleasing your ego. When you're experiencing worry, stress, or anxiety, then adjust your attention in the direction of how you can help someone else in need. It not only alleviates any negative emotions experienced, but it uplifts you to be able to help someone else. This raises your vibration, which then attracts more positive circumstances to you. Suddenly the worries you previously had will evaporate out of your aura and into the universe.

Having a connection with your Spirit team enables you to be able to help others in a positive way. When you're feeling out of sorts or unfocused, then reach out to others to see how you can assist them. This will help raise your vibration to a place of joy and contentment. You'll be on cloud nine when you are able to be of service and help someone out that truly needs it. At the same time be alerted to not be taken advantage of by others due to your kindness. You've got to be sensitively sharp and on the psychic ball to see through the dangers of someone taking advantage of you.

This is an egotistical world with a grandiose sense of entitlement, which is a negative side effect to the rise of technology and social media giving everyone a voice. There is a fine line one walks between believing you deserve something to carrying an arrogant air of privilege. If you do not merge into that middle ground mindset, then you'll get walked all over by everyone else.

Society, technology, your peers, the media and the Internet have trained humankind to display a self-absorbed aura. There are good selfless souls threaded around the world to counteract this attitude by being of service. This is not only to help others, but also to show that in the end good deeds prevail. No one warms up to a self-entitled brat, but instead they grow more distant to humankind. Direct your efforts into showing compassion and helping those in need or those who could use a friend and listening ear. This carries over to all aspects of your life.

Working For You

One awesome trait to successful self-employment requires that you be self-disciplined. You take your job seriously as if it were any other job. Instead of answering to someone else, you must answer to yourself. This is a good and bad thing depending on the dynamic. Who doesn't want to turn their hobby into a lucrative enterprise? One of the steps in doing that is to keep your side day job while you work at your hobby. If it truly is your hobby, then it won't feel like a drag to dive into it during off hours. This is another reason guides on the Other Side tend to insist on everyone taking care of themselves on all levels. This way you don't experience early burn out. You have more energy and stamina to do both the regular income-making job, while you work at growing your side hobby business. Taking care of yourself also gives you stronger psychic channels to pick up on the wisdom required.

Don't quit your day job until you know for sure that you are consistently making enough to survive with the incoming money from your hobby. Ask your Spirit team to work with you full time in building your side business into full time work. The Archangels to call on for Heavenly assistance with this are Archangel Gabriel *(motivation manager)*, Archangel Nathaniel *(life purpose work)*, Archangel Michael *(eradicate fear)*, and Archangel Ariel *(abundance and supplies)*.

Know that it may take some time before you are able to quit your regular day job. It could take years, but if you believe it in enough and enjoy what you do, then eventually results will be forthcoming. It also won't feel like work doing what you love on the side. Building a business is like climbing a mountain until you reach the top. It will be a struggle at times, but it is a challenge that you can overcome with an endless reservoir of persistence, dedication, faith, confidence, and passion. This same mindset is the way you rule your life. In a sense, all souls are self-employed at heart. You manage you, your life, relationships, and your entire surroundings with the same commitment and enthusiasm you would as if it we're your own business. You are the chief executive of your life.

Dealing With Life's Setbacks

Many have expressed frustration due to working so hard and contributing so much, yet they feel there isn't enough return or pay off. Maybe you're not being rewarded or compensated at all. While the work itself is its own reward, you live in a world that requires monetary compensation for basic necessities in order to survive. Have patience and keep on trucking forward. A winner perseveres regardless of setbacks, rejections, or delays. Heaven is aware of what you've been doing, and they want to see you be at a place where you're at peace. Know that they cannot wave a magic wand and the monetary success you desire comes flying into your lap. They cannot force your next love partner to knock on your front door. They do what they can from where they are to help make things happen for you as long as it's aligned with your higher self's path and not ego filled desires.

They give you clues and signs while attempting to communicate with you on what you can do to help make it happen along quicker through action steps required on your part. When you are in tune, then you are in harmony to the guidance and steps your Spirit team is filtering through you to assist you along your life's path and in conquering your dreams. Keep in mind they are also wrestling with the free will choices of those who can help you attain success.

Roadblocks can be something like you desire a love partner and your team has one in mind. The issue is that both you and this potential partner are not paying attention to your Guide and Angel. Instead you are both ruling through free will choice. One or the both of you might not be following the guidance you're being given. There is a gradual progression upwards towards your dreams as you move through life following the guidance your Spirit team is aiming you towards.

If you are an awesome and wonderful hardworking soul, then avoid allowing negativity to enter your field. Stay focused on what you need to do and be anchored by faith and passion. Circumstances may be dormant, but nothing relatively bad is happening to you, yet you feel stuck beyond comprehension. Look at how far you've come and the progress you've made, rather than why the things you desire have not shown up yet.

Heaven and the angels save you in a myriad of ways that sometimes might seem pretty small at the time, but in hindsight appear fated.

Rock singer Alanis Morissette has one of the bestselling albums of all time called, *Jagged Little Pill*. The album came out about a week after her 21st birthday in 1995. Two years before that she was in a different situation. She was nineteen years old and made a big move to Los Angeles when she immediately ran into some trouble. She was heading home carrying two bags with her. One of the bags had her money in it and the other bag had the lyrics to her not yet recorded album for *Jagged Little Pill*.

A thief was following her and came at her with a gun. She felt enormous panic and fear praying that this person would not take the bag that had her *Jagged Little Pill* lyrics. Guess which bag he took?

He took the bag with her money and not the bag that had her lyrics for *Jagged Little Pill*, an album that was bought by nearly almost everyone on the planet when it came out. It ended up selling over 33 million copies. It's been on numerous top bestselling lists. At press time of this book, it is the 13th highest selling album in history. What if the thief had taken her work instead of the money? There was a reason he was prompted to take the money instead of the art. At that time, she was broke and had not become a financially successful artist yet. The money taken was all of her funds. It was interesting that she was relieved that the money was stolen and not the lyrics.

As a creative artist, I understand how the art can overtake a financial situation. I was working on my computer when out of a clumsy reflex I smacked my tea, which fell onto the keyboard. Within minutes the computer shut down and did not turn back on. My heart raced with panic. This was not because I would have to shelve out money for another computer, but because I had spent the week producing so much writing work that I worried it was gone for good. There is no way I could repeat it word for word. I hadn't yet transferred the work out onto a flash drive for back up as I do pretty regularly. This is not the same as being robbed, but the point was that the money was less of an issue over losing my work. Luckily, the computer was saved as well as my work for a lower fee than anticipated. I also attribute that to asking for immediate Divine assistance and intervention by my team after the accident.

Money is a piece of paper that we apply value to. In the Alanis story she needed money, but it wasn't of importance to her when face to face with the thief. It was the creative art she feared losing. The money came to her later by not craving it on any level. It wasn't something she sought out.

CHAPTER SIX

*Optimistic Visualization,
Getting Enthusiastic and Taking Action*

The power of visualization has been known to create extraordinarily magical results in your life. What assists in contributing to making great things happen are a few central steps: Optimistic Visualization, Paying Attention, and Taking Action.

Optimistic Visualization Foresight

One of the tasks to put into practice towards accomplishing your goals is working on altering your perception into a positive confident mindset. This simple easy reminder is needed for when you stray too far off into negativity that it becomes your newly adopted personality trait. Positivity equates to you being a stronger abundance attractor, while reinforcing your connection with your Spirit team. This is because positivity and optimism reside in the higher vibrational energy field. It is the high vibrational state that allows an effortless connection with God.

Raising your consciousness simultaneously raises your vibration giving you a deeper awareness. This impeccable mindfulness helps in identifying the subtle cues coming in from the Divine that go unnoticed within and around you. Those cues are important because that communication is what is guiding you towards your purposes that need to be fulfilled in your lifetime. It is what prompts you to take notice of when a shift in thinking and feeling processes on your part is necessary. You were born able to access Divine communication effortlessly, but over time blocks rose up in your life that prevented you from having a crystal-clear connection with God and your Spirit team. One of the tasks of a spirit guide is to guide you through life to help it be less friction oriented, than it would be if they weren't around. They guide you towards experiences they know will help shape, mold, and evolve your soul. They want to see the student snap into soul reality and become blissfully aware of all that is greater than the limited of the superficial. This requires your work to tune into them and heed their guidance.

Having spent my lifetime studying the human condition to the point of hair splitting, I've noticed that those who are believers in a higher power and remain in that state have less of a hard time in life than those that don't believe. This doesn't mean that those who are believers are problem free, but life is not as dramatic without that connection. It's also why gossips and those that love drama seem to have little to no spirit connection while in that state. Their life also seems to be filled with daily negativity and drama.

Another way to achieve your dreams is to put it in your mind that you will obtain what you desire. This is pending that what you desire is not harmful to your well-being or another person's. It will be something beneficial for your higher self's goal and soul's growth. Nothing should stop you from achieving and positively attracting good stuff pending it's not harming yourself or another.

Fears, insecurities, or low self-esteem are abundance success killers. They were born out of the darkness of ego and the human development stage. God and higher evolved beings don't entertain the lower energy, even though there are religious groups that focus on those lower energy elements and then say it's from God. I don't know any God that enjoys the evil and darkness of lower energy. The lower energy is of the Devil and has the intent of sabotaging and criminalizing you. Occasional fears will creep in on you on occasion, but when that's all that plagues your mind daily dominating your thoughts, then it will take over and do its best to destroy your goal. The goal of the Darkness is to stop you from finding the Light. It will do this in ways that convince you that you're unworthy. Avoid allowing negativity to take over and drown you.

Believe you already have what you want. Even when it seems impossible to enter your life, imagine it's a part of your life now. In your mind, close your eyes, and visualize it in motion. Feel it in every crevice of your cells as if it's happening now. Feel the good feelings associated with how you would feel having what you desire. This energy expands and spills into your reality by helping to make it happen from this visualization. This visualization is something that should be done regularly until you have what you desire.

If you desire to buy your own house one day, then begin the visualization of having this house. You can close your eyes at least once a day and envision what this house will look like. You'll visualize its surroundings, the kinds of neighbors that are around you, the location, and everything about it. You'll then visualize yourself living in this house, walking around throughout it, sleeping in your bed in this house, making a meal in the kitchen, the kinds of friends you have visiting this house, or the love partner that is with you in this house, and so on. Notice your feelings and state of mind and how you'll feel while living in this house as this is happening.

You can apply this visualization exercise to whatever you desire, whether it's a love relationship, job, car, or anything you desire. This is pending it is aligned with your higher self's purpose and God's will. The benefits to this visualization exercise are that it programs your mind to move away from the doubts and fears that you'll attract this in. It also assists in getting the positive energy surrounding this visualization towards making it happen.

When you wallow in negative feelings and thoughts that you'll never attract in what you desire, then this creates a separation between yourself and this desire that grows wider and further away from you. When you think good stuff associated with this desire, then it starts to bring the aspiration closer to you through this energy. You're already creating with your thoughts and feelings anyway, so you may as well make it positive oriented.

Using your imagination visually paint the picture of what you desire. Experience feelings associated with confidence and enthusiasm surrounding this visual, as if it is real and here in your life happening now. Avoid allowing doubts or worry to enter your mind as that can negate the process. When you experience negative feelings, then this energy multiplies causing more of that pessimism to come into your vicinity.

Optimistic visualization is about believing that what you want is coming to you with great veracity. Some achieve this by creating a vision board. A vision board or visual scrapbook is cutting out photographs of ideas of what you would like to have in your life. Pick up magazines to find these images or print them off your computer. You can use the vision board for whatever you choose from the kind of house you would like to live in, to the type of love interest you envision having, or for any other desires.

The reason some put a vision board together is because it helps them focus on what they want without forgetting about it or veering away from it. If they wake up every morning and the first thing they see is the vision board they made, then those images continue to build and seep into that person's consciousness. This is the same as those that have empowering words carved out and hanging around their house. It serves as a reminder so that they don't forget. The world is a busy place and people are distracted and rushing around. You're focused on negative feelings or on mundane practical tasks that need to get done. Soon you find that you've grown stuck in that routine energy. If you have these images and words up around your home, on your computer screen, or in a specific place where you see it regularly, then this triggers the essence, energy, and vision of what you want.

You've had another trying day at work arriving home beat and defeated. The first thing you see when you walk into your place is this board you created reminding you of the things you desire. It uplifts you a bit to see these images. Not everyone will want to have this vision board up on the mantle in their living room where all who come to visit see it. Perhaps it doesn't go with your décor. Find a place where you remember to catch a glimpse of it or have access to it. You can certainly shove it in your closet out of view from visitors, but don't forget it's there. Maybe stick it in a corner in your room or any other place that you know you'll remember having it.

A vision board or motivating words on a mantel are a reminder to stay focused on your purpose and visualize what you want. The images you put on this board are right in front of you. Sometimes pulling the board down and gazing at the images or words at the end of the night or at the start of your day can help uplift you and put a smile on your face reminding you of what you desire. This uplifting feeling raises your vibration back up. What a great way to start each day.

The power of optimistic visualization is immensely helpful in obtaining your desires. Sometimes one can forget what's important when they are bogged down in the practicalities of their everyday life. They forget to daydream and visualize what will make them happy.

Daydreaming includes the dreams you have while sound asleep to the kinds of imaginative visuals you conjure up in your mind during waking hours. If you're someone that has frequent vivid dreams, then one of your dominant psychic senses is Clairvoyance.

Keep a notepad or journal near you to jot down key visuals that are in your dreams. Dreams tend to fade immediately or within minutes to an hour after waking. This is the benefit of writing it down quickly before you forget. Otherwise you'll find you're one of those people who later in the day says, "I had the greatest dream last night, but I can't remember any of it."

You only remember the feeling it gave you. Your subconscious mind is where the greatest psychic input resides because your ego is asleep at that time. It's not getting in your way of receiving heavenly guidance and messages to discredit it.

Souls with an active imagination prone to daydreaming are that much closer to understanding the process of manifestation. A jaded blocked adult might tell a child, "Get your head out of the clouds and quit daydreaming."

This is tragic since the child has a better shot at manifesting their desires over the cynical adult. Daydreaming requires one to be still and allow their thoughts to drift away from what is their current reality. Some daydream in order to escape an unhappy life. It's used as a safety device as they imagine what they wish their life would be like. Daydreaming is an escape in this scenario and used for their protection. If your home life is horrible or abusive, then it's not uncommon for that person to become a daydreamer of a life that is more pleasing to that person.

Daydreaming is also a great way to connect with Heaven and your Spirit team, since your thoughts are relaxed and moving towards what you desire. You're open to receiving psychic hits, messages, and guidance. Daydreaming is typically filled with positive wish-filled thoughts, which raise one's vibration and assists in manifesting good things in that individual's life. Great ideas come to you when you are in a daydream state since your connection to your Guides and Angels is stronger. You're not pushing for Divine information while in a daydream state, so it flows through you naturally.

Get Happy Now and the Rest Will Follow

Getting positive and optimistic isn't about covering up your negative thoughts with phony positive ones. The positive thoughts and feelings need to be authentic and unforced; otherwise it's just a negativity mask in disguise like hiding a cut behind a Band-Aid. Feel the good energy by partaking in fun healthy activities that you know will raise your vibration. Feeling positive thoughts and feelings authentically is experiencing those vibrations inside you.

Ask for Heavenly intervention and help through prayer, then pay attention to the guidance you're expected to act on and take that action. You may not receive an answer at the time you're praying, but ask God and your Spirit team to show you signs of what to do. Request that they continuously reveal this answer in a way that you can recognize it.

Divine guidance will usually come to you three times or more. It repeatedly enters your auric field through your psychic clair senses in hopes you'll discover that it's a message. When your psychic senses are strong, then you're more likely to pick up on the messages coming in. Your Spirit team will continue to give you the same signs until you notice it.

Bring in what you desire by allowing it to flow towards you naturally. You're not chasing your dreams in a panic. You're taking productive action steps through methodical movements with love to obtain what you long for. If there's someone you're interested in romantically, then ask them out whether or not you're male or female. Regardless of their answer, don't chase or burden them by staying on top of them relentlessly. When it's the right one, it will flow and merge with you naturally and organically. Placing any kind of demands will push it away. The same goes for work related endeavors or anything you have your eyes set on. The serious relationships I've had over the course of my life all transpired without effort. It came to be when I wasn't looking or longing, but when I was content. When I was frustrated or in a negative mindset, nothing came to pass.

Actress Nicole Kidman once said there was a time when her fantasy life was richer than her reality. She dove into working on back-to-back films because her real life outside of work was less than she originally hoped. Over time this was reversed where her real life became everything she dreamed of with the house, husband, and family. Those particular things may not be of interest to you, but the point was that she escaped into work not realizing these other things outside of that were being moved into position. She worked hard and the rewards she desired eventually one day came.

If you continuously fall into a negative mindset, then be aware of when that happens and mentally tell yourself something like, *"I need to adjust the vibration levels of my thinking."*

Follow that with shifting and raising the negative direction of your thoughts into optimistic ones. When you've been wallowing in negativity, then that can block good stuff from flowing to you. It's easy to fall into despair and frustration when enormous time has passed, and your desires haven't manifested into reality. When you look back on the passing time, it might seem that nothing in your life has changed. You feel stagnant like being indefinitely stuck in the mud. You crave positive change and stimulation, but good stuff ceases to flow in. There isn't anything bad or negative happening in your life, which is a blessing that isn't often appreciated, but there is zero movement with anything at all. You are not where you thought or envisioned you would be five years prior. This can put a damper on your faith as you wonder what you've been doing wrong. When this happens, revert back to faith and prayer to help re-align your soul. This is when you discover that the stagnancy is no accident. Even Jesus was in living in stagnant obscurity for a long period of time before that began to change.

Paying Attention

Pay attention to the guidance and messages that your Spirit team is relaying to you. If you're unclear on what your next step should be, then carve out some time where you can sit quietly in meditation. Meditation helps you pick up on the guidance from spirit coming in. Some have expressed uncertainty on how to meditate or what it is. You move into a slight meditative state as you drift off to sleep at night without realizing it. It dissolves or reduces your waking ego and brings forth your consciousness. The answers come in clearer when you are calm, peaceful, centered, and in a setting that matches those traits. This is one of the many reasons that the angels advise that human souls be outdoors in nature. Nature settings are calming, and it relaxes the mind. When the mind is relaxed, then the messages and guidance are picked up on in a clearer way. There is no distraction of the physical material world when you are hanging out in a low crowded nature setting. It takes some measure of discipline, since you need to shut off all noisy distractions such as television, cell phones, and boisterous people.

I've had cases where I sit down and Heaven's messages rush in out of nowhere, but then my phone buzzes near me and I have this urge to reach for it. After a number of times of being easily distracted I finally mumble, "Okay, that's it. This needs to be off."

I turn the phone off or put it in another room where I'm unable to hear it vibrating. My mind moves incredibly fast where I'm seeing and picking up on every nuance. I have to be disciplined about my surroundings when it's time for me to get down to psychic business.

If you have trouble meditating due to not being focused, then create an atmosphere that works for you. This would be one that is set up in a way that easily moves you into a peaceful state. One way to do this is to find a place where there are no obtrusive distractions. Play some soft background music, light a candle, then sit and focus on it. Allow any mindless chatter or distracting energies to evaporate. Sitting or lying down works, but you might find that when you lay down that you drift off to sleep. It is okay if this happens since your Spirit team embeds messages into your consciousness. If clairvoyance is one of your stronger Clairs, then you might get the messages and guidance while dreaming.

If you're new to meditation, then don't worry if you're not receiving anything right away. The first number of times practice meditating without any intention of picking up on your Spirit team's guidance. When you strain to receive messages, then this blocks you from obtaining anything. Sometimes the guidance can come in after you've relaxed in meditation. You might have spent about fifteen minutes in this meditation state where you've cleared your mind and then you get up to continue on with your life. It's not uncommon for there to be a delay before you pick up on the messages. As you're getting ready for bed later on, suddenly the crystal-clear Heavenly guidance comes rushing in through one of your Clair channels. You cry out, "That's it! That's the answer."

You're swiftly filled with excitement and optimism, which is another sign that you've received Heavenly guidance, since there are no doubts, worry, or any other negative feeling involved when it's guidance from Heaven.

Divine Guidance Through Action

You may start to fear that Spirit and Heaven are ignoring you or perhaps the non-movement is out of your hands. Consider the possibility that Spirit is diligently working behind the scenes throughout that entire time and have not had much luck getting things moving for you. They have to work with other people's free will choices that go against what is intended to take place. They're also putting up signs, guidance, and messages for you or others to act on. You or another might be ignoring those action steps; sometimes for years thus no movement happens during that time. They can't reveal the next step until the first action step they've been throwing in front of you is taken. It doesn't matter if that action step takes one month or ten years. The same repetitive action step will keep popping up in front of you for a reason until you notice it and act on it.

There can be cases where you have been putting in the tireless work and action steps. There is nothing you did wrong to cause your life to feel forever stationary. There could be other factors at play to consider. Some of that might be the maneuvering of the puzzle pieces your Spirit team is attempting to orchestrate to help move things along. There are also the free will choices you or another party is choosing that go against what Spirit is recommending. Spiritual teachings contribute Divinely guided information to help those interested in becoming clearer vessels for God, which simultaneously has a positive effect on your soul's consciousness.

In an earlier chapter I mentioned that it took me seven years to get into the film business. I was sixteen years old when I psychically knew that was going to be my next big move. It wasn't until I turned twenty-three years old when it worked out in my favor. That's seven years of what felt like stagnancy. What did I do during that time? I obtained my first regular job as a teenager at the record store chain when those existed. I simultaneously studied up on the creative side of the film business, I read and wrote in journals, I experienced life, perfected my resume, made lists of entertainment production companies and contacted them. My general disposition was that I was going to get in and nothing was going to stop me. I said, "I will never stop trying to get in. I will keep doing that until I'm eighty, I don't care."

I had the occasional doubt or frustration with, "This is ridiculous. When is it going to happen?"

Those negative moments were rare, because that wasn't my general disposition. 95% of the time I was focused on getting in with excitement. I kept working hard to achieve it, and then by the force of a miracle from above I got in. What are the odds that a movie star is going to hire some young punk kid with no experience? There was regular praying and taking action steps on my part until one day I received that surprise call back.

In fact, when the call came in, I was so stunned that it took me an hour to center myself before calling back. It seemed too good to be true that I went into this hazy state of shock not believing it. The point of sharing that tidbit of a story was that I was no one in particular, without any experience, but myself to sell. This means that anybody has the capability of doing it if they have passion, persistence, hard work, and a great attitude.

After talking to me, the production company discovered that underneath that punk rebellious aura there was as one of them put it, "…. a super high intellect that dominated…" the bosses. This was considered a strength and asset to the company. Use who you are, your personality, and those parts of you to showcase to the world. People love authenticity and originality. Those that make big decisions such as hiring gravitate towards someone different than the norm.

Act and follow the guidance that your Spirit team has relayed to you. Sitting on your couch all day waiting for a blessing to ring your doorbell is highly unlikely to happen. You meet your Spirit team halfway by asking them what steps you need to take next. Perhaps the message you receive is to re-send out your resume to a place you already sent it to, but received no response originally. Now your team is asking you to forget about all that and send it again. You send out your resume to the same place as your team requested, only this time you get a response asking you to come in for an interview or meeting.

Sometimes the messages and guidance might seem insignificant or trivial. I've relayed messages and guidance from my team asking me to discuss these basic steps of meditation and hammer home the nature setting again. That seems trivial initially, but as I illustrated it's for good reason that can help benefit your life. Rushing around stressed out wondering when your life will change is not going to allow you to pick up on Heaven's messages, which are delivered to assist in enhancing your life.

It is a tough process achieving what you've always wanted to do, but you can do it! Take it one step at a time and eventually you will master it. When it's something you really want to do, then there's nothing you cannot accomplish. It's that passion, drive, and persistence that is your winning card. It doesn't feel like a chore when it's something you love. You want to learn about the processes and different avenues you can take to reach that goal.

What you can do before you do anything is change your thoughts and get positive. Look at the bright side of what you have in your life today. Take a second and allow the good stuff to flush through you now. Visualize what you desire to see in your life, get optimistic and excited about it, ask for help from above, and then take action and work hard to achieve it.

CHAPTER SEVEN

Partake in Pleasing Work

Some believe that if you're given a gift, a particular talent, or a divinely inspired idea, then you should give it away without charging money for it. There's the romanticized old view of the starving artist pining away in a tin can, which is absurdly unrealistic. In today's age, unless you were born into money or you're living off a large trust fund, then if you want to survive, you'll need to work to make money. You have to charge for your gifts and services, not out of greed, but so you can pay for rent, food, and clothing. When those basic necessities are taken care of, then you're able to focus on what you love without worry or concern of survival.

If you gave everything away for free, then you couldn't survive. You would have to find a super uncreative full-time job on the side to pay your bills, but that could sap your creative energy and life force anyway.

There was a time when people would barter and do a trade with someone, but now necessities cost money. This is why spiritual teachers charge. The only spiritual teachers that don't charge are those who work in a church, but those are non-profit companies where they are receiving donations from members of the congregation to stay afloat. If they didn't receive donations, then they would close up and many of them have. That money goes into their paychecks and the upkeep of the church, so even they are charging essentially.

There are a great many talented healers and artists contributing positive work and efforts towards humanity and their life purpose, but sadly many of them are stuck in regular day jobs that suck up their time and energy. This makes it challenging to pursue their true passion and make a decent living out of it. What makes that feeling worse is that an enormous amount of these day jobs lowers their morale. This is because those jobs are bathed in toxic energy in one person or more around them that are disconnected from spirit and the bigger universal picture. If that's not the case and all are a pleasure to be around, then the lowered morale can come from your lengthy commute to the job, or because the job is not your passion. That alone can be the reason for the lowered morale. As a sensitive this can be exceptionally taxing on your well-being system, but this is tiring on anyone regardless if they are psychically in tune or not. Being aware of what's greater than your physical body makes it more depressing to be in Earthly set ups that bring you permanently down.

If you're in this kind of a situation, then you are aware that a high percentage of your time is connected to this day job on some level even when you're not at work. This can stall a talented person from working towards what they want to do with their life in the long run. They soon give up and lose faith believing that the Universe is working against them and that they're just not as lucky in the way that others are. Don't give up on the account of someone else. It can be tough at times, but you have to keep going and fighting to do what your soul agreed to do.

One guy informed me that when he's not at work he's sometimes having dreams at night that involves his place of employment or about his colleagues. It didn't start off that way, but when the feeling of wanting to do what he loved grew, then his hatred for his day job grew, which started to manifest into his dreams. This day job became embedded deeply into his consciousness. When you're asleep and having dreams about your job, then that's a problem. Your energy is too mired and infiltrated into something that doesn't mean that much to you in the end. You're not at work and you're still thinking about it! It's not even a job he likes all that much, but he's always there which means there isn't enough balance of personal and professional time. Most of his days are spent at his job the way most do. This is not entirely his fault as that's the way the current break-your-back mentality mindset of human physical life is at this time.

Find meaningful work at a place that excites you. Consider the steps you can take today to change this whether that is through job hunting or home and apartment hunting. Imagine how many years you can endure in your current state before your spirit is permanently crushed. Working with a weaker boss can add more frustration and stress.

A fearful boss that lacks in confidence will ask, "How did this happen?"

A confident assertive fearless boss asks, "How do we fix this?"

This is because the stronger boss is interested in moving things forward. The weaker boss asks how something happened to stall forward movement and to place blame, which doesn't improve momentum or morale.

"How do we fix this?" is someone looking to keep things going. They have the desire to get others to think outside the box and provide solutions to quickly remedy an issue without wasting any additional time on it. This is the same thought process to have in all of your dealings in life from your daily choices, to your love and friendship connections.

Most jobs require you to be in the office full time, which is currently set to five days a week – eight hours a day. This varies depending on what city or country you reside in. The time you devote to your job doesn't include the getting ready for work, and driving to and from your place of employment, or your mid-day hour break, which I've discovered many rarely take.

This is also connected to the break your back work mentality that egotistical human beings designed. They had no concept of balance when they set it up that way. No one is happy about it, and bosses and superiors are unaware of it or don't care. Part of that is because they choose their own hours where they may work from home for a few hours before going into the office, or they take their time going in. They receive a larger compensation for the work. When you get paid super well, then you're more gung-ho about your job. This is up to a point since those who have larger dreams of doing work they love will do it for free if they had all the time and energy in the world.

Increase Faith To Attract

In the films *Passengers* and *Cast Away*, both show one person functioning alone for a long period of time, and eventually starting to go a little mad due to not having another person to engage with at some point.

If someone showed up on Earth to find no other people, then he wouldn't know what he was missing. Because there is no material distraction, he would be more in tune to the Heavens unable to hear anything else. This is how human beings progressed in the beginning of civilization. They paid attention to the Heavens and their Divine senses to guide them on how to naturally progress.

Eventually as progression took place, so did material and physical drive. This expanded and exploded to the point of never-ending distractions. The more this chaos rose up, the less Divinely connected human beings became. There is no way to escape that and not be aware that it's happening, even if you live in the middle of nowhere. While you might be more connected to Spirit in those areas, you lose the connection when you turn your television on, you surf the internet, you read media stories, or you hop on your phone. Now you are no longer spiritually connected. You might be connected to one another through technological devices, but in a distant loveless way. You are not connected to God through those forms.

The entire planet is unsettled and distracted, which makes it near impossible to sense the Divine energy that way. Your subconscious is aware of it, even if you're not paying attention to it in the present moment. However, if you're a highly spiritually connected being, then you're versed and readily able to move in and out of the Spirit connection whenever it calls for it.

Your soul's life force dies little by little living a life you're unhappy with. Perhaps you feel emotionally dead as if you don't have much else to give anymore. You've asked for help for years, and became doubtful that it will ever happen at this point. You're waiting, hoping, praying, and taking action for years wondering if a miracle and blessings will reveal itself to you. It can make you doubt, lose faith, and question if there is a God. It sounds like a roller coaster ride of voices competing with one another from your ego to your angels, to your ego, to your angels.

It is not uncommon to feel disconnected from other people when your consciousness is raised. Suddenly human life appears trivial and superficial. You begin to isolate as a result of not feeling like you can connect with people that understand or can relate to you. Do an inventory check of how the months and years to date have gone in your life. Examine your triumphs, your sorrows, your successes, and your challenges. Look at what was lost and what was gained. You'd be surprised to find the hidden blessings you never thought much of until you look back on it. When things are going swimmingly, people don't often notice it as much as they do when things are going horribly wrong. One can take it for granted until you take a moment to ponder on it.

"Okay my rent gets paid every month, my health is great, and I have a working car that gets me to work."

Look forward to the coming time up ahead with promise and hope. Have faith and believe that it will get better by accepting nothing less than that mindset.

Success comes and goes the way fame comes and goes. One of the best dreams to come true is being able to turn your love and hobby into a financially lucrative career. You are closer than someone else might be because you understand the concept of manifestation and asking for what you want. If you're stressed out at your job regularly, is the job really worth it? Make wise choices in your life that do not result in leaving you in a bind where you're perpetually unhappy. Take a job for less pay, live beneath your means, until you find the work that makes you feel bliss again.

Looking to the future with optimism you might sometimes find you've been chasing rainbows that evaporate as quickly as the champagne fizzles in your glass. You need not search long and hard for some measure of magic to reveal itself since it's always resided within you. You are loved even when you doubt it, avoid it, shun it and do everything in your power to deny it. When you reach that threshold of completing your Earthly run, the only thing you take with you is love. If you gain anything while here, then remember to love more, give more, and have compassion no matter how unpopular it is. Only then can you truly discover that magic you secretly desire.

CHAPTER EIGHT

*You Are Worthy
and Deserving of Blessings*

It takes a warrior like effort to not allow anything to kill off your life force and prevent you from working on your passion and life purpose. There are a great many rags to riches stories that included people that were once struggling and wondering if they'd ever break free from their self-imprisoned life, but they kept working hard on what they desired on the side during their down time. Eventually, they transitioned out of that and into what they love.

Keep forging on ahead fearlessly and making a personal pact to contribute a little bit of what you love towards your lifelong goals each day for a minimum of thirty minutes to an hour. Whether that hour is used to read and research up on your areas of interest, or to devote positive action steps towards what will ultimately be your life purpose income, such as creating a website, a social media page, postcards, etc. Putting in a tiny bit of time is better than putting in no time.

Become an independent, confident, and self-sufficient self-starter that manages your life with enthusiasm and finesse. It's a world of workaholics plugging away at meaningless tasks that usually amount to a great deal of nothing in the end. This carries off into all aspects of your life, but is primarily beneficial for those in leadership or supervising positions.

When spreading yourself too thin, you want to ensure to be extra careful about what you're putting into your body. You might complain you're too tired or don't have enough time or energy to contribute up to an hour a day into what could potentially be your full-time job. This is a dilemma and a block for you, but if this is work you truly love, then it doesn't feel like work. It's something you enjoy doing, so working on it is rarely a problem. When someone cheerfully wants to do something, then they will do it no matter how tired they are. In fact, putting in work on your passion and love gives you a positive lift, a boost, and raises your vibration. All of which are ingredients in that recipe for attracting in positive circumstances, more energy, and abundance.

Raising your vibration is a crucial element in giving you greater energy and a brighter mood. This encourages you to make the time to contribute towards what you love. After a long laborious and tedious day at work at your day job, you may be sapped of life force energy to keep going with your passion. When you have more continuous energy, then that's energy to help push you to contribute towards work that you love, such as your life purpose passion work during those moments when you're not at your day job.

The reason you might be exhausted at the end of each day is not always because work is so tough at your day job, but it's because this job does not excite you on any level. When you experience excitement, then the feel-good chemical dopamine is released into your system naturally. When you despise what you do, then this depletes the dopamine chemical, which sucks the life force energy right out of you making you feel tired. You then reach out for artificial substances to create the feelings you need.

When I'm doing what I love, then the energy keeps going beyond twelve hours where I don't want to stop. It's a perpetual rushed excited high, because I'm doing what I love that it doesn't feel like work. It's fun and I'm getting paid for it too! On top of that I'm being extra careful with what I put into my body and system. You know that if you have a glass of wine or a beer in the middle of the day, then you're unlikely to put in any work into what you love. Do the work first, complete it, and then celebrate with your beer. Keeping your energy high and motivated on those days that you want to work on your life purpose requires taking care of all aspects of your body, mind, and soul. When you believe that great things will happen for you, then great things will happen! The ingredients in this recipe include having a positive attitude, strong faith, asking for help in prayer, and taking action. Like the Journey song title says, "Don't stop believing."

For some successful people, there will come that point when the floodgates of blessings and abundance open and it soars wonderfully into your world. Some personalities will allow the darkness of ego to rise convincing you to panic, fear, and worry that it's a fluke and will be taken away from you soon enough. Some form of worry could be considered understandable, but don't let it consume and drown you. Quickly move away from that way of thinking and receive the blessings with a positive spirit.

Whenever I started a new film production for the studios, people were unaware that I had the occasional minor fear briefly in the beginning years. I would worry the first few days that I might get fired. I would go into a serious meditation exercise the night before my first day on the job and be prepared to dive on in and hit the ground running. The minor fear or worry was so miniscule though that it didn't dominate, but was rather a fleeting thought that peeked its face in, then blew away just as quickly. After the first number of days on the gig the fears would subside, as I'd fall into the comfortable rhythm and groove of the job. Employers would later comment they were surprised to hear that I'd have doubts in the beginning because it never showed. It would pop in for thirty seconds, then pop right out as I'd re-align, let it go, and just do the best job I can do.

It's a wonderful and awesome thing when circumstances start flowing positively. You think, "Wow, I can't believe how great this is. I hope it doesn't go away and I don't lose it."

Don't doubt, just accept, and enjoy the wave of excitement and optimism. Allow any roadblocks in your life to fall away as you move into smooth calm waters up ahead.

Get optimistic, have faith, and trust in God and your Spirit team. When you're worried about something, then ask and pray for intervention to remove those worries. Make this prayer request daily if the worry continues. Don't give up or try to do it yourself, but turn your worries into prayer, since that's what can help lift the burdens that negative thoughts and feelings can produce.

Prayer is intended to help you move away from worry and fear. You invalidate a prayer when you continue to worry afterwards. The worry tells Spirit that you don't trust their intervention and assistance and so you will continue to worry as a backup plan in case God doesn't come through. When you receive repeated nudges after the prayer to act on something, then take action.

When circumstances become too great, then take some time out in quiet meditation or contemplation. Create a sanctuary ambiance at home or in your room. Disconnect from people and technology for several hours or even the day, and spend that time conversing with God, a higher power, and the universe. Go on a day or weekend trip with a positive friend or by yourself if you find that more beneficial.

Let go of feelings of resentment and jealousy about other people who seem to be more successful than you are at this point. This success may be in career, love, or life in general. You want to avoid falling into that kind of envy energy because that will ensure you stay single or will never be successful. It's understandable to a point that you are feeling frustrated because you are just as deserving of a good life as anyone else. Resentment builds and overpowers you and crushes your soul in the process.

The flipside is if you are financially successful, then don't feel guilty about making money in general, or making more money than others. Money is energy, so when you're being paid for services you provide, then that is an exchange of energy. Feel no guilt about making money or how you choose to spend it. You are worthy of making money for any work you do. Don't apologize for being blessed.

Avoid resentment, jealousy, worry, or fear associated with money. Visualize the awesome circumstances you'd be able to partake in due to making enough money. Imagine how many people's lives you'd be able to change and help positively.

Your imagination is a powerful divine instrument of God so use it to your advantage.

You're already spending the day thinking, perhaps thinking about useless chores and tasks, but how about thinking about something good. Pay attention to those ideas that enter your mind. A great deal of it is coming from above. Look at the great music, books, art, and movies over the course of history alone that started out with one person's idea and rapidly expanded to the point where there is a 600-man crew filming it into a visual story. It's awesome what people have been able to create over Earth's progression.

The angels don't want to see someone destined for greatness working in a day job that kills off their life force. They are not keeping you down and nor are they keeping you there to punish you. There could be various reasons as to why you're still there that is beyond your control. They could be working diligently behind the scenes with aligning circumstances that work in your favor to get you to work full time in your self-employed business.

Release any vows of poverty you might have made in a past life, regardless if you believe in past lives or not. It won't hurt you to verbally say, "I release all vows of poverty I might have made in this life or any previous ones, in all directions of time."

There are some circumstances, which cannot practically be understood by the human mind. Navigate through life with an open and awakened mind and consciousness over what is unseen.

Have no fear or doubts in believing in Heaven, God, Jesus, and your Spirit team. Believe that you are watched over and are not being ignored, even on those days when you just want to throw in the towel and permanently give up. Don't give up because there is a reason you are here. Spirit can see the good up ahead even when you feel like this is it.

The world spins around, circumstances change, friendships come and go, some stay, some leave, people pass on, life goes on for the soul. Study and read up on success stories that you can do it! Don't feel resentment or jealousy over someone else's work, but feel inspired and motivated by it instead. It's to help you feel those things so that you can believe that yes you can do it too.

When one thinks of success, they automatically equate it to money, but success is not always financial or monetary. The utmost form of success is how evolved your soul develops in one lifetime. Since this is the true measure of Spirit's view of success, then you should thrive to push the billionaire mark. Rise above the world around you and dive deep into the depths of possibilities by working to expand your mind and consciousness. Seek out the vast reservoirs of wisdom, knowledge, and intelligence that the Universe holds. Take that by the reigns and soar full speed ahead today. Make some great things happen in your life now.

Manifesting

One of the keys to manifesting is having an unwavering passion for a desire. You can have anything you want and can cause anything to happen when you have unbending passion for it. This is where you feel this passion for your desire all over you, within you, and around you. You feel and know it in your mind. You feel and know it in your heart. You feel and know it all throughout your body and soul. You know without a doubt that it will happen and that it is here now. It's allowing this feeling to build to the intensity of an erupting volcano. You feel this desire continue to rise with positive excitement from within. There are no negative feelings associated with this passionate feeling. You visually see what you want happening in reality with great optimism.

If you are having a passion for obtaining something, but you have doubts circling that, then the doubts will overpower the desire and you will receive the doubts instead of the desire. Experience inner peace and uplifting joy that you're living this vision as if it is real time. It is seeing this vision as if it is here and happening now. Hold this intention daily and avoid negative thoughts from taking over. It is not enough to visualize something you want, but to also take action steps to get there. When you have a passion for something, you naturally want to dive into that passion. Having passion is a joyous feeling. It's the key to manifesting positively.

Once this is complete, then the difficult step is to then let it go. It's to release this vision and desire of what you want to your higher self, God, or your Spirit team. It's completely letting go of this desire and not caring about it. It's releasing and surrendering it to the higher power. The reason this is a challenging step is because most people find it difficult to let go of something they really want. They fixate on it heavily never letting the desire go. This then moves into obsessive doubts and concerns that it will never happen. However, if this last step is not followed, and you do not let this desire go and release it, then the manifestation connection is not fully made. It may push the outcome further away from you. This gives you an idea as to why your desire is not coming to fruition. You must let it go and move onto the next manifestation. Do not concern yourself with the how or when a manifestation will occur, as this will block it. If you obsess over a desire, then you will block it from manifesting. Instead, you will receive negative manifestations, or you'll find that you're in a stagnant position where there is no movement at all.

I've always been manifesting, as everyone is manifesting whether they're aware of it or not. I've been manifesting since I was a teenager through this process I describe. One of the many secrets was by stepping into my Divine power as a fearless confident spirit. I had passion and a steady, calm, euphoric positive energy surrounding what I wanted. I use the word passion to describe this process. If you don't have passion for something, then it will show. It doesn't matter what your expertise is or what kind of degree you have. None of that matters because if you have no passion for what you're doing, then that will come through. You need to passionately want it, but then let go of knowing, how, or when it will happen.

When I first started out in the entertainment business, I had no skills or experience to warrant getting a job in that industry. All I had to sell them with was my personality, drive and passion. I walked in there and conveyed how much I wanted it and how right I was for the gig. There was no acting needed, because I genuinely wanted it with incredible veracity. I went after every job position with this same passion and I was hired. This same manifestation process was the same process for how I became an author. I knew I was going to do it. I clairvoyantly saw it up ahead.

I've been following my own Spirit team's guidance, messages, and steps relayed to me from as far back as a teenager. This equivalent method was also the case with all of the relationships I was involved in. I knew without a doubt that I would be with a particular person. Granted, I'm sure in hindsight, I might have paid bigger attention to the red flags presented, but the point is to be careful what you wish for. If the wish is felt with great positive veracity, passion, and steadfast intensity, then you just might get it. This includes what you don't want. If you are intensely worried about something, then you are giving that attention energy you don't want to be feeding it with. It will end up expanding and bringing on more of that comparable energy into your life.

CHAPTER NINE

Awaken Your Creative Spirit

When you cannot seem to shake the uncomfortable rut of negative feelings plaguing and dominating your life, then dive into a creative project or hobby. Creative pursuits raise your soul's energy vibration and lift the passion quotient within you. When you immerse yourself in a creative hobby, then this opens up your heart, enhances your soul, and brings more joy into your life. Since immersing oneself raises your vibration, this attracts in good stuff and optimistic feelings to you outside of the creative hobby. If you do not have any creative interests, then consider looking at obtaining one. Creative interests can be anything from picking up a paint-by-number set, to training yourself to play a musical instrument, to pottery making to taking an acting class. There are endless ways to awaken the creative part of you.

Diving into creativity is a great way to shake yourself out of any funk you experience. It helps you navigate through the treacherous waters of human life. It assists you in finding innovative ways to solutions, which can carry over to other aspects of your life from the business arena to love relationships. It helps you to think outside of the box and showcase your originality because everything you're doing while being creative is solely you. It pulls out the deepest parts of your soul. A photographer is being creative by taking pictures. They might spend hours taking a variety of photos of different flowers in a garden. By doing this they see the beauty around them, which is often overlooked. These creative gifts come out of you and mirror what you have within. Your true nature is revealed back to you as a result.

Your soul is magnificently wonderful and loved by God and the universe beyond measure and comprehension. How awesome is that to be unconditionally loved no matter how you're feeling? All human souls desire to be loved and will seek it out in friendships, family members, colleagues and lovers. This is with the hope that these other souls will give you that all-encompassing love, but always fall short in some people's eyes. The love exists within you to begin with and can be conjured up naturally. This is God's love for you.

Creativity is a great reminder of who your soul truly is. It brings this love back out of you. Creativity cures any boredom or lulls in your day while helping you to express yourself in positive ways. When someone is bored, they tend to reach for an addiction. They might log online, surf the Internet pointlessly, visit a social media site, or log on to a phone app for human contact and stimulation that ceases to exist in their physical reality. You feel even more lonely and bored after hours of being unproductive. This becomes a bigger problem when you discover that this is how you spend every second of your day. If you didn't have that one step to check your social media page throughout the day, then you fear you might lose out on life. I've had friend's say, "Okay I've been on [social media] too much lately. I need to take a step back."

They're going crazy inside realizing it's not fulfilling anything positive for them. This is more about someone that spends each day for months surfing the internet out of lethargy while accomplishing nothing.

Artistic creative souls also have a higher attraction to abusing addictions and toxic substances. The same goes for those who are sensitive or psychically connected. If you are a sensitive, psychically connected, artistic, and creative, then the odds of you succumbing to a toxic vice or addiction runs higher than if you are one or the other. In many cases, having all of these traits go hand in hand with the super connected.

If you're a creative soul that regularly dives into artistic pursuits, then it's likely you have deeper psychic gifts than the average person. You may be aware of it or you are about to begin realizing the connection between both. When an artist doesn't create for long periods of time, then it can feel like you're running out of air. Creative inspiration is heavenly guided and influenced by Spirit. Your Spirit team plays a hand in it as well as the Archangel Gabriel, who joins the creative soul being to assist in the inspiration and motivation process. Archangel Gabriel is the hierarchy angel that oversees all creative souls who choose to turn their gifts into a lifelong hobby or career.

Artists are sensitive and can access and channel this inspiration often without knowing it. Channeling comes naturally to them, regardless if they are a believer in something outside of themselves or not.

If you fit this description, know that you are immensely gifted rather than cursed. The curse is when you feel unable to control the access of information or creativity that pours into you. This ends up propelling you to reach for toxic substances that might be considered an addiction.

Part of your soul's growth is to gain control and master your ego. This may take a lifetime depending on one's individual journey. You can become a master at being disciplined and yet you still find yourself tumbling down the rabbit hole every once in awhile. When that happens, call on Heaven for support. Don't beat yourself up over it.

I have been a lifelong addict, but others claim or protest to view me as being completely together, strong, and independent. It doesn't matter, because the addiction gene runs right through the human development part of my soul. It's something I wrestle with no matter how connected I am. I do my best to stay focused and do what I need to do. Over time I learned to talk myself out of reaching for an addiction until the cravings grew to be less. Luckily, my hard addictions were in my early twenties. I got it all out of my system so to speak, yet the addictive behavior is still there just below the surface. I have mastered the art of keeping it tempered and quiet through daily work, discipline, and effort over the years.

Many well-known artists, musicians, and actors are unable to control the input of stimuli and information, which tampers with their psyche. This drives them to drug, alcohol, or any other addiction to numb it all. One of the ways to avoid falling into an ocean of addiction is to find avenues to channel your creativity and gifts in a positive way. Take up a side hobby to unleash your positive gifts through an artistic endeavor. I worked with a well-known actress for many years who paints when she's not acting in front of the camera. Painting is another form of creative expression and it keeps her busy during those lulls between films, since you're not working every single day as an actor.

Actors feel more in control when they are working and inhabiting a character on stage or film. This keeps them out of trouble to an extent. If they're not working, which many are not on a regular basis, many of them find other positive avenues of creative expression. When you are working on a creative project, you are less likely to resort to addictive substances during those lulls. Creative expression brings you joy and an internal rushed high feeling that raises your vibration. This rush that you experience is your natural connection line with Heaven.

You may feel like an oddball or weird, but avoid placing too much emphasis on labeling yourself. Others may ridicule or criticize you for being different. They might call you inappropriate names, but pay no mind. It is better to be different than to be a clone that follows the herd. If you have a high receptivity to your environment, then you will want to ensure that your surroundings are controlled and that you incorporate some measure of discipline. If you have too much rigid control, then this can inhibit your artistic creative side. Finding a happy balance with everything in life is what contributes to a positive energy flow. Be expressively creative while running your life like a strict executive.

The negatives that happen to this are that creative types are also all about experiencing and experimenting to one degree or another. It's best to work on keeping your research on a level that does not bring on an addiction. I am a writer, author, storyteller and entertainer. Couple that with research being my middle name and being a former addict with an ongoing addictive personality and you have a bit of rock and roll going on. I wouldn't just do something new a little bit. I would do it to the point of becoming an obsessive-compulsive mess. The one positive about that is I'd grow bored with it and kick it out of my system. If my soul is going to have an Earthly life, then it wants to know what is available in the physical world. This is to also have a greater understanding of the nature of it. One can study something, but it isn't the same as diving into it like a method actor.

Artistic pursuits and creative expression are a great way to reduce or eliminate abundance blocks in your life. It's a positive healthy way to channel and direct negative, stifled, and stuck energy. By diving into creative pursuits, you're releasing the negative energy and these blocks in the process. You're also awakening your inner child, which resides in a higher state than your ego. Consider finding a creative hobby or interest that brings you joy. Creativity enhances your life force and lifts your confidence level. You may even find that your creative project soon turns into life purpose work where it brings in supplemental income or it becomes a full-time self-employed career. Some creative pursuits can include hobbies such as photography, painting, writing, playing music, singing, dancing, puzzles, or any measure of arts and crafts.

Writing is a great way to be creative and express your inner self. You don't have to necessarily write a book. It can be something that you write for the sake of release. Writing is fantastic therapy! You can write your own manuscript or keep a regular journal. Join writing groups you feel comfortable in enough to share your work with others or to have a meeting with likeminded individuals that share your interests. If you're shy when it comes to in-person meetings or you don't have the time to travel to group settings, then look for online forums and groups where you can communicate on the Internet. This is one of the plusses to having access to technology.

You can keep a personal diary when you're going through transitions or just want to jot down day-to-day stuff. You can email it to yourself. For example, use the subject line: Diary+Date *(Diary 12-25-18)*. Jot down anything that comes to you about that day, what you're going through, and how you're feeling or anything at all, then email it to yourself. Create a folder in your email box marked "Journal" or "Diary" and file each one in there. Choose to do what you want with it at a later date or just keep it for your eyes only.

Every soul has some measure or range of creative gifts within them, even if you never honed in on that aspect of yourself. It might come out in ways that you never expected or in a manner that you wouldn't think to equate as one being creative. It comes out in a variety of ways such as being birthed out of the mundane and the practical. It can be the way you organize your house, to working on a puzzle, to taking that extra step to ensure that your emails are centered, justified, or in the right font. Creativity can be in the way you speak to others, whether that is on the phone, at your job, or on a stage to an audience.

Although the news media is responsible for a major influence on the darkness of one's ego in humanity, the media in general is a great outlet for a creative sensitive to pursue work in. Many have agreed to an Earthly life at this time in order to transmit their work in a much easier way than it would have been pre-Internet days. During pre-

Internet days other people had a hold on preventing any creative artist from getting their work out to the public. Now most anyone can get their work out there with strong effort, diligence, and hard work. Depending on what your creative work entails, you may still need a team around you to some extent such as an agent, publicist, manager, etc.

While in one sense you are the manager of your life and your work, but in another it is helpful to have supportive professional objective parties around you for feedback when unleashing your art to the world. A friend is great to bounce stuff off of as long as the friend is someone you can trust. They are someone you can take constructive criticism from without getting upset or allowing it to damage your connection. The flip side is this friend should not be the type who is negative or jealous of you either. You likely being a sensitive should be able to pick up on any hint of dishonesty or malice from anyone when it comes to your art. It should be a given that you surround yourself with supportive friends, but sometimes even with the best supportive friendships they may develop resentment when they witness your success.

The one drawback to being able to put your creative work out into the world is marketing dollars. You can put your art into the world for sale, but if no one knows that it's out there and available, then it might feel as if your work was done for nothing. Unless you've got a huge trust fund or have made enough money at your day job to be able to do your creative life purpose work, then it can be challenging. True creative artists enjoy doing their work regardless of that. It's certainly helpful to have marketing dollars to promote your work or to make enough money with it where you can quit your day job. The creative artist that lives and breathes their work will still do it because they enjoy it. It's fulfilling and rewarding to them even if in the back of their mind they would like to make enough money to be able to do it full time.

Even if you are not immediately financially rewarded, take the time to acknowledge and recognize the beautiful work you've accomplished, as that will be its own reward. Give to yourself in some positive way for every job well done. Celebrate the accomplishments you do including the small ones. This assists in boosting your self-worth and vibration, which are both magnets for attracting in good stuff!

Be your most genuine and real self, but this goes without saying that your work should also be authentic. Authenticity is you being your most honest self without fear of judgment or criticisms. Avoid making changes or compromising because someone disagrees with any part of who you are and how you choose to express that. At the same time understand the benefits of constructive feedback, but don't marinate in it to the point where you feel it's negotiating how you express your artistic truth. When you bargain this honesty, then the heart essence put into the work is lost. It doesn't feel right and nor does it feel like you. You want to step away from the drama surrounding that. This is in order to clear your mind when you find that you're moving into people pleasing to make others happy.

Find the right balance between accepting others feedback and keeping your work genuine. The point of getting a second pair of objective eyes on your work put out to the public is because when you're heavily mired in a project or anything for that matter, then you don't necessarily see the possible hidden mistakes that could be present. There is a benefit to having compassionate, yet helpful input. Ask your Spirit team to guide you to the right people who can give honest feedback. There is a surplus of websites and companies devoted to offering services of every variety for a small fee. Sometimes this is the best route over giving it to a friend or acquaintance, since that becomes a conflict of interest. The one hired is objective and emotionally detached from what you're doing. This makes it a great test to see how a stranger reacts to it since your work is going out to strangers in the end as it is.

There will be times where it can be challenging to get motivated to do something you love. There are a variety of factors that could contribute to a lack of motivation. You're overworked, tired, stressed, depressed or have no support system. You have too much going on in your life around you. This is tampering chaotic and distractive energy enclosing in on your mind that it's difficult to find that space where motivation resides.

Some ways to get motivated are through relaxation. Take a time out to clear your space and remove any excess noise and distraction energy around you whether that is from people, your schedule, to any technological devices such as your phone or Internet. Turn off or temporarily remove phone apps that you hang out on to the point that you find that it occupies a great deal of your time. These are time wasters that block creative flow.

Sometimes doing busy work can help motivate you to do what you really want to do, because it's getting your mind charged up. Creative people understand this concept, since they have wrestled with creative blocks at one time or another. A writer is ready to sit down and start writing, but experiences a block having no clue what to write about. What do they do? They might clean the house, dust, vacuum, and organize. There are positive benefits to this, which includes implementing Feng Shui.

Feng Shui is an ancient Chinese art that contributes to the positive flow of good energy moving through all aspects of your life including your home and your soul. Some hire a professional Feng Shui artist to help them organize their home. This includes setting up your furniture in a manner that assists in attracting in good fortune. In the case where you're doing the busy work that consists of cleaning your house, this helps with the positive flow of energy, but isn't necessarily the art of Feng Shui. It's still an encouraging step in the right direction.

Writing or creating in a clean organized environment contributes to more precise focus, relaxation, motivation, and it helps in attracting in success. You want to make sure you don't find that you've wasted hours on this busy work. You've grown so good at cleaning the house that the day is over, and you have no energy left to create. To get motivated takes discipline and you have to manage your life and the decisions you make like a top business executive.

Feeling overwhelmed can prevent you from finding that spark of motivation. You're looking far out in the distance at the end result of what you want to do. This makes the goal seem daunting or intimidating, so you talk yourself out of doing it and putting it off. Breaking your ultimate goal into baby steps is a great way to go.

I will at times call on the Archangel Uriel who lights the path that is unseen. Archangel Uriel will show me one step at a time when working on a book. I'll be asked to cover one topic, and then once that's accomplished, he illuminates the next step. Before I know it what I set out to achieve is complete.

Uriel offers awesome creative impressions by dropping these light bulb ideas into your mind. You might have a creative idea, but then you grow overwhelmed as to how you're going to accomplish it. This is because you're seeing it far out in the distance, which can feel overwhelming. Take it one small step at a time and try not to think of the end result. This is a delay tactic the ego will impose upon you by making you believe that it's not possible to do. A rock climber understands its goal is to reach the top, but they're focusing on one step climb upwards at a time. They're not thinking, "I've got to get up there to the top. That seems so far. I can't do it."

Others complain about what's going on in their life and how it is not up to their standards. I ask them if they've asked for help. They will say, "Oh you're right! Okay, I will do that."

Talk to your Spirit team regularly and ask for help as needed, including with creative ideas. When you notice there is no movement and you begin to feel discouraged, then ask Heaven to boost your faith and show you signs that movement is forthcoming.

Signs and symbols are put in your path by your Spirit team to let you know they are with you and do hear your requests. It can also be to give you clues as to what they are trying to communicate to you. When you're ferociously requesting help and wondering if you're being heard, they will do things such as drop feathers, objects of meaning, or coins around you to let you know they got your message. Since they cannot pick up the phone to call you or send you an email, they resort to manipulating the energy in order to let you know they hear you loud and clear, or to get a specific message across. You are not being ignored and that should bring you peace of mind.

The Personal Altar

Creating a personal altar or space is a wonderful way to rouse your creativity. Awakening the creative part of you is beneficial because it unleashes pent up closed off repression. When left unchecked this can be a breeding ground for illnesses, diseases, and other negative attributes. There are hundreds of ways to begin the process of setting the creative part of you free. Creating a personal altar is one way, as it can be used as a place of focus when you're in a scattered state. This altar can be used for whatever you choose. Many spiritual people like to create this space for prayer, meditations, or readings. You decide what you will use it for.

Find a space or a corner in your home somewhere to set up a small table, which you will use to place important sacred items on that have meaning to you. You can place candles on it, crystals, divination tools, incense, sage, flowers, and/or little statues of deities that have some significance to you. When you create your sacred space, you will want to cleanse and purify it on occasion. You can do this by sage smudging. Light a bit of sage and move it all around you, then the table and area. Say a mental prayer with the intention that you are clearing this space of any lower energies allowing only the light to enter. You can use this space for prayer, to connect, to meditate, to get focused, or for whatever you choose.

Because this is a sacred space, you will want to ensure that it is protected. This means not only clearing it through prayer or the occasional sage smudging, but avoid placing other items on it. You're rushing around or you come home from work and immediately toss your car keys onto the sacred space table. Treating the space as a sacred one means you keep it protected and clear of other energies. When you toss your car keys on it, you're contaminating the sacred space with any negative energy that latched itself onto the keys. When you're driving the busy roads, then you're picking up on other energies such as abusive drivers or toxic people in other cars passing you. Ensure that you avoid putting anything else on the table that is not considered sacred to you.

The Joy of Receiving

Give yourself a break and practice the joy and love of receiving. Many spiritual or compassionate people have the qualities of being a selfless giver. While this is a magnificent heavenly trait to have, you can create an imbalance when that is all you are doing. In order to bring balance into your life, be open to receive in your life as well. When someone wants to do something nice for you for a change, then welcome that with open arms. Those that are predominately givers tend to wrestle with the joy of receiving. They might fall into the category of someone taking advantage of them.

Receiving is also giving to yourself where you are the receiver. It's treating yourself to something you love such as a weekend getaway somewhere or a spa day if you enjoy being pampered. Whatever it is that makes you smile to receive, then go for it and give to yourself.

When you balance giving and receiving gestures, then this uplifts your mood, raises your vibration, and awakens your inner child that is bursting with creativity. If you are the kind of person who gives too much or receives without giving, then this creates an imbalance in your life. Work on balancing the giving part of your nature with receiving.

Sometimes you work hard feeling like you're being ignored, or that there are no blessings coming in from this hard work. A possible block is the negative feeling you're experiencing. Deep inside you feel undeserving of blessings on some level. Know that you deserve blessings of abundance and good. Allow Heaven to bestow you with compensation for what you contribute to others and the world. When you open your arms to receive abundance, then it is easier to assist others after you're taken care of first.

You also don't want to spread yourself too thin where you constantly drop everything to help a friend, loved one, or family member whenever they ask. If you're not taken care of or in a comfortable place, then you feel resentful for having to help. Receiving is just as important as giving. Therefore, ensure there is a healthy balance on both ends. Put down strict boundaries to ensure that no one takes advantage of your good nature.

CHAPTER TEN

Rise Into Creative Confidence

Introverted and shy people have a higher quotient of creativity flowing through their spirit. Someone can be an introvert, but not shy, whereas an extrovert can be shy. Someone shy might be misconstrued to be an introvert when that's not always the case. Introverts keep to themselves or prefer higher bouts of alone time than an extrovert. It can be difficult for them to connect with others even if they crave human stimulation once in awhile. They may also have trouble allowing their fearless assertive confidence to shine out, but the exception is when they are engaging creatively. There are many ways that an introverted creative soul can connect with other likeminded people. Technology has its cons, but there are the obvious benefits to devices such as social media or phone apps. You can take your time getting to know others on a phone app or a social media page before you are comfortable enough to take it to the next level. The next steps preceding that are personal email, text, and then phone conversations. If you cannot have a phone conversation, then how are you going to be making it through an in person hang out? The next step is followed by meeting in person. All of this can help ease someone into confidence.

Other ways of connecting with those like you is to take a class. This can be online or a physical classroom, which allows you to interact with other students. Taking a class in the area or genre of your interest assists in awakening the confident creative part of you. It also opens the door to getting to know others with similar interests.

When you communicate via social media or a phone app, then be sure to put in an effort with others by opening up beyond a few words. I've discovered through hands on research that people who reach out to me barely put in more than a one to five-word sound bite response that is similar to the person before them. If you're a highly creative soul, then this shouldn't be too much of an issue since you can find creative ways to string words together to catch the other person's attention. The most nerve-wracking challenge will be when you and this other person meet face to face, but by that time you'll likely be so familiar with each other that it won't be that difficult. This is pending you're not jumping to meet every single person the second they message you.

Some of the other positive benefits to following social media pages or taking classes in the area of your interest are that higher learning and interacting with other like-minded souls stimulates inspiration. It pulls you out of a lull you might be experiencing and activates your mind while raising your energy levels, and focus.

Inspiration is a key component to achieve when looking to get creative. Find ways to bring on inspiration such as taking regular time outs to walk through a nature setting. Take long weekend getaways to a serene place of your choice that can inspire you. Any place bathed in nature can help with inspiration from the beach, mountains, desert, lakes, or any open nature preserve with little to no people. Go to a museum, art gallery, listen to motivating music, read a book, or watch a movie. Those are some of the things I do to get inspired. I also find inspiration in other people. My love relationships, romantic dates, and friendships have helped me creatively by acting as a muse.

Expressing Your Soul Through Creativity

The soul starves for stimulation and creativity. Express yourself artistically without censure or fear that others will not approve or like what you do. You don't have to share your art with the world if you choose not to. It can be for your eyes only, something you share with a loved one, or your close trusted circle around you. This is assuming that those who are immediately close to you are people you can trust and express yourself freely with. I've discovered from being approached by readers that they've said they feel they can be more open with me who is a stranger than someone in their immediate circle. One should have at least one person in their life they can completely trust until the end of their days. Work on getting to know other people through social media pages, classes, destinations, and apps that promote positive common interests between you.

Unleashing the creative spirit in you contributes to confident soul success in your life. Creative people seek out ways to stimulate that part of their soul for the sake of release. When done positively you engage in activities that are stimulating to your mind. A successful soul reads, researches, and partakes in positive activities, while an unsuccessful soul is sedentary, surfs the Internet, or sits around drinking bottles of alcohol, watching television all day, or chatting with others on apps out of boredom. When the darkness attaches itself to you, then this expands the ego causing one to go on a rant, rave, and attacking frenzy on social media through comments and posts. Now you've officially moved into the darkness of ego.

The Darkness of Ego

I've been doing extensive research into the human condition since childhood. This is due to my fascination with the complexities of human beings the same way a scientist examines a specimen in a bottle.

Heaven watched the rise of technology bring down the masses. No one reads as much anymore, educates themselves, or takes the time to walk in someone else's shoes. If you believe in something they don't, then they take it upon themselves to send you a toxic negative diatribe against you. They follow and adopt whatever the media or their peers feed them and believe it to be Gospel. Many will read a headline and base their opinion on what the headline is telling them without researching the story beyond the piece. If you're that rattled about a headline, then it must be something that hits home to you. If that's the case, then why not research more heavily into that topic and make it your life's purpose work to help instead of attack.

There are few that can carry deep compassionate meaningful conversations even if you disagree with someone. Arguing and antagonism is at the forefront instead of calm, balanced, compassionate conversations about differences in views and opinions.

There is no exploration, intelligence, or branching away from the crowd to investigate, research, and discover the deeper answers because no one cares. Attention spans are stunted and posting sound bites is in to get likes and followers. Conversations fizzle out as quickly as they start up, which has all carried over to the demise of long-term love relationships causing many of them to be short lived.

People today have a harder time working together in a union for life. There is too much ego to include another person's feelings and desires. You get into relationships to help the soul learn valuable traits such as compromise, balance, love, forgiveness, and on and on. It should not be about what can you do for me, but what can I do for you and for us?

Arguments are made to justify egotistical selfish behaviors. It is designed to mask the fact that the reasons long term relationships don't last is because people have short attention spans and grow bored with what they have after five minutes. No one cares about anybody or anything anymore. They pretend to when someone famous dies for a couple of days, but then they're obsessing over the next big media story. They're governed by their ego and what they desire at that moment. If it's no longer on par with the one they're with, then they leave them instead of compromising and finding a middle ground. They end up with someone new that lasts for a short time and that ends the same way. It's a repetitive cycle that ceases to end. Those that are single want to be in a relationship and those in a relationship fantasize about being single. The ego wants the opposite of what it has. All of this strangles the confident and poised creative spirit right out of you.

Ignore the Critics

Healthy creative souls are the ones more likely to compliment others on their positive traits, while unhealthy souls will criticize you, and then post negative words online. The unhealthy unsuccessful soul sits around gossiping about people, while the successful soul is animated and excitedly discusses things they want to do and accomplish.

Diving into a creative project or functioning from the artistic side of you helps in removing blocks. These blocks prevent good stuff from flowing to you. It cuts off the communication connection line with your own spirit, and your team in Heaven.

If you're a creative soul that enjoys the creative process, but also sells your art to consumers, then you understand the dynamic beyond being creative in the privacy of your own home. Having a career in the creative arts makes you susceptible to criticism from the public. The irony is the creative person is also a deeply sensitive soul, so it's important to do your best in separating the reality of what you do from harsh critics. All that matters is you participate in work that is meaningful to you. The ones it will benefit will be guided to it. There will be always be negative naysayers that have something toxic to say about your efforts, but their opinion has no validity in the eyes of God. When you put your soul's expression out into the world, then release the desire to absorb any criticism that happens to come your way. As for any measure of success you crave from your work, side business, or hobby, keep the faith that it will happen.

Remain optimistic while you continue working at your hobby and art. If it's something you enjoy doing, then it won't feel like work to you. You'll do it regardless if there is any monetary gain in it. Many success stories from popular artists admit that the success came to them out of nowhere. Suddenly they began to see a gradual rise or immediate shot of financial success fly into their life. When you love and enjoy what you're doing, then you're infusing this love enjoyment energy into your work. This is a positive ingredient that will attract a like-minded energy to it. If you do your work with fear and worry, then you will attract that kind of negative crowd base to it. The energy will be a block that prevents success from entering the picture. Stay positive, optimistic, and joyful with all that you do when you can help it. At the same time the more successful you become, then the more good and bad you will receive. You grow to be exceptionally great at ignoring the critics.

I receive my fair share of criticism, although it is minimal in comparison to those that appreciate who I am or my work. I've been receiving harsh criticism from others since I was a kid. By the time I became an author, I was already indifferent and detached from those that take issue with what I do, how I do it, or who I am. I've never cared if someone doesn't like me or not. I'm not going to stop because of them. I own my life and I live it for me. If I don't care about something or someone, I don't give it any energy or attention. It's not interesting enough for me to bother.

I've worked with well-known talent during my tenure in the Entertainment business.

These actors have told me they know to stay away from reading gossip about themselves or read comments under articles about them. I've never heard of any cases where they fold and read any of that stuff. Most of them are too productive and busy to notice. When you're busy with life you don't have time for boredom that leads to reading negative stuff about oneself. Not only are the comments and articles not based in reality, but it's not healthy or beneficial for you on any level to soak in that energy.

I've witnessed what it's like from the perspective of a famous artist. To me they're no different than any other friend or colleague, but then you realize they are super popular and many in the world love and admire their work. There are just as many people in the world who despise or criticize them unfairly and negatively. They say things about them that are not true, but you ignore that and stay focused on what's important. It's like someone saying negative toxic things on the news about someone you're close to. You don't know why or where that's coming from. It appears bizarre and peculiar that a stranger is talking about someone they know nothing about personally. It's also always been inaccurate.

Avoid allowing anyone to stop you from doing what you love. Ignore the naysayers and stay strong in faith knowing that you are loved no matter what you do or who you are. There will always be a critic out there who has something to say.

Focus on your work, put confidence into what you're creating in life, then put it out into the world if that's what you choose to do. When you release it into the world, you're also releasing the need to concern yourself over anyone who happens to like it or not. You create your art for yourself, and then you share it with those in the world who are interested and positively benefit from it. There will always be someone who doesn't like you, or what you do, so you have to get over that. It's not your issue to wrestle with.

Steer clear of all drama and negativity in others around you. This includes strangers who criticize you – not to mention those who are allegedly intended to be close to you. There is a difference between helpful constructive criticisms from those around you as opposed to critical attacks from strangers. The difference is that constructive criticism is someone who is close to you who've you asked their opinion on something and they've given you a critique.

Constructive criticism comes from a place of love where the person wants you to succeed. The opposite side of this kind of criticism is someone who is jealous of who you are and what you can do. They attack instead of offering helpful comments that benefit, because they have venom over who you are and what you're accomplishing. The lower self is governed by the Darkness and wants to take you down, but the higher self is of God and the Light and wants to see you succeed.

There are some people that are afraid to dive into anything artistic related for fear of criticism. The more you do something, then the easier it gets and the better you are at it. This can be anything in life from a job you take that you've never done before. You dread being exposed and vulnerable as if you're in some form of danger due to your high sensitivity. This anxiety is part of your ego mind and not based in truth. Avoid altering your creative work to appeal to the masses or out of panic that someone won't like it. When you do that you are distancing yourself from authenticity. This is seen with popular music acts that conform to the current market to remain significant to popular culture at that time instead of creating authentically the way they did when they first started their career. They were a trendsetter and unique when they weren't attempting to people please.

Your creative spirit is intended to be solely you and who you are buried deep within, and not what someone else wants or will want to see. If they want to see something, then let them create their own thing. This isn't about creating art that you intend to sell, but this is anything you set out to do whether it's a job, a friendship, or relationship. Be your most authentic self since you can only fake it for so long before being found out. Your authentic self is far greater than any fickleness.

I've done work that I've kept on a shelf for longer than it should have due to my insane unrealistic need for perfectionism. It's a level that no one can get to. If I waited until that thoroughness was there, then I would never get any work done. My Spirit team taught me in the beginning of my days to release the need to be perfect. The only thing that matters is the content and what one chooses to say. While it should be somewhat digestible, avoid getting lost over the fact that something might be in the wrong place. Make it as good as you can and then move onto something else. If you get into your head wondering what if no one likes it, then just quit, lie down, and wait to die. It's a waste of time putting something off because you're not ready or it will never be perfect. What is considered perfect is based on human ego rules, which have no validity in the end anyway. You have your own individual stamp on what you choose to say or create. It is impossible to please every single person. It will never happen no matter what you do, so throw that idea out the window and just do what feels right to you in the end.

Be Your Confident Authentic Self

Your sensitivity is a gift that can be immersed into your creative work. Other sensitive's will pick up on if you're going against who you are to please the crowd as opposed to be your true self. They will be attracted to you and your work when you do not compromise your integrity. Not only will they be fascinated, but they will relate and enjoy you even more for this authenticity.

I was seventeen when I obtained my first job. It was the one I honed in on and wanted with incredible force. Not many can say that as a teenager. You usually just accept any job you can get. I thought, "I need a job and the one I want right now is that one." After much persuasion on my part with the supervisor, she folded and hired me. I wasn't worried if I could do the job, but instead I was excited to learn how to do it. Soon I was mastering it as I mastered all jobs over the course of my life. When I got into the film business when I was twenty-three, I feared I would be fired in the first week. The opposite ended up happening where I became a sought-after commodity behind the scenes for studios, production companies, and talent. This is because I was soon doing the job with extreme precision and confidence. Word was spreading fast in this circus of similar creative intelligent misfits. Incidentally some of the well-known movie stars I know and have worked with also shared with me that they also had worry in the beginning of a film shoot. Some privately admitted they thought they would get fired. This gave me piece of mind that if someone that worldly known at their craft still has those worries, then this is a human nature trait that can attack anyone of any stature.

The same fighting confident nature is applied to all areas of extracurricular work I've done. I wanted to try my hands at those jobs for the experience and knowledge it entailed ranging from real estate, to law, and to digital marketing. All of my past jobs were classes that I received financial compensation for. When I started each gig, I didn't know anything about the genre. I was hired based on my enthusiasm and creative nature. When I chose to dissolve the employment in those arenas I did it at a point where I was on top of my game and had fully mastered the genre. All of those classes infused creative knowledge that I could impart into my work as a self-employed author. Everything you experience helps you gain confidence, knowledge, and life lessons. These traits were applied to my past love relationships where I would give my full confident work into the connection.

You deserve all measures of success whether that is inner or outer achievement. You are a soul child born with an innate knowing how to create. When you're home in Heaven on the Other Side, you paint the pictures of what you desire with intention. It is almost like magic due to how effortless it is. For instance, in the spirit world, if you want to visit someone or go somewhere, you think it and you are instantly there. The soul is limitless in the spirit world, while the soul is imperfect in the physical human body. On Earth, you can't think I want to be in Bali right now and then get transported there. The manifestation process on Earth is you can think about being in Bali today, then eventually one day get there with fearless assertive confidence that you will. Your thoughts produce circumstances as long as it's consistent. When you think or dream positive things, then that energy is catapulted outwardly and returned back to you tenfold. This is why you want to make sure you stay as positive as you can. Release any negative self-defeating words from your mind and aura. Know that you deserve good just as much as anyone that has experienced popular success.

Unleash Your Soul's Creative Essence

Allow the vibrating power of spirit to flow through you and awaken the creative part of your soul. Take care of yourself on all levels inside and out. This will assist in giving you greater energy, stamina, and focus, not to mention a stronger connection with your Spirit team. Having a crystal-clear communication line with God will enable you to make sounder decisions in your life. It will assist you in reaching a higher vibration state than if you didn't have that connection. Creativity helps in raising your vibration into higher feelings of joy, love, and peace, while boosting your faith and optimism. Diving into creative projects or obtaining a creative slant in your nature and day to day dealings also help in lifting blocks that are in your way towards abundance enlightenment.

Pay attention to the guidance your Spirit team filters in through you. When you receive a sign or message that is continuous, then this is a clue that it could be Heavenly support coming into you. The message has a positive uplifting feeling to it and will not be bathed in fear or anxiety. Sometimes one can mistake a message for being heavenly support as opposed to their ego. Heavenly support has a high vibration positive feeling to it that benefits you and everyone around.

Expressing restlessness or any uncomfortable feeling through creativity is a fantastic way to release negativity from your soul. You can paint, draw, take photos, write, play music, games, make your own mix MP3's or CD's, re-organize your home, put puzzles together, make fun videos, sing, dance, or anything creative at all. All creative movements get the positive energy within and around you moving again.

Awakening the creative spirit in you is more than working on art projects or becoming an entrepreneur and opening up your own business. Those traits are part of it, but it is also unleashing that part of you that is connected to God. It is the creative part of you within that is in tune to all nuances in and around you. It is your inner child that is full of love, joy, and peace around the clock. This is why detoxing and watching what you ingest are beneficial. These all play a factor into what drains your life force energy zapping any ounce of creativity in you.

Take care of all parts of you. Watch what you ingest and the energy of the thoughts you put into your mind. Self-care is a not only a luxury, but a necessity. Love all that you are and remember to pat yourself on the back for any job well done. When you've accomplished anything at all, then treat yourself to something good in celebration. Whether that's a hiking sabbatical trip or that t-shirt or music album you always wanted. Go for it! Reward yourself. You deserve the endless reservoirs of success and prosperity in all areas of your life that exist. Never stop being creative and live your life from the heart. Create out of love and give out of love.

CHAPTER ELEVEN

*Balancing Healthy Selfishness
and Selflessness*

In the next two chapters will look at the differences between key traits that many vacillate between. When you understand the differences between something like healthy selfishness and selflessness, as well as aggression, passive aggression, and assertiveness, then the more you are able to stand in your own Divine confident power.

Coming to the end of the road as you close your Earthly life chapter up, you realize then if you hadn't before that it was always intended to be about love. Your soul was born from a source of love and you will die right back into that love. Love is the most powerful energy foundation that exists in all dimensions. It is what helps you manifest fearless assertive confidence from within. The only thing that matters in the end is love. The best way to channel energy positively is to remember all things connected to love. Love is what kills energy like anger, sadness, fear, and worry. Outstretch your arms, release any fears, and fall back into the arms of this love. Allow it to protect and guide you on your Earthly journey.

Bring your soul to that beautiful glorious space of centeredness, serenity, and peace. Ignore any drama swirling around you and view circumstances from an emotionally detached perspective without judgment. Increase your faith through prayer and regular conversations with the Divine, knowing and understanding that you are loved and watched over.

Every day should be the most magical time of the year, but the lack of love on the planet that continues to be prevalent makes it less enchanting. Love and accept others even if their values are differing from yours. This is easier said than done since many have forgotten about the basic concept of what love is. Humanity continues to have a long way to go before every soul on the planet is aware that it's about love. One might say that it's the other person that isn't displaying love, but two wrongs don't make a right. Someone has to get the ball rolling in displaying love.

Treat everyone with kindness and compassion even if they don't share your values. This goes for all sides of the spectrum since everyone becomes guilty of it at one time or another. It's not okay to treat others badly or to abuse the luxuries you've been given as a free will thinking conscious being. It's one thing to defend yourself from someone who has accosted or randomly disrespected you, but it's another to take it upon yourself to harass someone because they're different and not a clone of you. You reach no middle ground when you're that rigid.

The #1 trait that Spirit doesn't like to see is someone mistreating or disrespecting another person in any form. This means a certain amount of decorum and etiquette is something they prize. Mistreatment is considered one of the most distasteful quality traits for God to witness. Sadly, that's also the top trait displayed on the planet by humankind.

There are different shades of mistreatment and disrespect that exist. Someone treated you unkindly, then the natural immediate reaction is to be reactive or defensive, so you lash out in retaliation. There's also that fine line between how far you intend to go with mistreating another person to deciding to limit your reactions to slights on your ego by choosing your battles wisely and selectively.

Some refuse to give respect to those that are mean to them, which is not what Spirit is saying. Decorum and etiquette more or less point to the same thing. This is about exuding class, compassion, and grace, while giving off a certain level of respect towards others. Humanity has a long way to go with that. There are a great deal of tantrums and stomping around angrily when someone doesn't get their way instead of seeking out the middle ground in meeting others half way. Treat people with kindness and compassion, but it's understandable to defend yourself with assertive confidence if someone attacks you.

One hopes that with age comes wisdom and spiritual maturity, but as you know this is not necessarily the case. In your twenties, you are more likely to be angrily reactive over something than a wiser one moving into the thirties and beyond. This is because the older you get, whether in human age or soul age, you hopefully learned to incorporate more of the Divinely guided traits of patience, forgiveness, and humility. What can you let go of, get over, and move on from? The risk you run into when not getting over something is when you fall into perpetual antagonism. Not only does that create enormous weight on your spirit, which can cause damage to your health and Divine connection line, but there comes a point when no one is being helped by the repetitive antagonism.

On the one hand Spirit says to teach people how to respect others, but you also can't get swept away in the noise nonsense. The noise nonsense is ranting and raving with everyone else on social media over the top trending story. That kind of disrespect doesn't do anything except add to the drama and noise. The mistreatment and disrespect here in Spirit's case is primarily the one on one kind, even though all forms of mistreatment are unacceptable to them. This can be where someone has overstepped their boundaries or is not displaying appropriate compassionate assertive protocol.

The worst kind of mistreatment is abuse of any kind whether that's physical, emotional, psychological, and so on. This is what irks and pains Spirit to witness, because in the end whatever you're not able to get over doesn't matter in spiritual truth, since you and all of this will one day cease to exist. To God all that's seen is everyone disrespecting everybody else with no end in sight. That energy is darting all over the place. At that point, there is no valid reason for it so just stop.

The most spiritual evolved soul is guilty of it too. Every soul on the planet is at one time or another, but they're aware of what Spirit doesn't like to see and wants to see more of. This statement isn't cut and dry as it can go exceptionally in depth when looking at each case. The general consensus for Spirit has always been the same. Treat your neighbor with respect even if you personally disagree with them. That's a rough trait for all to observe, but one to remember to revert to whenever possible. This is not about taking abuse. This is for those that deliberately and intentionally cause turmoil in others. Disrespect and mistreatment should never be tolerated. If that means you need to rise into Divine warrior mode to stomp that out, then that is what you must do. You have to teach people how to respect you.

In a perfect world, you wouldn't have to teach someone how to respect others, but the reality is there are billions of children on the planet that haven't been taught the basic concept of respect. If it's not there, then you need to move on. This is also about someone that physically, psychologically, emotionally, or verbally assaults you, then they need to be taught the meaning of respect. This isn't through the means of violence. You have to stand up for yourself when possible.

A five-year-old boy was brutally tortured and abused by his parents to the point where he fell into a coma, then passed away. Those parents need to learn the art of respect and compassion for human life. Walking away from something like that is not an option. There are cases where certain behavior needs to be taught and corrected.

Avoiding someone that mistreats or disrespects you is always the first way to go. This is especially the case with online bullies that take it upon themselves to message a stranger through social media to attack them. You don't bother with that kind of nonsense, but block them instead and move on. Flick them off your shoulder as if it's a bee. When one is in situations where that's not feasible or logical, such as a continuously hostile boss, an abusive spouse, or someone you're living with that perpetually antagonizes you, then there is no choice, but to talk to them and train them how to respect you. Otherwise you will end up spending each day under the reigns of abuse, which ultimately causes all sorts of psychological damage that is difficult to repair.

If someone attacks you online, then you ignore that energy, you don't engage with it. You avoid, delete, block, and move on to more important things. If you did something that instigated mistreatment from someone around you, then be conscious of when you did that and take steps to mend or correct it. Sometimes one can unknowingly hurt someone's feelings without realizing that's what may have caused them to be disrespectful towards you. People are complicated beings and learning to discern when a situation warrants how you'll react in kind to a disrespectful person requires your keen intuitive radar where you also choose your battles wisely.

The ultimate reason all are here is to love and to learn how to love. You cannot learn that unless you're thrown onto a planet with others who are different from you. Learn to accept others and see someone's personal truth. You're not saying you agree with them, but a way shower illuminates the way by example.

Be the King or Queen of showing respect and compassion to others. These traits are not popular globally. This doesn't mean that if someone abuses or walks all over you that you take it lying down. Pick your battles wisely and use assertiveness over aggressiveness when slighted. The general demeanor to strive for on a regular basis as much as possible is respect and compassion. Being a compassionate loving person is what garners real attention and attraction from others. If that turns someone off, then don't allow them into your auric circle.

Divine Act of Selflessness

Being entirely selfless is an act that requires no personal gratification, but there is some measure of fulfillment with the act of selflessness. You require unconditional love in a relationship, but unconditional love is to love without conditions. Most everybody has conditions to one an extent or another. This is especially the case in intimate romantic relationships. You hope the person you're with doesn't cheat or isn't abusive. Those are highly reasonable and warranted conditions, but they are conditions. You can get close to unconditional love as much as you can get close to selflessness.

All human beings have both a light and dark ego. The light ego is connected to traits such as having confidence in your abilities, while the dark ego is bogged down in gossip, anger, judgment, or violence. The dark ego will aggressively attack someone, but a light ego will assertively communicate their point. Those who are typically giving by nature are not being altruistic for personal pleasure, but for spiritual nourishment. There are various levels of attainment when it comes to altruism. To be completely selfless is a Divine act possible to achieve. You are made in the likeness of His being. Therefore, you have the capacity of great love and immense selflessness built within you.

I've witnessed others reach that space of being completely selfless. They've personally done things to help others without the longing for any kind of gain. No gratitude is required in those instances. The selfless soul desires to make sure someone is taken care of without any fanfare or acknowledgment. Because why offer praise for displaying traits that are present in every soul on the planet.

At the same time, many long for some measure of approval from others. Even the most centered person on the planet doesn't mind the occasional validation, which acts more as confirmation that they're on the right track. This doesn't make them any less insecure, but it does serve as a reminder to them that the work they're doing isn't for nothing. They can more than likely live life without it after a certain point. When you're in your teens and twenties you generally long for more validation and approval than when you age beyond that.

Altruism or selflessness is part of the universal truth, but it's also a God given trait you were born with. It's universal truth only to the extent that humankind decided to make the act of being selfless a virtue. A universal truth is everyone agreeing to make something be of truth at that time in history. This has been altered as humankind progressed onward. Universal truth is subjective, but basic core values are innately built into a soul operating at full capacity with a high vibration at optimum levels. Parts of the consciousness are God given qualities, while other parts are astrological and part of that person's human life upbringing during the crucial developmental years. It's a cocktail of complicated composites within each soul's make up.

Basic God given traits are displayed while in a high vibrational state. High vibrational states are qualities such as love, serenity, peace, confidence, compassion, and selflessness. The angels are egoless and therefore selfless requiring nothing in return for being selfless. They have nothing to gain by that action. They can be selfless due to being completely egoless. Human beings have an ego, so although many human beings can be selfless, there are varying levels of what constitutes observing selflessness.

Bright Side of Selfishness

If you believe someone else is selfish, then you may be projecting a lack that exists within you. You feel everyone owes you something, which is what selfishness is. You're threatened by someone who says what they want, does what they want, when they want, and without any interference. The person who is confident and goes after what they want, and who toots their own horn isn't concerned over what someone else thinks about them, especially a stranger's opinion. It will not sway the confident person that governs its life under the jurisdiction of the Light. Tooting your own horn isn't a spiritual crime. It can grow annoying for some on the receiving end when it's constant, but it's certainly not criminal. Most anyone with a social media account is praising themselves on some level. This is part of self-love, which is the opposite of low self-esteem and having no love for oneself.

An authentic selfish person has confidence and persistence. They're also less likely to be taken advantage of or give up on their goals. Selfish people have no guilt over saying no, while a narcissus will become angry when someone tells them no. Human ego trained one another to view selfishness as something negative. What some people see as selfishness, Heaven sees as self-love. Anyone calling you selfish prefers that you put yourself second and put them first, which falls into narcissism. True dark selfishness would fall more into greed. This would be racing past someone in a restaurant to get that great table before someone else takes it.

The opposite of being selfish is selfless, but you cannot be adequately selfless when you've fallen into people pleasing or emotional neediness. While in that state you become resentful that you're doing things for others and receiving nothing in return, which is not authentically selfless.

A selfish person takes care of its soul by instilling strict boundaries that prevent negative toxic people and energies from intruding on its serenity. Only when the selfish person is taken care of can they take care of others. The selfish are confident in what they want and go after it without any resistance.

The angels are selfless because they have no ego and aren't struggling to survive on a physical climate that demands you to be selfish and take care of you first. When a high vibrational soul has all they need to survive, then their focus grows more outwardly looking to see who they can help. You cannot achieve great heights or survive on the planet by being entirely selfless. That's not realistic or practical in a world full of people who are untrustworthy and will take advantage of your good nature for being selfless. They'll do it in a myriad of ways from insulting you to displaying passive aggressive behavioral traits in hopes they can get you to do something for them. A true healthy selfish person can see right through both and will have no trouble saying no without guilt.

You're moving into greedy territory when you use someone for your own gain. Being selfish is not a negative trait, because then it becomes greed in that instant. When a narcissus doesn't get what they want, or things don't go their way, they'll insist it's everyone else that is selfish only caring about themselves. You are not a victim, and nobody owes you anything. You owe it to yourself to take care of you. You cannot place that kind of impossible demanding attention and love to be given to you by someone else. That's what God is for. Having confidence, integrity, strength, and going after what you want is healthy selfishness and self-love.

When you're selfish how would you know you acted selfishly? You are too self-absorbed and narcissistic to care. Learning to be selfless takes quite a bit of time. The selfish individual needs to want to become more selfless, but it's difficult for their ego to convince them that this is what should happen. There is a delicate balance between portraying both a healthy selfishness and selflessness.

How enticing it can be to attempt to keep people happy. Certain instances can call for you to people please, but if it means you're going against your higher self's integrity, or God and your Spirit team's warnings in order to do that, then you're heading down precarious ground. This will create unnecessary chaos that is avoidable when you follow the wisdom you receive from above.

CHAPTER TWELVE

*Assertiveness, Aggression,
Passive Aggression*

When one is angry or upset, the human ego will display three different traits: Aggression, passive-aggression, or assertiveness.

The highest and most effective energy form of getting your point across when you're upset or need to correct a wrong is by displaying assertiveness.

Aggression is being directly hostile when you confront someone. You're a militant bully with the mantra that it is your way or the high way and no other opinion is allowed. Aggression primarily comes from fear or ego. It is fear that you are not being heard or the person you're directing that aggression towards is not going to listen to you. It can also come from high anxiety brought on in artificial ways such as consuming too much caffeine where you're bouncing all over the place in agitated aggression.

Aggressive force is your ego wanting to make sure that the person you're directing this force towards understands that you are in charge. You will convey that point by any means necessary. It's attempting to dominate someone with severe force to get that person to go along with your point.

Someone that screams their argument at someone else while pointing their finger repeatedly at you is someone displaying aggression. When you're aggressive you have a sense of entitlement with some self-righteousness mixed in.

A man sees someone moving in on his love partner, and the man becomes a bully and starts to physically shove the person who is making the move on his mate. This is aggressive behavior that can also be someone with high testosterone. Testosterone is built into the chemistry of the male species. Some have more of it than others and this can show through in their aggressive behavior. It can take a great deal of focus and discipline to try and keep that under control as much as possible. I definitely understand since it's been known that I can be pretty aggressive at times. It is instinctual in the male species to react aggressively to ensure others understand you've marked your territory. It also tends to be stronger in men in their teens and especially twenties. As they age their testosterone begins to decline and so does their aggressive behavior.

Passive aggression is just as bad as aggression, except that passive aggression is indirect. You're upset with a love partner, but you don't say anything or tell them that you are angry or bothered by something they did. Instead you keep it bottled up until it explodes in underhanded ways. The passive aggressive person will pout and mope whenever you're around. You'll sense something is wrong, but when you ask them if everything is okay, they appear cold and distant holding in their emotion. They may bite back under their breath with, "I'm fine."

They throw up a wall that makes them inaccessible and thus becoming submissive. This person may have lower testosterone and more estrogen, but they could also be more sensitive or afraid of confrontation erupting. Your thoughts and feelings do matter. It's important to express them when possible by being assertive.

The male species typically has a good deal of testosterone and therefore comes off aggressive when upset, while the female species has more estrogen and therefore can come off passive aggressive when upset. Either gender has displayed both aggression and passive aggression regardless of how much testosterone or estrogen one has. The reasoning for laying out the examples in this way is a generality. This way of reacting to something one is upset about is part of the human make-up, but it is one that can be reined in. Men see a drop in their testosterone levels as they age, while women see a drop in their estrogen levels and rise in testosterone.

I was jogging through a quiet residential area at night and suddenly a dog came at me. I stopped abruptly thrown off guard and hopped back a couple steps. A woman yanked her dog back with the leash at the same time. The woman said with warmth and kindness, "Don't you mind him, he just likes you cause you've got a lot of testosterone."

When active men continuously work out and exercise it starts to raise their testosterone levels. This can also contribute to the aggressiveness that comes out at times.

The passive aggressive person doesn't necessarily communicate with you with words. When they do finally talk with you, they make comments that start to sound as if they are indirectly attacking you or giving you back handed compliments. It takes you awhile, maybe even weeks before you realize, "Wait a minute, you're mad at me. What's wrong?"

The partner exuding passive aggressive behavior is unable to articulate what's wrong, so they become aloof, cold, and distant with you. They might be sad and slouch whenever you're around. If you're a sensitive or someone in tune, then you can pick up on this energy like nobody's business. Someone not in tune has no clue the other person's mad, so it can take much longer to realize it.

Passive aggression also comes from fear where the person is afraid to voice what's wrong, as they don't want to rock the boat or start a fight. They're not fans of confrontation and it's easier to just not say anything and mope around the issue. The problem is that keeping this anger or upset inside for prolonged periods of time can fester and cause potential health issues. It's better to get it out even if someone doesn't want to hear it. You can articulate what's wrong with compassion and assertiveness.

If you're afraid to say something, then write it out. You don't have to email it to the person you're upset with. Email it to a trusted friend or to yourself. It's important to get those feelings out of you. Whenever one of my close friends we're going through a heartbreaking relationship split with someone who left them, they would have the urge to call the ex or send them an email full of angry and upset tirades. They would send it to me saying, "Should I send this to them?"

I'd of course say, "Oh no don't say that. Write out everything to your heart's content, but just send it to yourself or me, so you feel like you're getting it out of you."

Sometimes they would send it to me and then send it to their partner that left them as well. It always backfires in their face where they come back to me. "I should've listened to you. Now it's worse than ever!"

When someone has chosen to leave you, there is nothing you can do or say to change that person's mind. They've already decided and it's in motion. They've more than likely decided long before they took that step to let you in on it. It's best to give them what they want and that is to be separated from you. If it's meant to be, they will come back and then you can decide whether to go for another round or move on.

One thing to consider is that you should feel safe enough to talk openly with your love mate. A relationship is supposed to be you and this person against the world. If you can't talk about things openly with one another, then who can you talk to about that stuff?

Getting an aggressive person to calm down is challenging since the aggressive person is heated. When you are dealing with an aggressive person, you're dealing with someone disconnected from their centered higher self at that moment. They are in no position to reason with, so it's best to get out of their line of fire and wait until they cool off.

The passive aggressive person is challenging to deal with also, because the wall they put up is impossible to pull down in order to get them to open up. The person they're being that way with starts to feel rejected by them. This creates an even bigger distance between both people.

As I've grown older, I've found that I've been more successful at being assertive over aggressive, even though it will freely come out here and there. I've certainly also had moments of passive aggression, but that's mostly in past love relationships. I am a sensitive and did not want to rock the boat with the person I'm involved with. This stems from an abusive childhood where I was trained to go along with someone just to please the abusive person. It's taken a lifetime of working on dissolving that behavior.

In the end, most everyone displays aggression, passive aggression, and assertiveness at one time or another. Be aware when you are displaying aggressive or passive-aggressive behavior, and then begin the process of shifting that energy into assertiveness.

An aggressive person may get violent or into derogatory name calling to get someone to hear their point. They might say or write to someone on social media something like, "You're an (expletive)! Anyone with half a brain knows that doesn't work!"

Whereas someone that displays assertive behavior will speak the truth directly with strength, but it is intertwined with compassion and understanding where one is open to compromise. You're not talking at someone to force your beliefs down someone's throat. Instead the assertive person is talking with the other person as if they're on the same level.

An assertive person will say something like, "I understand your point, but it would be more effective if we did it this way, because then you're not excluding anybody."

A passive aggressive person wouldn't say anything even though they're bothered by something. They would willingly go along with what they disagree with even though deep down they're unhappy about it. No one would know they're unhappy about it, because the passive aggressive person isn't telling them they have a problem.

Assertiveness is the goal to thrive for when angry or upset about something. When you display assertiveness, then you accomplish what you want. An assertive person is firm, stands their ground, but they work with and include the other person they're attempting to come to a resolution with. The assertive person is calm, strong, and composed, but not unresponsive, which would be passive aggressive. They are also not a tough bully, which is aggression. The assertive person is a relaxed centered person who is also direct in their communication with what they want to accomplish. They speak clearly and concisely without being heated and slamming things around.

When there is conflict, the best way to handle it is by being assertive. Call upon your Spirit team to give you confidence if you're feeling passive aggressive. If you're feeling constantly aggressive, then ask your team to help you in relaxing. Request they assist you in stating your point without hurting, upsetting, or walking over anyone, but with assertive confidence.

During my Film Production days, I was working with a Production Supervisor on a Sony Pictures movie. At times of high stress, she would come off abusive with her staff. Ironically, she wasn't like that with me, but that's usually the case as I have low tolerance for abuse. I naturally have the stance of someone demanding respect that most people give that when I enter a room. I became close with her since I tend to get along well with the extroverted tempestuous difficult types that rub others the wrong way. When I noticed she first stepped out of line with a crew member, I pulled her to the side with calm assertiveness and said, "That was harsh."

She pulled back struck by the statement. Mist glazed over her eyes as she revealed vulnerability. "Was I?" She continued, "I totally respect you. This is why I need you to tell me and smack me into shape if you see me doing that."

Afterwards, when I noticed her slipping into rude, hostile, antagonistic, bullying aggression with a crew member, I'd walk in the room and she'd quickly grow quiet and look at me for validation if she took it too far or not. Soon she began to be cognizant of when she might be crossing the line on her own. It was a proud moment seeing that she wanted to change and become better at dealing with others professionally with assertiveness rather than aggression. It wasn't her intention to be nasty as deep down she is a good giving person, but needed to be taught tools and other effective ways of communicating that wouldn't alienate or turn others off. Unfortunately, spiritual concepts such as this one is not something that is taught in school.

There was one minor incident I recall that happened with a Production Assistant where this woman slammed at him about it just as I happened to be walking into the room again. Minutes later when she was alone with me, she asked me if she was too harsh there. I explained that she was and that she can get her point across with greater success by being assertive. People will respect you more and it'll boost morale.

After those instances, I began to notice her softening over the course of the film shoot. She grew to become friendlier, fun, giving, and all smiles with the crew. She was still as much in control and strong as before, but she didn't need to convey that strength through abuse. Before that, she was notoriously known as a mean taskmaster that was whipping the crew into shape as if they were slaves. Others started to mention that they really like this new her. I was proud of watching her shift from aggression to assertiveness in the way that she supervised the crew by the end of the shoot. Sometimes you are in a job or relationship for a reason, which is to allow who you are to rub off on others in a positive way. You might despise your job, but it's not always about you. You may be there to be a positive influence. If human souls kept their ego in check, there would be peace on Earth. No wars, fighting, hate, or causing others pain. It would be as if you were back in Heaven where those negative traits don't exist. Keeping your ego in check is by displaying assertiveness, instead of aggression and passive aggression.

CHAPTER THIRTEEN

*Step Into Your
Soul's Authority*

A guru in India sat on a stage and talked to the audience about someone who was stressed out at their job.

The guru's response was, "Okay, I hope that you get fired from your job."

The guy said, "Oh no, I don't want to get fired."

The guru explained, "You have a job and you're stressed, so I offer to take the job away from you, but now you're stressed about not having a job. It's all in your mind."

Everyone applauds.

How deep would the guru be in the practical world where he would have to hold a 9-6 schedule office job for years with all of the demands that are placed on his back, and all that it entails on his well-being. One reader said that it was easy to wear flowing clothes and sit on a chair on a stage with a turban and dish that out. It's another thing to preach on matters you truly understand because you had to live it and be immersed in it for a long period of time. I consider all sides to have a greater understanding of the physical reality that different people experience.

On the flip side to counter that the guru had a point, where yes to an extent the misery is in your mind. When you change your perspective to see that not having that job would be far worse than having it, then you lighten up about it and you shift your perspective on it to gratitude and acceptance.

Others may preach about what you need to do, but they may not have lived the kind of life you're undergoing. These can be social media mentors, gurus, or motivational speakers who don't understand why the rest of the world is going through what it's going through. They may not have had to work regular jobs they despise for decades unable to break free. They might not have had to endure child abuse or hardcore toxic addictions. Instead they might have got lucky early on with their self-improvement business.

This is intended to illustrate that sometimes you may be drawn to someone informing you about changing your circumstances, but they have not lived through enough turmoil and darkness to understand the nature of rising above it. It can leave you feeling even more confused and dejected unable to grasp why you're not moving out of a situation you feel stuck in.

Someone told me about a popular speaker lecturing the crowd on getting happy, but they added, "That's easy for her to say, she lives in a $10 million-dollar mansion and doesn't have to work a job she can't stand just to survive."

That comment made me ponder on a deeper level growing more aware and observant about each individual's life history. When you're battling with something you have trouble overcoming, you want to hear from someone who lived it rather than some medical doctor who never experienced it. Perhaps the person discussing it has empathy and understanding, or they might have strong psychic spiritual connections that can help, while other times they might have both. If you're seeking healing assistance or motivation, then you'll gravitate towards those that resonate strongly for you. In the end, the intention of all motivators is to motivate you, and if it motivates you to positively change regardless of what that instructor has been through, then they did their job.

As for this particular speaker, she indeed endured a heck of a great deal of trials and tribulations from child sexual abuse to working jobs that sucked out her life force. She had also spent many years putting off the Divine wisdom that was guiding her to make a big change. When she finally did take that step, she catapulted to the top of the charts.

Many well-known spiritual and empowerment related speakers and counselors have moved into the role of encouraging people to be optimistic this lifetime. They do an exceptional job reaching an enormous amount people by inspiring and helping them to initiate action that can lead them closer to achieving bliss, growth, and abundance. Every single person on the planet seeking assistance is not drawn to the same teacher or speaker, which is why it's necessary to have a large selection of teachers in this role. One teacher may work for one person, but not for another. They are aligned with communicating in a language or manner that translates best for you.

If you're new to improving your life, then you know when someone's work has assisted you in positively changing it for the better. Some students are inspired to make healthy life changes, some constantly struggle with it, while others give up.

A financially successful motivational speaker who encourages you to be optimistic can be an exceptional motivator. What others have said they take into consideration are two additional major factors associated with a great motivator. One of them is the speaker is financially successful and working for themselves. They have enough income where they work from home full time or wherever they choose. They don't have to slum it day after day forty plus hours a week sitting in traffic to get to and from a soul sucking job, they don't care about that is ultimately killing off their life force. It is easier for someone to tell you to get happy when that's the life they already have. How many people struggling in life will be able to tell others to get happy at that point? The energy discord between both is wide and takes some effort to put into practice.

Don't beat yourself up when you experience those periods of frustration, despondence, and pessimism. Be aware of those feelings, make your peace with them, and then begin the process of lifting your spirit back into inspiration and optimism.

Many employees work in harsh or toxic environments that do not promote positive morale or a flexible schedule that allows for abundant productivity. Some are working with a toxic colleague or more, or they are working for a superior that fits that mold. What's worse than that is if they work for both a toxic boss and a toxic colleague. The vibrational distance between being in that space compared to achieving what a financially successful motivating teacher has is super wide to overcome. It is not impossible to do when you see that someone else was able to make that leap and transition. Knowing your motivator was able to do that is an excellent motivation to have in itself.

The financially successful teacher has the life that others dream of, so therefore it's easier for them to be optimistic. They no longer have the restrictions that prohibit them from achieving easy bliss. They're no longer walking in the shoes of someone working a job they despise that is killing off their life force and preventing them from remaining optimistic. We're they this optimistic when they had to slum it in a job they despised in a crummy apartment? It was more than likely a huge struggle for them to get positive in that instant than it is now doing work they love. Even the most wonderful upbeat positive teacher will have some down feeling days too, but you're not seeing that on camera.

The other factor is that some speakers have a naturally sunny disposition. They could have been born bubbly, bouncy, and extroverted with fewer horrid experiences to overcome. These are things such as they're not battling with mental, emotional, or physical disorders, or addictions and abuse that make it challenging every day to have that award-winning bright personality that takes people by storm when they enter a room.

It's challenging to get someone suffering from daily anxiety or depression to shift that energy when they have what some might call a chemical imbalance. Maybe you consume substances that are not great for you thus altering your state of mind to something worse. You take those substances because it gives you a temporary high. Soon that high wears off and you're miserable again until you consume the substance again. This is in order to keep going.

It's easy to sell positive thinking when you're a million-dollar speaker or you work for yourself. I'm sure you would love to meet the 9-6 Monday thru Friday employee who works a job they don't care about for a paycheck and simultaneously pushes perpetual positive thinking. They are rare and some companies are lucky to have that one person in there that brings joy just by being a part of that staff.

Spiritual teachers, speakers, and motivators assist in guiding you in a more enlightened direction, but ultimately you are your own authority. You have the true answers within as to what changes you need to make for yourself to get happy.

I grew up being physically, mentally, spiritually, and emotionally abused by one of my parents. It was repetitive and severe enough that my soul consciousness broke and split apart into numerous selves. I ended up struggling through alcohol, drug, and pill addictions, which also transferred into broken relationships. While things are much better and at peace today than back then, I still struggle to forge forward battling the side effects it brought on at times.

Growing up, I wanted to hear from someone who is or has had to drudge it day after day for decades and eventually escaped that to do what they love full time. Or they were still able to be endlessly optimistic and naturally motivated while working that kind of job. I have never in all my years in the work force encountered someone who was permanently optimistic. Most of them appeared miserable or disappointed in their life.

There are a great many teachers, role models, and motivators threaded around the world with past histories that fit the rags to riches scenario. Those were the inspiring ones I desired to see. They were someone that rose up from the slums of their life to the one they had only envisioned in dreams of Heaven.

Many people look to motivational speakers to inspire them, give them great life tips, or just to hear positive words, but you create your own life. You choose how it will go. If you don't like your life, then take action steps to change it. Pull yourself up by your bootstraps and through faith become your own champion and motivator. If you feel that you can't change it, can't move out of the place you live in, can't leave the job you hate for financial reasons, then you will remain in that position until you take steps to change it.

The odds of winning the lottery jackpot are slim to none, so you can't rely on that, but certainly buying a ticket can increase the rare probability of winning. What you can do is take action steps towards making the life you want a reality. Many people have done it. They've worked jobs they've hated and eventually worked jobs they loved or moved into careers working for themselves.

Working for yourself where you call the shots can have its drawbacks. You still have to answer to yourself and ensure you have consistent income coming in so you can pay your bills. Prayer and positive affirmations help alter your perception, but it still needs to be coupled with action since it is rare that anything magnificent will land in your lap with no effort. Even just a little effort goes a long way as it gets that energy moving in that direction.

While many will talk about how you have to be happy first and then the abundance will come, it's easy to say that when you have the abundance, therefore it's not always entirely true. The reality is there are many miserable people that achieved financial abundance in their lifetime and were still miserable afterwards.

Be as optimistic as you can be in general, since no one is rubbed the right way being around a miserable grump, but it certainly won't play that big of a part in preventing what you want from coming to you. People that achieved what they wanted regardless of being miserable or optimistic is because they worked hard and went after it without stopping. It's hard work and persistence that helps you achieve. It's not giving up no matter how many setbacks or roadblocks get in your way. It is rising into your Divine soul power of fearless assertive confidence.

It's also more than practicing positive thinking and bliss in hopes of achieving the ultimate reward, which are abundance and endless blessings. Don't be mistaken by this message telling you to think negatively instead. By all means, positive thinking is always the way to go, but in the most efficient way. You cannot deny how you're feeling by masking it with false positive thinking in order to convince you that you are positive, when deep down you are miserable. You are miserable with where your life is at, miserable that you don't have a lover, miserable that you're not doing work that you love, miserable that your life is not where you thought it would be, and miserable because you feel perpetually stuck. Those are valid feelings that need to be addressed and dealt with one at a time. You can choose to be miserable for a lifetime that the lover did not come, or you can make the most of it and accept it by letting it go.

The problem with saying that positive thinking is not the way to go is that it confuses one by glorifying negative thinking. It's basically saying, "Hey, it's okay to be miserable. If that's how you feel, then let it out and be proud of that."

That's dangerous to say since people are miserable and negative enough. No one has any problem being negative. It takes work to be positive, but the positive feeling has to be experienced naturally. If it's forced, then it's still negative with a false layer of optimism.

Numerous studies revealed surprising revelations that successful business entrepreneur millionaires were those who had a tough time in school. They might not have gone to College, but might have graduated from High School with a B or C average and sometimes lower. Most were not "A" students with a 4.0 GPA. I remember before my days in the Entertainment Industry that in the 1980's it was known that bigwig producers would make someone with a College Degree serve coffee just to prove that in the end it doesn't matter to them.

This isn't justifying or discrediting school achievers, nor is it attempting to sway anyone from striving to be your best in school. This is illustrating to those who have struggled not to give up. Don't believe you won't amount to anything because you did poorly in school or didn't receive a degree. There are numerous examples of people who did poorly in school, came from a poor or middle-class background, yet ended up becoming millionaires. This is partially because they tried harder, while conveying passion and dedication. They used more mental prowess to succeed despite not having a degree or a high GPA. They were optimistic, persistent, and streets smart.

A top CEO of a well-known real estate franchise informed me that she never went to College, but instead received her degree at the "school of hard knocks". Her offices combined bring in over $150 million in real estate revenue. Not bad for someone who came from nothing, didn't do well in school, and with little education.

Everyone entertains doubts or negative thinking at some point, including the most evolved enlightened being. It is humanely impossible for one person to be 100% positive in thinking every second of their life. Earth is not Heaven, and doubts and negative thinking will creep up even with the most positive appearing person. If you think positive, then you will achieve blessings and rewards. This is not always true and can put someone into a dangerous predicament. The secret to achieving blessings is a combination of factors that include taking action as well as being optimistic that you can do it. You can't layer your negative thoughts with positive thinking. This is like taking a pill to numb emotional pain. It may numb those rough edges, but it doesn't get rid of the issues unless it's addressed and dealt with in order to heal and then release it. Then you have a clean slate to forge forward fearlessly.

CHAPTER FOURTEEN

Fearless Assertive
Confident Soul

Show your best self by becoming a fearless confident soul that walks in faith. Share your light with others whenever you can. Let it out and let it shine bright. This inspires a mighty movement of peace. The hardness and toxicity that has plagued humankind for so long is outdated. The light inside you must be allowed to breath freely. Allow it to shine outwardly by taking back the control of your surroundings. Be a warrior of light and do your best to stay in that space even when you stumble upon a roadblock or a difficult person. Demanding people are merely acting out from their ego, which has no power or validity with anything real or long lasting. The ego lives in fear and acts out in fits of temper much like a child having an outburst when it doesn't get what it wants. You find peace, joy, strength and love when you remain centered in the light.

When you lose your way, ask for heavenly assistance to get back on track. The more you ask for help and work with your Spirit team to reach this space of contentment, then the easier it gets. What can work for you might be lighting a candle and meditating on this light. Call in your Spirit team to begin the process of re-aligning your soul back into confidence. Empty out your negative thoughts as you focus on this candlelight. Close your eyes and envision that the flame of the light is taking over any negative thoughts and blasting it away while lifting it off your body. Make room in your consciousness to receive the messages coming in from Spirit to help you be at peace and feel encompassed by love.

I have crossed paths with a wide variety of people with different belief systems and values. I have witnessed those who might disagree with any of this or who find it to be ineffective. Yet, these are the same people that struggle in a constant uphill battle. Or they might be the ones who have been stagnant with no hope for escape. When in those states your ego dominates your life big time ensuring that you never progress.

Within you are the knowledge of all lifetimes. Within you is the knowledge of why you are here. Pay attention to your intuition as that is one of the many barometer gauges that exist within your soul that accurately receives heavenly messages. All human souls receive heavenly communication everyday without exception. It is irrelevant what the soul's personal values and beliefs are, and whether they're aware that it is indeed their Guides and Angels. Pay attention to the messages in order to help you navigate through life much easier than if you were not aware of them.

Keeping your vibration high takes daily work. It's a lifestyle and view change you're adopting. One day you are riding on cloud nine with joy, which raises your vibration. Your vibration remains high until a negative thought enters your mind thus causing it to take a dip again. The next day you go on a drinking binge. This drinking binge prompts your vibration to drop astronomically. It can be a struggle to raise it than it is to drop it. Raising it back up can feel like pushing a huge boulder up a steep hill. Those privy to this knowledge can raise their vibration much easier than someone unaware of what to do in order to get it there. Having an interfering culprit like the ego is what gets its kicks out of double-crossing you and ensuring your vibration stays low. It makes sure that you do not succeed. When you make a commitment to incorporating higher vibration methods into your life every day, then you will notice the changes in your life shifting in a more positive direction.

It's easy to lose sight of why you're here. The way human life has been set up and structured by the ego in others has caused enormous discontent. Human ego trained others to be unhappy and glum by thriving for nonsense. Not everyone is affected by the harsh energies of the planet. These people have adjusted their lifestyle choices. This includes living in areas of nature with little to no chaos and people. Watching what they ingest in their physical bodies and taking care of it through daily exercise. They ensure the people they surround themselves with are high vibrational. They avoid the negativities of social media, the internet, and gossip entertainment.

There are a great many positives to Earthly life. People took what they innately learned from the spirit world and built homes, created work and jobs for others, designed transportation, as well as an ease of communication through advanced technological devices. These are some of the fantastic concrete practical necessities for human life. These are practical ways of surviving on a planet that is spilling over the edges.

However, interpersonal relationships continue to suffer sliding rapidly on a decline. Love is lacking, while cruelty and unfriendliness is gaining steam. It is true that human souls manage to find the love when a crises hits. They intervene when they notice someone is being pushed down, but the love they exude in those instances is temporary. You grow lost in the nonsense of the noise of the ego. Some are consumed by jobs they're not happy in, or you're living check-to-check, or struggling to find work. Perhaps you're in relationships that are unsatisfying, or you're perpetually single longing for a long-term committed love relationship that never surfaces. You're forced to be in situations you do not want to be in. What an effort it is to get to a place of feeling eternally happy.

When you're faced with circumstances that do not jive with your higher self, examine how you arrived at that place. Look at the underlying cause that has prompted you to feel negative when this happens. Identify it and then dig deep into understanding why it has upset you. There are circumstances that no doubt have made you angry or prompted feelings of discomfort. Maybe you ran into someone at the store who was rude to you. You being a sensitive absorbed that like nobody's business. It ends up putting you in a funk for the rest of the day. For some sensitive's, they'll be angry for a minute, others for hours, or you could be one of those who immerses in the energy for the rest of the day. Avoid beating yourself up over it. It just means that you're a hypersensitive psychic sponge. You have compassion and love within you as all souls do, even though this might be difficult to grasp.

Whenever you witness ugliness in someone else, remember that they were born with the deepest love and compassion beyond measure. What you're observing with them is the darkness of ego at its worst. This soul has given its power away to the Darkness, their lower self, and ego. The ego cannot be reasoned with or convinced of anything, but of what it wants. The ego seeks to sabotage themselves or others. It can be someone who slanders someone they don't care for. A high vibrational soul that is not pleased with something does not waste its time resorting to negativity or in giving it any attention. It only focuses on the things it enjoys.

When you witness aggression or disrespectful behavior flying at you, then you will absorb that energy. It seeps into your aura and soul. It causes an array of negative circumstances and moods to assault you. Find positive exercises that can assist you in releasing it and letting that go. It might feel easier said than done, but when a slight happens in your world, your ego has trouble letting go of it. When you understand this concept of separating yourself from the troublesome ego, it becomes simpler to manage and temper it.

When you have a higher degree of sensitivity than other souls, then you are more likely to be affected by someone else's ego. You're a psychic sponge who easily absorbs the negative or off-putting energies in others. It is a gift, but at times it can feel like a curse when you enter environments with people that display low vibrational behavioral patterns. You absorb that negative energy which drops your mood affecting your inner and outer world.

When you grow negative, moody, or agitated, then this is a sign of two possible conclusions. One is that you've ingested low vibrational foods or drinks. Or you may have absorbed this energy from someone toxic you crossed paths with. It can be a stranger on the sidewalk who walked past you. If they're displaying low vibrational behavior, then that energy is lodged in their aura. As a tuned in sensitive psychic sponge, you've absorbed that into your aura sometimes without knowing it. The super tuned in psychic sponges are typically aware they just absorbed this energy from someone in passing.

The souls you absorbed this energy from do not always intend to have a low vibration. It's usually done innocently and naively, or sometimes in other words not knowing any better. Some souls have not evolved enough to be more in tune to something outside of themselves. This is partially why that particular soul is living an Earthly life.

Those in tune with the Other Side, the soul and spirit, are turned off by harsh people and energies. They steer clear of those that perpetually display low vibrational traits. This can be from the guy trying to pull a fast one by nickel and diming someone to buy a car. We call them pushy salespeople. They don't care about you, but what's in your wallet. On the flipside, they have a quota and if they want to keep that particular job, they know they need to do whatever it takes to sell a car. There are easygoing salespeople who do care about you and do not display shark attack like behavior. They don't attempt to find ways to sell you something when you're having doubts or feeling uncomfortable about it. This type of salesperson will simply say, "I'm here to answer any questions you have about any of this. If you're interested, then let me know."

It can be your employer or someone you work with who puts on the fakeness whenever you enter the room. As a tuned in soul you can sense them a mile away. They're threatened by your higher frequency energy. They subconsciously know that you're on to them. This also turns off a lower vibrational energy in someone else. Low vibrational human souls are threatened by someone that exudes a high confident vibrational energy. The low vibrational soul's ego feels out of your league. High vibrational people don't feel threatened by others unless that person is exuding negative energy traits. They're not threatened but repulsed. Sometimes it can also be that you and these other people you come into contact with don't know each other well enough to accept your differences.

There was another incident in my former film days where I was working for an employer who rubbed everyone the wrong way. I noticed others kept coming to me here and there to express how this woman upsets them. This wasn't the same woman in the earlier story. There was one day when someone pointed out to me something negative about her.

I responded, "Yeah, I'm hearing that quite a bit. It's best to ignore it."

They said, "I guess that's all one can do."

That banter got me thinking about this woman. I decided to make a pact to meet her halfway where I would throw on the charm and friendliness. The next day I went into her office unannounced and sat in her guest chair. She was all business asking if there was something I needed.

I said, "No, I'm just visiting. Wanted to say hi and see how you're doing."

She seemed a little stunned as if no one had bothered to do that before. Although the business armor and cold reserve was still up, I noticed she flinched and softened slightly allowing just a little bit of light out. She attempted to engage with me and make some small talk. For me personally this was an effort since I dislike small talk. Something miraculous soon happened where we started this lighthearted dialogue banter.

The next day I continued with the new pact to visit her and to get to know her more. I proceeded to do that every day realizing we were bonding and hitting it off. Soon it was no longer an effort for me to chill with her briefly or for her to engage. Both of our reserves were coming down. Once I tore down those walls and met her halfway, not only did the morale within the production company improve, but our connection improved as well. We were not just two cold ice conquerors going toe to toe. She started to open up a little bit more as time went by.

To make a long story short at the time of this writing, I've known her personally for over two decades now. Like many of the friendships I made throughout the business, we continue to talk and meet up for the occasional get together. She's a wonderful soul with an amazing generous heart. When others have asked how I met her, I go back into time and remember that it didn't start off that way. Sometimes when you take the time to know someone who has the cold reserve up, you discover they're not as hostile as they are coming off. It's human nature to instantly judge someone who hasn't spoken a word instead of diving into who they are.

This coldness and reserve has grown in others thanks to the technological age. Newer and future generations are being raised on devices that train you to be lacking in honest face-to-face soul connections. For those that have gone out on a date you've probably noticed some of the typical preliminary questions. They want to know what your job is or what kind of work do you do. What kind of car do you drive? These ego driven questions are externally based. Your job does not define you in real reality, but the human ego has set their life up in a way that their whole world revolves around what kind of job you do. Who cares what you do for a living? Unless you're working in a field that is your passion and it brings you joy, then it is irrelevant what kind of work you do. This passion is your life purpose, but many do not work in jobs that are their passion. For most people it is a paycheck that squeezes the life force out of that soul. They're usually under stress and grumbling about life in general.

When you absorb the ions of negative and cold energy around you, then this can put a damper on your spirit until you address it. You can sit around and hope that something amazing will happen around you that will suddenly raise your vibration, or you can address it and do something about it immediately. It can be going for a walk in a nature setting. This is followed by taking deep healthy breaths in and requesting that your spirit team release any and all negative energy that has latched onto your soul. It can be getting together with an optimistic friend who observes healthy life choices. It can be someone that lifts your aura just by being in your vicinity. You can throw on a funny movie or make love to your relationship partner. What you're trying to do is re-raise your vibration. Taking basic soul enhancing steps when an assault has attacked your aura can do the trick.

CHAPTER FIFTEEN

Live Your Life Be Free

Everyone has experienced some hard times at one time or another. You might have negative things to say about it. The ego fixates on the horrid that came out of something rather than the positive gained. Rise above your ego and ask yourself, "What greatness did my soul consciousness receive out of that experience? What was awesome about it?"

The soul's experiences happen for a reason regardless if they're challenging or not. It is not because you did something to deserve it, but because your soul is destined for greatness. It reaches those heights of greatness through the challenges. You're here in this Earthly life school to find ways that suit you in order to enhance your soul and spirit. You're not here to find out what the latest sale on jeans is or rip through relationships selfishly with no care in the world. In order to improve you have much to gain. When something negative happens in your world, work on looking at it from an optimistic perspective.

An exercise you can do is to pick up a journal or a notebook. Use that notepad as your diary to put in only optimistic viewpoints in your life. When you find that you're buried heavily in negative thoughts and emotions unable to break away, take a moment to pull the notebook out. Devote a page or more to whatever it is that is upsetting you. If it's a person you know, then write that person's name in your journal entry. Instead of focusing on what they did to upset you or whatever circumstance has upset you, shift that into something positive. Think about all of the qualities you love about the person that has angered you. Remove your ego from the equation and look at that person through the eyes of an egoless angel. How would they see that person's soul within? List everything that is positive about them and how that affects you in an optimistic way. I know some may grumble when reading that and believe me I understand. I have an ego too! When someone has hurt or angered you it's going to be difficult to see them through the eyes of love. Know that when you're looking at them through the eyes of love, you're not condoning their behavior, and nor do you have to remain buddies with them. You're doing this exercise as a release. It's for your benefit in order to remove that old, tired, angry energy you're carrying around that surrounds the person or circumstance. You do not need that energy, but in order to release it, acknowledging it with love is what raises your vibration. When your vibration is raised you are more apt to receiving clearer communication from the spirit world, which in turn assists you on your path towards abundance in all forms. It is what feeds this fearless assertive confidence into your spirit.

Your mind may begin to wander to all of the things you feel this person (or circumstance) has done that has hurt or upset you. However, you will not write those things down. Remember this is a positive journal. You will immediately adjust your thoughts back to the positive things about this person. Let's say it was an ex-lover who cheated on you, was abusive, or left you and the relationship. You will not write any of those things down, but rather will focus on their good qualities. If you're only able to come up with one good quality, then write that one down. It is an exercise that takes much effort in this case, because you're holding anger towards this person for doing one or all of the things I suggested. Your ego refuses to see the goodness in someone who has upset or hurt you, which is understandable, but we're working on letting it go here.

If it is a circumstance that happened to cause you upset, then you will write down in this journal the optimistic features that have come out of that. For example, you receive a traffic ticket. Instead of focusing heavily on how you have no time to take care of the ticket, or no money to pay for it, write down the positive benefits that you've gained from the ticket. You might write something down like: "This has taught me to drive more carefully."

That statement feels far better than saying, "I have no money. How am I going to pay for this! It wasn't even my fault!"

The ticket could've been a karmic thread reaction to another issue going on in your life that needs addressing. Usually there is a domino effect of events that are within the same energy vibration.

This exercise may not immediately change your life, but it will gradually guide you into positively taking steps in changing your life. It will assist you in getting into the habit of bouncing back from upsetting situations much more quickly than you normally would. It will help you to view circumstances and people in a more positive light. The key is if you're going to play this game, then you have to play objectively. Putting all things positive and optimistic in this journal is the exercise. Only write your blessings, appreciations and gratitude for situations and people in your life. This absolutely includes everything and everyone that causes you to feel negative emotions. This might be challenging, but in the end, it will be rewarding as you are re-training your mind to think positively. This raises your vibration in the process, which assists with attracting in positive circumstances and people to you over the course of time. Because it raises your vibration it also clears out the debris that accumulates in and around the communication line to Heaven and your Spirit team. If it doesn't do anything, but allow you to start shining your true loving light, then that is all that matters in the end.

The higher self is a problem solver, but the darkness of ego is a wretched problem seeker. It might appear to be louder than your higher self and your Spirit team of guides and angels. This is due to a couple of factors. The atmosphere of the Earth plane is extremely thick and dense that connecting to the Other Side through all of the toxic debris makes it challenging. Your guides and angels are louder and more powerful than any ego. Yet, when the soul is in the Earth dimension, the communication lines are heavier and dirtier. The ego easily rises through the dirt. It rises as soon as your soul enters into this human life. The ego is activated in a big way. When the soul is in the earth plane it's like roaming through life with ear plugs and blindfolds on. Anyone who has put on a blindfold and ear plugs to sleep at night may point out how they can sometimes faintly hear light sounds with them on. The higher self strains to hear Heaven through this muffled sound. When a human soul lives in a higher vibrational state, this allows light in, which gives rise to the higher self. Suddenly that soul is hearing their guides and angels more clearly than usual.

You are not alone as at least one Spirit Guide and one Guardian Angel surround you from your human birth until human death. They assist you down the right path in order to fulfill your purpose while here. When you are in your higher self's state you connect with your Spirit team on the other side with greater efficiency. When you are in your lower self's state or ego, then you block heavenly guidance and messages that keep you on the right path and assist you in achieving your desires. In my connections with Heaven, I've discovered that all are loved and seen through the eyes of love. Do your best to keep the darkness of your ego in check and exude love full time.

This is your life and you need to live it confidently for you. Let no one shatter your dreams, feel no guilt about who you are, and apologize to no one about your gifts and talents. Don't allow what other people say to tell you're not qualified for something if it's something you're passionate about inside. You're not here to live the way the critics around want you to live. Can you imagine taking what other people say to heart? You would never accomplish anything. God's sends His best here, which means He knows you are great enough to stomp out that darkness in other people and follow your Divine calling. He knows you are strong enough to withstand the forces of dark critics by ignoring it and forging forward and eyes ahead on what He's calling you to do. It's no one's business how you choose to live your life. You may feel indebted to certain people in your circle this lifetime, but in higher truth the only soul you are beholden to is your own and your Divine contract.

Live your life freely by confidently going after what you desire with passion, enjoyment, and enthusiasm. Life may have dealt you a challenging hand, but use that to your advantage. Challenges are not intended to punish you, but to strengthen you into a warrior. Take the hint and toughen up. Don't allow setbacks to keep you down. When you trip, stumble, and fall, then rise back up again ready to forge on into battle. Revert to faith by leaning on God and the Angels for strength, confidence building, and support.

Fight for your life! If there is something irking you about a decision or purchase or commitment made - then don't hesitate to take action or feeling guilty about canceling or deleting it from your life.   If a situation is leaving you to feel taken advantage of, then take steps to fix it.

Acquire knowledge and wisdom through the process of living and feeling good about how your life trajectory ends up. Make the decision to change your ships course and aim your soul towards the direction of your dreams. The things you say and do now set in motion what is to come six months to a year from that point, so be aware and conscious of what it is you are putting out into the Universe.

Take the occasional step back to retreat and take stock in how your life has gone to date. Notice all of what you've accomplished.   Examine your triumphs, your sorrows, your successes, and your challenges. What was lost and what was gained? Look forward to the next six months of your life and affirm that it will go with superior promise. You will do your best to ensure that it will be even better than it's ever been.

Every morning you wake up, have gratitude for what you have now, and then mentally say to your consciousness that you will make today count.

One exercise can be to find an empty jar or canister, get a stack of post-its or little notes, and leave those blank notes next to the jar. At least once a week write at least one awesome thing that happened for you that week or each day. Even if it was someone who showered you with a smile that stuck. Fold up the little note and put it in the jar. Every several months or so often pull all of the little notes out and read each one and notice the blessings and good things that actually did take place in your life that you might have normally brushed off. Some people focus only on lack or what went wrong, but one rarely shines light on all of the good that took place. Focusing on the good expands that energy into more good things.

Focus on the good that happens in your life that might seem miniscule because it's not the big lottery financial win. If you get a flat tire that ruined your day, don't talk about that aspect of it on the post-it, but instead mention who intervened to help your day brighten up, including if it was the tow truck driver that got you up and running again. There are blessings all around you when you take the time to notice them.

Derive pleasure out of the day with the things you love the most. Don't allow any stress or negativity to override this pleasure. This also means avoid engaging in anything that's going to bring you misery. Focus on the good and the uplifting. Go after what you want without reservation. The happier you allow yourself to become, then the healthier you turn out to be.   This equates to a longer more fulfilling, passionate, joyous life. This is what every soul wants and deserves, but it takes a bit of effort on your part to re-train your mind into manifesting that fearless assertive confidence within you.

Incorporate regular bouts of fun times, make and connect with friends, family, and acquaintances. Open up and be sociable with others without any demands. Connecting with others through lightheartedness gives you a joy boost, which then raises your vibration. A high vibration is what brings positive manifestations into your life. Being sociable has added health benefits including that of being a wonderful stress reliever. This version of sociability with others does not mean resorting to gossip, slander, and complaints, but rather choosing to enjoyably engage with other people's energies. Seek out camaraderie, community, and positive shifts. Open up your heart to others with love and affection. Taking care of your well-being from the body, mind, and your soul are important because it is your temple and vessel that you have been given for the sake of numerous purposes. You have to take of all parts of you and take that seriously. You are loved even when you doubt it, avoid it, shun it and do everything in your power to deny it. When you reach that threshold of completing your run, the only thing you take with you is love. If you gain any knowledge of value, remember to love more, give more, and have compassion no matter how unpopular it's become. Only then can you truly discover that magic your soul secretly desires.

If God raised you, then you would grow up to see the love in all souls. You would exude love and joy full time. The best parts of you are what God is, and the worst parts are the darkness of your ego.

Practice with starting each day on a high note, since that will set the tone for the next twenty-four hours. How often have you woken up in a negative mood only to find that's carried into the rest of the day? Your coffee machine won't work, you're running late for work, and discover the traffic is worse than it's ever been. You walk into work and thrown at you are one issue after another. By the time you get out of work agitated, you race home to have a drink. It take a great deal of effort to shift your vibrational energy back into confidence, but the tools to do so are already within you.

Rejoice, celebrate, and love all that you are inside and out. You are perfect and beautiful through the eyes of God and the angels. This love for your soul is unconditional. See yourself in this same light as Heaven sees you and remember to practice self-care. You are intended for greatness. If you never do anything else, but let your loving light shine through to the world, then that will be enough to help combat all the evil in the world.

Your life moves in cycles that fluctuate. You can detect when an official cycle is ending due to all of the back to back closing of doors that appears to be happening. This can cause you to be filled with enormous tension. Allow the doors that need to be closed to do so as it is prepping you for a new chapter. You can use that time spent retreating, laying low, gathering knowledge, purging, and centering, so that you may rise in strength with clarity for your next new chapter.

Personal changes are much like the cycles of the weather seasons that ebb and flow. You are moving through a series of chapters, peaks, and valleys every day. Those are great times to evaluate and probe deeper into what you've experienced to date, how you've grown, what you've learned, and how you'll choose to move forward. What will you leave behind and what will you take with you on the next part of your soul's journey onward and upward into Utopia and beyond?

The Metaphysical Divine Wisdom Collection

METAPHYSICAL DIVINE WISDOM
ON BALANCING THE MIND, BODY, AND SOUL

CHAPTER ONE

*Raise Your Soul's
Energy Vibration*

The mind, body, and soul is a genre that is widely accepted and known amongst all of the spiritual communities around the world. These key areas are the core parts of you to focus on improving if one were seeking to bring out your soul's profound state of happiness that exists in Heaven. The mind was put first because it is in the mind where all things become possible. When you expand your mind and consciousness, then the opportunities you can create out of this are infinite. When your mind deteriorates or functions on a lesser frequency, then being able to feed all other parts of you become limited, which has an overall effect on your health and wellness state to other important areas of your physical life. It is the mind that houses the dark part of your ego that runs rampant holding a loaded gun that aims and fires wherever it can. It is in your mind where you train yourself to either see positivity in your life or the negative. No one has any trouble being negative, but being positive takes enormous effort. When you alter your state of mind by the will of your thoughts, then there is no telling what you can accomplish when you set your mind to it.

Your soul's vibration is the overall energy that it vibrates at. When you have it set in your mind to take care of your physical body, then this is simultaneously taking care of your soul. Taking care of your physical body includes taking care of your mental and emotional state. You might be exceptionally physically fit, but if you're a toxic person, then you may as well be drinking as much alcohol as you can until you black out. It's that mental toxic state which creates the most damage to your soul. Being a toxic person is equitable to the high amounts of toxins that someone puts into their body.

One of the benefits to raising your vibration are that it assists you in picking up on

Divinely guided psychic messages more easily. When you are able to efficiently pick up on those messages, then this equates to making solid choices in life that bring you closer to the threshold of abundance attainment. Improving all aspects of the mind, body, and soul are all connected to achieving greater heights in life both physically and spiritually.

When it comes to psychic phenomena, one of the bigger enticements that many want is to communicate more efficiently with the Other Side. The top reasons noticed is to see what their future holds. When will I meet my love partner? Is this person my soul mate? When will I find another job? When will I buy my first house? These are all physical material life desires, but this is not the main reason to improving one's psychic abilities. When someone's life hasn't been where it wants to be, then it worries about the future wondering if anything good will ever happen for them. This prompts them to pull cards or go to a psychic reader for help. The answers to your future lie within the core part of your soul because it's in your soul contract that you have access to when you raise your vibration and tune in to what is beyond.

This is a world filled with beings that wrestle with that dreadful ego, which constantly gets in the way of our soul's success. It's one of the things we all must master while here. The core reason to being able to connect with your Spirit team is not for the sake of being shown what's in store for your future. It is to be able to pick up on the daily guidance given to you to make sounder choices that lead you towards what you desire. They'll help you in steps to get there, but they're not going to drop those desires into your lap freely. These guides are within reach for the sake of picking up on those action steps required by you.

Even if you are able to psychically connect with Heaven, it doesn't mean your future will be relayed to you. Connecting with your team is not for fortune telling purposes. In fact, that's one of the last things on their list for wanting you to be able to have a stronger connection with them. Your Spirit team of Guides and Angels do not live your life for you. What is conveyed is on a need to know basis that will enrich and grow your soul. They may relay advice that might be displeasing to you, such as living a healthier lifestyle and to exercise more. Some may not want to hear that, but your Spirit team knows that when you are physically healthier, then this equates to a stronger mind and soul. This combo is what also gives you immense reservoirs of energy to stay focused on fulfilling your purposes and goals. They might urge one to exercise because they feel that you'll need energy and clarity for the bigger desire they want to bring you down the line. At least one guide and angel are guiding every person on the planet, but that soul is also being pulled in another direction by the Darkness energies that rule and penetrate the Earth in a darker part of the spirit world that is separate from Heaven.

Every soul is communicating with the Other Side whether they're aware of it or not. I walk from my car to the elevators in a corporate building and Spirit messages are sifting through me mostly via clairaudience (clear hearing) or claircognizance (clear knowing). I'm not doing anything specific to make it happen. Nor am I attempting to conduct a psychic reading. I'm not asking my Spirit team questions as I walk hurriedly to my destination. On an hour to hour basis the messages naturally fall into my vicinity without me wanting or thinking about it. I was born with heightened psychic abilities that were bouncing off the charts by the time I was four. I've forever had one foot in this world and the other in the spirit world. It wasn't something developed over time or over an interest in the spiritual world. It's been this way for as long as I can remember. This is one of the reasons as to why I'm a neurotic all over the place mess at times picking up on every shred of nuance around me.

Some people connect with their Spirit team as naturally as you brush your teeth. Others struggle to pick up on messages or they feel they're receiving nothing. Your Spirit team never disappears or stops communicating with you. When you feel you are receiving nothing, then there could be a block in your life that you might be unaware of or your vibration energy has dropped. What lowers your vibration is also a block. It can be any negative feeling experienced, which is connected to your mind. It can be a particular bad food you ingest, which is connected to your body. Poor diets weigh you down over time. It darkens your aura colors and creates a layer of dirt particles that can only be seen by Heaven or a Clairvoyant, which is connected to your soul. An exaggerated entertaining image of this is the character *Pig-Pen* from the Charlie Brown cartoon moving about with the cloud of dust around him.

When you ingest a diet primarily of toxins, then the toxins become you. This contributes to blocking incoming messages from spirit. When you eat chemically processed foods on a regular basis, then this energy infuses itself into your soul. Think about what kinds of food might have existed at the beginning of humankind and you have a pretty good idea of what is okay to consume. It was over time that humankind began heavily processing foods with unnecessary chemicals, additives, and fats. Junk food didn't exist at the beginning of time. Eating a healthy diet of fruits and vegetables is what assists greatly in removing psychic spirit blocks. It is also awesome for your mental and physical health, your soul and physical body. None of the content we're going to discuss in this book should be taken as condemnation or judgment. It's about being more mindful about making sounder choices to improve your state of well-being by how you think, feel, and what you put in your body. When it comes to toxic foods and drinks that you love, then view those favorite guilty pleasure toxins to be used in moderation if you're unable to let go of it.

Not all toxic foods will create a psychic spirit block since everyone's physical and mental chemistry is complex. We're rattling off the potential basics that could be blocking someone from connecting with Spirit while weighing their energy and life force down.

It's okay to indulge once in a random while. My weakness in my early twenties was Pizza and Beer. As I changed and leaned more towards a healthier diet my cravings for Pizza and Beer were reduced to next to nothing, which means I don't crave it anymore. I'm not opposed to it, but my tastes and palette have changed. You train your palette to become used to what you're eating whether it's good or bad for you. If something tastes weird that's good for you, then it won't be long before you become accustomed to the taste where it doesn't bother you so much. It wasn't much of a fight when I began juicing cucumbers in my twenties. It's like drinking water where I can feel the nutrients spread out through my body every time I drink it. I had my first sip of carrot juice when I was seventeen. I made a weird face, but I kept drinking it because I knew it was good for me. It didn't take long before I craved carrot juice and I ended up loving the taste and have been drinking it regularly since.

One of the big ways of connecting with Spirit is by raising your vibration. Someone that partakes in fortune telling readings or is gifted with psychic foresight could have a low vibration or operate from their ego, but they are still able to connect effortlessly. Raising your vibration is much more important in doing beyond reasons of being more psychic. You pick up on heavenly messages when your ego steps out of the way of your higher self. Meditating and being in a still environment in nature is a great way to access Spirit much easier than when you're under stress or any other negative emotion. This raises your vibration and opens up your psychic clair channels, which also gives you more mental alertness and stamina.

Your vibration is an invisible energy field within the DNA of your soul, aura, and body. The ones able to see that the energy is not invisible are those in Heaven. An Earthly soul with dominate clairvoyance can see the energy field as well. A clairsentient will be able to feel this energy. The vibration energy is a part of you. It is made up of undetectable cells by the human eye that fluctuate and change colors depending on your mood, your thought processes, who you surround yourself with, as well as what you ingest into your body. Your soul and entire aura is an everlasting breathing energy field that has an effect on your state of mind. This is whether you desire to be happy in this life or miserable.

You can be a CEO that is a perpetual angry curmudgeon rude to the staff and only interested in making money in any way they can. This person might be financially successful, but they are spiritually bankrupt. Spiritual soul power has far greater beneficial force than finances in the end. An angry state lowers their vibration, which brings in an onslaught of negative circumstances and harsh health issues at some point in their life. This is due to the angry stressed state they've endured throughout the course of their human existence. It builds up like mold in a damp basement until the individual decides to eradicate it and make some healthy lifestyle changes. Many don't bother until they receive a major health scare that could result in death according to their Doctor. This shakes that person out of the way they had been living. Don't wait until later in life to receive a scare to snap into taking care of yourself. If angry businesspeople worked on well-being exercises, then this would help them be more in tune, which assists them in building their business to even greater success. In fact, I've conversed with many business executives that have admitted to me that they consult the Tarot on occasion for certain decision making.

You are in a temporary physical body with an inflated ego that pushes you to anger or sadness when life circumstances throw you a curve ball. This can be inevitable depending on the kind of life you live and who you surround yourself with. You could be a busy professional that works a job that drains your soul's life force. Working a job you despise will lower your vibration. It's been said that there are a whopping 70% of people that hate their jobs. You sit in traffic to get to this job you're unhappy at only to leave at the end of the day and sit in traffic to get home. This stress in driving in those conditions lowers your vibration. This is why it's vital to incorporate some fun in your life at least one to two times a week. Take frequent breaks throughout the day that includes getting outside to breathe in some fresh air. Heavens messages travel along the particles of oxygen that invigorates your life force.

The fun you inject can be whatever lightens your load. It can be getting together with a friend to go to a restaurant to hang out and shoot the breeze. It can be heading off to the beach or to go on a hike in nature. It can be watching a funny movie or playing a board game. It can be date night with your lover or releasing tension at the gym in a workout. Spirit won't point the finger and tell you not to drink a six-pack of beer to lighten that load. That's something only you can decide. Drinking a six pack lowers your vibration and you wake up feeling even more rundown. I know because I've been in that state myself. I was one of those party animals when I was twenty-one, which is so hard to believe today. I would have a drink, but then counterbalance it with one of my cucumber or carrot concoctions.

Every living organism, plant, animal, element, atom, and cell vibrates of energy. When you take a stroll through a garden or park, you'll notice an invisible heavy weight being lifted off you. You suddenly start to feel elated and more relaxed. This is an example of what it might feel like as your vibration begins to rise. But then you get a phone call from a friend who is a gossip and proceeds to tell you about how someone you both know did something and they angrily disapprove. Now your vibration begins to decline even though you didn't do anything, but answer your phone. You were on the receiving end absorbing the negative energy that your friend was outwardly shooting at your soul. Now your vibration has dropped down.

Some animals will dart away when they sense a hostile energy coming towards them. They're highly in tune that they guard their territory without thinking about it. The reason most animals have high vibrations is because they do not live the kinds of lives that human folk live. They're not stressing out over making money to pay rent. They're not thinking about where their next meal is coming from. When they're hungry they will seek it out at that point. They're not falling into emotional turmoil because a lover has left them. They eat, breathe, move, go to the bathroom, sleep, and then repeat.

A pet of an abusive owner will have a dropped vibration. If the animal has been trained by the owner to feel fear due to the poor abuse of that human owner, then the fear emotion drops the animals' vibration. Human souls are responsible for the havoc and destruction that happens on this planet. They're responsible for the harm done to people, animals, planet life, and so on. The other exception is Mother Nature. The weather on the planet can be uncontrollable and erratic in places. It can and will destroy anything in its wake. Earth can thrive and prosper rapidly without humankind tampering with everything.

The astrological sign of Pisces is considered one of the most psychic signs in the zodiac, because like the symbol of the fish they are born absorbing every nuance naturally. Like a fish in the water, when you attempt to get close to someone with Pisces in the top tier of their chart that person will evade or swim away. You have to keep at them if you truly care to ensure they know you're safe to be around. Feeling every nuance causes heavy burden on the backs of the Pisces. They can be prone to addictions to hard substances just to get rid of that feeling. When they evolve and become more aware that it is a gift and not a curse, then they can reach greater heights than anyone has ever dreamed of. We're using the sign of the Pisces as an example in order to demonstrate what it's like for someone who might have strong sensitivities and how they might navigate through life. This is regardless of what someone's sign is. Will it be addicted? Or will they choose to soar high above the clouds in spiritual transcendence?

When you welcome the hostile energy in someone else, then you become one with it. Becoming one with it is when you engage with someone that has hostile energy. This also includes engaging with hostile people on social media.

As I moved through my twenties, I grew to have a zero-tolerance policy for negativity of any kind. This means I'd cut out those that were perpetually negative. This isn't about not being a listening ear to the occasional negative experience a friend is having. This is about the offenders that reside in a 24/7 ordeal that is filled with constant complaints and negativity. There is zero positivity that rarely peeks out. They have no interest in shifting that mind set or taking steps to make positive changes in their life. When you move into that sort of negative state, then you've officially moved into the state of victimhood. You have the power to change your life by the will of your own thoughts. This is by seeing the good that is working for you more than the challenges. It is seeing the blessings rather than what you don't have. My entire spirit being repels negativity because the cells of my soul open up and drink that in, which is not a comfortable feeling. It's easier to rip that negativity out immediately rather than be tortured by it.

You might have a complicated life and therefore live in ways that are not conducive to raising one's vibration. Perhaps it's at a cutthroat stressed out environment at your job or with your home life. This is about being aware of what can and will lower your vibration while doing your best to avoid the negatives when possible. When your mind is consciously aware of what you need to do even when you're not doing it, then this is a step in the right direction. It becomes second nature to you as you adopt healthier life changes.

My most toxic addicted years were in my late teens to early twenties. I was drinking tons of alcohol, doing lines of cocaine, meth, smoking cigarettes, and marijuana regularly. As I was doing that, I was consciously aware in the back of my mind that if I'm not going to stop at that moment, then I better incorporate some healthy lifestyle choices. I'd do a line of cocaine and chase it down with carrot juice. This lasted until I started following my Spirit team's repetitive shouting guidance in my clairaudient ear that I needed to stop. I was listening to them during that time, but I was ignoring them like a spoiled child ignoring his parent's naggings. This was primarily during my rebellious punk years of the late teens to early twenties, which is pretty common for many around that age. It's when parents worry about their child the most, especially if they're as out of control as I was.

My Spirit team has always been igniting my inner life force to the point where I would crave toxic vices less to complete elimination of the toxic addiction. I knew I needed to stop with much of it, so I eventually folded and requested their help in doing so. It was after admitting that I needed their help did they infuse me with the discipline to do so. Alcohol in high amounts lowers your vibration, which I don't think is too much of a surprise to many. This does not mean that they are demanding that you stop drinking. Your choices to do, stop, dissolve, or reduce particular life choices that drop your vibration is for you to decide. If you enjoy drinking a bottle of wine every night and yet you regularly question why you're not content with your life, and nothing ever goes your way, then this would be one of the possibilities as to what is blocking what you desire from entering the picture. Since alcohol in high amounts blocks the divine and lowers your vibration, then you miss out on the messages and guidance from your own Spirit team. Having a drink once in a while is not going to kill you. This is about the repetitive regular abuse of toxins.

Some of the common messages and guidance I've received from Heaven are geared towards the importance of exercise and taking care of all things connected to your body. I've been into physical activity since I was a kid thanks to the urging of my Spirit team. Even when I fell off the wagon and into heavy toxic addictions, such as drugs, cigarettes, and alcohol as a late teen and young adult, I was still greatly aware of the importance of taking care of myself in the back of my mind. My Spirit team dominated my need to destroy my body and got me back into shape by focusing strongly on my overall well-being by the time I was twenty-five years old.

Raising your vibration is a lifestyle change that positively benefits your soul and all aspects of your life. There are values that need to be adopted or modified in order to reach a centered place that helps you be more connected. This carries over beyond what you're consuming and into what you're feeling and thinking. If you spend months obsessing over an ex-lover that is no longer in your life, then this is a block that lowers your vibration.

This ex has left you, moved on, or perhaps blocked you on social media or on a phone app with no explanation, yet you cannot find a way to let it go and move on, then this lowers your vibration keeping it there until you permanently extricate the ex from your aura. You are checking your ex's social media page regularly to see what they're up to. Are there signs they might be interested in you again? Who are they talking to? What photos do they post with other people in them? Could they be romantically or sexually connected to any of the people in the photos? What about those who comment on your ex's posts? Is something going on with your ex and that commenter?

Your ego is running the show that is your life. It is desperately curious to know or find out some clues about what's going on with this ex-lover. This lowers your vibration and creates a block. If someone is no longer interested in communicating with you, then that is your cue to work on moving on and walking away. I understand this as I've been there too. It's not something that happens overnight, and some people have a harder time letting go. The moment you visit this person's social media page to spy and read their posts with the intention of discovering new information that can benefit you, then your vibration drops. This isn't about checking a friend's page to see what they've been posting lately to find out what they're up to because you've been busy with work, school, or any other life activity. You don't have any emotional interest except genuine positive feelings to stay up to date on your friend's life. That will likely not lower your vibration unless you read a tirade of negative posts from them.

A low vibration is what makes you depressed, miserable, angry, or agitated. When you focus heavily on this ex, talking about them, focusing on it, and wondering, then this drops your vibration. Your vibration continues to drop whenever you obsess over their every move.

When you're still checking up on them months after they left you, then that's when it may be time to look at taking action steps to cut it all loose for your benefit. Talk to a counselor, therapist, healer, or join a support group and get outdoors more and connect with friends. Find ways to muster up the effort to continue on with life without the ex that left. It will be a struggle, but overtime it will get easier. The thoughts of them will dissolve gradually to the point where it's only once in a while. When they do pop into your mind here and there after you've healed, then the emotional quotient surrounding the thoughts and feelings won't be as intense as they once were. You can think of them the way you do anyone you were once close to.

It's natural to be going through all of those feelings, thoughts, and emotions after a breakup, but eventually you do it less as time progresses on. If you don't move through the grieving emotions, then after a year of this you'll find that it has ultimately destroyed your life force. This includes your work, friendships, overall soul's well-being, and creative pursuits to name a few. It stalls circumstances until you begin the process of re-raising your vibration again and getting back to that place of perfect contentment. You will get there with effort and discipline. It's a gradual progression as you deal with the death of what no longer is in your life to make room for what is. Your interest in the coming and goings of others will decline. You'll notice improvement and positive changes happening steadily as a result.

When your vibration is low it takes effort and work to re-raise it. You can raise it when you decide to move swiftly through making important positive life changes and adjustments to reach a place where you're content again. Somebody who is no longer a part of your current life is not your higher self's priority or concern. You begin to think of them less while diving into living life again.

Take frequent breaks and disconnect from technology and/or hostile people in order to re-center and gain perspective. Sometimes the most in tune person can be too close to the truth to pick up on it. Letting loose in a joyful hobby releases your soul from the clutches of the burdens of the body. It raises your vibration in the process. There isn't enough fun in people's lives these days and so this is much needed.

When you tune into your guides energy, write down any great ideas or dreams you've been thinking of no matter how big or small. It can be positive behavior changes and perspectives you want to begin incorporating into your soul make up. This is guidance being passed down to you in some fashion by your Spirit team. They might instruct you to make a pact to have weekend getaways at least once a month or every two months. It can be a business plan or asking someone out on a date. Incorporate these lifestyle adjustments one-step at a time and notice the positive effects that end up coming out of that.

CHAPTER TWO

*Fire Up
Your Inner Child*

You grow older, your body ages, and you become more hip to the idea that you need to be responsible and disciplined if you want to survive living on the planet as pain free as possible. You have bills to pay, clothes to buy, and food to eat. How far in before you've lost yourself in physical Earthly demands?

You know you're beginning to lose yourself when your relationships with those around you grow distant or fall apart. It's when you find that you've been running on empty, stressed, tired, or all of the above. The way human life is today is that you cannot permanently sit on the couch all day drinking beer, app chatting, and texting. You need to get a job, have larger goals, make money, live life, and support yourself. You'll want to keep a fine line between doing that and not losing yourself to the point where your inner child is trapped until its release when you pass on.

Your inner child is the person you were before age ten. It is the innocent all loving part of you as a child that had no judgment or criticisms of other people. Those criticisms came upon you through your environment and at the hands of those who heavily influenced you. If you grew up in a community where the people were racist, then the chances of you developing this racism trait are higher than anyone else. You were not born racist and nor were you prejudice against anyone and their life choices. This goes for any sort of bias from political affiliations, religion, or hatred of someone's sexual orientation. None of that exists with your inner child.

Your inner child is the part of you that has the strongest access to God. It is the part of you that is in an all-encompassing state of love, joy, and peace knowing how to stop judging and thinking negative thoughts and just have fun. The inner child longs for this release if only your ego would pull that part of you back out to play again. When the dark ego dominates and grows lost in the physical world, your inner child screams for attention and love. Diving into creative artistic pursuits is a great way to fire up your inner child. When your inner child remains buried under rubble, then feelings of emptiness and loss begin to rise. Some go through these feelings of being lost during pinnacle times in their life. It can be brought upon due to a loss of any kind. This might be the loss of a job, a friendship, a lover, or any other loss to something that gave you a sense of security or happiness.

Lost feelings for a prolonged period of time can also indicate that you're moving through a transition that will eventually lead to an awakening. This awakening is where you gain clarity on everything around you and what you need to do. There is no time limit when moving through a transition or a personal evolution. It can take one month, one year, or three years. Allow what is intended to evolve without interference. Go about life's business and avoid pushing for anything to happen in a stressed-out haze.

Your inner child is who you were before all of the layers of trauma and life experiences jaded you. It was when you saw life without judgment or critique. You saw life through the lens of pure innocence and love. It was before human tampering made you despise anyone different from you. Those who despise someone that is different we're not that way when they were four years old. It was their caregivers, peers, community, and societies influence that taught all of that stuff. If God raised you, then you would've grown up to see the love in all souls. You would exude love and joy full time. Seeing the love in all souls means psychically peering beneath their hardened cold and unkind exterior to see who they were at birth.

When you were born you were immensely psychic, and filled with overflowing feelings of love, joy, and peace. You were wide eyed ready to absorb everything around you. You saw the beauty in life, in the colors, and in the trees. You were also a sponge absorbing the environment you were growing up in.

If your parents were the type that would constantly argue with one another in front of you, then this hostile energy is absorbed and becomes a part of your consciousness. If your caregivers and the society you live in were prejudice in any form, then this rubs off on you and you begin to believe this is the way it is. If someone is different from you, then they automatically repulse you. Hate is not something you were born with, but your environment, society, and peers teach this to you. It adds another layer around your inner child until there are so many layers that your inner child is trapped within unable to get your attention.

The souls that enter into this life from the various realms in Heaven are born into an Earthly life for a bigger purpose. They evolve at a rapid pace than a newborn soul would. They're the ones that might grow up in a toxic environment, but have higher awareness and psychic intuition to know that the way everyone else is behaving or thinking doesn't seem to have any balance in it. The realm soul might be considered the black sheep of the family, or the outcast, or weird. You are and always will be a child of God with a greater purpose than perhaps someone having their first Earthly life run.

You may have a growing adult body, but inside this physical case beneath all of the layers of your experiences resides your inner child. Your inner child is buried underneath an avalanche of experiences, lifestyle choices, and human development interference. When you had a negative, toxic, or abusive experience, then this is seared into your consciousness even if you continue on with life having great times. This child within you cries out for fun whenever you're feeling any negative emotion. Your inner child is psychic always operating from a higher vibration than any other part of you. This is why Heaven urges others to find that part of you and bring them back out. Your inner child is pure joy to be around, so let this part of you run free once in a while in order to bring you back.

Energy Drainers

Energy draining people and lifestyle choices suffocated one's inner child. Have a zero-tolerance policy for any meanness, negativity, or drama from anyone. There is a difference between loving someone from afar without getting caught up in their drama or toxic energy, to choosing to keep them at arm's length if you don't want them to go away. It might be a family member, parent, sibling, friend, or colleague. It can be someone that is seemingly not easy to deal with, so you cut them out of your life permanently if possible. You love the goodness in them, but no one should put themselves in a position where they are a punching bag, which affects your self-esteem and your ever-growing consciousness.

Someone might not be mean towards you directly, but they harshly complain about other people to you. This causes you to end up feeling down or worn out after communicating with them. Having your energy drained by others is real. This is why those on the receiving end grow weakened, annoyed, or rubbed the wrong way. Those doing the energy draining are not necessarily aware they are, because this type of energy makes one clouded.

You can be an exceptionally good compassionate person yourself and not realize when you're in the midst of behaving in a negative way. You're having a physical human experience and it's going to happen once in a while. You want to be aware of that when it happens. This is about someone that is always negative or toxic every time you connect with them.

When negative energy from someone else is around you, then you want to steer clear of it and not become consumed by it. If you drown in it, then this will bring you down, darken your aura, and lower your vibration. All of these phrases mean the same thing. If you are a sensitive or in tune to energies beyond the physical world, then you cannot deny how it makes you feel when you're around someone toxic. You can have love for them and still choose to not engage with them full time. Connect with them in small doses and then wrap it up and excuse yourself that you need to leave. They might react in a tantrum, but don't fall into guilt. You have to think of you first.

Everyone is living their own path, and no one can live it for them. If someone chooses to head down a self-destructive path, then no one can stop them. They have to want to change on their own. You can be polite when they reach out to you, but blow in and out of there quickly. This way they're not around long enough to infiltrate your area with their toxins.

The key is to say, "I have love for them and wish them well, but we don't engage much. When we do, I stand in a place of emotional detachment."

Energy draining is a major issue in the lives of millions of people around the world. It pushes them to pop pills to sleep, or pop them to wake up to continue on. It lures them into toxic addictions such as alcohol, food, and even drugs. You can wake up feeling alive and joyful, then you get in your car to head to work and the traffic is so bad that by the time you arrive at work you feel drained and dejected. The planet is overflowing with people and so many of them understand the fight to keep on going everyday morning and night. Others underestimate how bad traffic can be when they find a job and a place to live. You might think you live fifteen minutes away from work, but that is until you neglect to consider that the commute can be thirty to forty minutes. And that's on a good day! This is a major energy drainer and so are some of the choices one makes in their life. This can be from who you associate with from friendships to love relationships. Working with one bad apple can spoil your work life.

When you notice these circumstances happening, then you want to begin the process of considering the options you can make to alleviate this kind of stress. What areas can you change today and what areas will take longer than that. You do not want to spend years in a situation that drains your energy since this is equal to draining your life force. Not to mention the long-term health issues that can arise, and the blocks erected between yourself and Heaven's guidance.

Hugging and Touching

Hugging and touching have immense healing properties to the soul. It awakens your inner child, which is also connected to the creative part of you. Are you overworked, stressed, depressed, or angry? Hug others more and allow them to hug you. Hugging lowers your blood pressure, relieves stress, and releases the brain chemical Oxytocin. This contributes to positive bonding or otherwise known as the love hormone. Hugging reminds you that we're all on the same side. Many of the cure all remedies for so many issues reside within you. Hugs are one of the various activities that promote positive health. And hugs don't cost anything. They're free!

Naturally, you're not going to randomly approach a stranger or someone at work to hug them out of nowhere since that would be inappropriate. Hugging is with those you know personally that won't be bothered by it otherwise ask, "Can I hug you?"

Of course, they might say, "What? No. Why are you acting weird?"

They're not used to that kind of affection, as it was absent during crucial moments in their growing up phase that they came to expect unkindness.

There was this story of a straight male father that went to a gay pride festivity wearing a shirt or t-shirt that said, "Free hugs". Random people were going up to hug him. He recalled feeling their emotion from one guy to another girl that wouldn't let go. He could sense they hadn't been loved in so long by anyone. They were likely thrown out of the house or ostracized from their family for being gay. The man acted as an angel to say, "I love you and you are accepted."

It's not like someone that needs to be hugged is going to go up to a total stranger to ask if they can hug them. People end up wandering life jaded, stressed, or feeling unloved when all they need to bring their soul back out is that hug. If you're willing to part with a hug, then do it more often. Hug your friend, your lover, and even your pet! Unless your pet is a goldfish, then you can just pucker up and blow kisses at it from the glass of the aquarium. Animals are souls and crave the hug of another. Hugging is one of the many great vibration enhancers. For a brief moment your soul can breathe while in the midst of a hug. It tears away any off-putting ions that latch itself onto the aura around your spirit. You experience release and you understand what freedom feels like.

Everyone needs a hug whether they like to admit it or not. The most toughened human soul needs that love to tear down the walls they've built around their heart. You've likely come across someone who you try to hug and they clam up or turn into a brick wall with harms falling to the side barely giving back a hug in return, or they give you that police pat on the shoulder during the hug, "Alright, alright, let's not get goofy now."

They're terribly uncomfortable being touched, as it's not something they likely grew up getting enough of. They hardened over time at some point in their life.

Many are angry, depressed, or feeling any other kind of emotion that disconnects your soul from a feeling of joy, peace, or love. Those qualities are traits, which are innate inside of you, but buried so far deep it can't climb out of the hole it's trapped itself in. The world needs a war on hugs. If you're going to complain about something, then complain that you're not receiving enough love, hugs, and kisses from the world. There are millions of nerve endings in the human skin and to experience touch activates these nerves prompting you to raise your vibration releasing your inner child out of its caged prison within you.

Bring on the Joy

Joy is one of the highest vibrating energies that exist next to love. When someone laughs into hysterics, you sense the infectious energy. Suddenly strangers around that person light up with a smile. Someone else's energy will affect others around them. If they're being negative, then that will transfer. If they're infectiously giggly, then that will transfer. Seeing the fun and lightheartedness in situations raises your vibration. It lightens the heavy loaded burdens of stress. When your vibration is high, you attract in brighter circumstances to you. If you're stuck in negative feelings, then call upon your Spirit team and ask them to help in elevating your soul into a happier space. Request they guide you to getting back into the joy of your life again. Radiating with joy is what brings more of that good stuff to you. No one wants to be around a miserable stressed out and depressed grump. Feeling joy while visualizing your desires is what helps the manifestation process take place more quickly too. Archangel Jophiel is the hierarchy angel to call on to bring more joy and beauty into your life.

The working class is breaking their back to put food on the table and take care of their families and loved ones. They're being run ragged into the ground. This is thanks to human decision to work people like dogs. I've had so many conversations with the working class over the years and I've heard their common understandable complaints. I wonder how many politicians have truly heard the stories I have or even care. If they have, then they would've implemented change by now.

I'm an advocate for hard work as are the beings in Heaven, but this means working hard while incorporating regular time outs to decompress and spend with your loved ones. This isn't about working one day a month while doing nothing the rest of the time. This is working smarter schedules. Although the five-day forty-hour work week is excessive, it was much worse pre-1900's when people were expected to work ten to sixteen hours a day. Soon it was realized that it needed to be cut shorter, so they implemented the weekend off to give people a break.

Now even that's not enough since lives are busier than ever. People are getting smarter and hip to the fact that the soul and body need more adequate time for rest and relaxation. It's currently not enough, because by the time the weekend comes around people spend the first day getting all of that practical stuff they did not have time to get done during the week. The second and last day is spent burned out lounging around. Finally, on the third day they're energetic and ready to do something fun, but alas it's time to head back into work.

At least several times a month incorporate playtime and personal time. This is essential to your overall health and wellbeing. This will also increase productivity and decrease health issues, not to mention help the crumbling of relationship connections. This personal time isn't used to go grocery shopping, gassing up the car, or gym time, which is a necessity and wasted on one of the weekend days off. It's to connect with loved ones, relax, rejuvenate, take a day trip, or any other fun activity that helps you let go and release.

Heaven watches millions of people rushing to and from a job burned out and running on little sleep. It saddens them to have this aerial view of so many detached souls that are unhappy deep down. It's no wonder there is a rise in disconnection from God. Heaven demands that all souls take a time out to enjoy regular bouts of personal luxury time. When you include fun and relaxation in your life, then when you head back to work, you're more energetic and focused. Your soul is crying out in pain when it runs on any permanent negative emotion. Stress, anxiety, and depression are examples of symptoms that crush your soul. This energy shoots into your physical body causing an array of issues. It also merges into your aura and touches other people's auras around you that absorb that.

Luxuries are a necessity for your soul so that it can be awakened out of its cold corporate prison that life circumstances have created around it. Let your inner child out and have fun once in a while. Shake off the seriousness and the constant critical gossip and judgments of other people and circumstances.

CHAPTER THREE

Nature Therapy

Improving your psychic senses simultaneously improves your spiritual connection with the Divine. Some find anything connected to psychic phenomena as being of the Devil, but the irony is having a strong connection with God comes through your psychic senses that everyone is born with including the non-believers or strictly religious. Some strict religious groups that disapprove of psychic behavior will talk about having a godly vision or that they prayed on something that helped. Where do you think that communication is coming from? It's coming through your psychic senses. Some might strongly disagree with something and call it evil without having any knowledge of it enough to be making a comment. That's been going on since the dawn of humanity. They may be confusing the possibility that having a strong psychic antenna can invite in negative spirits. Negative spirits will attack whoever they can get close to, including a non-believer, a believer, or someone psychically in tune, so that theory is null and void. There are also numerous cases of a dark spirit attaching itself to a devout religious follower, so the belief that a dark spirit can only be conjured up by a Medium also isn't bathed in truth.

Strengthening your psychic clair senses helps with increasing your faith and being able to follow the guidance coming in from above. Getting out into a nature setting can assist the soul in reaching a higher level of awakening. It is far easier for Spirit to access someone when they're in a calming environment such as a nature setting. Many purport to feeling much calmer after taking a stroll in nature. I'm a fan of all things connected to nature, which includes the deserts and badlands with its dry terrain and extensive geological erosions that cast into a breathtaking color display of volcanic rock, canyons, and mesas. Those areas have always proven great escapes to commune with my higher council through the winds as the sage Native American Wise Ones once did in massive numbers across North America. All that remains are the clues left behind in entombed sediments of extinct fossils of tribal skulls and dinosaur-like creatures that no longer roam the Earth, but whose presence is profoundly felt.

Spirit communication travels along the particles of oxygen, so where there is wind there is spirit in grave numbers. It gives you an opportunity for reflection, redemption, and answers. Just like Bob Dylan said in his song, "The answer my friend is blowing in the wind."

The Divine answers are travelling along with the wind. The sense of time while in those nature places is what hits you. You realize we have a short shelf lifespan. You hear that from others of older age that it flies by, so take advantage of the time you have while here. As a teenager at a party, I was conversing with this woman in her thirties. I remember her saying, "Make your choices today. I wish I knew then what I know now."

What she said forever stuck for me because I knew what she was talking about. I knew that a human life glides by faster than you would believe while in your teens and twenties, so don't waste one minute not getting into life's work and diving into your purpose. Otherwise you'll wake up one day and look in the mirror and wonder where the time went. I remember being in panicked mode around age fifteen and sixteen realizing that I need to get moving and get to work as my life is flying by. I was hyper aware as a teenager of what was up ahead while here. I've talked to people that reach older age when it truly hits them. They were young and vibrant with the whole world at their feet. After years of disappointments, what they once dreamed of seemed to grow impossible and unlikely to transpire. They may look their age, but inside feel as if they're still sixteen. Continue to expand your mind and consciousness beyond the routine, so that you can take advantage of every moment while here.

There are various reasons I love all nature power places. It offers quiet contemplation through Divine spirit connecting. It also gives you an injection of clarity along with a wider perspective that can easily get lost when you fall into the superficiality or the mundane of physical life.

When I was twenty years old, I knew those shallow interests were great for five minutes, but I needed to be challenged. I was a sponge screaming inside for more than what people gave me through Earthly patterns. There was no way I could endure living with a mediocre mindset, even if that meant I would be set apart from everyone else, which I was regardless.

In vast nature settings, your view broadens and opens up. You see who you are in comparison to this temporary home of a planet. Things like social media suddenly seem trivial in contrast. All of the wrangling on it does nothing to attract any kind of a positive abundant mindset, but instead dulls the spirit senses, your life force, and vibrational energy unless you are using it for good and positivity. Living hypnotized by the toxic allure and superficial triviality gossip every second can be depressing. Some believe it's natural to remain in a superficial state, because it's what's taught. Some of it might arguably be fun once in a while, but to endure that indefinitely can be primitively medieval.

Have faith and believe what you desire will come and that you are deserving of good. Be open and receptive to receive ensure you're balancing giving and receiving energy throughout your life. This is by not overdoing one without the other. This imbalance can block the positive movement flow. Examine what your desires are and what work you're willing to put in to achieve your goals.

Act and be persistent with it. Helping the movement along positively means putting in the work. Kicking back dreaming of desires to come to fruition doesn't help those desires come to life. Dreaming of desires is a great first step to take. It's the dreams in your mind and visions that start out like a seed. These dreams gradually begin to develop in your mind for a while, much like a human pregnancy until that moment when you give birth to your dreams, as if you're giving birth to a child. Once that happens, you initiate action steps that can help the dreams grow and evolve.

Have a plan and know what you want, so as not to confuse the positive attraction quotient. Take regular time outs, retreats, and vacations. This helps alleviate stress, opens your psychic clair senses, and brings great ideas in. It helps elevate your vibration since people tend to be in a brighter spirit when they take a break. Study, perfect, and expand your mind and consciousness. All of this helps in cracking open the door to abundance.

CHAPTER FOUR

Elevating Your Mind, Body, and Spirit

God, Spirit, and the Divine's energy moves through me in waves. I, and you, are one with God. From as far back as eight years old, I could feel His energy pushing me forward to take care of myself on all levels from the mind, body, and soul spirit. From as minor as going for a jog or a bike ride to delving my mind into study and learning. Since my childhood years, fitness and exercise have forever been a big part of my life's interests without ever fading.

I can remember teaching myself to learn to ride a bike the same way I'd teach myself to do anything and everything I was interested in. We couldn't afford much growing up, so when one of my childhood friends went out of town, he left me his bike to practice with. It was diving into the practice, which helped me to teach myself to ride a bike. There was no one walking me through the steps. The Internet and You Tube instructional videos didn't exist in those days. I grabbed the bike and practiced on my own. I fell off it a number of times, but I picked myself up, picked the bike up, and continued on with the persistent practice until by the time my friend came back, I was an excellent bike rider. This is how I trained myself to do anything and everything I had a desire to learn. It was through the avenue of tough no-nonsense streets smarts and practice that would carry with me throughout my Earthly life.

I learned things through the school of hard knocks. This was by jumping on in and doing the work without any formal training. Due to my inhibiting ADD/ADHD, learning anything was fraught with some kind of disability anyway. I couldn't retain by sitting in a class listening to a lecture. I had to dive in and actually do the work.

Since I was a teenager, the major jobs I received throughout my life consisted of me being the candidate with zero experience for the job being interviewed for. In the end,

I was the candidate they went with. I was able to convince them I could excel at whatever it was they gave me. I might be rusty at first, but give me a few trial runs and they will be unable to find a harder worker that can master it over someone with the education and experience. It was this passion coupled with my forthright fighting nature that was my winning card.

This proved true as many of those employers later commented long after I left the employment that they chose well when taking that risk to go with the person without the credentials or experience only to be blown away. These employers that remained in contact with me long after I left all had informed me, they were unable to find a suitable replacement that could do what I did for them.

The point of that is that it has been my long running mantra throughout life. Be a fighter in all you do. Have passion, persistence, drive, and a strong will to do the job fast and fearless. I've always had an interest in being completely aware, conscious, and driven to be the best I can be. My interest and focus on expanding my mind, strengthening my body, and nourishing my soul were present since childhood. I've persistently been a huge promoter of taking care of yourself on all levels. This advocacy includes the body through fitness, exercise, and nutrition.

Even when I fell into my young adult party days of alcohol, drugs, and cigarettes in my early twenties, I was still conscious enough to work out hard if I was going to be putting those toxins in my body. Luckily, the partying days evaporated by the time I was moving into my mid-to-late twenties. My main focus moved right into fitness and exercise in a broader way. I knew that a strong body was necessary. This had nothing to do with vanity, which is why some work out. There has been evidence that some people work out and take care of themselves more while single, but as soon as they end up in a long-term relationship, they get lazy about it. This is because they were working out to attract someone in rather than working out because they care about their overall well-being. My desire to exercise and work out regularly is partially because I always feel incredible afterwards. If I was feeling low or depressed, I would go for a run or endure a rigorous work out. Suddenly I was feeling stronger and more alive than I had ever been!

The stronger I grew through physical fitness; the stronger my Divine psychic connections became. It also helped me make it through the long days of juggling my day job work life to building my side business life purpose career.

I run into people today and many have commented, "You are so fit!" Never mind the positive side effect that it helps you look good, but what's more important is that I feel incredible! Today younger friends have told me that I run circles around them as well as those two to three times younger than I.

This isn't about being better than anyone else, but about motivating others to do the same and push yourself beyond the limits. You have to care about your body the way you care about other things you have interest in. One cannot neglect that physical vessel you were temporarily gifted with.

There will be a day when I may physically not be able to do certain things. Although, one friend once informed me that he and another friend of ours was in Joshua Tree National Park on a particular occasion. As it was getting dark, they noticed a female figure racing down the rocks from up high. She was incredibly fit racing towards them until she slowed down in front of them. He said she might have been in her sixties when they first noticed her. They talked to her and were surprised to learn that she was in her nineties! She's been doing that exercise for decades and feels great.

My mouth was on the floor, "Wow, that's incredible! I love hearing stories like that. I want to be like that if I'm still around in my nineties."

I received a huge rush of joy and excitement to know that it could be possible. God gave you this temporary body to house your soul so that you may live an Earthly physical human life full of lessons, experiences, blessings, missions and challenges. You have to take care of all parts of your body, mind, and soul. All three of these are what the spiritual genre was comprised of, but that's mainly because these are the important aspects that make up the totality of you.

Some people avoid exercise or express disdain and reach for those potato chips and ice cream day after day feeling even more lethargic than the day before. Many shun study and higher learning while instead trying to find their next conquest to have sex with. Some are surprised by the number of messages I receive from people regularly that send me inappropriate messages, as if I'm just a body to use. One would think you should be flattered. When you have an expanding mind and consciousness, but the intelligence is uninteresting to someone, then that comes off more offensive.

I'm highly aware of what people are interested in because I receive this from them every single week. They only have one thing on their mind. Attempting to have any kind of intellectual deep conversation is met with resistance through their one to two-word answers of disinterest in talking about anything beyond physical pleasure. It's about how quickly can you come here and give it to me, for lack of a better phrase. I've had some friends say in recommendation, "I feel like you need to dumb it down for some people."

It's never been said as an attack or harsh judgment, even though I was initially thrown off. I soon realized it was sage advice. They know having a raised consciousness and higher intelligence level in an Earthly world dominated and ruled by the darkness of ego, the superficial, and shallow can be a lonely place for that soul. This has been a common theme complaint from the spiritually based crowd. Many of them have been raising their consciousness and intelligence through knowledge gaining, study, and experiences. They've found it difficult to relate or connect to others that weren't interested in any of that. Some have disbanded friendships that were no longer on that same path.

On Earth, the more superficial you are, then the more popular you become. The masses love superficiality, shallowness, and a hyper focus on the exterior. They want to see hard young bodies, fancy cars and mansions. It doesn't matter what that person has to say as long as they fit that description. A social media user only needs to post something like that without any caption and it will garner thousands of people giving the thumbs up and applause. This isn't a criticism or judgment, but the current sad reality with the evidence being in plain sight for all to see. I've had discussions of this myself with other spiritual buddies. They've told me that people seem to pay more attention to their spiritual posts when there is a shirtless pic in it, and this is on a spiritually based account. Unfortunately, the reality is that is what sells, which is why I have sometimes done that on occasion. The photo is to get their attention in hopes they will see what's more important than the photo and that is the enlightening verbiage that accompanies it.

Many shun deepening their soul and consciousness through spiritual and religious studies coupled with hard driven life experiences. What good is life if the three components of body, mind, and soul that make up basic healthy survival are ignored and discarded.

Work on making healthier life choices. This includes your diet and drink intake as well as adequate regular exercise, pending you are physically able to. You might be someone physically unable to exercise due to human physical challenges this lifetime. This is not directed to those that cannot physically do it due to a handicap or physical issue. This is directed to those that are capable of physical exercise, but don't want to out of laziness or because they hate it.

When you take care of yourself on all levels, then this has an effect on your overall well-being. Having a strong well-being has a positive effect on your mood and thoughts. This simultaneously elevates the vibration of both your feelings and thoughts, which makes you a powerful abundance attractor. Joy brings in more joy and sadness brings in more sadness. Which would you like to have?

This isn't saying you're not allowed to have any fun. Having fun is an essential luxury. When you operate in high octane stress mode attending to daily practical matters, then you risk burn out. You also raise your stress levels, which drops your vibration. A low vibration can diminish the potential of attracting in positive blessings and abundance. Perhaps you don't care for the theory that pushes you to be positive and avoid negativity. How many people do you know that are perpetually negative, but are simultaneously attracting in all sorts of positive abundance? I don't know of many cases where that exists. I've heard of more cases where someone is a positive optimistic go-getter and is simultaneously attracting in awesome great things in their life.

Get up off the metaphorical couch and out of a dull mindset and get to work. Create a sanctuary in a private space in your house where you can connect to God and your Spirit team to receive profound insights, messages, and guidance that urge you to make positive changes in your life. Pay attention to these messages and act on them.

If your Spirit team is urging you to get outside and exercise, then follow that advice. They know that when you take care of your body that you become a ferocious Divine communicator that helps you make powerfully positive choices that bring your goals and dreams to fruition. Suddenly the flow of positive abundance and blessings starts to move in your direction. Fitness and exercise breathe new life into your soul. It helps dissolve or reduce any negative emotions such as depression or stress. You feel an uplifting crystal-clear calm focus that enables you to put action into your goals that makes great things happen.

Don't beat yourself up if you find exercise difficult at first. The more you do it, then the easier it gets where it eventually becomes like oxygen to you. If two days have passed and I haven't exercised, then I can feel it in a big way. I can feel it in my body and entire state of being. I can feel it in my psychic senses pushing me to soar forward freely in an exercise routine to re-awaken it. I have to dive on in before I go crazy. I'm then transported into the spirit of the Divine with this essence moving throughout my entire body. Great ideas soon rise to the forefront over what I need to do and accomplish.

Whenever I have an unresolved problem, I go directly to God the ultimate source of guidance. I don't rely on human beings to prop me up and change my life. I rely on God to help prop me up and change my life. He has that power having proven it to me time and again.

It's no one else's job to cheer you up, bring you joy, or lavish you with attention. Stop expecting other people to take on the responsibility of bringing you joy. Avoid being dependent on others to prop you up, fix you, and give you devotion. And stop getting angry when others are not catering to you the way you want them to. Doing that will only result in frustration and bitterness, which is the perfect breeding ground for the Darkness to grow. No one can fulfill that impossible demand. Anyone with any measure of a healthy self-esteem won't stick around and bow down to that kind of energy.

It is your responsibility to create your own joy and prop yourself up. Avoid relying on people to remind you of your worth. Pull yourself up by your bootstraps, stand tall, and know your worth by empowering yourself through Source. When you've excelled at reaching that space where you no longer need or require any of that from others, then does all the good stuff start to fall into place naturally on its own. And even if it doesn't, you could careless, as you're not craving validation anyway.

This joy seeking attention from others is more about the co-dependent and toxic like relationships that others rely on. It is not necessarily about the healthier balanced relationships where you feel joy being around your partner as they do with you. There may be some that fall into the space of needing constant attention from others, whether it's from a lover, friends, family members, or strangers. They love messages of joy, but fail to notice when they have been guilty of falling into the co-dependency aspect part of it.

It's sometimes hard to believe that I was once a co-dependent person while in my early twenties. I mistakenly put too much dependence on other people to prop me up and fix me. Luckily, it was only a matter of years in where I rose above it and realized that it wasn't working. People cannot fulfill that kind of unrealistic demand from another person. Today, one of the top keyword's friends have repeatedly used in describing me with others is independent. This is mentioned because it's dramatically opposing to what I once was in the earlier years. As you evolve your consciousness and all aspects of you, then you are also evolving out of co-dependency and into independence.

It's pretty common to seek out attention and love from external sources from the teenage years on up into one's early twenties. One hopes that by the time you begin moving into your later twenties, your desire for external sources to shower you with love fades and grows less enticing. You realize that the love you crave can be conjured up naturally by standing in your own power.

Exercise does a body good on all levels for this reason. It helps in raising your vibration, energy, and consciousness where you feel alive without the validation of others. You look and feel incredible. It cracks open the psychic line with the Other Side even more. It also helps you heal from illnesses that are healable much quicker.

The last time I was bed ridden with a dramatic flu was 2004. Technically when I was getting sick in those days it was usually from catching it from someone else that was around me. I eventually grew to be so strict that I refused to be around anyone that had a cold or the flu until they were better. It doesn't mean I'm unkind, because if they are someone close to me, I am buying all sorts of healing remedies and a goodie bag that I leave at their door.

This doesn't mean I don't get sick or haven't been sick since, but I just haven't been bed ridden for days or even a day for that matter. I have however felt the initial hints of a potential flu coming onto me. I'm highly aware when something with my body has suddenly shifted. I might have crossed paths with someone that was sick, so I start to feel a bit weak. The second I suspect anything, I immediately always up my game and begin the process of the preventatives, the exercise, the higher intake of vitamin C supplements and foods, and more water than usual.

I also pray to God and call in the healing Archangel Raphael to help prevent what I'm feeling to blow up into more. I believe in both medicinal healing remedies coupled with spiritual healing remedies, then I follow all of this by going to bed earlier than usual. Nine times out of ten I wake up the next morning energized and ready to seize the day. No signs of the illness anymore. It was completely knocked out of the park. This doesn't mean I couldn't suddenly be struck with an illness or that I'm invincible and immune to anything ever happening. It's just illustrating the point of doing the best you can to be hyper aware of your body within and without. When you notice an issue coming on, then do what you can to reverse it if it's a reversible issue.

This is all connected to being in tune to your body, mind, and soul. Be aware of everything happening around and within you every second. Notice all changes and shifts that take place within you. If it's a challenge coming upon you, then take care of you by taking care of it as fast as possible. Be disciplined about you, yourself, your body, mind and soul. Take it seriously and don't ignore the subtle hints and shifts within and around you, since those can be Divine guidance messages coming in.

CHAPTER FIVE

Expand Your Consciousness

Every soul has varying degrees of psychic abilities regardless if that soul believes in it or not. You are born with a strong degree of psychic clair channels, but somewhere along your human life development, these clair channels become clogged due to negative influences within and around you. The purpose of understanding this is so that you can be aware of what is and what is not dimming your communication with Heaven.

You can be completely clear minded, healthy, and doing all the right things to ensure you have crystal clear communication, but you still feel like you're receiving nothing or that you're being ignored. There is no such thing as Heaven overlooking you. When you feel you're being ignored, then something surrounding you is blocking the communication. When you push to receive a message from Heaven, then the communication is driven further away from you. Pushing for a message shoves it away. The pushing and hoping to make a connection blocks it because there is this anxious, nervous, frustrated, worry energy within. This can be where deep inside you feel you're not going to make that connection. If you're anxious to make a connection with your Spirit team, then this blocks it since it lowers your vibration. A low vibration is the equivalent to cutting off one's oxygen supply to breathe. In this case it is cutting off the oxygen supply to your soul.

Your psychic clair sense channels are telecommunication receptors you use to communicate with your guides, angels, and any in Heaven with. Your various senses are the phone lines to your Spirit team. Everyone was born with sharp senses, which open and close throughout the duration of your life depending on your lifestyle choices, surroundings, thoughts, and feelings. When your clair channels are free of toxic debris, then the clearer the messages and guidance is that comes in.

Your psychic abilities never go away even if it sometimes feels that way. They are under the surface and always accessible. When you don't feel psychic, it just means something is blocking it. Blocks can be certain foods, drinks, negative moods, bad energy, technological distractions, and other people. The closer you are to the physical Earth and nature, then the easier it can be re-awakened. This means anything that is not human made.

Some are drawn to the spiritual genre because they're interested in fortune telling. They're fixated on telling the future. Some do not want to know the future, while others are desperate to know the future. You want to know the future when you're in a place in your life that does not make you happy. Your dreams have not been realized. Perhaps you've been single for quite some time and you wonder if you'll ever meet the one.

Much of the time related future predictions are difficult to assess since the mass majority operate on free will choice above Heaven's guidance. This is shifting and altering one's course dramatically every so often. Being more psychic is to also help you make better choices in your life. It's to help ensure that you stay on the right path, which in the end will bring you to your destination of fulfillment on all levels. It's to bring you a healthier and happier existence.

Removing toxins in your life assists in opening up your psychic clair channels wider. There will be negativity that enters your vicinity, but when you're aware of when it happens, then you're able to quickly take steps to modify it and bring you back to that centered space. This is why Heaven advises that you take care of yourself as best as you can. They might guide someone to be alcohol free, since they believe that no one needs any toxic vice if they're governing their life from a place of joy, love, and peace. The high that comes with those traits are beyond what any addiction can satisfy. In the end moderation is important with anything and you're not going to Hell if you enjoy a glass of wine every night, so don't misunderstand this. They're merely explaining that it can block and dim the messages coming in if you're attempting to connect. They feel that toxins are not craved on a regular basis when someone is operating from a high vibration.

In order to be creative you need to have focus, stamina, energy, motivation, and inspiration. When you've been feeling sluggish for days and don't know why, ask your team for help to give you natural energy. You can ask them to guide you to healthy products or to give you the steps you need to take to regain your strength. They may give you a task that is telling you to go to the gym for an hour. After you do that, you leave the gym as if you're floating on air with natural energy.

A successful working Medium friend who assists with solving crime cases informed me privately that she would have one beer or two before she begins filming an episode on television since it relaxes her. She will not have any more than that because then she'll just be all over the place and way too buzzed to connect.

What works for one person will not always work for another. What my Spirit team advises is sometimes a generality. They also reside and operate from a space that is challenging for the ego to get to. They understand the struggles that human beings go through, but they feel that if everyone on the planet operated from the space they do, then there would be peace on Earth and toxic addictions wouldn't be desired. Everyone would be happy because no one is treating others disrespectfully or clawing their way to achieve or dominate. If everyone paid attention to Heaven, then love would reign. Unfortunately, this is not the world that exists today, and human beings are to blame for that design.

You have the ultimate say on what works for you. This is your life and you must live it for you and do what you feel is best. When someone that loves to cook becomes accustomed to how to follow a new cooking recipe, then they may start to alter it a bit and add things here and take away things there. My team relays a structure for you to jump off of. When they make recommendations to watch what you ingest from unhealthy foods, to drugs, to alcohol, then it is for various reasons that include helping you be a stronger conduit with Heaven, which simultaneously moves your life into a happier content place.

When you focus on a health issue, then you give more energy and power to it. This expands and makes it worse, which is what you want to avoid. There will be health issues you might be faced with. Your soul is separate from what's happening to your physical body. Avoid labeling and identifying with a health issue. Know that everything will work out in the way that it's intended to. In the end, your soul is always intact regardless of what is happening to the physical body you temporarily inhabit.

You Are What You Consume

The FDA *(Food and Drug Administration)* is indirectly responsible for the premature deaths of many human souls due to their abusive power and control on potentially lifesaving products that are considered illegal in some areas. They are deciding what they think should be approved and what you should or should not ingest in your own body. They are human beings and human beings are flawed. It is no one's place to decide how you choose to live your life pending it isn't harming anyone. The government regulating what others should or should not have needs to be equipped with spiritually based people who have a stronger connection and therefore will know what would be good or not.

At the same time there are products such as hair or skincare that is using ingredients that doesn't need to be cleared with the FDA in the USA at this point. There are activists attempting to get a bill passed where this needs to be the case. Therefore, on the flipside, the FDA can have some benefits if they're able to push cosmetic companies to be more transparent about their ingredients, but then let the consumer decide if they want to continue using it.

There is an excess of human made drugs, foods, or drinks that are considered toxic to your body when taken regularly or in large quantities, but these products are ironically considered legal by the FDA, so you can see how it's a bit of a flawed system.

Some see an issue with marijuana, but they have no issue with alcohol, which is responsible for more accidents, deaths, and harm on other people than weed. The only reason some find an issue with marijuana is because they were taught that it's an illegal drug. It's a plant that comes from the ground long before humankind existed. It is only illegal because the human ego made it this way for various reasons. The government made alcohol legal, which ingrained that into the minds of the human condition that it must be better than weed because it's legal. Weed is only illegal in places because humankind chose to make it illegal. Alcohol is far more harmful than weed.

Flawed human beings make decisions for you. Over time there have been products that were once legal before the FDA banned it and vice versa when they later discovered they made an error in judgment. Examine all of the atrocities and destruction created out of the choice's humankind thought to be correct in the past and you get a pretty good observation into how you are controlled.

This isn't advocating that you smoke weed or drink alcohol. This is illustrating the way human souls perceive things around them. Most of it can be connected to the way they were taught. If you started out on Earth alone with no one else telling you what to do, what to eat, what to drink, then it would be interesting to note how you view your surroundings and how you would survive.

I have had others ask me about what the angels think about eating meat. Angels have said that it's no good. I'm not a vegetarian, but I am fairly strict about what I consume to an extent. They went into that when you eat certain meat or anything that was a living soul, then you are eating that life force. The conditions of animals today in the way they turn them into food is horrific. This means you're also eating their trauma. They're showing me crammed cages in abusive environments. They also explained that it's not a sin to eat meat. They mean it's no good for the human's health long term. There are better exceptions such as if someone is eating meat that is organic, or where the animals are raised for food in loving conditions. There are certified organic farmland where no added growth hormones, pesticides, or antibiotics are used, which is certainly better than the other kinds of meat if you love meat. Things are slowly changing since you can find organic products in the stores now. The animals, plants, sea life, and all of that were partly put on Earth for human's survival. Humankind cannot survive necessarily by eating the leaf off a tree.

No one knows how an animal they're eating was raised. You're not going to Hell if you crave and eat a hot dog at a Carnival. Nor is someone who is a carnivorous eater their entire life going to be sent to Hell and damnation. Like anything that could potentially be toxic, meat should be consumed in moderation and caution should be adhered to with whatever you are ingesting. Ultimately, you make the life choices that feel right to you. Besides regardless of what is said here, your Doctor will tell you what to cut back on if they're detecting a potential health issue down the line due to what you're consuming.

There are many souls sent here to battle the food corporations to get them to make their products naturally or organically. They are also fighting to get food companies to reveal what the product is made of on the label. It is interesting that some of the food companies are fighting right back to avoid having to do that. If what you're using is good, then you'll be proud to show that to the world on a label.

There are organizations that use genetically engineered or modified seeds in their crops. This is otherwise known as GMO or Genetically Modified Organism. When human tampering starts genetically altering anything with chemicals, then you can guess what negative cons will come out of that.

One of the many issues that came out of that was the genetically modified soybean. It first came to light in the early 1990's. The soybean was said to be toxic to human health especially in Men. It drops their testosterone levels and raises estrogen levels at an earlier age than is typical. Estrogen is great in high amounts in the female body, but not the male composition. Examine the male species post 1995 and how they differ in comparison to those of pre-early 1990's. The bottom line is some of the food companies use chemicals that have a high level of toxicity when consumed. Most people are consuming it and not aware of the buildup happening in their body over time.

Food corporations make many products with all of these additives that are bad for you and create toxic build up in your system. This food didn't exist centuries ago and humankind thrived and survived just fine.

The food companies and corporations often make products with all sorts of dangerous additives and ingredients that no one can pronounce or say. You'll note the obvious red flag when you see a long list of ingredients on the package with names you've never heard of or can barely pronounce. These products become addictive because they artificially alter that person's state of mind or mood temporarily into a feeling of joy. The human being has been unable to replicate the kind of euphoric high they felt when back home in Heaven. It is challenging for them to get back to that state when they were a soul before they entered a human body. Therefore, they consume human made products to get there. They become attracted to other addictions to fulfill a hole of loneliness, boredom, depression, or any other emotional state. This is what emotional eating is.

Falling into Addictions

Most of the world's most successful people are goal oriented. They take action and go after what they want even when others tell them they have no business doing something. They pay no mind and continue to work at achieving their goals one after the other. You rarely hear about them succumbing to an addiction such as drugs, alcohol, or bad food. The ones that do fall into the realm of toxic addictions then start to see aspects of their life crumbling. The only addiction the rest of them might be guilty of is one of winning and accomplishing. They're too busy to fall into a depression or time waster. When you're doing work that gives you pleasure, then this raises your vibration. The vibration rises above depression and toxic addictions. You no longer crave those substances because you're high on life.

While disciplined individuals can reach this heavenly euphoric state naturally through spiritual practices, it is still a struggle for human souls to achieve overall in the practical Earth world. The rebuttal or a non-believer might say something like, "You take care of yourself and live nine more miserable years longer than I do. Big deal."

It is a myth to assume that someone who is regimented and takes care of oneself is unhappy. Someone that falls into the bell jar consuming an excess of human made addictions can be an unhappy camper, which is why they resort to toxins to give that artificial lift. Someone on cloud nine and feeling a natural love from within rarely craves a toxic addiction. I know what this is like since I've resided in both ends of the spectrum bouncing back and forth experiencing all of it.

We know I had a drug and alcohol addiction in my early twenties. After I was clean, I was involved in a love relationship in the past with someone who had an alcohol addiction, but craved the alcohol less while with me due to the natural feelings of love that were growing within while around me. When our connection dissolved, you can accurately guess that the craving for high amounts of alcohol rose up once again for this person.

When you're in a healthy long-term relationship, then that reduces or zaps away the desire to consume negative toxins and addictions in high quantities. The reason is love raises your vibration. When your vibration is high, then you don't crave or desire toxins. You are also less addicted to those substances. If you're someone battling addictions to something, then it is often likely you'll fall back into that path while in this healthy loving long-term relationship. This is because the love relationship can only sustain for so long before it is no longer in the newness category. An addicted person may grow bored or start to feel inadequate while in the love connection. They soon reach for the addiction in hopes it will remove those negative feelings. For some they may fall into that addictive behavior, but they're absolved in it far less than when they're single and unhappy.

You are not being criticized if you have an addiction to particular toxic substances and obsessions. As mentioned, I'm a lifelong addict and know firsthand what it's like to have an addiction to alcohol, drugs, vices, cigarettes, and sex. You name it and I probably became obsessed with it. Ironically food was the only substance I've never had an addiction for. With the assistance of my Spirit team over the course of my life I diminished the harder addictions while in my twenties. I became more of a disciplined bloke who worked day in and day out to make it through without succumbing to the addiction as best I could. I've fallen into the addictive behavior from time to time, but hopped out just as quickly, whereas in my twenties I climbed in and stayed in. I'm what some might call a dry addict. This is someone who is not using addictions, but still behaving like an addict. Moderation or elimination is the better alternative in avoiding the dangers of toxic addictions.

Addictions break apart positive connections with others. It has a negative effect on your life path trajectory. They bring on an array of diseases and even premature death. This is enough to scare some out of the addiction. In large quantities, the toxic addictions block and dim the connection with your Spirit team on the Other Side. This isn't in judgment again to those that are battling a serious toxic addiction and who are in and out of treatment. I've been in the trenches of toxic addiction in the past with the drug and alcohol addictions where I've also fell into the bell jar and off the wagon more times than I can count. I understand what it's like to battle addictions having gone through it myself. I also understand the fight it takes to get out of it successfully.

When you're in tune and connected to what's beyond, then your life begins to improve. When you're in tune to the guidance filtering through you from your Spirit team, then you make fewer mistakes. You pick up on the Divine guidance that might be guiding you to your dream job, or to a loving soul mate partnership, to the right car, home, roads to take, and so forth. Being in tune elevates your life in a brighter way. It raises your vibration, which is the space where you are experiencing feelings of love, joy, and peace naturally.

CHAPTER SIX

Detoxify Your Soul

How do you generally feel when you head off to bed every night? How is this feeling carried throughout the next day? What is the energy of the words that pass through your mind as that happens? Is it joyful, stressful, positive, negative, or full of sadness? What is your life like? Do you wake up in the morning and wonder what the point of getting up is? Or do you wake up and feel awesome ready to jump into the day with excitement? How long does that feeling last before you reach for something to give you a lift? What or who causes the feelings to drop? What can you do to change that? What about your thoughts? Are you generally a happy optimistic person or a down feeling kind of soul?

Many factors in your life will dictate the state of mind you will be in every day. If you're someone that desires a loving partnership and it has been years since that's happened, then you will move about each day with some despondence. Even when convinced you're enjoying life and you love your job, but then you head home and realize that you're single and there isn't anyone there to share your life with when you arrive. Maybe you live with a family member or you have a roommate. Those you live with can be a temporary distraction until you realize that ten years have passed, and you don't have a lover.

Perhaps you despise your job, but you're afraid to leave. You worry that you won't find another job and you have bills to pay. Human physical desires convert into toxins that buildup within your soul and this subsequently affects your physical body. It can leave you feeling consistently rundown. This is why it's beneficial to detoxify and cleanse your body and soul as often as you can.

If you're a busy professional always working, then this is especially important. These toxins can also build up if you're unemployed or if you're someone who lounges around the house all day bored with nothing around that excites you. The boredom feeling is what contributes to soul toxic build up. The fear energy of how bills will be paid when you're unemployed or if you will find another job can build up too.

I've had others approach me protesting that they've been drinking non-stop for days and need to stop. The great feeling they had when they started is no longer there. It no longer matters how much they drink because it is not helping. It's weighing them down causing them to feel agitated, lethargic, and unmotivated. You have one to two beers and you get a buzz. You start pounding back additional beers into you to the point that you start to feel out of it. The negative health risks also increase if this is a regular habit.

Pay attention to what you put into your body. Utilize self-control if you've been on a killer streak of consuming toxins in high quantities. When one is experiencing negative feelings or you're super sensitive, then you might reach for a toxic vice. This is more than just having a beer or a glass of wine. It's drinking a six pack or an entire bottle of wine regularly. You feel high for about an hour or two, then you start to come down from that and the feeling is much worse than before you had the drinks. You feel lethargic and it messes with your sleep. You wake up the next day feeling even more gross and sluggish. You count down the hours in the day before you can have another drink again just to make it all go away. Days and weeks have gone by and nothing has been accomplished. Not to mention that you've been unhappy throughout the whole process.

The super sensitive of the world are more in tune and connected than they might realize. You have a greater frequency of psychic reception than others do. Make lifestyle adjustments that are more conducive to your sensitivity levels. This is by being cautious with who you connect, communicate, or hang out with. Follow your gut if you're not feeling like going to a social event you've been invited to. Pick and choose which events you go to and what has the greater benefit to your overall well-being.

A positive way to deal with moodiness, sensitivity, or a rise in negative feelings is to dive into a creative project. Negative feelings are a sign that your soul is starving to create and express itself. It's a great way to unleash and release all of that built up negativity.

When a popular artist in entertainment culture experiences a painful relationship break up, then they often channel that pain into writing songs and making another record. Actors find characters to play that might be the opposite of who they are in order to release any repression and emotional toxins. You don't have to necessarily try to be an actor in films or a singer on stage, but you can take an acting class for the fun of it. You can find positive creative outlets to unleash your downward spiral of emotions. With the way technology is accessible today, you can film your own acting pieces or record it into a microphone even if it's just for your eyes and ears only.

There are times where nothing specific happened to contribute to mood decline. It is the result of a physically inherited genetic disposition. Other times something happened in your life that upset your world. The third way is that the mood decline is a result of what you're ingesting, be it food, pills, drugs, alcohol, etc. You could be eating something that you love, but happens to be high in sugar. It lifts you up only to drop you down to the floor an hour or so later. Keep an eye on what you put into your body regularly and test products out to assess what could be triggering a sudden mood drop. Do a daily test by examining and testing out what products you consume that could be the cause of regular lethargy or negative moods. The most obvious causes are alcohol or drugs, but sometimes it's food you wouldn't think to be the cause of. It can be dairy, too much caffeine, red meat, or the supplements you take.

Caring for Your Skin

When I see the human skin, clairvoyantly it appears to be covered with little cell like mouths all over every inch of your body. It breathes in the pollutants in the air, sucks in the energy of other people, and becomes clogged and closed up whenever any form of toxins hit it. Your skin craves the thirst from touch. It inhales the vibrations in its surroundings. Taking care of your skin and your body as much as possible is vital and beneficial. This means checking out the kinds of soaps, shampoos, and lotions you use to ensure they're not damaging. Some use natural essential oils, which are derived from plants. When anything touches your skin, then these cells drink all of that in. Ensure that what you're putting on your skin isn't toxic. My guides have said that if it is toxic, then it is the equivalent to someone drinking bleach.

Touch awakens these mouths over the skin. This can be through a lovers or friends touch or by the hands of a massage therapist. Massage therapist here means anyone who knows how to massage someone else whether it is a friend or lover. I've seen little kids playing around and massaging their parent's shoulders for fun after a long day at work. This is beyond a massage therapist, even though a professional massage therapist is ideal since they know the right points to hit.

The topic of tattoos has been brought up with me as well. Getting tattoos is a personal choice. I'm surrounded by family members, siblings, friends, and ex-lovers all covered in tattoos. I'm no stranger to it and attract those who are big on self-expression into my world. Tattoos are creative attributes that express one's individualism. There are risks involved with tattoos, such as injecting ink into your skin, which can cause an infection due to bad needles, which I'm sure tattoo enthusiasts are already aware of. There is no denying that puncturing the skin is going to have some measure of effect, but it isn't going to kill you. A needle is puncturing into the skin and depositing ink. There are other parts of one's body that is not tattooed that has just enough visible mouths for it to not be a problem. When one chooses to get tattooed, they should take precautions such as making sure the needles are sterilized and the ink being used is only for them and no one else. It should be looked upon that the work area is as clean and hygienic as anything else in your world.

If anything is touching your skin, you want to make sure it's not toxic. This includes the clothes you wear too. Some fabrics are made in toxic chemicals that touch your skin. Washing it before you wear it might not always help. There are also some laundry detergents that can be filled with toxins and chemicals, which cause you to break out. They can produce an allergic reaction after you put the clothes on after the wash. You'll want to be mindful of the soaps you use to wash your clothes too.

For women, certain underwear can cause an issue such as thongs, which can contribute to a urinary tract infection or vaginal problems. Certain tight underwear might be sexy, but if that's all you're wearing it can harbor bacteria. High heels are damaging to a woman's feet if that's all you mostly wear as well as constricting tight outfits.

For men, wear boxers more than underwear briefs. The male testes are outside of the body for a reason. It needs to move freely and not be restricted. There are exceptions at times such as if one is playing sports or being physically active, then it needs to be protected, but if you're sitting down all day, then wear boxers. This is more of a guideline of how often one wears boxers as opposed to constricting underwear. Underwear drops the male sperm count and it can take two to three months to reproduce and increase it. Wear that sexy underwear or those hot outfits, but in moderation to avoid potential issues.

Guilty Pleasures

Pray for assistance and intervention daily to be led to the right products that will not be damaging to your body. The obvious toxic culprits are vices or guilty pleasures like alcohol, drugs, nicotine, sugar, salt, fatty foods, and high amounts of caffeine. No one is going to reprimand you for eating a hamburger, unless it's a Vegetarian activist who sneers whenever you eat meat in front of them. The reason the angels are always preaching about avoiding toxins when possible is for your benefit. They know that consuming toxic products in high quantities will block the communication with them. This also contributes to you missing out on beneficial instructions given to you in order to achieve your desires through action steps.

Toxins are a breeding ground for harder health issues down the line. These products also dictate how you will feel. There will be an initial high the toxin gives you, but then it is soon reversed shooting you to the floor. It weighs you down and makes you sluggish, depressed, irritable, and so forth. Who wants to feel that way day in and day out? You reach for the toxin again to get that temporary high. Multiply that every day and visualize what that could possibly be doing to your insides and your aura. You might not think so or care at age twenty-three, but come sixty-three you'll be wishing you had done things a little differently in your life.

Toxins in life are regularly abused more than the good stuff. These are also toxins that the angels feel that no one needs if you structure your life in a way where those cravings are limited or not desired.

Can you blame the world though? Look at the kind of lives that human souls have created. It's been designed in a way that ensures people run themselves into the ground leaving them permanently exhausted, stressed, and dejected. It's a struggle for most to achieve profound happiness, so they reach for toxins in high quantities to help get through it.

You have some form of caffeine to get yourself going in the morning and you keep this momentum every few hours just to get through the day. When you're unhappy, then this drains your life force energy leaving you feeling as if you need high doses of caffeine to feel energized. I've worked with executives in the past who drink soda all day long to keep them flying. This isn't one soda, but many throughout the day. Multiply doing that by two decades and imagine what will happen to you. No matter how much caffeine you have, you're still feeling the constant daily crash. If you overdo caffeine, then this can cause more stress and anxiety within you, not to mention the damage it does to your heart and health over time.

There was a case of a man who abused caffeine to the point where he was diagnosed with liver cancer. Granted before he passed away, he admitted to drinking six to seven energy drinks a day and had a poor diet of pizza and burgers. This is far more excessive than the daily caffeine jolt. He passed away at the young age of thirty-nine.

If you're unable to quit a toxin right away or do not want to, work on reducing it so that you're indulging it in moderation. Moderation is having an alcoholic drink or a cup of coffee once a day, rather than drinking it until you drop. It's what it's doing to you or will do to you down the line if you're consuming large quantities of it daily. Reducing your toxin intake and balancing it with healthy stuff is a great step in the right direction to being happier, healthier, and more connected with the Other Side.

Let's say that you're unable to quit having a couple cups of coffee to get going in the morning, but you know you want to. Adopt a balance with some carrot juice, herbal teas, or tons of water preceding that as your day continues on.

Incorporate a detoxifying cleanse every so often. This can be where one day you shut off all technological distractions or time wasters. If that's impossible or difficult, then start small where it's shut off for several hours or your personal cell phone is off during your entire workday. Use your sound judgment on when it's practical to do so. You do not want to vanish for days on end when there is an emergency, crises or even death in your life and no one can find you. The technological detox can include spending this day away from stressful and drama filled people. Consume high vibration food into your system such as fruits and vegetables. Notice how you feel when you do this and compare it to those days where you're taking a pound of sugar in your coffee.

More people lead sedentary lives than ever before. You're either parked all day on your rear at an office job, standing behind a register, or plopped in a chair at home with little to no movement for hours on end. Over time this begins to increase the risks of health-related issues, not to mention your energy levels drop and your body begins to feel as if it's eternally out of whack.

Incorporate regular exercise at least once a day if possible. Take frequent walks, jog, or bike when you're able to. If you're suffering from a physical issue that makes exercise difficult, then add in certain exercises that are safe to keep the blood flow moving. When unsure of what you can handle or what is good for you, then talk to a medical or professional licensed expert when incorporating health, fitness, and nutrition related action steps into your life.

Regular exercise is one of the bigger guidance and messages I've received and have been preaching about longer than anything else. Treating the temporary vessel you're renting with the utmost compassion and care is always urged. If you poured something other than gasoline into your car, then it would tear your car up. Treat your body the way you would a car to ensure optimum performance.

Archangel Raphael is the healing angel to call on for assistance with all health and well-being related issues. Ask Raphael or your Spirit team to help in reducing your cravings for toxic vices or to eliminate it knowing deep down that you're ready. Your Spirit team will work with you on that after you have made a specific request to begin the process of reducing or eliminating something you're trying to control. Request to be guided to healthier alternatives and to incorporate a more balanced intake.

Fresh Air and Water

Fresh air is another top important element to awaken your psychic gifts. This is because spirit power is heavy outdoors. The messages from Heaven travel through the molecules of oxygen. Get out there in nature, amongst the trees, grass, flowers, sunshine, and take deep healthy breaths in. Open your windows at home daily allowing the fresh oxygenated air to flow in clearing out all of the toxins that build up in a home with the windows permanently shut. Fresh air means clean air and not smog polluted air.

Many human souls get up every morning five days a week to sit in an enclosed car to go to an enclosed office to sit in all day. They hardly go outside for their breaks. At the end of the day they climb back into their enclosed car to go to their enclosed home, and then repeat the next day. Many cities have built shopping malls, theater complexes, promenades, apartment complexes, and grocery stores on top of one another. It's grown to become void of quiet nature settings. Land developers don't care about trees. They care about building, which isn't a problem until you're building shamelessly and unwisely on top of one another.

Take steps to include more fresh air in your life. Make a pact to take breaks throughout the day where you can get outside and at least walk around the block. When you arrive back home, open all of your windows, and allow the fresh air to waft in if even for a few minutes. Go for walks after dinner, or get in a workout before dinner. Get plenty of exercise and fresh air. These are additional key secrets to integrate into your life in order to awaken the creative part of you, raise your vibration and consciousness, give you a clearer psychic line, and improve all aspects of your body, mind, and soul.

Water governs so much of this planet from the ocean, to the lakes, to the human body. Water is one of the most awesome detoxifiers. This includes bathing, swimming, or sitting in front of an ocean or lake if you're near one. If you're not, then the power of visualization can take you there. Open up ocean photographs on your computer or thumb through a photography book of beaches and meditate on them. Drink plenty of water every day to flush out the toxins in your body.

The world's oceans are critical to human survival and its habitat. It must be kept clean of toxins the same way you keep your physical body clear of toxins. The ocean is what contributes to the clouds that form in the sky, which produces the water your body needs in order to endure life in a healthier way. When one heads to a non-crowded beach, they have reported to feeling more relaxed and alive than they did before they went to the beach. Those that live along the coast have been reported to have stronger health than others might. The ocean breeze blows away smog particles that the rest of a big city would breathe in. It increases your body's ability to absorb oxygen. If you're not near an ocean, or lake, then the water comes to you by drinking it, taking a shower, bath, or through the power of visualization. The mind is a powerful device and can take you anywhere you want to go and bring you anything you desire including what you do not desire, so use it wisely.

CHAPTER SEVEN

Soul Cleansing to Motivation

Many sensitive's shy away or keep away from other people due to the negativity that they often associate with other people. It may not be that every person is bathed in negative energy, but a highly sensitive person is more prone to absorbing every shred of energy from all that it crosses path with that it can become unbearable. Some might call them anti-social or shy, which is the not thought out point of view because it goes much deeper than that. Not everyone is bouncing off the walls in extroverted spirits. Every person on the planet has a built-in composite of personality traits that they're born with, such as the genetic to the astrological, or it's molded into them by the events during their childhood. The highly sensitive person ends up seeing all people as risky to be near, even though there are good and bad energies within every person that exists. Because they sense every nuance, they absorb these energies that people emanate off of them more than other souls do.

There are good people threaded in the mix of the negative, but because both energies are so potent, the highly sensitive person is overwhelmed by the massive energies that dart towards them that it leaves them temporarily drained. Going to crowded places like a mall, amusement park, or grocery store can wear them out. This is why they have to run their life like a strict disciplined executive ensuring their soul and sensitive nature are protected. They learn to be careful about the decisions they make each day that could have an effect on their well-being. This is one of the pluses of being a highly sensitive person. It's that you're more likely to have a keen clairsentient clear feeling psychic channel where you can detect what to stay away from. While another person that isn't as in tune will dive right into danger oblivious of the consequences.

Detoxing your world when it comes to people means being mindful of who you allow into your auric circle. Keep those you see as antagonistic away from you or in small doses if you have no choice. Those you have no choice but to see might be family members or work colleagues. Surround yourself with optimistic positive people whenever possible.

When two positive optimistic go-getters join forces, then there is no telling how far you can both go. You feel inspired by one another, rather than brought down by them. Some of the personality types that can contribute to lowering your vibration just by being in their vicinity can be a gossip, negative complainer or someone that regularly makes toxic choices. When you're around someone like that every day, then this can unknowingly have an effect on you being a positive abundance attractor.

You may be a naturally positive person and feel you're doing everything possible to attract in good stuff, but find that nothing good comes in. One of the blocks preventing this good stuff from coming in can be something you were unaware of such as being around negative people. This will have an effect on what you are attracting into your life.

Being around a Debby Downer will only bring you down and stall you from moving forward. Focus on quality people to surround yourself with such as those that are mutually supportive of you as you are with them. They also allow you the required space you need throughout each day because they understand that you are a sensitive. Highly sensitive people need more time outs alone than others.

Eliminating toxic friendships also includes those on your social media page. The world is drama ridden and chaotic enough with all the daily gossip noise from politically hyped chatter to celebrity gossip. You've likely noticed whenever the latest scandal rises that every other person will post non-constructive words that come out in a negative toxic scream, whine, or complaint about the target. This does nothing to help anyone. It's toxic energy that fans those flames undeserving of attention. It brings you down, it lowers your vibration, it blocks good stuff from coming to you, and it puts a damper on your life. You then carry that out in the world and spread that to whomever you connect with. Those you pass it to then take that energy and spread it around as well. Soon the entire planet has erupted into nonsensical chaos that helps no one at all.

This isn't just practical advice from Spirit, but those sensitive and more in-tune than others have all vocally expressed having noticed this on their own. They know how it ultimately makes them feel, which isn't a positive uplifting feeling.

I've watched past acquaintances and friends on social media announce that their wall thread is too plagued with negative energy that they plan to take a break from social media. That's one of the great ways to detox from technology for a bit, but at the same time you shouldn't have to run and hide from your own page. Instead you can hide that toxic person's posts or remove them altogether. Some have gone as far as to deleting their account, which might seem extreme. There are ways around that if you want to stay on social media. This is by being exceptionally careful about the types of people you're allowing on your friend list.

One of the positive tools available on some social media sites now is you can unfriend people if you choose to, or unfollow them if you don't want to unfriend them. This way you can keep them in your friends list, but you no longer see their posts. This is beneficial for someone you like, but you can't stand the constant negative posts they keep putting up. I did this myself with people that continuously posted negative posts on the politicians and celebrities they hate everyday all day long.

Popular social media sites at this point are Facebook, Instagram, and Twitter. All three now have this 'hide' feature. Many social media sites are aware this is a problem, so the fact that my Spirit team and I are discussing it is nothing new. If at the time you're reading this, none of those social media sites are around, then there is likely something similar available that can apply to this.

It's rare for someone to post about the positives they like about someone. It's easier for the ego to gossip about who they hate. When someone is unhappy or unaligned, then they are more apt to posting negativity. Happy centered people aren't attracted to negativity and prefer to post constructive positive content.

By the time I was done hiding the repeat offenders on social media, I had a nice clean uplifting page with people that posted more engaging interesting content that was on the positive side. Letting go of negativity allows room for positivity. Positivity brings more positivity.

When detoxing from people and social media, you also want to detox from distractions and time wasters. These are distractions that eat up good chunks of your day from wasteful internet and social media surfing to chatting with random people on dating apps that you don't care all that much about. This is knowing that you have work to do or that you could be doing. It's not a crime to have a guilty pleasure you enjoy breaking away to for some fun, such as random internet surfing to chatting with others on a dating app. Chatting out of boredom daily rather than chatting with someone you genuinely have an interest in knowing can lead to more procrastination, non-productivity and laziness.

Clear the Clutter

Clearing the clutter is part of organizing your life. It's included as part of the detoxing process. Detoxing all aspects of your world prepares you to open the gates to abundance and blessings. The clutter clearing is beneficial since it cleans the energy and allows you to focus more clearly. Clear focus equates to a stronger communication connection with your Spirit team. As a writer, I will incorporate procrastination techniques where I need to make sure my space is completely clear of clutter before I fall into the zone to write.

When you walk into a messy room you immediately sense the chaos, which makes your thinking more chaotic and unsettled. Clear away the cobwebs and the clutter by boxing up or throwing away items you will never need or look at again. If it has deep sentimental value or attachment and you're not ready to part with it, then box it up and put it in a closet or storage if it doesn't need to be lying around.

Commit to simplicity and keep your surroundings organized and uncluttered. Extricate friendships that you don't consider to be true authentic friendships, but connections you keep around due to a fear of loneliness. If the friendship stresses you out, then it's time to begin distancing yourself from them. Friendships that are true and long lasting will place no demands on you or your time. They understand this and form naturally unfettered.

This all has an effect on the energy you're creating in your life. If your life has some unseen negative dents in it, then this can create a block to attracting in good stuff.

Detoxing your inner and outer worlds isn't just about detoxing your body of toxic addictions, bad foods, drugs, or alcohol. It's more than going on a fast or cleanse. It's also about detoxing every aspect of your life from clearing the clutter in your home and work life to detoxing the people around you. Do a thorough examination of the people in your world from family to friendships. Who brings you down whenever they come around? Work on eliminating and dissolving those in your life that do nothing, but bring drama and chaos to your world. Even if you don't extricate them, eventually the angels will remove people from your life that have fulfilled their purpose or contribute nothing of positive benefit, but stall you from moving forward. You don't have to wipe out best friendships or family members that you love on some level, but you keep contact with them in small doses. Generally, when someone isn't a fan of a family member, they're usually not spending every mind-numbing minute with them anyway, unless they live with them.

Get structured in your life and plan, schedule, and organize your surroundings. When you have a clear space, you have a clear mind. A clear mind helps you get focused while allowing your Spirit team's wisdom, messages, and guidance to come flowing in. This guidance helps bring you one step closer to achieving what you desire.

Be mindful of the daily or weekly purchases you make. There is a fine line between overspending on things you don't need, as opposed to buying the occasional gadget or item you would love to have. Buying something for you is part of self-care. It's when it moves into constant frivolous financial spending to fill an emotional void that you begin to block the flow of abundance. You may already know when you're spend-happy to make you feel better. When it becomes a regular habit, then it moves into toxic territory that can have an effect on what you're bringing into your life. Every atom, cell, and matter that exists is energy, regardless if it's physical material items or part of your feelings and thoughts. Breathe new life into all of the energy cells in your world to becoming a clear vessel of reception with God. All wonderful things end up coming out of that.

Get Motivated to Succeed

You might have other distractions such as work or family obligations that seem to eat up your time each day. This is to the point that you have zero time to devote towards your life purpose, passions, or in building your side business. That side business is the one that will eventually free you from the confinement restrictions of being unemployed or from working day jobs you despise. Daily procrastination techniques and distractions can eventually make you notice that a week has gone by where you've donated zero time towards your purpose. Sometimes your ego will have you push that away when realistically you could squeeze in a half hour to an hour each day that consists of one action step towards your passion and purpose.

In the past, I've made excuses that there isn't any time. After weeks of that I started to pay more attention to the downtime I did have. I'd say, "I have forty-five minutes with nothing to do before I need to leave for my dinner. I can squeeze in something important now."

All souls on the planet are worthy and deserving of blessings as any other. When you get into a position where you feel blessed for the good you have now, then this lifts your energy vibration to welcome in more. It also allows you to do good stuff for others when you are no longer filled with other practical day-to-day worries. Once you're taken care of, then it's easier to freely focus on others who could use your helping hand.

Everyone is born with special gifts in the areas of psychic abilities to creative skills. There isn't one person on the planet that doesn't have something extraordinary about them to utilize and contribute towards the betterment of humanity. At the same time, many distinctly amazing people struggle in low vibrational jobs to physically survive that they end up pushing their authentic talents down to continue on. The angels want to guide them out of that and can help maneuver circumstances to produce blessings to propel that soul forward. It can take them years to decades to help some people, while it seems others are blessed at an early age. It doesn't mean you're less talented or gifted than someone else.

Each person is a special case with varying reasons as to what the delays or blocks are. This is another reason clearing and detoxing your world is beneficial. It helps you become a stronger conduit with the Divine. When that takes place, then you're able to detect the answers clearly as to what is preventing the positive flow of abundance enlightenment.

Avoid placing a time limit on when good things can or will happen. It doesn't matter how old you are since you are not discriminated against from receiving blessings and miracles at any age. There are numerous factors that have to be considered that come into play as to why there are delays to witnessing a positive flow of abundance. Some of those factors require work on your part.

An older person might feel resentment when they see a twenty-two-year-old popular well-known entertainer purchase a mansion worth three million along the coast with a magnificent view. This doesn't mean this popular star is any more deserving or worthy of excessive material abundance over you. In one sense, it might feel like the luck of the draw, or that the maneuvering your Spirit team has been working on behind the scenes is taking longer than another person. It's super easy to fall into envy and resentment in that instance, especially if you've been working so hard and yet are seeing little to no return in the hard-working investment you've been applying for years. Believe me I as well as Spirit understand, but you don't want to wallow too deeply in that energy indefinitely since that will block what needs to come in.

The other side of that is you don't know the challenges and tough experiences the popular star is faced with behind closed doors. You may say you don't care, but despite their fat bank account, they could be battling with issues far worse than you could imagine. Some find it difficult to sympathize with anyone who doesn't have money issues, but when you do that then you're placing higher value on money. That person with money is human like anyone else and going through personal challenges you're unaware of. What matters to Heaven is what is in your heart and who you are regardless of what's in your bank account.

Heaven is also dealing with people that operate primarily from ego and free will. Your Spirit team could be frequently attempting to get the attention of someone important on Earth that can propel you forward, but that person is not picking up on the guidance. You suffer longer because the person intended to make an important offer to you that can change your life is not following the hunches periodically put in front of them. It can also be you who isn't noticing the guidance coming in or following. All of that can create an immense amount of delays.

Due to human free will choices consistently getting in the way of conclusive progress can create an enormous amount of delays to seeing your hard work not reap much reward. Never give up, never lose faith, and never stop believing. Keep telling yourself the breakthrough will come and it will on the wings of Angels. And so it is.

CHAPTER EIGHT

*Clearing the Chaos
Within and Around Your World*

Balancing all parts of the totality of your soul's self are the endless positive potential possibilities. You open up the universe to the blessings of abundance on all levels from the mind, body, and spirit. This is abundance within the soul consciousness mind, the spiritual awareness, and the most enticing to human beings, which are the physical blessings of abundance. This includes the necessary material comforts such as the home, the great job, plentiful finances, as well as friendships and a love partner. There's nothing ill about desiring physical comforts until it moves into greed territory and that it is all one desires. All other aspects need to be in play. For instance, when one's spiritual soul awareness opens up, then this simultaneously draws in positive experiences of abundance.

One of the steps to preparing you to open the floodgates of abundance and blessings and balance in your life may cause some fuss, but it is a simple task that anyone can do for free, nonetheless. This is cleaning and clearing the clutter in your life both internally and externally. It can be clearing out friendships that only bring you down and make you feel bad about yourself, to cleaning up and organizing your home life. Messy discombobulated surroundings can create a disrupted flow of positive blessings of abundance.

You can get into it by consulting with a Feng Shui expert. If this is too costly or doesn't interest you, then do some free research online to gain some basic tips. The clearing of the clutter doesn't need to be perfect, but you might feel you can get more organized than you might be right now. If you walk into your home and you see the disarray with items piled sky high, then take one section a day at a time to get your home organized, so that it's not overwhelming. Disorganization disrupts the energy flow in and around your life. When we say in and around you, then this includes the mind, body, and soul aspects.

Be mindful of the kind of people you hang around with as they can affect your aura and energetic field as well too. If you're around someone that is a perpetual toxic person, then you will absorb that into your consciousness being and will become one with it. Work on dissolving connections that offer you no positive benefit. You don't have to abruptly cut people out, but if you are looking to reduce your contact with them, or dissolve them out of your life, then work on dissolving people the way you dissolve any toxic vice, which is gradually, safely, and slowly. You are available for them less and less over time.

This isn't about abandoning people in a time of need. This is about the offenders that only use you to harshly rant and complain about something regularly that they have no interest in improving. You make constructive suggestions to help them, which is met with retaliation and resistance. Follow this by keeping your options open to add in brighter friendships with those you feel a stronger connection with that are enjoyable to be around and more aligned with who you are or are becoming.

The other benefits to clearing the clutter within and around you are that it contributes to helping you think more clearly. The flow of energy moves swiftly than if you were living in chaotic disarray. When the energy is moving positively, this brings in positivity. When you live in chaos, then that's what you invite in. After my father passed away, I was stunned to discover how he had been living in such disorder. Nonsense piled sky high covering every inch of space that could be found filled with something. I had always seen it and mentioned it to him over the years, but it was after the death when you're going through stuff with family members to sort out that you truly see the disarray.

Sometimes the clutter can come up in the least likely of places. One of the positives of the Internet is that you can purchase most anything you desire without so much as a thought. You can do that from anywhere, such as from your phone in bed in the middle of the night when you can't sleep. You no longer have to fight the traffic and crowds to get a good parking spot at a store, then spend all of that time browsing the aisles, and standing in line to purchase those items.

It's so rare and infrequent that I physically walk into a store. The majority of everything is delivered to me, including groceries! This isn't out of laziness, since others have explained I'm one of the least lazy people they know. Part of the delivery bit is the convenience, but the other part of it is due to my severe social anxiety and the tampering of chaotic psychic energies absorbed while going to a crowded place filled with disgruntled people like in a retail store.

The downfall to this ease of ordering stuff online is that there are now numerous statistics popping up all over the place indicating a dreadful vision. The world in general is hoarding more products they don't need due to impulsive online shopping.

There was a point I had walked into my place and noticed all of these items sitting around in boxes that were delivered. My heart sunk in a feeling of devastation. I couldn't believe what I had allowed to happen, "What is all this? How do I have all this stuff? For what purpose?"

I decided to give it away to people who could use it. Giving away clothes sent to me by that label that I never wore or took the tags off. Labels and vendors send me stuff on top of that due to the position I'm in. I had become what I thought I would never be…. a hoarder. Luckily, it wasn't a lifetime of collecting, but more like several weeks. This was several weeks too long that I had to get rid of it all. If I've never used it, then I never will. I then looked up local charities and places where people were suffering from material lack and brought it to them.

Most people admit that the stuff they buy they don't really need. They end up throwing it away creating a bigger trash situation. This is a planet of hoarding! It's become another addiction even for those who don't like shopping. They hit, "add to cart", and then click that "buy" button and a chemical rush of Dopamine lifts them up.

Dopamine is that high happy feeling one gets from things like food, drugs, alcohol, sex, shopping, and on and on. It is anything that makes someone feel good…. temporarily. Because once that high drops astronomically, which it will sooner than later, you crash suddenly feeling low again and are out in search of another fix. You race to get that addictive fix like a drug injection that gives you another temporary high to keep going.

Some consume this false happiness where they do this daily just to stay happy and keep going. It never lasts and winds up leaving you craving another fix. When the package you ordered arrives, then that dopamine fix hits you again to open that brand-new package. But what do you do with that package after opening it? I've discovered that some never even take it out of the wrapper. It gets tossed aside to sit on the counter for a week or two until you mumble, "I need to put this away. I never even took this out of the wrapper."

Because of the ease of buying online, you're not paying much attention to how often you add to your cart and click purchase. There are people who are exceptional at watching what they spend. Some don't have the money, or they don't own a credit card, and they're just trying to get by with the basics. For others, myself included, I've had to learn to be extra cautious. I'm usually cautious as it is, but sometimes I'm looking at what's being delivered and wondering, "Did I really need this contraption? What possessed me to buy this?"

It took some additional self-discipline to realize I was being sucked into the new trend of online shopping and hoarding without realizing it. Compared to others it wasn't as bad as I'm not that much of an impulsive shopper. I've never liked shopping unless there was something specific I needed. I wasn't one of those people buying additional pairs of shoes or clothes I knew I would never wear. I'm the opposite extreme where I've worn the same pairs of shoes until they grow torn. That's my cue to buckle down and get a better pair of shoes. I never bought the latest iPhone, but would use the same version for years long past its upgrade eligibility date. I'd keep using it until key features like the home button would stop working. That would be clue that it was time to buckle down and change the phone because the buttons are no longer working.

While some people revel in the latest gadget craze, I saw no difference. Plus, the hassle to transferring everything over to the new device was too much of a chore that was never worth it to me. If the phone still works, then I'm keeping it.

Other things to keep in mind are that manufacturers are using cheaper materials to make items, which means they break or tear sooner than later, so you have to keep buying the same gadget or item repeatedly over the years. I had regular oscillator fans that seemed less powerful in its breeze a year after it was bought. I soon realized I had to keep replacing them the way you change your tires or brakes regularly on your car.

Clothes are also getting holes or shrinking sooner than later after a few washes. You have to replace those regularly. While the trend to be more environmentally safe or conscious has risen, that hasn't necessarily shown when it comes to how much material is being dumped into landfills. According to many statistics, that number has increased astronomically, which means the environmental craze hasn't improved much.

Many Universities and Colleges have reported enormous shocking statistics surrounding how much waste students collect or are unused. Tons of waste is discarded or donated if the student hasn't bothered to do it after vacating their dorms. The waste that the planet tosses on a large basis can make anyone with a heart, soul, or conscious break down. It's an eye opener when you know about this massive waste and that there are people around the world struggling to survive barely able to afford food. The amount of waste that could be donated to organizations that can help people in need is staggering. There is no mobilization, protest, or marching over circumstances like poverty or child abuse.

A great deal of stuff donated to places like the Goodwill isn't getting sold there either. They end up getting dumped in a landfill as well in the end. You order something online because it's easy. You think it's no big deal if the item isn't what you wanted in the end because you can return it. When it comes to returning items bought online, a great deal of people admitted they don't bother, because it takes a bit more effort to find packaging for it, printing out the proper return slips and receipt, then driving down to the mail carrier service. Most people find it's not worth it to go through all that unless it was a super expensive item.

A messy house, aura, ambiance, surroundings, and life contribute to messy abundance attraction energy. It creates a block due to the restricted flow of your physical surroundings, which simultaneously creates imbalance. If you are a sensitive in tune being, then you no doubt have noticed that when you've walked into a cluttered filled room that you can feel the dark weight of that. When you walk into a space that is free of clutter, then this uplifting feeling rises inside you. Everything in and around you has an effect on your well-being state, including the things you would never consider to have an effect.

Conduct regular space clearing exercises where throughout each year you periodically walk around your house and examine what needs to be boxed up and put away. Look at what needs to be re-organized and set up in a better way. Move furniture around if you have to in order to create a more ideal set up, which can assist in the flow of abundance energy.

When you walk through each room of your house, how do you feel? Are you disappointed at the mess? Do you feel joyful and clear minded? Do you feel a heaviness?

Any negative feeling felt is a clue that some re-organizing needs to be conducted. If you find you're too busy or you keep putting it off, then set a disciplined schedule. This can be where you rely on the seasons changing to re-organize. When it's the first week of Spring, Summer, Fall, and Winter. Use those dates to begin the space clearing if you're someone that procrastinates or keeps putting it off. Light some sage, incense, or candles to help purify the air. Open your windows daily if for at least fifteen minutes to an hour to clear the old air with the new one. I know that can be tougher to do in colder climates, but do what you can and when you can. You know what you can tolerate and get away with without it harming your comfort or health.

When you sage your home, pay attention to corners of your house where energy gets stuck. As someone with Clairvoyance, I've seen darkness in corners of homes and buildings, which show up as floods of insects. There is trapped dark energy in corners more than in any other spot. Have the intention of ridding it as you sage and clear your space. Also pay attention to doorways, which can be entryways for toxic dark spirits.

Clear your aura and spirit, which you can do with sage smoke around your body as well too. You can take a cleansing shower or bath with Epsom salts and essential oils, or you can simply have the intention of clearing your aura by calling in Archangel Michael, Archangel Raphael, or Archangel Jophiel to clear you and your space of any toxic negative energy in all directions of time.

Part of cleansing you, your space and home with sage is also paying especially important care to your bed area. You most likely spend a great deal of time in bed. It's important to clear that energy regularly. If you go to bed in any negative state or if the night is met with tossing and turning, negative feelings, thoughts, or bad dreams, then ensure you clear the bed with sage or whatever tools you prefer to purify it as a precaution.

Sometimes all you need to do is sit or stand in silence and prayer, eyes closed, and mentally call in God, your Spirit team, and only those beings of the highest vibrational nature. You can say something like: *"Please clear me now of all negative toxic energy I've absorbed or created in all directions of time. And so it is."*

You might choose to create an altar or sacred space in your home used primarily for prayer or to help you get more spiritually focus. Burn candles and diffuse nice smells with essential oils to incense, sage, or cedar burning. Candles are great to help give you a focal point. The light of a candle is also welcoming for angels who enjoy the light that is not harsh or tampered with such as artificial or florescent light.

Be careful with your tech gadgets and how they're situated near your bed. There are also growing scientific statistics showing the negative effects on you and your well-being when tech gadgets are so close to you while sleeping. It's more likely than not most people tend to have their cell phones near them all the time. They've become extensions of us. Imagine what that's like and the repercussions that can come out of that. A great many people also live in smaller places or apartments where it's not realistic to hide where their computer equipment is situated. You can consider it covering it when it's not in use. You do the best you can with how you're setting it up, so that it's not affecting your well-being and sleep.

CHAPTER NINE

*Gossip Machine
to Centered Light*

Looking down on Earth it's deathly quiet from the vantage point of space, except for the subtle sounds of electromagnetic vibrations moving through the Universe. Circumstances on Earth appear trivial from that perspective. It's a similar view from Heaven as spirit beings take note of the low vibrational noise and bickering energy coming out of the billions of Earthly souls that put up endless resistance refusing to come together in peace. They want to see someone that is kind and compassionate, but shares a different viewpoint than you, and yet you still accept them for their differences. This is what brings about a Utopian paradise more than anything else. It's that one small step towards active compassion.

Spots of rose light mixed with tinges of white and gold are sprinkled around the planet in the higher vibrational souls that move about attempting to counteract and temper those that run their life from the darkness of ego, but the ratio to the darker souls is on the minimal side.

Part of creating more balance in your world requires talking about areas that are not considered joyful topics. When one considers improving your well-being in the spiritual genre it tends to stick to the airy-fairy light and sunshine bits, while ignoring the root of the issues that reside in the Darkness. Gossiping is one of the majority of these issues that human beings live their daily lives in unable to break free from.

The act of gossiping is one of the dominant forms of expression on Earth, but it has a damaging vibration energy surrounding it that feeds the Darkness. Gossiping induces a temporary joyful rushed high before you experience the inevitable hard crash leaving you wanting more of that fix. Certain personalities and dispositions become extremely addicted to it over others. The effects are similar to that of a drug, alcohol drink, or sugar high. The gossip is either unaware of its toxic effects or they don't care, which would then make them a sociopath void of empathetic emotions.

Gossiping is a lower vibration energy that does nothing to positively benefit anyone. The lower self and ego receive a quick high from gossiping that deludes them into thinking they have a superior voice. Someone with high self-esteem has no desire to gossip, because they are sure of themselves. When you are sure of yourself, you're not looking to engage in gossip, which is designed to cut others down to make you feel better.

High self-esteem people desire good vibrations in their life and will automatically throw up a wall around them when negativity or gossip is in their vicinity. Those drawn to gossip do so out of boredom. They're addicted to the high, because they're experiencing and battling with some form of misery inside. It makes them feel good to attack, lash out, or negatively gossip about others. Productive focused people are not drawn to gossip and are too busy to entertain it. Happy people live in joy and surround themselves with others that are optimistic, pleasant, and positive. They know gossip brings the energy down. You've likely witnessed this when you or someone else is in the line of fire of a negative complainer. You try to wiggle out of there and brush it off to get away from them. You can feel your joy filled serenity being tarnished and dragged down.

The same way there is a dark and light ego, there are also varying levels of gossip from the harmless to the dangerous. The harmless gossip would be you expressing concern for a friend you suspect is going through something tough they won't tell you about. A mutual friend informs you in confidence that this is taking place. This kind of gossip is to get to the bottom of what's happening with a friend with the goal and intention to help them. The dangerous kind of gossip is the lies or negativity that others spread about someone. "Loose lips may sink ships" was a popular phrase coined around World War II that ended up being about the dangers of gossip and how detrimental it can become.

Gossip is dangerous to your health whether you are the negative gossiper, or you are within the vicinity of a gossip. As an innocent bystander to gossip you will absorb that energy into your aura becoming one with it without intending to. This lowers your vibration and brings your energy down while blocking Divine guidance in the process. Eventually the gossip rush causes you to crash to the ground, thus driving you out in search of that quick fix again. The health dangers of gossip are destructive and damaging. Negative energy of any kind will affect your overall health and well-being in the long run. The same kind of rush that the ego receives over gossip is what drives one to obsess over the latest media stories propelling them to post about it on their personal social media accounts.

Common keywords in a media headline used to entice the ego are words such as,

"Outraged, blasts, blasted, slams, slammed, under fire, uproar, offends."

Gossip columnists and bloggers use low vibrational turmoil-ridden words to entice someone's ego and lure you into the drama! Notice how adding an exclamation point to the end of that sentence altered it into something uncomfortably dramatic. It gives you a rush of anxiety, nervousness, or adrenaline luring you into its web to pay attention. This is a goal that it gravely succeeds at. It can stop achieving this result when the masses wake up their consciousness and avoid giving it attention. Unfortunately, there are millions of souls threaded around the planet that reside right in the epicenter of that darkness. They're drawn to it on a daily and regular basis. Log onto any social media site and scroll to witness the endless gossip being darted out into the universe.

A realist falls between the optimist and a pessimist. The realist doesn't wear rose colored glasses and nor do they see things through a hazy filter. They see things as they realistically are. Being optimistic is a positive virtue and not necessarily a bad one, pending that the optimist considers all of the data that things might not go according to the way they want them to go in the end.

Life is brighter when you're in a positive optimistic mindset, which is certainly better than the mindset of: "We're all doomed!" Because that's not technically true. One could easily say the human race has always been doomed, but it's the human race that put itself in that position. If the end of the world were to happen, there's nothing you can do about it anyway, so let that go. Typing it out in a seventy something character bite on social media will not stop it.

The way to accelerate life on Earth towards Utopia is if every person on the planet resided in their soul's true nature, which is in a state of all love, joy, and peace. It's virtually impossible for millions of souls to exude that state around the clock in today's ego driven physical designed modern world governed by the darkness of ego. It is counterproductive to their true nature, so people live under constant stress as a result.

When there is discord, then one needs to remain neutral and objective while finding the right balance between opposition. Most extreme issues can be compromised on, which is the quickest way to success. A balanced judge or authority figure stands in the middle hearing everyone's point of view before deciding on the best course of action.

Balance in human lives is lacking and the world is plagued with division between opposing viewpoints not hearing or seeing the other person's point of view. Eventually or hopefully people will figure out that if you can't beat them, then join them. This doesn't necessarily mean agreeing with their stance. If after much discussion both come to some kind of middle ground instead of a rigid unbendable extreme viewpoint, then balanced compromise is reached. People are more likely to be happier and content on all ends when they're not attempting to oppress one side so that the ego can get what it wants with no care about anyone else.

I've conducted studies where I've locked two people in a room together with severely opposing views and values forcing them to connect. By the end of the day, it's not surprising to find that both people walked out of there having gained compassion and respect for the other person, even if they didn't necessarily agree with them. When you have a one on one civil calm discussion with someone with an opposing view, you make further headway than hiding behind the safety net of a mob with pitchforks emotionally ranting and raving about. People don't respond positively to anyone screaming at you, so therefore nothing is improved with aggression.

The mob mentality is predominately on the Internet and social media, which allows people to be louder than they normally would be in person. People band together with their pitchforks to spend a day vilifying someone with constant badgering over something that is generally a minor human crime that people can honestly get over. In the end, they do get over it and completely forget about it in a few days when another story to gossip about is thrust to the top with a bullet.

The mob mentality is associated with the same ones that engage in violent protests, which the world has witnessed all throughout Earth's history and on up into the post technology days. If you examine and study each of those protests to see if what they were protesting about worked in their favor, you will find it to be rare that anything good or positive came about from it post technology. It worked out to change policy by giving women the right to vote or during the civil rights movement, but not post technology. Most that make up a good chunk of the world see it as drama and tantrum energy, neither of which sways the opinions of the recipient or those who agree with the stance. The calm peaceful protests made better headway to successfully helping a cause, because most people respond to calm peaceful advocacy over violent outbursts.

If you genuinely care about an issue or don't like the way something is, then you find a positive action step to implement. Talk to Congress and peacefully explain why the change you wish to see is necessary. Get a job or volunteer in Government to work from the inside out. If it's something you passionately care about, then it could be connected to your life purpose. Destroying people and property over something you dislike is called war where no one wins.

The paradox is that the same people opposing war are the ones creating the destruction of innocent bystanders and property. In the end, what they were protesting about never positively changed anything. It creates a dramatic ruckus and soon evaporates dissolving away having accomplished nothing. The darkness of ego feels more empowered in a group, therefore the idea of roaming the streets in a protest sounds fun and exciting to it. That is until you have to get back to your regular life that entails becoming responsible by getting a job to be able to pay your bills.

Social media has its grand benefits of creating friendships and staying in touch with family, but the dark side of it is that it feeds the mob and the gossip machines. You have to leave it numerous times if you're bombarded with negativity in your thread. When it gets to be insanely bad, then take a breather or a technological detox. You've noticed the out of control gossip and negative ranting's that persists on people's pages. You end up hiding those people who are repeat offenders. They can't see how far they've fallen and are unable to get over whatever it is they are ranting about. It's their page, so they can post what they want, but you don't have to be subjected to it if you're not interested in the daily absorbing of it.

Follow this hiding or removal of repeat offenders by following and liking high vibrational happy pages and accounts, so that it will be what dominates your social media feed for the most part. You may let some negative posts go here and there as everyone has their bad days, but if you see the same person enacting harsh attacking energy on every single post for months on end, then temporarily hide them for a while until they calm down. Check back weeks or even months later, and then scan their wall to see if they're back to the person you once knew before they fell into the darkness of ego disguised through emotional and mental instability.

I've conducted social tests where I've hid repeat offenders, then gone back to their page after months or a year later to see if it was safe to see their posts again. Not surprisingly a year later the original offender was still negatively ranting about the media and politicians, but I also noticed their posts had little interaction on it. It had dropped off over the year because that many people got tired of absorbing the same demoralizing energy over and over. The only person oblivious to the drop off rate was the perpetrating offender lost inside the darkness, except now they were posting to no one. One of the offenders was ironically an angel card reader, which might seem unusual considering that your readings with Spirit are tainted while in the mind space of drama, gossip, and pessimism. After a couple years of that I noticed the angel reader was able to have that awakening moment where they discovered they had been out of control. They admitted the Darkness had got a hold of them, hooked them in, and kept them enslaved in that energy, until finally one day the Light came bursting in lighting his way out of that.

The other negatives perpetuated on the internet that affect the soul are reading fictional media pieces. Many websites contain recycled material that comes off more like a blog than a credible news source. Unless it is a prestige's journalist the rest of the journalists rarely do their research or homework anymore. They just lift the information off of other sites and put it on their own site. You later discover that it wasn't accurate to begin with. It's like someone in school copying another person's paper that also got the answers wrong. Before technology, newspaper editors would refuse to run a story if it wasn't fact checked to a hair-splitting degree as being verifiably true. Many stories were scrapped and not allowed to run if one fact was off. That's not the case today where they run it anyway. I've heard from media site editors that have informed their writers to just run the story regardless of the accuracy of the piece. This is because time is money and they have to keep posting to keep viewers going to the site. It's a business after all and the way to stay in business is to give your audience what you know they'll gobble up regardless of the content.

History has been erased and re-written to the point that some of it is no longer accurate. The media will take a story and begin altering it and passing it around as if it's fact. What originally happened is no longer part of the story.

It's important to discuss the dangers of the media because it is what dominates and controls the minds of the public. It is typically corrupt, malicious, biased, salacious, and feeding you altered truths that are sometimes manipulated until it isn't true anymore. Humankind has been doing that since the beginning of time. There are endless cases where a story was told in archaic days. Someone else takes that story and begins to alter it, and then another alters that one. Eventually the story becomes more of a fable than a true account of what actually took place. All throughout history this has been the case from the Bible, to the news, to celebrity stories, to school ground gossip. One of the ways the devil works through people is to destroy them through lies. Mentally question what you're reading and if it makes sense instead of following it because your news source of choice hates the same people you do. That doesn't make them accurate.

Remain neutral and balanced since you can't rely on your sources to be. Be the example and stand in the center in the middle hearing all sides, doing your homework, studying up, listening to opposing people objectively and without emotion. Move into the rational thinking part of your consciousness. Seek out media that appears to generally be objective and neutral where it seems the journalist is not taking a side, but merely giving you the facts and the story.

Many spend a good chunk of their time thinking about gossiping or judging others, including well-known people online or in person with anyone that will listen. I've worked in office environments before the author work and that was the top conversation that flies around. It was like that in each one, so it's safe to say that's the general overall way that people live. That's their main topic forms of conversation. Imagine sitting in that dark toxic atmosphere absorbing all of that undesirable energy all day every day. If you're exceptionally sensitive, in tune, and psychic, then you could agree that the energy surrounding them is permanently miserable. They're typically negative about everything beyond that. Now imagine being in that mindset day after day, year after year, and decade after decade until the end of that person's life. The only people that would want to be around someone like that are similar souls, which is why like often attracts like. You bring in the kind of people that match your vibration more or less. Those who are exactly the same would flock to that person.

If you're finding you keep attracting those types in and it bothers you, then take a step back, and adopt a higher view of yourself to see if you are guilty of it too. Sometimes one can easily find they don't like the drama, gossiping, and judging, yet they fall into that pattern when they're around certain friends or colleagues. It's easy for energy to stick to something, so in this case your energy attracts this person to you. You become one with it and then your energy gets stuck in that long after the conversation has ended. It takes work to pry it out of there and take a higher view.

Taking a higher view requires endless hard work that you have to do by the will of your thoughts and actions. The ego is trained to be attracted to the density of triviality and superficiality. It doesn't require much work to be in that space. Raising your vibration and rising above that takes more discipline than people grew up learning to do.

Spend at least a half hour or more without uttering or thinking words that are judgmental. Just 'be' and see what happens. To 'be' means to be still, be focused, and be present. Let go of any negative thoughts. Avoid judging yourself if you find that you're judging. Let it all go as if you're holding a bird in your hands cupped together. Lift your hands upwards and release the bird that takes flight away from you. You're letting go and releasing all of those thoughts, erasing the mental chatter, and the lists. Imagine you're walking through paradise breathing in the amazing fresh air breeze. Breathe in deeply and exhale out pessimism.

Choose to rise above negativity by showing some beautiful poised class. Stay centered in grace and love despite any whirlwind of darkness surrounding you. Nothing is truly as bad as it seems. When a line is crossed, then you graciously intercept it by focusing on solutions rather than creating unnecessary issues. What you focus on will multiply, so you want to make sure it's positive. If you find you fall into the epicenter of negativity, then work on moving past that and in bridging the gap between all souls, including the ones that hold a differing perspective than you.

Look at the positive aspects of a situation or walk away from it. Divert your attention to the blessings in your life, and steer clear of the intoxicating drama and gossip that attempts to lure you into its sticky trap. It does nothing to help anyone and improves nothing, but contributes more hopelessness to the nonsense.

While you're urged to be positive, this doesn't mean living in denial either. You will experience negative thoughts and feelings on occasion. Some will experience it more than others. This isn't about pretending those negative thoughts and feelings don't exist. It's about acknowledging it when it happens, and then take action steps to alter it into something positive and proactive rather than reactive.

Don't feel guilty for being angry that you're stuck in one-hour gridlock traffic driving to a location that is only fifteen minutes away. This is about recognizing when you're feeling that way and looking at ways that work to bring that back down. When someone is in a negative state, then more mistakes are made.

When a driver is angry, they become erratic and reckless. Minutes later in a fury they get into an accident. This is a perfect example of how a negative state can overpower you. This is about being more careful and mindful, but don't feel guilty for feeling negative. Be aware that it's happening and seek out ways to resolve what you're angry about to move past it. Focus on activities that bring you joy and peace rather than negative energy drainers.

To shield yourself from harsh energies, each day call upon the Archangel Michael to blast away negative harmful energy from your aura. Ask him to surround you with protective white light allowing only high vibrational love to enter. You can do this by mentally calling out to him and requesting it in your own way, since there is no right or wrong way. You are heard the second you call out to any heavenly being.

CHAPTER TEN

*Balancing Your
Inner Spirit*

One of the many ways to create more balance in your life is by dissolving toxic people. This is done safely and gradually in the same way you dissolve any toxic vice. Some people will be harder to remove if you feel attached to them or have deeper connections to them such as a family member or friendship that you've outgrown. You can't leave, but you can't stay, and so you're left torn not knowing what to do. Cutting a close connection out abruptly without warning can bother anyone on the receiving end. You eventually reach the point where you say, "I love you, but I love me more."

There are also the toxic people that are impossible to remove at this particular time such as those you work with. In those cases, you won't be able to kick them out of your life, but you can take some disciplined measures to protect yourself. These would be things like calling in the Archangel Michael to shield you with protective white light. That's what you can do spiritually. As for physically, you can keep your distance from them. Keep dialogue to a work related minimum and putting up a cold distant reserve. You're not doing this because you're unkind. You're doing this because you care about you.

You take care of your own well-being first and extract from your life whatever you feel is not jiving with your higher self. This can be whatever is stalling or keeping you from moving forward and upward, but it's not something that anyone can tell you to do. You already know what you need to do and how much you can tolerate before you've officially reached the limit. It's not an easy move to make getting rid of certain toxic people. It's one that you'll do when you feel totally amazing about it and are ready to do.

With toxic friends you once loved, but have found it's become consistently too much, then you can busy your life with other things. Grow more distant from them and be less available. If they complain or cannot handle that you're distant, then that is their issue to wrestle with. What are they going to do, sue you for being distant? This is your life and you are the owner of it.

Moving Out of the Dark Ages

Times have changed where children are handed a technical gadget early on over interpersonal bonding. This sets the stage for relationship suffering when they grow older. This is already seen post 2000 when Earthly life dramatically changed due to the rise in technology and commerce. Technology can be an issue when it dominates preventing anyone from having successful interpersonal relationships. If you use a technological device to post or comment something negative, then you are using the device for harm. It's like handing a psycho a loaded gun. When parents or teachers are dealing with a child that is restless or having a tantrum, they immediately hand it a technological device to keep it quiet so they can be in peace. From an early age, that child sees technology as the way to go.

I grew up in a time before cell phones, internet, and social media, which dates me. There were cell phones, but it was primarily only a small amount of super rich people that owned one and those were the mobile phones that were built into their cars. If you were trying to get a hold of someone, you'd try their home phone, pager, office line, or car phone if they had one. People had a long list of phone numbers in those days. The Internet and computers were coming out, but again that was also primarily used with the rich. There was no social media that gave rise to the darkness of ego and low self-esteem and unhealthy competition. I have the differing perspective of having lived before that time as well as what it was like afterwards. Today one has to watch what they say and how they say it. That's not the world I grew up in. You spoke your mind and people could take it or leave it.

Earth reached high noon on 11/11/2011 *(not 12/21/2012 as some believe)* when the light was equal to the dark. You'll notice how many centuries it took to reach high noon. Before 11/11/2011 is what was called The Dark Ages. After that date we began moving out of the Dark Ages, but it will still continue to be Dark for centuries before those violent dark times are over with. You'll note how many centuries it took to reach this high noon where the Light and Dark were equally balanced. This is about how long it'll take before the Light will be completely dominating. The positive to all this is that we're now going back in the other direction towards the Light. Humanity continues to have a long way to go before global Utopia exists on the planet. As long as love is non-existent in the hearts of the majority, then that is how long it will take to officially be in the heart center of the Light Ages. Having love in your heart means showing love to those who are different from you or who have a differing opinion than yours. What a challenging thing to do!

Humanity is gradually moving in the other direction where the Light is expanding greater than the Dark. It will take centuries ahead to reach that place where the Light dominates and has taken over. We're moving in the right direction, but when it's come to human evolvement it's at a snail pace.

You've likely noticed the tantrums around the world going on in places. They're not pleased with the Light taking over, but this is what is intended. You've got half the world with a consciousness that is rapidly raising, while the other half is settled into the Darkness. It is a war between the Light and Dark, but if there is any truth it is that the Light always wins in the end.

The light workers, warriors of the light, the realm souls, and light warriors, all of them are not exempt from falling into the darkness or into the ego on occasion. Some may be attracted to it more than others. When you're in a weakened state, you fall into the drama of the chaos, the noise, the media, and the politics. It's easy to become enticed by the allure of all that and then become one with it since it's all people talk about in an antagonistic way. To remain centered and balanced it's best to avoid it and not get into the attacks and gossip of it all, because in the end none of that matters. What's intended to happen or take place at this time will be. This is regardless if it's not what someone wants or not. You have to stay focused on what's important. It's understood you want to stay somewhat informed, but those that are attempting to stay informed wind up falling into the allure of the drama. It takes incredible self-discipline to rule your life in a high vibrational state as much as possible.

If you're on the fence wondering if the media and the news are beneficial to you, then try out this exercise. Keep a journal for a month and write down every single thing that bothers you. This means a trending topic you found yourself falling into. After enough time has passed revert back to that journal to see what you wrote down and notice if it has truly had any positive effect on changing your life, or if it was just another time waster you fell emotionally drawn to, but could care less about weeks later. It will be mind boggling to witness the long list of time wasters that prevented you from being happy, moving forward, and acting in life.

Focus on your life purpose rather than time wasters. Look to see if there is something specific in the media that deals with something you passionately care about such as immigration, gay rights, environmental issues, etc. If one of those feels like a stab to the soul whenever you hear it, then this is a sign that it could be connected to your life purpose and mission. If that's the case, then take action steps in doing highly valued research into how you can help surrounding the issues you care about that will create a change in policy. This does not include ranting and raving in attacks on social media.

What you set out to do in the realms of your purpose and life mission is creating change even if you don't feel like it is while in the midst of it. You may think that someone else will take care of an issue, but no one really is or does. If you need to go it alone, then you have to go it alone and tackle it one issue at a time. One small action step can get the energy flowing in that direction. Research and seek out ways where change can be made in the area of your interest that you strongly feel needs to be improved, otherwise let it go.

Stay Focused and Ignore the Noise

One of the purposes for some is learning to ignore harmful words said about or to you. Don't allow it to permeate your soul consciousness. People are going to say negative things at some point around you. It has nothing to do with you, but more to do with what they're battling with internally. If they're saying negative things about you, then they're more than likely doing it to everyone. That's their issue to wrestle with and not yours. You have a higher more important calling, which is to stay focused on your soul's Divine purpose.

Public figures have had to learn to ignore negative words from strangers, since they hear it through public forums more than anyone else. Because they're thrown into the public eye in such a severe way, many of them quickly mastered the art of ignoring it or not paying attention to it. Not all of them follow that mantra and will attack back, but in those cases, they're trying to defend themselves. If someone says something untrue or slanderous about you, then the natural reaction is to correct it. There's nothing ill will about correcting it as long as you remember to try and do it through assertive poise. The top choice is to ignore it and walk away, but that can be hard to do if the words are fictitious and affecting your good name.

Some public figures know to not log online and read stuff posted about them, while others have chosen not to have a social media account. Sometimes they might hear it from those around them personally and professionally, but the ones that master it are careful about who they allow into their private world. They also grow a thick skin in business learning to let certain things roll off. Despite all this they also wrestle with self-doubt like anybody else, but in the end, they ignore it and go after what they intend to regardless. They have a job to do and can't afford to drown in self-doubt that is powerful enough that it is paralyzing them.

When you make mistakes, you correct them, learn from them, and then avoid making them again. That's how you continue to grow and evolve. Everyone makes mistakes as that's part of life, but the crucial element is to learn from the mistakes. Work on avoiding placing blame on yourself or someone else for those mistakes. Mistakes are made to learn from in order to grow and evolve.

Self-Doubts

I've had my share of self-doubts in the past, but that was more so during my teens and twenties than any other age. By the time I turned thirty, I had become Divinely invincible to the point that others around me noticed the massive change that took place with me. I had a master class running big budget films for the movie studios throughout my twenties. The things you are doing now are preparing you for what's next. Whenever I'd start a new film production, I'd have minor doubts that I couldn't do it or that I'd get fired after the first week. After the first week or so those feelings would subside. The thoughts also weren't plaguing me into feeling paralyzed with fear. It was a small thought that might creep in for a second here or there, but then the drive and determination to do the job I was hired to do would overpower any negative thoughts and would quickly dissolve.

I refused to allow negative self-doubt or fear to overpower and cripple me, so the thought might enter and exit super quickly as I adjusted and focused on what I needed to do. When you're going to be one of the coordinators of a film production for a studio worth over $100 million dollars with a crew that will exceed 600 people, then some measure of adjusting to get into it is typical.

The night before every film production job would start, I would meditate for hours and move into the space of the role that I chose to take on. I would show up the first day on the job and immediately take over and fearlessly dominate my role. Any fear that might have existed before I started was non-existent.

I was also satisfied to know from some of the movie stars I was working with that they too had self-doubt and worry the first week or so as well. This was even more understandable considering that they know the movie production ultimately sits on how well they do or don't do their job in it. It doesn't matter how much experience one has under their belt because there will be some measure of self-doubt and worry that creeps in here and there.

The best you can do is to give it your best. I've always given until it hurts when it's something I'm interested in. That's when you give and you give until you can't give anymore, but then you give more.

Let Go of the Obsolete

There comes a point when you have to come to the reality that you cannot continue to keep watering a dead plant. This metaphor can be applied to anything from relationships to your job. Perhaps you've done this with actual plants by continuing to water them long after they've wilted into the dirt. It's on its last leg and you're not giving up. You will continue to breathe life into it hoping to wake up one day and find that it's spruced back up again. There have been occasions where it miraculously strengthens and blossoms right back up out of nowhere. It's able to carry on for another six months to a year, but then it officially dies completely limp stuck to the dirt and you can't figure out what happened. It was like one day you wake up to find it's dead and probably had been for quite some time. The only regret is you allowed it to drag on longer than intended.

This is a metaphor to how you work on relationships and circumstances. How long will it take before you realize there is no life left in a connection or a situation? Know when it's time to wrap something up and bring it to closure. This way you may begin a new chapter with brighter blessings and circumstances dying to enter into your life. In order to bring in something great, you have to give up something of value.

You've permanently lost the passion for something or someone, but you relentlessly continue to beat that dead horse against a rock. You hang on longer than you should. You're exhausted by it, but you keep drowning that baby with water in hopes it will reverse its dormant behavior. I've seen others do this with someone they're in love with where they're not getting any mutual love and attention. They attempt to donate wasted time, effort, love, money, and energy into something that has no return. This also applies to work efforts and project endeavors, to staying in a work position you've been over with for a while.

I'm also way too loyal and I don't change, therefore I will stick with something or someone continuing to fight until I finally realize it's a lost cause. If you've done this too, then you understand when you look back that you may have allowed it to drag on much longer. As a loyal fighter you have the hope of some miracle turnaround. This can apply to love relationships where you can't make someone interested in you. They either are or they're not. You don't want to waste valuable time on people who are not your match.

Love and Forgiveness

All souls incarnate on Earth for the purpose of love, whether that is to learn to love, to teach love, to express love, or all of the above. As you've probably noticed many people haven't been able to master the basic art of love. This includes the ones that protest they love everybody. Attacking people over a statement that messed with your delicate sensitivities is not love.

The hyper technological age has seen a rise in instability and a lack of clarity and depth. The only way to change the hearts and minds of others is to show them goodness. Stomping around in a tantrum making all kinds of noise only expands that creating more noise. It changes no one and offers nothing positive.

Everybody is mad at everyone else for not living the way they want them to live. They're angry that someone else isn't graciously agreeing with what their ego wants. You're mad that someone else hurt you without apologizing. You've held onto that hurt for years allowing it to ensure it becomes a part of your consciousness refusing to let it go. You decline to forgive the person for what they've done so that you can move on. You reject the idea of letting go of the anger for what someone else chose to do. The person it's hurting in that equation is yourself. The other person is certainly not losing any sleep over it.

Don't worry about justice being served or not served because all karmic energy is paid back on some level. Let it go and forgive them so that you can be released from the burdens it's placed on your back crushing you into the ground. It's stalled you from moving forward into the next chapter of your life with a brighter, rejuvenated, awakened, transformed, and renewed outlook.

Be like the egoless angels, filled with an all-consuming love and forgiveness shining God's rays of light down onto all those void of love and in great need of healing and clarity. In their eyes, you are loved without judgment. It is the darkness of human ego that harshly judges others. This doesn't mean that someone committing cruel crimes on someone else will receive a free pass of forgiveness, but in Heaven's eyes you are expected to correct poor choices. You are expected to ask for forgiveness and to correct any wrongs you've been enacting on someone else. This is part of developing a deeper conscious. Partaking in wrongdoing knowing you'll be forgiven doesn't count, since that deceptiveness is taken into consideration. It's like giving someone a gift with the hopes of getting something in return. This isn't authentic giving when you desire something back.

If you continue making choices that negatively affect you or another, then you'll notice the ripple effect of adverse energy roaring through your life creating even more issues until you snap out of it and realize that the way you've been living isn't working. When you ask the bigger questions, then you receive the bigger answers. You grow more open to the art of learning and evolving. Moving from a toxic monster to a centered Light takes enormous willpower, because your ego will do everything it can to hold you down. It will do whatever it can to ensure your soul doesn't rise up into the Light.

The Darkness of ego and the Devil are one in the same. It rules Earthly life with an iron fist working through so many people on the planet pushing them to cause some form of harm, hurt, or hate filled act on others. It will push someone behind a computer screen to post daily negative based words all over the Internet through social media and websites that allow comments and posts. It will cause you to act out against your soul's better nature. It brings out the Devil in some of the worst ways imaginable. There was a time when physical violence reigned supreme. While it still exists, the new violence that rules Earthly life is through words, thoughts, and feelings. This is how the Darkness does his work, which is through poisoning the soul. He knows this energy moves rapidly able to bring out the greatest darkness imaginable out of the once purest Light. His goal is to bring everyone down as quickly as possible. He's been successful at it for so many centuries. Become the example of love, goodness, respect, and light.

This is what always wins in the end.

You were born a pure Light of love, peace, joy, compassion, and understanding. You were filled with immense passion and love for all you came across. Throughout the soul's journey on Earth, it is faced with temptations, judgments, and harm by those around it that primarily function from the darkness of ego. It is your job to remember who you are and who you were when you were born out of God's love. It is one of your purposes and missions to rise above the hatred, darkness, and lower energies that assault you everyday. Move back into being the centered Light that you were made in.

Pay attention to the moments when you find you've become guilty of being a toxic monster. Climb out of that painful abyss as quickly as possible. Extricate the cause that triggered you to fall for the dark one's deception. Kick it out of your life for good. Don't forget who you are. You were born perfect in His love's Light. You have the power at your fingertips to create the most splendid magnificent life by the vibrational energy of your thoughts.

Move out of fear and toxicity by closing your eyes, taking a deep breath in, feel and experience His love light moving into and through you allowing it to become one with you. You have a centered Light within you that is waiting and willing to be ignited whenever you allow it. Make that choice today to become one with it once again. You have arrived in God's economy when you become a blessing to others. You are simultaneously becoming a blessing to yourself as well too.

When the lower energies and Darkness attempts to drown you in its dumps, then learn to pull yourself back up and climb out of that. Achieve laser focus by honing in on God and His Light. Rise up, stand tall, strong and centered in His grace. Revert back to the Light through regular prayer and faith that all will be well in the end. The more you do that, then the easier it becomes, and the less challenging life is as a result. You take things in better stride. Let go of the things you cannot change and positively alter and modify the situations that you can. Re-adjust the direction you were headed down and get back on that road that leads you towards your soul's purpose and goal. Rise above the mundane, physical, and superficial. Dive right back into the higher vibrational joy of your life. This life you've been blessed to have without losing sight of the grander Divine truths that are accessible within you.

CHAPTER ELEVEN

*Rise Above the Mundane
and Into the Divine*

Food and water are essential to human survival, but it is also common to rob yourself of much needed soul nourishment. Regularly hydrate your soul the same way you hydrate your body with water. The human race is trained early on to avoid putting themselves in the dramatic circumstance where they could be without water or food, even though many around the world suffer in this impoverished state with no evidence of Light at the end of that tunnel. It's easier for the masses to mobilize to protest or raise money for politicians or to voice their disapproval of a politician, but strangely nothing of such massive protest is ever made for causes such as child abuse or feeding the hungry. Food and water depravation cause grave damage to the physical body. Partaking in any kind of unhealthful activities for a consistent prolonged period amount of time will also do harm to the physical body. This simultaneously has an effect on the deterioration of the soul. When you nourish your physical body, then this has an effect on your state of mind and body.

God and all higher spirit beings love all souls equally and no one is ever ignored even when it feels that way. To Heaven, Earthly life is a blip on the radar, a millisecond compared to eternity. The perspective Spirit has is greater than imagined by the human mind. Experiencing that great love feeling from the Divine begins by increasing your faith and having regular daily prayer or conversations with God. Even if it feels like you're talking to no one, you are heard and responded to at some point. This is where you pick up on the messages and guidance immediately or further down the line. Sometimes you have to endure a rough patch before the light is shown. At the moment when the light appears, you realize why you were kept in a situation longer than you intended to be. This is that awakening moment when it all suddenly makes sense.

None of these statements are enlightening verbiage on a teabag for the soul. I can personally attest that the things I've asked for intervention or assistance with either came to me immediately or in the future on the outstretched wings of an angel. This means there have been circumstances that took years to transpire into fruition, but they did eventually emerge. I wouldn't feed anything to anyone that I hadn't experienced firsthand.

There were years that felt like an eternity wondering if something I desired would ever take place, but I believed in my gut that it would because I could also clairvoyantly foresee it visually in motion. This was the same foresight I'd see other things that would take place. It would eventually transpire and come to fruition. The question was always when.

A great deal of fearless confidence, persistence, patience, and progression were necessary traits to adopt.

Pray for a strengthening in faith when you feel like giving up and throwing in the towel. Ask for Heavenly help daily and believe you are heard. Request they help boost your spirit's fearlessness and bring you into the vortex of soul confidence. Pay attention to any guidance that could be coming in that is advising you on what to do. Praying, affirming, and asking for help daily is part of the equation, but so is taking action. It's that latter action step that many seem to ignore. They believe if they ask for help that they can then sit down and watch television until what they're asking for comes crashing through the ceiling and onto the couch next to them. You are expected by Heaven to put in the work as well too. It's not their job to sprinkle down blessings and gifts every single time you ask for something.

Can you imagine if a child was constantly asking their parent for a toy or a gift every single day? If the parent obliged to those requests, then they would have a spoiled child on their hands. That child will go through life expecting everything to be taken care of for it. When this doesn't happen, then a tantrum breaks loose, which is essentially what you're witnessing when some hide behind a computer or phone screen typing out words in an outrage on social media. It is impossible to have any clarity or psychic foresight when one is living on social media absorbing every bit of trending information and news story broadcast into your consciousness. It is designed to manipulate and hook you in, which it does successfully.

When you take a step away, then you are able to easily move into operating from your highest self's state of joy, peace, and love. That's when you are able to pick up on the divinely guided communication sifting in. You're also able to notice the Divine signs that indicate you're not alone and that you are loved and looked out for. In the physical world, the ego requires physical concrete material evidence of that love, but the love is felt from within like a great big warm hug. This is part of what having faith entails. There is nothing you can do to rescind that love. Spirit will not suddenly say,

"Oh you're hopeless I'm done with you."

They function like good parents guiding and pushing you to become an independent soul by doing things yourself, while occasionally stepping in to help when it's gravely needed. They are your partners in this life.

As challenging as it is to believe even the most heinous human being is loved. It is who the soul is deep inside that is loved. The intention is that the soul learns to reduce, dissolve, and limit operating from the darkness of ego. It is expected to awaken its consciousness to the spiritual reality they are bigger than the limited being they've chosen to confine themselves to. Heaven doesn't expect one to completely eliminate the darkness of ego, because even the most all loving and compassionate being on the planet will fall into the dark side on occasion. It's a limited rare occurrence that creeps up infrequently compared to the heinous dark human beings that have chosen to live a life ruled primarily from the darkest depths of their ego.

The dangers of a soul operating from the darkness of ego full time throughout its Earthly life run are that upon passing away the soul can get stuck in purgatory limbo between the Earth and Heaven plane or pulled into the back gate. This is no place to hang out where you run the risk of reliving bad Earthly experiences over and over again. The souls in limbo also make up some of the dark souls that attempt to attach themselves to Earthly loving souls. They will wreak havoc on that person's life or drive them to a toxic addiction. This could be the same addiction that the dark soul once formed a cord with while living in a human body. Your body will one day disintegrate into the physical Earth, but your soul consciousness remains, as it was upon the physical death, only now it's liberated and free from confinement.

To sense the encompassing love from the Divine it is necessary to reduce Earthly distractions in order to raise the voices of Heaven. Participate in a soul detox that includes limiting technological use on certain days, getting out in nature to clear the mind, exercising regularly, reducing toxic foods and drinks, and centering and balancing out your thoughts and feelings. I know that sounds like quite a bit of work just to hear God. I can hear the grumblings of some saying, "I'm not doing all that. I'd rather that everything I need just land in my lap while I relax nursing a margarita while YouTube channel surfing."

Use discipline when it comes to what or who you allow into your world. Your world is you as well as everything around you. Your body should be treated with amazing care. It's a temporary home you're renting, which needs to be taken care of and cleaned like any property you rent. Avoid gossip, negative news, and the media swirling around you when feasible. Detach and unplug anything and everything when possible. Get out into nature to clear your aura regularly. Shun getting caught up in time wasting drama that stalls you from moving forward. Have self-discipline to avoid time wasters in general. This is especially when you need to get to work on important matters that may include your life purpose goals, to connecting with others in healthy personal relationships for physical experience and soul growth.

Personal and Work Life Balance

How is your work life balance? There are far more people on the planet today than there were pre-technology days. This means more cars and traffic on the roads than there used to be. Work lives have grown busier and demanding due to technology. It's become easy to send a work email to someone off hours and expect someone to dive into work on it or to respond. Boundaries no longer exist as to what's appropriate work etiquette because everyone is doing it and not able to be strict about not doing it unless it's an emergency, then you move into what constitutes an emergency. When there is a small break to get away from that, no one wants to hop in the car and sit in traffic for an hour to have a lunch with someone they haven't seen in awhile. Universally we've become comfortable in the new rut of the way things are. Often, it's not done on purpose, but the masses have moved in that direction as a collective.

Someone sends a work email and they're red flagging it like it's an emergency. You look at it and read it wondering, "This isn't urgent. Why would you red-flag this?"

The mentality process of the way people work has been altered in a way that there isn't a centered balance calm in the reign of chaos. Some people are so used to living and functioning stressed out that they carry this over to every aspect of their life. Everything that goes on is blown up and out of proportion to what the issue is. They're on edge filled with perpetual stressed out anxiety that everything is urgent, when most things are not as insistent as they make it. Most everything is fixable no matter what it is. How you move through something that needs to be corrected determines how efficient you are in a crisis.

I've communicated with people who head straight home after work because they're too exhausted to go out after being up since 6:30 am. They end up going home to continue working, since they receive work related email into the night by others who have nothing else to do. They don't know about incorporating boundaries and balance. Boundaries and balance are mandatory well-being traits that are mostly never taught to each person growing up by their parents, caregivers, teachers, or society.

Luckily with the rising interest in spiritual concepts there are armies of light workers that continue to expand and grow in numbers. They are interested in anything that helps improve overall life on Earth and individual well-being traits. This is knowing that incorporating self-care balance into your world can greatly extend your life span. They will pass this onto their children if they have them. Those children will pass it on to their own and so forth. Over time a mighty movement wave of peace, balance and love energy will pervade the planet with greater magnitude. It takes many generations to start noticing the positive effects.

When you love what you do, it doesn't feel like work, and therefore you keep on trucking not realizing how much of the day has passed. In those cases, you're not immune to experiencing burn out and should attempt to incorporate some form of balance and breaks. This also helps give you more energy, clarity, and focus that can be positively applied to your business.

Design and structure your life where you are able to balance work and play. This means you are putting in an equal amount of work, as you are to letting loose, playing, and relaxing. Playing and relaxing are as essential as getting to work. Working too much will cause burn out and the suffocation of great ideas, but playing too much and not getting to work promotes an idle slacker mentality. Find the happy medium between knowing when it's time to get to work, and when it's time to put the work down to have some much-needed fun.

The noise and chaos that exists in the media around you change nothing and offer no success. It only expands that energy making circumstances bigger than they are in reality. Having worked with and knowing some publicly known people, I've seen the media and news reports of them that blow something false up to the size of a skyscraper. Yet, when I'm with them everything is calm and relaxed, nothing at all is close to how the media portrayed them to be. It's astonishing to see how wide that fictionalized account of them in the media is compared to being in the room with them on a personal level. They are just like anybody else I know except they happen to have a job in this lifetime that has propelled them to popularity in the media. Early on I could never figure out what propelled the journalist or blogger to come up with the lie they printed. We know it was to ultimately entice viewers and stay in business. They know deep down that the public's dark ego loves drama. Sell drama or fear and you'll be a success! This works because so many people buy and believe it all.

One of the goals of the ego is to blindside and distract. It's been effective with that on a global scale. It will not give an opposing view a flash of insight, nor will it enlighten. That energy isn't designed to sway anyone, but is intended to add to the noise. It deludes you to believe it's changing something until time passes and you look back on that incident and realize it changed nothing. Those that believe otherwise do so to be able to justify behaving badly.

I've never personally been able to get or understand the nature of Twitter for example, but I know some around me love it. Scanning it in the past all I saw were people moaning and whining about something they hate, or they were attacking someone they hate. Doesn't sound like a phenomenon of mind-blowing information, but seems to allow the darkness of ego a playground to create additional unnecessary gossip, noise, and chaos. Even more disconcerting was how much attention those that spread that kind of darkness were getting. I've attempted to use it on occasion to post up words of messages, guidance, and wisdom, which is typically unpopular because it's not attacking anyone. The majority of users tend to get high off drama, which is why they log-on in the first place. This isn't to say that every user does that, but it has been noticed that it seems to be in the higher percentage ranges. I need tons of time to discuss an issue or topic. I've never been able to successfully reduce what needs to be said into a limited character sound bite. When I did try that I found that it was misunderstood, because it's not enough information to dive in-depth to dissect an issue to a level that is Universally clear. It's got to the point where social media is now primarily used to crucify someone publicly because you don't agree with them. There is a judicial system and a court of law for that.

Compromise, cooperation, balance, and tolerance are what modify an opposing perception. It's meeting others halfway and seeing their point of view and goal while lovingly getting them to see your view through understanding and compassion even if they disagree.

The saying that states *let's agree to disagree* is a repetitive statement that one should use more often. It's to say, "I know we don't agree on this particular topic, but I respect you and your point of view, so let's move onto other things.

A toxic monster would never dream of saying something like that. It will continue to attack, threaten, raise its voice, and stomp its feet in a tantrum until you succumb into submission and bow to its whim and join it. Stories that move up the trending charts are the ones where the lynch mob demands that someone apologize for something they said. When and if the recipient makes a public declaration of apology, then it's found to not be good enough and the attacks continue on relentlessly. It could be bemusing to see people live comfortably in that permanent toxic state of mind. Imagine knowing someone like that personally. How is that an enjoyable connection? There is no shred of light, reason, or psychic clarity in those spaces. It is to live and reside in a suffocating darkness that will only continue beyond death. I've met people that have fallen into that abyss and they're miserable grumps in general about everything. There is always some kind of drama or negativity going on in their life on any given day. The way I clairvoyantly see someone infected is there are a mixture of dark cords and webs entangled around them. There are also disgusting creepy crawlies moving about over them that are seeping in from the darker part of the spirit world. It's a sad and horrifying sight to witness that which they cannot see that's on them.

Emotionally detach from chaotic events to come to a higher understanding of the greater picture seeing all sides like a balanced judge. Focus on love and your higher self's path knowing that all will result well in the end.

I've always trusted the Divine guidance coming in because it has never failed me. It has been consistently and dangerously accurate regardless if it's the popular view or not. I don't pay any attention to what's common in current Earthly fads, and nor do I care. While others have fallen into the black hole abyss of what's being fed to them, I have continuously stood outside of it clear minded and focused as if viewing it through a glass wall in front of me. One could easily fall into the deepest suffocating madness of human world events. Spirit trained me not to be swayed by the human illusion presented. If I did that, then there would have been no reason to come here since that would mean I'm not ready or strong enough to withstand that dark energy.

Don't allow negativity and drama to sway you from your purpose. You become a way shower and a leader by inspiring and enlightening others, as well as remembering to display assertive love and compassion. Don't forget who you are and why you are here.

The toxic monster receives a rushed high by absorbing negative energy. Once consumed by it, you're yanked even deeper into the dark void drowning into its web of deceit. Be a warrior of light who shines so much light, confidence, and love onto all sides that your body cannot contain it. Remain neutral and balanced steering clear of the noise.

The human experience can bring on extremely intense days. The intensities that wreak havoc on your life are generally human driven. This is either by your own fear-based thoughts or actions. It can be someone else's words or actions around you that ultimately cause distress to your comfortable world. How you choose to take in those actions is up to you since no one on the planet can tell you how to think or feel about a situation.

Some temperaments are naturally prone to more fear or worry than another person. Anything that isn't human made or motivated is not going to cause much of a damper except for the occasional shifts and changes in the Earth's climate that can cause weather disasters. Other than that, most drama is human related, so it boils down to how you choose to accept or react to something.

Some personalities may be more dramatic than others in reacting. When there is a fire drill, it is how you choose to move through it that matters. When anyone is dramatic, then that will have a ripple effect creating anxiety and stress in those around you. When there is a catastrophe, people feel safer and comfortable with someone present that is strong, cool, and proactive to resolve an issue. Many police officers or security guards tend to fit that personality. Those guys also tend to be Knights incarnated to another Earthly life drawn to job career positions where those gifts are best utilized.

The movement of the planets in the Heavens has influence on the energy on Earth, since all energy is connected. It's not planets that make things happen, but it is how someone chooses to react on a day when the energy is testy. How you choose to move with that energy will determine how smooth you'll glide through a circumstance.

Some people see being governed by the planets as nonsense, but those are also the same people witnessed to having a harder time navigating through the tumultuous waters when a planet is in a challenging position. They also haven't studied up on it to understand its nature, which is typically the reaction of human behavior. The ego will judge something without studying, diving in, or doing their homework on it. Reading a headline and an article doesn't equate to knowing or understanding what's going on.

Those living in nature or in the middle of nowhere have it down. I've taken retreats and been out in those majestic nature locales and there are no issues at all. It's permanently calming and uplifting without all the noise of human distractions that escalate when there are more people around. Having strong clairsentience, I can pick up on that humanity is chaotic in general thanks to the darkness of ego.

During a Mercury Retrograde planetary transit, I can be in a busy city slammed with people and notice rising intense energies all around where one thing after another goes wrong. I've been in vast spaces of nature with no people during a Mercury Retrograde and there are zero issues or intensity noticed. This is because there are no people around who don't know what the retrograde is or how to move through it in the right way.

If you battle mental health well-being issues, then you can still carry the turbulence with you into nature even if you're alone. The unsettling intensities are not as bad on you than if you were in a noisy crowd full of strong erratic feelings darting all over the place like weapons. Being in a nature atmosphere with little to no people will greatly reduce the emotional stress pending you're not reading or watching toxic media. You should be outdoors! Nature is a natural powerful healing medicinal remedy to help calm, relax, or lighten certain mental health issues, such as anxiety and depression.

CHAPTER TWELVE

*Cord Cutting, Shielding,
Grounding*

As you make positive life changes and adjustments that include modifications to your diet and your exercise routines, it is vital to be psychically aware when antagonistic energies are in your vicinity. Most people head to work on a daily basis only to be met with a colorful array of personalities. Some are good and some are shooting invisible daggers at you. If clairvoyance is your strong psychic sense, then you may see this energy. If you are clairsentient, then you are feeling what others are pouring into you as if you are a drainpipe for their pollutants.

There are techniques you can partake in that can minimize or eliminate the effects the damage causes you at the hands of others. You will need to keep an open mind about some of these methods described. Have trust and faith that it works, since these methods do and have worked for me and countless others. You need to be disciplined about it. You can always test my Guides and Angel's hypothesis before you discredit it. If you have an analytical mind that works in the same rational way mine does, then you may be skeptical about cord cutting. I've spoken with many others that were hesitant, but then decided to give it a try. They would report back to me later to say they started to notice positive changes and improvements in their lives after adopting some of these methods.

It can be challenging making the transition into a light worker or rising up into a warrior of light. Sometimes there are people in your life that hold you back from evolving. They get in the way, give zero support, or cause you grief. If there are certain people you wish would go away, then you can do so by what is called *cutting cords* or *cord cutting*. It is almost like magic in the way it astonishingly works.

Anytime you connect and form a relationship with or to someone whether that is a family member, friend, colleague, business or love relationship, you form an etheric cord of attachment to them. Clairvoyantly this looks like an etheric gasoline hose coming out of the other person and hooking itself onto you. For example, if the person is needy, negative, or always stressed out, then they are pulling high vibrational energy out of your soul. This feels as if someone is sucking the life force right out of you. This gasoline hose is actually a dark etheric cord that clairvoyantly looks like spider webs wrapped around this tube strangling it.

Whenever someone in your life affects you negatively, you can be sure you have a toxic cord attached to them. You will feel drained, stressed out or uncomfortable whenever they are around you. When the thought of them approaching you makes your stomach turn, then you can be sure you have a tough nasty cord connected to them.

This cord attachment is formed between romantic partners or potential dates as well. Let's say you are chasing a guy or girl who is not romantically interested in you. You start to check that person's social networking page daily for weeks. This is followed by a negative cord of attachment to that person. You grow to obsess over it to the point where it has taken over your life in an unhealthy way, which starts to darken this cord. Married couples, roommates, and anyone that lives together form cords of attachments. This is why some couples are so in tune to how the other is feeling. Both of the lights around your souls have connected and merged. The cord is still present even if one of you is living in another city. This is why you need to make sure that you and your partner are aiming to practice living a life of joy in your individual lives when possible, since you will have rough days just like anybody else. If one of you is experiencing constant negativity for months at a time, then the other partner will absorb that causing your cord between one another to become polluted. This is draining and can even cause you to have incessant arguments or to ultimately break up. One of the many points of a relationship is that you support and lift your partner up when they're experiencing discord.

It's important to cut cords regularly to certain relationships due to the buildup of dirty energy. This doesn't mean that you are cutting them out of your life necessarily unless this is what you choose. You are removing the dysfunction or toxic part of the relationship.

What I have discovered while cutting cords is that Archangel Michael will either remove and eliminate that person out of my life or improve the relationship. They eliminate them if they know there is no additional purpose or lessons needed to happen with that particular connection. Archangel Michael will remove the person in question if the lessons you need to gain with them are completed. They will also remove them if that person is still hanging around causing you turmoil. This can simultaneously hold you back from moving forward. Your vibration has risen while the other person remains buried under a lower vibration. They are not intending to deplete your energy, but this is what is happening regardless since you are made up of energy. If you are a sensitive person, then you are especially susceptible to the repercussions of forming an attachment to a negative and toxic person. I cut cords to certain people as part of my daily morning ritual. I mentally cut cords throughout the day if I need immediate cord cutting intervention with someone hostile or draining around me.

Sometimes when you work with certain toxic people, then it may be difficult to get rid of them. This is where some of the uninvited contamination in your aura happens. The second place is at home if you are living with others. This is why it is important to do your best to ask that you be guided to work or live with high vibrational people. If you are unable to live alone, request to live with similar higher vibrational people who are peace loving souls or to help alter the low vibrational person's frequency. You will need to raise your vibration and keep that energy in your vicinity in order to attract in someone of a high caliber. High vibrational people can sense someone who is not of integrity or who is going to be a problem from a mile away.

If you are in a loving, committed relationship with someone and you are living together, then you have formed a cord. If the relationship is based on 100% pure love and compassion, then the cord will not be as dirty, but there will be a cord. You still need to keep some form of detachment so as not to fall into a position of co-dependency since the cord can get dusty. Those that you have formed a cord attachment with are not purposely attempting to drain your energy or spit toxins into you. They are unaware they are doing this. You are your own barometer gauge to know how certain people affect you. This is your soul to protect and it is up to you to manage it. You have the assistance of God, your angels, guides, and archangels within reach for this process. All you have to do is ask for their help. You don't need to chant some complex invocation. Saying something like this below has invited in heavenly help:

"Okay, Archangel Michael I need your help with this…"

As you begin cutting cords, then you will find methods that you're comfortable with that work for you. You can think the word "angels" and you are heard and have invited them in to help.

Say, *"Archangel Michael I call on you now. Please cut the cords between (so & so) and I."*

List the people that you find to be toxic and draining. Say one person's name at a time. Take a deep breath in and exhale after each name. Do this by visualizing Archangel Michael taking his light sword and slicing the cord away between you and this other person. The people you list are those you know you will have to deal with or face that day and you definitely do not want to. Sometimes it might just be one person while other times it's a few. There are some whom you will have to cut cords with every single day for months until they are gone from your life or the connection improves. When you find a connection is putting you in a repeated negative place, then cut the cords immediately. There are those you love and are close to, and you do not want them to go away, but you do not want any pain or dysfunction in your world anymore either. For those cases you could say something like this:

"Please cut the cords between (the person) and I. Only remove the toxic, fear and dysfunction from this relationship, but keep the love and lessons."

When I've requested that the dysfunction be removed, I have found those relationships drastically improve or they elevate into something better. I hear Archangel Michael cutting the cords with one slash of his light sword. If it is a difficult cord that's hard as concrete, then he will continue cutting every day until it is removed. This can work with someone you're involved with romantically. If you find yourself not trusting them, and yet you have no valid proof to be reacting this way, then you will want to cut the cords with them. Some are afraid to do that because they fear that the person they love will be taken away. Having the cords cut does not necessarily mean they will be banished from your life. Your Guides and Angels will take care of the when and how. They will make the decision that benefits your higher self's path. All you need to do is ask for assistance. There is no reason to endure negative insecurities with anyone including a romantic partner.

I have had cases in the past where I was stuck having to deal with someone I did not want around me. This might have been an acquaintance or colleague that was toxic, negative or a gossip - all of which I will have no part of. It was pushed to the point where I was done with them. I had no interest and they offered nothing to me in the way of progress or growth, but merely contributed to heightened negative feelings. For those special cases I am quite firm in my cord cutting and even angry if nothing has been done about it. The angels are egoless and see your true light and nature. They don't take anything personally such as you stomping your feet in aggression. Not that I'm advocating that you do that, but there have been times where you are pushed to the edge and scream out for help.

"That's it! I want you to cut the cords between (the person's name) and I. Remove them from my life in all directions of time. Thank you."

I will immediately begin to see that our connection is elevated to a level that I can tolerate, or they are removed from my life permanently.

With some suspects, it can take a while to remove them out of your life, but you need to cut cords to them every single day. Do not give up or stop cutting cords until you feel the circumstance has improved. I have witnessed incredible results over the course of my life doing this for myself or I would not continue with it.

Sometimes it's a process to extricate some people out of your life. The improvement might not be right away. I have witnessed changes and shifts happen over a period of time for some cases. Suddenly that person is let go from their job, they decide to leave and move on, or you have been moved away from them. The angels are maneuvering obstacles in the way. This is in order to bring about the changes you wish for that benefit your higher soul. They might be working behind the scenes with the other person's guardian angels to enact positive changes that benefit all parties involved.

In the meantime, continue cutting those cords to that person every day until they are gone, or you are seeing an improvement in your connection with them.

Working lower energy jobs while attempting to grow your light and become spiritually evolved can be challenging. You might have to deal with someone that can be disconnected from the real reality and living in full on arrogant ego mode. They are extremely deadly to you, your environment, and well-being. You could be working at the greatest place on Earth with wonderful colleagues, but there might be one or two bad apples that you might love to toss out a window. Every time you turn around, they are standing there. They might be pushing your buttons in a negative way or getting under your skin. This is where cutting cords works beautifully. These are people you have to cut cords to every single day. They may not always be extricated from your life immediately, but you will start noticing them become a bit more tolerable and eventually off your radar. You form a cord of attachment to anything that is made up of energy. This means that cords can also be formed with material items such as your home, car or any other material items that you hold dear to your heart. You form cords to your feelings and emotions too. Cord cutting is a positive lifestyle trait you're adopting and incorporating regularly. Be aware of what you are attached to, as that is a clue as to where the cords exist.

If a loved one has crossed over to the Other Side, your cords are still connected. This is the case if you had a strong tie on Earth. These are energetic cords that both departed spirits and human souls share. Cord attachments are not always negative, but they can be. You would know if the cord has turned dirty. You might feel weighted down or lethargic when you think of that person. You feel negative thoughts or anxiety when that person is on your mind. This is a sign that their energetic cord is attached to you. You would need to cut the cords with that person, especially if it is preventing you from functioning or moving forward.

There is no difference whether the cord is connected to someone on the Earth plane or in the spirit world. It is an etheric cord connecting two souls. Your soul can have hundreds of cords attached to it since there is no limit. However, it is unlikely one would have that many at one particular time because you would feel it and know it. Your mind is not thinking of hundreds of people at once. If someone has not been on your radar for some time and you have had no communication for years, then it is not likely you would have a cord attached to that person since it has dissolved away over time. Unless this is a rare circumstance where you have been thinking of this person every day since.

These cords attached to someone else can be communication devices with that person. This is why married or committed couples for example know and sense what is going on with their partner without them uttering a word. The same goes for exes. I have communicated with exes and old friendships telepathically on occasion in the past. This was long before I controlled my thoughts. This communicating with them telepathically prompted them to reach out to me. Call on Archangel Michael to cut those cords daily.

These etheric cords grow and form between yourself and any object you place your focus on whether positive or negative. This object can be people, material items, or your thoughts and feelings. When you become attached to any of those things and it is bathed in negativity, then a cord is formed between yourself and the point of your focus. A dirty cord drains your life force and lowers your vibration, especially if it's negative. Not only do you lose the object of your focus due to the blocks erected as a result of your negative feelings, but it delays you from moving forward and brings in more negativity from other areas. It grows like a wild and unruly fire.

If you have constant disagreements with someone, then your connection with them becomes toxic. This is a sign that it is time to cut the cords between yourself and this other person. No one benefits in going back and forth to rehash an issue with anyone where two people are not compassionately seeing one another's differing point of view. This doesn't only apply to friendships, but rifts on social media between strangers not agreeing over a certain viewpoint. Calling people names because they have a separate view is not going to suddenly wake them up. This lowers both you and the other person's vibration while creating a cord attached to them. Who wants an etheric cord attached to an enemy?

Constructively explain to someone with compassion that hating anyone who is not like you is more likely to open their mind rather than sending a tirade of attacks. It also raises your vibration because you're coming at it from a place of love, then let it go, walk away, cut the cords and move on.

When you think about someone and your thoughts move to upset, depression, sadness, anger, or any other negative feeling, then you have formed a dark cord to this person. You pine over someone you have interest in, but become dejected when you come to the realization that they're not succumbing to your interest. This is a sign you have formed a dark cord to this other person. No love exists within that cord. This is why it is imperative to have those etheric cords cut.

Cutting cords does not always remove this person, so there is no need to fear that you will lose the person after you cut the cords. The only time the person is pushed away or removed is when your Spirit team knows that this connection is not beneficial to your higher self's goal in any way. In the end, the removal of this person or object is for good reason; such as they might have been abusive. Sometimes you have to walk away from someone you love because you know that the connection is toxic. There are no benefits for anyone in a connection like that. It endures the drama preventing you both from moving forward in your lives. You do not want ten years to go by when you realize how much time you wasted not letting that person go.

Cut the cords to anyone or anything that is toxic, not of love, or of benefit to your higher self's path. If you're wondering what cords you need to release, then examine the negative emotions you're feeling around anyone or anything. Are you feeling sad, depressed, argumentative, stressed, or angry? Whatever the upset is targeted to is a clue as to what you need to release. Let it all go, release it, or let them go. When you cut the cords and release it, then you open the door that brings in new good stuff! You also feel an uplifting surge of positive energy that raises your vibration.

Archangel Michael is the go-to higher being for cord cutting, but you can call on the Heavenly being or guide that you are most comfortable with. You can call on God, Jesus, or Buddha to cut the cords. Any higher being in Heaven can assist in getting these cords cut. If it's a stubborn issue, then you cut the cords to that object every single day until you intuitively sense that all is well again. If you work or go to school with that one person that rubs you the wrong way, then every morning as you begin your day, request that the cords be cut between you and this person.

Sometimes you're unaware that you've formed a cord with someone else. When you experience negative emotions over anyone or anything, then you're no longer seeing a situation clearly. The road up ahead is filled with a hazy fog that blinds you from reality. Perhaps you're hoping the object of your affections will return your interest, but none is given. This causes you to feel depressed and upset. A dirty damaging etheric cord has now wrapped around your soul and hooked itself onto this other person's soul. Cutting these cords releases the negativity associated with this cord. You do not need to be around someone who is constantly disrespecting you and causing drama. It's not worth it in the end when there are many wonderful peace-loving people in the world.

Cutting cords is a beneficial tool you can utilize daily when it comes to enhancing your soul. Your life could be a busy stress packed one where you're surrounded by energies that contaminate your aura regularly. This is where cutting cords can assist. You can cut cords to a former faith-based religion that was toxic to you. Some religious teachings within certain faiths have nothing to do with God. They instill traits in you such as fear, guilt, harm, or low-self-esteem. Those traits are dark ego teachings and not God teachings. You can be part of any faith you're interested in delving into. You will draw your own conclusions as to what feels right to you when it comes to what others are sharing. Bringing you closer to God should never be done by making you feel bad about who you are. True, honest, faith based spiritual teachings will have love and compassion with it.

Cutting the cords to family, loved ones, or those who have been close to you are the most difficult cords to cut. You can cut the cords without cutting them out of your life. It's the dysfunction that's cut. Sometimes you have to nip it in the bud and say enough is enough. It's time to cut the cords to this person or situation. My life is intended to be peaceful and not stressful.

Shielding

Follow the cord cutting ritual by asking God and Archangel Michael to shield you with protective white light allowing only those of love to be allowed to penetrate it.

I am a sensitive that grew to have immense social anxiety due to a volatile violent upbringing. With the help of my Spirit team I was able to bring my social anxiety down to a manageable level. I was also born and raised and functioning in an unpredictable and somewhat soulless city like Los Angeles. You take unstable people and give them a machine to roam around in and control, such as a car, then you have a full-blown battlefield on the streets. The energy is worse than the anger of a murdering terrorist. This isn't just my perception, but other Los Angeles natives have said the same thing. And now there are statistics citing Los Angeles as the #1 city with the most aggressive drivers in the United States. This is why it is important to shield yourself wherever you are.

Shielding is another beneficial process to incorporate especially if you are a sensitive person. Sensitive people absorb more energy emanating off of others like a muddy kitchen mop.

Take a deep breath in and exhale out. Call upon God and Archangel Michael. Ask him to shield you with bright white light for protection. Visualize a cocoon of white light surrounding you. This will keep out those nasty pests that insist on entering your field. The people you work for or whom you are around regularly can be the greatest people, but even great people get moody, agitated and out of line. You sense this energy and vibration and it suddenly lowers yours. See the innocence and humor in other people, and do not let their drama and moods affect you. Be wary of over shielding yourself or your business to the point where all are invisible unless that's what you choose. To avoid that from happening ask Archangel Michael to surround you with a white shield of light allowing only the love to infiltrate.

You can request and envision different colored shields of light around you as well too. These heavenly lights can be layered together or on its own. Your soul and aura is six feet tall, which is why your soul is literally too big for your body. It is important to be aware of it, sense it, and take care of what enters your auric field. The shields of heavenly light last up to twelve hours so you will need to do it daily as needed.

Cord cutting and shielding needs to be done daily when desired because the shielding fades after twenty-four hours. Cutting cords daily between yourself and a problem you're unable to remedy can benefit. The cords will dim or grow darker depending on the toxic people you come into contact with. Do this daily until you notice positive changes happening. It will be done with your higher self's best interest at heart. The connection will gradually begin to improve, or one day you'll find the person has decided to move away. It ends up being a blessing in disguise after they've gone away leaving you to discover you're officially at peace.

Light Shielding with Meanings

- White – Strongest light that protects you. Nothing can penetrate this shield.

- Rose/Pink – Offers protection while allowing only the love to enter your auric field.

- Emerald Green – Heals you in all ways such as physically, mentally or emotionally.

- Violet – Assists in raising your spiritual gifts and psychic sight.

- Gold – Incredibly powerful. Brings in God's love and light. Blasts away and repels all traces of negative thoughts and your lower self from your mind and body.

Grounding

Grounding is the process of connecting your soul to the physical world. You can lose yourself if you float too far upwards into the next plane. While this can be exhilarating, it is helpful to find the right balance between the spiritual world and the physical world. Grounding into the physical world helps you reap the benefits of the material world. This isn't saying to desire an overindulgence in material possessions, but there is nothing wrong with obtaining material necessities for your human survival such as a home, family, food, clothing, car, etc. When you're not grounded, you can be feeling out of sorts, chaotic, anxiety ridden, or unfocused. Grounding helps you balance that out so you're clear minded, focused, and full of life.

In order to ground your soul, find a place anywhere in nature, whether it's a park, beach, desert, mountain, or your own backyard. Connecting with physical nature helps to ground you. You can take a walk through these areas and breathe in deeply and exhale. Ask your Guide and Angel to work on grounding you while strolling through a nature setting. Take your shoes off and allow your body to connect with the Earth by planting your bare feet on the ground. This can be in the sand, on a beach, or on the grass in a park. Visualize white light moving from below the Earth, and up through your feet, then through your body, and out through the top of your head. Take deep breaths in and exhale out any stresses, worries, or cares by releasing it all out into the heavens.

Finding an area with little to no people if possible is extra effective, because you don't have the tampering energies of the noise of the crowds. It's perfectly fine to be with a loved one or calming friend who is looking to chill out in nature and connect as well. Lean your back up against a tree and allow the Earth's healing properties to work its way through your spirit. Working on a garden outside also helps to ground you. You're moving your spirit light into the Earth's light as you work your hands into the physical world. This merges the physical and spiritual part of you. The key is the contact between the physical earth and your physical body. Both simultaneously connect with your spiritual body and light, which assists in igniting your inner life force.

It is essential to ground and vital for the well-being of your overall health. Grounding is connecting with nature and the physical Earth. It can be walking barefoot in nature or anywhere the Earth can touch your skin, such as the woods, grass, lake, or beach. Grounding is helpful in obtaining a stronger frequency connection with your Spirit team. It's more than just putting your feet on the soil. It's planting your feet on the ground while sitting or standing. Close your eyes and feel and visualize tree roots wrapping around your feet and growing downward into the ground. Take at least a few minutes or longer if you prefer to do this.

There have been scientific tests conducted on individuals who were considered to be unhealthy. The test required them to go barefoot in nature to connect to the physical Earth. They used an infrared test that exposed them as they grounded. It showed that before they began grounding the cells in their body were dark. As they grounded, the dark cells lightened and showed fewer of them in the test subject's bodies. This isn't surprising since all living souls and organisms are made up of cells and energy that is constantly shifting depending on your lifestyle and those you surround yourself with.

Grounding assists in giving you a stronger connection with the Other Side. Close your eyes, inhale deeply, and then exhale. Do this exercise several times until you feel relaxed. Then, as you're continuing to inhale, imagine you are inhaling bright white light. As you inhale this light, allow it to move through your body and consume all of you inside and out. Exhale breathing out this light so that it is surrounding your body and growing larger. You might feel a little dizzy or lightheaded while grounding and connecting. This is releasing toxins out of your body and replacing it with Heavenly light. You are having high psychic input where it's bouncing all over the place. This is whether or not you hone it or take classes to keep the hypersensitivity at bay. Grounding can certainly help to bring your soul back down to earth. Have one foot in this world and one in the other.

Cutting cords, shielding, and grounding is a lifestyle you're adopting to ensure you travel along your path as serene as possible.

CHAPTER THIRTEEN

Vibrational Uplift

Millions of people around the world acknowledge holidays, their birthdays, or even the end of the year as a guide to see how far they have improved or progressed. They look at it as a time out to celebrate with optimism in hopes that the future will be brighter for them. It is when people will often say, "Next year will be better."

If you keep saying tomorrow will be better, then you will always be one step away from happiness. Feel peacefulness today and then your challenges will lessen.

You are being asked to examine your life in a deeper way in order to make significant positive changes. Many human souls have been waking up in the process. This transformation you have been going through will make the ego unhappy, because change is something different than what you are accustomed to. You get uncomfortable whenever there is a drastic adjustment that forces you out of your comfort zone.

There is often fear energy talk surrounding new diseases or an end of the world. These are all false fads that are beat upon society by human ego. There is never going to be an end of the world, but the negativity and the obsessive focus on that sort of talk amplifies the darker sides of the world's character.

Get unstuck so you can be at a place that benefits your soul. Evaluate your beliefs, values and ways of doing things and make significant changes in your life immediately. Shed all of that garbage from in and around you. This will open you up to be receptive to the wonderful circumstances headed your way. Be open to receive those gifts in the right spirit and start living fully today.

Daydream

Avoid getting caught up in the noise and drama of the world's often dark nasty behavior. Human drama flies out from all angles on a regular basis. It is erratic and unstable. It does nothing to help you or anybody. Take regular time outs than necessary and relax and smile more. Shun going to places where you know it is going to be taxing on your system. Go for walks alone, or with a love interest or friend, and daydream. Do this in a nature setting if possible. Daydream about beautiful, wonderful circumstances and feelings.

Think about the amazing blessings you currently have and then daydream about what you would like to see manifest next in your life. If your life is where you want it, then daydream about that more. Take walks in areas where you know it will not be crowded with people. I've witnessed others attempting to go for a stroll in busy cities only to dodge restless and reckless drivers nearly running them over. You're on guard and your heart rate shoots up on high alert every time you have to cross a busy street with impatient drivers. I saw a child leaving school alone and running across the street in the crosswalk in a panic because it sensed that toxic energy coming off the drivers. This is no way to relax and center your soul. It was devastating to see that a child was so aware of it. Venture off into a nature setting whenever possible for strong effectiveness.

Find a quiet place to focus or meditate on anything that is not human made. This can be something like a sunset, a plant, flower, or mountain peak.

Full Moon

The moon phases and cycles have a larger energy power behind them. The New Moon is a great time to start a new positive activity or regimen. This can be things like beginning a new relationship, job, an exercise routine, to sending out your resume. The New Moon symbolizes new beginnings. The Full Moon has immense manifestation power as well. The Full Moon is typically a nice phase to release bad habits, things, or people, while aligning your focus with what you truly desire. The energy is so powerful that it can pull uncomfortable things out of you.

Release that which has been delaying you and holding you back from positive progress. You likely already know what you need to let go of, but are procrastinating out of fear or indecision. It is anything or anyone that brings you down or prompts you to experience consistent inadequate feelings such as depression, anger or stress. This also includes foods and substances that are not good for you and cause your body to react negatively such as giving you low energy or irritability. This delays you from taking positive action and in moving forward. Release anything negative so that you can truly be free and soar upwards to where your higher self lives. When you release negative stuff, then you are on your way to obtaining your dreams. Your dreams come true as a result of this release, but you have to do the work. You have to release negative thoughts, patterns, lifestyle choices and people.

The Full Moon transit is a great time for releasing, re-aligning and then manifesting positively - so watch your thoughts! Many use the night of the Full Moon to release that, which no longer serves them or their higher self. You can do this mentally or write it down and burn the sheet safely. It's the intention that has the power. Release anything or anyone that you know is toxic and causes you to experience uncomfortable feelings. The energy of the Full Moon is potent, intense, and powerful. It brings up all sorts of feelings and thoughts. It has the force to magnify and direct your energy in large ways. This is why it is important to be crystal-clear with your thoughts in general, and especially on the night of the Full Moon.

Simply having intention can make this release happen efficiently. One way is by meditating or gazing upon the Full Moon for 5-15 minutes. Take a deep breath in, exhale, and repeat until you are fully relaxed. Breathe in and connect with the Moon so that you are one with it. You can do this longer than fifteen minutes if you choose. Sitting underneath the Full Moon outside in order to make contact with you is even better. Sometimes this is not realistic if it is a cloudy or rainy night, but as long as the intention is there is all that matters.

Mentally visualize what you would like to remove from your life. Follow that with what you would like to see come to fruition. This brings your Spirit team in by your side notating the work you are putting in to make healthy life changes. Archangel Haniel is the hierarchy angel who you can benefit from working with during that time. Ask her to be with you through the Full Moon releasing process. She awakens your third eye chakra, which opens up clairvoyance.

The New and Full Moon transits add extra manifesting energy to your thoughts. Be careful with your thoughts more than usual during those moon phases. Keep them positive and upbeat. If your mind goes into worry or something negative, then you are going to bring about more of that to you.

Check online or a planetary calendar for the dates of the New and Full Moon phases. Most calendars have those two transits listed each month.

Flowers

Flowers raise your vibration, so fill your surroundings with flowers. Purchase flowers or put up photographs of flowers. Having the real thing is the most beneficial. If the only option is a framed picture of a flower due to severe allergies or other circumstances, then that's better than no flowers. If you have allergies, call on Archangel Raphael and ask him to reduce or eliminate the severity of the allergies. Pay attention to the guidance he places in your path where other alternatives to having a flower can come into play.

Lean into the flower and breathe it in. If this is a photograph of a flower, then envision that it is real as you lean in to breathe it in. Notice how wide open the flower is with its arms outstretched. Take it all in allowing it to awaken and open up your mind and senses. Meditate on the flower or image and take a deep breath in. On the exhale release any negative thoughts or lower vibration words that you have been using. The flower's arms expand wide giving you a big hug.

The flowers, trees, plants, grass and all of nature are gifts from God to help you relax and connect with your Spirit team. God created flowers for numerous purposes. One of them is to surround you with beauty. Beauty and flowers both raise your vibration. It's a double whammy! It is not okay to destroy nature and this world through greed and naivety. Flowers keep this planet alive and to keep you feeling alive. Flowers are little reminders of the beauty that exists in the Spirit world, which is abundantly ripe with flowers. Nature is a powerful sense awakener with immense healing properties. When you take in a huge inhale of a flower, then your spirit feels invigorated. Your mind opens up becoming clear, focused, and stimulated. Absorbing nature regularly prompts you to experience the natural uplifting feelings of well-being.

Placing flowers around you can invite positive circumstances into your life. Each color tends to bring in specific energy into your vicinity. The darker the shade of that particular color, then the more intense it will be. The lighter the shade of that color, then the softer the energy will be. If it is a pink flower, then it can bring in more love into your life. If that pink is a deeper rose color, then the love will be heavier and more intense. The lighter the pink is in that flower, then the softer the love is or subtle it is.

Here is an example cheat sheet of the healing properties that the color of a flower can give off. Place these flowers around your space if you would like to invite in a higher energy for a specific desire:

- Red – passion, romance, sexiness, deep relationships and commitments

- Pink – Love, beauty, attractiveness

- Yellow – Joy, optimism, success, ideas, positive thoughts, friendships

- Green – Healing, releasing, cleansing

- Violet – Spiritual awakenings, protection, third eye opening

- White – Harmony, Purity, vibration lifting, hope

- Orange – Growth, vibration raising, empowerment, expansiveness, career

- Blue – Strength, courage, calming, honor, creativity

Rainbows

The Rainbow colors are a mixture of colors that different hierarchy spirits exude and radiate. They are high vibrational colors and lights. Archangel Raziel shows up wherever rainbows or rainbow colors are. There is nothing negative or cryptic about a rainbow connection. They are reflections of light created as a message from Heaven. They are one way that someone on the Other Side is sending you a message if you are seeing the same symbol repeatedly. Heaven will communicate through repeated symbols and signs that have the same pattern. It would depend on what type of help you are asking for if any to decode those symbols.

If your question or request for Heavenly assistance were in regard to a work promotion or something having to do with material success, then the rainbow would be a sign that the pot of gold is coming up or good news is on the horizon. The rainbow can also be a bridge or a passage that things are looking up. It also means hope and assurance that God is indeed present. Whenever God is present it is always a reminder that you need to be exuding love more often. He is always present, but when He is showing signs of His bigger presence, then it would show up in many forms including rainbows. He does not reveal his presence through violent acts despite what some might believe. Those are the acts of human ego. God is all love.

Awaken Your Inner Child Through Joy

It is inevitable that you will hit a rough patch in your Earthly life. This might be where your soul feels lost, overly emotional, or lethargic. Sometimes these feelings signify that you are on the precipice of grand changes needing to happen in your life. It is a transformative period prompting you to be more introspective. What matters is how you work through the issues that this energy is bringing out of you. What it creates within you might be uncomfortable as it is asking you to examine where you are at in your life. This can be in any area such as career, relationships or health.

Learn from your current circumstances, choices and experiences. Avoid remaining mired in negative feelings and thoughts. Heavy emotions force you to be hyper-focused on where you are at. This prompts you to feel stuck as if you are trapped in an eternal prison. Uncomfortable feelings stall your progress and forward movement. It becomes difficult to reach a place of happiness while in that state.

In order to work through these feelings and thoughts, you have to examine them with a fine toothcomb. Look for the underlying cause and message that continues to prompt you to obsess over thoughts, which have no basis in reality. What areas in your life are provoking you in a negative way? Those are areas, which require a necessary change. Ask your Spirit team for assistance and follow their guidance even if they push you out of your element. Know they do this for your own higher self's good. It is a sign that it is a time to move on to the next plateau. See only the love and lessons in the experiences you are asked to modify or leave. Make your peace with it in order to move to a brighter, content life.

Inviting laughter into your life is crucial to your well-being. It opens up your heart while awakening and unleashing your inner child. It has profound health benefits next to love. Love and joy are two of the highest energy vibrations in the universe. The entire Spirit world is bathed in the wonders of exuding those powerful feelings eternally. These are some of the biggest most recurring messages I receive. The messages sound easy enough, but why is it so hard for some souls to live in that space 24/7? Many lives are full of stresses, toxins and disappointments. You have no problem living in those conditions and choosing grief instead of harmony. This way of living is thrust upon you by others. It is a learned trait because you certainly were not born that way. You come into contact with someone that is negative or toxic and you absorb that energy. You end up taking it out on someone else and they pay that forward and so forth. Your aura and soul darkens along with your state of mind. Soon you are behaving like that too. You pass it around to one another like contagion. This is what gets passed around when it should be lightheartedness, optimism, love and laughter. Many choose a path of deep anguish where they allow that distress to drop to a level where no one can reach them.

I sense every range of energy in the air without escape and we are indeed stressed globally. There are evolved souls in this lifetime spreading humor and joy, but it's not enough to get the tides moving fast enough. Get everyone to join in!

It can be challenging being around others who are permanently mired in negativity and you cannot get away from them. They may be a romantic partner, family member, roommates and the worst offenders, which are colleagues. The reason they are the worst offenders is because many people spend most of their days with those they work with. You cannot escape them. If that one draining apple exists in the bunch, they have the power to shift the entire mood within the work environment. Typically, that one sour grape is keen on spreading it around to others who are not interested. This causes a decline in productivity and morale. It takes great effort to raise it again. This is carried over into your daily personal life when you head outside, brave the streets, and eventually head home. You pass that energy to your friends and loved ones. You suppress it or feed it by getting your hands on a toxic addiction.

A friend sent me one of those fun social media tests that allow you to check to see what your mental age is. I scored the lowest in our group showing that my mental age is nineteen. I joked that I am either immature or young at heart. This is an example of keeping your responsibilities and commitments balanced, but also remaining young at heart. Take some time out daily to see the humor in life. Make light of situations that would otherwise be distressing. You might have put your body into a tense position, or perhaps you are stuck in a rut without realizing it. You can get unstuck if you remember to have fun and unleash your inner child. You remember that kid when it was little. You saw the wonder and joy in the smallest things. When you laugh and have fun it opens up your heart Chakra, which not only invites romantic and loving situations into your life, but it also enables you to manifest your glorious dreams. The Heart Chakra is connected to Clairsentience, the psychic clair sense.

Do whatever it takes to get you to that place of feeling happy and content. This can be anything small from watching a funny, uplifting movie, to hanging out with a cheerful friend who always makes you laugh. Place your work and worries aside and celebrate your life. Be grateful for what you currently have. See your soul and where you're at in a positive light. See the blessings that you have in your life right now. Do not think about or worry over what is coming next or what is not here. Put that all aside and let loose and enjoy yourself. Learn to celebrate this life and insist on having more good times.

Get Unstuck from the Rut

Many around the world continue to feel stuck. They are in the middle of a transition or they're at a crossroads evaluating all aspects of their lives that cause unhappiness. They know changes need to take place in their lives. There is going to be quite a bit of moving on as far as changes go for them. Leaving one way of life and into another. This includes a great deal of people walking away from their current employment and into another one, or leaving one relationship and into another. Many will be making moves to improve their lives. This includes adopting a more balanced point of view.

It is time to work on getting unstuck and work on changing your perception of world events as well as personal ones. Incorporate positive healthy life changes and viewpoints. Tune into the higher vibrations of spirit to see the truth of why events and circumstances take place. Negative anything harms your health; whether that is your feelings or thoughts, so always revert to shedding the negative layers you continue to add around you.

Cause and Effect

Model yourself as the creator and as the angels do. They love you without conditions, which means there is nothing any being can say or do to stop that love no matter how horrific. This doesn't mean negative actions are without consequence since each being is creating their own reality every day. They are paying for both positive and poor actions previously made.

What is put out into the Universe is flipped around and multiplied right back to you in this lifetime, the next, and the other worlds and planes beyond. It's the nature of the way that the Universe is laid out. The energy will catch up with you whether you choose to follow the herd as a collective and partake in negative actions, or out of your own independence. The ego drops down into darkness when it has a group to feed off of. It is more likely to contribute negatively to the violent energy being emitted outwardly into the Universe when joining a group to hide behind over hitting the pavement solo.

Every action made has an effect, so in essence the actions you make today are bending the energy around you forming new circumstances that are of equal or greater value to that energy. Regardless if the energy you send out into the ethers is positive or negative, it will multiply. Sometimes what is manifested from that energy can happen almost immediately, while other times it can take anywhere from three to six months on average to transpire.

CHAPTER FOURTEEN

*The Balance of Masculine
and Feminine Energies*

Part of incorporating balance in your life includes balancing the masculine and feminine energies within you. In the next couple of chapters, we'll dive a bit more into what this all means and how it can positively or negatively affect your soul connections with others.

All souls have both masculine and feminine traits and energy within them. When you exude one trait over the other, then you create an imbalance that can lead to complications or challenges. This is similar to giving and receiving gestures, which are both masculine and feminine energy. This doesn't have anything to do with what gender someone identifies themselves to be in this lifetime. When you give you are operating from the masculine energy and when you receive you are operating from the feminine energies.

Masculine energy is external. It is about giving, action, security, and protection. It's putting outward energy into something or someone. It can be promoting yourself and your work. It can be putting effort into a relationship.

Feminine energy is internal. It's about receiving, nurturing and caring. It's being open, compassionate and receptive. It is kindly accepting praise, compliments, or monetary payment for your work. It can be accepting gifts of any type graciously from spirit. It's receiving love with joy from your significant other and showing compassion for them.

When you have trouble with some of the core examples mentioned, then this can indicate the areas where you need to work on increasing your masculine or feminine energies.

Selfish and self-centered behavior isn't masculine or feminine, but one's ego ruling the roost. If there is too much of either a masculine or feminine energy trait in someone, then the scales tip creating an imbalance in your world. An imbalance blocks the flow of positive abundance and blessings to you. It creates other issues such as the selfish and self-centered tendencies example.

Keys to successful relationships sustaining the distance beyond basic attraction, compatibility, and values are balancing these giving and receiving energies. A successful couple is happiest when they exude both masculine and feminine traits. This is regardless of the genders involved in that relationship.

If you have two love partners that are both dominating with too much yang energy or yin energy, then imbalance and issues can arise. It helps when one is more yang (masculine) and one is more yin (feminine) to one extent, but both know to incorporate an efficient amount of masculine and feminine traits. This applies to all couples regardless of their sexual orientation or gender. When looking at power couples that seem to have it down, you'll notice how effortlessly they do this dance of the masculine and feminine energy. It is vacillating back and forth with an equal balance. The more evolved your soul becomes, then the more balanced you become. This balance is balancing both the masculine and feminine energies within you.

American men have the stigma of being previously trained not to show emotional vulnerability. It was insisted by society that they behave in ways that are considered all masculine traits. Their life expectancy ended up being shorter than women since withholding and internalizing emotion can cause health issues later in life. Now it's become more on an equal footing where the life expectancy for both is relatively similar. History has shown this is becoming increasingly less common with the newer and future generations of souls. The younger generations of men display and express more emotion and feeling than the generations of long past. This is creating a more optimum balance within the composites of many men. In fact, some have pointed out there is more emotion in younger men than younger women. Several European countries and other cultures never had the odd stigma of how a man needs to behave and how a woman needs to be based on society's acceptable norms of that time period. They are more soul evolved in that respect.

Everyone has the masculine and feminine traits within them. The traits are perfectly balanced when you are born into an Earthly life. Once society, your peers, and communities get a hold of you with the wretched ego domination, then they can cause future issues within you that can be difficult to reverse through this imbalance of energies. This is through human ego tampering. You've got a required list of rules by society that dictates how you must behave and live your life, which is still going on today in a sense. Except today you just get harshly criticized through social media. They cement it into your psyche on what activities you must partake in. This luckily shifts when your soul leaves the Earth plane and crosses over into the next room. This is when your soul is restored to optimum levels before human tampering entered the equation at that point. This is why it's important to be focused as much as possible now.

Avoid falling into the trap of believing what society and your peers say you must do or how you must act. Refrain from following the herd just because everyone else is doing it. Avoid being influenced by gossip and negativity. Just because a large percentage of people follow and believe that something needs to be a certain way doesn't mean it's true. You are a full-fledged thinking human soul and have an accurate barometer within you on what is right for your soul's journey.

Balancing the Energies in Relationship Connections

When a soul is born into a human body, it has an equal amount of both masculine and feminine traits. A relationship has a brighter chance at success when both partners exude more of one or the other. This has nothing to do with the genders involved. If a girl asks a guy out, then she is the male/masculine energy. When the boy agrees to the date and allows the girl to plan it, then he is the female/feminine energy. It is irrelevant if his overall nature is typically the masculine energy. Masculine/Male energy is the one who initiates, gives, or takes action. The Feminine/Female energy is the one who lets in, receives, or surrenders.

The best scenarios are the couples that have the balance of both energies intertwining. This is by alternating from the masculine to the feminine. Vacillate from being receptive and going along with something (feminine) to the one making the decisions, initiating, and taking action (male).

If the relationship connection is a partnership where you're both the same gender such as two males and two females, then this still applies. One of you needs to be the masculine energy while the other is the feminine energy in order to create a balance within the duo. Human life has trained the masses to see masculine as a man and feminine as a woman, which creates confusion when talking about those energies in spiritual context.

If you have two people exuding masculine energies in any kind of connection, then they might experience some level of discord, arguments, or conflict. If you have two people in a relationship exuding feminine energies in the connection, then nothing gets done and no one asks anyone out or is proactive. There is no movement or anything taking place. You need to have an initiator and a receiver. This also applies to business connections as well as friendships or family member dynamics.

The best of both worlds is where you are alternating between both energies throughout the course and duration of the connection. When one of the partners is always initiating (masculine), then they risk growing frustrated as if they're the one doing all the work. There are cases where one partner initiates and as soon as the other partner finally initiates too, then their mate rejects that initiation. This is because they're both in the masculine role.

When a woman contacts or messages the guy she's interested in to plan to go on a date, then she is now exuding the masculine energy. It may not usually work if the man does not move into the feminine energy as the receiver who accepts her offer at that point. If he's typically used to being the masculine energy, then he will be turned off by a romantic interest being the initiator.

If two people have a romantic interest in one another, and they're both sitting around waiting for the other to make a move by calling, texting, or emailing, then they are both residing in the feminine energy at that moment. What do you think happens in that instance? Nothing. They will wait an eternity for the other to initiate contact. In the end, they may grow frustrated, disheartened, and might temporarily lose interest and move on altogether unless one of them steps into the masculine energy role and takes charge.

Incidentally, I conducted several online polls with single gay men to find out if they preferred to ask a guy out or if they preferred the guy to ask them out. 89% preferred to have the guy ask them out. When you expect someone else to ask you out, then you are operating from the feminine receptive energy. If 89% of the prospects are in the feminine energy, then no one gets asked out. 11% get asked out if there is a match to begin with. The majority of those polled were single and frustrated over having no movement in the love and dating department for a lengthy period of time. They are all waiting for each other to ask the other one out, but there is no one stepping into the initiating masculine energy. There's going to be quite a long wait until that happens. This would also apply to gay women as well too.

The best-case scenario is where the feminine energy person merges into the masculine energy by biting the bullet and going after the one they have their eye on. The other person is still in the feminine receptive energy and therefore accepts the proposal. Now the connection has been made. Movement continues to happen and grow pending they both vacillate between one another's energies accordingly from masculine to feminine.

One woman is the primary breadwinner and makes the bulk of the survival income. She is an executive that runs her own company. Her husband works from home, but doesn't make as much money and takes care of the children. The wife in this scenario is the masculine energy, while her husband is the caring compassionate feminine energy. This doesn't make him any less of a man or her any less of a woman. This relationship works because they have incorporated the right balance of energies.

If a couple is two people of the same gender, then this balance law still applies. If you examine successful long-term unions, then it is likely that you will be able to notice that one of the partners tends to exude the masculine energy while the other is the more feminine energy. They might flip flop where it toggles from masculine energy to the feminine energy field. This is depending on what's going on or what needs to get done. Exceptions can always be made to a generalization.

There is the stereotype that women are looking for emotional support while men are looking for sex. A woman might have a difficult time connecting with a man if she hasn't connected with him on an emotional level. A man might have a difficult time connecting with a woman if he hasn't expressed himself through sex.

This concept applies to the masculine/feminine energies. If a man or woman is exuding the feminine energy, then he/she will want to connect on an emotional level first. However, a man or woman is exuding masculine energy if he wants to connect on a mental level first. If he feels the person is a buddy type, then he's more open to sex or a relationship with that person.

Same sex couples offer another challenge. Two people of the same gender may seem to be a super easy connection due to both genders understanding what it's like to be that gender, but that's a myth since all people are complicated regardless of their gender or orientation. You could have one male being the more emotional one craving (feminine) emotional support from his partner, while the other (masculine) is less talk and more action. The latter guy is the more masculine energy of the two partners. Two women would be the same concept.

One heterosexual man attempted to debunk the myth that men do not expose their feelings. He is a heterosexual man who said that some have called him sensitive while others have said passionate. He added that he's the type of guy who will fly his fist into a wall, but on the flip side he can write a poem. He wondered if he was too sensitive.

Some women/men want a guy that is sensitive and passionate, rather than distant, aloof, and insensitive.

Sensitivity and being passionate can go hand in hand, but are quite different. Being sensitive can mean that you have an artistic creative side and are in tune to others feelings as well as your own. Passionate is taking that sensitivity to another height. It's sensitivity with some fiery emotions or temperament. It can be someone who is hypersexual and prefers the long sensual kind of lovemaking. It can also be someone that puts their whole selves into whatever they undertake whether it's a career or a relationship. The sensitive more passionate partner is exuding the feminine energy in this state.

If a man in the relationship doesn't feel the support from his partner, whether the partner is a woman or a man, then he will shut down and distance himself. He needs to know his partner is fitting the definition of a "partner". This means the potential mate is much like a business partner where both work together as one having a sense of camaraderie. You offer mutual support the way you would with a best friend.

Relationships reach a place of strain when both partners don't understand when to willingly and graciously give the other partner space as required. Many men primarily need constant bouts of space otherwise the connection will suffocate and so will he. This is why you sometimes hear stories about the guy going out with his buds to have a beer, watch a game, or tinker around with gadgets in the garage. The man in this instance is exuding the masculine energy of strong silence and not needing any kind of emotional distraction, but seeking out an outlet for action. The woman or feminine energy desires to talk about a situation, therefore this person is exuding the feminine energy. This person ends up calling up a friend to gab about it. This energy vacillator applies to all connections regardless if it is romantic, friendship, family, or business, and whether or not it's coming from the man or the woman.

The genders of human souls have drastically shifted to be equal across the board, which means it's now more common to see some women also desiring this space and not wanting to talk about anything serious, while the man wants to talk about it. This is the role reversal of energies we've noticed evolving. Women tend to want to bond even closer to their partner when they're having troubles. The differences of the genders involved are especially evident here. The feminine energy wants to talk about it, while the masculine energy wants to take action to fix it and move on. You also have astrological factors and one's upbringing to consider when studying the complexity of an individual.

With same sex couples there is another rough dynamic depending on what kind of energy the partners exude. I've consulted with same sex couples where there were two males and one of them was the more emotional one demanding constant attention from the other. The more he did that the more the other guy withdrew and grew more distant and less talkative. Pressuring the non-communicative guy to talk will only shut the communication down. A non-talkative guy doesn't open up to emotional demands regardless of his sexual orientation. You likely wouldn't charge at a friend that way, so you'll want to consider approaching the guy as you would one of your friends.

I've also received cases where it's a male-female dynamic with the female wanting to talk to her guy about something, but the more she does, the more the guy pulls further away. The one pulling away is the masculine energy that requires space. The more you hound that person, then the worse it will be. This is because the male/masculine energy prefers to take action to correct something rather than talk about it. It's the same concept as someone who doesn't care for repetitive work-based meetings. They find it to be a waste of time and a bunch of nonsensical hot air blowing around instead of getting to work and doing the job.

During my past work endeavors I was never a fan of the meeting. I found them mostly to be mundane and counterproductive in general. I exude the masculine energy in this case where I prefer diving right on in and doing the work immediately. There are exceptions where sitting down to have a meeting about something is necessary, otherwise give me the bullet points quickly and let's move on and not dwell on it. This is more along the lines of daily meetings as opposed to beneficial once in a while meetings.

There are also male-female dynamic relationships where the female is the one in the masculine role and needing that space, while her man is in the feminine role demanding emotional attention. I've had married men reach out to me to talk about how their wife is dismissive about his feelings, which further points to the energies and how times have changed. Usually it was the wife feeling like the husband was dismissive. This doesn't make anyone less of a man or a woman. This has to do with energies and ensuring that it's balanced within the relationship.

Is there also balance with your work and personal life? One reader named Missy explained that her boyfriend Tom is distant and cold. Tom has compassion and cares, but he doesn't express it the way Missy would like. There is no reassurance about their connection coming from Tom. Missy heads to work where her colleagues are distant and cold as well too. This isn't in a nasty mean way. Her colleague's personalities happen to be the quiet serious distant types that do their job and leave. There is no balance within the team where another personality in the mix offers warm and cheery sociability.

When Missy leaves and goes on a date with Tom, she finds Tom has the same energy as her colleagues. There is no cheer in Missy's life as she prefers a little enthusiasm and personality at some point in her day. This can cause one to feel glum, even if everything in your life is going well. Missy has a job that pays her bills. She has a boyfriend to go on a date with, but she still feels despondent about it. There isn't enough balance of cheer from either her colleagues or the guy she's dating.

Missy used to work the late afternoon shift at work. The team at the company that also worked the afternoon shift was always cheery and sociable brightening up her day. She explained she now works the morning shift where her teammates are quiet and keep to themselves. She said that all would be well if either her current morning shift teammates were bright and cheery, or if her boyfriend was. This is playing a part in the lack of balance in her life. When you're experiencing unhappiness where the source is not understood, then look at the masculine and feminine energies around you and adjust where necessary.

CHAPTER FIFTEEN

*Twin Souls
Yin and Yang*

God's bright uplifting blinding Light fills the planet, the Universe, all the Galaxies, planes, dimensions from here and beyond. The one area the Light rarely touches are the spaces and pockets of Darkness. It's not that He avoids it like the plague, but there is no love in that space. It's not a pleasant space to reside in for anyone. The exceptions are when a soul cries out for help, then does this Light begin to penetrate the Darkness.

There are two different types of Darkness. There is the Darkness that exists on the Earth plane in a human body within the human ego. There is also the Darkness in the Spirit planes. It is what some have used various names for like Hell, Purgatory, or Limbo. Regardless of the label used to describe it, it's not a place one should desire or thrive to live in. The pain associated with it is unbearable for a soul. There are entities governed by this Darkness that puncture into the Earth plane to enslave as many human beings as possible. You know this has happened when you see a human go corrupt in some way. This is through the avenues of negativity, violence, or hatred of any kind. It is the Darkness that enflames the ego into Darkness.

There is a Light at the end of that Dark tunnel. This is where He exists ready for all that call on Him. Like a stern but loving parent He is always there. He created every space available in all dimensions from here and beyond. He created every living soul and breathed magnificent life into every one of them. He created every soul and every species. Within every soul that incarnates into a human body, He created each soul with the intention of breathing glorious life into them. It may appear to be a complicated design to create a Universe with one planet filled with billions of living souls. This planet whirls around in a vast space filled with billions of miles of other planets and stars soaring for all infinity with no other visible soul or life form except on Earth. This doesn't mean this is the only life form that exists in the billions of infinite miles that go on for an eternity. None of this is an accident and nor is the soul in a human body an accident. The soul came from somewhere important as much as some would like to believe the theory that human beings evolved through the evolution of animals. The animals came from somewhere as did the infinite miles of black space. The consciousness within the soul is the part of you that develops reasoning discernment and skill. It has the capacity to psychically see beyond the surface and what you see or don't see or comprehend with your physical sight.

The soul chooses to incarnate into a human body for an Earthly life for various reasons and purposes. This includes you choosing the two souls that will be your human parents. This is regardless if the child is given up for adoption, raised by a single parent or guardian, or two people of the same gender. It doesn't matter who will raise them, but who they will be born from and why. This is knowing the consequences and risks that will come along with that.

During some human pregnancies, there will be times when an egg is split producing two offspring. These are Earth born siblings called twins. Human twin siblings tend to be exactly identical, nearly identical, or nowhere near identical. They may be identical in looks and/or personality, even though they were split from the same egg, but some human twins also look nothing alike, but may display comparable personality traits. This is similar to the concept of how twin soul flames are born. Human born twins can be twin flames, but this is a rare occurrence unless they tend to share a high measure of spiritual instincts with a deep running psychic line between each other. This same deep running psychic line runs between twin flames. It is one of the reasons they are in tune to each other when they first lock eyes.

The most accurate label is twin souls, but many in the spiritual community are accustomed to calling them twin flames, so we'll continue alternating the label for the sake of comprehending. Twin flames have a shared ongoing sentiment and quest from the moment they're a spark shooting out of God's love that explodes into a blinding white fire that breaks apart causing one to be two until two become one again, separate and whole, and back around again. Each flame understands what God meant when He said, "I am You."

This is because looking into the eyes of your twin flame is like looking into the eyes of God. You can actually see God behind one another's eyes. Suddenly human life makes sense if it didn't before. All souls were born out of His love and will fall right back into that love before being re-born again into that love.

All souls spark out of the same source of energy. This energy source is what some call God, the Light, Energy, the Source, All Knowing, the Creator, the Force, and so on. Differing groups, religions, sects on Earth that choose to follow their own belief system will call it one thing while another will call it something else. It doesn't matter what name a human being chooses to call it and nor does Heaven care what someone calls it, because all that is understood is what is.

When a soul is conceived from this source, it splits into two souls in the same fashion that human twins split off from the same egg. Twin flames are one soul split into two souls from the same source of energy at the same time. All souls are made as one, but then split into pairs for the purpose of having a partner that each soul calls home. Sometimes they connect on Earth and other times they separate to have distinct soul missions.

Yin Yang and Masculine Feminine Energy

Like human twins, twin flame souls also share the traits of being exactly identical, nearly identical, or not identical at all. One half of the twin soul may exude more yang/masculine energy, while the other twin soul half displays more yin/feminine energy. They both vacillate equally between the pair. It doesn't matter what their human gender is as we're talking about energy, which has no physical anatomy.

Within these split aparts, both souls conceived have an equal amount of yang/masculine and yin/feminine energy. This means that all human souls are born with a balance of both male and female energies within them. The goal is to keep that balance present throughout the duration of your Earthly life. This makes for a well-rounded put together human soul operating from the highest consciousness level possible they can achieve under the circumstances.

There are human developed traits that will prompt someone to display more of one gender energy over another. For example, human men tend to have more testosterone, which causes them to display more male dominated energy, while human women tend to have more estrogen, which prompts them to display more female receptive energy. This varies and moves up and down as the person ages, and depending on that particular person's make-up.

Typically, this energy reverses as one moves into the human thirties and beyond. Men see a significant drop in testosterone with a rise in estrogen, while women see a drop-in estrogen and a rise in testosterone. Part of this change can also be due to environmental factors as well as diet. This definition is separate from what the male and female energy is within the compartments of one God created soul.

There are also men who may exude more feminine energy, while some women may exude more masculine energy. This doesn't make that person any less of a man or a woman. Those myths are due to human ego being taught one thing growing up only to discover there is more going on in the world than they imagined or understood there to be. The energy in the human man or human woman is the gender energy they mostly convey, which has nothing to do with the anatomy you were born with.

Someone in the creative arts will tend to display more feminine energy because creativity is in the realms of that jurisdiction, while someone in construction, building, or the areas of physical sports and activity will display more action masculine oriented energy, regardless if the person was born this lifetime as a man or a woman.

There are also people who may exude a steadiness of both energies, which is the ultimate goal for each soul in order to achieve spiritual balance. This might be where they dive into the creative internal expression world on one day, but the next day they're playing in a sports league to express themselves through action.

Running your own business would fall into the realms of masculine energy, because you're taking action. Taking action is the masculine energy, while thinking creatively outside of the box would fall into the feminine energy side. The best of both worlds is when you are vacillating back and forth between displaying all facets and possibilities that your soul is capable of. This is what the twin flames convey while in one another's presence. When you reach that balanced energy state in life, then it becomes more likely that you would cross paths with your twin flame. Some souls may come exceptionally close to revealing this balance, but then once they bond with the twin flame does that rise to a fuller balance in both parties. This doesn't mean that every single soul that attains that balance will connect with their twin flame, since most twin souls are back home where you are with them indefinitely. There would be little reason for them to incarnate at the same time.

"You complete me" is a famous romantic cliché line that has a measure of truth with all soul mate connections, but even more so with the twin flames.

All souls are expected to find a happy medium where they display an equal amount of balanced masculine energy with feminine energy. Masculine energy is associated with words such as action, giving, aggression, control, and domination. Feminine energy is about traits like receiving, caring, compassion, creativity, and passive aggression. When all human souls show an equal amount of both energies and know when or when not to display one over the other, then you have reached the center and space of where your soul is the most content in its consciousness. It is when your soul is as whole as possible as it was when it was born into an Earthly life.

An interesting example of who displays this balance of twin flame masculine and feminine energy regardless of energy, would be those fictional female outlaw characters in the film, *Thelma and Louise (Susan Sarandon and Geena Davis)* In the film it became Thelma and Louise against the world mirroring one another's personalities like twin souls do, then swapping identities where one is the more masculine energy and the other is the more feminine, only to re-calibrate and re-balance that out by switching and exchanging personality roles in an effortless fluid transaction. The Thelma character becomes the more masculine energy when Louise has fallen into the feminine energy of emotion that causes her to give up hope in that hotel room after discovering their hard-earned money has been stolen by the cowboy drifter *(Brad Pitt)*.

Thelma and Louise were inseparable best friends lacking in the deep kind of romantic love they had with their boyfriend or husband. It was with each other that they had that kind of love that transcends beyond the physical attraction you have between yourself and the mate of your choice. Thelma and Louise become liberated and experience a soulful kind of freedom neither had felt before. Coming together in the way they did coaxed their true natures to take flight just by being in one another's presence in an unforeseen dramatic circumstance.

This has nothing to do with the fictional crimes committed in the film or the fact that they were fleeing from the law. This went deeper and beyond that part of the story, but the underlying focus was rather the spiritual essence moving between their souls that propelled them to keep going and soar off that cliff in the end of heightened transformation that only a twin flame union could produce.

It's helpful to describe the energies by using two people of the same gender. Using the general accepted point of view with the image of a human man and a human woman coming together causes confusion leading one to believe this is the vision of a twin flame. To see the twin soul, one must look beneath the human anatomy and gender to note the soul's overall energy force.

CHAPTER SIXTEEN

Blissful Happy Place

Use an equal balance of logic and emotion. This isn't to be confused with being closed off emotionally with others. This is about avoiding the long fall into the abysmal whirlwind of wasted emotions over something trivial such as a news story, unless you're able to practically do something positive about it. The complaints and constant attacking of others that so many partake in today do nothing to help anyone, except contribute to the noise.

There will continue to be a greater divide, opposing viewpoints, arguments, conflict, and challenges brought on by the darkness of ego. Earthly life will continue to be more of a repeat for those stuck in that rigid mindset. None of that will help to bridge opposing viewpoints until those who are guilty of it learn about the true meaning of having compassion and displaying respect for others. This also means showing those virtues to those you disagree with. It's looking for ways to meet an opponent in the middle.

Avoid obsessing over a media headline as that lowers your vibration, which creates a block. There is nothing positive gained by becoming emotionally invested in a news story. That is the overall theme of modern-day life today in the post technological age. It's time to move the held back consciousness away from that.

There are those who spend each year wishing the previous year would go away. Reality is what you make it, so if you choose to see a year as being miserable, then that's the energy you'll continue to bring in. Moving forward is not going to change anything until you decide to change.

What is one of the steps in Alcoholics Anonymous? God, grant me the serenity to accept the things I cannot change. The courage to change the things I can and the wisdom to know the difference.

Have the perception of a great actor, which is to walk in another's shoes as if you are part of their consciousness. All of this can help in raising your vibration, which will give you stronger psychic input.

Thinking and speaking positive words is preached in nearly most every spiritual or religious circle or group. Overall this wisdom might sound cliché and vaguely generic, but there is a reason this tip is so popular. There is some basis of proven truth to it. Understand the depth of the meaning of thinking, speaking, and feeling positive words. This is telling you that the majority of the time your thoughts and feelings should be on the positive side if you are intending to make a desire come true. You are thinking positive thoughts and speaking positive words whenever you can.

This isn't telling anybody that it's a crime or a sin to fall into negativity on occasion because you will. You are a human being having a human experience that entails all of the colorful ranges of emotions and thoughts based on your current experience.

General spiritual practitioners preach that you be all love and light. If every person on the planet exuded that state, then there would no doubt be peace on Earth. Since this is not a realistic or practical request that the billions of people on the planet are capable of following, we have to examine this on a deeper realistic level. Some recipients have found they've fallen into the cracks of negativity when attempting to move into a permanent love and light state. There are people born with a naturally genuine bubbly personality, but not everyone wakes up in laughing joyful upbeat hysterics ready to seize each day in this manner. In fact, some people might even become a bit skeptical of a personality that exudes that infectious joyful state all day long, while others might say I'll have what that person is having.

Earth would be a blissful awesome place to reside on if every human being on the planet were able to achieve that bright, joyful, goofy, loving life state all day long. Imagine yourself walking around in that state feeling that energy essence throughout each day. It can make you feel good, and bring in more of those good vibrations to you, but that is also not a realistic practical demand to place on a human being.

Every person on the planet is having a specific human experience with trials, tribulations, and challenges, coupled with varying measures of success, good times, and blessings. Everyone would love to have the latter kind of life and state of mind and being where you are filled to the brim of good feelings. Why wouldn't you? Who wants to feel a heavy weight of ugliness sitting on top of you day in and day out? It's an exhausting way to live with such a heavy burden sitting on top of your back.

Find the healthiest balance you can between making changes in your life through baby action steps that will help you achieve a more positive state. At the same time be realistic that you will have setbacks and challenges thrown at you out of nowhere that can throw your life off balance. That equation is inevitable and a part of life. Those types of rougher challenges help you grow, evolve and change.

It's also not a realistic demand to place on the masses to be joyful every second, especially for the millions of people around the world battling mental and emotional health issues and disorders. This is something that touches me on a more personal level. Some were born with that in their disposition, while others developed it over time due to traumatic life experiences. As someone who is included in that statistic of battling mental and emotional health issues, I understand how difficult it can be to keep yourself in balance. Who more appropriate to discuss this with you than someone that understands the nature of the beast by battling with that in daily life.

Bouncing around blissfully all day long is a wonderful space to reside and view circumstances in, but that's not what helps you grow and evolve. It is the hard times and the tough experiences that shape you. That is what assists in the soul's evolving process. This can be seen in the many success stories out there. When you investigate that person's past, you discover they came from some measure of abuse or trials and tribulations that seem more severe than others. They tend to appear composed, centered, and strong with a warrior like stance.

It's inhuman and impractical to be positive and optimistic 100% of the time. Your thoughts and feelings fluctuate throughout each day depending on your mental, emotional, and physical state. The more positive you are, then the better the results. You can get by as long as the ratio of positive is larger than the negative. For example, it can be 75% positive and 25% negative, then the chances of you making a stronger matched vibrational connection with the positive flow of abundance is greater than if those numbers were reversed. If the percentage of negativity you give off is greater than the positive, then it is the negative that will expand and bring more of that to you.

If you're generally a positive person with the occasional negativity that's on the bare minimum side, then the positive quotient is strong enough to make some traction. If you're always negative or you are more negative than positive, then you'll need to work on that. The negative essence is too great and overbearing to bring in something positive. The consequences are that more negativity comes into your life. The more positivity you can conjure up, then the more likely you will be in a state of positive abundance reception.

I've witnessed those who are perpetually negative where they always seem to have one thing going wrong after another in their life. I've also observed those who are typically positive people, and they always seem to have great things going on for them. It's too consistent not to notice this pattern. Many others have noticed this design too, especially abundance preachers, which is why it's one of the hotter tips always made in abundance circles. And that is to be positive!

Being optimistic includes looking for that silver lining when in a crisis. Not only does that help with the abundance attracting business process, but it also helps in re-training your mind to finding creative solutions to issues that arise in your life, rather than seeing the constant bleak hopelessness of where you are currently at today.

It's understood that a major crisis is expected to create upset. It also depends on what one views a crisis to be. In the latter years, any crises and drama that has taken place around me throughout the course of my life was taken in stride. When I was younger and immature, my reaction was more aggressive and erratic. That's one of the things you hope tempers with age or during your soul's evolvement progress. A legitimate major crisis would be losing a loved one, but a false major crisis might be one's obsession over a gossip media story that pushes you to see it as the end of the world. It's generally not the end of the world and you move onto the next gossip media story.

Many around me have commented that I seem to be the calm inside the storm or that my emotional reaction to things is on an even keel, while others might have a harder time with managing dramatic curve balls thrown at them. Their stress, anger, and upset will shoot from 0-100 in the span of five seconds. Others will skyrocket past that as you may likely recall seeing them in hysterics making all kinds of noise.

You might also be aware and conscious enough to notice some that rise in anger and upset tantrum energy. They are catapulted into the sphere of creating a domino effect of negative circumstances into their life preceding that. When you then look at those that reveal a calmer demeanor while in crises, you may note how strong and in control they are over an issue. Circumstances tend to go much smoother for those personality types. They also make exceptional leaders who can take care of emergencies as swiftly as a Fireman answering a bell. Obviously, the latter tend to be people that are destined trailblazers.

A great leader has calm strong composure most of the time like my 15th second cousin Queen Elizabeth I, who also shared my life path number 1 for those numerology lovers. When the life path number 1 is showcasing the best parts of themselves, they are ordained to lead in some way. The negatives are the opposite of that which can be domination, but don't worry I'm pretty regal and composed like Elizabeth.

Human beings were designed to be a fully-fledged thinking feeling consciousness. We get moody, stressed, upset, depressed and on and on. This isn't about denying those feelings and thoughts when you move into that space. Feel your feelings, think your thoughts, and be aware and mindful of them. Don't feel guilty about experiencing rough feelings. This is about having the additional awareness of everything that is happening around you. This helps in being completely conscious of when you've hit a negative state. Look at what can be done about it. Examine what caused it and what you can do to remedy it.

Don't fake positivity if you're not feeling that. Avoid kicking or beating yourself up if you find it impossible to pretend to be happy if that's not your current disposition. It takes time to work on becoming more of an optimistic positive person. Cut yourself some slack and focus on working on being more aware of your overall thoughts and feelings. If it's always negative, then work on attempting to shift that into something positive at least once a day if even for a few minutes at a time. The more you put that into practice, the easier it gets before you find it happens effortlessly and naturally.

When you're asked to be positive and optimistic, this also means that you need to be more positive than negative. This is cutting you some slack and giving you a bit of leeway to be negative on occasion. This doesn't mean be negative deliberately because you're allowed.

This would apply to those who are told, "You're too negative."

They're response is, "I don't care, I'm mad and they all need to know."

Do they really need to know or is your ego bruised about something? The Devil works in mysterious ways as God does. The Darkness ensures you remain stuck in a negative state. The Darkness part of the Devil is not to be confused with the Dark that some light spirits reside in because they understand it well. Statistics have revealed that a higher number of people believe in the possibility of God, but a far lower number believe in the possibility of the Devil. How can one witness the dark demonic behavior of humankind day after day and not suspect that there is a something more sinister interfering? The sinister energy comes from within the darkness of ego that resides in each human soul.

When you fall into negativity, then recognize when you have. Work on improving that state again without guilt of having fallen into a downtrodden state, since guilt can lower your vibration. Your overall demeanor is content and at peace, with the occasional hiccups that come in here and there. Involve prayer, meditation, and quiet retreats into your life. You can do this anywhere that helps you move into a more serene state, such as at home in a private space or go to a quiet nature locale.

You can get to an optimistic space easier if you take a step back to acknowledge the positive things you're grateful for in your life today. You can move closer in that direction if you focus on hobbies and activities that make you smile, rather than doing things that aggravate your natural centered state of being.

Acknowledge the blessings you have today that may sometimes be taken for granted until it's taken away. Are you able to live in the place you currently live in comfortably knowing your bills are getting paid? Then that's something to be grateful for. You're not on the streets with nowhere to go and no one to turn to. Do you have a car or a mode of transportation to get you to work and other places you need to go to? That's another blessing.

Make a list of the things you're grateful for in your life today. Type it out in an email to yourself. The benefit of that is it helps you to take a few minutes to think about the things that are working in your life. If it's something that seems insignificant, write it down anyway. As you're writing it out, you're taking that moment to acknowledge its existence through focus while marinating in that thought and feeling of gratitude. You start to feel a bit better in the process. You might even have that moment of clarity that you do indeed have some things that are working.

It's human nature to constantly seek out and obtain things. You obtain one thing, then you're quickly onto the next. This is followed by disregarding what you just achieved instead of taking that extra moment to realize how grateful and blessed you are in that moment for obtaining what you originally sought out.

I thank God and my Spirit team daily for the blessings that come into my life. If I need assistance with something or someone, I will request it in prayer. Once it pans out well, then I quickly thank my Spirit team. I've said things like, "I don't want you to think I don't acknowledge what just took place. I am highly aware of how you've just helped me with this, and I thank you. Thank you for putting up with me and for helping me with this."

Because I know what a pain I can be at times, even though from spirits perspective they are unfazed about that.

You can have whatever it is you desire, pending it is aligned with your higher self. You are a master magician able to create all of the wonders you've always longed for right there in your mind. This is the first place that the manifestation process begins. What an amazing power you have to be able to access all of that right within you. You don't need any divination tools, nor do you need to recite any special invocations, unless that's something you enjoy doing, but in the end it's not necessary. Move the thoughts in your mind right into your soul's spirit. Use those psychic clair sense channels you have built into you since the birth of your soul that allows you to have a direct communication line with Heaven any time, day, or place. God gave this to you so that you can access Him whenever you like. It's like a good parent that gives you a phone line to them whenever you want or need it.

Feeling positive and optimistic means not only are you thinking and speaking positivity and radiating optimism, but you are also feeling positive and optimistic. You feel this energy essence all throughout your body, mind, and soul. Feel and experience God's white light energy throughout your body now. This means allowing yourself to feel it within and around you and your aura. This uplifting positive white light energy is rising from the Earth's ground, through your entire being and spreading throughout all your senses. It expands to ten feet, then twenty and thirty feet around you. You feel this on a massive level as it blasts out of you and upwards making a solid connection with God and with Heaven.

Imagine this light clearing away anything considered negative or toxic. This abundant uplifting optimism moves through your physical body. It penetrates your mind awakening it. Your perception grows to become more transcendent and deeper than you've ever experienced. Your spirit and soul are blasted with white light raising your vibration into the Heavens, which balances all aspects of your mind, body, and soul. You have now moved into the realms of becoming a powerful positive manifester!

KEVIN HUNTER

The Metaphysical Divine Wisdom Collection

METAPHYSICAL DIVINE WISDOM
ON INCREASING PRAYER WITH FAITH FOR AN ABUNDANT LIFE

KEVIN HUNTER

CHAPTER ONE

The Power of Prayer

They say ask and you shall receive. I've been a strong advocate for prayer and asking for Divine help since childhood. It's been one of my longtime goals to devote a book that primarily points to having faith and asking for Divine heavenly assistance because of the endless miracles I've witnessed come about whenever I'd pray as opposed to not praying. My mother taught me to pray before I was five years old, but she wasn't religious or particularly a big believer. It was just standard practice by many families when I was growing up. Still her coming into my room every night as a young child before bed to pray was enough for me to take that and run with it more than anyone anticipated.

I was a strong promoter for prayer by the time I was seven years old. This was long after my mother stopped the nightly prayer ritual. I continued with it because I was seeing positive results come out of it, especially as I grew older into the teenage and young adult years. A great deal of my psychic and mediumship lessons was during my childhood years. My teachers were my Spirit team council of guides that have been around me since childhood as well too. I was seeing and hearing spirit naturally from a young age that it was enough for me to be convinced of a life beyond this one. I'm someone that is naturally skeptical and analytical before anything else, but it has been my repetitive testing of my Spirit team that has kept my faith. A great deal of what I discuss in many of my spiritual works are things that I was taught by them. This is why sometimes it might seem familiar and other times it might feel as if I've gone rogue from what people expect in the spiritual related genre.

One of the many things I've learned from my Spirit team was that the entire time I was talking to them that it was also considered prayer. Whether you are having a conversation with them, making an affirmation or statement, then you are essentially praying. When I have a problem I immediately go directly to God and my Spirit team to discuss it. If I'd need an answer that wasn't forthcoming, then I'd continuously ask them, "You've got to give me something on this. Anything."

Within a few days the answer would come in that was pleasing enough for my ego to drop it for awhile. It gave me the comfort and peace of mind that would remind me to relax and understand that things are moving towards the wanted desire. When it's time for what I want to surface, then it will take place on Divine timing. Eventually I'd see it surface and I'd quickly be grateful and blessed.

I'd say, "Okay, I'm sorry I'll never doubt again."

That of course is a lie. Because once my ego rises again on something, I want that isn't happening fast enough, I'd repeat the cycle with them. I'm certainly not exempt from watching my ego rise. The difference is that I'm hyper cognizant and aware I've moved into that space. If the ego is strong enough, I'll rebel and say, "I don't care right now. I need to stomp around and get this out of me."

As my soul's consciousness evolved over the years, the tantrums grew less as I learned to be more patient than I normally was. The majority of the time I've learned with maturity to bring it down quickly, then of course again I'm apologizing for my behavior. They're unfazed by it and understand that I'm wrestling with the dreadful dark human ego. I'll pray to help relax and contain it, then help me get re-centered again into warrior mode. As I've grown older it's become easier to master.

Friends and family could be having an issue and I'd interrupt to say, "I'm going to stop you right there. Have you prayed for help with this?"

Ah-okay, you're welcome.

Sometimes I'll receive silence for a beat, then the other party meekly says, "Well no because...".

I interrupt, "Okay well do you want help or not? Look, nothing else you're doing is working right now, so what do you have to lose by asking for heavenly help in prayer?"

I've had some ask, "How do I pray? I don't know how."

They've never done it before or might not have grown up in a house that believed in prayer or considered it, so therefore they weren't taught to know how easy it is. I've had those same people come back to me weeks later, "You're not going to believe this, I finally got a breakthrough! The praying actually worked! I can't believe it. You were right."

Some never believed in prayer or bothered with it much because they assumed it was something that only the serious religious do. Prayer is not a special act that belongs to any particular group. Prayer is allowed to do by anyone at any time regardless if you are a believer or not. You might ask God or your Spirit team for something in prayer verbally, but in your heart, they know what you really want. It is what is in your heart that Spirit reads.

You might ask for something less than what you desire, because you fear asking for too much. You desire that home of your dreams in a certain area, but you ask for something smaller because you're afraid to go big. With that scenario some have become surprised when they asked for one thing, but received something even better. When I started praying for help on certain things I desired, I'd watch one year go by, then another, and another. I didn't give up hope or stop praying. Years from the point when I started praying, I finally got that breakthrough and that long running desire I wanted was granted.

There is a reason God delays certain blessings. He may have something much bigger than you had in mind and that takes longer to make happen. Do you want something menial that will be disappointing in the end right away? Or do you want to wait a bit longer for the big gold that ends up lasting? I'll be patient and wait a bit longer.

I've had someone tell me he was having constant issues at work. I asked him, "Have you prayed for help with that?"

He asked, "You can pray for something like that?"

I said, "You can pray for anything you like. There are no requests that are exempt from being asked for."

He asked, "What if it's not something God approves of or it's something greedy?"

I said, "Then He won't give it to you."

One of the other things I've been taught from my guides is that while prayers help for other people to an extent, the daily prayers coming directly from the person in trouble is a hundred times more effective. When you're praying for other people, you're driving at 25 mph, but the person that prays daily for their own stuff increases that speed to 60 mph. This is to breakdown the discord in understandable terms. If you're praying for someone that isn't a believer or isn't bothering to pray, then the effectiveness is only a mild improvement that could increase if the other person does it too. The exceptions would be someone that is incapable of praying such as if they are in a coma.

Sometimes heavenly assistance is not forthcoming for a variety of reasons. It could be you are being guided to take action steps that will help move you out of the stagnancy you're in, but you're either not picking up on this guidance, or you have fear about making this move because it might feel that it's moving you out of your comfort zone and into a negative repercussion. God nor any high vibrational spirit being in Heaven will guide you into a disaster. What might seem like a scary move could be the one that ends up propelling you upwards into the sphere of Divinity.

This doesn't mean that God and your Spirit team sit back and act like Genie's in a bottle waiting to grant your wishes. If one is only praying for abundance and gifts, but isn't doing the soul growth work, then this will play a part in whether or not blessings will come.

Playing on your phone and surfing the Internet all day blocks divinely guided psychic messages. It's a distraction that pulls you away from heavenly communication that is attempting to filter in. This isn't said with the intention of instilling guilt feelings for being on your phone. This is about counter balancing some of those moments by devoting at least a few minutes to ten minutes a day to communicate in prayer. How often have you reached for your phone out of boredom instead of taking a few minutes to give God some of your time?

Praying persistently and daily isn't just praying for blessings, money, love, or a new job. This is also about offering gratitude and humility. You express your appreciation for the things that are going well in your life. It also helps in establishing a stronger relationship with God and your Spirit team. In order for any relationship to thrive and grow stronger you have to show up. You have to put in the work and communicate with one another. The same goes for God and your heavenly guardians. You don't want to turn into an entitled soul only going to Spirit with a list of daily demands.

Imagine that you have kids if you don't, and every time they walk in the door, they're only asking you for things. They never talk to you unless they need something from you. You would get annoyed pretty fast that that's all they see you as and that they have no interest in spending time with you at all. This is to offer some perspective of God as the parent and you as the child. He nor heavenly beings mind it when you ask for blessings or help with things that give you comfort such as security. They'd also like it more if you were interested in spending time with them because you want a relationship, and not because you want them to keep giving you presents and opening doors to abundance.

You can put in requests with Heaven for blessings and desires, but also offer gratitude, be grateful, and see how you can positively be of service to them. Blessings won't automatically land on your lap with the snap of the finger. They may be planting action steps into your consciousness for you to take that should be adhered to. When you're receiving nudges, signs, and symbols of the same thing repeatedly, then don't ignore that. The Devil, Darkness, and your lower self's ego will do its best to sway you from acting through procrastination and negative thoughts and words. I've learned that the hard way during my days of human adolescence.

The Devil's goal is to wear people out, which he can do by attacking your mind. Those negative thoughts that talk you out of good things are the Darkness getting in there to prevent you from moving forward. God and the Light want to see you prosper, evolve, and thrive on all levels. While the Devil and Darkness prefer the opposite where they help you to create your own self-sabotage and downfall.

The Darkness will infect your mind with lies. This soon affects your thoughts and then your emotions. The dark energy wants people independent from God's will. That's why he grows angry when someone defies that and doesn't fall for his deceit, because then he knows he lost another soul to the Light, which he can't stand. The way to anger the Darkness is to stand strong in the Light.

The Darkness can work through other people to attempt to stall you from moving forward. It's the same way the Light can work through people. I've definitely spent this lifetime having the enemy attempt to stall me by using other people as pawns, which is super easy to do. Luckily, the Light has countered that by then working through other people to undo whatever the Darkness just tried to do. This is the moment you feel Divine empowerment.

Some look at empowerment as a negative word. Empowerment is not about gaining fame or financial success. Empowerment here is more about feeling soul and spirit empowerment because God is working through you from the inside and out. The side effect would be success on some level, but that's not the goal. Empowerment is waking up each day with a bright new optimistic outlook. It's a sign the angels are working on you and your consciousness is receiving that in the right spirit. I know that feeling well as it seems to naturally move within me regularly. When I've had those lower moments in my past such as a relationship break up or any disappointment, then deep down I know there is that warrior soul strength that is lit by the Divine. It always eventually rises up back within me prompting me to stand tall preparing to aim, seize, and fire! The empowering moments continue to rise and rise again.

CHAPTER TWO

*Be Vigilant with
Prayer and Affirmations*

So many struggling to make ends meet, struggling to get by, struggling uphill period. This isn't unusual, as humankind has infinitely struggled throughout Earth's history to achieve peace and happiness. That's one thing that most everyone can agree on. The goal is the same for all and that is to be happy. Even the permanent miserable grumps deep down in their soul essence long for that joyful content feeling. It makes you feel good and blasts away any moody irritable unhappiness.

As you read this now, I surround you with the Light of the Holy Spirit as well as angels who are of 100% pure uplifting love and to help in raising your vibration and to assist you along your life's path and purpose.

When in doubt, ask for help from above, even if you don't see evidence of movement. If your faith wavers due to lack of evidence, then ask to have your faith boosted. Miracles happen daily as Guides and Angels in Heaven work tirelessly guiding every soul on the planet to make life a little more pleasant. That's seven billion souls living an Earthly life with at least one guide and one angel per person. That's at least 14 billion spirit beings guiding every human soul on the planet. They can only do so much. Their job is to guide you, not hand you everything the second you ask for it. They are also dealing with the free will choice of human beings. Most people are not that in tune to the guidance and messages coming through from above, nor do they understand how to recognize it, yet each and every soul has the strong capacity for receiving incredible psychic hits.

It's not like Heaven can drop a bucket of cash on everybody's doorstep as much as many people would rather enjoy that. What would everyone learn if that were the case? Those who are well to do financially are also not exempt from troubles I can assure you.

If something isn't forthcoming, then there are reasons beyond what you cannot comprehend or understand at the time. There are also circumstances and experiences that you need to be enlightened about on your own.

Sometimes heavenly assistance is not forthcoming for a variety of reasons. It could be that you are being guided to take action steps that will help move you out of the stagnancy you're in, but you're either not picking up on this guidance, or you have fear surrounding this move since it might feel like it's moving you out of your comfort zone. You fear a negative repercussion, but no high vibrational spirit being in Heaven will guide you into a disaster. What might seem like a scary move could be the one that ends up moving you upwards.

I have forever believed in the power of prayer. This is not because it's taught in some circles to do. This is because I have witnessed miraculous intervention and changes in my own life as well as for others only after I prayed. When I did nothing, then nothing changed. When I asked for assistance or prayed, then I noticed positive changes come about. I wouldn't continue with anything unless I knew it worked. This is one of the many reasons I have been a lifelong advocate of prayer.

Sometimes Divine intervention happens immediately, while other times the assistance isn't forthcoming right away, but with those cases I have noticed it eventually comes to fruition at some point. I have incorporated daily prayer throughout the course of my entire life because it works.

Many are usually surprised over the humor that pops in and out at times while talking to Heaven. That's because Heaven is not some stern, harsh, cold place. It's filled with uplifting love, peace, and joy. Those are qualities that all beings in Heaven exude. They are bathed in those energies, which equates to also having immense humor. You can then likely gather that this is how they view circumstances in the practical based Earthly world. They see most of what goes on in a humor filled light rather than the tragic offended manner that many on Earth view circumstances around them in.

Some atheists or non-believers do not accept prayer as anything that works, but they're also unaware that they are praying without realizing it. I've heard of cases where a non-believer takes time out each day to sit with their thoughts. In that instance, they are communicating with God whether they believe they are or not. You are a piece of God. Every atom and cell that exists in all dimensions is Him.

You can use prayer to boost your faith, reduce fear, and give you crystal clear psychic perception. Prayers are much like affirmations in that it is the intention behind the words that have weight. The stronger your intention within your prayers, then the brighter the light around it is.

Heaven sees affirmations and prayer as lights being shot upward into the Universe. These lights are of varying shades. Some prayers have a brighter and stronger light around them, while other prayers appear dimly lit if it's a prayer or affirmation that has ego-based property energy within it that benefits no one except the ego. Other times the dimly lit prayers can be a request that is not considered urgent. It could be you really want that brand-new tech gadget that the store just received, whereas a brighter lit prayer would be coming from someone who is in immediate physical danger.

Children's prayers tend to have some of the brightest lights around them. Part of that has to do with the fact that most Children have not become jaded and believe in a higher power, whereas an adult might have some doubt energy within their prayer, which actually darkens the light being shot into the air. Asking for a boost in faith strengthens this light within the prayer.

During the early childhood days when my mother was praying with me, one of the things that stood out was there was no judgment or negativity associated with these prayers at all. She is an incarnated angel, so those prayers were bathed in 100% compassion for all people. My mother's faith eventually waned over the years and my father struggled to have some resemblance of faith. It was ironic that in an extended family that I had the most faith that would only grow stronger as I moved into adulthood. Part of this was due to the fact that I could hear my Spirit team, so I knew there was something bigger than the physical plane that existed. I mainly grew up in a home of atheists and agnostics, but as I grew more vocal with my teachings many of the family members slowly awakened their skepticism. The point of that is I wasn't influenced by anyone around me growing up when it came to my spiritual beliefs. It was Heaven that heavily influenced me.

Many people sometimes feel as if the Divine does not love them, or that they're being ignored, neither of which are true. All are loved and no one is ignored. When it feels that way, then that has to do with your feelings, which ebb and flow. Feelings are not incessantly accurate when it's a reaction generated by the ego. The best way to feel loved by the Divine varies from one person to the next, but you can start by increasing your faith, having regular prayer and conversations with the Divine, even if it feels like you're talking to no one. You are heard and eventually you start noticing the signs that you're not alone and that you are loved. In the physical world, the ego requires physical concrete material evidence of that love, but the love is felt from within like a great big warm hug.

I find all forms of prayer have worked and have been equally successful for me. This is regardless of hands clasped together, in meditation, in writing, or while in motion. There hasn't been one method that works better than the others. This is because it doesn't matter how you do it, but that you do it. The most immediate way of receiving answers in a prayer is while in a calm state of mind, which means that sometimes the response will come about long after the prayer was executed.

Have the intention that you will clearly hear, see, feel, and know the messages and guidance Heaven wishes to relay to you. Visualize crystal clear bright white light shining onto your soul in order to awaken it from slumber. Imagine the white light blasting away any and all of the toxic dark debris that may have accumulated on or around you.

The psychic clair senses within all souls are nothing unusual, because it is through those senses that the spirit and soul communicate with one another back home on the Other Side. Soul mates or couples that are super tight on Earth have a telepathic communication between one another where they are able to sense what the other is going through or thinking. Some people have joked that they wished they could read someone's mind. Well, back home in Heaven that is how others communicate with each other. There are no lies created, because everyone already knows the truth.

You may also call upon a specific Archangel to assist in opening up your various psychic clair channels. Below are the top four psychic clair senses that all Heavenly beings communicate through you with. Call on these Archangels for assistance in awakening that particular clair:

Archangel Uriel: Claircognizance (clear knowing)
Archangel Haniel: Clairsentience (clear feeling)
Archangel Zadkiel: Clairaudience (clear hearing)
Archangel Raziel: Clairvoyance (clear seeing)

CHAPTER THREE

*Ask for Divinely Guided
Angelic Help*

No one is ever truly in any kind of danger and all is always well in the end. You have Earthly life challenges that hinder your movement from day to day events such as getting your brakes fixed on your car. Now that's another expense you have to deal with. Other challenges such as figuring out how you're going to get out of work early to make it to your son's baseball game, to wondering if your love mate is cheating on you. You have larger challenges such as the death of a soul close to you leaving you to wonder how you'll continue on. A physical death is not the end as hard as that it is to accept and understand when moving through the grieving process. The soul simply moved onto more magnificent destinies that await it. Earthly life is the most limited restricting destiny that it truly is a soul relief to graduate from it.

Signs and symbols of angelic help are all around when you take the time to pay attention and notice it. The top important step is to ask for help, since no being in Heaven can intervene or offer assistance to anyone who doesn't ask for help. Some people may not believe that's possible or they have stopped believing, so they continue to suffer. It doesn't take much effort or time out of your day to stop what you're doing and ask for assistance from above. What do you have to lose by asking? If nothing else you've tried has helped, then what could it hurt to say the words?

Another step beyond asking for help is to be aware by paying attention to the repetitive action steps you may be guided to do. You might say, "I've asked for help and heard nothing."

Sometimes you're not going to hear the answer audibly or verbally. You might be given messages, answers, and guidance through nudges, signs, symbols, or other ways that can get your attention. Perhaps after you've asked for help, you're invited to an event or party, but choose not to go because you're uncomfortable with social settings. You failed to notice the synchronicity that took place following you asking for heavenly guidance. Your Spirit team may have been orchestrating a meeting between you and another person who will be at this event. This other person could end up being someone that is connected to a future job you'll have, or they could be the next relationship partner or a new friend. Instead you chose to stay home alone when you were being asked to follow this guidance with an action step.

Asking for help can also entail asking another person for help since God and the angels also work through other people. You might be afraid to ask someone for assistance because you're shy or you don't want to bother or burden them. You might have a great deal of pride and are used to doing things yourself. Even the most self-sufficient person can use a hand occasionally. Sometimes the support can come in the form of helpful words of advice from another person. If you're down and out, then just talking to someone can be a great way to access support.

You might ask for Divine assistance, but then you start visualizing how you expect the answer to come in. The visualization soon forms into worry, which is a prayer killer. When you ask for help, step out of the way and busy yourself with other things. Meanwhile, allow the prayer request to come into your life the way it's supposed to on Divine timing. This is the same way you ask a friend or anyone else for help with anything, but then you end up getting frustrated. You then take over and do it yourself instead of allowing and trusting the other person to handle it in their own way. When you ask for Divine guidance or assistance, then let it go and step out of the way without interfering so God can handle it.

You could feel guilt or unworthiness about achieving success, which also creates a block. You see other successful people and the lower self part of you brings you down, "I'm nothing like them. Look at this woman. She's so good looking and this is why everyone is buying her products. And look at me, I don't have that look that people are attracted to."

Everyone has something of value to offer the public that helps them in some way. Looks will only get someone so far. Eventually looks fade, so if they don't have something else going for them, then they'll end up being a flash in the pan. Many have found this out the hard way. They were bowed down to for their looks in their twenties, but when they move into their thirties, forties, and beyond, they notice people are paying less attention to them. They discover society shuns or ignores them the way some do with older people on the sidewalk or in passing.

Abundance is not automatically granted to those that seek and ask for it. There are numerous factors that have to come into play. Sometimes life lessons and experience need to happen before the rewards come in. Sitting around wishing and hoping for a miracle will generally not bring in the miracle. Tough times are part of the soul's growth process before the floodgates of abundance and blessings are cracked open.

You pray for help, follow the guidance coming in, and then put in those action steps. Putting in action steps towards your goals can increase your odds of bringing in what you desire. This is due to a combination of factors from action movement to the positive excited feelings you have building up inside of you about the endeavor. The universe detects this optimistic energy you radiate outwardly. As you partake in endeavors that have a positive meaning for you, then playing an active role in the process will help over doing nothing. It's like the old saying that if you want to increase your chances to winning the lottery, then you have to buy a ticket. It doesn't mean you'll win the lottery, but you have more of a shot than if you didn't buy a ticket. This metaphor is similarly aligned with your dreams and goals coming to fruition.

If you don't ask for help, then how can the doorway to bring in help be forthcoming? Asking for help includes inviting in God and your Spirit team in your life to work with you daily. Working with you doesn't mean to grant all of your wishes. It is to guide you towards what you need to personally do to help move things along towards positive blessings. This includes the life lessons that will move you towards that doorway of light.

You can verbally ask for God and your Spirit team's help out loud, mentally in prayer, or you can write it out. It doesn't matter how you ask for heavenly help, but that you do. This is due to God's universal free will law that says no higher spirit being in Heaven can assist any soul unless they've been given permission to do so. This doesn't automatically mean that what you are asking for help with will happen or that it will happen right away. Be as clear as possible with your request, because your Spirit team follows what you ask for. If you are not specific, then you might be surprised by what comes in or doesn't come in. If the request sounds wishy-washy or unclear, then something else may come in that you don't want, or nothing at all will come in. You may even wonder why something came in that you didn't want, but then you recall what you asked for and realize that you indirectly requested it without realizing it.

Part of helping prayer requests along includes to think about what you'd like to have or what you'd like to accomplish. Visualize it happening in your mind, then put in daily practice of keeping it there. Let it overflow your entire body, mind, and soul with the essence of that desire. Make a pact to do this daily. You can do this at the start of the day upon waking, at night upon falling asleep or both. It won't hurt to do it more than once a day.

I was training with weights in a workout with a fitness friend. As I'm lifting, I asked, "Should I do another rep?"

He said, "It can't hurt."

This is similar to making your dreams come true. It cannot hurt to give more than you typically give.

Don't worry about not asking for the right thing because requests are not automatically granted like Santa Claus with a sleigh full of gifts. If something is not aligned with your higher self, or if it's something bathed in greed, then it is unlikely to transpire. If it does, then it isn't long before something upsets that balance. This has been witnessed in cases where the greedy that achieve through deceitful means meet their demise at some point in their life.

Ask for help and have crystal clear intentions about what you desire. If you feel unsure of what you want, then this can create unsatisfactory results. If you fear asking for the wrong thing, then it is this fear that can manifest into a prayer block. Other blocks can be fear that you don't deserve help or fears of being selfish. Be sure of what you want and don't hold back for fear of asking for the wrong thing. Don't worry about whether or not your request is a selfish request or not. Your request may be selfish, but your Spirit team might not think so. If the request is considered selfish or not aligned with your souls' purpose, then the wish will unlikely be granted anyway.

Attracting in abundance and the laws of attraction believe that you can manipulate the energy in your life by the power of your own thoughts. It is much more complicated than that in Divine spiritual truth. The real truth is that if you work hard enough with persistence, passion, and optimism, and you couple that with prayer, then you have a far greater chance of achieving and reaching your goals. If you don't try, then you won't have a shot. If you battle with feeling depressed, worthless, or have low self-esteem, then the first steps will be to work on improving your well-being state. If your well-being state is perpetually in a negative state, then first focus on ways to improve that. This is not about someone who has the occasional drop down into negativity, but rather about those who battle uphill in life in that negative state every single day.

You can pray to God to improve your emotional state. If you're trying to accomplish something or you feel stuck and this is draining your life force, then pray to have your faith boosted and your emotional state brought to the heavenly dominated traits of love, joy, and peace.

Working on improving life's matters requires your dedication and persistence one day at a time through prayer and following the guidance given. You implement new strategies and techniques to apply to your life that help dissolve those negative feelings and thoughts you carry around. This is also why taking care of yourself on all levels possible is beneficial. It helps to keep you working on optimum levels while cracking open the psychic communication line with God. All of this is included as part of the process towards slamming that soul enlightenment door wide open.

CHAPTER FOUR

*Turn Prayers
Into Manifestation*

We are in a critical state as a human race. Many are unhappy with where they are at in their lives attempting to reach for a miracle or an answered prayer. You wake up in the morning and your mind immediately moves into worry or something negative. You know how this makes you feel and it's not pleasant. This is how you have set the tone and theme for your day. I have certainly had those moments in my past. Every morning my eyes open I move into a Divine channel and communicate with God and my Spirit team.

I may ask them, "Is there anything I need to know right now or is there anything you would like to discuss?"

I will also let them know what I am grateful and thankful for. This is followed by positive affirmations, which have a higher frequency vibration when you say them.

Read this line: "I'm broke and never have any money."

How does that feel to you? It feels heavy doesn't it? I felt that just writing it. Well, guess what you're summoning? You're bringing in more of that broke stuff to you.

How about instead you say something like: "I have plenty of money flowing into my world that never stops. I am taken care of and my needs are met in all ways."

Notice how saying that makes you feel.

Your lower self is the imposter self that will chime in at about this moment.

"Yeah, well I don't have a lot of money. I wish."

The Darkness will feed you self-deprecating thoughts such as, "I'll never get that job. I'm too old. I'm too fat. They want someone younger and better looking."

When the Darkness and lower self runs the show that is your life, then it seeks to undo the greatness that you were born with. It does not want to see you happy or succeed. Whereas God and your higher self knows there is plenty to go around and works with you to ensure you are taken care of and guided to circumstances that bring you closer to hitting gold.

When you say something like, "I'm never going to get that job." Then it feels as if there is a heavy weight of an elephant sitting on you. It makes you feel low and worthless, which subsequently begins to bring in that same energy into your life. What spirals in is a domino effect of more negative things that only increase those feelings of low self-worth.

Now firmly say believing it: "I WILL get that job."

Much better.

Now say: "I HAVE this job, and all is wonderful."

Even better!

Say it as if you have it and mean it. Even if you don't have it yet, say it every day as if you do. Never stop saying it or believing it. This is what a positive affirmation is. It trains your mind to be in that space more than when it's not.

The main aspects where people struggle the most are the areas of career, love, finances, home life and health. These are the areas that people often want to look at when they get a reading or consultation with a professional. It's no surprise that they are all connected to physical human survival and happiness, so it's understandable to long for those basic human desires. It's difficult to comprehend that in order to begin reaching those physical desires, one must start within by working on their soul's consciousness and change their perception and outlook while including a boost in faith.

When you fight needlessly against the current, then your circumstances grow worse. This is due to the energy you are putting out there. Because your soul often feels trapped in human form in this heavy and dense atmosphere, your lower self and ego rises and becomes attracted to material and superficial things. Your soul is limited in its body for a reason, but the angels, guides and spirit souls are unlimited. You lose yourself in outside events forgetting who and what you are.

If you use negative affirmations, thoughts, words and feelings, then you end up bringing more of that negativity to you. You are always manifesting throughout your life whether you want to or like it or not, so you may as well manifest what you want. Use positive affirmations and words when you speak, think, or write so that you can attract that same energy in. Try it out for a week and observe how things improve for you. You will discover that this will take practice since no one likes to try to be happy. That takes too much effort. It isn't long before the ego grows angry attempting to take over once again. It doesn't matter if your ego fights you on it. Because you can train your higher self to take it right back. Always revert to seeing things as working out positively in your life in amazing ways.

Perhaps you've experienced a situation where your work life is on cloud nine, while another part of your life suffers, such as love and relationships. It may feel like one area of your life is mastered while the other areas are lacking in positivity. If you excel and shine with confidence whenever you are at work, then this is a great example of where it comes to you naturally. This state is a positive form of manifesting. Your lower self does not question it or think about pulling you down. This is the same as creating a vision or dream board. You are saying the magic words without realizing it.

Look at how self-assured you are when you are at work or doing what you love. You can do it effortlessly and blissfully. This is the state where you manifest positive circumstances in other areas of your life. You have the positive visions and attitude in your mind and know how to accomplish what you need to when you are at work. This is how I obtained the things I wanted in my work life. I saw it in my mind's eye beforehand, even though it would seem impossible to someone else at the time. I prayed on it and asked for repetitive help. I knew and felt it in my gut and every cell of my body that what I was asking for WILL happen. I paid no mind to anything else including the critics or my lower self, and I eventually obtained what was envisioned and asked for.

Never discredit the power of prayer. I've spoken to others that have no belief in prayer. They do not believe in God or that there is any kind of higher power, or they may not pray because their prayers had never been answered before, so they gave up on that. However, those same people may suddenly call out to God when something detrimental happens to them or to someone close to them. God notices that you will cry out for him suddenly in a panic. He wants you to always communicate with Him, and not only when there is a dire circumstance begging for His intervention. He wishes to have a closer relationship with you beyond only needing help.

Prayer has provided miracles over the centuries to millions of people. I have witnessed the marvels and wonders that have taken place by praying. It is not enough to pray, but to keep an optimistic mindset and take action steps where you're guided. If you pray, but continue to fall into deeper despair, then pray for help with your emotional state. Once your emotional state is back to full power, then you are in that space where you can pray with detachment for the outcome of your desires.

Pray with intention, which means you are experiencing the prayer coming true through all parts of your soul and physical body. Prayers are also positive affirmations contrary to some beliefs. The positive affirmations have an even more powerful effect when you work with God on the affirmations.

For example, "Thank you God for empowering me to do what you've called my soul to do."

It does not matter how you pray or whether you recite positive affirmations. It all has the same energy intention. God, the angels, and your guides are with you hearing every word.

There is no wrong way to pray. Traditional religions have shown one often depicted as kneeling down by a bed with their hands clasped together while others may bow. It does not matter how or where you do it, but that you do it. Prayer is great because it can be done from anywhere. You can communicate with God mentally in prayer as you are walking to your car to driving or sitting at a spotlight. Of course, you won't have your eyes closed and hands clasped together in those cases. You are building a stronger relationship with the Divine through prayer. It is beyond praying when nothing is going right in your life, but it is praying to acknowledge when things are going right.

Prayers are communicating to God and your Spirit team out loud, mentally, or in writing. Prayers are asking for help or thanking God and your Spirit team for their assistance. Praying is praying for other people too! You do not want to be slacking in that department either. If someone is cruel to you, it is easy to want to lash out or become negatively affected. Try praying for that person instead. Request that they receive intervention and assistance to find the love that exists somewhere within and operate from their higher self.

Atheists have protested that they do not believe in prayer. They may however sit with their own thoughts and ponder about their life at some point. They will feel grateful for what they have, what is to come, or what they would like to have. Without realizing it they are praying in those instances. They are reciting or conducting positive affirmations and prayer. It is the same concept and intent regardless of what title you use to describe it within your personal belief systems. All thoughts, affirmations, or prayers are heard by God and your Spirit team depending on what it is.

A non-believer might say something like, "How can they talk to someone in the sky who does not exist?"

To them He does not exist, but to others He does. I do not blindly know that He, my Guides or Angels exist. I have experienced great circumstances firsthand by being connected to them since I was born. This was by repeatedly testing them out whenever possible. I have requested specific Divine assistance only to witness it come true not long afterwards. I've tested them by saying, "I'm going to test you on this."

They would then make the small request happen to give me that boosted faith that the larger requests that are taking forever are being worked on. I am always communicating with Him daily and subsequently receiving results. If I never did, then I wouldn't bother with prayer.

Prayers are not always answered in the way you expect or hope. Sometimes they are answered in another way you never thought of. When it comes to all things beyond the physical world it is important to keep an open mind. You can add in your prayer requests that you wish for a desire to come to fruition pending that it will not put you in danger or cause more issues. I have mentally asked for help in prayer, and then watched it eventually come to fruition. Sometimes it is immediately and sometimes it is far off in the distance, but I never stop praying or believing. I know that there are reasons that nothing is happening right away, because there are certain pieces of the puzzle that have to come into place first.

Many long for practical security-based things because this is a physical world that requires those necessities to survive or make life a bit more bearable. Let's say that you are wondering why the right love partner has not come into your life yet. It may be that you are ready, but perhaps your love partner is in a place where they are not ready to meet you yet. They may currently be involved with someone that will not last. It might also be that you're not ready and have more soul growth work that will bring you to the level of the partner that God wants to bring you. Keep an open mind and consider all the possibilities as to why certain prayer requests are not coming to fruition.

Always say thank you for being helped as well, and not just I need I need. The angels love it when you show gratitude and express thanks for what you currently have. You don't want to become a spoiled child of God who takes and asks constantly. You are blessed in many ways so take time out to say thank you. Every morning when I'm getting ready for the day I'm communicating with my Guides and Angels. There is not a day that goes by where I am not. Some of the things I say to them are things like, "Thank you for my health, thank you for the place I live in, etc."

I move down the list letting them know how grateful I am for the blessings I currently have. I feel more alive and alert when I start my sentences with, "Thank you for…."

Those words have ferocious power!

Focus on being grateful and saying thank you for what you have and watch how much lighter and happier you start to feel. You'll find that your life starts to feel less tumultuous in the process. Being grateful and saying thank you raises your soul's vibration and consciousness to the level where positive Divinely guided manifestation occurs. Your prayers are ultimately answered in ways that benefit your higher self. You may need to get knocked around off your high horse a bit and dragged through the mud before you can see your prayer answered.

It seems challenging to break out of a cycle of negative thoughts and words used. It feels far easier to think and speak negative thoughts and worry. How about saying something positive? Choose not to live your life in misery. Basking in God's love helps one live with gratitude and more joy. Choose not to allow your lower self to have control over you dominating your thoughts and mood.

You can pray for other people and send angels to intervene with someone else, but that person has to also want help. The angels will definitely be by their side. They will give them love, offer assistance and nudges, but if that person is not paying attention or wanting it, then there is only so much that can be done. God and the angels will stay by that person's side continuously trying to get them to notice. They do not give up on you, but do you just give up?

Here are some examples of positive affirmations and high vibrational phrases:

"I am worthy."
"I have strong health."
"I am loved."
"I have a financially successful career."
"I live in a beautiful house in the countryside."
"I have a loving and loyal relationship partner."
"My opinion is just as valid as anyone else's."
"I am taken care of in all ways."

Don't shortchange yourself or be embarrassed as if you are not deserving of a great life. Heaven and your angels know you deserve it. They want you to be at peace so that you can fulfill your life purpose. You do not have to be on this planet to suffer indefinitely.

Make a list with your own positive affirmations and recite it every day either mentally or out loud. Do it before bed or when you wake up. Keep doing it until you have obtained your dreams. God, the angels and spirituality are like vitamins. You have to keep at it daily before you begin to notice the much-needed improvement and changes shifting in your life.

Everything you desire will not happen right away. Sometimes for certain things there are life lessons that you must go through and be enlightened about on your own before the next step is shown. If you are feeling stuck at a dead-end job and nothing is moving forward, then look at the lesson that is surrounding where you are at and acknowledge this. To do this you have to be completely unbiased and remove your ego from the equation. Look at this dead-end job in a positive light and ask yourself, "What have I learned while I have been here? How am I being of service to others while there?"

What positive trait or traits did you gain while working this particular job that you did not have before? This is your answer to absorb and learn from. Acknowledge it so that you are open and ready for your next step.

You can write to your angels about anything you want in a prayer. This is by writing it to them in a notepad or in an email that you email to yourself. Tell them about your fears, issues, and circumstances you would like to change. When you pour your heart out to them with great purpose and intention, then you are truly heard. Then release it and move on with living life graciously and positively. Have patience with the outcome. Watch the miracles and changes happen in the coming months that follow as you continue with this positive mindset.

When you pray or recite positive affirmations, I will conclude it with: "This - or something better God."

Because they may have something greater than you imagined in mind and you don't want to limit yourself. Your dreams and wishes come true, but sometimes not the way you requested. It will be in an even greater way than you expected. It can be a major change, or it can be subtle. Sometimes you will find you're still at the workplace you complained about, but then you realize that you're perfectly content there. They are keeping you somewhere for a reason and to fulfill a purpose such as getting along with a particular colleague. The delays can be that they have much to maneuver beforehand or have a grander plan that you cannot see yet.

Remain optimistic and open minded to the outcome of your prayers. Know that there is a reason for everything that is happening for you in your life at any particular time. Know that you also have the power to change that simply by adjusting the way you think and feel about it.

Ask and you shall receive. Pray about the changes you'd like to see happen in your life. Have faith and believe in it. Focus only on what you desire to see happen and not what you don't want. For example, say something like, "Please guide me to friendships with like-minded interests."

Also add in, "Thank you."

Be grateful for what you have.

"Thank you for keeping my body healthy in all ways. I'm grateful that I have shelter, etc."

Shifting your outlook can take practice and time, but before you know it, you will start noticing the positive changes happening in your life.

Ask Archangel Michael and/or Jesus Christ to surround you with white light protecting you from lower energies when you pray. Praying for others has therapeutic effects. When you send positive words about someone else whether in the form of a prayer, affirmation, or a statement, then you are raising your soul's energy vibration. This process not only results in additional healing light sent to the other person, but this same light is magnified and re-directed back onto yourself as well. This only solidifies the theory that your thoughts do produce things to an extent, whether those thoughts are of yourself or someone else.

When someone upsets you and you find yourself complaining about them, you are not only sending negative energy to that person, but that energy you're toying with acts as a mirror reflecting the same energy right back onto your soul. Many have admitted that when doing that they noticed it was one negative thing after another preceding that. This is why it is important to catch yourself when you discover that you are spending more time using negative words about a situation and quickly modify them to be optimistic. Sending prayers or positive words to someone else is a win-win situation because it not only has the added benefit of elevating the other person's soul, but it also improves yours.

Sending positive prayers and affirmations to others will help as much as the other person allows it to. They have free will choice to go against the prayers and override any heavenly assistance offered. If they are choosing to stay in a negative space or they're making choices that their ego insists on, then there is little you or Heaven can do. When you send prayers to another person, the angels will continue to uplift that person's thoughts and nudge them in the right direction continuously hoping that person will notice.

Sometimes you pray for change with little to no instant results. When you notice that nothing has happened, your ego kicks in and causes you to worry. The ego wants things immediately. You start to lose faith when you notice nothing has changed. Your unanswered prayers sometimes have other factors that need to come into play first before you notice changes.

There are times when your prayers are answered. The way it is answered might not be in the manner you expect it. You fail to notice the blessings that have indeed trickled into your life. There are the repeated signs you ignore that your Spirit team is asking you to do. It could be something as simple as signing up to take a particular class or go to a location you're guided to. They put these Divine signs in front of you. For example, you might notice that you continue to notice the same seminar flyer, but you never act on it or equate it to Divine orchestration. Sometimes your Spirit team has to maneuver certain pieces of the puzzle before you notice the changes. Other times they want you to endure a particular experience as part of your karmic thread, life lesson, and soul's growth. The insight you gain in what appears to be a less than stellar situation carries over into your new situation. You have the revelation of why the experience was necessary, then it all eventually makes sense.

A Prayer

"I'd like to thank God for creating this planet and its entire habitat, plants, wildlife, animals and the beauty of all of the nature surroundings. Help me to take care of it and never take it or my life for granted. Thank you for providing me with all of the necessities I need to survive in a human body such as food, clothing, housing and finances. Help me to align perfectly with my higher self and its purpose while here. Thank you for assisting me to revert to living in and expressing love full time."

CHAPTER FIVE

*Create an Abundant Life
With Faith*

Having an abundant life can mean many things to different people. It can be something that makes you happy and gives you daily pleasure. It can be filled with good positive-minded friends that accept you unconditionally no matter how many skeletons you reveal. There is nothing you can say that would make them write you off. Your mutual loyalty is sacrament to the both of you. I would be the first to help a friend bury the body, which I know select people can truly jokingly say that and mean it. Especially today where people are quickly writing one another off if a flaw is revealed or if their choices are not exactly like yours. If they vote politically a certain way or have a different spiritual view, you could be kicked out of someone's life with the snap of a finger. They quickly write others off when what they believe to be any imperfection is revealed. That's not mafia like loyalty at all, but a loyalty riddled with conditions. Having that kind of rigid stance with your own clan will ensure the instability continues on in other areas. This attitude blocks the positive flow of abundance from coming in.

Some of my best friends may partake or have participated in behavior that I don't condone, but I don't write them off. Accepting people's differences takes an immense amount of work. No one is exactly like anybody else and people are going to do things or believe in things that are disagreeable to you. How you choose to accept that and not take it personally can have an effect on how successfully you navigate through those Earthly life hiccups and challenges. One of the repeated phrases I've heard from friends and those around me are, "I feel I can always tell you anything and you don't have any judgment at all. I don't know anyone else that's like that."

An abundant life today can be about having more good times, fun, and laughter. Laughter raises your vibration up into God's vortex. You can feel your vibration has risen when this happens. Your vibration is your overall well-being and energetic state.

Your physical self and spiritual self work in tandem with one another. If you're feeling low, then your vibration is low. If you're on cloud nine and filled with happiness, then your vibration is high.

You've likely had one of those laughing fits at some point in your life. You were also able to detect how that made you feel, and the feeling was good. You could feel it through your entire being. Suddenly you were walking on clouds happy in life. Some have commented that they could sense that infectious wonder just by hearing someone else's laughing fit in the vicinity. Maybe it happened while you were at a restaurant, in a movie theater, or at work. You smile and look at whomever you're with and share a telepathic acknowledgment that this laughing fit you're hearing is irresistible.

The laughter and joy are an example of what raises your soul vibration. When your vibration is raised, then it reaches that threshold where abundance and blessings flow in. This is why it's important to bring these little things up as reminders as to what can help in accelerating the flow of good things in your life. It doesn't mean you're going to be drama and challenge free.

God can mean diverse things to different people from a higher power, the Light, Spirit, the Universe, and so on. My own life was less dramatic and less challenging when I devoted my life to God full time. It included incorporating these little tips to the point that I noticed a grander shift happening. It was too obvious not to notice the positive changes and results that were surfacing.

An abundant life can be about partaking in work that excites you and brings out your passions. This is also similar to finding your life purpose and diving wholeheartedly into that in the right spirit. It enables you to have enough time outside of that work you do to spend with friends, family, and loved ones, or whatever activities you find pleasurable. This is pending it's not harming you or another person.

Some find anything associated with the word pleasure to be evil. You're not intended to have a miserable life. Pleasures and playtime fun are essential in making sure you're not overloaded with constant stress or that you don't experience burnout. This isn't about the kinds of pleasures that are considered toxic, dangerous, or unhealthy. It might be to go on a hike with a friend, or a fun road trip to a destination far enough away from home to feel as if you're getting away, but close enough to get to. It can be that you have enough time to take regular breaks and see places you've always wanted to visit and explore. It can be watching a movie that entertains, inspires, and helps you escape a hard circumstance for a spell. It can be spending intimate time with a lover. You have that beautiful blissful loving soul union relationship with someone, which makes your life feel abundant.

Having an abundant life can be having enough income to be able to live problem and worry free without fear of never being able to pay your bills or purchase practical necessities to survive. You've reached that place in your life where you are no longer struggling. You can choose the area you've always wanted to live in. You can buy that home of your dreams. You can and may even obtain all of that and much more, but you may still feel unfulfilled. Without a strong spiritual connection with something greater than yourself, you can be left feeling empty even after achieving and obtaining those material physical pleasures and desires. There are countless cases of people who fought hard to achieve materialistic abundance, but were still left feeling just as empty as they were before obtaining those things.

Some people seek out and chase fame and fortune. They achieve that and more in a big way, but have admitted to still feeling empty, low, unimpressed and unsatisfied. There are similar cases reported where someone was chasing material physical pleasures and desires. This is because true authentic happiness and joy comes from within rather than what you can get your physical hands onto. The latter kinds of happiness are short lived and operate more like a drug that might satisfy for a quick moment, but then like any drug the high soon wears off and you're left where you started.

Many purported to say they found that happiness in a strong spiritual connection, whether that is a connection with Jesus, Buddha, God, the Universe, or Spirit. It doesn't matter what you call it even though in some spiritual circles they may do their best to make you feel guilty or bad, and might even bully you for not following who they personally follow. This is not about them or what they want for you. This has been especially the case in extreme organized fundamentalist religious organizations. That behavior is what has chased followers and people away from those systematic human made created religions. Because of their self-righteous and judgment on others claiming they are doing it out of love, they have pushed people away from Christ and the Churches. Now people hear the name Jesus Christ and they cringe. They assume he is the one casting the judgment, when his love is all love. The harsh judgment casting was coming from his misinformed followers that wallow in the darkness of ego. Out of thousands of pages in a book, they only follow a few passages that were added at a later date during a superstitious time. They only use those passages to use as ammunition to attack and condemn others. This is not being spiritual or of Christ. You are a flawed human being and every soul will transform and evolve on their own timing. Forcing them to do that will never end well.

Statistics have popped up showing a never-ending decrease in religious followers because of all of this. They've chased some people to the further extreme of atheism. Although now more people today are finding a stronger connection with God in the spiritual communities, which angers extreme religious followers and atheists. Extremist religious people have great disdain for anyone that is not strictly and religiously following the Bible word for word, even though many of them cherry pick and choose what they want to follow themselves anyway. They will use the excuse that it is okay as long as they ask God for forgiveness for their wicked ways.

There are a great number of people that walk in both worlds of the spiritual and religious. They are some of the most content and centered people I've met because of that balance. They might praise Jesus while being supportive of people no matter their race, political affiliation, gender, sexual orientation, and on and on.

Some of the extreme sides of spirituality or religious disagree with someone being able to walk in both worlds, but that just means they're unable to or choose not to. They don't have a say in what you decide is best for you. This is your life and when you walk with God, you are able to be more of an efficient manager and owner of that life. No one else can claim that power, even if they use the Bible as an excuse to justify their insistence on you changing to bend to their ways. They don't have the market cornered on what God wants for you. It is your journey to discover God's ultimate purpose and guidelines for you.

Regardless of your spiritual beliefs, you are trained early on by society and your peers, to achieve a high status of popularity and fortune. Some abundance teachers and motivational preachers ask you to pay large amounts of money and sign up for their seminars so that you can work where you want and still have enough time to travel the world freely. People chase those practical monetary dreams only to find that it never pans out that way. While a small percentage might achieve it, they continue to fight to achieve more physical desires long after the achievement. Many remain unhappy and stressed out throughout life. They haven't figured out that this is not working for them. They're unhappy because they're merely going along with what they were trained early on to seek. At the same time, you understand the need or desire to at least be making enough of an income that you can live comfortably without fear of not being able to pay your bills.

Perhaps you have a large calling and purpose guiding you to partake in work that is not only your passion, but it is a purpose that has a snowball positive side effect of helping others. The problem is you don't have enough time to devote to it, because you work a full-time day job that does not fulfill you in any way. You want to quit that job so you can participate in the work that means something to you. You can't quit that day job because you need an income to be able to pay your rent, buy food, clothing, and practical necessities. You know you have to quit in order to focus solely on your passions and life purpose, but that is not a realistic move, so you wind up feeling stuck. You could look for another job to get out of the life force draining one, but you also know you may end up moving from one poor circumstance to another.

Money doesn't solve the problems of happiness, but it does help to have enough to physically survive. And in that scenario described, having enough income where you don't need to work a time and energy sucking full time day job with toxic people is not an outlandish desire for a physical being.

The good news is there is a glimmer of light at the end of that dark tunnel. Devoting just a small amount of time each day or week towards your passions that you desire to be lucrative can give you something to look forward to. There are many success stories where someone lived that way and reaped in positive benefits. Add to that daily prayer and asking for heavenly guidance gives this a greater shot and making this dream come true.

There are also stories about those who were in a situation like that for years. They worked hard on their passion and purpose on the side while at a day job they despised. Once enough of a steady income was coming in with that passion purpose side work, they were able to comfortably quit their day job without fear or worry, and partake in the work that truly is their passion and love.

Regardless of what your finances are like, you are the manager and creator of your life. When you team up with God and your Spirit team, then there is no telling what you can accomplish. You can decide how you will act or react to something someone says or does. You can choose the job you want to look for to an extent. Sometimes you may end up accepting a job you don't really want because you have bills to pay. You are still choosing to make that temporary sacrifice by accepting that blessing of a job. No one is putting a gun to your head. You are doing the best you can in managing your life with the resources you have at this juncture in your life.

Achieving a utopian abundance life state is what the soul desires because it reminds it of home where everything was blissful and peaceful. It's like you moved from a mansion overlooking paradise in Heaven to a rundown apartment on Earth for a brief time in your soul's existence. You did so for the sake of evolving your soul. Your soul doesn't evolve much unless it has to endure rough experiences for the purpose of lessons learned. When you learn a lesson on Earth, then that means you learned from the mistake. When you learn from a mistake, you grow and work on not doing it again. Some get stuck in that cycle of repeating the same mistakes until they notice the pattern and snap out of it. This way they can move onward and forward.

Even the most miserable person on the planet longs for happiness deep down inside the core of their soul. Happiness being subjective since one person's version of the happiness they desire could differ from another ones.

There are people who have evil fantasies of world domination and that would make them happy. This of course is not the kind of abundance God and my Spirit team speaks of or the kind you're even thinking about. This is also what they mean when they say happiness is individual based.

One person could desire a home, the love soul mate marriage partner, the kids, and a good job. Those requests would fulfill their physical desires. For another they may not care about any of that, but want the freedom as a single person to roam about the world and travel to see the different parts of the globe and dive into higher culture learning.

Longing for that authentic abundant life feeling starts from within. You fill yourself up with overflowing happy thoughts of Divinely guided enlightenment and abundance. Your emotional state feels like you're riding sky high above the clouds. It's to live a utopian existence that would be possible if people acted from their better nature and fought to function through life in a high vibrational state. Most of the chaos and turmoil created is at the hands of other people or conjured up within you. Your goal should be to reach this utopian paradise state, but then transcend even higher than that. When you are in the epicenter of that vibrational energy, then there is no telling what kind of bountiful abundance would come flowing in.

CHAPTER SIX

*Increase Faith to Accomplish,
Achieve, and Persevere*

Craving human interaction and social stimulation is something sought out by many, while other people prefer to function alone. When you have a strong connection with God and Spirit, then you never feel lonely. Loneliness is ultimately longing for a connection to fulfill you that can only truly be satisfied by God. To have a mutually reciprocated blissful love union with another person is to know God, because a soul's best qualities are parts of Him.

Since it's sometimes difficult for a human soul to have a connection with God, the ego part of one's self will crave love, attention, and admiration from other people. It's temporarily fulfilling because no one can ever fill that space within you except God. God in this case is not that cliché image of a man with a beard sitting on a chair in the sky. This is the image that non-believers tend to overuse, which has no basis in the reality of the massive energy force that created all that IS.

All souls desire some form of companionship with at least one person. Some people might disagree, but they do crave some form of a relationship based in love if even through a social circle of friends.

A businessman might say that he only cares about work and money, yet he is cut off from the Universe and the Divine. If he didn't have to get it from some source connected to another person, then he wouldn't crave it at all. He needs other people around him. If they weren't around and all people were taken away from him so that he could be completely alone, then it wouldn't be long before he begins to go crazy and start to miss that stimulation and crave another person.

If this businessman showed up on Earth to find no other people, then he wouldn't know what he was missing. Because there is no material distraction, he would be more in tune to the Heavens unable to hear anything else. This is how human beings progressed in the beginning of civilization. They paid attention to the Heavens and their Divine senses to guide them on how to naturally progress.

Eventually it expanded and exploded to the point of never-ending distractions. The more this chaos rose up, the less Divinely connected human beings became. There is no way to escape that and not be aware that it's happening, even if you live in the middle of nowhere. While you might be more connected to Spirit in those areas, you lose the connection when you turn your television on, you surf the internet, you read media stories, or partake in toxic timewasters. Now you are no longer spiritually connected.

You might be connected to one another through technological devices, but in a distant loveless way. You are not connected to God through those forms. The entire planet is unsettled making it near impossible to sense the Divine energy that way. Your subconscious is aware of it, even if you're not paying attention to it in the present moment. If you're a highly spiritually connected being, then you're versed and readily able to move in and out of the Spirit connection whenever it calls for it.

Your soul's life force dies little by little living a life you're unhappy with. Perhaps you feel emotionally dead as if you don't have much else to give anymore. You've asked for help for years and became doubtful that it will ever happen at this point. You're waiting, hoping, praying, and taking action for years wondering if a miracle and blessings will reveal itself to you. It can make you doubt, lose faith, and question if there is a God. It sounds like a roller coaster ride of voices competing with one another from your ego to your angels, to your ego, to your angels.

I love films from all genres, from horror, to intense dramas, to frat boy comedies, and to films with an uplifting spiritually based message like, *The Shack*.

In *The Shack*, the character Mack is a Man that grew up in a home full of physical and emotional abuse. As a Father in present day, one of his youngest daughters is abducted by a serial killer that rapes and kills her. Something this extreme and bleak had to take place so that viewers can understand how this man's faith and trust in God and life are gone.

He endures emotional and mental anguish, horror, anger, and a loss of spirit. He's led to the shack where his daughter was killed by who he believes is the killer. He's in for a powerful awakening when he discovers it's the Holy Trinity, but taking the form of people. Jesus and the Holy Spirit are there along with God Himself, who takes the form of a woman.

The man is confused and says to God, "Do I know you?"

God chuckles, "Not very well." And then with firm inviting comfort, "But we can work on that."

I loved the film from that point when the man gets to hang out and develop a stronger relationship with the Holy Trinity. They take the form of a warm cozy family that feels like a Hallmark card feeding you spiritual wisdom that isn't that far off from the truth. Through this relationship, they help this man regain his faith and hope in himself and life again.

Some strict religious people found this to be heresy, while some non-believers found it to be like a church sermon. As usual, I don't hang on either side and found *The Shack* to be uplifting, truthful, with a Universal message of love. It feels like taking a warm bath in the Paradise of Light with Heaven's greats that is moving, joyful and empowering.

Focus on your Soul's Purpose

When your consciousness is raised, it is not uncommon to feel disconnected from other people and view human life as trivial. This is when it's time to do an inventory check of how the months and years to date have gone for you. Examine your triumphs, sorrows, successes, and challenges. What was lost and what was gained throughout that time. You'd be surprised to find the hidden blessings you never thought much of until you look back on it. When things are going amazingly, people don't usually notice it as much as they do when things are going horribly. One can take it for granted until you take a moment to note, "Okay, my rent gets paid every month, my health is great, and I have a working car that gets me to my job."

Look forward to the coming time up ahead with promise and hope. Believe your life will get better and accept nothing less than that. Celebrate your wins and accomplishments to acknowledge what you've done. This also helps lighten the burdens of life that you experience on occasion.

Success comes and goes the way fame comes and goes. One of the best dreams to come true is being able to turn your love and hobby into a financially lucrative career. You are closer than someone else might be if you understand the concept of manifestation and asking for what you want. If you're stressed out at your job regularly, then is the job worth it? Make wise choices in your life that do not result in leaving you in a bind where you're perpetually unhappy. This might mean taking a job for less pay and living beneath your typical means until you find the work that makes you feel bliss again.

Looking to the future with optimism you might sometimes find you've been chasing rainbows that evaporate as quickly as the champagne fizzles in your glass. You need not search long and hard for some measure of magic to reveal itself since it's always resided within you. God loves you even when you doubt it, avoid it, shun it and do everything in your power to deny it. When you reach that threshold of completing your Earthly run, the only thing you take with you is love. If you gain anything while here, then remember to love more, give more, and have compassion no matter how unpopular it is. Only then can you truly discover that magic you secretly desire.

Keep a journal for a month and write down every single thing that bothers you. This means a trending topic you found yourself falling into. After enough time has passed revert back to that journal to see what you wrote. Notice if it has truly had any positive effect on changing your life, or if it was just another time waster you fell emotionally drawn to, but could care less about months later. It will be mind boggling to witness the long list of time wasters that prevented you from being happy and moving forward.

Focus on your life purpose rather than time wasters that act as a procrastination technique to prevent you from getting to work on what you desire. The tiny action steps you make are creating change even if you don't feel like it is while in the midst of it. You may think that someone else will take care of an issue, but no one really is or does. If you need to go it alone, then you have to go it alone and tackle it one issue at a time. One small action step can get the energy flowing in that direction. Research and seek out ways that change can be made in the area of your interest that you strongly feel needs to be changed.

Sometimes healthy time wasters have good mind enhancing properties, such as those card games like Solitaire or emailing or texting friends back to get you out of a procrastination cycle. You just want to make sure you don't fall too deep into the time wasters that you find four hours have passed and you have yet to get to work on your dreams. Even just a small amount of time working on action steps that can one day bring you what you desire will make all the difference in the world. It's definitely more advantageous than contributing nothing towards it. As always follow this all up with regular insistent prayer knowing that something good will happen for you.

CHAPTER SEVEN

Complaining Into Abundance

There is the reality that you may not have a choice and will have to accept what is coming your way. This is part of the physical survival on Earth, but one that is also contributing to your soul's growth and evolving process. This may come in the form of accepting any job position to ensure your security. You have to do what you need to do in order to stay afloat without worry.

During my day job tenure, I accepted any old job that I wasn't all that happy with, but they did give me some measure of flexibility. It was close to home and the safety net of that job enabled me to find an even better job that I truly wanted months later.

When you feel worry and stress over your day job, or not having enough money to work on your life purpose, then you risk moving into worry or complaining territory. Complaining is an abundance, prayer, and blessing killer. If you spend your life complaining, you will guarantee that you will be given more to complain about.

Several of my friends and I have a pact where we step in if we see someone falling into perpetual complaining. This is pointed out to help one another stop the runaway train downwards. This is not done insensitively or to quiet one's voice from expressing itself. It also doesn't mean ignoring a problem one is experiencing. This is about taking a step back to evaluate what can be done about the issue that is causing the person to complain for days, weeks, and sometimes months.

When you are fearful about something, then it will cause you to vent and complain about that. This isn't telling you to suppress your worries and fears, but rather get to the level of realizing when it's happening, have your quick complaint about it, but then shift that into something positive like an action step that can be done to help move out of that dirty cycle of complaining.

When I've prayed or asked for Divine assistance, then that was when the assistance eventually came. I wouldn't force-feed you prayer if it never worked for me. When your thoughts move into a plea or gratitude, then you've moved into prayer. You might call it an affirmation or just something you were thinking about, but it is a prayer that the Universe and Heaven are hearing come out of you. They will also hear you when you're incessantly complaining whether out loud or to anyone listening. Complaining that nothing is happening or changing for you will not suddenly bring in the blessings.

Complaining your way into blessings and abundance will not result in success. If you're going to continue complaining about something, then don't bother praying for it since the complaint will negate the prayer anyway. You ask for heavenly help, but nothing comes around as quick as you'd like it if at all, so you assume you've been given up on. You might play the victim card that no one was able to help, you're being ignored, and woe is me. God is attempting to train you to stand tall, pull yourself up by your bootstraps, and forge forward fearlessly with faith as your anchor. When you pass on, you're not taking anyone or anything with you. You will be making the journey home solo with the exceptions of God and your Spirit team that are ushering you into the Light.

Learn to get to know and lean on your Spirit team for assistance when your faith and well-being are wavering. Work on being grateful for the blessings they've helped you with to date. Do you have clothes, food, and a roof over your head? Then say, "Thank you."

Some people are under the impression that the job of heavenly helpers is to grant your desires like a genie in a bottle. When that doesn't happen you automatically assume, they must not exist, or you're being ignored. You're expected to participate and do the work yourself as well too. Sitting around on your couch drinking a beer all day watching a sports game hoping gifts will fall from the ceiling onto your sofa is never going to happen just because you've asked for it. It's also not Heaven's job or anyone else's job to constantly tell you what to do, where to go, and when to do it. It's your job to do those things. You're given what you need, not necessarily what you want. Needs are the essentials such as housing, food, and clothing.

Spirit guides will step in when necessary to nudge you to move in a certain direction where the most benefit for your soul's growth exists. They will not live your life for you. You're not a puppet on a string that they're controlling. They are like any good best friend who taps you on the shoulder to get you to notice something important, but it's not their burden to carry if you fail to detect it. They can put the same repetitive cues in front of you to get you to see something, but there's nothing more they can do if you're not paying attention to it. If you don't make moves and go after what you want, then nothing will happen because they are not going to do it for you. If you don't have the confidence to go after what you want, then confidence gaining skills is one of your life purposes to master. This can also be added to your prayer requests, which is to help be given more confidence. Avoiding an action step towards making something happen is something you must learn to overcome and master.

Complaining is surrounded with undesirable energy that lowers your soul's vibration and opens the gate for the Darkness to ensnare in its trap that block even more goodness. Negative anything will manifest into health-related concerns down the line. Sometimes you fall into perpetual daily complaining that you don't even realize you are doing that because it's become habitual.

If everything that comes out of you is toxic or a harsh assaulting judgment, then that energy will grow and manifest into more of the same. It marinates into the cells and pores of your physical, emotional, and spiritual body making you permanently one with it. You may know someone like that, and you know they're a challenging person to be around.

The largest culprits put that energy out into the Universe by posting words aligned with toxicity on their social media accounts. They're not aware that the Darkness has enveloped them. Having an understanding that the person can no longer help it can offer some measure of light in how you navigate around someone like that. The best thing to do is avoid or ignore them as much as possible. This is unless absolutely necessary such as in the workplace where you have no choice but to face them. Limit contact to work related dialogue in those instances. Being around someone who is perpetually negative and toxic will affect you, your energy, and vibration. This has an effect on how things go in your life by negating the positive process from working in your favor. Call in the Archangel Michael to extricate toxic people from your vicinity.

This doesn't mean that there isn't anything to complain about. The most enlightened being is mumbling a harmless complaint to themselves on occasion. The difference is that they are aware of when it happens, and they shift that complaint into a positive action effortlessly. People want to be comfortable and when they feel their comfort is being messed with, then they will complain. Evolving souls prefer to hang around people that complain less over the toxic complainer.

There are different levels of complaining. Some of it is harmless like, "Oh wow it's cold out here I need my jacket."

A toxic complainer is someone that is negatively ranting and raving about on social media or with anyone that will listen to them. They are always complaining about something that they're a drag to be around. It just brings you down.

Day to day issues happen to everyone all around the planet. Some of it can be extreme enough to push you to vent. Even the nicest, sweetest, most compassionate soul complains. This isn't about that, but about being aware and conscious of when you fall into a dark pattern of daily repetitive complaining that it's become all that you are. You know it's an issue when someone you know sees you and they turn the other way to avoid you. Because they know it's going to be the same sad or angry bitter song being played.

When you find that you've fallen into perpetual complaining that it's now annoying you, then work on turning that complaint into positive action steps. An action step can be choosing to stop complaining. It can be to look at what you're complaining about and finding creative ways to resolve whatever it is you're complaining about. If it's something that is not realistic or possible to correct, then work on letting it go. Divert your focus towards positive beneficial activities to distract your mind from the negative while adding what you desire to your prayer request.

Positivity Vs. Negativity

You will experience negativity on occasion throughout your life. It's not insisted that you be positive every single second, since that is not realistic or practical for a human being. It is about being mindful and aware of your overall state of mind. This means that as long as you're more positive and optimistic, than negatively stressed, depressed, and angry, then the positive quotient is high enough to pull in positive blessings. You're in the clear if most of the time you're a fairly positive and optimistic person.

When people like you they will say, "He/she is a joy to be around. I just love them."

You know you're in trouble if how they think of you is, "He/she is always complaining about something, I can't stand them."

The dangers of pretending to be positive when deep down you're not is that God and your angels see how you're feeling. You could put on the façade that you're optimistic and positive, but if what you're feeling underneath is struggle and negativity, then that is what is pulled into your life. This is because that is the overall nature you're conveying, not the deceptive friendly face on the exterior, but your soul's entire energetic well-being and state.

Some have said, "I'm not naïve for being positive and optimistic. I just choose to look at the bright side of things."

This is a fantastic mantra to have as long as you're not falling into denial over an abusive situation that's taken place. This is also pending that what you're being optimistic about is aligned with God's will for your soul in the end. Looking to have your ego stroked or having a distorted excited goal of being popular is not aligned with the Light. It's losing your way and falling into the deception of the Darkness.

Deception is not going to be obvious, which is why it's called deception. Deception shows up as something that can easily entice and lure you into its trap. It has to be something or someone attractive enough that it causes you to light up with excitement. This is the danger of deception, because it shows up in this attractive form pulling you in until you later realize that you've been had. "How did I not see this?"

It's because the Darkness shows up in this way. Its goal is to pull you in and drown you in it. You later realize after much time has passed that you got sucked into something that had deceived you. This can apply to anything such as when someone promises you all sorts of stuff that never pans out. You find out you wasted hundreds or thousands of dollars on something pointless that had no positive benefit.

Deception can show up as a hot looking guy or girl you find attractive. You become blinded by their beauty bending over backwards to cater to their every whim. One day you wake up and realize it was always you being the giver. They were consistently taking advantage of that by receiving and never giving. You obtained a temporary rushed high from the object of your desires positive reaction over what they received from you that you continue to keep giving and giving. That is until you hopefully wake up and realize that there is a grave imbalance in the connection. You could discover they were never truly that interested in you, but couldn't say no to the constant kindness you kept bestowing on them. This is how one gets taken advantage of, which can also lead you to feel resentment.

This is why it's called deception, because deception is not going to show up as deception. It's going to show up as something attractive enough to lure you in and pull you down. It's designed to trick and deceive you into falling for it. When you discover you were deceived, then you look upon it as if you had been out of your mind while the deception took place.

A positive person can fall into despair every now and then, but it is not their permanent daily state. If you're complaining every single day about the same issues for months on end, and there is no positive change, then take a look at that.

There is no doubt that on my journey towards accomplishing what I wanted to, there were moments I ignored my Spirit team's guidance and fell prey to the allure of the Darkness convincing me that I will never obtain what I seek. In younger naïve days, I have been led astray down a different path that looked like it was filled with glitter, but wound up full of deception. I've also fallen into daily complaining about an issue until I received that eye opener. It prompts me to say, "I'm starting to annoy myself. I need to stop this at once. How did I allow this to endure for so long?"

You're suddenly sounding like a broken record at that point, even to yourself.

When you're in tune, aware, and conscious of what's happening around you, then you are also more in tune to picking up on how complaining can make you feel. It doesn't feel good, it lowers your vibration, and you feel this ugly weight on you afterwards. This isn't telling you to never complain as everybody whines on some level. This also isn't saying that there isn't anything to complain about. You could easily find at least one thing to complain about daily.

The moments I'm alone, productive, and working, there are no complaints filtering through my mind. When I'm with a fun positive uplifting friend, there are no complaints moving through either of us, so it is something that can be done. It doesn't even cross our minds. It's only when certain personalities come around that it moves it into a complaint, then I find I've become caught in its web if it continues indefinitely. Find people that tend to move into positivity to connect with.

Generally, it's other people that can infect your aura, specifically the gossipy complaining ones. Sometimes it's just good humor and harmless, but other times it's bathed in hostility. You likely know that one person in your life where every time you bump into them, they are harshly complaining about something. If you're a clairsentient sensitive empath type, then you can feel your entire body shift, stress, and tense up. You end up walking away from that person feeling low. When before you encountered them, you were doing great and riding on cloud nine.

There is also that one friend you may know of that every time you bump into them there is some kind of gossip. They see you and shout, "There you are! You are not going to believe what I just found out about Karen."

No one needs to hear about the gossip you've dug up on Karen. Worry about your own life and work on fixing that, because generally if someone's life is that dull, they will negatively fixate on other people's lives. The obsession some personality types have for gossip is also what made the tabloid industry a billion-dollar enterprise. They have enough people wanting to follow the lives of the rich and famous to comment on it. Buying tabloids or frequenting gossip sites is not usually to get inspired, but to either falsely worship a celebrity you don't personally know or harshly criticize them. Neither does well to open the floodgates to attracting in abundance and blessings. This is due to the energy involved with gossip and complaining about them.

Everyone complains on some level, which usually comes from the inner feelings experienced. I feel this, I feel that, I feel I feel. Feelings are the culprit for a great deal of unhappiness. It drives one to an addiction. Some complain about their jobs, others complain about the daily traffic, some complain about their friends, family members, lovers or a situation that happened while out at a store.

Become self-aware and mindful of what you're complaining about. Is complaining about it helping to resolve an issue or is it just splattering negative gossip energy around? Notice how you feel when you're complaining as it's happening. It may give some people a rushed high at first, but like sugar or alcohol, you inevitably feel that low drop in energy causing you to crash to the floor. If it's continuously bringing your energy down when you're done venting, then work to detangle from that and let whatever it is bothering you go.

Choose your battles wisely. What situations can use your warrior like vigilance in correcting and what can you foresee as being a complete waste of time. Sometimes it helps to complain about something with someone in order to come to a resolution. You're having relationship issues and don't know what to do about it. When you have the goal of wanting to correct the issue, then complaining can be temporarily warranted. Talking it out with someone can help you come to a resolve that will work. Complaining wanders along that fine line of helpful to toxic. Is the complaining constructive in order to reach a positive resolution? Or is the complaining taking place because you're dying to harshly trash someone because you hate that they're doing well in life while you've been struggling? The latter is non-productive for you since it's not hurting or harming the target, but your own well-being. This is part of taking care of you, so that you can stay on track and on path towards accomplishing your ultimate goals in life. This is whether spiritually, emotionally, mentally, or physically.

Humanity would be a step closer to a Utopian world if everyone would stop ranting and raving about. The repeat offenders don't know to stop and are unable to get over whatever they're constantly angry about. Some of the largest complaining noise happens on social media, which is often used as a public diary to air your venting about what happened when you were trying to get into a parking space at the grocery store.

You likely know there are social media accounts that are filled to the brim of some kind of non-constructive rant about someone or something they despise. This isn't about the occasional slip that an overall positive person falls into where they suddenly take a moment to complain about something. This is about the regular offenders where the majority of their posts are negatively based every hour of every day. It doesn't do anything to help matters. It certainly doesn't contribute to bringing more love into the world. Someone looking to bring more love into the world already knows this won't help their causes.

There are now statistics and scholar studies surrounding the negative effects of social media with sites like Twitter. Twitter has grown to be a platform for predominately negative energy rather than positivity. There is also growing evidence that social media contributes to increasing anxiety and depression symptoms in some people.

There is something eerie about having an unqualified suspect posting something that can negatively destroy someone's well-being by accusing them of a crime they never partook in. This is how dangerous social media has become. Those guilty of it don't feel they're contributing anything negative. When you're buried that deep into it, then it's difficult to see clearly. This is why gossip is considered one of the toxic addictions and part of the deadly sins. This is due to the array of negative issues it causes both to the sender and any recipient. The Darkness wins by using the naïve and guilty as his pawn towards humanities destruction and downfall.

The limitless statistics repeatedly popping up cite and illustrate that many people are finding this to be a growing problem. I also hear from many people informing me they're either distancing themselves or shutting their social media accounts down due to this happening, because it is an epidemic. There are the usual offenders that you know will quickly jump on board with every single daily top trending story that exists. Some of them have hundreds of thousands and millions of followers that bow down to their every word. It's like the pied piper leading them all to slaughter.

There are moments I've fallen into a complaint, but I'm fully aware of it. I've said, "Okay I need to wrap this up and move on, because I'm just irritating myself now."

Dwelling in that kind of toxicity doesn't help anything. Release any anger and resentment you have towards whoever or whatever it is you're complaining about. Let it go because you don't need it. Carrying the pain or heaviness of the complaining energy is not harming the target of your complaint. It is just a toxicity festering inside you that has been scientifically proven to manifest into health issues down the line.

Can you not feel that energy while in the gossip complaint? Are you not tired of living like that? You don't need to carry the unnecessary pain. Give it away to Heaven to transmute and turn it into gold. Pray to be helped from incessant complaints. Ask your Spirit team to help you turn your complaints into positive action.

Do you complain about having no money? What action steps can you do to change that? If the answer is nothing, then that's an action step you're choosing to make. Making no move is making a move.

If your thoughts are filled with negative talk, you may as well work on shifting that to something positive. Since you have thoughts racing in your mind as it is, wouldn't you rather listen to good stuff than bad? No one is forcing you to think a certain way. You have control over what you're thinking. That's one of the things you actually do have control over. You can spend your life regurgitating negative things about yourself, or you can begin the process of adopting more positive things to say about yourself. No one else can control that except you. Look at the good you have now, because you have more good in you than you realize or are willing to admit or notice.

I'm not immune to the occasional negative thoughts and feelings either. It was much more prevalent when I was younger, but as I grew older, I learned to stand into my own and appreciate the good aspects of me. It wasn't an overnight change, but a gradual one as I had God and my Spirit team work with me to put this into practice. I don't remember my negative self-talk being particularly severe or damaging. It wasn't as bad as the words my now deceased father said to me growing up that had more of a permanent psychological impact. Ironically, I was particularly loving and supportive towards myself, which no doubt was coming from God.

My motto as a teenager was that if no one will support me, then I will support myself. That still holds true today. By the time I was sixteen, I knew that if I was going to survive on this physical plane that I better find a job. My family was poor, and we grew up with no money, so I knew the only way to not allow that to continue was to fight to make it on my own. I ended up doing that successfully. I prayed, connected to God and my team daily, and followed their action steps. They showed me one thing, I accomplished it, then they showed me another, and I accomplished that, and so on. This is how God works. You'll continuously be shown the same thing for days, weeks, months, and even years until you finally notice the synchronicity to make that move. You delay that move out of fear or by not realizing that it was a psychic hit from Heaven.

I've heard from others who informed me of their day-to-day negative self-talk that is more along the lines of self-cruelty. Mine was more along the lines of, "Why did I say that to that person?" Or "Now why did I do that?"

I would acknowledge that for a second, but then move on from it and onto other things quickly. It doesn't mean I'm perfection, far from it, but I do my best to be aware and mindful of those moments that any negative feeling or thought I've conjured up isn't real. I realized that most of those feelings and thoughts were ultimately not based in reality, but my own personal human perception.

Imagine spending your days saying sentences like, "I have no talents, I'm not good at anything, no one likes me the way they love others, I'm unlovable, I'm hideous, why would anyone hire me, why would anyone want to be with me, I'm useless, I can't do anything right, I'll never amount to anything, I have nothing to be grateful for, my life sucks, it's always one thing after another going wrong, I'm too young, I'm too old, I'm too fat, I'm too thin…."

That must have annoyed or brought you down to read. As an ever-inquisitive bee having communicated with so many people over the years I've discovered that everyone has those negative thoughts about themselves to one extent or another. For some it only enters their mind once in awhile, and for others it's a constant daily attack of badgering of themselves. Their perception of themselves is negatively skewed.

Where can it get you to sit around all day thinking low thoughts one after the other?

Love yourself because you are created in His image. You were born out of love from the creator who loves you unconditionally. Those negative words you tell yourself are untrue lies fed to you by the devil's darkness. They seem or feel true from your own current reality and perception, but not in the eyes of God. Not in the eyes of those in Heaven. Your soul is perfection in every way and loved unconditionally for all that you are, including your strengths and what you consider to be personal flaws. Love, accept, and appreciate you, because you're a gift!

CHAPTER EIGHT

*Taking Action
on Divine Guidance*

You've done the visualization exercises, the dream boards, prayed and asked for help, yet nothing has moved in your life or has been forthcoming. Take a step back for a moment and look at any repetitive ideas that may have continuously entered your mind urging you to take action on. What repetitive feelings or thoughts have been hitting you, but you've brushed it aside, ignored it, or not followed it. This process requires your intuitive powers to determine whether the action step you keep getting is one generated from your ego or is divinely guided.

Generally, a divinely guided idea or action step will come into your consciousness several times or more, whereas something from your ego may come in an inconsistent way. A Divine impression that sifts into your soul would be an idea that harms no one including yourself on any level whether emotionally, physically, mentally or spiritually.

Ideas that are manufactured from the ego would be things like get rich quick schemes or a longing for public notoriety, popularity, or fame. Fame is usually just a side effect that happens out of one's talent or gifts, but it's not something the talented person seeks out. They just want to be able to participate in work they love. Any fame or fortune that enters the picture is a side effect of diving into that passion, but it is one that the talented person could do without as long as they can do their work without fear of not having enough money to pay their bills.

Your Spirit team steps in to assist you while on your journey. They guide you towards particular accomplishments at the right time. They could be helping you with a specific issue indefinitely for awhile, but then there are times where they step back and allow you to make a free will choice. They can't live your life for you and make every single shred of decision making. You would never learn anything or experience life if they were continuously making all of your choices for you. Since most people don't typically listen to other people, it's unlikely they would listen to their Spirit team.

Your Spirit team may guide you by getting you to notice someone or something that can help you achieve a particular desire. It could be by implanting the information into your consciousness where you can sense you're supposed to take action on something. They will continue to offer the same action step indefinitely until you finally take it. It doesn't matter if one week passes or one year. That same action step will be put in front of you until it's taken. Once you've taken action on that step, then they will show you the next step and so forth.

When it comes to matters of love, they will put particular soul mate choices in your path intended to connect with you, but then it is up to you and/or this other person to notice it and act on it. They work with the other person's guides to guide that person toward you, while your own guides are guiding you towards them. That's quite a bit of guiding going on behind the scenes in hopes that both parties notice. They'll get you in the room alone together to face each other, but then it's up to the both of you to do the rest of the work. If neither of you do, then it's back to the drawing board for both sets of guides to continuously work to orchestrate the meeting again and again in hopes that action will be taken. This can only go on for so long before the moment passes, and neither is unable to keep the orchestration from happening. At that point a lost opportunity has passed for both parties.

Perhaps you are afraid about taking that divinely guided step, or you don't know how you'll do it, or you've already tried that, but it didn't work. The idea is still coming in trying to get you to notice it for a reason. Don't discredit those divinely guided ideas that require you to take action. Taking action is another key step to opening the floodgates of abundance and blessings in your life.

Act on the continuing positive nudges you receive and follow it. Don't allow worry or fear to set in blocking you from moving forward. Avoid inviting in more of that negative worry stuff to you. Some people choose to create a vision board, images, or positive words posted around them that remind them of what they want. This assists in implanting the ideas into your mind, which will help direct the energy towards making something happen. The goal is to fill your life with positive words and phrases that are aligned with abundance.

Affirm only what you desire and not what is lacking or missing in your life. The more you affirm what you don't want, then the more likely you will bring in that which you don't want into your life. Since that's the case, you may as well work on affirming positive thoughts and feelings. It's easy to live in negativity since that's what the Darkness drives each soul to reside in. No one is exempt from the ego taking over and talking you out of positivity.

If you perpetually keep displaying negative thoughts and feelings, then changing that process will take daily practice to re-train your mind to think differently. Don't feel discouraged if you find that you keep reverting back to negativity or that it becomes difficult. Notice when the negativity comes in, pay attention to when that happens, and shift the energy into positive thoughts and feelings. It also helps to work with a close friend where you can both catch each other when taking things too far into negativity for too long. At the same time that doesn't mean to pretend you're fine when you're not feeling it. It takes a great deal of work to lift your vibration out of the doldrums and upwards into God's light. It may take you months as you implement this new mindset into more optimism than pessimism. Practice altering your thoughts and feelings to positive ones. Being mindful and aware of when you fall into a negative pattern can help accomplish this.

Pray Instead of Worry

Challenges can be easier to move through when you pray and ask for daily help and guidance. This must also be followed up with you paying attention to the repetitive guidance coming in, then you take action on that guidance. Often when you ask for help in prayer you will be guided to take action on something to help it along. Pay attention to the recurring guidance asking you to take action on something. It will continue to come into your aura indefinitely until you do it. This taking action step will never ask you to harm, hurt, or hate anyone including yourself.

Prayer is intended to help you move away from worry and fear. You invalidate a prayer when you continue to worry afterwards. The worry tells Spirit that you don't trust their intervention and assistance and so you will continue to worry as a backup plan in case God doesn't come through. When you receive repeated nudges after the prayer to take action on something, then take action.

Worry is a negative based emotion that makes you believe that something is not going to go according to plan. Sometimes that can create a self-fulfilling prophecy and push what you desire further away from you. You want to ensure that your thoughts and feelings remain positive that you will obtain what you desire.

Most don't favor constant change as it disrupts the momentum they've become comfortable in. All human beings are equal in the end regardless of what they look like, where they are from, or what lifestyle choices they make. No one is better than anyone else even though each of the ego's attempts to scream the loudest to let others know their way and opinion is the best route. In the end, all the world hears is noise. There is no Divine energy light that exists anywhere within that noise.

Others choose not to believe in a higher power when their prayers have gone unanswered. I've had my own share of roadblocks, but there are numerous unseen reasons as to why prayers go unanswered. When it's a human souls time to pass on, praying can alleviate any hardship for that soul crossing over, but it won't necessarily stop them from passing on, because eventually souls will pass on. That soul might have agreed to pass on during that time in that way for a lesson they chose to learn.

There are various reasons that Heavenly requests are not always fulfilled. Sometimes what you're requesting isn't aligned with your higher self and may cause unseen harm or turmoil. Other times there are pieces to the puzzle that need to be adjusted before something can come to fruition. They may also have something better in mind that you're not seeing. One of the other reasons is you're being guided to take specific action steps to help something come along, but you're not pursuing it. Follow the repetitive guidance and messages you're receiving by taking action with the steps you're given.

You're wrestling with an issue, so you request heavenly intervention and assistance mentally or out loud in a prayer. It feels rushed or forced and your ego gets in the way convincing you that no one can understand or hear you from above. You are heard regardless of your state of being at that moment and whether or not you believe your request for help sounds messed up or garbled. With intention simply saying, "Heaven help!" has already formed the connection.

Observe humility, appreciation, and gratitude. When you experience testy times, it doesn't help when your focus is on the drama swirling around you. When you shift that energy into something positive, then the drama grows less hostile as your higher self rises back up and takes charge. Your higher self is the part of your soul that is the most connected to God.

Be appreciative for the good you have in your life now. This is shifting negative complaining words and thoughts into something positive. What you're thinking and feeling now is what dictates the direction of how your life will go in the coming months. Sometimes you can get caught up in what you don't have instead of the good that you do have.

It's easy to get caught up in the good that comes in. This is where you ignore where these blessings are coming from. The feeling behind being grateful is a high vibration energy, which attracts in more of the same. Gratitude goes a long way towards manifesting higher soul feeling experiences.

Pay Attention to Divine Guidance

Maybe an action step you're guided to make is taking you out of your comfort zone. You're afraid of making a drastic move that you know deep down you desperately want to make, but you're fearful of what will or will not come if you take action. Trust the continuous guidance your Spirit team is giving you. This is putting your faith and trust in God and the Universe that there is a Divine plan laid out to assist you. You will never be guided into something that God doesn't think you can handle.

You want to be realistic and practical while making Earthly decisions, such as you want to be careful walking away from a job when you don't have another one lined up. There are a great many success stories that include someone taking a huge risk by walking away from a job before they found another. Still you want to move cautiously with that kind of a major decision.

A reader named John owns an art gallery selling expensive art to high end clients. Before he was doing that, he was a salesperson for a company. He would work from home most of the time, but wasn't putting in much of an effort as a salesperson. His heart wasn't in it, so instead he dabbled around with this art selling idea. Eventually the company he was a salesperson at let him go when they discovered he wasn't putting in any effort. After he was let go, he dove head on into his work as an art dealer. He opened his gallery and ended up attracting in all sorts of clients and buyers that his side business started booming. He now owns this successful business. He was also able to buy his own home and he's never been happier.

The way he told me the story had struck a positive inspirational chord, as I've listened to other similar stories. Sometimes getting fired, laid off, or quitting is the severe push one needs to completely focus on their side business and making it a full-time money-making business. It's true that it can be risky doing it that way, but many have been successful at that. They're no longer being weighed down by this day job that drops their vibration making them miserable. That state is not helpful in building your side business.

When they were let go from the day job, this put them into high gear where they kicked up the action efforts into their side business. They had a bit of a financial cushion to give themselves a few months to dive into building this side business without fear of not being able to pay their bills. In John's case, he was able to increase the income as an art dealer to the point that looking for another day job was no longer necessary. This isn't advising you to quit your job if that's a concern. Always move cautiously with big decisions weighing the pros and cons before acting. When in doubt revert to prayer for guidance.

Maybe your Spirit team continues to nudge you to apply for a job you always wanted, but you had already applied at that same place a year prior and received no response. Months or a year later the job is still on your mind. Many companies are open to people re-applying or re-submitting their resume or credentials every six months. You may have received no response the first time, but the repetitive Spirit guidance coming in on it again may be no accident. You're being asked to try again, as they see the timing is now right. Your name also becomes more familiar to the employer that does the hiring. They are more likely to call a familiar name to come in for an interview over a name they don't know.

This same scenario has been true for me. As far as with the jobs I've had in the past from the record store to the film business. I was turned down initially or I received no response from them. I tried on numerous occasions on a later date and received no response or they'd say something like, "Sorry we're not hiring right now".

I tried again at a much later date and that was when I struck gold. This time I received a response to come in, met with them, and was hired on the spot. Imagine if I didn't follow the hunches to try again.

Perhaps you were turned down or you turned them down, but the hunches kept coming in stronger over time, so you try again. It's the trying again part in the equation when it all comes together.

Sometimes you're supposed to be at a specific job at a time in your life for a reason that might not be understood while it's in motion. You may be longing to quit this day job for some time and cannot understand what the delay is. You could be gaining skills at this day job that you will be utilizing later. You may not think so at the time you are working the job. It's only in the future when you're at the next gig or chapter in your life that you look back and realize why you were there for the time that you were. This concept goes for relationships of all types from friendships, business, to love as well too.

You could be single and constantly bumping into the same person in passing or while out and about getting you both to notice one another. You and this person may secretly be developing a crush on one another that you start to pick up on with the mutual warm smiles and hello-how are you's. As time progresses you both gain confidence to say more than hello and strike up longer conversations. This is how I've met some of the ones I ended up with in long term love relationships with in the past.

There are times where you've been psychically blocked or you're not receiving a crystal-clear Divine answer on something, while other times it will slam into your consciousness in a matter of seconds. For those times where nothing is coming in, it helps to pray, connect with God, ask for intervention, signs, messages, and guidance. Ask your Spirit team to help you notice what these messages could be.

Before bed and drifting off to sleep, ask your Spirit team to come into your dreams and communicate with you there. Your ego is asleep, and your consciousness rises leaving you more receptive and open to receiving the Divine content while in a dream state. Ask that they help you remember the dream, because sometimes the dreams can be so vivid, but the second you wake up it's gone and vanished. Keep a journal or notepad within reach while asleep so that when you wake up, you can quickly jot down the images you received in the dream as soon as possible before it's gone. Even if it has no meaning to you at that point. Jot it down as it could have significance later.

Dreaming is also connected to Clairvoyance, which is clear psychic seeing or clear viewing. Many that have vivid dreams regularly tend to have strong Clairvoyance. Clairvoyance requires some decoding on your part, since the messages come in as visuals that are more symbolic than a direct message. Write down everything you remember seeing in the dream, even if it was a color. Colors have symbolic meanings as well too. There could be some important clues in your dreams that were planted into your subconscious from Heaven to help you.

CHAPTER NINE

Gratitude and Optimism

Gratitude is one of the greater ways to increase bounty in your life. This is not fake appreciation with the hidden goal of obtaining increase, since Heaven knows when you're being deceptive. It has to be a genuine gratitude where you truly do feel this gratitude within every cell of your being. Gratitude is a challenging trait to display because the darkness of ego part of someone desires to be thankless preferring to be greedy. In America, on Thanksgiving the tradition is everyone gives thanks and gratitude to those around them. The irony is the next day is Black Friday, one of the larger shopping days of the year causing a rise in greed and violence. If you do an internet search of, "Black Friday greed" or "Black Friday violence", then no additional proof or validation of this greed is required. You'll find endless pages of it.

Be grateful for what you have in your life here and now. Living in a miserable or pessimistic state blocks the flow of abundance and increases the challenges in your life due to God's law of the universe.

You could be struggling in life and facing insurmountable challenges, but everyone is battling something. Some of those challenges they're battling with could be considered as being worse than someone else's depending on whom you ask. Any form of uncomfortable struggle still counts as energy in the eyes of the Universe.

This isn't telling you not to fall into pessimism or negativity, because everyone has some measure of struggle. Even the most optimistic person will experience some browbeaten feelings and thoughts. No one is exempt from challenges. This is just explaining what can block the flow of positive abundance, blessings, and answered prayers.

All energy expands regardless of the tone of that energy. If you're positive, then this positive energy will expand. If it's negative, then that's what will expand and bring more of that to you. Since this is deemed the case, functioning in an optimistic state when it is possible will have more benefit than not.

Don't force positivity if you're not feeling it. Avoid beating yourself up if you're battling negatively. Take your time being aware of the moments you're in a negative state. Look at what is causing it, then examine what action steps you can take to relieve that stress. If you are unable to do anything about it, then work on letting it go.

You could be sitting in daily traffic that doesn't move, which always angers and upsets you. Sitting in your car in upset will not lighten the traffic. It also won't help in getting to your destination quicker. All it does is attack your soul and pull you down. You arrive at your location stressed and edgy. When you look at the detrimental effects it places on your back, then it's easier to move out of that.

Mentally say in prayer, *"I don't want to live in misery. I need to shake this off. God please help me move out of this stress and back into joy."*

When I've been in those situations, I've worked extra hard to move my angry stressed thoughts into something more productive. Use that time to mentally communicate to God and your Spirit team to help alleviate the stress you continue to feel over circumstances you cannot do anything about. In addition, ask for Divine help in mending the areas that you are able to. Ask God for help and to put ideas in your mind that you can take action on to fix a situation you'd like to see positive changes with.

It can be easy to fall into a state of pessimism when nothing good is going for you, but if you're breathing and you're alive, then that's something to be grateful for. Do you have a place to lay your head, food on the table, clothing, and the basic practical survival necessities needed? Then that's something to be grateful for. Imagine having one or all of that taken away with no one to turn to, because this has happened to a great number of people all across history. How would you feel if that happened?

Statistics have revealed that more people than not despise their job. Many people rightly complain about their job, especially if you're working in an abusive environment with toxic people. It could be a soul crushing job that kills off your life force. You could work with one or more difficult people. You partake in work that doesn't inspire you to want to do it, but you do it for the paycheck to survive. You're not partaking in work that you're passionate about. When you move back into gratitude, you're able to observe the job from a higher perspective. The more challenging plight is when the job is toxic or abusive. Pray daily for a way out into something better and more improved.

Otherwise say in prayer, *"I know I sometimes complain about my job, and I do want to make a positive job change, but at the same time I am grateful that I have a paycheck coming in. I know if I didn't have that, then who knows what would happen. In that respect, I am grateful for this job. I'll do my best to look at it positively while I'm there until I can find another change, I can make to move out of that."*

State that kind of a positive prayer affirmation by not just saying the words, but realize how the words ring true. Feel the gratitude that you have this job and are genuinely blessed. Through that move you are raising your vibration again. The vibration is being raised to match the level of the type of blessings you wish to attract into your life. You are the magnet and the abundance is the steel. You are drawing it towards or away from you depending on your actions, thoughts, and feelings of every moment of every day.

Heaven and the Universe, which we use interchangeably, ensure your basic needs are met. They help with what you need, not always necessarily with what you want, especially if what you want is not beneficial for your higher self. If they do see that it will benefit your growth and higher self, then they will work with you to help bring that which you desire to fruition. All potential and possible factors would need to be examined for each person.

There are various time delays per person as to when particular blessings are bestowed on that soul. Each person's trajectory is different from another person's. It's not that one person is more worthy of blessings over another soul. There are various factors that have to come into play as to what is delaying blessings and miracles.

For every soul on Earth, the desire for blessings and miracles have many factors which come into play to determine whether they will be granted. For someone in the United States, they may have a middle class somewhat comfortable lifestyle as opposed to someone born in a country or area where restrictions, suffocation, bondage, and resistance are evident. There are third world countries where people live in inadequate and unsafe conditions. They may never know what it's like to be able to manifest what they desire.

At the same time, many are brought up in these conditions where they know no other way. They may not have television or internet and have no idea of what is happening in other parts of the world. They may be perfectly content because it is all they know. They weren't brought up in a country or city that displays a desire for excess in front of them around the clock. What they choose to desire may not be as high as what someone else desires in a wealthier city.

The person in a Third World Country may desire to attract in enough food for one night's dinner. Whereas in another part of the world, that wealthy person is bombarded with imagery that you can be whatever you want to be and achieve whatever you want to achieve if you set your mind to it. Maybe you will, but will that bring you ultimate happiness?

Ultimate happiness is the state of high personal soul power. It's climbing beyond the superficiality and the physical to achieve an absolute transcending spiritual life force that is perfectly aligned with God.

The positive side effect to that utopia reached is additional physical manifestations, blessings, and abundance flowing in. Many that reach a higher soul spiritual level no longer desire materialistic excess. This is not limited to the basic human survival needs of a home, food, and clothing. Add to that good friends or a loyal loving love partner, pending you desire the latter. Some spiritual soul achievers tend to be perfectly comfortable alone.

Sometimes it can be that you are indeed ready for blessings. You've done the hard work and experienced what you were intended to in order to bring you to the place you're at today. You have consistently maintained this hard work ethic, but still nothing has transpired to help you have that breakthrough you've long desired. You've done everything right, but nothing has come to pass. In those cases, there are other elements at play preventing the blessings from coming in.

It can be your Spirit team is working diligently behind the scenes with you, but there are free will choice delays that have taken place. It can be that those who are intended to notice your hard work are not paying attention to it, even though the signs have been in front of them forever. Other times it can be that you're doing everything right, but you express no gratitude. Complaining and worry just tells the universe bring me this thing I don't want as fast as you can. All it does is reverse the positive manifestation process into negative manifestation.

Work on being grateful for what you have now. Being ungrateful will block and delay what you desire. It's that negative energy that stalls forward movement. It's understandable to feel frustrated when you've been doing the hard work for so long and yet nothing has come to assist and give you that big miracle breakthrough you long for. It's not like you're being punished, and that God is purposely withholding blessings from you while granting it to others that you feel are less deserving of it. Feeling envy blocks the flow of abundance. It's also not anyone's place to decide who is worthy of what and when. There are varying time limits for each person that determine when and if abundance will flow in and what that will entail.

You're going to feel negative feelings on occasion in terms of what is or isn't coming in. You'll feel frustrated and envious of others that seem to get blessed instantly. This is about recognizing when those feelings hit you and working quickly to eradicate it and move back into a positive alignment. It takes practice and discipline to re-train your mind into a new way of thinking and seeing things. Changing your ways will not drastically happen overnight. It's a gradual methodical process that will take work and focus on your part.

Whenever you notice anything good happening in your life, whether or not it's big or small, remember to say daily, "I Am Blessed!"

You are blessed in the smallest of details, the smallest of ways, there is that glimmer of light that attempts to crack its way in to help you remember to believe again. If you're interested in attracting in positive circumstances, then be genuinely grateful in prayer for what you have now.

CHAPTER TEN

Grieving, Depression, Suicide

Perhaps you are battling with emotional or mental challenges. You reside in a cutthroat ego dominating world that has the attitude of kill or be killed. This hyper technological age has diminished face to face interaction and trained others to conduct themselves like cold aloof robots. The more sensitive souls struggle to stay afloat while battling a consistent array of depression or anxiety symptoms in the mix of this warzone.

There is a difference between being born into this life with a brain chemistry imbalance to feeling the occasional depression blues. Depression blues that hit you once in a rare while can be triggered by poor lifestyle choices or a negative circumstance that knocks you off cloud nine. Those that experience the rare blues usually bounce back if their innate personality is typically upbeat and optimistic. There are those that have always suffered from depression and anxiety symptoms their entire Earthly life.

Depression and anxiety symptoms that develop and remain within the composites of your soul in this lifetime don't have to be seen as a curse. Some of it is connected to your sensitivities, which are connected to your Clairsentience psychic clair channel, which can be channeled positively through artistic and creative pursuits.

Your sensitivities are a gift from Heaven to use towards the self-improvement of your soul as well as the betterment of humanity. Many with heightened sensitivity and stimuli have been able to turn their sensitivities into a successful career in the creative world. They are the artists of the world, such as actors, entertainers, painters, singers, writers, photographers and the list goes on. When they channel their sensitivities positively, there is no telling what they can accomplish. Unfortunately, the downside is when they're unable to channel it positively or they vacillate back and forth from channeling it positively and producing striking work to falling into the darkness of depression symptoms. Some depression symptoms are terribly severe that it leads that human soul to suicidal thoughts.

If you battle with emotional and mental issues in this lifetime such as depression and anxiety, know that you are more psychically in tune than you realize. There is assistance out there in finding healthful ways to temper it or control the onslaught of depression emotions experienced.

Many well-known artists such as actors and singers have resorted to suicide, which has devastated the world prompting a discussion in many circles to take depression and suicide seriously. On the flipside, there are the negative critics popping in that are lucky enough to be cruising through life as happy campers. They've made erroneous statements such as suicide being a selfish act or that if you're depressed to get over it. These people are disconnected from their soul consciousness and anything outside of their physical body. They have been blessed enough to be removed from the imbalances created in more sensitive beings due to the harshness of the Earth's environment.

I'm often asked how is it that a person's guides and angels don't stop something like suicide from happening. This is asked as if Heaven isn't doing anything on their end to stop it. They're merely sitting around twiddling their thumbs. Human souls have free will choice in order to learn and grow their soul. Free will choice means that no heavenly being can intervene without the person's expressed permission. That means if the person is feeling suicidal, then a simple prayer and call out to God can help get the ball rolling.

Where suicide is concerned, the soul's guide and angel are doing what they can to ease that soul's heart and convince them not to do something that will prove fatal. However, as many sensitive beings understand, when you're experiencing negative emotions such as depression, anger, fear or upset, then you're not picking up on anything outside of yourself, let alone your own Spirit team's communications from Heaven. You're only hearing the shouting negativity of your own thoughts which spreads in your mind like a poison.

It isn't uncommon for artists of all types to suffer from depression. They are highly tuned in psychic sensitive sponges able to walk in someone else's shoes. They hold the least amount of judgment by being able to look at a cruel person and find that person's heart when playing a character. Having grown up and worked in the entertainment business, I see them as just like everybody else. They have immense success and talent, but they are struggling with more internal issues and demons beyond the public's comprehension.

A great deal of human souls born into this lifetime and those beyond are ultra-sensitive. They've been planted on Earth or we should say plopped in the middle of a battlefield. Hostile and barbaric human souls surround the sensitives in this world. They tamper and wreak harsh energy that causes long term side effects on the more evolved and evolving souls.

Someone that was bullied growing up by other kids will choose to turn the dark into something light. They'll make light of the darkness by making jokes about it and everything else. For some this might not be enough if the internal turmoil goes untreated. Others resort to drugs and alcohol to quiet the inner demons and to feel happy if just for five minutes. The physical life at times becomes too overbearing on souls battling with ongoing depression.

One's life rarely stays the same and circumstances are always changing. Although it can be tough navigating through life's pitfalls and challenges, you do not have to do it all alone. Prayer is one of the greater ways to help temper all of this as much as possible. You can pray for healing or to be led to help calm any depression and anxiety down. You can pray to be guided to the right Doctor, Counselor, or Healer that can take care of you through the right professional medical care. There is nothing off limits when it comes to prayer, even if you're praying for world domination. This doesn't mean a prayer like that will be answered, but the point is there are no exemptions on the list of things to pray for. This is one of the greatest things God has given and that is a direct line to Him and your Spirit team 24/7 free of charge.

The doorway of communication to Heaven is always open to speak as freely as you choose, and you will never be judged. How awesome is that to actually be able to say whatever you like to them and there is no risk of being judged, attacked, or harshly critiqued the way you would be on this Hell on Earth by other people?

Call on your heavenly team of guides and angels who are on standby to partner up with you in order to make some of these challenges in your life more manageable.

It's important to take depression seriously and get the treatment necessary to continue on. It's also important to remember the body of work that one has donated for the improvement of humanity. This is what will remain alive in years to come, rather than the matter of how one's soul moved into the next plane.

There are sometimes many violent ways in which a soul's life might end in its lifetime. When someone takes their own life via free will or due to a chemical imbalance with their mental health state, then they do so before their time. When this happens, their soul goes into a state of shock as it crosses over. The state that you're in upon suicide as you cross over could stay relatively the same for some. If you had a large ego, then that large ego is still intact as you're crossing over.

If you were suffering from depression and you took your own life, then the state you were in when you took your own life is still present as your soul is crossing over. It's not a pleasant way to cross over because you took your life for the hope of release, but you're not released long after your soul has been extricated from your temporary body. There is a process that takes place in restoring that soul to full capacity. There's a delay before that happens. Sometimes the soul that took their life is disoriented. At the same time there is no pain when crossing over. Any pain that exists is only when in the physical human body. If a soul committed suicide, then like any soul crossing over there are angels and guides surrounding that soul to usher them through the difficulties it might be having.

There are other things that the soul agreed upon as well when they entered this life. If they take their life prematurely, then many end up having to incarnate into another human body and go through similar issues and circumstances all over again. Therefore, it's only bad from the perspective of that soul. It's not bad in the way others preach how you're not supposed to take your own life, or you go to Hell. It's that you had a contract agreed upon to fulfill. If nothing is fulfilled, then it just gets added to a new contract.

Grieving

Human life is accustomed to losses that cause a heavy dark cloud over one's heart. Losses include the human death of someone close to you or the loss of a deep love relationship that ended. Any loss that causes prolonged grief is included. From the perspective of spirit, there is no real loss in this scenario. These losses are part of the human soul experience, but this is an illusion. They do not exist in the bigger reality of why you are here.

Everything you have ever loved or missed comes back to you when your Earthly class is complete. Those grieving over the human death of a loved one must understand that it is not a death in the way that you know it. That soul simply graduated from their Earthly class life run. The uncomfortable heavy weight of the human vessel they occupied was shed off of them. They soared effortlessly into the next room where you will one day re-unite with them. The transition for most is incredibly smooth! There is no pain since pain exists in the Earth's atmosphere. This Earthly life school is equated to boot camp for the soul!

The exceptions are the souls that reside in negative dark energy that have enacted hatred and violence on others. They endure a different process than other souls do, which often requires being diverted into the back gate or left door, which is not a door any soul should desire to go in.

The feeling of grief where you have lost someone you deeply cherished and loved can be challenging to overcome. It is more that you are afraid of the unknown or not seeing concrete proof that your loved one is still around. The ego mind that is detached from spirit conjures up all sorts of conclusions of the worst possible scenarios that there is no next life. As a human soul, it is a process of adjustment when the one you love is not in front of you. It doesn't mean that they're gone in the reality sense. You will be seeing your loved ones again when your Earthly run is complete. All that you loved and lost will be present when your class here is over. As your grieving dissolves you grow more in tune to your surroundings. Grief blocks heavenly communication and you're unable to notice when the loved one is communicating with you from the Other Side. Over time as you raise your vibration from grief, you'll notice the signs and ways your departed loved one is saying 'hello' or communicating with you in the interim.

Often times when a human soul is grieving over the passing of a departed loved one, it pulls the departed soul back into the Earth plane. When you make peace with the one that has passed on, then you release the grieving attachment to them that might keep the soul stuck in this plane. See the soul as exiting through an etheric doorway of heavenly light where they will be doing fantastic! You will see your departed loved one again when your lifetime is complete. In the meantime, they will be with you, watching you, and working with you as one of your guides from time to time. They will be there to greet you when you enter that doorway of light yourself.

When feeling the heaviness of grief, revert to prayer to help you cope and continue on. Ask in prayer that signs of their soul's existence be shown to you. And as always seek out professionals such as grief counselors, support groups, and friendships and family members you trust to be rejuvenated to continue on knowing your loved one is still with you and helping you heal.

CHAPTER ELEVEN

The Significance of Spirituality

There have been numerous polls over the years showing that more people identify as "Spiritual, but not religious" as opposed to those that identify as atheist or strictly religious and not spiritual. This is one way that the repetitive scientific data is indicating that their truly has been a rise in spiritual interests since the 1980's. It accelerated post 2000 as we moved more into the technological era with social media. This is one of the positives of the Internet, technology, and social media.

Part of these findings may be due to how easily information is accessed now online. Before that time period, many people secretly wanted to be more spiritual, but feared ridicule so they went along with pretending to be a hardcore religious person when in the company of other religious people. They didn't have access to communities that had a similar mindset before the Internet domination. Some of the content I talked about during that time was that people were moving away from the fundamentalist religious belief systems and atheism, while becoming more spiritual. We're now seeing these findings to be true.

Without people knowing what I do upon first meeting they would be talking about God and faith, but then would quickly say, "I'm spiritual but not religious." They're saying that to inform the other person not to worry they're not judgmental and full of hate and condemnation the way one expects a religious person to be. Saying that you're spiritual but not religious shows someone has a strong faith-based belief system, but without all of the hate filled dogma that one would associate with a fundamentalist preacher.

Because of this rising spiritual but not religious mindset that has grown astronomically post 2000's, some churches have begun to adopt more lenient policies to welcome more patrons since they started to simultaneously witness a decline in fellowship. This is especially the case for gays who face so much hatred, wrath, and condemnation from some people. All of this because they cannot but be attracted to someone of the same gender. It was how God made them, but they are faced with backlash over it. I've heard of many churches that have become more welcoming for gays, which naturally has also drawn ire from the more fundamentalist patrons. The greatest irony is the fundamentalists go to a house of worship to be taught to remember God's top mantra of love, but are unable to extend that love to all people from all walks of life.

Spirituality is asking the bigger questions and being open to the understanding that there is much more to an Earthly life than the physical material world of narcissism created by human ego. Someone can consider themselves spiritual if they are religious and go to Church regularly. They can also be someone who enjoys going to New Age stores, playing with Tarot cards, or reading self-help books. The spiritual person can be someone that is solely interested in improving one's well-being and subsequently the way they live and their quality of life. The list is long as to how deep the spirituality genre can go and what that individual soul identifies it to be for them.

Someone that considers themselves to be a spiritual person will more than likely be curious, interested, or at least open to all facets of the genre. This is one who is interested in deeper philosophical knowledge as to why they are here or how everything was created. They want to know how to improve themselves and this world. Their belief in God will vary from believing in some form of higher power to not believing in any type of God, Light, or spirit. They might follow and enjoy all facets of spirituality, but will not believe there is any kind of God. God also has different meanings for people depending on who you talk to.

A spiritual person that does not believe in any kind of God is not to be confused with an atheist who tends to not believe in anything, except that when you die, you're done and all goes black, the end. An atheist does not believe in God, an afterlife, or any form of metaphysics, spirituality, new age, religion, or God. Even though they might lump the entire spiritual genre together, generally they take issue with organized religion, God, the Bible, and religious dogma. They find the mere mention of an afterlife to be hogwash, and any hint of spirituality to be New Age phooey. An agnostic is someone more open minded to the possibility of some form of God or afterlife, but they do not fully believe in it, yet they also do not fully believe that there is nothing after this either. They hang in the middle requiring physical evidence to convince them. They're more likely to be open to spiritual pursuits in order to assist them on their quest for this knowledge.

I've witnessed atheists transitioning into having more of an open mind when they get their toes wet in any level of spirituality that they feel some form of comfort with. They receive a big enough jolt in their life that leads them to begin questioning and thus becoming more of a spiritual person or agnostic. There are atheists who might not believe in any of it, but are still drawn to spiritual or self-improvement books and interests. In a sense, they're not realizing at that moment they're moving from atheist into an agnostic. Many tend to use labels on themselves that they don't truly understand the meaning of. All human souls are spiritual beings regardless if they believe in that or not.

Earth and all of the planets came from somewhere. They did not suddenly appear in a perfectly orchestrated solar system that affects the energies in humankind depending on its planetary path. An explosion did not create a setup of planets that circle the Sun in a flawlessly designed fashion and then permanently stayed that way. Pluto is the only planet farthest from the Sun to be detected by humankind. This does not mean there are no other planets or galaxies beyond that, as there most definitely are. Humankind is just unable to detect that. No other life form outside of Earth has been detected scientifically after eons of centuries gone by. As big as the universe is, all life forms seemingly only inhabit Earth, or so one believes.

Almost eight billion people on Earth in this solar system at this time in Earth's history are not an accident. This also gives you some perspective as to how miniscule humankind is in the grand scheme of things. You venture off into space to planet Jupiter or Neptune, then suddenly life on Earth appears immensely ridiculous and trivial from that distance. All of the fighting, disagreeing, pollution, harm, and negative words darted back and forth to one another make humankind look rather silly. You can get a pretty good idea as to how Heaven views the planet from where they are. All of the nonsense that goes on means nothing to them. They watch everyone hate, hurt, and harm one another and roll their eyes with indifference so to speak.

Others find it difficult to believe that God, the archangels, and the angels are unaffected by the harm people are doing to one another. This is thinking from the ego and in a limited way. God, the archangels, and the angels are egoless, which means they have no ego. When you have no ego, then you're unaffected by anything. It does not mean that you do not care, but you are not ruffled emotionally. An egoless being witnesses harmful destruction and feels nothing. You have a detached perception. You view things from a higher perspective. This is not to be confused with a murdering terrorist or serial killer who is without a conscious. They have a dark ego that governs their life demanding they kill. They want control, which is an ego trait.

When you're upset, then this is your ego. God, the archangels, and angels do not get upset because they are egoless. Someone might say operating from ego, "God will punish you for that." This is that person's projection of hoping that God will punish that person, but God does not chastise.

There are ego beings in Heaven, but their ego is not out of control the way it would be in the Earth's atmosphere living a human life. Go back through centuries of history to the beginning of Earth's conception and the start of humankind. At least one man and one woman would have needed to be present in order to multiply. It is not by chance that they were suddenly here and figured out how to mate. They did not evolve out of apes and then stopped evolving out of them. They did not rise from the dirt and appear. There are circumstances existing that are larger than the human mind can comprehend. Science has attempted to make sense of it all, but without much luck enough to convince every person. This is going back to the initial creation of life, the planets, people, animals, plants came together in ways that a non-believer wouldn't be able to fathom or comprehend. There is no data that exists of when the first man walked the Earth and what that was like. There was no language or concept of anything being what already is. The spiritual connections were stronger at the dawn of humankind because there were limited distractions and blocks that the darkness of ego would later create within them.

It was human instinct to connect sexually and suddenly people were being born and multiplying at a rapid rate out of that. They soon believed that it was God's purpose for them to continuously procreate. Breeding intelligently is one thing, but multiplying to eight billion people shows that most reproduce out of ignorance, naivety, and to fulfill ego desires. Earth is a rapid ant farm with people screaming and starving for attention, power, and domination. If this increases, it will have catastrophic consequences.

Every living soul is a descendant of the first man that walked the Earth. No one is separated by color, culture, or any other factor. The darkness of ego caused separation from one another. When someone is not evolving, then they view their surroundings and other souls in a limited way. They are uncomfortable with anyone that identifies as different from them being in their vicinity. The ego will grow angry and cause them harm, hurt, or hate just because the other person is not an identical clone. The ego sees this person as threatening, instead of viewing others with understanding, love, acceptance, and compassion.

You move into the realms of spirituality when you start asking the bigger questions such as, "Why am I here?" and "Why are some people different?" or "Is Heaven Real?" You understand there is much more to life than the mundane physical existence that has been structured and set up by human beings of years past. As a spiritual person you have a belief in a higher power, energy, light, spirit or life force. You have a belief that when your life run is complete that it is not the end. Someone spiritual has their own personal barometer on how things should be. They might not necessarily believe in God. The teachings within the spiritual and religious genre tend to differ while other times you'll find there are some common parallels aligned with one another. The similarities are give and take by varying degrees.

One who is interested in spirituality is open to expanding their consciousness and seeking out the solutions unanswered for them. It is an individual quest to align your soul with energy bigger than the material plane. This is working on your soul and becoming a better person in the process. You want to be connected to what's beyond the current life you're living.

Sometimes one is not born spiritual, but as they evolve over the course of their life, they grow to become spiritual. They might have hit rock bottom moment in life, which prompts a major transition that awakens that soul and raises their consciousness. They could have been raised in a strict religious upbringing that felt wrong to them if it was enforcing shame, guilt, and other negative feelings that are not aligned with God. To their subconscious this feels dishonest as they recall their connections while in Heaven and where they came from. They do not remember it to be a place of hate and assault. Suddenly they find themselves hip to this reality. Why do people commit horrible deeds? Why are others cruel to one another? These are some of the questions that one desires answers to that can make some measure of sense to that soul. If God exists, then how can He allow bad things to happen?

I have deep connections and communications with spirit beings that consist of guides, angels, saints, and archangels. This is no different than what anyone else can do when they elevate their consciousness, raise their vibration, and tune in to what's beyond. It is true some people are more strongly connected than others, but all souls have the capacity to elevate their consciousness, vibration, and psychic clair channels to be equally connected. Every soul connects to the Other Side whether it is believed you are in communication with your Spirit team or not. Sometimes you think that the accurate information you're coming to is your imagination or you second-guess it. Examine all of the varying belief systems that humans have designed and invented. From that point you connect the dots to where the truths within each belief system reside. There are some common denominators and similarities such as all paths lead to God. What others feel God to be is up for individual debate. The higher evolved human souls' sense that in the end it's all supposed to be about love. The further you stray from love, the more disconnected you are from spirit and God.

There are teachings that instruct you to not crave material wealth as that is a detachment from God and that the only way to true happiness is from within. While this has some measure of truth, many shun this belief just as much as they reject strict religious doctrine that insists you will go to Hell for something like French kissing. These dogmas need to be corrected and illustrated in a way that is easily digestible. The detachment from materialism needs to have the right balance, because the way Earthly life is designed today is by prospering the economy. This is the current Earthly life reality whether you agree with it or not.

Human beings need to make money to survive, to eat, to be clothed, and obtain housing. People designed it this way over the centuries of history. They implemented new ways of finding work through the rise of supply and demand. In the process, they grew detached to anything outside of themselves. You get up every morning to drive to a job to make money to be able to pay your rent or your mortgage. Most people spend the majority of their waking hours at work. This is more than at home with family, friends, and loved ones. You're taught to meet someone, get married, move in together, and start a family. These are the basics, which sound easy enough, but in the current modern-day world it's grown much more complicated than that. People have a difficult time finding a partner in crime to be with for life in a love relationship. And when they do finally find that person, it doesn't always last until the end of their days together on Earth the way it used to.

Humankind is taught how to function, and the mass majority moves along with that trend. They're taught to go to school, graduate with a High School Diploma, and start thinking of College or look for a job. They're taught to hate others who are not like them, and pass judgment, or cause harm against those who live life differently. You can be spiritually connected and still thrive to find great work that fulfills you in order to make enough to live comfortably on this planet. There are differences between becoming obsessively money hungry that you are viewed as an angry miser, to being someone who works hard, and does their job well, but you're not ruled by this job.

When you remember who you are, and you have a stronger connection of what is beyond, then the answers become clearer and God comes rushing in. Your consciousness is its own thinking, feeling, and soul inhabiting a human physical body. You are bumping into other souls inhabiting a body as well. They are also their own thinking and feeling soul inhabiting a human physical body. Why are you here? What does your consciousness remember from before your human birth? Your consciousness is the part of your soul that continues to grow wherever it moves along its life path. Your soul has been to many places. One child recalls repeated dreams of seeing both a red planet and a black one. Another child vividly remembers Christ making him.

In essence, when any soul is born, they are spiritual at heart. They are 100% in tune and psychic. They are full of immense love, joy, and peace. The soul knows where it came from. As the child grows, its environment trains them to be who it prefers it to be rather than who you really are. At that point you stray further from your soul's essence. You're having an individual spiritual journey. If you're an atheist, then that is your current spiritual journey. This is the same if you're Buddhist, Christian, Catholic, Muslim, Agnostic, and so on.

The kind of spirituality we promote is where you get to be yourself as long as it's not hurting you or anyone else. You get to be as raw, crass, and different as you like. In some spiritual circle's others have mentioned that they feel judged by someone who is on a different journey than they are. Slamming others, harassing them, and name-calling is not being spiritual or a good person for that matter. This is different than the ego rising up to resort to reacting out of anger because someone has attacked them. We're talking about those who go out of their way to attack someone for not doing something the way they might do it. This is not someone operating from their higher self. Everyone is on a different spiritual journey including a non-believer. That is their journey they've chosen to go down. As long as no one is hurting anyone, then allow that soul the freedom to explore what works for them.

Warrior of Light

There are souls living a human life that are threaded around the planet called Warrior of Light's. A Warrior of Light is a strong soul that fights in the name of Heaven, God, and the light. They are often the darker souls that ferociously defend and teach in the name of the Light. They are typically unwavering and unbending. As representatives of the Light they have no problem rising to head into battle, which they're called upon to do often even when they don't want to. Archangel Michael is the General of all Warrior of Light's. The Light is God and God is the Light. They are interchangeable energy and the all-knowing source. A Warrior of Light is someone that is a fighter or soldier for God and Heaven.

Imagine a company created by Heaven called, "The God Organization". You are one of the employees. When you need supplies, you ask God for these supplies. Sometimes He might temporarily deny the supplies due to budgetary constraints, but He is a fair boss and will provide what He believes is best for you at that time.

The Warrior of Light is not a role I'm playing, but rather it is a part of me. I do my job when I can as if I'm working for anybody else. I have off days as any human being does. The difference here is that I love this employer. When you like your employer, then it's not a drag to do the work.

CHAPTER TWELVE

Spirit Is In Your Corner

We've discussed the free will law that says no spirit being can intervene with any soul to make choices and decisions for them unless that soul has specifically requested it. This means when you desire something or you need help with anything, you send out a request to Heaven. This can be done in prayer, mentally, in writing, or out loud. If you don't ask, then they are not allowed to intervene in your life unless it is to prevent a life-endangering situation that might result in death before your time. Other than that, you're on your own until you ask for help.

Your Spirit team will guide and nudge you along your path, but unless you're paying attention to these cues there is little they can do. There are some that don't believe in any of that, but the irony is they remain in a stuck and miserable position in life. If you're already stagnant and feeling hopeless, then what could it hurt to say a little quick prayer asking for help. You're already saying and thinking words and thoughts anyway, most of which are unhelpful. You may as well say a few words in prayer. No special words or invocation needs to be said. Simply saying words like this can get the ball rolling, "God can you please help me with this."

You can call upon whoever you're comfortable with communicating to such as God, Heaven, your Spirit Guide, Guardian Angel, departed loved one, Archangel, Saint, or Ascended Master. You can do this at any time or hour of the day. Whoever you are choosing to communicate to is still heard by God since there is no escape from that. Heaven understands what you desire in your heart, but they also need to hear you make the formal request. It's much like the mythological image of the Vampire, where they cannot enter your house without an expressed invitation from you. Or when a friend or employer knows you want to ask for help with something, but you're not saying anything. They wait for you to finally approach them and ask for the help you desire. This is similar in how Spirit beings in Heaven work. You need to invite them into your life if you want them working with you.

It doesn't matter how you ask, but that you do ask. You can say something like, "Please help me find another job." Or "I need help finding a love partner". You can ask them for anything. It doesn't mean that they'll always grant it, but it also cannot hurt to ask.

If you need help looking for another job, then discuss with them in prayer the kind of job you desire, but avoid laying out how you want something to come about. Leave the how and when up to them. They will orchestrate what needs to happen when the timing is right. This is pending that it is aligned with your higher self's goal. Your higher self uses the least amount of ego. While your ego might desire something, your higher self isn't interested in triviality or superficiality. You can pray to be guided to the right love partner.

Have faith and a strong belief that Spirit is in your corner, even if it feels like there is a long delay or stagnancy period going on before results appear to be forthcoming.

When I was sixteen, I knew that I was going to write books one day. I wanted to write, and no one was going to stop me in working at my passion and purpose. I knew I had to get a regular job first. I had a strong connection with my team of guides and angels when I was a child. From adolescence, I had been working with them, communicating with them, and following their guidance. I asked my team for help with getting this first job at a record store. This was back when record stores existed and were as popular as an amusement park. My team guided me in steps to make that happen.

I wanted to get into the film business not long after that, so I asked my team for help with that. I followed their guidance in trying to get in, and then the lucky break took place. All great things came down from that point. It took years for something like that to happen, but it did end up happening in an even bigger way than I expected. This is an example of Heaven intervention and assistance coming through regular prayer. When I asked for help in prayer, then it eventually came to light. When I did nothing, then that was exactly what I got. I've been testing them out my entire life through trial and error. This has helped me learn the process of how they operate.

When you ask for help, guidance, or intervention, then step out of the way and allow the assistance to come about. Release and let go of the need to push for an answer or the need to control a situation. When you call up a friend you don't repeat the same phrases as if they didn't hear you the first time. You say it once and then move onto something else.

You can repeatedly request something to your Spirit team, but it will only make you grow aggravated and frustrated when you receive nothing right away. Days pass and you're feeling miserable wondering what's going on. You might say to yourself, "I don't get it. I've been praying and repeatedly asking for help with this, but nothing is coming. Maybe this isn't real or they're ignoring me."

Those in Heaven view circumstances on Earth from a different perspective than human beings. They do not get caught up in the human ego drama and tantrums that we sometimes fall into. If you feel you're being ignored, then it's likely the ego that is having a fit, which Heaven is indifferent to. They are not fazed or affected by the ego's spectacle the way we can sometimes be.

All of the stuff in the media, human politics, and people arguing with one another is seen as triviality and a waste of time and energy from the perspective of those in Heaven. Being caught up in that space is what can cause a long delay of inactivity until you step away from being completely absorbed in pettiness.

What Heaven pays attention to is someone that has a huge growing light around them. This is someone contributing to humanity in a positive way. It is someone doing their best to be a compassionate loving person. Those are the ones that widen the eyes of a high vibrational spirit in Heaven. They want to help that soul, but sometimes they have to maneuver situations that require another person to pay attention.

For instance, you want a job at a specific company. You've put in a request for help from your Spirit team, but time has passed, and nothing has surfaced. If it doesn't come about, then take into consideration the possibilities that you're not privy to. One of them is that the person responsible for hiring staff is not paying attention to the guidance from their own Spirit team to bring you on. Another reason is that this job would not make you happy, even though you cannot see that right away. Your Spirit team can see how it would end if you joined that particular company. It would not end well in your favor, so they keep it from happening and continue to guide you to the place of employment they see you joining and being happier at. There is also the possibility that they have something greater in mind for you that is further out in the distance and you're required to have patience, faith, and trust that things are in motion behind the scenes. This concept is applied to all aspects of one's life including a desire for a loving relationship partner or a new place to move to. They might keep you away from someone you have a love crush on because they know it would not benefit your higher self. The person might be abusive in some form that would cause you prolonged heartache. When one has a love crush on someone, they don't truly know that person. They've developed an ideal fantasy image over how great their crush must be while being blinded by any potential red flags. Later down the line, you connect with someone out of this world that is better than the one you had the crush on.

Putting a request into Heaven in prayer once a day can be sufficient for a desire. Put in at least one request for them on a matter before they can intervene and assist.

You're allowed the freedom to live your life the way you see fit pending it's not hurting yourself or someone else. You place your prayer request with Heaven and then you walk away. You busy yourself with other things and don't fret or think about the request you made. Let them help while you focus on something else. This is why they are called your Spirit team, because they are your team who works with you helping out where possible. You are also helping them out by taking action when they push you to. Avoid trying to think about how a prayer will be answered, because often times it's answered in a way that you do not expect.

Sometimes prayers are answered immediately and other times it may be delayed for a reason. If there are life lessons you must endure in a particular circumstance, then this could be one reason for a delay. Notice or pick up on the guidance they continue to filter through you as to why

You might find yourself saying, "I kept getting this nudge to call this person up and I continuously brushed it off. I finally called them and what I wanted came to be!"

This is an example of your Guide or Angel nudging you to make that call. Heaven communicates to you through your etheric psychic clair senses. When your senses are clear of debris, toxins, and blocks, then the clearer the messages are. This is one of the reasons they insist that everyone work on being clear minded, exercise regularly, head out into nature, take time outs, avoid negative people and choices, and watch what you ingest into your body. Those action steps contribute to you being a fine-tuned up communication machine with your Spirit team. Being in nature is one of the greatest healing places to be in. The messages come in clearer in those areas.

Your Spirit team of Guides and Angels are at your disposal. Ask for help and intervention with anything you desire. Understand that there may be delays to fulfilling your request or they might have something better in mind for you. They will also only deliver what is aligned with your higher self. Develop a daily relationship with God, Heaven, and your Guides and Angels.

They can help by giving you strength in a tough situation, motivating you to write that letter for the job you're interested in, or to obtain that potential love mate you have your eye on. If it appears that what you desire is not happening, then take into account the various possible reasons for that. When you are tuned into Spirit, then the reasons as to why will filter through you effortlessly. Centering yourself and getting your ego out of the way helps you to be more able to pick up on the possible explanations. This can be that what you're asking for is not aligned or beneficial to your higher self's growth and path. There are circumstances that need to be maneuvered in order to make it happen. Your Spirit team has a list of variables in the way that are challenging. This can be something such as working with someone's free will choice including your own.

Many human souls no longer pay attention or listen to their Spirit team's wisdom let alone believe in a higher power. Those that believe in a higher power are unaware they have a Spirit team they can connect with. They might believe the process to be associated with witchcraft or hocus-pocus. A lack of faith in your team blocks the incoming messages and guidance. Your Spirit team is relaying action steps you need to take through their guidance, but you're ignoring those steps, or brushing it off due to assuming it is wishful thinking, laziness, or procrastination. Your Spirit team will continue to give you the same guidance repeatedly until you follow it. Once you realize that the same synchronicity is continuously being put in front of you to take action on, and then you take action on it, then your Spirit team will show you the next step to take and so on as you travel along your soul's journey.

CHAPTER THIRTEEN

Be Your Own Messiah

As life on the planet continues to evolve and progress, so do many of the souls who choose to enter into an Earthly life. These souls are easy to spot since by the time they're about eight to twelve years old they have begun questioning the chaos that surrounds them. They consciously know a great deal of the madness is perpetuated by the darker sides of one's self. Discovering early on that perhaps others do not have the market cornered on the point of humanity's existence. These particularly young people are extremely sensitive and may be seen to others as different or the outcast that are hip to deception. Hence an Earth Angel is born.

Earth Angels have a larger faith-based belief system beyond what organized religion has offered the previous generations. Organized religion has infused fear, doubt, guilt, and low self-esteem into others. These are qualities not aligned with God. The traits associated with Heaven are love, joy, and peace.

This isn't saying that organized religion has no light in it, as there is good in all groups and sects. The public only hears about the bad elements from each category of people. There are good people within the confines of organized religion that accept and love all with compassion as well too. Every soul is moving through a different class education level of spiritual growth regardless of their religious belief or non-belief. When one chooses to associate with a particular religious belief, they are moving through that level of spiritual lessons intended for that soul. Atheism is also choosing a belief system of non-belief, which is also a spiritual lesson they are moving through.

Growing up, I loved going to the church I was a part of and had no complaints about it. There was no talk of a vengeful God and nor did anyone affiliated with the church hate or disapprove of anyone that wasn't like them. I quickly and rapidly graduated beyond that as a teenager when I realized that my connections with God were happening no matter where I was. I didn't need to go to a particular place or be around a specific group of people to connect with the Other Side, because my Spirit team was moving around with me wherever I went.

When I went to Church regularly growing up, I never recalled anything negative at all associated with it from the destructive words we hear today to the negative people who claim to be Jesus followers, but are in actuality buried under the reign of the Darkness. Either I was lucky to not have heard any of that or I was just going to the right more accepting joyful churches that are based in all love. Then again, I grew up during a time when there was no Internet and social media. You could be living in a bubble thinking all was well not realizing there was a great deal of condemnation and hatred going on. The public just wasn't hearing about it the way they are today.

If I ever did hear any form of hatred, lies, or damnation, I would've left immediately anyway. I don't tolerate that today and most certainly didn't tolerate it then. I have no negative memories of that at the churches I went to. I also didn't grow up in that kind of a household. I was the unusual spiritually connected one, which reveals that I had come to that conclusion on my own without any family interference or influence, but rather through my Spirit connections that have been around for as long as I can remember.

There is also quite a bit of abusive organized religious sects that condemn everyone and everything in their path. They are permanently judgmental, angry, and disrespectful lacking in compassion. Bathed in lower energies, they come from a place of fear and ego, instead of God and love. They are responsible for the massive growing number of atheists threaded throughout the planet.

Many organized religious groups have been and are so abusive, negative, and hateful that they created a vast disconnection and block with God. Instead they created a closer relationship with the darkness of ego, otherwise known to them as the Devil. They were successful in spreading false judgment out of ancient superstition that they birthed the atheist movement through this negativity. As a result, it spiritually blocked many people that grew up in that environment. You have the hate filled organized religious groups on one extreme side and then atheists on the other extreme side. Extreme sides don't bridge the gap that unites the planet together as one in compassion, unity, and love.

Someone asks their church a question about something that appears to question certain text or scripture, and no answer is given, but a generalized statement telling you to just read the Bible and follow Christ.

This is no longer an acceptable answer to the hyper intelligent souls incarnating into an Earthly life demanding answers and solutions. Because all Earth Angels operate on a higher frequency than the norm, they're suspicious and see right through organized religions that lambast and judge others that are of a different race, gender, or sexual orientation. Naïve human adults cement this into their consciousness, as if it is true

Gospel.

The Bible has beautiful passages written about showing compassion and love, but then there are texts clearly written by someone residing during a superstitious time period that no longer coincides with the awakened consciousness way of thinking. Many of my guides are from the archaic days of biblical times. Some of them made significant contributions to the Bible at that time when they were living an Earthly life, such as Luke and Matthew. Much of what they discussed in those days have been modified to one degree or another, or misinterpreted.

Mother Mary, Saint of Inner Strength

Saint Mary, Mother Mary, the mother of all Mother's often depicted with the Archangel Gabriel announcing to her of the child she would deliver to humanity. They were and are both symbols of love.

In my connections with Mother Mary, I immediately discovered what a strong ferocious soul she is. This is nothing like what is depicted in man's artwork of her, which conveys a softness. She is bathed in compassion, but nowhere near being like the passivity that is portrayed of her to be. Her light and presence are immense, stable, forceful, full of overflowing love, and strength like her Son's.

My relationship with Mary dates back to childhood where I would obsessively pay homage to her image whenever I'd excitedly arrive at church as if I were going to a nightclub. A different and contradicting child, I was draped in rosary crucifixes, a filthy mouth, and a young cocky arrogance that I will do what I want, when I want, without interference.

Mary appears with this inspiring feel good inner warmth that continues to expand bigger than all the compassionate maternal beings of the world put together. The blazing sparkling rose and white light of love that shines around her outwardly like the sun is so intense that it overpowers her tiny 4'11" frame that fades into it.

The long running connection with Mary might not be surprising considering that one of my main guides Luke, who is of the Gospel of Luke, discusses Mary more than any other writer in the controversial loved and hated book. His portrait of her is layered in detail with the most quotes than any other. He's also the most educated, observant....and like myself - long winded. His stories tended to be filled with the goal of ultimate healing, which shows he had more compassion for others than some of his counterparts in the book with their superstitious fear-based dogma. When touched by Mary's power, like her Son, it is unconditional love experienced that no words can describe.

Mary urges you to be strong and persevere. When you feel like crawling into a hole, you're drained, over worked, or stressed, then call on Mother Mary to help you in healing. She coaxes you not to hide and or play the victim. You will rise up and dive straight on into battle. She believes you can do it and are stronger than you may give yourself credit for. Mary has never been passive, and she demands that you don't be either. When you draw from the Light, there is no telling what you cannot do. The Light helps you forge on even if you feel you're unable to. Let your connection with the Divine be the source of your pillar of strength.

Archangel Raphael, the Healing Angel

Archangel Raphael is known as the healing angel. This is because he has performed miraculous healing for physical, emotional, and mental issues when others have requested his help. The light that consumes him inside and out is bursting with emerald green light. Whatever he touches with this light begins the process of healing.

Call on Archangel Raphael whenever you are experiencing any issues related to physical, emotional or mental well-being. Visualize his healing green light being showered anywhere that requires attention. Understand that he may guide you to the answer that can remedy any issue. This may be from being guided to the right medical specialist or to healing medicinal properties that can assist in a medical related issue.

Raphael works alongside Mother Mary and Jesus Christ during great catastrophes where souls are extricated abruptly leaving them disoriented for a bit. The disorientation is not painful, but more of a confusing amnesia where your soul is not quite sure what's just happened.

I'm a super physically active soul and with that I've faced some physical consequences. One of them included an incident where I felt this sudden pain in my right arm or what is called the *flexor carpi radialis muscle* in the human forearm. Days passed and the pain still flushed in and out without any sign of healing. This was when I realized I needed heavenly intervention.

I called in Archangel Raphael before I went to sleep. I rubbed my hands together until I felt the heavy friction between them. I pried my hands slowly apart and clairvoyantly saw an emerald green light fire bursting between them with energy. I took that light and began hovering one of my hands over the area where the pain is. And it is done.

When I woke up in the middle of the night there were still signs of slight pain here and there, but I headed back to sleep anyway. I woke up the next day and discovered that the pain was gone. I twisted and turned my forearm and noticed no signs of any agitation or anything. Days passed into weeks and I realized that the pain had evaporated and never re-surfaced.

I believe in the power of prayer because I've witnessed and personally experienced countless and endless miracles over the course of my life as a result. When I don't ask for help, then help is not forthcoming. I've always followed and adhered to faith healing combined with medicinal healing. This is by bringing in prayer over an issue, while being guided to medicinal or herbal remedies to assist in bringing the body back to tip top form. Some only believe in faith healing, which has resulted in harm and even death, while others will pop a pill, and not bother to include Divine intervention. Their illness persists for much longer as a result, and sometimes they never get better.

Removing blockages can be done through body movement and physical exercise, which Raphael can also help with. What kind of health issues does one have that prevents them from regular exercise? For some it's...dare we say it, laziness, but for others there are some in this life that are genuinely authentically physically crippled and absolutely cannot. This applies to those who are physically capable of exercise, but just don't want to. Exercise helps in dissolving blocks with the Divine.

Archangel Gabriel, the Angel of Creative Expression

Another way to dissolve blocks is through creativity. Dive into creativity, creative pursuits, and projects when you find you're falling into a blockage. You've lost energy, passion, and a zest for life. Creative expression can assist in reopening that pathway to Divinity again. Archangel Gabriel is the one to call on to help with procrastination and in awakening your creative gifts. All Angels and Archangels are genderless and have no anatomy, despite artists depicting them in various physical forms in paintings and art. It is true they may take certain forms in appearing in ways that are recognizable to that person.

Archangel Gabriel has a feminine energy because she assists others by pulling things out from within, whether that is creative expression, passion, nurturing your inner child, mothering Children, pregnancies, or the birth of a project or endeavor. The uncertainty of how Archangel Gabriel is perceived has carried on for many centuries. This goes back to how life was lived during biblical times. Centuries ago the world was a male dominating patriarchal society, and the female form was considered forbidden and secondary. For that matter, the Catholic Church changed Archangel Gabrielle to Archangel Gabriel and demanded that she be seen, depicted, and perceived as a male. The only female deity allowed at that time was Mother Mary and that was because she gave birth to Jesus Christ.

No one can control the free will actions of mankind. This change has caused confusion over the centuries where some believe Gabriel to be male. The church eventually corrected this perception, but by that time the world was already training one another to continue to see "Gabrielle" as male.

Gabriel is an egoless genderless being unperturbed by the false beliefs of man, since all human souls have free will choice to believe what they want to believe. The "Gabriel" name may have a masculine tone to it, but gender identity is strictly reserved to human beings that have been taught and trained to separate male and female. This has also caused quite a bit issues among humankind.

Archangels and Angels will appear in a form that the individual is used to in order to be recognizable, even though it is not their natural appearance. They can morph in and out of a light source as a spirit.

It wasn't until the 1900's and beyond when women in some countries were allowed to vote or have an opinion. It was taboo for women to get a divorce or even work. Gender equality didn't really move full steam ahead until beyond the 1970's. In some countries, women are still forced to take a back seat specifically in third world countries. Therefore, it's not surprising to know that during biblical times man did not want a female deity figure.

Archangel Gabriel is my agent guiding and moving me along my career path since I started the workforce as a teenager. Luke, one of my guides, works along with her on all career work related endeavors. My writing work is done with the both of them present.

Gabriel has clairvoyantly appeared numerous times over the course of my life. Her physical appearance is neither male nor female. The shape of her face is not like a human face, but the structure of it is soft and on the feminine side, almost androgynous. She drops down into my space in a bright copper colored light with white sparkles and wears a light blue cloak that covers everything except for her face. The cloak is dominating and flowing. She also doesn't have wings even though that's how artists paint her.

When she moves into my space, I clairaudiently hear music rush up emitting out and around her. There is a sudden intoxicating joyous uplifting feeling that soars through me. The lyrics to, "Hark the Herald Angels Sing!" were words that she whispered into the consciousness of the writers of the song. She communicates predominately through me clairaudiently and telepathically. Telepathy is one of the primary ways of communication on the Other Side.

Mother Nature's Wrath

When violence is placed upon the backs of anyone, then that can shake one's faith. There are good and bad people in all groups, except for terrorists who are against any and all that don't subscribe to their way of life. There is no room for light in that darkness. The real followers of God are peace loving people rather than fundamentalists or terrorists that scream the loudest and get the most attention from the media. They don't know God and are blinded by the infusion of Darkness. Deep down somewhere in that terrorist's soul is someone born with goodness and love inside. This concept has been brought to light in entertainment. Look at the *Star Wars* films and the character Darth Vader who was once good, but crossed over to the dark side and became evil. It wasn't until his deathbed when the goodness he once had finally came back out.

There are some that believe that Mother Nature is attempting to tell humanity something important through her majesty's destruction. They find it disheartening to see so many souls passing on as a result. This includes what some consider nature's fury and anger through Earthquakes, Fires, or Hurricanes.

From a higher level, Earthquakes and other natural disasters have to do with the construction of the Earth. God or any being in Heaven doesn't make natural disasters happen nor do they prevent them from happening. Human beings are given a place to inhabit so it's up to them to ensure it's livable. You're given a massive planet to have life on.

Like every being that exists on the planet, the planet Earth is a living-breathing organism made up of energy as every cell and atom that exists is. Energy fluctuates and compresses every second of its life reacting to the energy around it. Negative energy will aggravate all living-breathing organisms around it in a negative way since energy creates a domino effect with all that it touches.

If someone is joyful and positive, then this will uplift those around, but if they're negative and toxic, then this will bring everyone in the vicinity down. People chose to build homes on top of one another and in environments or areas that are prone to natural disasters. This isn't God's fault since He metaphorically more or less sits back and allows all souls free will to choose how they want to live life on Earth.

Nepal once experienced a bad Earthquake that caused massive devastation. Many skeptics protested to ask, "Where is this alleged, God?"

My Spirit team pointed out that those areas that were destroyed were buildings that were human-made and not up to code to withstand a catastrophic Earthquake, let alone a small Earthquake. This is all due to human decision and error, not any being in Heaven. Many people procreated at an expedited level and then inhabited areas that cannot withstand a natural disaster. The lives lost we're not lost in spiritual truth. They passed on from this plane as a collective. When catastrophes happen, it is the job of all Earthly souls to examine why and how it happened, rather than having the mindset that they're being punished.

The Archangel Michael can help with fear in any situation, but no one in Heaven can stop the Earth's plates from shifting. Earthquakes have been going on since the beginning of Earth's conception. Although some might claim that God controls natural disasters causing them to happen as punishment for some of the human sinners, which is ludicrous because the entire world sins. If he were controlling natural disasters for that reason, then He would take down the entire world in one clean swipe.

Planet Earth is an energy vessel and a ticking time bomb aggravated by the billions of energy atoms that encompass the souls that inhabit it. Regular disturbances such as hurricanes, fires, and earthquakes are not unusual, even though it's been extremely volatile. It cannot be denied that it's been shifting abnormally. God is not bringing in storms. It's the climate and nature that creates hurricanes. God doesn't care about possessions and homes. He cares about someone's character. When it is your time to go, then it's your soul contracted time.

There are also some that believe that God must love and prefer people that live in First World Countries who have access to 21st Century medicine over those that live in Third World Countries. This has been stated due to how privileged some of the rich and money hungry dominate in America primarily. God doesn't control, give, or deny anything. Tragic situations happen due to human free will choice or human incompetence. Those in First World countries are not exempt from catastrophes as they've had numerous disasters all throughout history. Some claimed that God must've hated the people of Nepal by allowing a major Earthquake to happen in 2015. The plates shifted and the Earthquake took place before anyone had a chance to pray.

It's naive to believe that God will sit there ready and able to push a button to stop a potential disaster or harm from happening simply because you want Him to. This way you can kick back, relax, and enjoy life while God sits around controlling everything to make it as pleasant and easy as possible for you. Naturally, He wants human life to be pleasant, but it's not His fault that human beings choose to govern their life through free will choice and the darkness of ego, which as a result backfires and creates harm. Who do they blame when that happens? God. He can take it regardless that it's not true. This is similar to Children that blame what's wrong with their life on their parents. Since God is much like a parent figure and we are His children, then this metaphor is no different. Challenges are inevitable on Earth and most of the time they come about due to human free will action or through a natural disaster.

Deep Thoughts on the Universe

The first man and woman that walked the planet spoke no words, but figured out what was needed to survive. They were guided to find food, shelter, and figured to clothe themselves. It isn't like the first person that roamed the planet stood up and tried on a suit. Clothes didn't exist and there was no shame with that. At one point, this changed where it was guessed, "Hmm, perhaps I should cover these areas."

What made him/her decide this is what should be done? If the first people that roamed the planet didn't know any better, then how would they know to do that? Where did the first man and woman come from?

Some will cite the Bible with Adam and Eve; others will cite evolution or have various other theories. No one has the market cornered, except that there had to be a first man and woman popping up from somewhere. It wasn't like, "Poof! There they are." Did they first show up as babies? Who put them there?

Those that don't believe in a higher power are unable to answer the question in a way that would make logical sense, but the extreme side has also been unable to answer it in the same logical way. This is because there is no logical understanding for the human mind to grasp how the universe came to be. This planet has grown to have nearly eight billion people on it that descended down from two people, meaning we're all descendants of what some refer to be as Adam and Eve. We are all related when you go back into time to the beginning of humankind.

The first two people on the planet we're unable to read, write, or form words in speech. Language has shifted and changed over the centuries taking on an entirely different life of its own. People set up life, dictated how it should all go, and everyone else followed.

How perfectly orchestrated it is that the planets seem to glide around the sun for billions of years in a calculated succession that has been measured in technological degrees by astrologers. A human being didn't create that orchestration. A big bang theory couldn't create a perfectly orchestrated set up with planets circling the Sun for centuries never being knocked off its axis. Besides walking on the moon, no one is up in space able to accurately detect what is going on and into the further it goes.

There is this orchestrated design of the planets swirling around the Sun never being knocked off its axis where it could hurl aimlessly through space. One of those planets contains humankind, a species that has multiplied astronomically out of control into the billions. Everything is being held together by what humans call gravity, but this is a name they gave it.

How far deep into space can you go before you hit a wall? It ends at some point and circles right back around. When you come to the awareness that this universe is dangerously deep, vast, and endless, then you realize that the noise on Earth is trivial, petty, and insignificant. None of this seemingly complex design is by accident.

Astrologers have measured how the planets seem to move in particular calculated ways around the Sun. The Universe expands and goes on for eons with numerous portals that break through into the next dimension and beyond. Where did it all come from? Who set it up that way? You can't say there is no higher power and not have a valid justifiable reason as to how this Universal design exists in its exceptional perfection. Once you believe in the higher power, then you move into where the higher power came from and what it is.

Why are eight billion people sitting on one planet alone in a Universe with no other visible life forms anywhere else? Why do those eight billion people share that space and spend it fighting, bickering, complaining, whining, posting, commenting, and attacking each other over ridiculousness? Human beings created that nonsense that has yet to lighten up. This antagonism has been going on since humankind came to be. A higher power and otherworldly figures have no time or interest for such menial trivial circumstances. They desire to see every soul raise its consciousness.

One clap in the Universe, and the Earth and everything will cease to exist. More people are growing angry in the way that others are behaving. They are welcoming something that extreme to happen to make it all go away as they've had enough. It is perplexing as to why a soul chooses to reside in the darkness of ego state around the clock. How exhausting it must be to live your life eternally in that space.

All of that and more should be the questions that every living breathing human being should be considering regardless of their personal belief systems they've chosen to follow and trust in. The answers to these questions come to life when you tune in or as you cross over back home. When that happens, you realize how superficial and trivial life was on Earth. In hindsight, you kick yourself for having been sucked into it more times than you wish you had.

It is only love that matters in the end. If parents and teachers around the world all banded together to do their job of teaching love from early on, then that would bring more love like behavior to the planet. While every bit helps, every soul on this gigantic rock needs to partake in it or the collective consciousness will be no closer to peace and love on Earth than they had ever been.

CHAPTER FOURTEEN

*The Commanding Function
of Prayer*

The power that comes with prayer is out of this world. Ask God and your Spirit team for guidance in prayer, through an affirmation, out loud, or in writing. There is no wrong way to pray. The traditional ways others have prayed are with your hands clasped together, kneeling down in a Church or by your bed. It doesn't matter how you pray, and you won't be penalized for not doing it the correct way because there is no right or wrong way. Prayer is having a conversation with God, which can be done from anywhere and in any manner.

God knows what's in your heart, which means you can say one thing while attempting to shield what you truly desire. What is hidden is what God and your Spirit team already knows. This is why you cannot get away with a lie in Heaven the way you can with others on Earth. They see, know, feel, and hear all. If you're doing something you know is making you guilty inside, then this guilt is a Divine nudge to honor that. At the same time, the guilt can be coming from the Darkness as well too.

The Darkness is known as the Devil in some circles, but there is a dark area in the Spirit world that runs parallel with Heaven and Earth. It is ruled by what some refer to as Lucifer, but no matter what you call it or him, the Darkness is real, and it is a place that no soul should desire to be in. I delve much deeper into this Darkness in my book, *Stay Centered Psychic Warrior*. For the purposes of bringing it up here it is to illustrate that the goal of the Darkness is to enrapture as many souls on Earth as possible. He does this because it is so extremely easy to do, as you've likely noticed if you're a psychically in tune sensitive.

One of the ways that the Darkness can get to an innocent person is by poisoning their mind with lower thoughts. It might make you feel guilty for desiring something good in your life. It will attempt to sabotage your prayers by making you think things like, "Why am I praying? This doesn't work. My prayers will never be answered."

All of the possible self-sabotaging thoughts you experience are connected to the Darkness, which doesn't want to see you or anyone else succeed. Those that are able to wipe that away through a strong faith-based system are readily able to move back into the Light of love whenever the Darkness attempts to ensnare you.

There are endless cases over the course of history and the centuries that have passed revealing how prayer has worked and been answered in miraculous ways. One of the top steps to take when praying is to ask, but another step is to believe that your pray is being answered. You believe it with every ounce of your entire being. This is part of what having faith is.

You are always communicating with God whether you're aware of it or not. Sitting quietly with your thoughts to anyone that will listen are prayers too. When there is trouble in your heart, then this is picked up on the Other Side. They desire to step in to help you. This can be seen when that person is troubled and feeling beaten down, but then suddenly lights up and says something that sounds like an answered prayer. They might say something like, "I just got an idea. You know what I need to do…"

Or they might get up to find an email, phone call from a friend, or be directed to something that turns everything around. Where do you think that sudden revelation came from at just the right moment? It's no coincidence that Divinely guided spirit guides and angels are actively working for God on the Other Side to help people on Earth through their often-tumultuous challenges. It would be nice if they could receive a bit more praise and acknowledgment for all of the hard work they do, but luckily for them they don't seek praise or validation the way someone on Earth might for a deed well done. They know who they are under God and have no ego filled desires that plague human beings.

I made it through the difficulties in my life through my fervent active prayer. I was praying knowing within my heart that what I needed help with would be taken care of through my faithful heart. I would eventually see what I was praying about for guidance or help with would transpire. Sometimes it was right away while the tougher long-term dreams naturally took a bit longer to maneuver. I always knew there was a reason for prayers being delayed beyond what I could see. I knew that if it was Divine will that eventually what I desired would come true. I also knew that I would need to help those prayers along by believing it would AND doing what I could through action steps. Many will pray or ask for help, but then they go back to the television set or their phones to play on them thinking that will do it. Then they later wonder why the prayer isn't getting answered. No being in Heaven is going to sprinkle blessings on a lazy or passive person that inactively waits for something to happen while mumbling complaints on it when it doesn't.

Some people pray through the act of bowing down or head down, which for some may be a sign of respect. Others may pray and look upwards because this is a position of standing in confidence allowing the power of the holy spirit to move through you. It's not because they think someone is sitting there in the sky. I've never met any faithful believer that actually believes someone is sitting in the sky on a throne. The only ones that seem to believe that delusion are atheists and non-believers. As someone with lifelong Clairvoyance and Clairaudience, spirit has always been beside me, not above or below, but next to me the way any faithful loyal friend is. The position the body makes during prayer for some is about how that person is feeling at that moment. This is the much deeper reason beyond what non-believers assume. This is also why in the past we've said that non-believers could move into believers if they moved beneath the surface of the physical and into the depths of the truth of spirit. It may seem they are incapable of great depths, but in spiritual truth they are extremely capable, but they just have to do the hard work to puncture past the physical, which takes immense mind discipline and lifestyle changes and adjustments to awaken that part of their consciousness.

More atheists than hardcore religious followers have attacked me. I've had atheists specifically send me condemning messages while telling their peers that it would be like clubbing a baby seal with me because of my own strong Divine belief systems that I broadcast to the world through my work. As a Warrior of Light, you are exceptionally cognizant that you when you incarnate into a human body on Earth that you are officially on the Devil's playground. He has the most control over people in this atmosphere. God wouldn't have sent you if He didn't think you could handle it.

I have always had a scientific analytical skeptical mind and I've been testing and communicating with my Spirit team since I was a child. When I say I test them, this means that I would report on when I've prayed and when I haven't. When I prayed, then what I asked for would soon come to fruition. When I did not pray, then I would notice that nothing has happened. I wouldn't continue with something if there were no results. There are more people in the world than not that believe in some form of prayer, which means that there are non-believers or people that are not religious that pray too. I've also heard from those on the fence of being a believer by folding to pray. They would say, "I've been battling this issue that I need to pray on, because I don't know what else to do."

They receive that sudden nudge from their guides that puts it in their mind to consider prayer. This nudge is coming through Claircognizance, which is the psychic sense of picking up on Divine guidance through the act of knowing. You're not hearing or seeing what you need to do, but rather you just know what you need to do. Claircognizance tends to be one of the stronger psychic senses in people that are not necessarily particularly believers, but have an analytical mind. They receive light bulb moments of ideas that end up being an answer that filtered into their consciousness from the Divine.

Praying has nothing to do with religion. Anyone can pray from an atheist to a spiritual person and you are being heard. Sometimes non-believers are praying without realizing it. They've admitted to sitting quietly with their thoughts at night with the things they desire or want to see happen. Through that act they are praying. Many of them will fall down to pray when they are in a traumatic circumstance that cannot be helped by any person, but they now realize they're only hope is that there is someone out there beyond the physical plane that can help. It's usually those deeper profound moments that suddenly snap them into believers of something beyond.

Praying is also connected to the law of attraction in some ways. This is where you are believing with all your might while praying that what you desire is here now and will come to fruition. Some of the law of attraction theories has grown out of hand as we moved into the hyper social media age where anyone qualified or not can post whatever they like. Some of them master social media by amassing a plethora of followers only to feed them half-baked truths. The laws of attracting in abundance are one of those things. Because attracting in abundance and the laws of attraction are beyond just thinking positive. There is a great deal more work involved than forcing yourself to try and come off like a happy camper high on life even when you don't truly feel that way.

You ask for help in a prayer and it doesn't come to light, then you immediately believe Heaven is ignoring you or God doesn't exist. You help some of those prayers along by taking action where necessary. This is also by paying attention to your Spirit team in order to follow any instructions given. They may give you the answers you seek by communicating it through one of your psychic senses.

In some religious circles, they believe that delving into psychic practices are of the Devil. And in some atheist's circles, they believe that psychic practices are fraudulent and not real. You cannot be too extreme in anything because then it blocks you from the truth. The religious will pray on something hoping to receive an answer. They suddenly receive a positive feeling to something that tells them this is the answer. That feeling is coming through your psychic sense channel called Clairsentience, which means clear feeling. This is how the messages come through from any being that is not a physical human being. Non-believers may scoff at psychic phenomena, but the irony is they too have psychic clair sense channels built into their soul which is guiding them along their Earthly journey to make what some can call good or poor decisions depending on how they choose. The ones that are open to psychic phenomena tend to be in the middle, which is the most balanced place to be indicating they have it down.

The second you demand something in prayer will not always mean it's going to be instantly granted. The direct line to God isn't for the sake of gifts, abundance, and blessings. This is where some in the spiritual communities may receive the most criticisms. It tends to be those in that area that move to a spiritual belief system after becoming enticed by an abundance and law attracting meme. After spending years reading book after book on the law of attraction and becoming nowhere near to attracting in abundance, they become skeptical and even hyper critical denouncing the entire movement of spirituality. When the truth was, they were blinded by the deception of those cute memes and positive words in a book like *The Secret*. There is more to life than trying to gain as much finances as possible like it's a big lottery win. God isn't going to be helping with things like that. Soul consciousness growth work is included in the ingredients to attracting good things. He will help with some of the gifts and blessings to those that do the work.

Sometimes life lessons must be endured before those gifts and blessings are bestowed. There are other reasons for a delay with the blessings. For example you could be asking for help in getting the big career work position you desire, but your guides are waiting for you to wrap up a toxic relationship and bring it to a close first before they guide you towards this work position desired. Sometimes there is something that has to end before something good in another area transpires. You may be perpetually guided to move to another city, and it is something you want to do, but you've been procrastinating, which delays it out for months and sometimes years. Your Spirit team is waiting for you to make this big move they've been guiding you to where what you want is waiting for you. It could be a new love interest or job that is ready for you, but not until this move is made. Perhaps the new long-term love interest is in this new city. This wouldn't be a fleeting love interest that lasts less than a year, but the love partner that lasts indefinitely.

The angels will never put you in a situation that will end up having a negative impact on you. You make choices that sometimes seem as if you were reading the signs correctly only to later discover you made an error in judgment. The more you work with them, then the easier it gets in deciphering what is indeed your Spirit team and what is not. While it's important to keep one's heart open to others, you also need to be on guard to an extent so as not to be taken advantage of.

With the angels it's about letting go of the control and allowing what is intended to fall into your lap naturally. If you feel the slightest bit of doubt or a tinge of an uncomfortable feeling within, then that would be a sign to back away from something. You would also need to pray on it and trust your Divine instincts if the doubt is the Darkness or your ego attempting to convince you that you're not deserving of good in your life. God and your Spirit team can be super subtle in Divine communication, which is why they push for you to be clear minded and to watch what you ingest as your psychic senses are highly calibrated at that moment. When your senses are calibrated, then so is the communication with them.

Let's say that your guides give you information that will come out as if it is a future prediction and then it doesn't come true. You'll begin to believe it was your imagination. If you went to a psychic reader and a prediction did not come to pass, then you would believe they were wrong and denounce all professional psychics. Psychic readers and mediums are not God, and neither is your Spirit team. They have no control over what someone does or doesn't do. They only see the projected outcome and can guide accordingly. This outcome changes from one day to the next pending on anyone's free will. While there are some psychics interested in taking advantage of a client, this is not the case with every single one. Just like any group there are both good and bad involved. The best psychics and mediums are only about 70-80% accurate on a good day. Even though like you, the soul part of themselves were born 100% psychic. Due to the heavy Earth plane with all of its toxins and blocks has dimmed that considerably. It blows right back up to 100% when you cross over back home to Heaven.

There is a job you truly want and so you ask your Spirit team for assistance in obtaining that job. If your Spirit team knows that this job is aligned with love and your higher self, then they will get to work in helping you attain this job. How they might do this is by connecting you with the person at this job who would be responsible in hiring you. If you're paying attention to the guidance of your Spirit team, then you will discover who the appropriate person is to contact at this job. You meet your Spirit team halfway by getting your resume together and forwarding it to this employer.

Your Spirit team then contacts your employers Spirit team behind the scenes through their psychic clair senses. This is in order for them to begin nudging this employer in getting that person to notice you. They may keep dropping clues in front of the employer such as getting your resume to the top of the stack. If this employer is not paying attention to the nudges and guidance that their Spirit team is putting in front of them about you, then it becomes challenging. As a result, you start to believe that your Spirit team is ignoring you and not helping you get the job. You have to keep an open mind and understand that this is not always the case.

There are several factors that come into play as to why the job offer is not happening. One of them being that this employer is not paying attention to the messages and guidance being put in front of them about you. There are a great deal of human souls who are now disconnected to anything outside of themselves, including the assistance of their own Guides and Angels. They do not have to believe in Heaven to notice the messages. Employers have pointed out that someone's name was constantly being put in front of them and they did not understand why, but it did make them take notice. They went with it and called that person anyway to offer them a job realizing it was a good move after hiring the candidate.

Your Spirit team is wrestling with someone else's free will, which people use quite bit of. Don't just ask for help, but believe that it is forthcoming and already here. If you feel abandoned by God and your Spirit team, then ask them to boost your faith. Those in Heaven would never desert the soul they're assigned to look after and guide. The reverse is that many people abandon God and head down the path guided by their ego.

It's also important to know that Heaven cannot fix everything that comes at you. You are placed in situations that you put yourself in based on past decisions. Your team will keep you away from eminent danger that could result in extreme harm or death before your time when you work with them, but they cannot ensure that everything is in working order and tip-top shape. You can drive your car all over creation every day and hope that nothing ever happens to it, but eventually something will. It will need to be serviced or the tires will need to be rotated and changed. Some of the work is up to you to take the bull by the horns and take action on.

You have a love crush on someone and want to run into them again. You ask for help and continuously run into this crush every so often. You both stare at each other with interest, but say nothing. You grow depressed thinking maybe that the crush isn't interested. You ask for Divine help in prayer again. Your Spirit team can get you both in the room together, but they cannot make you talk. That's up to the both of you to do. It's like someone can get you a job interview, but it's up to you to get the job. You're a self-sufficient thinking human being. You're not a puppet on strings that Heaven is controlling or making you walk and talk.

Your Spirit team and the object of your affections Spirit team work together to get the both of you in the room together by communicating to the both of you through your psychic senses. If you're both paying attention to your senses, then the quicker you'll have your answer on whether or not this is a positive go. If one of you isn't paying attention to their guides, then this can delay the process of bringing you together pending this is indeed the divinely guided soul mate relationship intended to happen.

Your team works with the object of your interests Spirit team to place the claircognizant idea into your mind. When this happens, then you suddenly say something like, "I need to go to the store today."

You hadn't planned to go to the store, but felt like you had to. You head off to the store only to turn the aisle and run smack into your crush.

This is also why it's important to work on raising your vibration and watching what you ingest, since a raised vibration equals clearer psychic communication with God and your Spirit team. You're able to pick up on the messages and guidance filtering into you from your team such as when to go to the store to bump into your crush.

Mark, a reader of mine in his twenties, moved into an apartment where a neighbor's cigarette smoke was blowing in the wind and into his place. He was annoyed and didn't want to close his windows since he enjoys fresh cool air breeze blowing in, but not mixed with nicotine smoke. He asked and prayed for some kind of resolve. He said, "I like this person, but I can't do the cigarette smoke."

Gradually over the course of several months he noticed the cigarette smell was gone. Eventually the neighbor ran into Mark and informed him that he quit smoking recently. He added that he was suddenly being nudged to quit. Over time the prayer helped as Mark saw the results. This is an example of a prayer being answered, but down the line. And this prayer request ended up benefitting two people. This was both the one that didn't like the smoke as well as the person doing the smoking, since it would improve the smoker's health by stopping.

Some people pray once or maybe twice, then they give up and chalk it off to not being heard. When you give up that quickly, then it's seen that you don't care about the issue being resolved all that much. You have to be fervent and consistent in your prayers.

When a catastrophic situation happens in your life, then the immediate emotional response is panic and anxiety. While in that state it lowers your vibration and cuts off the communication from Heaven. Not to mention you forget to ask for help while in that state of mind. Simply crying out with the word *help* during a state of panic can bring in heavenly assistance.

Jennifer, another reader of mine, has been in those situations where a circumstance like this has happened and she's moved into panic mode. She immediately asks for help in an alarmed state. She realizes she needs to calm down and trust that help is forthcoming. She thinks to herself during those panics, "I need to quiet my panicked mind knowing how devastating this situation is at the moment. Close my eyes and ask for help calmly."

Within the hour of the prayer, the situation is miraculously resolved, and all is well again. She admits to feeling foolish afterwards for having panicked in the first place.

There have been numerous statistics and studies that have shown that those that pray or have a stronger faith-based system than those who do not, tend to also have a stronger well-being. Prayer has immense health benefits beyond just using prayer simply to get material things. If that's all you're praying for, then the prayers may go unanswered for some time. Prayers have immense health benefits on your soul in that it also acts like therapy being able to pray with every part of your being that it's activating those dormant dopamine cells. Prayer can ease the mind and soul when you come out of the prayer.

CHAPTER FIFTEEN

Divine Assistance

There comes a point where you've done all you can do and others are using your vessel as a sponge to absorb their drama, but won't take heed of the guidance coming in. It ends up backfiring on them when you do the opposite. They come back around, "Now what do I do?"

Well, you broke the glass on the floor, so now you need to sweep up the mess. When you move through a time of having a lack of clarity and a rise in anxiety, then this will cloud the Divine messages coming in. You're not seeing the picture clearly except what your ego wants to do.

Ask for help from your Guides and Angels. Even if you've been asking for help, you haven't seen results, and are losing faith – keep on asking and putting that energy out there. They are not ignoring you. If it is not happening right away there is a reason, but it will happen. There are obstacles and barriers being removed that are in the way to get you to that place you want to be in. Pay attention and listen for the signs that they might be giving you as well.

They may be answering and advising you, but you are not paying any attention to it as you're expecting the answer to take a different form. If you are receiving a repetitive sign that happens more than three times and benefits your higher self, then you are receiving heavenly messages. They want you to feel at peace. They want you to have enough time and resources to be able to focus and work on your life purpose. They do not want you to feel stuck at a dead-end job struggling to make ends meet for all eternity.

Communicate with God, Heaven, and your Angels daily. Pour your heart out to them in any manner you prefer, such as out loud, in prayer, in writing, in an email, or journal. Keep an eye out on any self-destructive tendencies you have a habit of doing and ask for Heavenly help with it. Taking it easy as much as possible is the best way to make it through.

I head out into nature regularly where all of the taxing physical energies are lifted off me. Partake in healthy activities that make you smile, whether that's cranking up some uplifting music, or watching a funny movie, to some lighthearted banter with a friend.

Don't give up, but keep chanting the common phrase, "This too shall pass. This too shall pass."

Because that saying is true, since everything eventually shall indeed pass away. No circumstance lasts for all eternity. When there are testy energies swirling around you, then that's a sign to take a step back and bring in God's wall of light around you to block that out. You fall into your day to day life patterns and realize, "Wait a minute. Snap me into spiritual truth."

I've certainly had those moments where I'm struggling with something for some time, then I hear one of my spirit team members say through Clairaudience, "Do you plan on ever asking us for help on this case or are you going to continue to struggle with this on your own?"

To which I pull back, "Oh! Right. Okay."

Suddenly after asking them to help with it, it's corrected then and there by me granting permission on it.

If every single person on the planet knew or understood that there are heavenly helpers around them, then their lives would be significantly more manageable. They would view circumstances in a broader way by making sounder choices that will enhance their life even more. Having pride is by being your most authentic self and owning it.

When it comes to prayer and asking for Divine intervention and assistance, several things must be taken into account. For one, faith should be part of the equation. When doubt is included behind your words, then this can block the outcome. Include genuine gratitude for the blessings you currently have. When your prayers are all about what Heaven can give you, then how do you think that looks? What are you contributing to help matters along?

Another factor is to pay attention to what you're psychically or intuitively picking up on from God and Spirit. What action steps are you being asked to do? Sometimes you may be asked to step outside of your comfort zone. This can create fear and anxiety prompting you to procrastinate and push off doing it. This is because you're too full of anxiety surrounding that action step. Have no fear and charge on in with what you want. This is your life and you are the owner of it. If it's another job you want, then your guides may push you to make a call, or send an email to someone that can help. When you play the game of life, then you're more apt to receiving your wishes and blessings. Ask for an increase of faith from above when you feel it waning.

Call in the Archangel Michael to extract all fear and anxiety from your aura if you're called to transform into a warrior and grab what you want without hesitation. Don't allow other people to hold you back from your dreams and desires.

Stay strong in faith knowing there is a plan. Pray and ask for help daily even if the answer isn't forthcoming right away. This isn't some blanket statement or enlightenment on a teabag, but through repetitive experience.

In an earlier chapter, I mentioned that my first job was when I was seventeen at a popular top record store chain back when those existed. Years in I was worried I was going to be there forever and would ultimately die there. Obviously, that wasn't the case, but I still remember that fear feeling would plague me once in awhile. It wasn't that I hated the job. I actually did like it at the time, but it wasn't my life purpose. I had bigger dreams that I wanted to get started on. This fear feeling was a nudge telling me to not get too comfortable at that place because there is a bigger quest coming up. That's just one example out of many throughout my life. I remember feeling that stagnancy at some point fearing I'd be stuck. I prayed daily and have since I was a child. It's not just to help me with this or that. It's also to express gratitude for what I have at that time in my life that's working.

There were days that went by where I prayed, and nothing would come to light. Months would pass and still nothing. Months turned into years and suddenly out of nowhere the answer that came in was lit up like a Christmas tree and I was placed in an even better set up. There were varying time limits as to when a prayer was answered. For some instances it was immediate, while others took much longer.

If you're in a situation that you don't care for, then consider the reasons for it. Sometimes you're in a situation longer than you intended, but you're acquiring skills and traits that God needs you to collect, because it will be useful and beneficial for what's to come next. If you were thrown in what's to come too soon, then it would fail. He knows when it'll be time for the next chapter. You'll look back and then realize, "Now I know why I was at that place."

Everything I've gone through both and good bad ultimately had a benefit I gained that I was to apply to the next chapter of my life.

You work your day job to survive, but meanwhile you work on your life purpose and passion on the side. When you devote thirty to sixty minutes a day towards your purpose, then eventually that will grow over time. One day you are making enough income with that enabling you to survive doing it full time. If it's your life purpose work, then it doesn't feel like work. This is because it's your passion and it's enjoyable to dive into.

One of technologies benefits is you can watch instructional videos, seminars, read books, or listen to motivational podcasts right on your computer or phone. You can do it kicking back on the couch after a long day at work. If you're too tired after work to put any effort into your life purpose, then you can do those little action steps where you're gaining knowledge kicking back and watching, reading, or listening to motivational pieces.

Another positive beneficial reason for taking care of yourself on all levels is that it gives you more energy in the day to dive into your purpose work, even after working at another job. There are people that work more than one job. Look at your life purpose as a second job if you already have a primary job. Another benefit is that work lives are inconsistent and unstable. No one knows when the job will suddenly end and if you're able to find another job. Creating something on the side that can generate some income early on can ensure you have that extra stability should something happen.

You are sometimes thrown into situations with people that have no connection beyond anything but the superficial. It feels as if you're being tested, but there is a deeper reason for it. You have a light that is working through others even if you don't see that as it's happening or while you're in that situation with them.

I've always been super guarded and cautious over who I allow near me. I can come off aloof and cold when I truthfully have no interest in inviting in those who choose to live in harshness or meanness. I can't even force pretend that I care. I have to keep my own light protected from that darkness.

It's okay to ask for heavenly help in guiding you to an improved situation with loving people you feel more comfortable getting along with, because you deserve it. You deserve to have your prayers answered. Notice any signs or synchronicities of God's help that can sometimes come in a form you weren't expecting as well. It will keep showing up until you notice it and take action on it.

I work for God and his company we jokingly call *God, Incorporated.* Ultimately the abundance is filtered down from Him and into my life in many ways. When I need supplies, I put in a request with Him. Sometimes He grants it and other times He doesn't. I'm made aware as to if it's just a temporary delay and to be patient, or if it's because He sees that this particular supply I'm asking for will not benefit me positively in the end. My own vision may be limited to the results of what would happen if I received that particular request. Sometimes it's my own ego that desires something, not realizing I could be harmed in the end. Other times there is a temporary delay, or He plans to bring in something better that is taking a bit longer to fulfill. This also applies to you as well as anyone interested in how God works.

The enemy will always try to get in there and undo all of the work you've been doing on yourself. You cannot allow that to happen. The enemy is the darkness, the devil, the ego, or the lower self. It doesn't like progress, so it does what it can to stop you by getting into your mind and making you doubt or experience fear. You don't have to endure life alone, since that's where God comes in free of charge whenever you ask.

There is a song by Sade called "King of Sorrow", where the lyrics she sang were, "I've already paid for my future sins."

The story in the song describes someone who was working hard and not getting anywhere, but secretly longing for some kind of positive breakthrough release.

Continue to keep the faith and know that things will change one day. Sending you

Divine help as you read this now and wishing you the awesome best in life, because you deserve it.

Fear Not, Because I Am With You

Who is this being of Light so great it has conjured up centuries of endless controversy and hatred in the darkness of human ego. The irony is that He is nothing that comes close to that limited view. His light has the opposite effect when you are truly standing in His presence.

Despite the toxic noise that pervades Earth by humankind, this most holy child of salvation's eminence never stops illuminating love and healing energy light off his radiance. His power and Light are so magnificent and intense that I've had to stop whatever I was doing when he's entered my vicinity because his presence is so overwhelming that it's paralyzing. Words to describe what's taking place never do it justice. It's a sense feeling of the highest most impossible love that I've never seen another human being give, but he did, and he does.

If you're down and out or experiencing any negative thought or feeling, the love of Jesus can wipe that away just by walking into your room and standing next to you. Find that space where his love resides and bathe in its vitality. The planet could learn a little something about this unconditional healing love he continuously gives without censure in a world devoid of respect.

Out of the deepest dark shines the purest light that blasts away all traces of negativity, anger, sadness, confusion, and stress from your being. If there's anything good that happens in life, it's from God. He is present for all who call on Him regardless of who you are, what you believe in, or your souls' choices this lifetime. No matter your race, gender, sexual orientation, belief or lack of belief, all are welcome to His love without judgment. You have His uncompromising permanent compassion and friendship. You are loved in ways your ego is incapable of understanding or comprehending. Those without love, those who are troubled, those wrestling with demons, you are forever loved by this being of Light free of charge. Hookers and drug users have someone who loves them unconditionally, because no one on the planet is exempt from His love.

It's less shocking to the soul that has crossed over to first see a figure they identified with on Earth. To go from a human life on Earth to human death is surprising for some. The deity they believed in or followed on Earth will appear first after death to ease them into the other plane. If you followed all deities on an equal measure, then all of them would surface. Heaven knows your consciousness and the one you would gravitate towards when it is your time to cross through the gates back home.

Why am I here? There's little that's pleasant about this place. One of the messages

Jesus said was that even just a tiny bit of faith that you can spare will move mountains.

"Nothing would be impossible."

His love for you is boundless regardless if you're a believer or not. He doesn't need faith to believe in you. He already does. It already is.

What did God say?

"Fear not, because I am with you."

There's nothing you can't do when you've got your Spirit team in your house.

Affirm always: I am worthy. I deserve good. I deserve blessings. I deserve love. I deserve to be happy. I deserve peace.

CHAPTER SIXTEEN

Scripture Reminders on Faith and Prayer

The purpose of this chapter is to reveal some of the more positive enlightening texts in the controversial book that can be pointed to how having an increased faith and regular prayer helps improve your life in so many ways. It doesn't matter if you're not religious or not that spiritual, but that you do believe in the power of prayer. You don't have to be religious or spiritual to partake in prayer. This is one of the great things about prayer. It's not a private club that only a select group can partake in, because anyone can partake in it including a non-believer.

In Mark 11:24 he said, "Therefore I say to you, all things for which you pray and ask, believe that you have received them, and they will be granted you."

This goes back to the mantra of ask and you shall receive, but it's more than just asking and receiving. It's also believing that you HAVE what you're asking for. This means even if you don't have it yet, you are asking as if you already have it. You can feel that you have it today. Your faith in that which you are asking for is strong enough to make it happen. God knows that you believe that He is working to help you attain your desires, pending that what you are asking for is not something that will bring about your soul's down fall. Don't worry if you think you're asking for something that will bring about pain, because He is not going to give you something like that even if you think what you're asking for will be beneficial to you. Higher beings see more than we can see at times.

In John 10:11 he said, "I am the good shepherd; the good shepherd lays down His life for the sheep."

This is more symbolism and analogy. Jesus is the shepherd that watches over the sheep. A good shepherd is devoted to the sheep and will die for them. That's how loyal and devoted he is. In this case, Jesus is the shepherd and the sheep are everyone that puts their trust in him. When you put your faith and trust in him, then he will not disappoint, because he values loyalty. This isn't to be confused with a master servant situation or that he has an ego and demands this love. This is more about being a devoted loyal person that has a tight relationship with God. This carries over to all aspects of your life if this is your overall character. People will disappoint you and betray your trust, but God's devotion is constant.

When a good person knows that someone loves them, then they will do whatever they can to appease that person. When employees at a job know they are taken care of and adored by their employer, then those employees tend to work harder with a happier disposition because somewhere in the employee's soul they can feel the goodness that comes with respect and loyalty. This same concept can be transferred to prayer and your relationship with God knowing that you have someone that loves and adores you and wants to see you thrive, but also wants to see you put some fight into your life too.

In Luke 6:45 he said, "Good people do good things because of the good in their hearts, but bad people do bad things because of the evil in their hearts. Your words show what is in your heart."

This can be applied to critical complaining. The complainer is showing what's in their heart through these complaints. Witness all those rants on social media. Each of those posters reveals what is truly going on inside them. You may ask for something and believe you're good, but if you're complaining then you are showing yourself to be a critical soul, which doesn't bring in anything good.

If you are out in the world doing what you can to help others in some positive way, and you are praying for blessings, then these good acts you've been doing count in the doing good equation. Those prayers tend to get answered quicker over the lazy passive soul's prayers that pray once or twice, then they go to crack open another beer and sit on the couch day after day waiting for the doorbell to ring with that good news. God wants to see you get up and put some fight in your life!

In Luke 11:9 he said, "So I say to you, ask, and it will be given to you; seek, and you will find; knock, and it will be opened to you."

This means you ask in prayer for your request and it is done, but the scripture goes further, seek and you will find. Sometimes what you're looking for is right in front of you. When you take it a step further beyond just asking for something and begin seeking it out on your own as well to help it along, then this shows God and your Spirit team how serious you are about receiving this blessing you are asking for.

Knock and it will be opened to you. When you knock on a door, you are knocking more than once, but a few times until someone finally opens it. You are being requested to ask in prayer for what you want, but also seek what you desire through action. This is showing God what you're willing to do to get what you want. Notice the feeling of a door opening wide to what you've been asking for and how that will make you feel.

In John 14:27 he said, "Let not your heart be trouble neither let it be afraid."

In Mark 5:36 he said something similar, "Be not afraid, only believe."

And in Luke 12:32 he said, "Fear not, little flock; for it is your Father's good pleasure to give you the Kingdom."

All of those scriptures point to boosting your faith and knowing that all things are possible through faith. You might be feeling fear, doubt, or anxiety about something good never happening for you, but those scriptures point to you experiencing those traits as being a candidate for blessings.

In Matthew 9:22 he said, "Be of good comfort; your faith has made you whole."

This is saying that by increasing your faith and believing that through God and spirit all things are possible. This is because it is this boosted faith, which fills you from within that gives you the courage to rise up into warrior of light mode knowing that you are being guided purposively. There is nothing that you cannot do, accomplish, and gain through faith.

Matthew also said this again in 19:26, "With God all things are possible."

In Luke 6:38 he said, "Give, and it shall be given unto you."

This is hammering home the idea that it isn't always about praying to get prayers answered. What are you giving to the world to positively better humanity and others?

Humanitarians have quite a number of Guides and Angels that have entered their life to work with them. When the humanitarian has those frequent moments of wanting to throw in the towel or they doubt God, then that persons Spirit team lifts their heart and mind in order to motivate the soul to continue on. Sometimes they do this by infusing a sudden burst of energy that is an uplifting motivating feeling within you. This is after hearing your prayer or cry out for help.

For some, you agreed to an Earthly life for a specific purpose geared toward the world at large. When you falter on your path, then your Spirit team coaxes you onward. This is also why your soul's purpose can never truly go away, because it is innate in your soul's DNA. It's part of your contract, which you have access to in the deepest regions of your psychic mind. One of the roles of your Spirit team is to make sure you fulfill elements of your soul's contract. Your purpose is part of the giving in the giving and receiving equation. When you give then you will receive.

In Luke 6:37 he said, "Forgive, and you shall be forgiven."

If you have any pain in your heart, then through prayer ask for forgiveness if you feel you've done something to warrant that guilt. You don't need to drone on about it falling to your knees in dramatic ways. Simply stating that you'd like help with them lifting the heavy burdens of guilt from your heart will work in your favor.

In Matthew 26:41 he said, "Watch and pray, that you enter not into temptation."

This also has to do with praying and asking for blessings, but then you go off and partake in activities that you know are harmful to your soul. If you pray, then you go over to social media to attack people and complain, then you've missed the point of prayer. You're not doing the work and walking the talk of having complete spiritual faith.

In Matthew 7:7 he said, "Seek, and you shall find."

This has been said numerous times throughout the holy book and takes on endless meanings. In this case it's about delving deep to reach those Divinely guided answers. It's you venturing on that soul spiritual quest to uncover truths that can help expand your soul and propel you further into enlightenment.

In Matthew 5:14 he said, "You are the light of the world."

Don't forget you have agreed to an Earthly life to shine that light of your soul onto the world through the compassionate acts and deeds you put forth in your life. This can also be by being your highest best self whenever and wherever possible. You are helping someone out there even if you're telling your story. You are motivating, inspiring, and encouraging someone else. You are treating others with kindness and compassion, while steering clear of those that have hate in their hearts.

Last but certainly not least in Luke 21:36 he said, "Pray always."

I don't think you can get any clearer than that. Make prayer part of your daily life. Don't just pray whenever you need something. Pray to develop a stronger relationship with God and your Spirit team. Prayer is like vitamins that you have to take daily before you begin to see positive results within and around you. It's not for the sake of blessings, but to completely transform and evolve your soul consciousness in being one with the Light. You were part of this Light upon your soul's conception, but might have lost your way in the dark regions of Earthly life.

You may ask for certain material blessings, but how long will those physical materials last? When you pass on from this life, then those material items will become obsolete and meaningless, but where will your soul be? You spent your life demanding you receive material items in prayer, but where's your heart and your soul in all this?

It's okay to ask for material necessities such as things that can help you survive such as a steady income, a place to live, food, clothes, etc. Those are necessities a human being needs to survive on this plane. God understands that, but it's more than just asking for material abundance. It's also asking to be awakened to the light and diving deeper beneath all of the physical longings. The material that comes into the faithful warrior heart is a positive side effect to evolving your soul consciousness.

Pray always, pray daily, pray with passion, pray with intent, pray with action, pray with faith. Prayer is one of the most powerful spiritual things you can do to improve you, your soul, those around you, circumstances, and your life one day at a time.

The Metaphysical Divine Wisdom Collection

The Metaphysical Divine Wisdom Collection

A PRACTICAL MOTIVATIONAL GUIDE TO SPIRITUALITY SERIES

METAPHYSICAL DIVINE WISDOM

ON UNIVERSAL, PHYSICAL, SPIRITUAL AND SOUL LOVE

KEVIN HUNTER

The Metaphysical Divine Wisdom Collection

METAPHYSICAL DIVINE WISDOM
ON UNIVERSAL, PHYSICAL, SPIRITUAL AND SOUL LOVE

CHAPTER ONE

It's All About Love

The point of all existence in the end is connected to love, whether that is love for another person, self-love, or universal and spiritual love. One of the main reasons all souls are here is to learn the nature of love. Perhaps you're incredible at running a business, accumulating money, and helping people physically survive by keeping them employed. This is one of your life purposes, but when you pass on you will not be taking any of that with you. If you haven't learned anything about love, then what was the point?

In one of the episodes of James Lipton's *Inside the Actor's Studio*, he interviews actress Sharon Stone. She tells him a story about a friend of hers that was dying of AIDS. She explained that she would visit him regularly in the Hospital. There was a point when he was cutting in and out of death. When he cut back into this reality his whole expression changed. He said, "Oh my god, oh my god!"

Sharon was filled with emotion, "What? What is it? Tell me?"

He said, "It's all about love."

Sharon grabbed her chest choking back tears head slumped down with emotion.

It's all about love.

Some souls choose to incarnate into an Earthly life in order to experience all of the Earthly physical pleasures from sex, food, and music, making love, falling in love, loving love to spreading love. Love is an in-depth complicated word with various meanings beyond being in a love relationship. Love is difficult to pin down since the meaning is much deeper than the surface. It can be an intense satisfying appreciation or approving supportive expression for someone or something. Love can be putting passion and heart into whatever you do in life. It's making choices from the heart, rather than rationalizing it through the mind, which can talk you out of doing something you are more than capable of.

Love is to understand that even the most heinous person in your eyes has love built into them deep down in the core of their soul. When you are in Heaven you truly understand what Universal love is like. While on Earth there is no such thing as Universal love when it comes to human beings thanks to the domination of the Darkness that controls the human ego. Human beings are the one species incapable of displaying Universal love. Some may claim to love everybody, but when you dive into the governing human ego, then it's easy to detect that this is just not true. There are exceptions moving about on this planet. They are the rare people that see the good in all they come across no matter what. We call those spirits Incarnated Angels living in a human body, because their compassionate personalities are like that of an angel. Angels are egoless and see the love within all souls including the most heinous human being on the planet. This doesn't mean they're approving of that person enacting violence or hatred, but they have this keen psychic ability to see beneath the surface. They know who that soul was at its conception, which was 100% love.

It's an impossible request to demand that someone with an ego that is constantly susceptible to being captured by the Darkness display Universal love. It's almost an unreasonable request to place on a human being to show love for someone that caused harm on another person. One Mother was somehow able to do that with her son's killer demanding that instead of condemning him to punishment that he be treated for his "sickness". Many applauded that Mother for being able to do something that almost no one can do.

It is not unreasonable to request that someone show love to those you don't understand. Skim all of the attacks on social media accounts like Twitter and you'll find that 99% of them are misplaced and unnecessary. It's all bathed in dark ego, anger, stress, and lower distracting energies that change no hearts or minds. Sadly, it is also what is popular on social media. The dark ego is fed through drama achieving a drug like high off it. This is what fills social media accounts to the brim of some kind of non-constructive rant about someone or something they despise. This isn't about the occasional slip that an overall positive person falls into where they suddenly take a moment to complain about something. This is about the regular offenders where the majority of their posts are negatively based every hour of every day. It doesn't do anything to help matters. It certainly doesn't contribute to bringing more love into the world. Someone looking to bring more love into the world already knows this won't help their causes.

You may find someone to be monstrous, while another person has a deeper understanding of that person. Someone tells me about someone that enacted a horrible crime. Others will immediately jump into the hang him rhetoric, but I want to understand what propelled the person to do something. I've forever been fascinated with the complexities of the nature of human beings and all of the details that it encompasses. This includes wanting to understand what makes someone on Earth the way they are, because they certainly weren't born that way.

While human beings are flawed and will inevitably mess up when their ego rules the roost, it is spirits love that is constant and unwavering. When I connect with God and Spirit, they pull me up into a wave of love that is better than anything I've ever experienced, and I've experienced plenty! I couldn't write thousands of pages of text without them, especially with my restless ADD *(attention deficit disorder)*. We found that the one area my ADD is not present is when I'm writing, which is no doubt a sign of Divine intervention and guidance.

If one is too absorbed on the surface of things to comprehend what's going on beyond the physical, then it is unlikely they are in touch with the psychic touch. The touch is being in tune to spirit and the vibrations from beyond. It doesn't mean they are incapable of that kind of deep spirit connection, because they do have the power deep down within them to access it. Every single soul has that same power, whether they know it or not, and regardless of their human belief limitations.

It would be awesome if every single person on the planet was keenly aware of their innate psychic abilities built into their soul's DNA, because then Earth would be as close to Heaven as feasibly possible. There would be never-ending joy, peace, and love for every soul. Everyone would be operating from a higher vibration while moving mountains in the process. We see this kind of amazing uplifting joy in others when they're in a high vibrational state. Because this is not the current reality where everyone is functioning in that space, this makes Earthly life more challenging than it should be. It is either us or other people that create the majority of problems that happen in the physical world. Once in awhile, Mother Earth creates catastrophes, since this rock we temporarily inhabit has a life force of its own. If you want to see a horrific allegory symbolism that proves it's point as to how Mother Earth is a living breathing organism, then watch a film like *Mother!* with Jennifer Lawrence. It was a film that was both supremely loved and venomously hated. You know a piece of art did its job when it creates such opposing reactions in people.

The dead are amongst us on Earth, but they're not dead in the way one might believe them to be dead. They're no longer weighed down and strangled by this ego dominated false reality that force-feeds a fictional superficial shallow view of human life. The real death and Hell are living on a planet that lacks in love with minimal to no awareness or mind-blowing perception. This isn't saying that no one is like that because there are a great many souls on the planet that are filled with love, operate from love, and give love. They also have enormous awareness and mind-blowing foresight. The majority on the planet does not reside in that space. Because if they did, then that would be evident in the physical world's culture and it's not. The dominant rule on Earth is the darkness of ego. This is why one quarter of the planet is here with a purpose to counter that with their Light. You are a way shower in this manner even if it changes one person that ends up changing another and so forth. This is how a mighty positive love movement of change happens Universally.

We have been moving into a period where more souls are incarnating with this grand awareness of love. There has been a growing movement of people seeking ways to find fulfillment and happiness. Some call this the New Age, but it's not New Age but the soul's reality. If the New Age is about displaying love, then feel free to drink a healthy helping of it. The New Age teaches about self-love and that you are your own authority. To one extent this is true, but there is a higher authority that some call God, the Universe, Spirit, or however you choose to label it. Many will fidget or grow uncomfortable when the word God is said. This is due to the excessive negative way it's been used in horrific ways by Nazi-like fanatical religious groups. They will hide behind the God or Jesus Christ name to harm, hate, and harass other people claiming they're doing it out of love. Regardless of what label you choose to use, God is the ultimate authority to partner with in order to find that eternal love within that brings true soul happiness. Human beings cannot do everything alone and why would you want to when you have willing spirit guardians around you on call and available to help, protect, and guide you to become a stronger person and a more evolved soul in the process.

Being all love and light is a great quality to have, but you also cannot be naïve to other elements that are alive and affecting a great many souls around the planet. There may be quite a bit of the love and light stuff being pushed into the ethers. Being happy and filled with joy and positivity is a wonderful state to achieve, but ignoring everything else as if it doesn't exist can cause problems too. You cannot fully understand the Light if you don't have an understanding of the Dark. Life is not all cute stuffed animals, flowers, and cuddles.

The Light souls on Earth do their best to stay away from anyone that resides in a lower energy space. They can detect when to steer clear of the dark energies due to having a vastly tuned-in calibrated psychic antennae. They move towards those that reside in a higher vibrational Light state, while the darker human soul attracts in others that reside in a negative space. Their negative energy grows more repressed as the Dark energies take over, while the stronger sensitive soul rises like helium above the Darkness and into the vortex of the Light where love resides.

A person's Guardian Angel and Spirit Guide are always near the person they're assigned to in many ways on varying levels. Being connected to them is like having a best friend in another dimension. Like God, these are beings that know everything about you including all of the good and the bad. They know your thoughts and feelings, the things you hide, the things you reveal, and yet they never leave your side. They continue to love you unconditionally no matter how horrific a human crime you've done, which isn't saying that you won't need to pay for that crime depending on the severity.

One of their jobs is to support and guide you on the right path. This includes through paying for karma created. When you act out and cause trouble in school, then you're sent to the principal's office to be disciplined. The soul class works in a similar way, but some of the soul crimes are not all the same as the Earthly crimes. If you're headed towards danger, then they do their best to stop you or steer you away from that. This is why it's important to be clear minded and to develop a strong connection with them. It helps you decipher between a good decision and a bad one when you're tuned in to them daily.

I was never trained to call on the Angels, Archangels, or Guides, nor do I practice yoga or meditate, not that I have any problem with anyone that does, because I have many friends in the spiritual communities that do. We all respect our own ways of doing things with love and without judgment. As a restless driven warrior soldier, my soul's physical energy charges forward with more energy than those decades younger than I. It's always been like that and hasn't stopped yet, but this restless fighter soul energy from back home in Heaven is infused into the human part of me. This makes it challenging for me to sit still and meditate or do yoga exercises, because it's not how my soul was made. When I'm in nature I may sit or lie down to kick back and absorb God's uplifting healing love energy for a bit, then I'll stroll on foot to breathe it all in. This is how I personally connect with Spirit to have their love envelop me, but what works for me may not work for you.

I grew up in a volatile abusive home that was lacking in love. Something like that would break most people. When it broke me, it would only do so for a minute or two, but then I'd be lifted back up. God and my Spirit team would reappear refusing to allow me to be broken down by any of the poor human circumstances I was stuck in at the time. God loved and strengthened me back to life and into complete spiritual centeredness. Every day when I wake up from sleep it feels like a new dawn where I'm renewed with feel good feelings of love again. This is regardless of what my state was in the day before. If it was a bad day the day before, then I pray, go to bed, I wake up fully healed and restored with an optimistic attitude ready and revved to go again. One of the first thoughts to my Spirit team is, "What do you want me to accomplish today?" To this day, I still converse with God and my Spirit team each morning.

Having been raised in a violent abusive household with parents that struggled with money adds to the differing perception of human life than those growing up in a less dysfunctional environment. Growing up not loved by any human being gave me an enlightening lesson. I didn't need to be loved by anyone, because the love I was getting from above was stronger, loyal, long lasting, and more powerful than any human being is capable of giving. This empowered me to rise up in warrior mode. If I have to go it alone, I'll go it alone, I've done it before and succeeded.

Every soul is made by God, which is why some see Him as their parent, rather than their own parents. Souls reside in different areas, realms, and dimensions in Heaven. Some call it the spirit world when there are more spirit worlds than just one. Spirits are not all in the same place as they are on Earth. Even though all souls can travel wherever they choose to be. They still like to have one place they call home even on the Other Side, just like on Earth. If a soul is a free-spirited soul in Heaven, they may have a place they call their home base, even if they're out and about traveling through all of the infinite vast spaces that exist in Heaven. Souls look to see where they can be of use, since all souls love to be of service in some way. On Earth, you may be trained to serve yourself, but in Heaven we serve others under the Light.

Some people will continue to repeat another human life the way you go to another grade in School to continue your education. This is with the hopes that the soul will have that breakthrough into their consciousness that prompts them to evolve out of the limited consciousness they were previously residing in. Regardless of which part you reside in Heaven, all souls are free, courageous, and fearless. They all display joy, love, peace and high-octane upbeat energy always. It's what truly being alive feels like if one could get that way naturally without any toxins or substances.

When it came to my spiritual work, I was more interested in helping people learn to make sounder choices in life, love more often, live more peacefully, joyfully, and obtain their goals. I knew that if they were connecting to a higher power themselves that it could positively help them reach those things, while also knowing there was more to life than the physical mundane trained early on.

Earthly life is tough for more people than not, but it is especially tough on the sensitive souls. It is the ultra-sensitive that psychically see, feel, know, and hear more than the average soul. It can be challenging to stay centered in a world that doesn't believe in that, understand it, or care for that matter. This is a clue that you came here for a reason, even if that reason is to shine that bright light of love that is your basic nature to all you encounter.

The highest vibrational energy that exists is love. This isn't to be confused with the kind of love bond two people have, but this is more of a universal love. To understand love is to be able to peer into the heart of a human being. The heart part of you is your soul. It is who you truly are behind the physical and personality part of yourself. This means judging anyone in anyway on appearances means you will have to take accountability for that one day.

The physical limitations can make it challenging for someone to break through human superficiality and get into the soul of another person. Only an accelerated soul can get in there and be able to see who someone is. It's being able to see the true soul of the cruelest man. That's not a task that the ego has any interest in. When you judge on the surface, then you can't protest to know about love. Being unable to see the truth and soul of the most difficult person destroys your own spirit.

Love is the most powerful vibration that exists throughout all of time and space. One of the reasons that many don't show love on Earth is because to show love takes effort. Showing hatred is easy, but love...that's something else entirely. Love will always cost you something, whether that's time or energy. Love will cost you pride when you need to not let your ego dominate and let certain things go that someone else did.

Many experience difficulties in the world. Maybe your situation is financial, or you've lost your job and need another job. The good news is God knows it. He knew it before you ever entered into that struggle and He has your big break on His mind, which is all part of the plan for you. Things that happen to you might surprise you, but your Spirit team is never surprised. Like God, they you, know you, care about you, and will come through any struggle and challenge thrown at you. Never give up on life, because you are loved in a way that is bigger than your problems.

Many shun deepening their soul and consciousness through spiritual and religious studies coupled with hard driven life experiences. What good is life if the three components of body, mind, and soul that make up basic healthy survival are ignored and discarded.

Your emotional and mental well-being state is important for numerous reasons. When you're happy and healthy, then the more love and abundance you attract in. This also raises your vibration, which awakens your intuitive psychic connection with Spirit. It is that connection which helps you receive divinely guided information and inspiration designed to keep you on the right path towards soul enlightenment and beyond.

Others have also purported to say they found that happiness in a strong spiritual connection, whether that is a connection with Jesus, Buddha, God, the Universe, or Spirit. It doesn't matter what you call it even though in some spiritual circles they may do their best to make you feel guilty or bad, and might even bully you for not following who they personally follow.

General spiritual practitioners preach that you be all love and light. If every person on the planet exuded that state, then there would no doubt be peace on Earth.

Since this is not a realistic or practical request that the billions of people on the planet are capable of following, we have to examine this on a deeper realistic level. In the coming chapters we'll look at all things connected to love, which includes spiritual soul love, self-love, as well as physical love such as dating and relationships, which is something of major interest for so many people.

CHAPTER TWO

Creating the Life You Love

Ultimate authentic success surrounds your soul's growth and evolving process. It's when you realize that none of the physical ego driven desires matter in the end. You can work hard to make sure you stay afloat, you're able to pay your bills, and support yourself and family, but you're not chasing friends, likes, followers, fans, or people to prop you up. Any amount of goodness displayed from your heart is the true measure of real accomplishment. An overflowing feeling of optimism and love coupled with faith and action is what increases the chances of attracting good things and positive loved filled experiences to you.

This is a physical world that requires money to survive on this planet. It's misguided to believe that money isn't everything. It is true that money is not everything compared to love, great health, and good loyal friends that understand you and have your back, but the reality is that money is required to survive on the planet. Find that steady balance where you gracefully thrive to achieve to make enough money to be comfortable enough where you no longer have worry of not being able to pay your bills. At the same time avoid getting too carried away with it that you fall into greed territory, which is an abundance killer.

Abundance is more than monetary and financial increase. It can also be about reaching an awe-inspiring optimistic heavenly well-being state of joy, peace, and love. This positive emotional mindful state simultaneously attracts in blessings.

It is not immoral to desire to live securely enough where you have a comfortable place to live, a career, job, and/or hobbies that fulfill you. Your bills get paid without worry and you have a love partner or a healthy social circle. When you're taken care of with your physical needs, then it is easier to focus on what others need. When you feel safe and secure, then your vibration is raised within that comfy nest. This makes you a joy to be around and a powerful abundance love magnet at the same time.

If you desire to buy your own house one day, then begin the visualization of having this house. You can close your eyes at least once a day and envision what this house will look like. You'll visualize its surroundings, the kinds of neighbors that are around you, the location, and everything about it. You'll then visualize yourself living in this house, walking around throughout it, sleeping in your bed in this house, making a meal in the kitchen, the kinds of friends you have visiting this house, or the love partner that is with you in this house and so on. Notice your feelings and state of mind and how you'll feel while living in this house as this is happening.

You can apply this visualization exercise to whatever you desire, whether it's a love relationship, job, car, or anything you long for. This is pending it is aligned with your higher self's purpose and God's will. The benefits to this visualization exercise are that it programs your mind to move away from the doubts and fears that you'll attract this in. It also assists in getting the positive energy surrounding this visualization towards making it happen.

Bring in what you desire by allowing it to flow towards you naturally. You're not chasing your dreams in a panic. You're taking productive action steps through methodical movements with love to obtain what you long for. If there's someone you're interested in romantically, then ask them out whether or not you're male or female. Regardless of their answer, don't chase or burden them by staying on top of them relentlessly. When it's the right one, it will flow and merge with you naturally and organically. Placing any kind of demands will push it away. The same goes for work related endeavors or anything you have your eyes set on. The serious relationships I've had over the course of my life all transpired without effort. It came to be when I wasn't looking or longing for one. I was in a perfect state of contentment desiring nothing. When I was frustrated or in a negative mindset, then nothing came to pass.

When spreading yourself too thin, you want to ensure to be extra careful about what you're putting into your body. You might complain you're too tired or don't have enough time or energy to contribute up to an hour a day into what could potentially be your full-time job. This is a dilemma and a block for you, but if this is work you truly love, then it doesn't feel like work. It's something you enjoy doing so working on it is rarely a problem. When someone cheerfully wants to do something, then they will do it no matter how tired they are. Putting in efforts towards your passion and love gives you a positive lift, an energy boost, and raises your vibration. All of which are ingredients in that recipe for attracting in positive circumstances, love energy, and abundance.

Raising your vibration is a crucial element in giving you greater love energy and a brighter mood. This encourages you to make the time to contribute towards the things you love. Even after a long day at work at what you might consider to be a day job, when you have more energy, then that's energy to help push you to contribute towards work that you love. Putting love into your work counts as part of the love feelings you are utilizing from within. Love applies to your passions, endeavors and purposes. When you enjoy doing something, then you are putting love energy into it. This expands that love energy making a great deal more.

The reason you might be exhausted at the end of each day is not always because work is so tough at your day job, but it's because this job does not excite you on any level. When you experience excitement, then the feel-good chemical dopamine is released into your system. When you despise what you do, then this depletes the dopamine chemical, which sucks the life force love feeling energy right out of you.

When I'm doing what I love, then the energy keeps going for hours where I don't want to stop. It's a perpetual rushed excited high, because I'm doing what I love that it doesn't feel like work. It's fun and I'm getting paid for it too! On top of that, I'm being extra careful with what I put in my body and system. You know that if you have a glass of wine or a beer in the middle of the day, then you're unlikely to put in any work into what you love.

Human beings have been trained and taught to accumulate material and physical gratification over anything else. Thriving to create and produce what you love is one positive element to abundance, but this is about the obsession to achieve more finances. Chasing a dollar to have more money you do nothing positive with is not a goal to thrive for, but squeezes any love energy right out of you.

For some it becomes hyper mania to obtain additional finances even though they are already financially comfortable enough for life. If there are any positives to chasing finances, then it is to improve the quality of life for yourself, which subsequently enables you to be free to help others. This might be done through things like humanitarian work, charity giving, or you have a staff to employ and need to take care of. By that turn, you're ensuring the survival of more than one person that relies on that paycheck to pay their bills. You are showering love to others by this act. At the same time, chasing anything pushes it further away from you. It's the nature of the way energy attraction tends to operate.

The soul has the capacity to absorb a wealth of knowledge. It has the power to bring in what it desires into its current reality. This starts with a thought, a dream, and a foresight that begins to grow and expand into an intensified crystal-clear vision. What many are longing or fighting for in this human jungle is a profusion of love and abundance.

The traits of happiness and love are traits that every soul on the planet personally longs for. It's become a struggle for many to reach that state of love happiness. They wind up chasing after butterflies and mirages that appear to be enticing as the answer to revealing these riches. The density of the Earth's atmosphere places enormous pressure on the soul that causes communication blockages with the Divine. It messes and tampers with your emotions in trying to find that centered space of peace where you have everything you could ever want. You spend your entire life pursuing those pretty dreams hoping and praying for some blessing or miracle. The answer is in your hand, in your mind, and in your feelings. It is in your soul burning like a raging fire screaming to make that Divine connection where you are transcended into an authentic feeling of joy, love, and peace.

True abundance is living an existence where you are functioning in the highest soul love vibration possible. You are filled with God and Spirit's love. It is overflowing to the point that you experience upbeat high vibrational emotions. It is impractical in today's world to be in that state non-stop every second, even though you can imagine how awesome life would be if that were humanly possible. Many attempt to artificially create that feeling through toxins.

If everyone followed the mantra of functioning without stress, obscenity-ridden judgments, and instead chose to live in a joyful peaceful compassionate state, then this would be a utopian paradise. This is unlikely to happen anytime soon. Especially considering that the planet is centuries and more into humanity's progression and life on Earth, and yet the globe is still unable to revert to love as the core manner of communicating with others. Discord has been ripe with relentless fury since the first human beings walked the Earth. It has never lightened up.

Humanity has a tough time in thinking and feeling in love. This isn't about being 100% positive 24/7, as that is an impossible feat even if your general disposition is a happy content positive one. It does mean going back to the mantra that if you don't have anything nice to say, then don't say anything. When you're experiencing negative or challenging anything, then take the time to move through that. Examine what it is that took place in your life that threw your world off kilter.

CHAPTER THREE

Self-Love and Self-Care

You must love yourself first before you can faithfully love another person. It might seem to be there is quite a bit of self-love going on in places like social media, but when you're posting content with the ultimate goal of gaining accolades, comments, likes, and followers, then that is the opposite of authentic self-love. It is placing the responsibility on other people to fill you up with the kind of love that no human being can give. You are reaching out to external sources to boost your self-esteem, which is never permanently successful.

There are endless studies and statistics that have indicated how social media has crumbled one's wholeness and well-being state. There have also been numerous interviews of some of the world's popular social media influencers that have admitted to the depressing loneliness they experience. They've illustrated that their social media accounts give people the false illusion that they're popular due to the one million followers they have, but if they were in a personal crisis there is no one around them they can truly call a friend.

This is because the kind of love the soul part of you is attempting to grasp is reachable within you. This is where the Divine source of love is that lifts you up into the heavens while raising your vibration and consciousness. It is the source of true authentic love that increases your self-esteem, self-love and independence from the toxic addiction of relying on external sources for this impossible love.

One of the ways to find this kind of love is to practice self-love and self-care. It is paying attention to what you need rather than what others can give you. The more you raise your self-love awareness, then the more opened up your world will become. There is no telling what you can accomplish and attract in when you have built up that inner confidence through this act of self-love.

Participating in self-love and self-care means to also give you personal time. This is a much-needed intermission your soul needs regular amounts of in order to recharge and decompress from the stresses of the physical life. It is time devoted to you alone or with a loved one. When you're alone sitting in a park, in meditation, or in nature somewhere, you're able to clear your mind and allow perspective and additional Divinely guided ideas to flow into your soul without any physical distractions. It is what fills your soul up with the love you've been struggling and fighting to get from external sources. You gather up the newly gained incoming ammunition and tools and store it away for future use. This is when you re-emerge from your personal soul time and back into the next phase of your physical world action momentum. You take the tools and knowledge gained from this personal soul time and apply it towards your next new chapter of forward motion. Practicing self-love and self-care enables you to accomplish your life purposes. You take your time and enjoy what you're doing without the desire for external praise and adoration.

You're not intended to have a miserable life. Pleasures and playtime fun are essential are all part of self-love and self-care. One of its necessary functions is that it ensures you are not overloaded with constant stress on your body and overall health. Self-love and self-care are necessities that prevent you from experiencing burnout. This isn't about the kinds of pleasures that are considered toxic, dangerous, or unhealthy. It might be to go on a hike with a friend, or a fun road trip to a destination far enough away from home to feel as if you're getting away, but close enough to get to. Give yourself enough time to take regular breaks and see places you've always wanted to visit and explore. It can be watching a movie that entertains, inspires, and helps you escape a hard circumstance for a time period. It can be spending intimate time with a lover, a best friend, your pet or family member. Giving to you is part of self-love and self-care. By taking time out of your busy life to play has many positive health and success benefits.

Self-love includes loving all that you are. It is to love and accepts how you look, which is something many suffer from including those that you wouldn't think to be the case. Those that primarily post one photo of themselves after another are seeking love or praise from others. This isn't about the occasional photo one posts, but rather those that crave external validation and approval. This includes those who appear hot in the eyes of others. I've seen some posters post one hot photo of themselves after another with some inspiring words. They either likely know that is what will attract in praise and followers, or they are seeking external approval and validation.

The ones that aren't seeking that out are the ones that unsurprisingly are not as popular when it comes to social media domination. They're not playing the game of approval seeking, which is what attracts in popularity. The ego in humankind is attracted to pretty people with beautiful sayings. In mythology it was Narcissus who saw his hot sexy reflection in a pool of water and fell in love with himself. Due to this extreme form of self-love he ended up killing himself because he could not attain that person in the reflection. This is a symbolic metaphor for human behavior on social media today.

With anything in life, you want to keep it balanced and in moderation. This goes for self-love where you give yourself just enough self-love acceptance where it raises your self-esteem, but isn't pushed past that breaking point into narcissism, because then you've aligned yourself with the Narcissist that fell in love with his own reflection that it caused his demise. What you might perceive to be a flaw in your appearance is subjective. Even the hottest person on the planet isn't attractive to every single person that exists. Most everyone I've ever talked to has opened up about what they feel is their flaw. This includes from those that you would think have people lined up outside their door because of how good-looking they are. I've heard those same good-looking people tell me random things out of nowhere that they perceive as a flaw. Things like, "My nose is too big." Or "My ears are too small."

These are things that no one notices in the way they do. They see what they feel is a problem about themselves and they magnify it to the point of extremism.

Learn to love everything about you flaws and all without the need for external approval. Change the things you're able to change about yourself that you feel could use an adjustment. Love and accept the areas that you know you will never be able to improve. The things that you perceive to be as flaws are qualities that God loves about you. All heavenly spirit beings see you as pure love inside and out. They have a hard time grasping why so many people spend each day longing for constant validation and approval that will never come no matter how hard they try. It feels like an exhausting way to live inside one's head demanding that endless craving of love and adoration that comes from above, not from human beings.

Where can it get you to sit around all day thinking low thoughts about yourself one after the other? Love yourself because you are created in His image. You were born out of this love from the creator who loves you unconditionally. Those negative words you tell yourself are untrue in the eyes of Heaven. They seem or feel true from your own current reality and perception, but not in the eyes of God. Many that seek out this external love do it in frustration only to be met with disappointment. They are usually people that don't have a higher profound faithful spirit belief and connection, which is why they chase human beings for it down here. Your soul is perfection in every way loved unconditionally for all that you are, including your strengths and what you consider to be personal flaws. Love, accept, and appreciate you, because you're a gift!

External human validation isn't something I require, because I know my worth through God. I know who I am, what I can do, and what I've done. Believe in yourself and give yourself credit when you do good things. Praising yourself is considered self-love that lifts your vibration up into the vortex of attracting in more good stuff.

Most people are only super close to a few others in person that you can count on one or both of your hands. Everyone else outside of that is extended friends, family, or acquaintances. These are people that you are friendly with when you bump into one another, but they don't necessarily know about every shred you're going through on a daily basis the way the super close ones do. Authentic love comes from those that know everything about you and are still with you. They never criticize you, but support you and stand by you as you do with them. You both know how to give this love authentically.

Someone might have hundreds of acquaintances, business associates, and appear to be super popular in person or on social media, but in the end the super close ones that know every shred of breath they utter are on the minimal side. Those people are the ones that would be there during your most dire of circumstances. They stand by you when you're at your best as well as your worst. They are the ones that have your back while supporting your endeavors. They will offer constructive criticism, which you can handle if you're headed for a cliff you cannot see. In the end, what matters is the quality of people around you and not the quantity.

This is also true for those people with thousands of likes on their social media accounts. I have friends who are exceptional masters on social media with the tens of thousands and millions of followers and likes, yet knowing them in person they have a small number of quality friendships that know the real deal and day-to-day nitty-gritty happenings going on with them behind closed doors.

This is also true for well-known celebrities or public figures who have followers and likes in the hundreds of thousands and on up into the millions. Knowing some of them in my personal life I can tell you that they are no different than any other friend. In the end, they are surrounded by a small number of quality people in the real-life reality outside of the media platforms. They are not as big as the public believes them to be in their personal life.

The media and social media recycle this false deception to the public. Even if you're unknown to the world, you choose what you decide to post on your social media. It's never enough for anyone to know the real you because you're controlling what is out there. It's all an illusion and you have to be careful not to get swept up in that fiction believing this is the way to obtain love.

It might seem as if some are more loved than others, but popularity is an illusion because the love you think they're receiving is a superficial one. People may love that person's work or the way they look, but they don't know who that person is deep down on a daily and regular basis. Will they be by their bedside upon death's door?

Perhaps you long for strangers to like you. You will do anything to grab that adoration, idolatry, and admiration. Who cares if anyone likes you? Focus on your purpose and don't worry so much about being propped up by others. Lean on Spirit, God, and Heaven in order to prop yourself up and stay focused on what needs to be accomplished while on your path.

Some people might reach a higher popularity than someone else making it seem as if they're more worthy of popularity, but popularity doesn't matter in the end. No one will remember much about anyone presently popular one hundred years from now.

What is in your heart and what you set out to do is what matters. If your heart and soul is bathed in negativity and hatred, then your soul light is a flicker ready to go out leaving you in darkness. The popularity is insincere and fleeting on Earth. Someone outwardly unpopular on Earth is in actuality more popular in spiritual soul reality if what they put out into the world is authentic.

Your strength and gifts are much needed to help move humanity through the next transition and into the next plateau. Make good with your intentions, follow through, take action, cut out those that are perpetually negative, bullying, or abusive. None of the noise around you is important. What is important is your character, your soul's true nature, and what you intend to accomplish while here. Stay focused on the job at hand, but also remember to inject regular breaks, fun, and relaxation. Your soul will always thank you for those gifts of leisure. It makes you that much stronger and ready to forge forward fearlessly after having rested up and re-charged.

Current human life has propelled others to become obsessed by youth and exterior appearances. For some it is to the point where reality has fazed those that have fallen into the epicenter of this superficiality. There was a time pre-technology days when you respected your elders. Now many disrespect those older because they are ageist and under the delusion they are untouchable and exempt from aging. Popular culture in Entertainment became more about visual appearances in the music industry, rather than making and playing great music. Magazines airbrushed their models and celebrities almost to the point of making them unrecognizable in some cases. Even the most amateur photographer on the planet that enjoys taking their daily selfies will ensure that the filters are just right. The photos must appear attractive enough to post for validation and praise. This all stems from the soul's core desire of longing to be loved, admired, and praised. Many desire this deep down, but some take it to the furthest extreme more than others.

Some desire praise and attention more than others to the degree of extremism. They cannot help it because they desire and crave admiration and love. A soul was born out of love and will die right back into that love. It moves about in a human body longing to be hugged, cuddled, and loved up. When that love is starved from their existence, then they may harden and toughen up, become distant, aloof, cold and indifferent. Or they may head in the opposite direction and compensate by trying anything and everything to find ways to gain that praise and admiration that never sticks. It only lasts for a millisecond until they notice that people have moved onto other things and no longer have any interest in them again. It's dangerous to place your well-being state in the hands of others. Relying on people online and around you to continuously prop you up and feel good about yourself can become tiresome from all aspects. Love yourself and all that you are now.

The body is temporary, and it is aging each day until it stops working and ultimately disintegrates as your soul leaves it and soars into the other world. This scares some causing them to be unsure of what happens after that. They may believe there is life after death or they're hesitant because they don't see it with their own eyes. The one thing everyone agrees on is that we will all cease to live on this planet forever. Those that invested deeply into the physical material world may have the greatest fear involved. The reality check will hit them on their deathbed when the material fades away.

As you grow older, you want to reach the realization that you don't have a choice and you have to strengthen your faith and resolve. This is partially why you may have noticed that as one grows older their spiritual belief system seems to become stronger. This is the case even if they were a non-believer in younger age. Perhaps they won't suddenly believe in God, but they will grow more open minded of the possibilities of something good beyond their Earthly life. They subconsciously know that their body will permanently stop working for good. It will shut down and become lifeless. They may hopefully see that their soul and consciousness is somewhere in there and that it will continue on. The struggle for likes, followers, and praise suddenly appears trivial in comparison to what is coming up for every single person on the planet.

The human bodies were not designed to live forever. You reach older age signified by your physical body aging, and eventually shutting down. The body will die, and the soul will exit and move on to new destinies. There is no way around that. No one would want to live on this planet forever since back home is where the true fun and serenity exists full time. You are with those in your soul tribe, whereas on Earth you are mixed in with all souls in various levels of growth. Many souls in a human body use enormous amounts of dark ego, which dominates their higher self. This is what causes so much unrest, a lack of love, and unhappiness on the planet. The ever growing and expanding spiritual metaphysical movement has been helping to make one another's souls more aware, conscious, and enlightened about life beyond the physical and superficial. The goal of spirit is to bring all into the highest vibrational love state possible around the globe, so that Heaven can exist on Earth.

Other ways of inviting more self-love is not only giving to yourself, but it includes giving to others. It is also about receiving from others in the right spirit. Give and receive throughout the course of your day-to-day movements in order to increase the balance of feelings of self-love and Universal love. Giving is not necessarily giving money away, although giving something to your favorite charities counts. Giving is also the giving of a small positive act to another person that has the potential to brighten their day, such as a smile or a compassionate complimentary word or more.

Sometimes it's the little acts of kindness that might go unnoticed, but which are actually creating a wave of love. One person makes one small kind move to help someone, then that person carries that act of love and compassion to another, and so on until it wraps back around reaching the original person again in the end.

What you put out eventually comes back to you. This is seen on the planet with the dark energy, but rarely shown are these small moments of love from others in the seemingly smallest of ways. I notice those little small acts of kindness from others that come through out of that one amazing person out of hundreds.

Once I had dropped a huge wad of cash not realizing it. This guy jogged after me and said, "Excuse me."

I turned around and he had a smile, "You dropped this, here you go."

I said stunned, "What? Thank you. Wait a minute, who does what you just did?"

I handed him some of it as a reward.

He put his hand up refusing it and said, "Just pay it forward."

I smiled, "I will."

Another incident, I was standing at a urinal and this guy tapped me and said, "I think this is yours."

It was my driver's license. These things might be small, but you'd be surprised how rare those small acts of kind gestures are. There are people with ill intentions that might steal it, throw it away, or not bother to say anything.

At one point in my life, I ended up on crutches for six weeks after tearing the tendon on my foot during a bootleg camp work out accident where I landed on a jump wrong. Everything is fine today as if it never happened, but back then I was balancing on the crutches and putting groceries into my car with another hand. This well-to-do rich woman in her thirties with one of those massive SUV's was loading up her car before she caught my juggling act. Like a fireman answering a bell she gasped and quickly jogged over to me to help. Again, you'd be surprised that those little things are rare, so when they happen you do feel the magic of humanity's compassion that is in there deep down.

Use God's mantra of remembering to spread more love, more kindness, and more compassion, even in those tiny gestures like a smile to a stranger. They add up and do mean something in the eyes of God and the Universal energy. You don't do those things for fanfare or attention, nor to get something in return. You do it because you have a strong willed compassionate sensitive part of you that cares wanting to be of service. In Heaven, all spirit beings want to be of service. They don't have the massive dark egos that human beings have where there often seems to be an ulterior motive that isn't aligned with the soul's higher good.

Being of service are the little gestures that are actually large blessings you're giving to other people. It doesn't take much to brighten someone's day just from a simple move. Because there isn't enough of it as it is, that when it does happen, whoever is on the receiving end notices it.

I've had people tell me that only one person smiled at them throughout the day, and it was that one person that stood out enough that it uplifted their energy after that. They could feel it shift just from a stranger's random genuine smile. Sometimes those reminders are God working through other people to reach out and make that positive move towards someone that could use it at that moment.

Give yourself a break from the struggles in life and practice the joy and love you can feel from receiving. Many spiritual or compassionate people have the qualities of being a selfless giver. While this is a magnificent heavenly trait to have, you can create an imbalance when that is all you are doing. In order to bring balance into your life, be open to receive in your life as well. When someone wants to do something nice for you for a change, then welcome that with open arms. Those who are predominately givers tend to wrestle with the joy of receiving. They might fall into the category of someone taking advantage of them. Never mistake kindness for weakness.

    Receiving is also giving to yourself where you are the receiver, which is part of self-love and self-care. It's treating yourself to something you love such as a weekend getaway somewhere or a spa day if you enjoy being pampered. Whatever it is that makes you smile to receive, then go for it and give to yourself regularly to increase your self-love and self-esteem.

CHAPTER FOUR

Karmic Soul Connections

After you've mastered the art of regularly incorporating self-love, then you are ready to move into the world of relationships. From a young age, I had quickly begun the process of studying the human condition as well as the various relationship dynamics that exist between others. I can remember being a love bug Don Juan Casanova type from as far back as five years old when I recall developing my first crush. I've spent a great deal of my life experimenting and experiencing every kind of relationship dynamic possible, including but not limited to witnessing my parents own Karmic Relationship to the deep Soul Mate love relationships I've had that were filled with the kind of love you find in a romantic novel or movie. I've also experienced my own personal Karmic Relationships with less than suitable partners when I was in my twenties. These were partners I had intended to marry at the time; therefore, you can understand how deep each and every love relationship partner I've had has been romantic, passionate, and intense. It comes with the territory when you're with me. As I grew older, my partners grew more stable as did I. Hence, the karma was being balanced out to the point that there were virtually no real major issues in the latter relationships and years of my life.

You romantically dream it up and I likely experienced it from the kissing in the rain to the cathedral like set up when getting proposed to. Love has been my overall nature and it stays locked up only displaying it on those trustworthy enough for that kind of intensity.

In my late teens and early twenties, I started writing column pieces on love, dating, sex, and relationships. That became the genre I primarily chose to gravitate towards and focus on. I've also always been in love with love. I've been around the block my friends have said. This is through the life course of studying, reading and psychically scanning others that pass me, while avoiding anyone that I pick up on as dangerous, while welcoming in those that are filled with love.

There has no doubt been a rise in a great dividing intolerant wave of hatred that is completely devoid of love around the globe. There is no Light and no psychic intuition in that space. I've been versed in the nature of soul connections since I was born and understand it all well. This is because like you, I am a child of God. I'm also a Warrior of Light, a channel for the Divine, a lifelong psychic and medium. Since I was four years old, my focus has primarily been aimed at the Light. The endless exactitudes I've protested over the course of my life have led myself and my Spirit team to discuss the truths and mythology over some of the spiritual concepts made popular over the years. This includes karmic relationships, soul mates, and twin flames. Some believe in all of those things, some of those things, or neither of those things. Regardless if one believes it or not, we're going to use those terms in the coming chapters for the sake of easily identifying the differences. Irrespective of what it's called they are some of the varying soul connections that exist on Earth.

This planet is still having a tough time moving into that love space after all these centuries of Earth's evolution. In the end, your soul's life was born out of love and it will die right back into that love. Love is the only power that can kill the demon, the ego, the devil, and the darkness in one big bang.

You could possibly be part of the many around the planet that have been in the kind of love relationship that transcends time and space. This love lifts you up into the Heavens and transports you to places you never thought possible to reach. It's a mutual deep physical attraction sensed upon first sight with another person. Before you know it, you're dating and quickly falling into an immediate love connection. You've been waiting for this your entire life and now it's real and in motion. Life couldn't be any better!

As your relationship connection continues through its initial beginning stages, your intensity for this person never wanes, but instead grows to an obsession. This is the one you've been waiting for without a doubt in your mind, because no other relationship has been this intense before. You've finally found that love paradise that artists write about in romantic novels, films, and songs. This is the honeymoon period of a love connection.

The honeymoon period in a love connection is the initial beginning stages of two people coming together romantically. The honeymoon period can last from one week to around eighteen months. This is before the honeymoon blush begins to gradually wear off if it hadn't already by that point.

After the blush has dissolved, then that is the moment when both partners begin to know if the relationship is truly working or not. Most relationships have a hard time making it to the end of that period, which has been made clear through endless statistics being polled. The couple will be hot and heavy the first few weeks to a few months upon meeting before watching the connection dismantle. One or the both of them realize that now that the newness has subsided, they're actually not that into the other person as much as they thought.

It's a testy time for relationships in general. Most relationships today have a challenging time lasting until death do either of you part. If you are one of the exceptions at this point, then treasure what you have to the greatest of your ability, because you have what many either long for or are incapable of sustaining.

If someone is physically attractive, then the relationship might last a bit longer due to the lust filled magnetism had with the attractive person. You're not necessarily truly compatible with the person you have a physical attraction for, but because you find them physically attractive, you're pulled in for longer than it should've been. Being with a physically attractive person is like witnessing a beautiful butterfly flitting around you. That person can do no wrong when you've got those rose-colored glasses on. Look at how society puts attractive people on a pedestal just for looking good. They treat them with more love and compassion than someone they don't find attractive or see to be average. Attractive people surmount a huge amount of likes and followers, even though they're not really selling a product except endless selfies. Beyond physical attraction there is no other chemistry to keep the connection cemented and enduring.

If you've fallen into the drunken hazy love of that kind of adoration for someone way too good looking, then you need great will power to take a higher step back to truly examine if they're a good person for you or not. Are you brushing aside certain behavior traits they do that you normally wouldn't be so forgiving with if it were someone else?

Enormous deception is the challenge of walking into the beginning stages of a bright new love connection. One day you wake up to find the relationship has abruptly broken apart. You wonder how this is possible as you were sure this person was the one.

One of the two in the partnership starts to display an eerie disinterest that builds causing them to pull away or ultimately walk away from the connection. This leaves you with this dark heavy pain that burdens your heart and simultaneously places a huge weight on your soul. Some justify the reasoning the partner left being due to the runner part of the runner chaser equation theory pushed in twin flame circles. It's the only way to help you make sense of why the person you thought could be the love of your life turned their back on your comfortable love nest. You cannot understand how this could happen because this person was supposed to be the one.

The intense love feelings were there, but those intense love feelings are present for most every deep romantic love connection in the beginning stages. Your feelings cannot always be trusted when you fall in love with someone. Falling in love puts you into a joyful happy place, but it also places rosy glasses over your psychic visions. Suddenly all of the rules are thrown out the window and Divine instincts are reduced. This evidence is present and all around through the millions of deep intense love relationships that break apart sooner than later causing the person that was blindsided to note that in hindsight the red flags were there, but they chose to ignore them. They believed their mate was the one to the degree that the infatuation carried them away on that love causing them to brush any practical sense aside.

Since most relationships have trouble lasting until the end of their days, the odds of it being a twin flame connection will be slim. An authentic twin flame soul connection tends to last indefinitely. We say it tends to because there are rare cases that a twin flame relationship will break apart and stay apart. The truth is the relationship just described at the start of this scenario was actually a Karmic Relationship.

Karmic Relationships

Every soul on the planet is developing and creating karma every day through their actions, thoughts, and deeds. Karma is being created quickly with the relationships you have with others including friendships, family members, business colleagues and lovers. We're focusing on the love-oriented relationships in this example, but it can be applied to other types of connections as well too.

Karmic relationships can start off exceptionally deep and intense. God and your Spirit team bring the two souls together in a radiant attractive enticing shower bathed in enormous intensity. This is to make the two inseparable for the purpose of balancing out past karma. If they have an intense draw to one another, then they are more than likely going to come together to take care of soul business. If there is no intensity, then it is unlikely to draw them in, thus leaving the karmic pattern stuck on pause. They come together intensely until they are no longer inseparable and the restraints they formed have been broken. The connection and interest in one another begin to dissolve.

What happened was the karmic thread had completed and been balanced out. There was nothing left to learn with this person. If the person comes back, then that could mean the connection had not balanced out the karmic thread completely the first time around. Usually a partner will come back at another time allowing the opportunity for both people to balance out the Karma and produce healing, which is then followed by official closure.

You will know that the karmic relationship is complete when you have both moved on your separate ways. You have no negative thoughts or feelings about them. This means any previous animosity, anger, or sadness attributed to thoughts or feelings about them have dissolved, or they've been significantly reduced you hardly notice it anymore. You are in a place of peace and contentment with the fact that you are no longer in that partnership anymore. There is no feeling of something missing after they've gone. In fact, you don't care whether or not they come back. You are open to new experiences and relationships.

All souls are developing, creating, mending, and balancing out karma. Whenever you come into contact with someone and have any kind of relationship, then you are both creating karma due to the actions on both of your parts. Karmic relationships may start off amazingly hot and heavy, but eventually they tend to be bathed in some kind of turmoil, drama, or chaos. Some are more extreme in this than others.

Many karmic relationships are displayed in all its nonsense and glory on social media or in the media. This is because the public's dark ego receives a rushed high over drama and watching the theatrical lives of others. Dramatic and chaotic relationships love to use the world as its stage. This is also why tabloids became a billion-dollar enterprise. It's why reality television and reality stars were propelled to celebrity status. It was due to the public's obsession with drama fueling all of that to the top of the charts.

There is no God or spiritual essence in drama, because that is where the darkness of ego resides. Every person on the planet has had or will have a karmic relationship with someone else, whether it be a friendship, colleague, neighbor, love connection, and so on. There is no limit to the dynamic that the relationship will form.

Karmic connections can be a soul mate partnership as well too. The difference is that soul mates are not perpetually antagonistic. They might have the occasional antagonism, but not to the daily or weekly degree that a karmic relationship does.

Soul mate partnerships are a give and take, whereas a karmic relationship tends to mostly be a taking kind of relationship. It's always about me or what you're not doing for me. Karmic partnerships tend to complain incessantly about their partner with anyone who will listen.

The karmic soul partner may show up in the beginning putting on the act of a chivalrous Prince or Princess, but as the connection grows you begin to notice little red flags popping up. You may eventually believe them to be sociopathic or narcissistic. These red flags are those warning signs that something is not right. You might brush off the first few red flags. Some will even brush off the first few dozen red flags, but their friends won't. Someone's good soul mate friendships tend to see that this relationship is a problem long before you do. You don't see the love relationship the same way they do because anybody you're romantically connected with is the world to you. You're just happy as a clam to be entangled with someone in a love connection that you'll accept the drama over being alone.

Millions of souls crave love and companionship, which is why they seek out committed love relationships with one another. Everyone has challenges they endure and there will be trials no matter how spiritual or put together you are.

Karmic relationships end up being the ones wrecked with some kind of negativity, drama, or endless challenges. There are more people in karmic relationships today than in any other kind of relationship. This is partly due to the ego driven modern day world that life on Earth has become. It's a me-first attitude and this is taught in almost every circle. If someone doesn't get what they want, then they throw a tantrum, or they take to the streets or social media to protest and complain. There is no love in any of that space. What you have is new karma being created. The positive that comes out of that are lessons and potential soul growth. Having a genuine love relationship requires sacrifice and compromise.

Because there are more karmic relationships than any other kind of relationship, then that means that many karmic relationships have been mistaken to be twin flame connections. Some may explain away that their twin flame turned out to be a narcissus, which is unlikely to be the case. It's not that twin soul flames are above or below being a narcissus, but the odds of the twin flame being a narcissus is on the slim side. This is due to the twin flame having evolved more rapidly on their soul's path in terms of spiritual growth that succumbing to narcissism is also rare. If they do fall into some narcissistic tendencies, then it's so miniscule compared to others that it's almost never a problem.

The narcissus terminology gained steam when social media, technology, and the Internet took off. Many will use the sociopath or narcissistic word if someone leaves them, but they do not truly understand its psychological definition. Because in its definition most everyone can be accused of vacillating between the humble to narcissistic on any given day. If a partner was indeed a narcissus based on the psychological definition, then they were more than likely in a karmic relationship.

CHAPTER FIVE

*Soul Mate
Soul Connections*

Heaven understands the negative challenges that people are assaulted with on a regular basis. No one is exempt from challenges, because if you don't have challenges, then you don't grow. Your individual Spirit team works to assist in bringing soul mates into your life with the goal of assisting you in various ways while on your journey here. One soul mate might have one purpose to accomplish with you, while another will have several. Some of them help out by offering mutual support as you endure these challenges.

These people are called Soul Mates. The word *soul* describes the part of you that is separate from your body. When you pass onto the Other Side, your soul exits your body, and your physical body disintegrates into dust, but your soul and consciousness carry on and move onto other destinies in the next plane back home.

Mate can mean a love partner, a companion, a friend, or a business associate. It is a pair of two people joining together for a purpose or purposes. This would be someone who is comparable to you. Soul mates are other souls you cross paths with for a specific purpose or purposes that are aligned with teaching or learning something from this person and vice versa. Everyone has something to teach one another and learn from, even if it's not evident at first.

Soul mates can be a lover, a friend, a work colleague, a pet, a parent, a sibling, a neighbor, an acquaintance, or even someone you crossed paths with for several minutes. This might be someone that says a profound line to you in a quick conversation that makes you think or propels you to make a positive change in your life.

Perhaps you strike up a conversation with a stranger in an elevator. During that short ride that stranger manages to say something that makes you think about something in a deeper way. Sometimes the stranger can act as a catalyst that prompts you to action. Often a spirit guide or angel will have other soul mates deliver messages to you in this way. The soul mate will offer you challenges to overcome that enable your soul to grow and evolve.

A soul mate friend will pull you out of your comfort zone and toss the metaphorical ball to you to take and run with it. Your guardian spirit is right there on the field coaxing you both along to be proactive in your life.

When you evolve out of karmic relationships and into selflessness in love, then you are moving into what you can do for your partner and vice versa. This is when you have a greater opportunity to graduate into healthier soul mate partnerships. Healthy soul mate partnerships praise and uplift their partner, rather than complain or beat them down. This also means it's a mutual reciprocation, because if you're always doing something for a partner who doesn't reciprocate that, then that's called co-dependency which is an imbalance.

Co-dependency can point to a lack of self-love, therefore you look to others to receive that love and become co-dependent on it. There may be some that fall into the space of needing constant attention from others, whether it's from a lover, friends, family members, or strangers. They love messages of joy, but fail to notice when they have been guilty of falling into the co-dependency aspect part of it. People cannot fulfill that kind of unrealistic demand from another person.

It's pretty common to seek out attention and love from external sources from the teenage years on up into one's early twenties. One hopes that by the time you begin moving into your late twenties that your desire for external sources to shower you with love begin to fade. You realize that it can be conjured up naturally by standing in your own independent soul power and connecting with the Divine.

The soul mate will offer you challenges to overcome that enable your soul to grow and evolve. They might be someone that shows up at just the right time it is needed to offer love and support, such as when a parent or child passes on and a soul mate shows up in the form of your pet dog to give you that unconditional devotion and love you crave during that grieving period in your life. Or your best friend calls you regularly to offer cheering support about something. This person is also your soul mate. Your love mate stands by you through this time of grieving. They are also your soul mate. Your soul mate will also push you out of your comfort zone coaxing you to go after someone or something that you are fearful of. They can be someone that happened to show up at the time you needed it in your life most, then they evaporate away.

This might be an acquaintance that temporarily befriended you. You realize they helped you through a tough time in life, but then as you healed the connection dismantled gradually. This is because the purpose was fulfilled. God and your Spirit team are sending soul mates to others for the purpose of guiding them through a tough challenging time in life or for something specific. Once that mission is complete, then the connection becomes moot.

Soul mates are not interested in holding you back or pushing you down. They're typically not abusive, but they may give you tough love. Tough love is someone that may push you out of your comfort zone to get you out there on that stage and display your talents. They may shine the spotlight on both your strengths and challenges or as some call flaws. Their motive is to coax you on to become better than you are now, even though they also see you as perfection in their eyes the way God does. They understand there is always room for anyone to improve. They understand you have dreams and they want to help you go after them, but you are the same way in return for them too. The soul mate friendships in my life helped me become who I am today. When I was in my late teens and early twenties, I was much darker than I am now. You know the look of a punk kid with a skateboard and the dark black hoody over my head. The kind of dark character that Tim Burton would have a field day creating in one of his masterpieces.

One of my soul mate friends who are still around today is a confident physical fitness trainer. He had told me something interesting once when I was in my early twenties. He gave me this long talk that people keep telling him how deep and intense my eyes are. The issue is that I would avoid looking at people or I would hide them behind gigantic dark jet-black sunglasses the way Anna Wintour does. He explained that my eyes are one of my winning cards and that he noticed the moments that my gaze is held on someone he would see them grow intimidated and suddenly melt. He was trying to get me to understand to use my eyes on people more because the effect is so powerful. I had never heard that before, so I decided to practice doing it for fun to see if he was right, and he was. Doors were opening and my world was becoming more successful. I thought how odd all for just doing that one move of using my eyes as weapons so to speak. This soul mate friend indirectly wound up being one of the many that helped me rise up into that warrior confidence that so many comment on today. This story is to illustrate that I wasn't necessarily showing that constant warrior like confidence. It is also explaining how a soul mate is someone that can provide some tiny shred of advice that you take to heart and end up running with it. Think back to those moments when someone said some compassionate words of recommendation that propelled you to incorporate into your life. This is an example of the role of a soul mate. They are unknowingly working through God and Spirit to relay information that they are helping you to do in order to become who you truly are.

Soul mates will not always have something in common with you. This is why some soul mate connections might seem challenging because perhaps one of you is extroverted and the other is introverted. Some introverted souls are rubbed the wrong way when in the presence of an abrasive outgoing soul, while the extroverted soul will feel as if they're working overtime to bring the introverted person out of their shell. When you give the connection a chance, you both discover that you end up admiring this outgoing cheeriness in this extroverted person, while they admire your put together more introspective and creative part of you. These are souls that challenge you in a positive way to open up and come out of your shell, while you enlighten the more outgoing soul. It might at first make you feel uncomfortable, but then as you think about it and remove your ego from the equation you realize that perhaps they might be right.

Soul mates direct your attention towards something or someone in a loving compassionate way. They might be the best friend that has your back and coaxes you to excel in ways that you normally would not have done had you not had that supportive push.

When you have that realization moment in your life that positive changes need to be made, then it is expected that you would pull yourself back up and release that need to give someone else power over you. While it's nice to have that great time with someone else, it's even more profound when you let go of the need to rely on them to prop you up into happiness.

Everyone on the planet comes across dozens of soul mates throughout the course of their lifetime. You might have formed soul mate friendships that were instant simpatico upon meeting. You both knew you were meant to connect with one another. There can be the fleeting soul mate connections where someone showed up just as you needed it most. They might have offered wisdom that helped you move to the next level in your life or helped you get over the pain of an event that left you broken.

Another example of a soul mate is someone that tests you, pushes your buttons, or supports you and teaches you things you hadn't considered before meeting them.

Soul mates can also be people you've never met such as your favorite entertainer, artist, actor, singer, photographer, or writer. The benefit the teacher has as that person's soul mate is passing on wisdom or inspiration through their work, since soul mate relationships happen in order for the purpose of teaching or learning. If someone pushes you to success even if you don't know them personally, then that person acted as a soul mate without realizing it.

Another best friend of over twenty years at this point is one of my many soul mates. He is outgoing and a strong forceful character. He is also someone you don't want to get into it with, as there have been times where he will dominate and win a debate.

When I was talking to a close relative of his about him once I said, "He and I have never got into a fight in all these years."

This relative said matter of fact and with surety, "That's because you two are soul mates."

I had never given it that much thought until that point. The soul mates in my personal life are all around me on a personal level, while I'm simultaneously awakening parts of souls whom I do not know simply through my writing work and teachings. This has been one of my life purposes in that respect. It is to help others be better people, make sounder choices, connect with their Spirit team more efficiently, and to awaken parts of their higher self's soul that may have been asleep for some time. This doesn't mean I'm infallible and without challenges. I too am a constant work in progress and continuously learning through God and the guidance of my own Spirit team. There is no way I would protest to be all knowing since no human being is all knowing. You cannot be your own God. The work my Spirit team and I do is also for me too. If no one cares about our preaching, then I'll preach to myself since the work is helping me grow my consciousness in the process. I've seen my earlier work and cringed while being able to detect that I'm no longer that guy anymore. I've graduated over different levels in the process of the work. It's also a bit eerie and interesting to see that it's all displayed publicly at the same time.

You have many soul mates throughout the duration of your Earthly life. There is no limit or number to the amount of soul mates you will cross paths with. When some think of a soul mate or twin flame, they automatically equate it to a passionate romantic relationship where you're making love on a white sandy palm tree lined beach in paradise for the rest of your lives. This beautiful mythological notion has caused great turmoil in others who long for this person that fits the description of a lothario character in a romance novel. It is also an unrealistic and misguided interpretation of the soul mate and twin flame dynamic.

Clearing up some of the myths while revealing tips on how to recognize these unique soul connections can be somewhat simplified. All human souls desire some measure of unconditional love and attention deep down within including the most jaded and hardened criminal like mind. This admiration craving is a detachment from God. God being the omnipresent energy space that fills up every cell that exists. He breathes life into every space filled in all existence and all dimensions into infinity and beyond. The stronger your Divine connection with the Other Side is, then the closer you are to understanding the true nature of love and love connections.

It's a basic human desire to long for some form of a companionship. It is the deep love connections that many crave more than any other. There are people who would like that friend companionship in one person, but it doesn't necessarily need to be a passionate love connection. In the end, a passionate sexual connection with the same person for life is rare, because even the most passionate couples experience lulls in that department on occasion. This may turn many off insisting that they will never allow that to happen.

That would be beyond your control. The human body ages and develops issues whether physical, emotional, or mental that creates roadblocks cutting off that passionate supply link you have with another person. What matters is the strong bond and companionship you have with that one person. As you age into your senior golden years, what many end up longing for at that point is someone just to have dinner with once in awhile, or perhaps to hold hands gazing out at a sunset perfectly content in one another's spaces. If you're unhappy with your current partner, then there is someone that would be happy to take them off your hands and they will accept your partner as is just to have that companionship.

Your life doesn't have to end as you move into your golden years. Many have announced they've noticed friends have moved away or passed on. This leaves little human contact from someone in the form of a friend. Sex drives and sex interests decline leaving one to experience loneliness or boredom if there are no hobbies or activities that you enjoy filling in those empty spaces. Many desire someone else to fill this missing void that seems to have been extracted from you, yet is alive and well deep inside burning like the embers on a log. You may be like me - a romantic at heart who revels in the idea of being swept up in blissful love feeling.

The overall energy of the planet is cold, dangerous, erratic, and hostile. The darkness of ego in humankind has created an unsatisfactory turbulent life for so many that it's simultaneously hardened the hearts of souls who were born awakened and receptive to love. Somewhere along the way of their developmental stages as a child, this love was stomped out by the cruel ego in others. This made many on the planet unreceptive to love while deeply longing for it.

Someone gives you that rare smile as they walk past you and you don't know how to receive it. You're shocked that there was one person out of over seven billion who chose to warm up slightly in your presence. Because you don't know how to receive it due to not being used to it, you walk past them realizing you never acknowledged them back. It was only after you continued walking that you realized you couldn't believe you didn't smile back, but instead glared at them angrily annoyed. That's not receptive or being open to love at all. Who can blame you when Earthly life has beat down on your soul to the point of becoming closed off. You place your happiness on other people to prop you up and love you up, but that's an impossible demand to place on a species that is incapable of giving that unconditional love every second. Even the most compassionate loving person would desire a day off to not have to spread love on you. Only God and higher spirit beings are built to shower that undying, unwavering, and unconditional love on another full time every second of every moment of existence.

Every soul is born completely in tune, stress free, and filled with overflowing feelings of love, joy, and peace. As you coast through an Earthly life you come face to face with hostility, sometimes as early on as childhood while on Earth's elementary school playground. Most of this hostility is executed by another human soul through the darkness of their ego. It might be someone jaded and cut off from Spirit and God. You seek to find that one person on the planet that can give you that unconditional undying love that you crave only to be disappointed in the end.

When you have a mutual love with another person regardless of their gender, only then do you understand what God's love can feel like. This essence of God's love breathes life into your soul. It awakens and lifts you up to the most incredible euphoric high that is better than any drug or addiction. In fact, many who have been addicted to alcohol, drugs, food, or any other toxic vice have proclaimed to have lost interest in those addictions while in the throes of a beautiful mutual romance with someone else. This is partially because they're receiving the Dopamine chemical rush through true love feelings, which can be an addiction in itself, but it is less harmful than putting toxic substances into your body.

It's easy to grow lost and addicted to love. As a love addict, I know and understand all of the pitfalls and challenges that come along with that desire for love that never seems to reveal itself. Spirit understands this desire and craving human souls have for companionship with at least one person. This is a reciprocated companionship where the positive feelings for one another are mutual, rather than an unrequited love that can only cause heartache. This is one of the reasons that soul mates are put in your path. Spirit understands the desire that human beings have for a close companion and confidante. Even better is when that companionship is also passionate like in those romantic novels.

The human soul is not intended to endure a solo life even though most do or will end up doing into older age. This is why there are soul mates you cross paths with over the course of your journey to offer companionship and vice versa. You have more than one soul mate as all souls do. You ride up in an elevator with someone who strikes up a conversation with you. They end up saying something to you that has a positive impact. It could be a statement that changes your life. It gets you thinking, or it is an answer to an issue you needed solved. This is someone that was a soul mate in passing.

Soul mates come into your life for the purpose of your soul's growth. This might be done through teaching or offering you life tools that become helpful for you at a later date. A soul mate is the listening ear of someone you feel comfortable enough to talk to about a life issue. They help you through rough times where it would have been more difficult to get through had they not been there. I've certainly had more people than I can count tell me, "I honestly don't know how I could've got through that time in my life if it weren't for you. You were there for me day in and day out in ways that no one else was."

Soul mates are not all blissfully and unrealistically perfect. They challenge you and prompt you to look at the darker aspects of yourself that you would prefer to keep hidden. The soul mate helps to bring that out in order to help you improve, grow, change, and evolve. They do not bring these things out in an argument or out of cruelty. It is done out of love and with compassion because they care about you.

Potential soul mates' cross paths with you for a variety of reasons. Most of them are with the intention of offering mutual soul lessons and growth. Some soul mates are intended to test you, coax you on, support you, and challenge you. Some of them might be to offer reminder blessings upon you such as in the form of positive optimistic words that help you to achieve something of importance, whether it's in the areas of work, spiritual, or personal life. Sometimes it can be to gain emotional traits that you didn't have before you met that person.

The purpose of other soul mate relationships is to offer you that mutual companionship that helps strengthen and support you along your Earthly journey. Some souls accomplish more while in a loving connection with another person. This helping you is a reciprocated one where you both learn and gain knowledge from one another that neither had before. Sometimes the soul mates' goal is simply to remind you how to love. They are the catalyst that prompts you to change from being closed off and into a soul being that is open and receptive to love. Love is what keeps the Earth soaring around in the Universe and there isn't enough of it going around.

If you look back on all of the people you had connections with, you'll note some of the lessons learned while with them. There is always a lesson learned even if you don't believe there is or are unable to detect what that could be. If you don't know what the lesson is or was with a particular soul mate, then you'll be consistently met with the same situations being repeated and set up over and over again until you do. This is why some people have stated, "Why do I keep attracting in the same types of people into my life?"

Because the same lesson those mates are offering have not been fully realized and learned from by you. There is no time limit for learning lessons that contribute to soul growth. One specific lesson can take a week while another will take your entire Earthly life.

Other soul mate pairings grow to be doubly challenging where they show up in the form of a karmic relationship, as mentioned in the previous chapter. Karmic relationships tend to be bathed in antagonistic ego more than soul mate partnerships. They're usually unhealthy addictive connections that both partners cannot seem to stay away from. While at the same time there are still lessons and growth involved in those types of connections as well too.

Soul mates tend to challenge you and get you to notice things from a different perspective. This isn't to be confused with someone who is heartless or abusive. Abusive tempestuous connections formed with others are karmic relationships, even though not all karmic connections are abusive. This is where there is unfinished business that needs to be wrapped up with that soul. You'll continue to incarnate together until you gain wisdom from it or gain strength to eradicate the connection.

There are cases where both people in the karmic relationship gain and learn from it, while both evolve out of that and into a healthy positive soul mate connection with each other within the same lifetime. The connection dynamic shifts halfway through. Many couples that have lasted a lifetime together may appear at peace and contentment with one another in older age, but they may admit that it wasn't easy in the beginning. This could be because they started out as a karmic relationship that eventually graduated into a soul mate relationship.

CHAPTER SIX

*Twin Flame
Soul Connections*

We've looked at karmic relationships and soul mate connections. The final spirit soul type of union is the twin flame. In Heaven, the twin flames are actually called twin souls, because they are souls that were made as one, but split into two. A great deal of people around the world can accept the idea of soul mates existing, but may not necessarily buy or believe in twin flames. Still we're going to look at them anyway since it's the third type of soul connection that can exist on Earth.

God does not have hard and fast rules jotted down on stone like the Ten Commandments when it comes to twin flames. What is discussed here about the twin flames is a generality of what most twin flame connections are like. You may see that you and your partner or potential friend of interest may fit some of the traits, but not all of them. This is about the personality traits fitting into most of the general guidelines my team has given me, but not necessarily every single one. It's to give you an overall idea of the nature of twin flames and how they are slightly different than the soul mates and karmic relationships you have throughout the course of your life. The twin flame is the highest form of a soul mate, which means the lessons they teach is enormous. You have numerous soul mates you cross path with, but only one twin flame.

There is quite a bit of contradicting information surrounding what a twin flame is, which has simultaneously caused all sorts of confusion. The reason it's caused misunderstanding is because when many talk about the twin flames today, they are discussing the feelings and emotions one feels when they meet their twin flame for the first time. The reason this causes misperception is because those intense feelings and descriptions are vague enough that they can be attributed to every single love relationship someone has ever had over the course of their entire life. Those feelings tend to exist for most anyone that has fallen in love or developed a love crush on another person. What makes the twin flame connection different than a love affair is the additional revealing stand out signs beyond the intense feelings one has. It is true the feelings for a twin flame are often intense, but that doesn't necessarily equate to a romantic union.

The feelings currently described for a twin flame are the same feelings used to describe when someone comes into contact with their soul mate or karmic relationship. Once that soul mate trend kicked in and grew to popularity, people started pining and longing for that one special love soul mate to come into their life and sweep them off their feet. Hollywood films then began to perpetuate the notion of finding your lifelong marriage love affair soul mate partnership through silver-screen stories. Romantic comedies in general have made billions of dollars displaying those stories on the big screen. They've made an enormous amount of money for the studios, production companies, and stars, because most everyone longs for that special love just like in the movies. They crave that one person they can live and mate with until death do you both part. The soul longs for the transcending kind of love that lifts them up into the clouds. Even the coldest person wouldn't necessarily shun some kind of positive attention from another person, since positive attention can be seen as love.

Everyone has more than one soul mate, which is becoming a bit more understood than it was pre-2015. It hasn't fully taken global understanding and effect yet. There are still people out there that are unaware they have more than one soul mate. These might be people who haven't necessarily studied up on it or connected with God for answers on it. Others don't believe in it or care much about it, but they have heard of the word phrase floating around. The most jaded non-spiritual person may admit to saying the following statement upon meeting someone they deeply and intensely gravitate towards: "I think this guy/girl is my soul mate."

In the spiritual communities, the concept of understanding that you have more than one soul mate has become accepted and understood as the years progressed since my earlier books on soul mates and twin flames came out. This is mostly due to how easily information is now shared across the Internet. The negative side effect to that is false information can grow like wildfire on the Internet leaving masses of people to believe in something that isn't true. There is quite a bit of enormous confusion that starts to also rise as a result of that.

As people began understanding the spiritual truth that all souls have more than one soul mate sifting in and out of their life, then it became, "Well, that simply won't do. That takes away from the specialness of me being in love with that one special person for life that needs an appropriate label."

They then took the meaning of soul mates and transferred it over to be about twin flames instead. This is the same way man specifically altered the Bible in places in the later additions to fit a new narrative of life at that time, which would include all of the superstitions believed during that century.

Many have begun to understand that there is more than one soul mate, but only one twin flame. Since there is one twin flame, the thought has become, "Ahhh, well that sounds more distinct and I want something special."

They moved the feelings for the soul mate and transferred them over to mean about the twin flame. That notion has been lifted up and trended massively by those who are great at social media and getting their blogs noticed and picked up by websites. Now the latest growing trend is everyone is searching for that one special twin flame to fall in love and marry for life, except there are several issues with that. One of them being that your twin flame may not be a romantic partner nor will they be living on Earth at the same time you are.

Your twin flame is like a karmic or soul mate connection where it can be a friendship, family member, business partner, or lover. The reason twin flames don't necessarily incarnate at the same time as you is because you spend eternity with them back home on the Other Side. If you're spending an eternity with someone, but you embark on a separate soul mission to incarnate on Earth, then why would your twin flame follow you? There are rare circumstances where a twin flame will incarnate relatively in the same lifetime.

The latest trend has taken the truths about twin flames and swept all of those big hearts longing for love into a frenzy causing all sorts of confusion in the process. Everyone is now looking for that one twin flame to complete them the way Tom Cruise protested it to Renee Zellweger's character in the film *Jerry Maguire*.

Except in spiritual truth a soul is already complete before the twin flame merges with their split apart. Your soul is in a place of feeling complete and whole with a raising consciousness beyond the superficiality of the physical life before the twin flame shows up if they are going to show up at all.

This is why for so many people if the merging is going to take place in their lifetime, it typically happens later in life after a great deal of maturity, unless there is a large age difference, but even in those cases the younger duo of the partner has exceptional maturity for their age.

Twin soul flames are not always romantic in nature, as much as some would love to believe that the pretty imagery in some twin flame drawings and photos matches the romance novel kind of love found in those books. There are millions of people in the world that will never have a romantic partner. Many of them have accepted that. There are different reasons for why that is and many of them know and understand this reality. To have others shove an unrealistic truth and belief that every person on the planet will meet their romantic twin flame in their lifetime creates a deceptive dangerous situation for the receiver. To believe that everyone has a romantic partner waiting to unite with them is a delusional myth. Every person on the planet deserves love, but that doesn't mean that will realistically come about in the form of a love partner. It's mistaken to assume that everyone will meet someone in a passionate love making romantic relationship like in the movies, as wonderful as that idyllic dream might sound.

Like soul mates, your twin flame can be a different gender or sexual orientation than you, which would make the love relationship bit impossible and unrealistic to take place. It won't however change the binding feelings you have for one another because the twin flames are indefinitely inseparable in spirit. This is beyond any physical attraction.

This isn't to say that twin flames cannot be sexually and physically attracted to one another, but that's the least of their interests because the connection they have is a soulful one with a higher life purpose. It is their souls that are drawn to one another beyond the appearance. They can sense something strong within one another that pull them towards each other. They feel as if they are looking in a mirror at themselves from a soul sense.

Having a mutual sexual physical attraction for someone is called lust. Lust for another person blinds you to the red flag warnings about someone else deceiving you into thinking you're in love with someone you just met. When you fall in love with someone you've just met, then it's more often than not a lust attraction first. This is why lust filled attraction relationships also tend to start up with this great passionate intensity before ending sooner than later. When it ends sooner than later, then that can indicate it was a lust filled physical attraction that had taken place and not a deep love. A deep love never wanes, dissolves, or goes away even if the two part indefinitely. It also endures throughout the years without ever faltering. A physical attraction can be deceiving into making you believe you're with the one only to discover the other person was never truly all that into you. Physical attraction can fade to some degree, whereas true deep love rarely fades.

The long running person you have more in common with on all levels minus the physical sexual attraction is more likely to be the twin flame over the person you have a lust filled sexual passionate physical attraction for. If twin flames coming together in their lifetime is due to assisting one another in a mission or purpose, then receiving that kind of support from someone you enjoy going to bed with to make love to because you find them hot, sexy, handsome, or cute is unlikely to be able to fulfill the demanding purpose of the twin flame.

Twin flames come together when they are rapidly evolving beyond the fads and trends of current modern-day society. Current modern functioning resides on the surface, but spiritual growth is higher up beyond the physical surface. The twin flames tend to be old souls regardless of their physical age due to the many lifetimes they've endured.

As a soul incarnates enough times, they grow to be more intelligent with a higher consciousness. God needs those souls to send on missions back to Earth to help usher in change as leaders, warriors, love showers, and teachers. That may not end up being the case as much as you or I might not want to come back while insisting this is it. Your perspective as a soul back home is much broader than it is on Earth. You take the mission of coming to Earth seriously before you incarnate again. In one sense, it is almost as if you are going off to fight a war or head to battle, because you know that is what it will feel like by agreeing to an Earthly life. You will be navigating a battleground on a rock consumed and dangerously susceptible to being attacked by the dark energies.

If a twin flame connection is going to happen for someone, then the union doesn't necessarily happen right away. While their mutual private draw to one another may be silently explosive, they move and come together at a slower pace than other relationships. This is partially because evolved souls understand there is no rush when it comes to a serious connection. Other less disciplined souls will rush passionately into a hot romantic interlude that quickly fizzles sooner than one or both may have preferred. Twin flames are in a place of deep spiritual maturity before they come together. They will never rush into something overnight, nor will they push to make a connection happen as fast as possible. They move methodically and at a slower pace. With spiritual maturity and a raised consciousness, one has also grown more patient about certain things including life circumstances and coming together with someone.

If twin flame souls incarnate relatively around the same time, then they do this within the span of eighty years. This means they can show up when you're eight or when you're eighty. There tends to be a generational gap or age difference of about ten years or more give or take between twin flames. If it's a love relationship with a wider age gap, then this is sometimes a source of conflict in this ego-based world. The conflict is not necessarily between the twin flames who are equally evolved regardless of their age, but the conflict may come from outside influences that have placed a stigma on any kind of age gap, which is called ageism.

Most of the time there is an age gap that is largely considered to be against what some cultures or parts of society believe in, especially in the United States over any other country. The gap can extend extremely wide into decades, which would make it even more unlikely that the two will form a love relationship, but a deep friendship instead.

Another newer theory perpetuated is to believe the twin flame is primarily a physical sexual love connection. This was spread by those that fell for those artistic memes and images posted by others that show a man and a woman intertwined with the phrase *twin flames* above it. This is despite its offensiveness to some by using a man and a woman as the depiction image of a true authentic deep romance. Twin flames can be the same gender and are not always romantic. This information can be easily retrieved through any higher Divine related psychic communication.

There may be the obvious initial challenges between twin flames such as age related, gender, cultural, and so on. They may even be confused by the connection if it's moving into love relationship territory, because they've never felt that intensely for anyone before. Both partners experience this intense draw that never wavers.

Your twin flame can be of a gender that you're not attracted to. It's not necessarily a deep love relationship, but it is a deep love and adoration between those two people without the sexual component. It can be a parent-sibling connection, it can be lifelong business partners, and it can be siblings or best friends. It doesn't matter if someone is your twin flame or not because no one is going to get a special medal for re-uniting with their twin flame. Are you happy with someone and they're happy with you? Any healthy positive loving connection between two people regardless of their gender or label is what is important above anything else. It is the love that God and the angels adore seeing on a planet that is generally devoid of love.

A soul may choose to incarnate as gay or homosexual at any particular time in history. Some say it's not a choice, but the soul did choose to incarnate as homosexual in their soul's contract for various purposes knowing of the challenges that will arise in that role with current society, which still views gays through a primitive archaic lens. The soul may also have chosen to incarnate as straight or bisexual, but at around a certain age in their human life they'll change their sexual orientation. The media has shown the polar opposites of humankind not evolved enough to accept that all people are equal and deserve love. The ego would rather see homosexuals harmed or executed, which is not someone evolved or of God. Those that believe the twin flame connection is between a man and a woman in a romantic love relationship have no understanding of what a twin flame soul connection is, nor do they have any authentic connection with God, because when you do have that strong Divine connection, then the truth is in plain sight. It's all about soul love regardless of your outdated human belief value systems.

More people than not used to have hatred towards anyone who had a same sex attraction. Once they realized that every other person they loved around them fit that description, they gradually changed their tune realizing they made a mistake about their hatred, and just didn't know any better. Now it's becoming increasingly common, loved, and accepted, but there are still those living in the stone ages with a limited view that have yet to gain love for those not like them. They believe that the planet is normalizing same sex gay love, as if love between two people isn't normal. Sounds ironic considering that the reason all are here is to learn to love. You would think those that hold the biblical book so close to their chest could've gained that small amount of wisdom from it. Using Biblical text that was added in at a later date by superstitious fearful men isn't a good excuse, since God created all breathing life this way for a reason. God doesn't have hang ups about two souls in love with each other regardless of their gender. Love is what He desires to see, so in that instant when two souls are in love, He is pleased. In fact, God has disdain for those that express hatred over two souls in a committed love relationship. Jesus Christ was the same way. His complaint was over adultery and not about committed love between two souls. There are also non-believers that have hatred for gays, but the media gives the religious the hate card. Prejudices exist within all groups that exist on the planet.

When you're not evolving, then the potential possibility of connecting with your twin flame is non-existent. It is the evolving souls that unite and merge with a twin flame partner for the purposes and goals of moving up to the next soul plateau beyond the physical realm.

One of the goals of all souls is to learn to accept all people in love. It is to learn to love and to give love. You learn that when you are thrown together with people who are not like you. You're not going to necessarily learn much by hanging around people that are your tribe and clan. People mark themselves off and stick to their own kind thus staying exactly where they are in their soul's growth process. It's human nature to behave in this primal instinctive way. It goes back to grade school when those who are like each other hang around one another in their little cliques and packs the way animals do.

When your twin flame is on the Other Side in the spirit world, they may work as one of your guides to bring soul mate connections into your life. They don't want you spending your days longing for love and companionship, so they assist in the process of bringing you potential lovers, friendships, colleagues, or acquaintances for soul mate connections.

Not everyone will experience a romantic love partnership, let alone one that lasts until the end of their days. This leads to the myth that there is someone out there for everyone, which is a misguided romantic notion that doesn't ring true for every single person on the planet. It's also a fictitious impractical assumption to feed the masses with. There are millions of people that will never obtain a love partner, or they may not be looking for one.

The twin flame is the ultimate deep love that transcends all. One of the common reasons all souls incarnate into an Earthly life is for the purpose of teaching and learning. The twin flames are together on the Other Side for all eternity, so there is little reason for both of them to incarnate into an Earthly life as well too, unless there is a larger reason, purpose, goal, and mission to do so. This would be one that requires the both of your Divine powers. The purpose of re-uniting on Earth isn't to be in a love relationship. There has to be something else that both are doing that points to their soul evolvement process.

The twin flame connections are not always love related, which on the one hand may be a blessing for some people. This is because if the two incarnate relatively at the same time during one lifetime and fall in love, then it will be more intense than if your twin flame was a best buddy or a business partner you've joined forces with for life.

Those around that witness a twin flame connection when they are together will point out the natural ease, they notice both have as if they are made for each other. They will point out that they have the same essence, movements, and moods to one degree or another. And others may point out that they seem like they even look the same, even if they are physically different in appearance. There is something about the cosmic kismet like feeling that shows them to be two peas in a pod. Once together on Earth they never leave one another's side even if they break apart. The break might seem permanent, but more often than not it ends up being temporary. They wind back around to each other at a later date as if the break never happened. This is due to the strong running soul pull between the both of them that never seems to leave even while physically apart.

The twin flame connection intensity is not necessarily a fun feeling to be in. It's uncomfortable and confusing for both people at times that sometimes it feels easier to just leave or keep their distance, so they don't drown in its intensity. That is until both are mature enough to ease into this intensity so that it works for all parties involved.

There are rare cases where the twin flames never unite back into a romantic relationship due to the self-sabotage or disruption that one of the partners executes, but they will never truly disappear. Instead they will forever pop up from time to time with a text, email, or phone call throughout the duration of both of your lives. You'll both wonder why it never transformed into something more again if it doesn't seem to. The exceptions are if the twin flames are not lovers, but friends or relatives, or if the age gap is so wide where one is twenty and the other is seventy years old. The deep connection love is always present even if it's not romantic due to a variety of human physical factors. It is rare for a twin flame soul connection to break apart in any other duo except love. Love relationships are always more challenging than any other connection in general, so it's no surprise that this is doubly so in a twin flame connection.

There isn't necessarily an order of how any of these types of relationships come about. Those who are in one dysfunctional relationship after another are typically encountering karmic connections. Some people will have several long-term love relationships that were soul mate connections, but ones that didn't go the distance. If a twin flame connection is to come about, then it will at some point later into adulthood after other relationships have been experienced first.

There are a great many people who meet someone in High School and get married and remain with that person for the duration of both their lives with little to no karmic issues. These are the general soul mate relationships. There are people that never have the luxury of being in any kind of long-term love relationship, some by choice and others because it just never happens for them.

This higher mission is not about coming together in humankind's holy matrimony, even if the twin flames are romantic in nature. There must be a higher mission beyond coming together that transcends a human relationship. This longing you have for your twin flame is a longing for love to fill the aloneness you might sometimes feel. This can be remedied with a stronger connection with God, Divine and Spirit. It can be relieved through the various potential companions God places in your path.

More often than not, one's twin flame is on the Other Side working with you to bring in soul mate relationships. They are in charge of the love relationships you have throughout your life because they know it contributes to your soul's growth. They will sometimes also work with your own guides on helping you fulfill your purpose.

Like God and your Spirit team, you can call on your twin flame if they are on the Other Side for assistance in the areas of love, but also when it comes to your mission. They are more than happy to come in and help because they are a part of you, and you are a part of them. They know when they are helping you that they are simultaneously helping their own evolvement process.

If they are on Earth during your lifetime, then you'll find that there is an eerie kind of mirror action going on with your twin flame. It is like a push and pull running and chasing situation happening. This doesn't go on indefinitely. It can go on as long as it needs to before you two come together. This means it might take one month or it might take many years. There is no set timeline especially with twin flames. Because the connection is felt deeply on an intense level it can go on for a bit before the union has lift off. This is regardless if it's a friendship or potential love relationship. The deep intensity is across the board regardless of the physical nature of the union.

If you travel to centuries past and you got married to someone, but then met your twin flame it would've caused confusion and torment. This is especially due to the time period frowning on divorce. If you got married to someone and met your twin flame back in history, then you ended up having to either let them go or have a discreet affair that ended up causing all sorts of Earthly controversy. It was frowned upon if a man had a deep love for another man and a woman had a deep love for another woman. This is still frowned upon by half the world, but the other half of the world has been awakened enough to fully understand that it is God's will that souls learn about love in ways beyond their primal archaic mind can fathom.

There is a serenity feeling for both partners in a twin flame connection, but that's not always experienced right away. When they first run into each other, they have an immediate curiosity with one another needing to know who that person is. Their mutual eye contact says it all. This part is like the movies in the beginning where they see each other from across the room. They might be talking to someone else, but find themselves constantly looking over with a smile or dancing eyes, and you're doing the same thing. It isn't so much the physical attraction, but a cosmic soul attraction. Both partners feel this exceptionally strong pull they've never felt before in that way with anyone to that degree. It's unexplainable for the both of them and they mutually want to get closer. This is regardless if the person becomes a love relationship, friendship, or any other dynamic. The intensity for both is the same.

The twin flame connections have a push and pull situation going on at first, but this isn't to be confused with co-dependency. Co-dependency exists primarily in karmic relationships. With twin flames it is that the feelings for one another are too intense for the both of them. Neither partner is used to feeling a love that deeply with someone else before. This pushes the ego reaction to shun it, hesitate, or move super slow in coming together. The feelings are too overwhelming in ways that neither felt before. This brings on a certain excitement enveloped with fear as well too.

When twin flames come across one another for the first time they both immediately notice that there is something different about the other one that feels awfully familiar on a soul level. Even if it's not an immediate romantic love feeling, there is something emotionally strong and unexplainable, because as previously stated twin flames are not always love relationships, even though there is a great deal of love and respect moving between them. It's beyond the physical and the first thing they both notice is the telepathic emotional sense picked up on, rather than the guy or girl is hot, since the latter is typically a lust filled physical carnal attraction and connection. The attraction between twin flames is beyond a physical attraction, even if that part of the equation is present. It is primarily a soul attraction above anything else.

CHAPTER SEVEN

*Benefits and Challenges
of Technology Dating*

There can be nothing greater than in-person soul connections uniting in the physical world. This is where you can go to the movies with someone, go to dinner together, talk face-to-face with them, or kiss and hug a mate. In-person connections build a deeper soul history filled with profound memorable nostalgic experiences. When you spend the day at an amusement park or a nature retreat with a lover or a friend, then more often than not you find you've grown closer and more connected with each other by the end of the trip. This is because you were building a deeper in-person connection and having a three-dimensional experience.

Deeper chemistry is created when you're hanging out with someone physically in a space together. This has grown more challenging to do with the rise of technology. The benefits to technology are how easy it can be to connect with most anyone. The negatives are that people often complain that it either doesn't move into an in-person connection or doesn't measure up to what they thought it would be in-person. Technology gives one an illusion of who people think you are only to be stunned at how dramatically different the person ends up being in-person.

I started out in the film industry working, conversing, and being friends with hundreds of well-known talents. This was throughout the 1990's and into the 2000's before social media became a thing. Whenever I would meet one of them for the first time, they were always much more dramatically different in appearance and personality in-person than the images of them on screen, in the media, in the news or in magazines. It was like sitting with anybody else, except they looked familiar, but on a smaller level. By the time the Internet took off with social media and dating apps, I was already versed in this interesting phenomenon of how dramatically different someone is in-person. But now the rest of the world was becoming privy to this notion through the use of the Internet, social media, and dating apps. You are building someone up online who you think is one way only to find that they are much different in-person. The real clue as to if it is a connection that will go the distance is when you spend numerous times in-person.

Sending a text, chat words, or email comes off distant and transactional. It dehumanizes others where you end up treating them as if they're a robot without feelings or emotions. This is why it's so easy for others to ghost, block, or ignore you online or on an app. You're no longer a living breathing soul in that person's eyes. You're just a picture with a name on it is all. They're not necessarily doing this with malice. They don't realize the deeper consequence to their behavior that's being tallied up in your soul contract as to how you may or may not be dismissing others. This has added to an entirely new set of lessons for soul growth being applied to humankind.

Ghosting is when you're dating someone, and then you end the connection by disappearing without a trace. No warning, no words, and nowhere to be found. This isn't to be confused with someone you have no interest in engaging with and nor is it saying to force an engagement when you're not feeling it. This is more of a generalization as to how the behavior is overall. It's easy to dismiss, drop, and eradicate someone via technological means. I had an ex break up with me twice via impersonal means. The first time was through an email message on the social media site My Space when that site was the #1 social media site over all others. The second time this ex broke up with me was years later via a handwritten note left on my door. As you may or may not have likely guessed, this particular ex was obviously around for many years leaving me in this same way, but never truly leaving.

There are a great number of people that are left in similar ways never to hear from the person again. It's easier for someone to leave people today through the impersonal technological ways. You lose the risk of in-person confrontation or having to deal with how the other person might react knowing that it might not be good. If it's someone that once meant the world to you one might think the diplomatic choice would be to at least talk to them in-person. That's how it used to be done before the days of technology. Some call it the cowardly way out or being disrespectful, but some do it to avoid confrontation. This doesn't make it okay, but it is the world we live now.

With technology you're treated like a no name suspect even if they know you. You're just a digital name on the screen at that point. As a result, the emotional factor underneath an email or a text on a screen can be misinterpreted. This is also why it's never wise to have serious discussions via text or email. It is also why many people have complained about being discarded by potential friends or lovers they've connected with online by being ghosted. If they're lucky, then they might receive an email, letter, or text. Sometimes there is no explanation, but the person gradually distances themselves and shows less interest in the person. When this happens, then some will take it harder than others to have their ego bruised in what they deem to be a hurtful way.

There are common behaviors that have become more acceptable etiquette even if it bothers some people. For example, if it's someone you were chatting with online or on a dating app for a few weeks and they suddenly drop the ball and move on, then you move on. Developing intense love feelings over someone you've never met and have only been chatting with a short amount of time can lead to a dangerous outcome. The person that drops the ball in the chatting is also chatting with many others at the same time. They don't owe you anything if you haven't met in person and have gone on at least a number of dates. It's become acceptable behavior in the dating app sphere to drop the ball in communication for good if you don't actually know each other.

This also goes for business relationships. Because so much business is done online you may find that your sole connection with colleagues or clients is through email, phone, or a chat program. This diminishes the quality of the connection into something colder and distant. Imagine the entire planet communicating this way and you can see how that has hardened and chilled the world to love. Love has a challenging time penetrating the technological sphere.

Technological connections have a remote distance to them because you are controlling what you're putting out there into the world. You decide what to type to another person in a text, an email, in a comment box, or on a social media post. This gives the illusion of having a deeper connection that may be one-sided. You're not absorbing the three-dimensional aspects that make up a person when you're in the same room with them.

Another reason it is growing increasingly rare is due to the domination of the darkness of ego. Many lack follow through with the endless choices at their fingertips. It is easy to discard others when you have a technological device. There have been numerous studies indicating that people don't know what to do when they have too many choices. Having a few choices is one thing, but you're twenty-seven and you have 1,600 matches on your Tinder dating app, but no love relationship and no prospects.

Some think if they swipe yes/right on as many people they initially find attractive that one of those thousands of matches is bound to be a match, yet this isn't necessarily the case. I've dove into the dating school of hard knocks to try it both ways. The first was to collect as many matches as possible to see if that works. Thousands of matches later, I was overwhelmed at the number of messages pouring in. I couldn't keep up and grew stressed out over it because I'm someone that likes to get back to people in general. When you have dozens of people messaging you at the same time each day, then it can quickly become overwhelming. One of the other issues I was faced with was the shotgun way that matches were attempting to go about it. They would message me with the initial *how-are-you's*, and then I'd message back with the same. They'd come back with, "Would you be interested in meeting up?"

I'd yank my head back…umm, no. I just said six words to you. From those six words you already want to meet up? This tells me you're basing your interest on me due to your physical lust filled attraction. That does not automatically equate to in-person chemistry in other areas. Communication style, values, and interests are what bond people together. If you're incapable of communicating with the person you're communicating with on a dating site or app, then how are you going to transfer that to in-person success?

The shotgun method potentials were physically attracted to me, so in their eyes they wanted to nail me so to speak. This isn't just one person immediately asking to meet up in this way. There were dozens coming in at the same time on a regular basis. I thought if I dropped everything to meet up with every single person that was saying hello to me and asking to immediately meet up, then I'd never get anything done. For the purpose of research, I did try out the method of agreeing to meet those shotgun people to see if maybe it could work. Unfortunately, I found that meeting that way ended up being a waste of time. When you don't take the time to get to know someone first with some communication banter, then you are unable to detect if it's someone you'd have a good camaraderie with.

When you are engaging in banter with someone on an app or online before meeting it's not always to waste time without ever meeting. It's to see if you have anything in common and a flowing rapport before meeting in-person. If you're both incapable of online app banter, then the likelihood of carrying that into an in-person meeting will be high. It will be unlikely that either of you will have much to say and there's nothing worse than sitting there struggling to say something that would be of interest to either of you. Meeting the shotgun way typically ends up being disastrous. Whereas the ones that engaged in app banter because they genuinely enjoyed communicating to you and getting to know you ended up translating successfully in-person.

The other extreme are those that chat for months and months, but have shown no interest in meeting. When you've brought up getting together at some point, then that was shut down, brushed aside, or excuses were made. This is a sign they are currently just interested in online communication banter. Some do this out of boredom, others delay meeting due to a shyness and uncertainty about the connection, while others do it because they're hiding something. If they do show interest and admit to wanting to get together at some point, then they've shown interest in taking it to another level....one day. There are also the busy professionals. If you want someone that is independent and has their own life, then you expect that the person will be busy often, which tends to be the case with professional achievers. It's either that or go after someone who has nothing going on in their life. Every time you message them, they quickly message back because they are never doing anything, which is the other extreme.

If you're in a rush to seal the deal with anybody, then continue chatting and dating around keeping your options open. You should be doing that anyway until you've landed on someone that piques your interest as much as you do with them.

I've also tested out the dating apps where I would only match with a select small group of people. This is by keeping the match list under twenty instead of into the thousands. I would then focus on developing a connection with each of them to see how conversational style is on the dating app. If they are giving one to three-word phrases, then they're showing they don't have enough energy to muster to communicate with someone properly. This will carry over to the in-person meeting, which would be a waste of time. The same goes for those that drop the ball in the online app banter which shows they've grown bored, distracted, or moved onto someone else on the app as does tend to be the case, so don't take that personally.

I would also give people time to respond before unmatching them. The date of the last communication is on there so I would look to see if it's been over a month since our last communication before unmatching them. Some people unmatch way too soon if they don't get a response within a day or two, which is unreasonable and unrealistic in today's world. I'm being super generous by giving them a month. People get busy, lives become a distraction, others get consumed over matters not realizing time has passed. Someone is not going to make a stranger a priority. I've also had people come back to me weeks later after they were going through something, then we just pick up where we left off. Many of those people ended up becoming friends or great dates, because they also weren't under the pressure of giving someone twenty-four hours exactly to get back to them, otherwise you've blown it. I've also met those that are that strict unable to accept that it may take some people time to get back to them. Those same people have also been single and living on these apps indefinitely. It hasn't sunk in that this rapid-fire way of demanding one keep messaging you is not working. That's not an inviting warm person that many would feel comfortable knowing or getting to know. I've had more success with having a smaller match list over having a larger match list. You put in more effort with people when you have a few to focus on rather than collecting matches for reasons that have no benefit at all.

The current dating app at this time that may have the edge is Bumble. Bumble keeps your match list clean to an extent. It works in the same way that Tinder and OK Cupid does. This is where you both have to swipe right on each other's profiles before you end up in one another's match list. Only when you're in each other's match list can you then message the person. I like this feature because you're not having random people hitting you up out of nowhere. If someone messages you, then you know you already matched with this person, which shows an element of interest present due to being matched.

Bumble takes it a step further where it gives you a short amount of time to send a message to your new match. If neither of you send a message within about 24 hours, then you will both expire from the match list and eventually drop off the grid. This works since many have found the method of Tinder to not be as effective. Tinder keeps your matches in your list until the end of time or you delete them or your profile. It's pointless having a large match list if no one is messaging one another. There is no edge or advantage to that.

The negative about Bumble's method is the amount of time allotted to message a new match is super brief. It's not always enough time especially for a busy professional. The quality matches for a long-term relationship tend to be people that are independent and professionally driven. Someone that doesn't have those qualities leans towards the co-dependent. When someone has too much time on their hands, they will demand more of your time, or they will seek it out by continuing to chat with others who can satisfy their boredom and feed them the attention they crave.

Bumble also works on algorithms where it shows you the matches they think are quality matches first. How do they determine what a quality match is? They base it on the profiles that get swiped right more than others. Of course, we know that the profiles that tend to get swiped right the most are the ones where the person appears physically attractive in some way to the user. This does not necessarily equate to long-term material and compatibility. It also further emphasizes the truth that people look at physical appearances first before even bothering to pay attention to that person.

These apps and this concept may be outdated if you're reading this at a later time in history, but there may be something comparable you can apply it to. If anything, you can know what was popular when I was around.

Trading long chats, texts, and emails with a potential friend or lover can help both parties get to know one another before meeting and connecting in person. The danger is if one places more emphasis and feeling on the fact that this person is sharing so much with them that they have a shot at developing something more serious. That is until you find out the person you've been sharing emails with had no deep interest in you and was merely an exceptional conversationalist via email. The other danger is you fill in the blanks of what you believe this person's motive is or isn't only to discover they're married or have no deep emotion for you. The positives to technological conversing with people you know is keeping in touch, especially if you don't physically live near one another.

In-person connections are rare since most people today remain in contact through the technological ways available. This has made others lazy in connecting in-person. There are other reasons that prevent in-person connections from happening that are valid such as you work a hard job professionally that demands a great deal of time from you. It's easy to connect with people via technology, text, email, or social media today, but more challenging to connect in-person. Why would someone connect in-person when they have so much to do and it's far easier to hop on a quick phone call with them?

Some have become pickier about what they desire in a love partner. There is nothing wrong with having high standards to an extent, but you also don't want to have them so high that you rule out potentials sent your way. I've come across men and women who have the long lists of what they do or do not want on their dating profiles. These are those super restricting stats of what they want in a potential person for a relationship. I've read profiles that might say, "No one under thirty." Or, "Your body and weight should be proportioned." Or, "I'll know what I like when I see it."

People really do put that and much more in their profiles, which in one sense is wise because then you know what you're getting if you choose to engage with someone like that. They will inevitably be negatively criticizing and critiquing how you look and what you say or do. I've also found those with the strict lists of what they want also end up unable to find anyone that fits the bill. They also live on the dating apps and sites indefinitely.

If something like someone's physical fit appearance is important to you, then the appropriate phrase should be something like: "I'm a physically active person and enjoy sports related activities. I'm looking for a partner in crime with similar interests in that arena to share that with."

At the same time, I've had people inform me that they'll have someone they matched with tell them they are interested in something like hiking in the way they are. But they discover this isn't true when they end up going on a legitimate hike only to find the person cannot hack it so to speak. This is because the other person that said they loved hiking was confused by what a genuine hike is. They assumed it was the kind of hike that posers see as a hike where you stroll in nature with a friend to chat. Serious hikers are hiking in rougher inclines in a nature setting that can last several hours and sometimes a good chunk of the day.

If deep down you know that you cannot handle anyone not fitting the bill of your picture-perfect ideal messaging you, then make that list for yourself, then file it away. Jot that down in an email or notepad for your eyes only. Don't put it in your profile, but make the list of the traits of the kind of person you'd like to be with in a relationship. Write that letter to God and your Spirit team, then email that to yourself and let it go. Allow what the Universe is intended to bring you to come to fruition.

You can have the secret mental list of what you desire, but when you let it go, you also let go of those restrictions. You keep an open mind in accepting the partner that is intended to match up with you, even if they don't match your statistical requirements. I've made those lists in the past and ended up with people that didn't necessarily fit the description, but we met and fell in love. When it comes to love in the end, those lists are discarded anyway. Ultimately, the one for you is not what you will be expecting. Many have admitted that their current life love partner was not someone they were typically attracted to or would have gone after, but now that they're with them they wouldn't have it any other way.

There are the more reasonable requests such as wanting to date a non-smoker, or if you're in Alcoholics Anonymous, then naturally you may not want to be in a potential relationship with someone that is a heavy drinker. There are the deal breakers that you know you cannot accept at all. Then there are the rules that you're relaxed about. These are rules that you know you could fold on and accept about someone in a relationship. If you won't fold on any of your rules, then you could end up single until the end of your life. You need some measure of compromise knowing that there is no perfect person that is interested in every single thing you are. Compromising is one of the bigger traits that are going to be required of anyone in any kind of connection.

Placing any kind of demand on others to give you the attention and love you crave will only end in disappointment. Souls are flawed and imperfect as people. They will disappoint especially when you are expecting them to be a certain way. When you want others to adapt to you, then you can be sure they will steer clear of you in the end. When you try to push someone to be your friend, then the more you push them away. No one will be your friend because you're demanding them to be your friend. Don't chase after people to give you what you crave. This is the same way you can't force someone to be in a relationship with you. When you push your mate for a stronger commitment with a list of demands when they're not in that space, then this turns them off causing them to eventually distance themselves from you. No one likes the idea of being caged or boxed in to do something out of force. The same goes for friendships or acquaintances. The successful connections that take place happen organically and naturally without force.

Nothing in the physical material world will fill up any emptiness in you. Certain aspects might temporarily fulfill someone for a brief spell, but it will not last longer than a day. The true measure of success is where your soul's growth is in moving through its personal transformation and evolution. Avoid getting caught up in the fantasy that is revealed to you through technology. Instead focus on your soul's personal journey by finding ways to awaken and open up your consciousness to the love that exists within the Light.

One of the positives of technology is that it has brought transparency to light in a manner that has never before been seen in history. In Heaven, no one can get away with a lie the way they can on Earth, but this is gradually shifting as everything is being pushed into the spotlight. The difference between Heaven and Earth in that respect is that beings in Heaven aren't dishonest in character. All spirit beings in Heaven are bathed in compassion, strength, and love full time. Whereas on Earth, a great many human beings are operating from the darker side of their nature.

The smaller percentage of the population that expresses compassion and understanding most of the time tends to be Earth Angels. They see the good and the best in others, but have great distaste or offense towards anyone that displays toxicity. Some of those personalities are Wise Ones that might be a younger appearing person who has exceptional poise that they come off as if they're hundreds of years old. This is because their soul is much older than their human years. They have chosen to incarnate on Earth for various purposes that include bringing much needed love to the planet.

There are good and bad elements to anything that was created. If two mature thinking evolved beings can find each other on an app and forge a lifelong committed relationship or best friendship, then this is the positive side to connecting on a technical app. When you find that great big rare love, then treat it like gold because it is a rarity.

The two evolved souls that reside in the space of love will find one another regardless of the obstacles put in their path of the current modern-day human climate, which has been as tumultuous as it was centuries ago.

You have free will choice, which can negate and alter what is intended to take place. Your soul contract may reveal a particular love soul mate that will show up at a particular time in your life. Due to free will choice on your part and/or this other person's part, it can alter and change both your paths pushing the connection further out or from happening at all.

Sometimes the future soul mate love partner will show up while you're still in a love connection that was supposed to end. You feel a strong gravitational pull towards that new person even though you might not romantically act on anything with them. Both teams of guides from your side and this other person's side are aware that the old connection is going to end, so they jump the gun and orchestrate the bumping into part of this new person knowing nothing might take off for awhile.

For some people connections take time before having full lift off that it's safe enough to bring the newer soul mate in and let it take its time evolving into more down the line. Meanwhile, the former love connection has fulfilled its contract agreement and begins to disband. It isn't long before the new love interest begins to have lift off.

When two souls are ready and evolved enough, then the lifelong love partnership will happen when either expects it. You will both be placed on the same path where it is orchestrated perfectly to the point where you're both standing face to face. There is no way either of you cannot see it.

You might be afraid to approach your crush for fear of being rejected, but if it's someone you can't get your mind off of, then take the risk to at least say hello to this person. Gauge their interest level after saying hello and notice if they seem standoffish because they're not interested or unfriendly due to shyness. Some people have given up a potential love interest that is intended for them out of fear, or they'll avoid approaching a potential partner out of fear. Fear is one of the greatest causes of human sabotage holding people back.

CHAPTER EIGHT

*Single and Longing
for a Relationship*

It's the human condition to feel bouts of loneliness or crave a passionate merging with a love partner. Being single for a prolonged period of time sucks for some people, while others have an easier time making the best of it and will live their daily life without that craving for a love relationship. The rest struggle to survive being alone.

If you can't change your relationship status tomorrow, then get with the program of the current dating market and protect yourself with the way it is now. Have a greater understanding of how the modern-day world of dating and relationships are at this point in Earth's history. Do your best to make the most of the state you're currently in. This is about making sounder decisions and learning to treat others with respect. This carries far into one's life where you can apply common sense etiquette to most anything.

You might be someone that loves being single and has no problem with it or you might desire a love partner. The longer it takes to obtain one, the more it feels as if you're trying to survive being single when you anxiously want to be in a relationship. You desperately wish you had a lover who loved you back with equal fervor, yet any and all potential prospects constantly evade you.

One of the ways of surviving modern day dating and relationships in a loveless world is by armoring yourself with knowledge. This includes knowledge over the way things currently are. You can read all of the love and relationship self-help books available on the market and still feel nowhere closer to obtaining a love relationship than you are now. You've went to psychic readers, you've cast spells, you put yourself out there, did the vision boards, the crystal meditations, and other love rituals presented to you, but you still find you're desperately wishing the person of your dreams was here already. You begin to grow more cynical as you grow older feeling as if it will never happen and that you just have to accept the fact that perhaps it's not in the cards.

You've grown permanently negative about not being able to attract in a love partner, so you debunk the tips that all of the love related self-help books have offered you. You're angry, frustrated, and over it. It's understandable that you've grown weary from battle in the love department, but this is not going to attract a stranger to you who could be the potential mate. You'll also stop bothering to put in an effort, as you've grown exhausted over the process. I don't blame you as I've been there too. I've had periods throughout my life where I've had to survive being single. When each of my past long-term love relationships ended, I would believe that was it. There would be no one else after that. As time progressed on and I seemed to be in a place of contentment, then a new soul mate would enter the picture. Rinse and repeat. It was anything but over for me.

Love is where all human souls are intended and expected to be, but most have strayed as far away from that space as possible. They've fallen victim to the mundane practical stresses of life, struggling to make a living, pay bills, buying groceries, and whatever it takes to survive in day-to-day functioning. Secretly somewhere deep down in that person's soul they long for some measure of a personal life that brings in a welcome relief and release in the form of a love partner. By the time you're done working you're too exhausted to sit face to face with another stranger, so you take the slim pickings that come to you seriously. You won't go out with just anyone who hits you up simply because they're attractive.

During my dating research moments, I've found that the some of the potentials that hit me up seemed to have too much time on their hands. They limit their messages to you in a series of one to three-word sound bite phrases while expecting to meet in ten minutes. This shotgun method of connecting with others doesn't work and nor does it bring you quality connections. For one, these are prospects that don't have anything going for them, which is why they have an abnormal amount of free time on their hands. Usually when someone wants to meet that quickly is because they only have one thing in mind and that is to ultimately get it on. This is one of the pitfalls to the dating app method of connecting. There is no way to filter out prospects by professionals or those with likeminded interests. You basically get everyone and their family hitting you up.

The love market has changed drastically as it seems to every ten years. The 1990's were the final decade where love and relationships would never be the same again. The technological age took off bringing the masses gained access to computers and cell phones, which later brought about dating websites, social media, and phone apps. There are definite pros to this as well as the cons to consider as there are to most anything. Having all of these fantastic choices around you sounds awesome initially, but humankind has a built-in ego, which causes one to wrestle with and vacillate between making decisions that work and ones that backfire. What came out of the technological age post 2000's is that it became easier to find sex than to find love. Love grew to be lacking more than it ever has in Earth's history.

There are more singles around the world than those in a relationship. Post 2000's was when the shift began to happen. The media, popular culture, and the high accessibility to technology heavily promoted sex instead of love at a rapid rate. The more a pop artist bumped and grinded on stage or in a video wearing little clothing, then the more popular they became. Popular culture was feeding and selling sex to the point where it was suddenly boring and unexciting.

After talking to and interviewing countless people, I discovered they all desired a long-term love relationship, but it was constantly evading them. It was difficult to understand, as they were independent, good looking, had a great personality, had their own money, we're caring, and compassionate. What was missing?

The main reason all exist is to LOVE. What else did you think you were here for? Is it to work a job? A job that will one day vanish once your run is complete? Jobs are a necessary means of physical survival, but it's not why you're here unless the job is connected to your life purpose. One doesn't need to be married to their job to the point where they have no personal life. Hopefully, you find meaningful work that is your passion, but that's not the sole reason you are here. In the end, it's all about love, yet that seems to be a major struggle to achieve for most. Wallowing in perpetual negativity, sadness, hate, bitterness, and deceit seems to be a much better space to live in. This must be the case since the energy saturating the primary masses around the world swim in the epicenter of its toxicity. Notice the continuing noise of the media and social media with all those negative words being darted at one another. This gives you a great clue as to where humanity is at in the love department.

While the challenges to finding love have increased, it's not impossible to find that one person for life who desires what you want with you. Attracting in a suitable romantic partner entails loving yourself like nobody's business and believing in all that you are. This is all part of the self-love we discussed earlier in the book. Confidence is one of the key traits that attracts in others to your light and overall essence and energy. This doesn't mean you won't be attracting all sorts of prospects from all avenues, even from those who are not looking for something serious. It includes those unwanted proposals that see you primarily as a piece of meat to help them get off. You have to weed out a great deal of people while on the hunt for love. The potential partner is the needle in the haystack and the diamond in the rough that stands out. The majority of prospects seem to only be interested in sex rather than forming a soul mate love connection with someone. You have to have faith and patience that this soul mate love is out there.

Giving up on love is understandable and certainly not uncommon. Many have protested they've hit a point where they announce that love might not be in the cards for them. They've reached a place where they accept that. It's been years and all they have witnessed is one loveless situation after another. I came across someone who had gone ten years without ever having dated, and then out of nowhere met someone they fell in love with and ended up getting married, so love can happen when you least expect it.

Everyone is having a difficult time where love relationships are concerned because you've got part of the world desiring a love relationship, are already in a relationship, or want to be free. The best freedom in the world is when you're in the right love connection with someone who understands you and supports you, while you give that to them in return. Live life for you with just enough room for another loving soul to merge in with you.

You have more people than ever operating from the selfish ego. There is no room for another person when you're in that space. You're expecting the most perfect love partner to enter the picture that bows down and caters to all of your needs. I often hear others tell me what they will only accept in a partnership. It's this long list of outlandish requests, which limits the possibility of inviting in the right person. It should be about what you have to offer someone else and not what they can give you.

Let's say that you are spending your days longing for a romantic partner. If your Spirit Guide and Guardian Angel are working with you on other day-to-day situations, then you may have another guide or angel who joins you in your life assisting you on your search for the kind of soul mate that would be beneficial for you. This Spirit will work with your soul mates Spirit team in order to bring you two together.

You could be a busy professional and not active in the dating world aside from joining dating sites and dating apps to get to know potential suitors. Or perhaps you have done that, and it resulted in disappointment. This assigned "love guide" works with this other potential's guides to help you two to connect. You find you suddenly start crossing paths with the same person repeatedly at the store, at the gym, in an elevator, or even in a parking garage. There is a reason behind running into this same person consistently out of the blue. You are attracted to them, and you notice they seem to be taking notice of you in a positive warm way, yet you both brush it off or do not act on it. This is partly due to your ego, fear, and partly how technology has trained others to communicate via technical devices, but rendered them incapable when face-to-face. Both of your Spirit team's will continue to work on getting you both together. Yet it is up to the both of you to do the rest of the work. This work includes something that might be difficult for some such as saying hello.

If you find that every time you run into this person the butterflies rise, you grow nervous, or feel inadequate, then mentally in prayer ask God and your Spirit team to help give you confidence and courage to communicate. What's the worst that is going to happen if you make a mistake by saying hello? The other person says nothing or reacts in a way that wasn't what you were expecting. At least you did it rather than spending your days, weeks, and months wondering what if.

It is difficult for two people coming together in this day and age where primary means of communicating to each other is through technological devices. Now you're standing in front of someone and you're suddenly a mute. This other person is likely just as nervous as you. They might be kicking themselves for not responding adequately. If you continue to run into this person, then you'll both grow more comfortable with the other one being around. It will get easier to begin conversation even if it's always a *hi, hello, how are you.*

There are no missed opportunities. If the soul mate you are intended to connect with is meant to happen, then it will. If it doesn't, then another soul mate will be brought to you to match where you are at on your soul's evolution.

Desiring a love partner should not be misconstrued to be co-dependent. The human soul desires the company of other human souls, even if it's just one person in a companionship setting. This is why many support groups consider solitary confinement to be inhumane. If you were deserted on an island, then no matter how much you love yourself you would start to go crazy after a while. This is despite those who are independent and prefer to be alone. I've come across quite a number of people that prefer a solitary life, but even they have those moments where they are surfacing and desiring some attention from another on occasion. To equate a basic human need with desperation is absurd.

Some people have stronger emotional endurance when it comes to being alone. There are also many people who do not cope well with loneliness. Some of them resort to suicide, while others resort to drugs, alcohol, or sexual promiscuity.

Studies have also indicated that infants who do not receive touch in orphanages have a higher mortality rate. The same goes for senior citizens in care homes. This evidence suggests that human souls need both friendships and camaraderie, not to mention love and intimacy companionship.

You find that you've been doing the work by focusing on hobbies you enjoy and self-improvement activities, but this still leaves you wondering if a love partnership will ever happen. Love circumstances happen when you least expect it. When you fixate harshly on it coming about, then it delays and frustrates the love from entering the picture. Attempting to rigorously find a love partner generally results in disappointment. I've had many serious long-term relationships and every single one of them came about naturally and without effort. They came about when I wasn't expecting it or looking for it. Each partner showed up out of nowhere and then the union was driven in full speed motion. It was almost as if they fell on my doorstep when I wasn't looking for a relationship. As cliché as it might sound, they were chance encounters where we turned the corner and bumped into one another physically, "Oh! Sorry. Are you alright?"

Dialogue happened and the communication sifted effortlessly and excitedly back and forth. Boom! The connection was made, and phone numbers were exchanged.

I wasn't actively looking for a love relationship or waiting for one when all of my past partners showed up in the form of a dating or a love relationship. We bumped into one another randomly or they discovered me through other avenues. Our communication began to build into something more over the course of many months.

I haven't run into any cases where someone was deliberately and desperately searching for a love relationship and then it came to them. At the same time putting in an effort is better than sitting on your couch waiting for your next soul mate to ring your doorbell. Love connections happen when you least expect them to. When you expect a love relationship to happen, then that prevents, delays, and blocks it from happening. It also creates frustration energy, which pushes it further away from you. Love can never be forced, but at the same time you put in a bit of effort while keeping your heart and mind open to all possibilities and prospects.

Incidentally, I've reviewed cases where those that were happy, single, and not interested in a love relationship were the ones that effortlessly ended up in a love relationship. When you let go of the need to be in a relationship, then the closer you are to being in one.

Some cultures still prefer on deciding within the family unit who they think you should marry, but this is imposing your free will on another. Love cannot be rushed or forced, and nor can it have burdens placed on its back such as having someone else decide for you. Get to know someone gradually first before jumping into marriage or a committed relationship with someone you don't know.

There are those rare cases where someone has deliberately raced out and nabbed the person they want to marry and it's worked out, but generally you cannot push or force someone to be with you. It will only be met with resistance and disenchantment. During the rare times this has worked is because both people were physically attracted to one another, but a connection based on lust does not always go the distance. A physical attraction is connected to a lust attraction, because you don't know this person well enough to be in love with them. The person's physical exterior beauty and looks blinds one to the truth about them. Having some measure of physical attraction at first is a good start, but being attracted to one's exterior does not guarantee personality chemistry. Eventually the lust filled physical attraction begins to wane if there aren't common interests, communication styles, and similarities between one another. The connections that began as a one-night stand or a physical attraction that have stood the test of time were because both partners had similar interests, values, and communication styles outside of that.

Imagine that ten years can go by and yet no lover has presented themselves to you. If most of your thoughts during those ten years are expecting this lover wondering when they will surface, then this prevents it from happening. It's one of the many laws of the universe in the way that things come about. At the same time, you do not necessarily need to be a passive observer putting in zero effort. If you stumble upon someone on social media, or at the gym, the grocery store, or anywhere and they interest you, then smile and say hello. See where that "hello" can go. Even if it goes nowhere, it at least gets your energy out there in a positive way. This would seem like common sense, but you would be surprised how tongue-tied two people can be when they're both attracted to one another. They feel that it's one sided or part of their imagination. They worry that the other person would never be interested in someone like them. They might feel that the person is out of their league. You don't want to spend the rest of your life wondering if something could've formed with a potential mate if only one or the both of you made a move.

Those who are single and struggling to find love want to know if there is some magic secret to attracting in love. Be a good person and allow that to shine outwardly. Improve yourself on all levels. This means feeling truly whole and loving all that you are. It is accepting all parts of you especially the uncomfortable parts. It is raising your self-esteem into a warrior like confidence that you are content being alone. This is not to be confused with being lonely.

Loneliness and being comfortable alone are two different scenarios. You are in a perfect space of peace. Only when you love yourself in this grand way can you be more than ready for the soul that matches that kind of vibration. Of course, you will have the occasional low periods in life as everyone does. It's human nature to experience ups and downs. You will have those random feelings of low self-esteem or feel tender about the way you look or certain parts of your personality. Optimism attracts in a love partner more than negativity.

Both good and bad people attract in potential love partners everyday. Relationship partners have no prejudice when it comes to the type of person it chooses to get involved with. Good people also get involved with bad people. They might ignore the red flags when seeing this new person through the haze of romance. The reality dawns on them, as they are knee deep in the relationship.

When you meet for the first time, you're secretly looking to see if it's a potential match, marriage partner, date, or even friendship. When there are more meetings or regular conversations with the person after that, then you know that you both like each other enough to get together. You soon start to get a sense over time as to how you want to define the connection. This is whether it's a friendship or if it's a more serious relationship potential, dating, friends, friends with benefits, or the romantic kind of love.

Love is something that takes time to happen and build. If you're immediately in love with someone after you meet them for the first time, then you're not in love, but in lust. There's no way you can love someone you don't know in a deep way. If you've been with them a year and you know their quirks, flaws, challenges, and yet you still love them, then it is real love.

Your Spirit team would never plant your only potential soul mate in one state and then let you lose out on love because you had to move to an entirely different state. There are many potential soul mates, men and women, who could fulfill you spiritually, emotionally, and physically. They are waiting for you in every city, occupation, and social group you might possibly choose to be in at some point in your life.

Forcing love to happen pushes it further away. It brings up fear that it won't happen and frustration that it isn't happening. This energy repels others whether it's a potential partner or someone you're dating. It puts stress and strain on a relationship with its intensity of trying to keep the connection going out of an obsession to hold onto them. The reasons behind this behavioral reaction often have to do with psychological build up from childhood of losing something you wanted whether physically or metaphorically. It can also point to having been denied love growing up, which breeds co-dependence. The other reason is that you've become so excited to have a new love partner that it feels as if you found the one and don't want to lose them. You overcompensate to the point of smothering the other person, or by becoming completely co-dependent that it begins to suffocate them. The other partner ends up retaliating angrily, pulling away, or ending the connection altogether. This could be applied to someone who isn't normally co-dependent by nature. A great deal of independent detached professionals announced that the times they have rare co-dependent feelings rise are only while in a love relationship.

When you develop strong feelings for someone you've recently met, then this is a combination of lusting after them or falling in love with the idea of them, but it will not necessarily equate to long-term love. True love is developed over time for someone. The more you bond with them and appreciate all aspects of them, then the more love can develop. Take the time and get to know someone before jumping into something serious.

You're on a hamster wheel when you continue to repeat the same patterns that lead nowhere. You continue to attract in the same types of mates, or you have no forgiveness in your heart with a past flame. The mate that is the keeper and the one you'll end up with for good is often the one that's different than what you're used to. That is if you can break the karmic cycle of attracting in the same types of mates that add toxicity to your vicinity. Forgive yourself and any past lovers that have caused you ill will. Otherwise these obstructions can prevent a new connection from entering the picture and blossoming out of the dating stages. You cannot force someone to change and suddenly want you, since you cannot force anyone to do what they don't want to do. Never wait around for someone who is unsure about you.

When it comes to matters of love, your guides and angels will put particular soul mate choices in your path intended to connect with you, but then it is up to you and/or this other person to notice it and act on it. They work with the other person's guides to guide that person toward you, while your own guides are guiding you towards them. That's quite a bit of guiding going on behind the scenes in hopes that both parties notice. They'll get you in the room alone together to face each other, but then it's up to the both of you to do the rest of the work. If neither of you do, then it's back to the drawing board for both sets of guides to continuously work to orchestrate the meeting again and again in hopes that action will be taken. This can only go on for so long before the moment passes, and neither is able to keep the orchestration from happening. At that point a lost opportunity has passed for both parties.

Some guides and angels might agree to show up at a certain juncture of someone's life, such as when major life changes are taking place. They leave once it's calmed down and heavenly help is no longer needed for that circumstance. A spirit guide may be sent to you to assist in preparing you for a particular love relationship partner, or to help you find a specific job where you will learn valuable lessons and skills at in order to utilize later in your personal and/or professional life. Once you and this love partner have connected or you obtained the job you desired, then that particular guide will leave.

Some people have made poor choices out of being deeply in love with someone. Heaven applauds love feelings for another person, but they know one of the side effects of intense obsessive love could fog up your psychic vision and divine connection. This can contribute to you making choices you might not have ordinarily done if those rose-colored glasses weren't tightly on.

Some people have been in a love situation where they were in love with someone who wasn't as in love with them back. This continues until they find out they were being taken advantage of by that partner. They look back and start to recall the many red flags and Divine signs offered to them about this new prospect. Those signs had been in front of them all along, but because they were in the deep blinding haze of being in this kind of love attraction, they failed to notice it or brushed it off. When you're that in love with someone you let them get away with murder, until they react cruelly to you in a way that snaps you back to reality. You realize you knew all along they were wrong for you, but you had been deceived by the dark ego.

CHAPTER NINE

Love and Relationships

When two people merge into the right healthy committed loving union, both of the lights in their souls expand and their vibrations rise. There is no limit to what you are able to accomplish individually while in that soul connection. Love is the main reason all are here. People gravitate towards this concept because deep down most everyone longs to have that kind of a connection if they don't already have it. Most everyone has made that one bond with somebody that pulls you out of yourself completely. Some have that one great love that is never experienced again, while others move through life and never connect with another human soul in an intensely deep way. This is about reciprocated relationships and not unrequited ones.

Unrequited connections are where you have a crush or romantic interest in someone who does not share the same feelings and attraction for you. It can be someone you are in a relationship with who either was never fully into you and settled, or their feelings shifted over the course of the relationship where they no longer have romantic feelings for you. Love relationships experience peaks and valleys, so there will be moments when you both feel as if you're stuck in a rut. This is why relationships take work and effort to continue to keep it interesting, passionate, and thriving.

A requited deep soul connection is where you understand one another more than any other experience you've had with anybody else. It is the kind of union that you never forget, and nor does it ever go away no matter how much you attempt to disregard it. This is the kind of rare soul connection that leaves you haunted by it decades later long after it ends. Your mind always drifts back to that profound tie you had with them. It is one that is never repeated with anyone else. The relationship might not have lasted due to various factors, but often times it's something trivial where one or the both of you allowed your ego to rule your life. When you use little ego, then circumstances function with minimal issues and relationships end up lasting.

The ego is selfish and makes decisions based on self-centeredness that can result in crumbling a union. There is a great deal of self-centeredness in the world today, which is why many struggle to keep relationships going. Before the technological age people were staying married or together their entire lives. Today they're out the door at the slightest sign of it becoming dull or antagonistic. No one usually leaves their long-term job that abruptly, but they have no problem walking away from deeper soul connections.

Selfishness is one of the top causes of relationship sabotage. Selfishness comes from the dark part of your ego. There are varying shades of the ego that range from the light to the dark. The light side of your ego believes in yourself, loving all that you are and having confidence. Relationships require selflessness, which is a quality lacking in today's modern-day world in general, let alone in a love relationship. The ego wants what it desires, even if it triggers damage to a deep soul connection. Soul connections are no accident, but are predestined and determined to make contact with one another this lifetime. A soul mate is a soul connection that pushes your buttons and helps you positively change and grow. Soul mate soul connections assist in one's personal and spiritual growth.

It takes me a long time to come around, but all of my romantic connections have always been forceful and intensely close. This is what happens when you merge in with a love addict. I use the term love addict loosely and in an exaggerated way to imply that I love being in love and being in positive love relationships. The true meaning of the love addict is someone who is in love with the intoxicating high of the initial getting to know someone part, but then once it grows familiar, they discard them and move onto the next victim. I've never done that, but rather have grown stronger and more connected with the one I'm with.

The reason it has taken me time in the past to come around is because I've never jumped into a relationship with anyone on a whim. I've taken my love relationships seriously including the coming together part. I need to be sure about them before I commit, because when I do it's for life. However, in the past, I had found those that rushed the commitment were just as rushed to end it. They did this with all those they were with; therefore, do not take love relationships seriously. It is impossible to be with me and not believe it's going to be deep or intense, because it will be. It's just the way it is. The love continues to grow more concentrated as time goes by. If a connection moves into superficiality or distrust, then it will break apart. Have zero tolerance for superficiality in love. Have the mantra of putting in all or nothing. This means you put in 110% into whatever you choose to commit to or don't bother. Don't waste energy on something that you only have half an interest in because it will show.

I can psychically see what is going on underneath and what is unsaid with someone. This has its positives and negatives. The positives are that it tells me what the other person needs. The negatives are when you see something that can make you question who you're with. One of the worst places to be is in a loveless relationship. This squeezes out all traces of oxygen and ultimately brings about suffocation. It is one of the worst love crimes you can commit next to cheating and abuse of any kind.

Those in healthy long-term love relationships report to being happier, calmer, more motivated, and less stressed in their life in general than those who are single. Note the word, "healthy", because being in a drama ridden love relationship, or unrequited one-sided love connection, is just as bad on your health than being addicted to a toxic substance. You might as well be single and develop a healthy social life instead.

Long term love relationships between two people facing in the same direction that have each other's backs tend to be less depressed, have less anxiety, and lowered blood pressure than those struggling alone with no social support system or a love partner for life. The loving soul connection motivates both parties to accomplish more in their life. They tend to live longer happier lives, rather than short miserable ones. The immense benefits in a healthy long-term love relationship are endless. There is no telling what both partners can accomplish while in a loving partnership.

This is not intended to imply that in order to be happy that everyone should jump into a long-term love relationship. There are some people who are not cut out for it, are not ready for it, or they genuinely prefer to be alone and single by choice. They are perfectly happy being single.

It is unwise to jump into a love relationship when you're not in the right space to be in one. It is also not fair to the person you're pushing to get involved with when you're not ready. If they're pushing you and you're not ready, then it is reckless to go along with it knowing that they want what you do not want.

To an extent, realizing your dreams first before getting into a love relationship is ideal, but if you wait for that to happen, then you might be waiting forever. The right partnership gives you that push to conquer your goals by giving you the space and freedom to explore your dreams. Without love within or without, then one's talents and accomplishments mean nothing. Love is the reason all are here bridging souls in one long thread of interconnectedness.

When an entertainer receives an award, nine times out of ten they mostly include their love mate in the speech. Some even go as far as to say how much their mates love is instrumental. Their lover's immense loyalty and support means the world to them. This is because they are aware of how the person closest to them has been their biggest support system and fan than any other. It's a stronger love than any fan because it's personal. This love partner knows who they truly are behind closed doors rather than the persona that the public thinks of them to be like.

How will you know if your relationship has served its purpose or if it is at the end of its tenure? If you have to ask, then it's over. Preoccupying oneself over whether or not a relationship has run its course indicates that you've already got one foot out the door. When doubt exists in your mind, then this is what shall come to you. Letting go of anyone or anything means you first let go of it in your heart. Once that happens, then the energy is activated and heads in that direction without you realizing it. This same process is applied to attracting in a love partner. You feel it in your heart that the love partner is already here. Use your imagination and visualize that it is in motion by believing with cheerful might that it is here now.

No matter how many love experiences gone bad it is worth the risk to open up one's heart to allow love in again, otherwise a missed opportunity can take place. When your heart has been bruised and battered, you subconsciously put up a wall that makes you inaccessible to anyone, even the right one. The warmth is what the right one will be drawn into and not the hostility. It can take a long time after one heart breaking connection has ended before you safely drop that wall of horror to allow someone new in.

When it comes to a love partner, one assumes this person has their back. They are merging spiritually, mentally, emotionally, and physically with this person on all levels. It is considered a big deal to give all of oneself in that way. When your life mate cheated on you, or was physically or verbally abusive, then it can be difficult to reach a place of forgiveness, although it is necessary for you to heal and truly move on.

The world is suffering where love relationships are concerned. This is an ego-based planet that includes ego-based pursuits, which have taken precedence over merging a duo in a beautiful long-term supporting love relationship. The ego contributed to the downfall of relationships. It's the ego that will jump into a relationship quickly and end it recklessly, or the ego will avoid a connection altogether as it dislikes feeling tied down.

When you fall in love, this releases the hormones dopamine and oxytocin. These are feelings that create an overall sense of positive well-being. You're basically high on life! You're suddenly focused and energetic able to accomplish things that you had previously put aside before you fell in love. This is also why being in love and having a love partner is beneficial to your heart, health, and overall well-being. It's also why those who are in love with you can stop at nothing to get you or be with you. This is because in essence love is like a drug. It gives them that natural high where they'll stop at nothing to obtain. The danger of this is that you may be in love with someone who doesn't share those feelings. There is nothing worse than being in love with someone and they're denying it because they're not interested. You'll notice that it doesn't necessarily detour someone from giving up. They will grow miserable or depressed not being able to be with you. Someone might start lashing out or resort to stalking behavior to get as close to you as possible.

There is no fixed formula for making a true unconditional relationship work since it's a mutually agreed upon and understood formula made by both parties. Unconditional relationships are also not 100% accurate, because unconditional means without condition, and you have conditions when in a relationship. You have conditions that your partner doesn't cheat on you. Right there you now love with conditions. But you can get as close as possible to unconditional love while easing up on issues. Unconditional love is a difficult trait to reach. Everyone places conditions on love to one extent or another. You want someone who is loyal, in it for the long haul and sticks around. As soon as you have the lists, then you love with conditions. If you can get pretty close to unconditional, then that is miraculous.

Love can come close to perfection when all of its imperfections are loved and accepted. Be honest with yourself and with others surrounding your intentions. Follow the wisdom of being authentic and real.

Deep down at the soul's core, the soul desires love, companionship, and commitment. The poor influences over the course of one's life confuse that craving with wanting more selfish self-gratifying longings. It has been taught that there is always an easy way out.

When two people merge into a healthy committed loving relationship, both of the lights in their souls expand and their vibrations rise. You know the meaning of the word God while in a healthy committed love relationship. Love and joy are what lifts you into that space. There is no limit to what both people are able to accomplish individually while in that match.

Being in love is a thrilling, joyful, and exciting feeling that only those who have experienced understand the depths it can reach. This is why so many people long to be in a love relationship or have a lover, because they crave that consistent feeling of happiness that the experience brings. In essence, when you are in love with someone, it is the same feeling as having a crush. Crushes never seem to be as intense and profound as they are when you're a teenager.

You've likely felt those strong intense crushing feelings over someone who has no idea you feel that way. You wonder if you have a shot at obtaining them or if they even feel the same way. The idea of having a crush sounds exotic initially, but they're called crushes because they can crush and hurt you emotionally. This is especially the case if the person you have a crush on doesn't return those feelings.

It may be a loveless world, but there are still a great many souls coming together in relationships everyday within the confinement of it. You cannot ditch love entirely, because love is present beneath the layers of all souls regardless if they choose to find ways to access it or not. Love never dies in this sense. You can say you want to focus on work or on yourself, but the bottom line is when a relationship is intended to happen, it will come about unexpectedly regardless if it messes up with your goals to achieve. You can still succeed while in a relationship. Being in the right connection motivates you to accomplish more and reach higher heights, so it's a win-win.

Cuddling, hugging, and touching have immense therapeutic properties. These acts assist to bring down your cortisol levels more rapidly than anything else. When you engage in these activities with someone, or your romantic partner, it assists in lightening the load or dissolving traces of unhappiness, stress, or upset. It raises your vibration and boosts oxytocin levels, which is the love drug hormone that calms your entire body and expands the soul's light. Even if you don't have a love partner, then hugging a friend or a pet can offer the same benefits.

Being physically touched and kissed repeatedly is like oxygen to me. It has the same endorphin release one gets through exercise. I am a walking love bug Casanova after all, which in the past has been a handful or detrimental when I placed it in the hands of the passion-less, the unromantic, or the non-committal.

Partaking in love activities such as regular touch can open up your clair channels to receive clearer guidance and messages from above in this state. Being in love releases the dopamine and oxytocin hormones. What have erupted are upbeat feelings that create an overall sense of positive well-being. You're basically high on life! You're more focused and energetic able to accomplish things that you had previously put aside before you experienced Earth's saving miracle called love. Love is like a drug, but a healthy one that gives you a natural high that no vice, cigarette, drink, drug, or bad food can offer or reach.

Like the song, remember to let your love flow like a mountain stream…

CHAPTER TEN

Love is a Battlefield

The relationships you have with others make up a big part of your life. These relationships can positively or negatively affect who you are and the overall state of your well-being. This is why you will want to ensure that you work on raising your vibration in order to invite in higher vibration souls into your vicinity. Avoid or distance yourself from those who are harmful and toxic to you. It can be challenging for someone with a low vibration to connect with a high vibration person, because the high vibration person can sense someone who is not of integrity or who has a low vibration. They will steer clear of someone with a low vibration. High vibration souls are extra sensitive and avoid participating in situations that will wreak havoc on their system. This includes being around toxic people.

When you get close to a high vibration person, you will discover they tend to mostly be friendly, compassionate, loving, and supportive people. The reason we say mostly is because they are ultra-sensitive. If someone crosses them or they sense harsh tampering energy on their soul's system, then they may grow frustrated and lash out, or they take off staying far away from the low vibration soul. This is the fight or flight response that those with higher psychic sensitivities have. The way that spirit beings are attracted to the light around any soul, the high vibration human soul is attracted to those with a large light as well.

To those that know a high vibration soul personally, they will say they're good people and not gossips or prone to following the crowd to fit in. They are into improving or taking care of themselves on some level. They are confident and comfortable with being alone and rarely fall into bouts of loneliness. If they ever do, then it comes and goes quickly. It is not part of their basic human nature. When the soul is operating from its higher self, then loneliness doesn't exist in the equation. Loneliness is a trait that comes out of the human condition.

This isn't to say that high vibration people do not drop their vibration or feel lonely from time to time. On average their vibration is dropping and rising all throughout the day. They are aware when it drops, and they begin the immediate work to raise it again naturally. They know what to avoid and what will negatively affect them in order to do this. Whereas someone that functions primarily with a low vibration tends to stay on that level until they have that awakening moment where they realize they need to make healthy life changes.

The human soul that has repetitive negative critical statements to say about someone is operating from a low vibration. A high vibration soul is not the one who congregates around the water cooler to gossip and spew negative words. They're the ones that distance themselves from that. This isn't out of shyness, but because they're not attracted to energy drainers. They don't need it or crave it on any level.

Feelings of loneliness will make you feel empty and miserable while lowering your vibration in the process. It can come upon someone who is bored, feels a low sense of self-worth, or craves a higher amount of social stimulation from others. Another person cannot fill these feelings up since this is something that needs to be developed from within you. A high vibration person operates from a higher space and usually does not desire curing someone of their boredom or boosting up someone's self-esteem. This doesn't mean the high vibration person does not desire a love relationship. They crave someone who is on their wavelength and of a like mind. They may complain that the suitors they connect with tend to be of a lower vibration. Low vibration suitors might cheat, are non-committal, or emotionally unavailable. They might be someone heavily addicted to a harsh toxin such as drugs or alcohol, and are uninterested in reducing or eliminating it.

High vibration people are catches for someone who wants to go the distance in a love relationship. They attract in others of varying vibration levels including those on a lower vibration. Getting involved with someone with a permanent low vibration is not suitable, as it can affect you and drop your own vibration in the process. It's like a fitness guru who is into nutrition and health, and yet they fall for and get involved romantically with someone who drinks alcohol in large quantities daily. It can be someone interested in going to museums and art galleries, and yet they get involved with someone who loves hitting the clubs or bars on a weekly basis. Once they are both deep into the connection, they secretly wonder how they ever got to together to begin with since their life choices are completely different from one another. They might have been compatible from an astrological, soul mate, personality standpoint, yet they partake in opposing activities. This can become frustrating from both sides if neither can accept their differences. It is something that should have been addressed in the early dating stages. Human beings are trained to put on their best face forward when meeting someone. This is a sense of deception, because you can only keep your best face going for so long before your true colors reveal itself to one another.

There would be a running joke in the past with whoever I was dating that I was revealing all the worst aspects of me immediately. This natural method of mine made those potential suitors even more attracted to me. I wasn't hiding anything and allowed it to all hang out on the surface. I joked, "If you can survive this, then we'll get along real well."

This kind of openness rarely pushed them away or turned them off, but instead ended up having the opposite effect. Each of the potential suitors would later say, "You started out by showing me your worst traits, but as I got to know you, I realized how amazingly compassionate and loving you are. You mask it with all this other stuff."

I explained I wasn't masking anything, but being my true self by revealing all facets of me up front. This method is the reverse from the norm where you're trained to put on the deceptive face to lure someone into your vicinity. Six months pass and the other person feels deceived as they learn things about you they're not comfortable with. Those who put on a deceptive face up front eventually discover that they have been found out.

I've heard others say that you treat a romantic date as if it is a job interview. This means you show the best parts of you up front. While this is true for a job interview it's not true for a romantic date. This isn't to say that you behave like a pig as you're getting to know this date, unless being a pig is your natural self. You put on your best face for a job interview, because when you are working at a job you're wearing a different professional hat that you maintain while at that job. It's a hat that does not include your personal life or who you truly are. A potential romantic partner needs to see and know the real you. The real soul mate that is intended for you will love all parts of you, as you will equally with them.

You check certain aspect traits of yourself at the door when you walk into work to focus only the job you've been hired to do. If this interferes with certain belief systems, then it's time to find a job that jives with your morals. You keep your professional and personal life separate at work. You date someone because you're looking to discover if you and the date will be a match for a potential long-term love relationship. If you're hiding important aspects of yourself with this date and you grow closer and deeper with them, soon enough these hidden aspects will come out. When it comes out, your mate will see it as dishonest. For those who have experienced this, they understand that it's a total blow to not have known the person they were seeing was a certain way until far in with them.

Joining into the most perfect romantic duo you will find that issues arise both big or small. What ensures a successful partnership is that both people love and respect each other enough to compromise. The ego does not like cooperation. It only wants what it wants and does not care what you desire. Relationships can go the distance when both people temper their ego and work together as a team communicating effectively.

Modern day love relationships are happening during a time of narcissism running high. This has caused love relationships to be massively short lived or to not come about at all.

Everyone and everything are made up of energy. This dictates the kinds of people you will attract into your area depending on the energy you give off. If you're someone who is always negative, then you will bring in those who are the same. The ones that find they're stuck with a negative person will find a way to break away from the connection when they develop the nerve.

Love and relationships are obsolete to the ego. The ego wants control, and this is witnessed with the current state of love relationships. By the time the Internet and social media became prominent, it was discovered that there are more single people than those in serious love relationships for the first time in Earth's history at that point. Many prefer hooking up with someone rather than developing a meaningful connection with them.

Technology has killed the long-term love relationship. Before the Internet, social media, and dating phone apps existed, human souls took their connections seriously. They never took them for granted the way many do now. When they would meet someone pre-technology days, they took that person seriously because there was no Internet or phone app to quickly log on and try and meet a replacement. They were grateful for the rare connections they formed. They cared about them and were interested in making it strong and long lasting.

Social media, dating sites, and phone apps are a candy store to the ego. The ego knows that if there is one tiny flaw in someone else that it doesn't like, then it would just log right back onto the app and chat away with more strangers in hopes of finding a replacement or at least a one-night stand. Before the rise in technology, people did not have that luxury. They took those they met seriously and developed long term love relationships and friendships for life. Their egos didn't have it that easy to leave everyone on a whim and start chatting around again online or on a phone app. The ego is unable to connect with one person throughout the duration of its Earthly life. It will find excuses to sabotage connections with others, give you reasons to cheat, or prompt you to govern your life from a place of selfishness. On the flipside, someone ruled by their ego full time is not someone ready to be seriously dating or getting involved with another person on a considerable level anyway.

There is nothing wrong with not desiring a love relationship. Some may not want one for good reason. Perhaps they're in no position to be in a love relationship. They might not be able to remain faithful to one person or they are battling addictions. They're uncomfortable with love, emotionally unavailable, or they're not where they want to be in life. You can still find meaningful relationships with others outside of monogamous love connections such as friendships, colleagues, acquaintances, and family members.

When you join another soul in this life, you are forming a partnership and a team.

Teamwork involves working together efficiently as if it is a growing and prosperous business. Each soul brings something to the table that the other soul might lack. You and this partner are both Teacher and Student where you switch and reverse the roles. When two people have gone into business together and face issues with their company, they don't immediately walk away from it. They sit down together to brainstorm ways of building it and making it stronger. It is interesting that others do this with work, but that it's not considered to do with their relationships.

In the end, the soul longs for companionship or a love relationship on some level. It wants to grow older with someone they feel a strong attraction for. It is the ego that does not desire this. The ego prefers freedom to hook up with random people or not fully commit to anyone at all. Technology and the media have both destroyed the possibility of deep long-lasting love relationships. It's not the technological gadget and the media that did that, but it is the individual ego working in the media, or who has access to technology that did. You give an ego power such as a fun and curious toy to play with and they will break it sooner or later.

I've received cases from those who hook up regularly. After talking with me about it, they admit to doing it for attention and love. In these cases, they expressed that they've been perpetually single and desire companionship, but that it has not surfaced. In the interim, they seek it out through meaningless hook ups. There is no judgment if this is what someone chooses to do, so don't misunderstand if you enjoy hooking up with others. What this is about is the common complaint expressed from someone who hook-ups regularly that they tend to feel even lonelier not long afterwards. Like any addiction or drug, they log back onto the phone app or website to find another hook up to temporarily satisfy their need for love. The suitors they connect with for a hook up mean nothing to them. It's a cycle they struggle with breaking. The others who hook up do so because they want to. They do not want to feel tied down to one person and crave variety. The others who do it are driven by a strong carnal sexual nature to begin with.

Technology is cold, aloof, and distant. This is how others are in the dating sphere. There is a detachment in texting and chatting that translates to how relationships function today. Technology has trained the ego to not develop emotional intelligence nor to dive beneath the surface.

Long-term monogamous love relationships are possible to have despite how it might seem. There are many happy couples that have gone the distance and last until the end. They are loving and compassionate with one another. They communicate regularly and support each other on all levels. Others around see them as a power couple, a success story, and one to dream and thrive for. In a successful love relationship, it is you and this other person against the world. You understand one another's strengths and weaknesses. You fill in the gaps that help one another grow and prosper. You take care of each other until the end of your days in this lifetime.

Everyone is in survival mode and it can feel unusual to the soul to have to endure difficult times alone without any support. This is where you ask God and your Spirit team for intervention during those times of struggle. Your team is loyal to you and present for you beyond measure.

Avoiding relationships does not help your soul grow. Necessary tools are gained when you join in any kind of connection with someone else, regardless if it's love, friendships, colleagues, or even acquaintances. After the rise in technology, it became incredibly difficult for human beings to connect with one another in relationships.

You desire a love companionship, but have found it impossible to obtain leaving you frustrated and dejected. To an extent there is a certain measure of pickiness. Technology made everyone a star, which expanded the human ego. They have the long lists of what they won't accept in someone else without any room for compromise or movement. If one is that strict over every little thing, then they'll be looking at a life of single-dom.

Others refuse to date a quality person who might either be too young, too old, too short, or too tall and so on. While some are looking for some perfect Adonis or Barbie looking person that appears as if they jumped out of a model magazine. These are all ridiculous qualities to have on one's list of what they're looking for. You rule out quality soul mates due to trivial fetish traits and therefore end up single indefinitely. Most of the time people end up with those they would not have necessarily been attracted to. There are cases where someone has a strong attraction for tall brunettes, but in the end they find that the person they ultimately fall deeply in love with for life is a short blonde.

There are common sense qualities that most do not want in a potential long-term love relationship. These are traits such as you don't want to be involved with someone who has a drinking problem, does drugs, is emotionally unavailable, is violent, or has a tendency to cheat and stray. At the same time for some people, when you're in a healthy long-term relationship, then that reduces or zaps away the desire to consume negative toxins and addictions in high quantities. The reason is real authentic love between two people raises both of your vibrations. When your vibration is high, then you don't crave or desire toxins. You are also less addicted to those substances. I've also personally found this to be the case ending up with those that battled those kinds of addictions, but they were reduced and diminished initially during our honeymoon phase. Part of this is that love raises the Dopamine chemical in your brain that makes you feel good. When you feel good naturally such as in a love high, then you're not craving toxins to get that artificially. You don't need it anymore, because you're already getting the chemical high through love.

An addicted person may grow bored or start to feel inadequate while in the love connection. They soon reach for the addiction in hopes it will remove those negative feelings. For some, they may fall into that addictive behavior, but they're absolved in it far less than when they're single and unhappy. If you're someone battling addictions to something, then it is often likely you'll fall back into that toxic path while in this healthy loving long-term relationship. This is because the love relationship can only sustain that for so long before it is no longer in the newness category. The honeymoon love high will eventually wear off for that individual, then the hard work comes in. Many leave the relationship when it gets to that point, because they want to continue feeling good and will seek out another new person to get it from.

Quality suitors want someone who is decent, cool, and a loving, supportive partner like friend. They desire someone who is in the connection with them and has the intention of going at it together for life. This is someone you can freely talk to and open up with about anything. It is someone that loves you and who you love right back without hesitation. It is not one person always being the listening ear, but it is a give and take. Even when you do not feel like it, you drop everything to listen to your partner. This is why love relationships are work. You have to put in the work as if it is your job, except you love this job because you love this person.

Some of the highest vibration qualities that exist are activities such as mutual hugging, cuddling, loving, and touching. The soul longs for air to breathe and these actions awaken your soul. Perhaps you had a lover who reached over to hold your hand and you know how amazing your soul felt to be that close to them. It feels as if you're soaring above the clouds and all you feel and know are love. You discover what matters while here and that is love. Love yourself first and you will be closer to inviting in someone who is the same.

CHAPTER ELEVEN

*Seeking Love Through
External Validation*

It can be challenging to find any love essence on a planet that is primarily ego driven. Reading stories laden in protesting gossip has no love within it. Focus on the positives of a situation, rather than dwelling on matters that are desperately out of your hands. Take the stance of an egoless angel who sees the love and positives of a circumstance. They understand that the way things are laid out is designed and soul contracted for a reason, even if the dark part of your ego has a tough time coming to grips with that reality. When you detach from the noise and drama of the bitterness in the hearts of those on the planet, then your consciousness is raised enough that it allows God's love filled light to come rushing in. This is followed by the higher Universal truth coming into view.

Resistance does nothing to move humanity forward. Having understanding, tolerance, compromise and meeting in the middle is what bridges the wide gap. This is the space where Universal love resides. Resistance is having a tantrum that creates a block stemming from the darkness of ego. It's stubborn and unwilling to compromise, which keeps others separated and divided. Resistance is not interested in working with others. It's defiant, it's rigid, it struggles, it impedes. Positive energy doesn't flow through having resistance. Resistance is restricting, which blocks Divine love communication from sifting into one's consciousness. There is no love or God existing in resistance. This doesn't mean you're siding or condoning what you believe to be bad behavior in someone else. It does mean you are taking the angelic perspective into peering into the complicated composites of the person you disagree with through love and not anger. This can also be applied to interpersonal connections.

The opposite of resistance is peace, cooperation, compromise, and meeting in the middle. One is more likely to listen to and warm up to someone that negotiates peacefully to find common ground over being aggressively stubborn and resistant. The answers can be found in that centered space where peace, joy, and love reside. When has war, fighting, anger, and resistance won the collective over? It's created more friction, more war, more anger, and more fighting. The ones falling into that venue are the ones protesting that it's getting worse and it's everyone else, but they're not taking the higher view to see how they've contributed negatively to that energy.

Absorbing yourself in negativity doesn't help anyone. It's understandable to be concerned about issues you were brought here to improve, but to dwell on negativity is called drama. No one likes it except those that stir it up. Residing in drama is the opposite of love. Focus on action that will improve a concern while debunking those that stir up spectacle and negativity. Regularly ranting on social media at others is not action, but toxic drama and gossip. If you preach about love or the light all over your social media, then walk the talk in all areas of your life.

For centuries, the Internet, technology, and social media never existed. People lived fulfilling deep and profound lives in person with others without any issues.

If all you care about is being loved by others in-person or online, then you risk getting carried down in that tide of caring about what someone else thinks. You can always count on Heaven to love you. When you are in the mode of appreciation and reciprocating that love, then you are in harmony with the Divine. When you lose yourself to what it means to truly love, and you despise those that have disagreeing opinions from you, then you disconnect further away from the source that the Light resides in.

Having true compassion and tolerance is by embracing and including those who are in opposition. It's the way to begin the process of bridging the gap of divisiveness laid out by the individual ego. This is a trait that the planet desperately needs to learn. They've always been divisive, but now it's at an alarming rate due to the way word travels through the Internet waves.

In order to walk the talk and walk in someone else's shoes, you have to be able to metaphorically walk in someone else's shoes. You have to know what it's like to be inside their consciousness. Otherwise, you'll never understand or have empathy to what they are experiencing. A great actor can do this able to play a vile monster of a character while not losing sight of their humanity. Many actors have acknowledged that yes the character is evil in the moviegoer's eyes, but they cannot personally look at the character as being evil while playing it. They have to understand the character's viewpoint and find the humanity no matter how monstrous that person is to others.

Social media is a playground for the ego. There are different measures of how the darkness of ego comes out in social media. Some of it is worse than others. You know what is along the lines of what is and what isn't. Unless social media is being used positively to bring light to important issues, then it tends to be used for some form of attention. It depends on how extreme or severe the need for attention is that it can be corrupting, which ultimately delays and holds that soul back from true accomplishment.

Human souls crave love, appreciation, and acknowledgement. The soul wants to be loved because it knows it flourishes when being radiated with love. It cannot breathe without love, so it will do whatever it takes to obtain that love in anyway it can. It craves God's all-encompassing love, which is lost in the dark banal physical existence. To put that kind of demanding expectation on other people to fulfill is putting too much burden on others who cannot satisfy that unnerving requirement.

The way to accelerate life on Earth towards Utopia is if every person on the planet resided in their soul's true nature, which is in a state of all love, joy, and peace. It's virtually impossible for millions of souls to exude that state around the clock in today's ego driven physical designed modern world governed by the darkness of ego. It is counterproductive to their true nature, so people live under constant stress as a result.

Choose to rise above negativity by showing some beautiful poised class. Stay centered in grace and love despite any whirlwind of darkness surrounding you. Nothing is truly as bad as it seems. When a line is crossed, then you graciously intercept it by focusing on solutions rather than creating unnecessary issues. What you focus on will multiply, so you want to make sure it's positive. If you find you fall into the epicenter of negativity, then work on moving past that and in bridging the gap between all souls, including the ones that hold a differing perspective than you.

Look at the positive aspects of a situation or walk away from it. Divert your attention to the blessings in your life, and steer clear of the intoxicating drama and gossip that attempts to lure you into its sticky trap. It does nothing to help anyone and improves nothing, but contributes more hopelessness to the nonsense.

Warrior of Lights and spiritual helpers contribute their part to spread love around the world in hopes it will raise the Universal consciousness, but it will not be an overnight effort. It will still be centuries of slow-moving progress in baby forward steps to Universal love.

The Divine loves all souls equally and no one is ever ignored even when it feels that way. To Heaven, Earthly life is a blip on the radar and a millisecond compared to eternity. The perspective Spirit has is greater than imagined by the human mind. Experiencing that great love feeling from the Divine begins by increasing your faith and having regular daily prayer or conversations with God. Even if it feels like you're talking to no one, you are heard and responded to at some point. This is where you pick up on the messages and guidance immediately or further down the line. Sometimes you have to endure a rough patch before the light is shown. At the moment when the light appears, you realize why you were kept in a situation longer than you intended to be and then it suddenly all makes sense.

When you're operating in your highest self's state of joy, peace, and love, then that's when you are more able to notice the Divine signs around that you're not alone and that you are loved and looked out for. In the physical world, the ego requires physical concrete material evidence of that love, but the love is felt from within like a great big warm hug. This is part of what having faith entails. The Divine has no judgment and all are loved. There is nothing you can do to rescind that love. Spirit will not suddenly say, "Oh you're hopeless, I'm done with you."

As challenging as it is to believe, even the most heinous human being is loved. It is who the soul is deep inside that is loved. The intention is that the soul learns to reduce, dissolve, and limit operating from the darkness of ego. It is expected to awaken its consciousness to the spiritual reality they are bigger than the limited being they've chosen to confine themselves to. Heaven doesn't say to completely eliminate the darkness of ego, because even the most all loving and compassionate being on the planet will fall into the dark side of the ego on occasion. It's a limited rare occurrence that creeps up infrequently compared to the heinous dark human beings that have chosen to live a life ruled primarily from the darkest depths of their ego.

To sense the encompassing love from the Divine, it is necessary to reduce Earthly distractions in order to raise the voices of Heaven. Participate in a soul detox that includes limiting technological use on certain days, getting out in nature to clear the mind, exercising regularly, reducing toxic foods and drinks, and centering and balancing out your thoughts and feelings.

Don't allow negativity and drama to sway you from your purpose. You become a way shower and a leader by inspiring and enlightening, as well as remembering to display assertive love and compassion. Don't forget who you are and why you are here. Be a warrior of light who shines so much light and love onto all sides that your body cannot contain it.

A parent disciplines their child out of love in order to differentiate between what they believe to be an acceptable mode of conduct as opposed to a disagreeable one. This isn't to be confused with blatant abuse. There is a difference between discipline and abuse. A good parent faces the student soul in the direction of love at all times.

Don't pay attention to the screaming noise of the ego, but stay centered and balanced in the whirlwind of Heaven's love instead. The truth of your purpose for being lives deep inside you. When you stop to clear away the metaphorical cobwebs and the noise, then focus inward and then above allowing the truth to rise up so you can see it with exceptional Divine clarity.

Being loved feels incredible because it is the one area that all souls desire, even if it seems to manifest itself outwardly in the physical world through disentangled misguided means. You may post one selfie after another on your social media account for external validation that gives you temporary satisfaction. You post another and another constantly seeking out love and affection from anyone willing to give it. The love you receive from that is temporary, so like any drug you experience withdrawals, then wind up using the vice again. You quickly head to your social media account to post away for more adoration in the form of likes, comments, or for anyone interested, even if it's just for yourself.

As with many things in this Earthly life there is a gauge between the healthy and unhealthy. The healthy side is posting selfies to have fun on social media. Done in moderation is a form of self-love, but where it gets into dangerous territory is when it's used all day long every day for external validation from others. This is where you risk bordering on narcissism or the opposite of that which is low self-esteem that manifests into an unstoppable craving of love and admiration from others. God and your Spirit team love you around the clock free of charge. When tuned into the Divine you can access that love knowing that it exists within you.

Narcissism isn't as dangerous as having low self-esteem, but it is toxic in higher amounts. Most everyone can be accused of being narcissist today. If you have a social media account that you post on regularly about what you're up to, then that is a form of narcissism, yet it depends what the content is. Posting stuff about you that can help others will fall into the realms of motivational self-improvement. It's contributing positively towards the betterment of humanity one person at a time. It is encouraging content intended to inspire others or to put a great idea in their mind to act on. Maybe it's to cheer you on to exercise more, or offer awesome healthy related cooking recipes, to delving deeper into higher learning.

Sometimes when you're posting random nothingness one after the other, then you end up spamming people with it. This might be done out of boredom or for driving desire for praise and external validation from others. There is a longing desperation to connect. This is about diving deeper to see if you're falling into perpetual non-productivity to cover up other issues that could be related to loneliness, lack of drive, or any other hidden emotional matter.

Social media helps give the lonely an outlet to connect with the outside world, which to another extent is positive if it gives the soul a healthy boost to engage. If you're a shut in and afraid to leave your house, then social media can help you connect with others from your personal computer or cell phone. In that respect, you are teetering on that fine line of having a healthy outlet to connecting with others to desiring false attention.

The real people that know you in person are the ultimate genuine beings that love you for you, because they are with you no matter what. They know and have seen you in person and they still stick around and remain loyal. There's nothing you could do that could take away that love, which is the closest one can get to unconditional. At the same time, there are people who feel isolated or live that kind of existence and have no authentic in-person relationships. Social media and apps can help give that person access to engage with other people, so long as it doesn't further isolate you from reality or cause depression.

Numerous studies have been conducted over the years indicating that lower social media usage is good for one's well-being, but higher social media usage has led to a higher rate of anxiety and depression. Those that struggle with social anxiety specifically had a stronger well-being when they engaged positively in social media on a minimal level. However, those that struggle with other anxiety related disorders and/or depression were more likely to overuse social media. Their usage borders on abuse whether it's constantly logging on out of boredom, or the abuse comes out towards others such as in comments, posts, as well as mentally comparing themselves to people. The ones that were comparing themselves tended to post more negative comments. With that said it could be safely understood that all those people that function from the darkness of ego and post negative attacks online are also battling some form of mental health issue. This could easily make sense considering that generally happy people with a stronger well-being state don't usually resort to posting negativity whether in posts, comments or online messages.

This could go even further as you psychoanalyze the human condition. Most human beings desire social interaction including the loneliest shut in of a recluse. If you're shy and find it tough to make genuine in-person friends, then social media can help you come out of your shell a bit. Where this gets into a problem is if your whole life and state of being relies on strangers to prop you up and give you the thumbs up or approval. That puts too much pressure on other people who can't provide that constant validation and love giving to one person indefinitely.

Inevitably you will be let down when you post something one day that doesn't garner that much attention. You wonder if you blew it or went too far or if people had enough of the spamming post. Weeks later you post something else that is #1 with a bullet and you're riding on cloud nine again with all the attention. It makes you feel as if you're a loved celebrity where you are popular for a day. This gives the ego a nice stroking making you feel good…. temporarily. Because if your self-esteem is not in check, it will come crashing down when that validation starts to dissolve all over again. It's a cycle that goes on indefinitely until you wake up and realize how much you've been relying on attention from others on social media to continuously validate you. Some have gone further by wondering whether they want to be on social media anymore, as it's become too much work and a drag to partake in.

You know you've gone too far when you realize you post something nearly every hour of every day and you're not selling a product. This becomes overkill for those that follow you prompting them to like your posts less. What a beautiful awareness level to reach when you can safely say that your desire for praise and attention from strangers on social media no longer matters. This is when you no longer seek love from external sources. You can conjure up that love from within the deepest part of your soul that is aligned with God who is all love.

CHAPTER TWELVE

Divine Soul Love

Connecting with source feels as if you're floating high on life and love. It's like a huge Dopamine rush that happens naturally without having to self-medicate with anything. Imagine being in that state around the clock in Heaven, because that's what it feels like back home. It's just a natural uplifting high.

Humanity is gravely obsessive over their physical appearance because the ego in humankind harshly judges one another by what they look like. The perception of who is considered beautiful or good looking would be vastly different if people saw one another's soul instead of the physical vessel they temporarily inhabit. Relationships would last longer because people would be merging together based on soul attraction rather than physical attraction, even though it's understood that in this world it is physical attraction that helps at first, but that's only the start of coming together. Physical attraction fades no matter how good looking someone is. When you're younger you base the quality of a potential love partner solely on their physical attractiveness to you. As you grow older and more mature, the quality of a potential love partner is based on personality chemistry and the companionship factor. You feel a natural easy soul rapport.

Craving human interaction and social stimulation is something sought out by many, while other people prefer to function alone. When you have a strong connection with God and Spirit, then you never feel lonely. Loneliness is ultimately longing for a connection to fulfill you that can only truly be satisfied by God. To have a mutually reciprocated blissful love union with another person is to know God, because a soul's best qualities are parts of Him.

Since it's sometimes difficult for a human soul to have a connection with God, the ego part of one's self will crave love, attention, and admiration from other people. It's temporarily fulfilling because no one can ever fill that space within you except God.

God in this case is not that cliché image of a man with a beard sitting on a chair in the sky. This is the image that non-believers tend to overuse, which has no basis in the reality of the massive energy force that created all that IS.

All souls desire some form of companionship with at least one person. Some people might disagree, but they do crave some form of a relationship based in love if even through a social circle of friends.

You might be connected to one another through technological devices, but in a distant loveless way. You are not connected to God through those forms. The entire planet is unsettled making it near impossible to sense the Divine energy that way. Your subconscious is aware of it, even if you're not paying attention to it in the present moment. If you're a highly spiritually connected being, then you're versed and readily able to move in and out of the Spirit connection whenever it calls for it.

Looking to the future with optimism you might sometimes find you've been chasing rainbows that evaporate as quickly as the champagne fizzles in your glass. You need not search long and hard for some measure of magic to reveal itself since it's always resided within you. You are loved even when you doubt it, avoid it, shun it and do everything in your power to deny it. When you reach that threshold of completing your Earthly run, the only thing you take with you is love. If you gain anything while here, then remember to love more, give more, and have compassion no matter how unpopular it is. Only then can you truly discover that magic you secretly desire.

More often than not, you agreed to have a physical life for a variety of purposes. Everyone is on the planet with the goal of spreading the three biggest traits aligned with God: Love, joy, and peace. All words affiliated with those three words describe what Heaven is like. You may look around and wonder how humanity grew to be removed from those phenomenal traits, but it is the reason you are here. Life is rough for some and reaching that state of being can be challenging, but it is not impossible.

All souls have access to the deeper parts of their consciousness. When you are born, you are 100% psychic and in tune to all things around you, beyond, and on over to the Other Side. Gradually, your caregivers, peers, and the society you grew up in began to have a larger influence on your human development. They train you on what to like, what not to like, and how to think. The ones who break away from that cycle know they have an important mission or purpose here, even if it's to spread compassion, love, or joy to others in some manner.

When any spirit being in Heaven communicates with you, the tone is direct, full of love, and uplifting, even if they are warning you of danger. They communicate firmly, while your ego communicates with uncertainty, anger, or any other disapproving emotion. Your Spirit team will never advise you to do something that ends up hurting you or someone else. This can be something such as developing a sudden urge to recklessly pack up and move away all of a sudden. It can be leaving a soul mate connection that was intended for you in order to go after someone else. Notice around you whom it might hurt including yourself. Typically, rash decisions tend to come from the ego since the ego is impatient. It believes the grass is always greener elsewhere, but where it currently is.

Every living soul is a descendant of the first man and woman that walked the Earth. No one is separated by color, culture, gender, sexual orientation, or any other factor. The darkness of human ego caused separation from one another. When someone is not evolving, then they view their surroundings and other souls in a limited way. They are uncomfortable with anyone who is different from them being in their vicinity. The ego will grow angry and cause them harm, pain or hatred just because the other person is not an identical clone. The lower evolved self sees this person as threatening, while the higher evolved self views others with understanding, love, acceptance, and compassion.

What others feel God to be is up for individual debate. The higher evolved human souls' sense that in the end that it's all supposed to be about love. The further you stray from love, the more disconnected you are from spirit and God.

Bringing yourself to your natural state is where you see things through the eyes of love. Your higher self requires nothing because everything is as it should be. If a mistake is made, your higher self learns from it with indifferent emotion and moves on. Your higher self efficiently corrects the mistake without drama because it knows that all is well. This is just an Earthly life run and should not have to be so complicated. It becomes complex when you are mired down heavily in physical desires and functions. You have to get a job and go to work to make money to survive. It's understood that this is how physical Earthly life is. You can still go after the physical necessities you require without getting obsessively bogged down in it that it stresses you out or makes you permanently unhappy.

Heaven understands you're going through human experiences they cannot relate to since it is not the world they live in. They reside in a place that is all love, all knowing, uplifting joy, happiness, serenity, and peace. There is no antagonism, bullying, domination, and unkindness where they are.

It doesn't matter what someone believes or does not believe, because God grants all living energy free will choice. The purpose for that is to help your soul learn, grow, and evolve. When you have free will choice, then you are more likely to make mistakes to learn from. You don't learn, grow, and evolve unless you're granted the freedom to choose and experience things for yourself.

Everyone is connected to God because there is no way you cannot be. God has the highest vibration traits possible and imaginable. It is easy to determine who is picking up on the voices of God and who is not. This means when someone exudes high vibration traits such as love, joy, and peace, then they are connected to God in that moment. When you exude traits that are the opposite of that such as hate, pain, negative feelings, and emotions, then you are disconnected from God. What this also means is that someone can be a practicing religious person who goes to Church regularly, or works in a Church, and yet they are unaware they are disconnected from

God.

What a spectacular gift it is to have the luxury of life everlasting. Your life is intended to be about love. Your soul in your body craves this love full time. Say goodbye to the dead part of you, and all that no longer serves your higher good, and welcome in a brand-new Phoenix rising gradually emerging and bursting out at the seams dying to get out and soar into freedom. You are alive, awakened, ignited, and ready for the most incredible ride up ahead. Make everyday count and spread love like you never have before.

No one who has been paying any attention can deny that Earth has been in a permanent state of disarray at the hands of corrupt people. The higher your psychic awareness is, then the more conscious you are of the disintegrating state of the planet. You cannot be in denial of this reality. You can be optimistic that there is serenity up ahead for life on Earth, which is why many sensitive strong loving souls incarnate into an Earthly life. It is in order to help move humanity along towards that goal. The struggle for them is that Earth is not an easy place for them to live on. They are aware of Earth's decay and have great distaste over the toxic behavior of humanity as a whole. When you are conscious of that feeling, then that is a sign that you are called on here to rise up and fight to bring love to Earth. Your goal is to help raise the consciousness of all souls back into its original state of being that is love.

There are no limitations beyond the physical world. The freedom to appear how one chooses back home on the Other Side is limitless. The only thing that doesn't change is the soul's consciousness. The soul's consciousness grows and evolves, but the essence of that soul remains relatively the same, which at its core is all love. If the soul's consciousness hasn't evolved, then it goes through specific training that takes place as a human being having an Earthly life, which is filled with challenges. Earthly life is made up of teachers and students in various levels of spirit evolvement.

The brighter the light is around you, then the easier it is to communicate with those on the Other Side. This light acts as a portal to connect with your Spirit team. They are with you from your Earthly birth until your Earthly death. Upon your human death is when you pass on through the tunnel doorway back home to stand face to face with your Spirit team. Those who work with angels, guides, or any being in Heaven on a grander level tend to have more spirit beings around working with them. Those who have larger purposes to help move humanity forward towards the ultimate goal that is love will also have more guides around helping them with this purpose.

I've forever heard the voices of Spirit since I was a kid. It was never unusual and has perpetually been a part of my everyday life for as long as I can remember. I was having conversations with those I could not see. Sometimes members of my Spirit team speak individually and other times it's in unison or harmony. The voices are slightly different from my own voice, although occasionally it might even sound like my own voice coming in from an alternate Universe. Growing up, I also did not know there was a name for it. It's not like this is studied in schools growing up, although spiritual studies should be a big part of the education system. It is non-denominational and helps in empowering and inspiring every individual to Universal love. It would definitely assist in altering the world for the better by teaching others class etiquette. There would be less negativity and hostile ego bullying, with more love and joy on Earth being exuded.

Spirit beings in Heaven see the light of love within you and ignore the range of wasted emotions, because to them everything will always end up being alright as it should be.

When circumstances grow extra intense around you, then issues or concerns that were doormat rise up to the surface in a big bad way. Use those moments to release anything that doesn't benefit your higher self. Find a spot in quiet nature to detangle and detach from the negative energies you've absorbed. Breathe in the love deeply and exhale out any stresses and concerns giving it to God and your Guide and Angel for positive transmutation.

All souls should utilize shielding methods to keep toxic energies at bay. This can be by saying something like this at least once a day:

"Archangel Michael, thank you for surrounding with me white light. Allowing only the love to penetrate."

Your gut feelings and hunches are connected to having clairsentience. It can sometimes be tricky deciphering what is real and what is imagined. The ego and lower self conjure up imagined or fear-based energies, while Divine communication is uplifting and full of love.

When it's your Guide or Angel, then you will hear the word, "You". It will be direct and immersed in love and optimism. This voice will say something like, "You will obtain that job as you are more qualified than you realize."

The guidance, information, and messages from spirit have high vibration energy to it. It is also filled with uplifting love that assists you or someone else in a positive way. If you are riled up in anger, then that is your ego, since heavenly communication is bathed in calm love even if it's a warning. The chatter in your mind causes confusion and chaos pushing you to act on the voice of ego. If you feel you're receiving messages urging you to create negative disruption in your life, or to hurt yourself, or harm someone else in any fashion, then that is the chatter in your mind and not God. Voices from spirit are direct, optimistic, and filled with compassion and love, even if it's sending you a warning.

Many are usually surprised over the humor that pops in and out at times while talking to Heaven. That's because Heaven is not some stern, harsh, cold place. It's filled with uplifting love, peace, and joy. Those are qualities that all beings in Heaven exude. They are bathed in those energies, which equates to also having immense humor. You can then likely gather that this is how they view circumstances in the practical based Earthly world. They see most of what goes on in a humor filled light rather than the tragic offended manner that many on Earth view circumstances around them in.

Many people sometimes feel as if the Divine does not love them, or that they're being ignored, neither of which are true. All are loved and no one is ignored. When it feels that way, then that has to do with your feelings, which ebb and flow. Feelings are not incessantly accurate when it's a reaction generated by the ego. The best way to feel loved by the Divine varies from one person to the next, but you can start by increasing your faith, having regular prayer, and conversations with the Divine, even if it feels like you're talking to no one. You are heard and eventually you start noticing the signs that you're not alone and that you are loved. In the physical world, the ego requires physical concrete material evidence of that love, but the love is felt from within like a great big warm hug.

Every soul has clairs (clear psychic senses) and chakras (soul energy points) that move up and down, and expand in and out. It acts like a gauge depending on where that soul's consciousness is at and what kind of emotions that soul is experiencing at any given moment during its existence. If you are riding sky high on love and joy, then your vibration raises. When your vibration rises, then so does your psychic antennae. If you are in the throes of any negative emotion, including complaining or whining about someone else, or what's being done to you, or how something upsets you, then this drops your vibration, and lowers your psychic frequency. It's just the way the soul is designed vibrating with varying colors and shades of the rainbow. It can glow a vibrant green color as it experiences healing, to an uplifting joyful bright yellow, to a purifying white, and then to the darkest shade of toxic black. This is all in the span of an hour depending on what that soul is experiencing in its life. If their emotions and moods fluctuate, then so does the psychic antennae.

Your soul at its core is a high vibrational being filled with ever flowing love, joy, and serenity. Don't forget who you are. Don't get lost in the negative toxic energy of the physical world. Take care of yourself, which means taking care of your soul and body on all levels as much as possible. Incorporate healthy life changes you can make today that will help you in awakening the parts of you that existed from the conception of your soul. These are the parts that can help you be happier, stronger, and that much more powerful.

You were born a vessel of love. Even if you do nothing with the gifts that exist within you, you will at least be shining that bright light of high vibrational energy onto all those in your path, which in turn tempers the severity of the bullets firing all over the place by the darkness of ego. The ego may have tantrums and cause all sorts of noise, but contrary to belief, love is more powerful than any other energy that exists on any plane in the end. Let your love flow and shine outwardly wherever you go. Revert to love, joy, and peace when possible. Take regular action steps that can help bring you back to this natural state of being whenever you falter on your path. Be conscious of who you are and the reservoir of gifts moving through you. This world needs more love and light in it. It is up to you to help guide others in that direction by doing the individual work to evolve and raise your consciousness. The planet doesn't need a ruler, since change starts with each individual shining this radiant love from within.

CHAPTER THIRTEEN

*Love Yourself
Back to Life*

You were born psychic and in tune to all that is beyond the physical world. This is the natural state of your soul. You were also born operating with highest vibrational qualities imaginable. All of this begins to fade in varying degrees due to human tampering and distractions during adolescence and your early human developmental years. These surroundings contain your caregivers, peers, the media you watch, and the community you reside in. All of this influences you on how to think, and what to follow, or what to believe in.

Having confidence in YOU is having confidence in God. The best parts of you are what God is. He is not a man with a beard sitting high up on a throne looking for ways to judge you. The ego and the Darkness are what judge others negatively. God is made up of energy that has the highest vibration traits imaginable. Because His vibration is so high to the point that it's not comprehensible, this makes it difficult for human souls to reach Him. You cannot reach him when exuding any measure of negative emotion. As you dissolve negative feelings and thoughts at any given moment, then that's when your soul's vibration begins to lift up and raise into love where your psychic abilities grow stronger.

Others have been turning their backs on any mention of the word God because of the stigma that misguided souls have preached. They insist that God disapproves of you, which could not be further from the truth. His immense love for you is unconditional. He only expects that you put in an effort to be a better more loving and compassionate person. Evolve your soul in order to move onto brighter destinies. This isn't any different than what a good parent desires for their child.

The Earth plane is a school for souls that take on the roles of student or teacher. The teacher souls vacillate between the role of student and teacher because they are evolved enough to understand that soul growth and learning will never cease to exist. The student souls are what we call Baby Souls because they are newborn souls that sparked out of God and immediately incarnated into an Earthly life to begin their first life run in soul school. They are easy to spot because they tend to be more naïve and innocent, yet some of them are filled with hate and destruction because they have not gone through enough soul training to be able to master the ego. The ego became this way due to how they were raised in their human environment. Hate and negativity are passed down into the human child. When you train your child early on to have love and compassion for all souls, then they will grow up this way evolving rather quickly. In that respect, the child's particular parent has the important mission and purpose of raising their child's soul consciousness. Teacher souls have an ego as well since all souls on Earth have an ego, but the teacher souls are a bit more advanced in that they are instantly cognizant of when they are going too far when it comes to ego.

Some souls are experiencing a repeat life in order to continue their soul's education so they can continue to expand and evolve into more love. They cannot move on to new destinies until individual soul lessons are learned, gained, and accepted.

God loves all souls more than can be comprehended. This includes even the most distasteful human being is equally loved. It is the same way a parent who has several children that are each different, but all loved equally.

Your soul is awesomely wonderful and loved by God and the universe beyond measure and comprehension. How awesome is that to be loved no matter how you're feeling? All human souls desire to be loved and will seek it out in friendships, family members, colleagues and lovers. This is with the hope that these other souls will give you that all-encompassing love. The love exists within you to begin with and can be conjured up naturally by doing the work to revert to love whenever possible.

When you are experiencing a block, then this could be a sign that the soul is starving for stimulation and creativity. Express yourself artistically without censure or fear that others will not approve or like what you do. Allow the vibrating power of spirit to flow through and awaken the creative part of you. Take care of yourself on all levels inside and out. This will assist in giving you greater energy, stamina, and focus, not to mention a stronger connection with your Spirit team.

Having a crystal-clear communication line with God will enable you to make sounder decisions in your life. It will assist you in reaching a higher vibration state than if you didn't have that connection. Creativity helps in raising your vibration into high feelings of joy, love, and peace, while boosting your faith and optimism. Diving into creative projects or obtaining a creative slant in your nature and day to day dealings also help in lifting blocks in your way to love. When you are enjoying your life, then it shows, and this is a powerful attractor for good things including a potential love partner.

Awakening the creative spirit in you is also unleashing that part of you that is connected to God. The creative part of you within that is in tune to all nuances in and around you. It is your inner child that is full of love, joy, and peace around the clock. This is why detoxing and watching what you ingest are important. It is because these all play a factor into what drains your life force energy zapping any ounce of creativity in you. Take care of all parts of you. Watch what you ingest and the energy of the thoughts you put into your mind.

Self-care is a not only a luxury, but a necessity. Love all that you are, and remember to pat yourself on the back for any job well done. When you've accomplished anything at all, then treat yourself to something good in celebration. Whether that's a hiking sabbatical trip or that t-shirt or music album you always wanted. Go for it! Reward yourself. You deserve the endless reservoirs of success and prosperity in all areas of your life that exist. Never stop being creative and live your life from the heart. Create out of love and give out of love.

I've always felt alive diving into artistic endeavors and in unleashing my creative spirit. When I was moody, depressed, or angry, I'd find something creative to do that dissolved those blocks and lift me back into the higher dominions of joy and optimism. Escaping into a creative world is where I've always been happiest. The world is a tragic place thanks to the darkness of ego in humankind, but in the creative world is where all love and pure enjoyment exist.

The same way your life force is ignited is the same way that your creative spirit is unleashed. It's a lifestyle change you adopt by changing your attitude, feelings, and thoughts to that of optimism. It's finding a love and passion for something and diving into it. This is getting back into the joy of your life, which is an inspiration in itself. It is the beginning stages of pulling that tiny spark out of you that grows dim due to life circumstances. Light a match on this ember and allow it to inflame into creation. Escape into the magnificent worlds your mind daydreams and visualizes. Find something creative you enjoy doing and master it. Immerse your whole being into the revelations that come to you. Apply it to your daily life by coming up with new pioneering ways in excelling. This assists you in your soul's growth and raises your vibration to the place where the connection with Heaven is made. You are creatively powerful! Activate, awaken, and ignite this part of you. Experience the exhilarating love high that comes with creativity.

When you love and enjoy what you're doing, then you're infusing this love enjoyment energy into your work. This is a positive ingredient that will attract a like-minded energy to it. If you do your work with fear and worry, then you will attract that kind of negative energy to it. The energy will be a block that prevents love success from entering the picture. Stay positive, optimistic, and joyful with all that you do when you can help it.

Diving into creativity is a great way to shake yourself out of any funk you experience. It helps you navigate through the treacherous waters of human life. It assists you in finding innovative ways to solutions, which can carry over to other aspects of your life from the business arena to love relationships. It helps you to think outside of the box and showcase your originality because everything you're doing while being creative is solely you. It pulls out the deepest parts of your soul. A photographer is being creative by taking pictures. They might spend hours taking a variety of photos of different flowers in a garden. By doing this they see the beauty and love around them. These creative gifts come out of you and mirror what you have within. Your true nature is revealed back to you as a result.

Creativity is a great reminder of who your soul truly is. Diving into creative and artistic pursuits brings this love out of you. Creativity cures boredom or lulls in your day while helping you to express yourself in positive ways. It gets your energy moving to see things in a different way. When human souls are bored, they tend to reach for an addiction. They might log online, surf the Internet pointlessly, visit a social media site, or log on to a phone app for human contact and stimulation that ceases to exist in their physical reality. You feel even more lonely and bored after hours of being unproductive with that. This becomes a bigger problem when you discover that this is how you spend every second of your day. If you didn't have that one step to check your social media page throughout the day, then you fear you might lose out on life.

Diving into artistic pursuits helps awaken your inner child. Your inner child is the person you were before age ten. It is the innocent all loving part of you as a child that had no judgment or criticisms of other people. Those criticisms came upon you through your environment and at the hands of those who heavily influenced you. If you grew up at the hands of bullying or any form of abuse, then this has a detrimental effect on your inner child. If you grew up in a community where the people were prejudice or racist, then the chances of you developing this racism trait are higher than anyone else.

You were not born racist and nor were you prejudice against anyone and their life choices. This goes for any sort of bias from political affiliations, religion, or hatred of someone's sexual orientation. None of that exists with your inner child. Your inner child is the part of you that has the most access to God, because it is all love, joy, and peace. Your inner child is the one who knows how to have fun and can see the innocence in people without criticism. It is jaded adults that did not evolve that spend their days attacking and judging others.

The inner child has no interest in lower energy behavior. It doesn't even cross its mind. Your inner child longs for release and fun if only your ego would pull that part of you back out to play again. When the dark ego dominates and grows lost in the physical world, your inner child screams for attention and love. Diving into creative artistic pursuits is a great way to fire up your inner child. When your inner child remains buried under rubble, then feelings of emptiness and loss begin to rise. Some go through these feelings of being lost during pinnacle times in their life. It can be brought upon due to a loss of any kind, such as the loss of a job, a friendship, a lover, or any other loss to something that gave you a sense of security or happiness.

Your inner child is who you were before all of the layers of trauma and life experiences jaded you. It was when you saw life without judgment or critique. You saw life through the lens of joy and love. It was before human tampering made you despise anyone different from you. Those who despise someone that is different we're not that way when they were four years old. It was their caregivers, peers, community, and society influence that taught all of that stuff. If God raised you, then you would've grown up to see the love in all souls. You would exude love and joy full time. When you were born, you were immensely psychic, and filled with overflowing feelings of love, joy, and peace. You were wide eyed ready to absorb everything around you. You saw the beauty in life, in the colors, and in the trees. You were also a sponge absorbing the environment you were growing up in.

Hug More!

Hugging and touching have immense healing properties to the soul. It awakens your inner child, which is also connected to the creative part of you. Are you overworked, stressed, depressed, or angry? Hug others more and allow them to hug you. Hugging lowers your blood pressure, relieves stress, and releases the brain chemical Oxytocin. This contributes to positive bonding or otherwise known as the love hormone. Hugging reminds you that we're all on the same side. Many of the cure all remedies for so many issues reside within you. Hugs are one of the various activities that promote positive health. And hugs don't cost anything. They're free!

If you're willing to part with a hug, then do it more often. Hug your friend, your lover, and even your pet! Animals are souls and crave the hug of another. Hugging is one of the many great vibration enhancers. For a brief moment your soul can breathe while in the midst of a hug. It tears away any off-putting ions that latch itself onto the aura around your spirit. You experience release and you understand what freedom feels like.

Everyone needs a hug whether they like to admit it or not. The most toughened human soul needs that love to tear down the walls they've built around their heart. You've likely come across someone who you try to hug, and they clam up or turn into a brick wall barely giving back the hug. They're terribly uncomfortable being touched, as it's not something they likely grew up getting enough of. They hardened over time at some point in their life.

Many are angry, depressed, or feeling any other kind of emotion that disconnects your soul from a feeling of joy, peace, or love. Those qualities are traits, which are innate inside of you, but buried so far deep it can't climb out of the hole it's trapped itself in. The world needs a war on hugs. If you're going to complain about something, then complain that you're receiving too much love, hugs, and kisses from the world. There are millions of nerve endings in the human skin and to experience touch activates these nerves prompting you to raise your vibration.

Unleash Your Inner Joy!

Joy is one of the highest vibrating energies that exist next to love. When someone laughs into hysterics, you sense the infectious energy. Suddenly strangers around that person light up with a smile. Someone else's energy will affect others around them. If they're being negative, then that will transfer. If they're infectiously giggly, then that will transfer. Seeing the fun and lightheartedness in situations raises your vibration. It lightens the heavy loaded burdens of stress.

When your vibration is high, you attract in brighter circumstances to you. If you're stuck in negative feelings, then call upon your Spirit team and ask them to help in elevating your soul into a happier space. Request that they guide you to getting back into the joy of your life again. Radiating with joy is what brings more of that good stuff to you. No one wants to be around a miserable stressed out and depressed grump. Feeling joy while visualizing your desires is what helps the manifestation process take place more quickly too. If everyone exuded their soul's natural state, then there would be peace on Earth. Everyone would be happy because no one is treating others disrespectfully or clawing their way to achieve or dominate. If everyone paid attention to their Spirit team, then love would reign. Archangel Jophiel is the hierarchy angel to call on to bring more joy and beauty into your life.

The Heart Chakra

The Heart Chakra is the fourth chakra energy center part of your soul. It is located in your physical heart and chest area. It is also in the middle of the eight core chakras blending both the physical and emotional/spiritual parts of you. It spins more rapidly than the previous three chakras illuminating a beautiful emerald green light.

As you might likely guess, the Heart Chakra is connected to all things having to do with love. This includes your love relationships and connections with others including friendships, family members, and colleagues. If these connections are toxic or cause you ill will feelings then this breaks your Heart Chakra.

An ex-lover has pulled a number on you leaving you saddened and moving through all of the various states of emotion from depression to anger to revenge. While this is a natural reaction to having a love relationship end, it also muddies up your Heart Chakra. This blocks love from coming in.

The Heart Chakra is connected to issues with all relationships from love, personal, business, to your negative states of emotion. When you cut off love and do not allow love in for fear of getting hurt or any other reason, then you clog up the Heart Chakra.

Ways to clean and clear the Heart Chakra is to remember to get back to that place where you can love again. When you forgive a partner, you begin the process of cleaning the Heart Chakra. Perhaps they cheated on you or were abusive. Both of which are difficult to forgive or forget. Regardless, in order to clear the Heart Chakra, you must reach that place where you forgive them for yourself and for your own benefit.

You can mentally say, "What you did to me was not cool, but I forgive you so that I don't have to carry this pain anymore. And now I release you from my aura permanently."

The Heart Chakra is also connected to your Clairsentience psychic clair sense. Having a strong Heart Chakra awakens your Clairsentience. This is your psychic feeling sense. Activate your Heart Chakra by lifting your emotions and feelings to that of love, joy, and peace. This will bring on a crystal-clear communication line with Heaven through your Clairsentience. Visualize healing green light shining onto it blasting away any and all negative toxic debris, and then exhale that burden out of you.

Those with a strong Heart Chakra are warm, friendly, and open. They hold no judgment or criticism. You can likely guess that all of those people that post negative words, attacks, and comments online have a muddied down Heart Chakra.

Other ways to awaken your Heart Chakra are through having a healthy loving relationship or by expressing kind words to those around you. Being supportive, loving, and partaking in self-care activates this chakra. Do things that give you a euphoric happy feeling of love including watching a romantic comedy. Love all that you are inside and out. Love is the reason all are here and this is why having a beautiful radiating Heart Chakra is especially vital to your overall health and well-being.

Archangel Raphael, Archangel Jophiel, Archangel Haniel, or Archangel Chamuel are the hierarchy angels to call on to assist you with your Heart Chakra. They work with you on matters of love, healing, emotions, and attracting in high vibration connections.

CHAPTER FOURTEEN

Bring Out the Good Vibrations

Show your best self by becoming a fearless confident soul that walks in faith. Share your love light with others whenever you can. Let it out and let it shine bright. Visualize yourself surrounded by a massive pink rose light that vibrates with white sparkles as you move about this creation. This inspires a mighty movement of love and peace. The hardness and toxicity that has plagued humankind for so long is outdated. The light of love exists inside of you. You must allow it to take back the control of your surroundings and burst on out of you. Be a warrior of light by doing your best to stay in that space even when you stumble upon a roadblock or a difficult human soul. Demanding people are merely acting out from their ego, which has no power or validity with anything real or long lasting.

The ego lives in fear and acts out in fits of temper much like a child having an outburst when it doesn't get what it wants. You find peace, joy, strength and love when you remain centered in the light. When you lose your way, ask for heavenly assistance to get back on track. The more you ask for help and work with your Spirit team to reach this space of contentment, then the easier it gets.

What can work for you to bring in your Spirit team might be lighting a candle and meditating on this light. Call in your Spirit team to begin the process of re-aligning your soul. Empty out your negative thoughts as you focus on this candlelight. Close your eyes and envision that the flame of the light is taking over any negative thoughts and blasting it away while lifting it off your body. Make room in your consciousness to receive the messages coming in from Spirit to help you be at peace and feel encompassed by love. You can call on them any time, day, or night. There is no special invocation that needs to happen. You can mentally communicate with them while you're brushing your teeth, taking a shower, getting dressed, and walking to your car. The more you do it, the more you'll find the most effective way that works for you.

I have crossed paths with a wide variety of people who have different belief systems and values. I have witnessed those who might disagree with any of this or who find it to be ineffective, yet these are the same people that struggle in a constant uphill battle in life. Or they might be the ones who have been stagnant with no hope for escape. When in those states, your ego dominates your life big time ensuring that you never progress.

Within you is the knowledge of all soul lifetimes you've endured. Within you is the knowledge of why you are here. Pay attention to your intuition as that is one of the many barometer gauges that exist within your soul that accurately receives heavenly messages. All human souls receive heavenly communication every day without exception. It is irrelevant what the soul's personal values and beliefs are, and whether they're aware that it is indeed their Guides and Angels. Pay attention to the messages in order to help you navigate through life much easier than if you were not aware of them.

Keeping your vibration high takes daily work. It's a lifestyle and view change you're adopting. One day you are riding on cloud nine with joy, which raises your vibration. Your vibration remains high until a negative thought enters your mind thus causing it to take a dip again. The next day you go on a drinking binge. This drinking binge prompts your vibration to drop astronomically. It can be a struggle to raise it in the Earth's dense filled plane than it is to drop it. Raising it back up can feel like pushing a huge boulder up a steep hill. Those privy to this knowledge can raise their vibration much easier than someone unaware of what to do in order to get it there. Having an interfering culprit like the ego is what gets its kicks out of double-crossing you and ensuring your vibration stays low. It makes sure that you do not succeed. When you make a commitment to incorporating higher vibration methods into your life every day, then you will notice the changes in your life shifting in a more positive direction.

It's easy to lose sight of why you're here. The way human life has been set up and structured by the ego in others has caused enormous discontent. Human ego trained other souls to be unhappy and glum by thriving for nonsense. Not everyone is affected by the harsh energies of the planet. These people have made adjustments to their lifestyle choices. This includes living in areas of nature with little to no chaos and people. Watching what they ingest in their physical bodies and taking care of it through daily exercise. They ensure the people they surround themselves with are high vibrational. They avoid the negativities of social media, the internet and gossip entertainment.

There are a great many positives to Earthly life. Human souls took what they innately learned from the spirit world and built homes, created work and jobs for others, designed transportation, as well as an ease of communication through advanced technological devices. These are some of the fantastic concrete necessities for human life. These are practical ways of surviving on a planet that is spilling over the edges.

However, interpersonal relationships continue to suffer sliding rapidly on a decline. Love is lacking in others while cruelty and unfriendliness is gaining steam. It is true that human souls manage to find the love when a crises hits. They intervene when they notice someone is being pushed down, but the love they exude in those instances is temporary. You grow lost in the nonsense of the noise of the ego. Some are consumed by jobs they're not happy in, or you're living check-to-check, or struggling to find work. Perhaps you're in relationships that are unsatisfying or you're perpetually single longing for a long-term committed love relationship that never surfaces. You're forced to be in situations you do not want to be in. What an effort it is to get to a place of feeling eternally happy.

When you're faced with circumstances that do not jive with your higher self, examine how you arrived at that place. Look at the underlying cause that has prompted you to feel negative when this happens. Identify it and then dig deep into understanding why it has upset you.

There are circumstances that no doubt has made you angry or prompted feelings of discomfort. Maybe you ran into someone at the store who was rude to you. You being a sensitive absorbed that like nobody's business. It ends up putting you in a funk for the rest of the day. For some sensitive's, they'll be angry for a minute, others for hours, or you could be one of those who immerses in the energy for the rest of the day. Avoid beating yourself up over it. It just means that you're a hypersensitive psychic sponge. You have compassion and love within you as all souls do, even though this might be difficult to grasp.

Whenever you witness ugliness in someone else, remember that they were born with the deepest love and compassion beyond measure. What you're observing with them is the darkness of ego at its worst. This soul has given its power away to the Darkness, their lower self, and ego. The ego cannot be reasoned with or convinced of anything, but of what it wants. The ego seeks to sabotage themselves or others. A high vibrational soul who is not pleased with something does not waste its time resorting to negativity or in giving it any attention. It only focuses on what it enjoys.

When you witness aggression or disrespectful behavior flying at you, then you will absorb that energy. It seeps into your aura and soul. It causes an array of negative circumstances and moods to assault you. What is important is that you find positive exercises that can assist you in releasing it and letting that go. It might feel easier said than done, but when a slight happens in your world, your ego has trouble letting go of it. When you understand this concept of separating yourself from the troublesome ego, it becomes simpler to manage and temper it.

When you have a higher degree of sensitivity than other souls, then you are more likely to be affected by someone else's ego. You're a psychic sponge who easily absorbs the negative or off-putting energies in others. It is a gift, but at times it can feel like a curse when you enter environments with human souls displaying low vibrational behavioral patterns. You absorb that negative energy which drops your mood affecting your inner and outer world.

When you grow negative, moody, or agitated, then this is a sign of two possible conclusions. One is that you've ingested low vibrational foods or drinks. Or you may have absorbed this energy from someone toxic you crossed paths with. It can be a stranger on the sidewalk who walked past you. If they're displaying low vibrational behavior, then that energy is lodged in their aura. As a tuned in sensitive psychic sponge, you've absorbed that into your aura sometimes without knowing it. Although, the super tuned in psychic sponges are typically aware they just absorbed this energy from someone in passing.

The souls you absorbed this energy from do not always intend to have a low vibration. It's usually done innocently and naively, or sometimes they do not know any better. Some souls have not evolved enough to be more in tune to something outside of themselves. This is partially why that particular soul is living an Earthly life.

Those that are psychically in tune beyond the physical are turned off by harsh people and energies. They steer clear of those that perpetually display low vibrational traits. It can be your employer or someone you work with who puts on the fakeness whenever you enter the room. As a tuned in soul, you can sense them a mile away. They're threatened by your higher frequency energy. They subconsciously know that you're on to them. This also turns off a lower vibrational energy in someone else. Low vibrational human souls are threatened by someone that exudes a high vibrational energy. The low vibrational soul's ego feels out of your league. High vibrational people don't feel threatened by others, but instead repel the lower energies.

This coldness and reserve have grown in others thanks to the technological age. Newer and future generations are being raised on devices that train you to be lacking in honest face-to-face soul connections. For those that have gone out on a date, you've probably noticed some of the typical preliminary questions. They want to know what your job is or what kind of work do you do. What kind of car do you drive? These ego driven questions are externally based. Your job does not define you in real reality, but the human ego has set their life up in a way that their whole world revolves around what kind of job you do. Who cares what you do for a living or what you have in your possession. Unless you're working in a field that is your passion and it brings you joy, then it is irrelevant what kind of work you do. This passion is your life purpose, but many do not work in jobs that are their passion. For most, it is a paycheck that squeezes the life force out of that soul. They're usually under stress and grumbling about life in general.

When you absorb the ions of negative and cold energy around you, then this can put a damper on your spirit until you address it. You can sit around and hope that something amazing will happen around you that will suddenly raise your vibration, or you can address it and do something about it immediately. It can be going for a walk in a nature setting. This is followed by taking deep healthy breaths in while requesting that your spirit team release any and all negative energy that has latched onto your soul. It can be getting together with an optimistic friend who observes healthy life choices, or someone who always lifts your aura just by being in your vicinity. You can throw on a funny movie or make love to your relationship partner. What you're trying to do is re-raise your vibration. Taking basic soul enhancing steps when an assault has attacked your aura can do the trick.

Everyone has experienced some hard times at one time or another. You have negative things to say about it. The ego fixates on the horrid that came out of that. Rise above your ego and ask yourself, "What greatness did I get out of that experience? What was awesome about it?"

The soul's experiences happen for a reason regardless if they're challenging or not. It is not because you did something to deserve it, but because your soul is destined for greatness. You're here in this Earthly life school to find ways that suit you in order to enhance your soul and spirit. You're not here to find out the latest sale on jeans or rip through relationships selfishly with no care in the world. In order to improve, you have much to gain. When something negative happens in your world, work on looking at it from an optimistic perspective.

An exercise you can do is to pick up a journal or a notebook. Use that notepad as your diary to put in only optimistic viewpoints in your life. When you find that you're buried heavily in negative thoughts and emotions unable to break away, take a moment to pull the notebook out. Devote a page or more to whatever it is that is upsetting you. If it's a person you know, then write that person's name in your journal entry. Instead of focusing on what they did to upset you or whatever circumstance has upset you, shift that into something positive. Think about all of the qualities you love about the person that has angered you. Remove your ego from the equation and look at that person through the eyes of an egoless angel. List everything that is positive about them and how that affects you in an optimistic way.

When someone has hurt or angered you, of course it's going to be difficult to see them through the eyes of love. Know that when you're looking at them through the eyes of love, you're not condoning their behavior, and nor do you have to remain best friends with them. You're doing this exercise as a release. It's for your benefit in order to remove that old, tired, angry energy you're carrying around that surrounds the person or circumstance. You do not need that energy, but in order to release it, acknowledging it with love is what raises your vibration. When your vibration is raised you are more apt to receiving clearer communication from the spirit world, which in turn assists you on your path towards abundance in all forms.

Your mind may begin to wander to all of the things you feel this person has done that has hurt or upset you. However, you will not write those things down. Remember this is a positive journal. You will immediately adjust your thoughts back to the positive things about this person. Let's say it was an ex-lover who cheated on you, was abusive, or left you and the relationship. You will not write any of those things down, but rather will focus on their good qualities. If you're only able to come up with one good quality, then write that one down. It is an exercise that takes much effort in this case, because you're holding anger towards this person for doing one or all of the things I suggested. Your ego refuses to see the goodness in someone who has upset or hurt you.

If it is a circumstance that happened to cause you upset, then you will write down in this journal the optimistic features that have come out of that. For example, you receive a traffic ticket. Instead of focusing heavily on how you have no time to take care of the ticket, or no money to pay for it, write down the positive benefits that you've gained from the ticket. You might write something down like: "This has taught me to drive more carefully."

That statement feels far better than saying, "I have no money. How am I going to pay for this! It wasn't even my fault!"

This exercise may not immediately change your life, but it will gradually guide you into positively changing your life. It will assist you in getting into the habit of bouncing back from upsetting situations much more quickly. It will help you to view circumstances and people in a more positive light as well as re-training your mind to think in a different way. The key is if you're going to play this game, then you have to play objectively. Putting all things positive and optimistic in this journal is the exercise. Only write your blessings, appreciations and gratitude for situations and people in your life. This absolutely includes everything and everyone that causes you to feel negative emotions. This might be challenging, but in the end it will be rewarding as you are re-training your mind to think positively. This raises your vibration in the process, which assists with attracting in positive circumstances and people to you over the course of time. Because it raises your vibration, it also clears out the debris that accumulates in and around the communication line to Heaven and your Spirit team. If it doesn't do anything, but allow you to start shining your true loving light, then that is all that matters in the end.

The ego is a wretched problem seeker. It might appear to be louder than your higher self and your Spirit team of guides and angels. This is due to a couple of factors. The atmosphere of the Earth plane is extremely thick and dense that connecting to the Other Side through all of the toxic debris makes it challenging. Your guides and angels are louder and more powerful than any ego. Yet, when the soul is in the Earth dimension, the communication lines are heavier and dirtier. The ego rises through the dirt. It already rises as soon as your soul enters into this human life. The ego is activated in a big way. When the soul is in the earth plane it's like roaming through life with ear plugs on. Anyone who has put ear plugs on to sleep at night may point out how they can sometimes faintly hear light sounds with them on. The higher self strains to hear Heaven through this muffled sound. When a human soul lives in a higher vibrational state, this allows light in, which gives rise to the higher self. Suddenly that soul is hearing their guides and angels more clearly than usual.

You are not alone as at least one Spirit Guide and one Guardian Angel surround you from your human birth until human death. They assist you down the right path in order to fulfill your purpose while here. When you are in your higher self's state you connect with your Spirit team on the Other Side with greater efficiency. When you are in your lower self's state or ego, then you block heavenly guidance and messages that keep you on the right path and assist you in achieving your desires. In my connections with Heaven, I've discovered that all are loved and seen through the eyes of love. Do your best to keep the darkness of your ego in check and exude love full time!

Abundance Profusion Exercise

The following is an abundance visualization exercise that you may choose to do to help train your mind to welcome in blessings in any form, whether that's love, career, finances, or stronger health. You may also choose to expand on it and create your own exercise that works for you.

Find a comfortable undisturbed space to lie down on the floor or in a nature setting, such as a patch of grass in a park or your backyard. If you're in a room, then look up at the ceiling. If you're outside then look up at the sky, pending the sun is not in your eye line.

Imagine the sky or your ceiling opening up letting bright Heavenly Divine light in. It breaks through blasting away all negativity and debris in your midst. Now visualize the sky or ceiling cracking open even more. Visualize infinite money bills falling out of it and on top of you while you lay there. You can create an ambiance of candles and listen to some good music as you lay there with a smile visualizing all these riches falling on you from above. These riches also equate to feelings of a strong powerful positive well-being, good friends, great health, lovely home, and a beautiful radiant love partner that you match with the same veracity. You can substitute the money for other desires. If it's love you long for, then visualize red roses dropping down on you.

Think about the roadblocks that constantly get in your way of attracting the blessings you wish would transpire. It can be your own thoughts and feelings or another person. As you think about each roadblock that stops the flow of positive abundance, begin putting into practice a visualization exercise. This is one where you close your eyes and imagine those blocks being blasted away with white light. This allows the block to disintegrate and fall away from you to reveal what you've long desired. Imagine each of these roadblocks dissolving away out of your aura.

Remove all mental obstacles of lack and begin to visualize what you want. For example, if you want a house, then visualize this house and the surrounding area of what you would like it to be. What kind of house is it? What does it look like in your imagination?

Visualize yourself walking through the front door of this house and moving through it. Who is in this house with you? Is it a love interest? A man or a woman? What are they like? Are there other people there or is it just you?   Imagine this desire as if it's happening and has come true now. Surround yourself and your thoughts with this image in your mind. What you visualize and envision you eventually receive. Through the power of your thoughts and feeling energy, you are bending towards that dream coming true. Do this regularly until the dream has become a reality no matter how long it takes.

The human ego mind sees things as fear based and riddled with negative emotions such as anxiety or depression. The higher self soul sees the potential and capabilities of achieving abundance. Allow abundance to come crashing into your life with welcome open arms.

Tell yourself daily that you are worthy of receiving abundance. You are qualified, worthy, and deserving of good.   You are filled up with a never-ending overflowing cornucopia of abundance. The floodgates have opened and the door to abundance has slammed open. Light is soaring in with abundant energy all throughout it. This light surrounds you like a great big hug. Abundance is all that it entails from a wonderful relationship, magnificent health, good friendships, etc. It can be feeling abundant spiritually and emotionally.

Move into the alignment that you believe you have everything you could possibly want in your life. See it as if it's live and in motion now even if it hasn't transpired yet. Allow your mind to see that it is. Allow your feelings to sense the great feelings associated with how you would feel to have that life. See and feel it as if it is here with you in your mind now. What will your state of being feel like?

Find that optimistic uplifting space knowing you have all that you could ever want and more. Get your energy into this positive alignment with God now. It surrounds you in a magnetic powerful way that you can feel it as you move about through life. You feel God's magnificent presence working with you to keep this momentum going. You are a powerful magical manifester with the ability to create all that you desire by the actions and energy of your thoughts and feelings. This is your winning card in attracting in blessings. You have these skills within you. Start taking action steps towards attracting what you desire today.

CHAPTER FIFTEEN

Universal Spiritual Love

All souls incarnate on Earth for the purpose of love, whether that is to learn to love, to teach love, to express love, or all of the above. As you've probably noticed, many people haven't been able to master the basic art of love. This includes the ones that protest that they love everybody. Attacking people over a statement that messed with your delicate sensitivities is not love.

Be like the egoless angels, filled with an all-consuming love and forgiveness shining God's rays of light down onto all those void of love and in great need of healing and clarity. In their eyes, you are loved without judgment. It is the darkness of human ego that harshly judges others. This doesn't mean that someone committing cruel crimes on someone else will receive a free pass of forgiveness, but in Heaven's eyes you are expected to correct poor choices. You are expected to ask for forgiveness and to correct any wrongs you've been enacting on someone else. This is part of developing a deeper evolving consciousness. Partaking in wrongdoing knowing you'll be forgiven doesn't count, since that deceptiveness is taken into consideration. It's like giving someone a gift with the hopes of getting something in return. This isn't authentic giving when you desire something back.

All human souls have an ego with varying shades of light and dark. It's the darkness of ego that causes the most unnecessary chaos. It prompts others to antagonize, attack, criticize, judge, hate, and all the cousins of those words. The world in general is loveless. This is primarily witnessed and absorbed on a massive scale all over the media. Comments posted are filled with bickering, attacking, confronting, and disagreeing with hostility and negativity. It's all noise that does nothing to positively serve, assist, or change anything. None of that is helpful and nor does it convince someone who disagrees with one's argument. All it does is breed negativity, which is absorbed by others and then passed around to one another like poison seeping into your soul.

If this is what the current general population of humanity is like, then it's no wonder there are many struggling to find love in any form. Being in that space does not attract in love. There is no room for someone else's opinion or choices that differ from your own to begin with. Having a warm inviting openness is what attracts in positive love circumstances to you. You start within you and then work your way out. You change the way you view circumstances and project that outwardly. You accept others for their differences, values, and choices even if you personally or morally disagree.

You can stay stuck in a negative mindset and despise other people, but the only person it hurts in the end is you. This negative energy weighs down your soul and stalls it from evolving movement, because it's dead set on holding a grudge. There is no clarity when the ego is running the show. At the end of your life run, the truth becomes clear as you are shown images of all your human years on the planet and what you did or did not do with it. You're shown what you said or did not say to someone. This includes how that affected you and the other person, whether it was a loved one, or an acquaintance, or stranger. You experience those emotions through all perceptions. It would be more beneficial to grow more aware today through psychoanalysis work.

There was a time when physical violence reigned supreme, and while it still exists, the new violence that rules is through words, thoughts, and feelings. This is how the Darkness does its work. The Darkness knows this energy moves rapidly able to bring out the most heinous ego imaginable out of the once purest Light. His goal is to bring everyone down as quickly as possible. He's been successful at it for so many centuries. Become the example of love, goodness, respect, and light. This is what always wins in the end.

You were born a pure Light of love, peace, joy, compassion, and understanding. You were filled with immense passion and love for all you came across. Throughout the soul's journey on Earth, it is faced with temptations, judgments, and harm by those around it who function primarily from the darkness of ego. It is your job to remember who you are and who you were when you were born out of God's love. It is one of your purposes and missions to rise above the hatred, darkness, and lower energies that assault you everyday, and move back into being the centered Light that you were made in.

Pay attention to the moments when you find you've become guilty of being a toxic monster and climb out of that painful abyss as quickly as possible. Extricate the cause that triggered you to fall for the dark one's deception. Kick it out of your life for good. Don't forget who you are. You were born perfect in His love's Light. You have the power at your fingertips to create the most splendid magnificent life by the vibration energy of your thoughts.

Every soul on the planet experiences fear throughout their Earthly life. It is the one common trait that everyone has listed in their soul contract before incarnating into an

Earthly life. You're a feeling, breathing, thinking consciousness moving about in a physical vessel for a variety of reasons. Every single person on the planet has a reason for being here, even if you have no clue what it is at any given moment. It is up to you to discover your numerous purposes that are connected to one singular intention. There are the default motives that all are here such as learning to love, but there are other goals outside of that even though love is always at the top of the list in the end.

Fear stalls humanity from evolving as witnessed in the centuries of evolution on the planet. While progress continues to be made in diminutive trickles, improvement still moves at a glacial rate thanks to humanities fear. It should not take hundreds of years to advance in the tiniest steps despite taking what we can get. This is due to individual fear resisting against changing their perception and awakening their consciousness to that of love. Finding the space of love and respect is challenging for the mediocre mind. Training every breathing organism to snap out of it takes an army of lights to do their part. Extricate fear from your aura and become unstoppable.

Move out of fear and toxicity, and close your eyes, take a deep breath in and feel and experience His love light moving into and through you allowing it to become one with you. You have a centered Light within you that is waiting and willing to be ignited whenever you allow it. Make that choice to become one with it. You have arrived in God's economy when you become a love blessing to others. You are simultaneously becoming a blessing to yourself as well too.

When your vibration is low, you feel and experience negative feelings such as anger, depression, stress, irritability, and so on. When your vibration is high, you feel euphoric feelings of joy, love, peace, and contentment.

A vibration in spiritual concepts is your overall emotional well-being and energetic state. Feelings such as depression, anger, and guilt lower your vibration, but if you're feeling joyful, in love, and centered, then your vibration begins to rise. The lowest vibrational state includes feelings of anger, stress, or depression. Watch out if you're experiencing a combination of all three at once.

The highest vibrational states are feelings of peace, joy, and love. Experiencing all three of those states at the same time makes you a high vibrational powerhouse! Love is the highest vibrational state possible, so always revert to raising your emotional state to that of love.

The lifelong battle with demons in my personal life is always matched with those from beyond the veil consistently pointing me towards the Light. When touched by the power, it is unconditional love experienced that no words can describe. The soul is overwhelmed in that radiance when enveloped in its arms. The answer to the question of the meaning of life is always the same. The answer is LOVE.

The more enlightened you become, and the more you raise your consciousness, then the better off you'll be. This doesn't mean that you'll be stress free, but you'll certainly experience less stress while being able to efficiently navigate through the treacherous waters of the practical world easier than if you did not have that raised consciousness.

Imagine if every human soul found the gift of love within them. No one would need to be here since that would be Utopia. When you find the space of love and learn to keep it there and revert to it when possible, then the closer you are to creating Heaven on Earth. It's a beautiful thing when one soul awakens another in a positive way just by being in their presence.

Deep down every soul longs to re-attain and achieve that blissful excellence that gives the impression of unabashed joy and serenity. It is a condition where unwavering love and harmony surround you in a protected cushion. Transcending beyond the dull insensible frustrated Earthy life and into the natural condition the soul once habited is a goal that delights. It reminds the soul of where it came from. You runaway and travel around the globe searching for a sign of this utopia, only to be consistently left with disappointment. This is because utopia begins and ends inside the spark that burns within your soul like a pilot light.

The spirit worlds are the ultimate Utopian paradise that is an unbelievable spectacle. It mirrors the nature settings and natural wonders on Earth, but is even more vibrant, lush, and magical than the human mind could comprehend. It would have to be because why would a place full of 100% uplifting joy, love, and peace be less than the physical Earthly plane? The Earthly plane is a school set up that house's spirits of every variety in a human body.

Human beings ruling their life from the darkness of ego cause the majority of misery experienced. If every single soul on the planet were in tune and connected with the Divine full time, while using their God given born traits of love, then Earth would be as blissful as Heaven.

Coming to the end of the road as you close your Earthly life chapter up, you realize if you hadn't before that it was always intended to be about love. Your soul was born from a source of love and you will die right back into that love. Love is the most powerful energy foundation that exists in all dimensions. The only thing that matters is love. The best way to channel energy positively is to remember all things connected to love. Love is what kills energy like anger, sadness, fear, and worry. Outstretch your arms, release any fears, and fall back into the arms of this love. Allow it to protect and guide you on your Earthly journey.

Bring your soul to that beautiful glorious space of centeredness, serenity, and peace. Ignore any drama swirling around you and view circumstances from an emotionally detached perspective without judgment. Increase your faith through prayer and regular conversations with the Divine, knowing and understanding that you are loved and watched over.

Every day should be the most magical time of the year, but the lack of love on the planet that continues to be prevalent makes it less enchanting. Remember to love and accept others even if their values are differing from yours. This is easier said than done since many have forgotten about the basic concept of what love is. Humanity continues to have a long way to go before every soul on the planet is aware that it's about love.

Treat everyone with kindness and compassion even if they don't share your values. This goes for all sides of the spectrum, as everyone becomes guilty of it at one time or another. It's not okay to treat others badly. It's not okay to abuse the luxuries you've been given as a free will thinking conscious soul being. It's one thing to defend yourself from someone who has accosted or randomly disrespected you, but it's another to take it upon yourself to harass someone because they're different and not a clone of you. You reach no middle ground when you're that rigid.

The ultimate reason all are here is to love and to learn how to love. You cannot learn that unless you're thrown onto a planet with others who are different from you. Learn to accept others and see someone's personal truth. You're not saying you agree with them, but a way shower illuminates the way by example.

Be the King or Queen of showing respect and compassion to others. These traits are not popular globally. This doesn't mean that if someone abuses or walks all over you that you take it lying down. Pick your battles and use assertiveness over aggressiveness when slighted. The general demeanor to strive for on a regular basis as much as possible is respect and compassion. Being a compassionate loving person is what garners real attention and attraction from others. If that turns someone off, then don't allow them into your auric circle.

All human beings have both a light and dark ego. The light ego is connected to traits such as having confidence in your abilities, while the dark ego is bogged down in gossip, anger, judgment, or violence. Some dark egos are power addicts. They are much worse than others where a result is desired for individual egotistical advantage. The result can be damaging even if the effect is not in the form of monetary gain. You can still receive a high soaring feeling of emotional satisfaction. Those who are typically giving by nature are not being altruistic for personal pleasure, but for spiritual nourishment. There are various levels of attainment when it comes to altruism.

To be completely selfless is a Divine act possible to achieve. You are made in the likeness of His being. Therefore, you have the capacity of great love and immense selflessness built within you.

Transforming your soul includes evolving in order to see the broader picture. This helps in stripping away the ego, which causes the majority of the sabotage. When you view things from the perception of an egoless being, then you receive that clarity.

There are numerous soul lights threaded around the world doing what they can to offer reminders of the soul's path and to help other souls evolve. This may come in the form of correcting disrespectful behavior, teaching compassionate common-sense etiquette, helping someone through suffering, teaching positive spiritual concepts, helping others have a more peaceful and content life, giving and displaying love, shining at your brightest, and to allowing those in the vicinity to soak that up.

Only love matters, and if parents and teachers around the world all banded together to do their job of teaching love from early on, then that would bring more love like behavior to the planet. While every bit helps, every soul on this gigantic rock needs to partake in it, or the collective consciousness will be no closer to peace and love on Earth than they had ever been.

When you exit this Earthly plane, you leave all of your belongings behind from your job, clothes, money, and all other material possessions. What you recall and take with you on your journey home are the lessons, growth, and connections you made. Whether you are a believer of a higher power, an afterlife or not, why would you waste time not finding a space where love exists? There is nothing joyful about hanging out in an area that has zero love, yet the space that others fall prone to is one of negativity.

Life can be a struggle as you forge on, head down, eyes forward, moving with determination to survive. Your soul desires the kind of rejoicing release that love offers. When you're operating from a high vibration state, then you can come pretty close to that all encompassing all giving love that is fired off from the source naturally. Human souls rely on one another to prop each other up and give a little of bit of that love essence that exists when you reach that high state, but that puts too much pressure on connections that cannot withstand the kind of love that is required as fuel to carry on. You have to stretch higher than that in order to touch the tail end of it. The Earth's dense atmosphere compresses this love due to the domination of the darkness of the ego. It's only when you've re-entered the gates of home does your soul explode by the infusion of this love that permanently baptizes you in its light.

It is the ultimate hope that if you take anything away from this entire piece that you take away love. Love is a simple word that has the power to defeat and kill the Darkness. Whenever you feel like you're struggling or full of stress, anger, or sadness that remember that your soul was made from love. Before you incarnated into the temporary human body you are currently renting, understand that you were made from this love with a purpose. His purpose for you was to carry this love with you while you travel along your soul's many journeys on into infinity and beyond. It is the ammunition you were given to succeed.

As you move about any lifetime in any dimension, you are gaining wisdom through the challenges and experiences you endure wherever you are. This is whether that is through your work endeavors to the various kinds of relationship connections you have from friendships, love, colleagues, acquaintances and family members. When you pass on from this life it is the lessons, knowledge and the love you take with you. It is hoped that as you are crossing over that you understand that Earthly life was the gift in intended to help you remember what love truly is. It is taking the higher angelic view of the superficiality and Darkness that plagues the planet while avoiding getting caught in its web like trap. When you defy the Darkness, then it erupts in anger to see he's lost one of God's warriors to the Light. Become a warrior of love and shine that wherever you roam. When someone agitates you, then re-center and re-align your soul by imagining this love growing bright within you to know that none of that matters. The only thing that ultimately wins in the end is love. Love often, love freely, love bravely and always return to love when you've lost your way.

Acknowledgments

Thank you to God, my Spirit Team Council, and to all of the loyal readers that have hopped on this awesome train ride of mine and stayed on. I am forever blessed and grateful for your eternal support of the work we do. Thank you also for supporting the arts and the artists of the world.

ALSO BY KEVIN HUNTER

Stay Centered Psychic Warrior
Warrior of Light
Empowering Spirit Wisdom
Darkness of Ego
Realm of the Wise One
Transcending Utopia
Reaching for the Warrior Within
Spirit Guides and Angels
Soul Mates and Twin Flames
Raising Your Vibration
Divine Messages for Humanity
Connecting with the Archangels
Monsters and Angels
The Seven Deadly Sins
Love Party of One
Twin Flame Soul Connections
A Beginner's Guide to the Four Psychic Clair Senses
Tarot Card Meanings
Attracting in Abundance
Abundance Enlightenment
Living for the Weekend
Ignite Your Inner Life Force
Awaken Your Creative Spirit
The Essential Kevin Hunter Collection
Metaphysical Divine Wisdom (Six Book Series)

ALSO AVAILABLE BY KEVIN HUNTER

Books that Empower, Enlighten, Educate, and Entertain!

Just as your body needs physical food to survive, your soul needs spiritual food for well-being nourishment.

The Metaphysical Divine Wisdom Collection

STAY CENTERED PSYCHIC WARRIOR
A Psychic Medium's Trip Through the Darkness and Light of the Spirit Worlds, and Other Paranormal Phenomena

In *Stay Centered Psychic Warrior*, metaphysical teacher, psychic, medium, and author, Kevin Hunter talks about what it's like battling between mental health issues and the deeply potent psychic input that continuously falls into his soul's consciousness throughout each day. He offers plenty of examples and discussions of his brushes with spirit, seeing and hearing the dead, the power of the Darkness and the Light in both the physical and spirit worlds, along with sharing his numerous personal psychic and mediumship essays, glimpses of the Other Side, near death experiences, past lives, soul contracts, traveling to and from the Spirit Worlds, spirit guides and angels, recognizing your own psychic gifts, and much more!

This unique autobiography focuses on psychic and mediumship related content coupled with the soul's journey and purpose. Stay Centered Psychic Warrior is an intensely forceful and revealing read that doesn't shy away from the uncomfortable, the Darkness, abuse, mental health issues, while uplifting it with the many blessings of the Light and intriguing day to day psychic phenomena all in one. Allow it to inspire you to recognize your own psychic gifts knowing there is much more to this Earthly life than can be seen or comprehended. Be empowered to break through the rubble and stand strong and centered under the powerful Light that shines through any Darkness.

THE ESSENTIAL KEVIN HUNTER COLLECTION

THE ESSENTIAL KEVIN HUNTER COLLECTION

Featuring the following books:
Warrior of Light, Empowering Spirit Wisdom, Darkness of Ego, Spirit Guides and Angels, Soul Mates and Twin Flames, Raising Your Vibration, Divine Messages for Humanity, and Connecting with the Archangels.

Kevin Hunter an empowering author specializing in a variety of genres, but he is most notably known for his work in the realms of spirituality, metaphysical, and self-help. He has assisted people around the world with standing in their power, and in having a stronger connection with Heaven, while navigating the materialistic practical world. Now some of his popular spiritually based books are available in this one gigantic volume.

The Essential Kevin Hunter Collection is the spiritual bible that contains over 500 pages of content geared towards improving and enhancing your life. It is for those who prefer to have everything in one gigantic book. The content included in this edition are from the books: *Spirit Guides and Angels, Soul Mates and Twin Flames, Raising Your Vibration, Divine Messages for Humanity, Connecting with the Archangels, Warrior of Light, Empowering Spirit Wisdom, and Darkness of Ego.*

THE *WARRIOR OF LIGHT* SERIES OF POCKET BOOKS

Spirit Guides and Angels, Soul Mates and Twin Flames, Raising Your Vibration, Connecting with the Archangels, Twin Flame Soul Connections, Attracting in Abundance, Monsters and Angels, The Four Psychic Clair Senses, The Seven Deadly Sins, Love Party of One, Abundance Enlightenment, and *Divine Messages for Humanity*

About Kevin Hunter

Kevin Hunter is the metaphysical author of dozens of spiritually based books that include *Warrior of Light, Transcending Utopia, Stay Centered Psychic Warrior, Metaphysical Divine Wisdom Series, Empowering Spirit Wisdom, Realm of the Wise One, Reaching for the Warrior Within, Darkness of Ego, Living for the Weekend, Ignite Your Inner Life Force, Awaken Your Creative Spirit,* and *Tarot Card Meanings.*

His pocketbooks include, *Spirit Guides and Angels, Soul Mates and Twin Flames, Raising Your Vibration, Divine Messages for Humanity, Connecting with the Archangels, The Seven Deadly Sins, Four Psychic Clair Senses, Monsters and Angels, Twin Flame Soul Connections, Attracting in Abundance, Love Party of One* and *Abundance Enlightenment.* His non-spiritual related works include the horror drama, *Paint the Silence,* and the modern-day love story, *Jagger's Revolution.*

Kevin started out in the entertainment business in 1996 as the personal development assistant guy to one of Hollywood's most respected acting talents, Michelle Pfeiffer, at her former boutique production company, Via Rosa Productions. She dissolved her company after several years and he made a move into coordinating film productions for the studios. His film credits include *One Fine Day, A Thousand Acres, The Deep End of the Ocean, Crazy in Alabama, The Perfect Storm, Original Sin, Harry Potter & the Sorcerer's Stone, Dr. Dolittle 2,* and *Carolina.* He considers himself a beach bum born and raised in Southern California. For more information and books visit: www.kevin-hunter.com

www.ingramcontent.com/pod-product-compliance
Lightning Source LLC
Chambersburg PA
CBHW080717300426
44114CB00019B/2408